Documenting the Documentary

NEW AND EXPANDED EDITION

Documenting the Documentary

Close Readings of Documentary Film and Video

NEW AND EXPANDED EDITION

With a Foreword by Bill Nichols

Edited by Barry Keith Grant and Jeannette Sloniowski

Wayne State University Press
Detroit

18 17 16 15 14   6 5 4 3 2

Library of Congress Control Number: 2013948532
ISBN: 978-0-8143-3971-8 (pbk: alk. paper)—ISBN: 978-0-8143-3972-5 (ebook)

∞

Designed by Keata Brewer
Typeset by E.T. Lowe Publishing Company
Composed in Scala

For
Bob, Millie, Jessica, and Xena

and for
Zoya Sloniowski-Kiff and Ethan Pano-Sloniowski,
Grandchildren extraordinaire

CONTENTS

FOREWORD TO
NEW AND EXPANDED EDITION

Bill Nichols

This volume arrives as a genuine gift. Anyone seeking to study the subtleties and complexities of the documentary film will want to see as many of the best examples of this form as possible. And anyone who sees a good range of outstanding examples will want to know what others who have taken the time and effort to examine them closely can reveal about why they possess the power and fascination that they do. *Documenting the Documentary* gathers together an exemplary set of essays that do exactly that. It is a great boon to teacher and student alike.

As an anthology it follows in a long lineage of collected essays on the documentary that go back to the middle of the last century, but its predecessors were mainly a mix of interviews with filmmakers and relatively casual commentaries. The interviews always revealed important qualities of how the filmmakers approached their subjects and achieved their goals, but they were inevitably short on any close analysis of the actual workings of the films. The commentaries usually indicated something about the film's subject matter and whether it succeeded or failed in engaging the commentator. This format bore more resemblance to a film review than to film criticism. Film reviews help us decide what we want to see, but if we have already seen the film, film criticism can help us see it in fuller, more complete ways.

The essays collected here revise assumptions, share insights, and provoke thought about what the nature and purpose of documentary film as an overall enterprise are. As such they belong to the great flowering of documentary film theory and criticism that began in the early 1990s. Prior to then the rigorous study of documentary was severely underdeveloped compared to that of narrative fiction film. Documentary tended to be regarded as important when its subject matter was important, such as recounting various aspects of World War II, or if it demonstrated the potential of fresh technological innovations, such as the arrival of synchronous sound recording for real-life settings. Narrative fiction film had received extended examination in terms of genres and directors, studios and nationalities; it had been put under structural, post-structural, semiotic, psychoanalytic, formalist, feminist, and Marxist lenses. A great body of work had arisen, and it enriched our understanding of fiction film immeasurably.

It took several pioneering works in the early 1990s to bring a similar degree of rigorous scrutiny and fresh insight to documentary film. Virtually all of these essays are a product of that renaissance in documentary film study, some by authors who might even be considered a second generation of documentary film scholars working in the new paradigm informed by the broader field of film theory and devoted to probing the intricacies of this remarkable film form. These essays represent the voice—a clear, compelling voice—of film scholarship, and what they share is a heightened awareness of the complex ways in which all films attest to both the historical world from which they stem and the specific, complex, and sometimes contradictory ways in which films regarded as documentaries activate that framework for their own ends, be it in sharp distinction to fiction or close alliance with it. This activation raises distinct questions of ethics, structure, and strategy, especially the rich array of rhetorical strategies where a persuasive or compelling goal complements the aims of storytelling.

Bear in mind that when we speak of cinema we often think of feature fiction films, and when we think of fiction films we think of a form quite distinct from the documentary. This is largely a function of where film theory made its initial impact most strongly and the historical prominence of the feature fiction film in the social imaginary. And although fiction films are fundamentally storytelling machines, storytelling does not belong exclusively to fiction. We find both narrative fiction and narrative nonfictions. Storytelling pervades our culture far beyond the bounds of fiction proper. It is no surprise that the in-depth exploration of fiction films would eventually spill over into the study of documentary as well.

Historical writing, anthropological or sociological studies, news reporting, legal arguments, and case studies in medicine and elsewhere, for example, all possess storytelling qualities that are bounded by additional disciplinary constraints, many of which involve the proper use of evidence and the application of rhetorical as well as narrative principles. For documentary film, these constraints have sometimes been thought to stem from journalism. Hence some place an emphasis on neutral reportage, objectivity, truth, balanced treatment of both sides of an issue, and so forth, and yet these qualities, although present in different films to varying degrees, are seldom at the heart and soul of documentary as the essays collected here demonstrate. Documentaries, like essays, poems, polemics, and advertising, normally represent the world from a distinct point of view or perspective. They speak with a singular voice that addresses us about the world we share, ideally in a memorable form. They are not neutral sources of information transfer but galvanizing agents, capable of prompting us to see the world, or some specific part of it, in a new way.

As in previous anthologies, it is what have become "classics," if not the canon, of documentary study that these writers address here. The addition of five new essays gives a good sense of how this canon continues to evolve. (This process not only adds new work but often subtracts older work although that part of the process is not demonstrated here.) Films like *This Is Spinal Tap, Culloden,* and *Borat: Cultural Learnings of America for Make Benefit Glorious Nation of Kazakhstan* may even expand our conception of what a documentary is or of what an effective parody or critique of documentary is.

Surely the essays on some of the earliest documentaries such as *Nanook of the North, Man with a Movie Camera, Que viva México!, Las Hurdes* (aka *Land without Bread*), and *Song of Ceylon* make clear how a canon begins to arise and then transform and grow. All of the later films discussed in detail here amplify on what it means to speak in a singular, compelling voice derived from this inaugurating set of works in the 1920s and 1930s, whether it is the politically impassioned voice of *Hour of the Furnaces,* the ironic, surreal voice of *Blood of the Beasts,* the highly submerged but still distinct voice of *Dont Look Back,* or the wildly irreverent, provocative, and distressingly hilarious voice of *Borat.* They are not reports, journalistic or otherwise. They are the vital, engaged voices of filmmakers of richly varied preoccupations and goals striving to help us see what we have already seen or could see in other ways, their way, a way that corresponds with the vision and passion they bring to their chosen subjects.

Some essays prompt us to ask "What is a documentary?" and "Is this film a documentary?" be it the entirely reconstructed account of the battle of Culloden in *Culloden* or the priceless mix of social satire and mockumentary in *This Is Spinal Tap.* Other essays take up how documentaries can address the mix of history and memory that goes into our construction of the past, be it in the allegorical references to French colonialism in the rituals performed by the Hauka of Ghana in *Les maîtres fous* or the personal memories of the Nazi concentration camps that underpin the voice-over commentary in *Night and Fog.* Questions of ethnicity and race come to the fore in yet other essays addressing films such as the powerful exploration of black, gay identity in *Tongues Untied* or of the struggle for civil rights in the face of shocking acts of hatred in *4 Little Girls*. And no survey of documentary would be complete without giving attention to the highly personal but socially attuned perspectives of filmmakers such as Werner Herzog in *Grizzly Man*, his fascinating study of a man who went into the wilderness to protect bears only to wind up eaten by them, or the poetic musings of Agnès Varda as she explores the phenomenon of gleaning both by others and by herself as a filmmaker in *The Gleaners and I.*

Documentary filmmakers, following in the tradition of explorers, missionaries, colonialists, tourists, travelers, and ethnographers often choose to live and work among others. And if they do not literally live among the people whom they also film, they do set out to grasp the issues that confront their social partners in the construction of reality. They often come from afar to understand the problems that plague their subjects, the institutions and practices that confront them, and the pleasures that engage them, even if it must be from across the span of history, culture, or geography. But whether they come from afar or begin close by with friends, family, loved ones, and self, documentary filmmakers then must find ways to represent what they discover and believe, and want others to discover and believe as a result of their own representations. These discoveries are what the essays so brilliantly gathered together here share enthusiastically.

The complex, fuzzy boundary to the enterprise of documentary filmmaking is well registered in the striking absence from the first quarter century of cinema (roughly 1895 to 1922) of any single word for what we now call documentary. There was no clear frame of reference for its production or reception, and its existence in this period can be considered debatable. Even after the word "documentary" began to designate something that looked like a distinct filmmaking practice, cinematic tradition, and mode of audience reception, it remains, to this day, a practice without clear boundaries. How might we represent the lives of social and historical others in film form? This is a question with no single answer, in narrative fiction or nonfiction. Documentary filmmakers may now be more self-conscious of their specialized calling and craft than were their turn-of-the-twentieth-century predecessors, but how they choose to undertake the act of representing themselves and others remains open to extraordinary variation. For this reason alone, the careful reflection on the precedents for and principles of this formidable challenge provided by these essays is of genuine value both to students of documentary and to its current and future practitioners.

Put another way, the question may be not only how do we discipline ourselves to write responsibly, rigorously, and usefully about the documentary tradition but also how do documentary filmmakers discipline themselves to live among others, fathom personal experience and historical events, and represent them in ways distinct from those of a sociologist, journalist, historian, traveler, or cultural anthropologist? If anthropology is fundamentally, in the words of Margaret Mead, a "discipline of words," documentary film is most fundamentally a discipline of audio-visual representation.

Documentary film calls for special techniques to give cinematic embodiment to lived encounter and historical events, personal experience and social structure, research and argumentation, vision and poetics. It, like ethnographic fieldwork, calls for specific ways of being among and apart from those ultimately represented in words or images. It calls for an ethic of responsibility, an aesthetics of film form, and a politics of representation.

These are among the dimensions of documentary filmmaking and criticism the essays here so memorably address. They are radical essays in the etymological sense of returning to the historical roots of documentary and to the concepts and issues that have informed its growth. What these authors also share with their predecessors from previous generations is a distinctly unembarrassed insistence on the valued status of the amateur author or *auteur* (amateur in the root sense of one who pursues an interest from love rather than for gain). They write to share their passion and insight, and we all benefit from it greatly. To combine livelihood and love in one profession is an achievement devoutly to be wished; we have here evidence that many scholars and documentary filmmakers had managed to do exactly that.

Bill Nichols

PREFACE TO FIRST EDITION

Documenting the Documentary is for students, teachers, and scholars. We believe that the essays collected here offer a significant contribution to the critical literature on the documentary, providing the kind of concrete analyses of important texts that too frequently have been lacking in discussions of this crucial form of cinema. The reader will find in these pages a welcome balance between theory and criticism, abstract conceptualization and concrete analysis. One can only come away from this volume with a new appreciation of the nonfiction film's textual sophistication, as well as of the range of aesthetic and social issues documentary addresses.

As a result of the impressive heterogeneity of the close readings our contributors presented us, after much deliberation we decided to sacrifice the imposed organization of a sectional structure for the simpler arrangement of placing the essays in chronological order according to when the films discussed were made. Such an arrangement is an invitation to readers to move around in the book as they might wish, while also affording instructors (who, in any case, usually adapt textbook sequencing to the particularities of their own courses) greater freedom in the order of selection. In addition, there are more documentaries discussed in this book than are likely to be contained in any one course, offering instructors more latitude in programming screenings than textbooks normally afford.

Of course, no single book about documentary film and video could ever be truly comprehensive. But we think we have met the challenge of filling the need for a book that offers solid critical readings of important individual documentary films while at the same time addressing the wide range of issues surrounding documentary as a specific form. We encourage our colleagues who choose to use *Documenting the Documentary* as a class text to share their experiences with us.

Readers who want to learn more about documentary might begin by consulting the general bibliography of this book.

ACKNOWLEDGMENTS

For the preparation of the first edition, we would like to express our gratitude to Dr. John Sivell, former Dean of Humanities at Brock University, for his consistent support of this project and our research in general. Undergraduate student Stephen Lenz helped with sleuthing in the library. Lesley Bell of the Visual Arts Program, Brock University, Mary Pisiak of User Services, and Jenny Gurski and Joyce Hasty of the Secretarial Services Department all provided invaluable technical support. For the second edition, we are grateful to the support, patience, and encouragement of Annie Martin, senior acquisitions editor, and the entire staff of Wayne State University Press for bringing it into being with such care and commitment. Jennifer Backer copyedited the second edition with great care.

Matthew Bernstein's "Documentaphobia and Mixed Modes: Michael Moore's *Roger & Me*" originally appeared as "*Roger & Me*: Documentaphobia and Mixed Modes," and is abridged from its original publication in *Journal of Film and Video* 46, no. 1 (1994): 3–20. Copyright © 1994 by Matthew Bernstein. Reprinted by permission of the author and *Journal of Film and Video*.

Virginia Bonner's "The Gleaners and 'Us': The Radical Modesty of Agnès Varda's *Les glaneurs et la glaneuse*" originally appeared in *There She Goes: Feminist Filmmaking and Beyond*, ed. Corinn Columpar and Sophie Mayer (Detroit: Wayne State University Press, 2009), 119–31. Reprinted with permission of the author and Wayne State University Press.

David T. Johnson's "'You Must Never Listen to This': Lessons on Sound, Cinema, and Mortality from Werner Herzog's *Grizzly Man*" first appeared in a slightly different form in *Film Criticism* 32, no. 3 (Spring 1980): 68-82 and is reprinted with permission of the author and *Film Criticism*.

William Rothman's "The Filmmaker as Hunter: Robert Flaherty's *Nanook of the North*" appeared in slightly different form in William Rothman, *Documentary Film Classics* (New York: Cambridge University Press, 1997). Copyright © 1997. Used with permission of the author and Cambridge University Press.

Vivian Sobchack's "Synthetic Vision: The Dialectical Imperative of Luis Buñuel's *Las Hurdes*" is a revised version of an essay that first appeared in *Millennium Film Journal* 7–9 (Fall–Winter 1980–81): 140–50. Copyright © 1981. Reprinted by permission of the author and *Millennium Film Journal*.

Robert Stam's "The Two Avant-Gardes: Solanas and Getino's *The Hour of the Furnaces*" originally appeared as *The Hour of the Furnaces* and the Two Avant-Gardes" in *Millennium Film Journal* 7–9 (Fall–Winter 1980–81): 151–64. Copyright © 1980. Reprinted by permission of the author and *Millennium Film Journal*.

Leshu Torchin's "Cultural Learnings of *Borat* for Make Benefit Glorious Study of Documentary" is a revised version of an essay that first appeared in *Film and History* 38, no. 1 (2008): 53–63. Reprinted with permission of the author and *Film and History*.

Thomas Waugh's "'Men Cannot Act before the Camera in the Presence of Death': Joris Ivens's *The Spanish Earth*" originally appeared in a somewhat different form as "'Men Cannot Act in Front of the Camera in the Presence of Death': Joris Ivens' *The Spanish Earth*" in *Cineaste* 12, no. 2 (1982): 30–33, and no. 3 (1983): 21–29. Copyright © 1982, 1983 by Cinema Guild. Reprinted by permission of the author and *Cineaste*.

Linda Williams's "Mirrors without Memories: Truth, History, and *The Thin Blue Line*" appeared originally as "Mirrors without Memories: Truth, History, and the New Documentary," in *Film Quarterly* 46, no. 3 (1993): 9–21. Copyright © 1993 by the Regents of the University of California. Reprinted by permission of the Regents and the author.

Stills are from the Museum of Modern Art, National Film Board of Canada, St. Nederlands Film Museum, and the authors' personal collections, except the following: images for *Titicut Follies* courtesy of Bridgewater Film Co.,

Inc. (Zipporah Films, Inc.); for *Finding Christa*, Camille Billops; for *The Act of Seeing with One's Own Eyes*, the Canadian Filmmakers' Distribution Center; for *Les maîtres fous*, the Center for Visual Communication, Misslintown, Pa.; for *Tongues Untied*, Frameline Distribution. Photos for *Finding Christa* by Kira Perov.

INTRODUCTION

When the first edition of *Documenting the Documentary* was published in 1998, Michael Moore's *Roger & Me* (1989) was the most commercially successful documentary of all time. Since then, fifteen documentaries have earned more at the box office, including *March of the Penguins* (2005), *Earth* (2007), *An Inconvenient Truth* (2006), and Moore's own *Fahrenheit 9/11* (2004) and *Sicko* (2007). Also since then, the documentary impulse has continued to inform countless events and news stories, from the inconsequential to the important, including the clandestine cell phone footage of Mitt Romney speaking about "the 47%," the hidden camera photos of Kate Middleton and the bare-bum shots of Prince Harry, the fall and resignation of congressional representative Andrew Weiner, and the role of social media in the political conflicts in the Middle East. We argued in 1998 that interest in documentary was the most intense it had been since the 1930s. Things have changed only to the extent that documentary has become even more popular and controversial as we write this in 2013.

In 1998 we were at the beginning of the proliferation of Reality TV, as well as continuous news channels like CNN. Reality TV is now the most popular staple of prime-time television. There are television channels that show nothing but documentary programming, and even fiction filmmakers are remaking documentaries as successful docudramas, as with *Grey Gardens* (2009). New filmmakers (over 700,000 of them) exhibit their documentary work on Internet venues like YouTube. Clearly interest in the "reality genres" is greater than ever with the advent of inexpensive filmmaking equipment (now we can even make documentary films with our cell phones) and freely accessible online exhibition sites where one's work always has the potential to "go viral." But more than the result of inexpensive and accessible equipment alone, there is now an intense global desire to record, examine, and exhibit "the real," from the massacre in Tiananmen Square to the violent death of Neda Agha Soltan in Iran or the terror of the massive earthquake and ensuing tsunami that struck Japan in 2011. Scholars remain as interested as the general public in this burgeoning of documentary, and the wave of new books on the genre continues unabated. Visible Evidence, devoted exclusively to the topic of documentary, has been a significant annual scholarly conference for the last two decades.

Of course, all of this is made possible by the documentary films and videos themselves. From those first actualités of the Lumière brothers, documentary makers have maintained the form's vitality. Nevertheless, much of the critical writing on documentary—both the old and the new—ignores or undervalues the significance of aesthetic pleasure and complexity that distinguish many documentaries. Certainly they have received nothing comparable to the critical attention given to the minutiae of narrative cinema. Instead, in the case of documentary, most often the apparatus and conditions of production are privileged to the extent that, as Annette Kuhn has written, it becomes the "determining feature of documentary film texts" (75). That is to say, documentaries tend to be discussed as documentaries rather than closely read as rich works of cinema. Yet even at the level of information, the documentary appeals to us through what Bill Nichols calls "epistephilia," the "pleasure in knowing" (178).

The reason, likely, is the different ontological status of the documentary image, its closer indexical relation to the real—that is, its more intimate connection to the real world, the physical world in which we live. In fiction films, no matter how realistic they may be, some form of "suspension of disbelief" is always operative. By contrast, documentary appeals to us precisely because of its truth claims, whether at the level of fact or image. Because it is the form of cinema that is most closely bound to the real world, to actual personal and collective problems, hopes, and struggles, it is understandable that concrete issues of ethics, politics, and technology (the physical apparatus) would take precedence over the intangibles of aesthetics. Yet as we increasingly garner our news and information about our world—indeed, our very perception and comprehension of it—from the visual media, it is more important than ever to understand the textual strategies by which individual documentaries are organized.

We hope that, like the first edition, this second edition of *Documenting the Documentary* will be a significant help in achieving this goal. Gathered here are essays by thirty-one scholars, employing a wide range of critical and theoretical perspectives. Together they cover the significant developments in the history of documentary, from the first commercially released feature (*Nanook of the North*, 1922) to contemporary independent film and video productions. The works discussed also include representative examples of many important national and stylistic movements and various production contexts from mainstream to avant-garde.

The essays by William Rothman, Barry Keith Grant, and Jeffrey K. Ruoff on, respectively, *Nanook of the North*, *Titicut Follies* (1967), and *An American Family* (1973), address the relation of documentary to fiction, seeking to elucidate both their differences and similarities—what Nichols calls "a fiction (un)like any other." But, as well, both Charlie Keil's formalist analysis of *The Plow That Broke the Plains* (1936) and *The City* (1939) and Thomas Waugh's account of *The Spanish Earth* (1937) point out how politically motivated documentaries have borrowed techniques from fictional film practice. In their essays, Jeanne Hall, Carl Plantinga, and John R. Cook consider the importance of performance, usually associated with acting in fiction films, to *Dont Look Back* (1967), featuring a young Bob Dylan; *This Is Spinal Tap* (1984), a fictional parody of the rockumentary genre; and *Culloden* (1964), an experimental documentary using local citizens to re-create the slaughter of Scottish Highlanders by the British army in 1746. Performative documentaries have become, in the view of these authors, not only more common but crucial to the ethics of revealing the conventions with which documentary constructs its powerful "truths."

Yet documentary, because of its impressive stylistic heterogeneity, also has a place within the avant-garde, a category often perceived as in stark opposition to, if not the antithesis of, commercial film. Several of the essays that follow are about films and filmmakers generally associated with avant-garde and experimental cinema at least as much as with documentary. Seth Feldman situates *Man with a Movie Camera* (1929) within the movements of constructivism and futurism, Bart Testa contextualizes Stan Brakhage's *The Act of Seeing with One's Own Eyes* (1971) within several traditions of avant-garde cinema, and Catherine Russell explicates Bill Viola's art video *I Do Not Know What It Is I Am Like* (1986) within the domain of ethnographic documentary. Surrealism provides a context for both Vivian Sobchack's analysis of Luis Buñuel's *Las Hurdes* (*Land without Bread*, 1932) and Jeannette Sloniowski's reading of Georges Franju's *Blood of the Beasts* (1949), although the directors of both films are more commonly associated with narrative cinema. And David T. Johnson raises issues of realism, focusing on the use of sound, in Werner Herzog's *Grizzly Man* (2005), a film about the shocking death of Timothy Treadwell, the "self-appointed savior to the Alaskan Grizzly Bear." Together these essays push the boundaries of documentary and offer a series of test cases.

But the textual emphasis of this book should not be taken as an aesthetic hermeticism—in other words, that issues surrounding documentary films as objects in the real world are devalued or avoided in these pages. Indeed, questions of ethics, ideology, power, race, gender, and representation are continually and emphatically addressed by these writers—but always in terms of how they arise out of or are involved in the reading of specific documentaries as particular textual constructions.

Of course, several of the documentaries discussed here have overt political agendas. *Triumph of the Will* (1935), as Frank Tomasulo's careful reading shows, methodically constructs a mythic representation of the führer in relation to the German people for the purposes of political persuasion. Jim Leach's analysis of *Listen to Britain* (1942) considers a colonial power's attempt to construct its own cultural myth during a time of national crisis. Robert Stam discusses the Argentinean film *The Hour of the Furnaces* (1968) as a significant example of the politically engaged sensibility of "Third Cinema." And Paula J. Massood analyzes Spike Lee's historical documentary *4 Little Girls* (1997) in terms of its re-creation of the racist history of the American South through moving, and sometimes enraging, interviews with the murdered girls' families and with the outspoken segregationist and former governor of Alabama George Wallace.

For many critics, ethnographic documentary most acutely foregrounds issues of colonialism, power, and appropriation of "the Other" through cinema's visual and aural means of representation. Rothman finds this tension at the heart of *Nanook of the North*, as does Joanne Hershfield in her analysis of *Que viva México!* (1932). Similarly, in his discussion of *Song of Ceylon* (1934), William Guynn suggests that in mythologizing a "primitive" culture, Basil Wright opens up ideas around colonialism and the representation of the Other that endorse the interests of Britain as the colonizing nation. In her discussion of Viola's video, *I Do Not Know What It Is I Am Like*, Russell suggests this appropriation is the inevitable outcome of any such endeavor at ethnographic representation. By contrast, Diane Scheinman praises Jean Rouch's cinematic expression of a "shared" ethnography in such films as *Les maîtres fous* (1954). Lechu Torchin's essay on the controversial *Borat: Cultural Learnings of America for Make Benefit Glorious Nation of Kazakhstan* (2006), featuring the British comedian Sacha Baron Cohen, notes the documentary/mockumentary divide, generic expectations, and cultural assumptions that structure depictions of the Other. Torchin finds a similarity between Borat and Rouch's ethnofictions, as well as ideas on the importance of performative documentary.

Yet even the more intimate autobiographical mode of documentary is political at the same time that it is personal. Matthew Bernstein's analysis of *Roger & Me* (1989), Lucy Fischer's of *Sherman's March* (1985), Joan Nicks's of *Daisy: The Story of a Facelift* (1982), and Virginia Bonner's of *Les glaneurs et la glaneuse* (2002) all trace the correlations between the films' personal stories and larger political and social issues through the various ways in which the directors construct and insert their own presences into the texts. Autobiographical documentary also allows people who are generally marginalized and disempowered to gain a voice by making documentary films about their own lives. Thus Julia Lesage sees Camille Billops's personal story in *Finding Christa* (1991) rich in implication about both the politics of black family life and the cultural conception of motherhood, and Sheila Petty discusses the personal struggle of gay black filmmaker Marlon Riggs in *Tongues Untied* (1989) to get his story told as resonant of the wider struggle against both a heterosexist white society as well as a frequently homophobic African American community.

In her analysis of *The Thin Blue Line*, Linda Williams argues that the aim of contemporary documentary filmmakers is to seek the "reverberations and repetitions" that reveal multiple and contingent "truths" rather than a unitary, unproblematic "Truth." Indeed, while each of the essays in this collection is distinctive in its emphasis and approach, ideas do reverberate and repeat throughout the book in provocative ways. This is particularly apposite, given that they all examine documentary, a visual mode that, as Williams suggests, reveals such "reverberations" to be inherent in reality itself. Thus Sandy Flitterman-Lewis finds a hopeful truth in *Night and Fog* (1955), which, given its subject—World War II German concentration camps and the Holocaust—would seem to suggest a much darker view about the human spirit. More recent documentaries, as several of the essays show, interrogate traditional depictions of the truth as stable, objective, and knowable, even suggesting that identity itself is shifting and fragmentary. Caryl Flinn considers how *Paris Is Burning* (1990) unfixes traditionally stable notions of gender, and *Daisy*, as Nicks shows, questions the physical authenticity of being when the body can be sculpted by elective surgery.

In the end, it would be impossible in this brief introduction to do justice to such a rich and varied group of essays, much less to the documentaries themselves. Indeed, no single reading, regardless of how persuasive it might be, can ever hope to be definitive. In any event, we leave it to readers to engage in what we see as the pleasurable task of sorting out in more detail the numerous "repetitions and reverberations" contained in this collection. But whatever relations different readers perceive, we hope all will come away from this volume with a profound appreciation of the aesthetic complexity of the documentary form.

WORKS CITED

Kuhn, Annette. "The Camera I: Observations on Documentary." *Screen* 19, no. 2 (Summer 1978): 71–83.

Nichols, Bill. *Representing Reality: Issues and Concepts in Documentary.* Bloomington: Indiana University Press, 1991.

Documenting the Documentary

NEW AND EXPANDED EDITION

Chapter 1

The Filmmaker as Hunter

Robert Flaherty's *Nanook of the North*

William Rothman

The field of film study has only recently shown significant interest in documentaries. In part, the scarcity of critical studies of documentary films is indicative of film study's general neglect of criticism, a consequence of the revolution undergone in the past quarter century by a field that accords precedence to what it calls "theory" and (more recently) to what it calls "historiography." There has been a special animus, though, in film study's resistance to devoting attention even to great works within the documentary tradition. It derives from the claim sometimes made on behalf of documentary films—less often by their makers or admirers than by detractors who invoke the claim only to repudiate it—that they are capturing reality directly and thus are inherently more truthful than fiction films. From the standpoint of the field's dominant theoretical frameworks, such a claim seems intolerably naive. By the late 1970s, the prevailing view within the field was that all fiction films are really documentaries and that all documentary films are fictions, hence that they do not fundamentally differ. Documentaries and fiction films are equally liable to be instruments of repressive ideology, hence equally to be resisted.

The publication in the early 1990s of Bill Nichols's *Representing Reality* (1991) and Michael Renov's *Theorizing Documentary* (1993) marked a shift. For both books, the starting point is the recognition that although documentaries are not inherently more truthful than fiction films, there are important differences between them. Reflecting on those differences is a major starting point for such reflections, because nearly all documentary filmmakers claim its inheritance, and because it marks a moment before the distinction between documentary and fiction was set.

The widely distributed videocassette of *Nanook* prefaces the film with a title stating that it "is generally regarded as the work from which all subsequent efforts to bring real life to the screen have stemmed." The implication is that fiction films are not "efforts to bring real life to the screen"— they are efforts, perhaps, to bring to the screen the imaginary life of fantasy and myth. Yet fiction films do bring real life to the screen; their characters are imaginary, but the camera's subjects are real. And documentaries are steeped in fantasy and myth.

Filmmaker Robert Flaherty actively involved Nanook and his family in the filming, often telling them what to do, directing their performance for the camera. (There are illuminating accounts of the production of *Nanook* in Barsam, Calder-Marshall, and Rotha and Wright. See also Flaherty.) Much of what is on view is typical behavior for Nanook's family (making igloos, lighting campfires). Some is not. Flaherty had his subjects revive a dangerous method of walrus-hunting that Nanook's people had abandoned when they became able to trade pelts for guns.

Although *Nanook of the North* (1922) accurately illustrates aspects of its protagonist's way of life, its primary goal is not to contribute to a body of scientific knowledge of human cultures; it is far from an ethnographic film in the current sense. For its own purposes, the film underplays the complexity of the social structures, different from ours, specific to Nanook's culture (he seems to have more than one wife, but no title acknowledges that Nyla is not the only woman sharing his bed). It also underplays the encroachments of the modern world, which gives Nanook's family no choice but to be part of it. Flaherty portrays Nanook's way of life as timeless, unchanging, when the way of life the film portrays was already succumbing to a mortal threat (more accurately, that way of life never existed, for no way of life is timeless, unchanging). And nature itself, the environment on display in *Nanook*, was—is—mortally threatened. (On *Nanook's* relationship to ethnographic film, see, for example, Winston, who wonders how different—and how much better, in Winston's judgment—the history of documentary film would have been if an anthropologist like Franz Boas, not a self-styled artist-explorer in a colonialist mold like Flaherty, had created the paradigm.)

Flaherty had a vested interest in portraying his subjects' way of life as timeless and unchanging. If Western civilization is destroying Nanook's culture, the filmmaker's own project is implicated. The video version contains a title noting that "the film was made possible by the French fur company Revillon Frères," but Flaherty's titles credit only the "kindliness, faithfulness and patience of Nanook and his family." Paired with his failure to note that his film was sponsored by a fur company, Flaherty's acknowledgment of his subjects' participation may seem disingenuous. Yet there is no reason to doubt his sincerity when he expresses appreciation for his subjects' human qualities or declares that he could not have made *Nanook* without their active participation. That Flaherty appreciates his subjects does not mean that his relationship to them is an innocent one. But who are we to judge Robert Flaherty?

In part, Flaherty distorts the real way of life of Nanook's family in order to tell a story about a man's heroic efforts to keep his family alive in a harsh natural environment, not about his conflict with villains or his quest for romantic fulfillment (or, for that matter, the destruction of his world by forces he does not perceive as threats). The story Flaherty tells is quite different from those his contemporary D. W. Griffith was telling. But Flaherty's story, like Griffith's, did not really happen; it is literally a fiction. And insofar as Nanook is the protagonist of such a story, he is as fictional as any Griffith character.

Nanook claims that its protagonist is a real person, not a fictional character. However, real people, too, are characters within fictions (we are creatures of our own imaginations and the imaginations of others). And real people are also actors (we play the characters we, and others, imagine us to be, the characters we are capable of becoming). As opposed to playing a character, *Nanook*'s star appears as himself or, as it might be more apt to say, plays himself (as opposed to playing a character other than himself). Yet the "self" this man plays and the "self" who plays him do not simply coincide.

Within the film, this man is called "Nanook," although in reality he bears the marquee-busting name "Allakariallak." Flaherty's titles characterize Nanook in mythical, fantastic (and contradictory) terms; Nanook thus emerges as a character created by and for the film in which he appears. But in the face of the camera, Nanook is not a mere "persona"; he is a human being of flesh and blood. The "real" Nanook—the man Flaherty films—is himself a character, a creature of myth and fantasy in the sense that all human beings are, but he is not a textual construct that serves a narrative and holds no further claims upon author or audience.

Insofar as he participated in the making of *Nanook*, the "real" Nanook has a relationship to the camera that is part of his reality, part of the camera's reality, part of the reality being filmed, part of the reality on film, part of the reality of the film. *Nanook* is an expression of real relationships between camera and human subjects, relationships that in turn are expressions of, hence capable of revealing, both the camera and its subjects. Yet Nanook also emerges as a fictional character with no reality apart from the film that creates him. Being filmed has no more reality to Nanook-in-his-fictional-aspect than to a character in a fiction film. But this means that the fictional Nanook has no reality to the camera. (Between a fictional character and a real camera, what real relationship—what relationship capable of expressing, hence revealing, the subject's nature, or the camera's—is possible?)

In a fiction film, the camera's revelations about characters are also revelations about the real people who incarnate them, revelations that express and thus reveal the real relationships between camera and human subjects. The prevailing fiction is that the character, not the actor, is real. What is fictional about a fiction film resides in its fiction that it is only fiction. What is fictional about *Nanook* resides in its fiction that it is not fiction at all. Both exemplify Stanley Cavell's maxim that the only thing that matters in film is that the subject be allowed to reveal itself (Cavell 127). This essay will reflect on three passages—the introductions of Nanook and Nyla; the scene in which the trader, "in deference to the great hunter," explains to Nanook "how the white man cans his voice"; and the thrilling passage in which Nanook, in the act of devouring the walrus he has killed, pauses to confront the camera's gaze—that achieve this revelation and thereby anticipate such issues, which have been central to the documentary tradition.

THE INTRODUCTION OF NANOOK AND NYLA

Nanook opens with a title: "The mysterious Barren Lands—desolate, boulderstrewn, wind-swept—illimitable spaces which top the world." This title is followed by two views, evidently taken from a boat, of the sublime, melancholy northern landscape that, on film, is an enduring wonder of *Nanook*. These views testify to the reality of the windswept lands Flaherty's words invoke. They also testify to the title's claim that these lands are "illimitable," "mysterious"—they are as fantastic, mythical, as any our imagination can conjure. The following title asserts that the humans at the center of *Nanook* are as real and fantastic as the lands they inhabit: "The sterility of the soil and the rigor of the climate no other race could survive; yet here, utterly dependent upon animal life, which is their sole source of food, live the most cheerful people in all the world—the fearless, lovable, happy-go-lucky Eskimo." Eskimos, as this title characterizes them, survive by subsisting on animals they kill. They are also fearless heroes who stoically endure rigors "no other race" could survive. Part savage, part hero, they are at once "lower" and "higher" than we. Eskimos are like children, too, the title patronizingly suggests ("lovable," "happy-go-lucky," "the most cheerful people in all the world"). That they also possess the qualities of civilized adults is asserted by the next title: "This picture concerns the life of one Nanook (The Bear), his family and little band of followers, 'Itivimuits' of Hopewell Sound, Northern Ungava, through whose kindliness, faithfulness and patience this film was made."

This title, the first to refer to the film's dramatis personae, characterizes the figures to whom it refers, much as a Griffith title might. But Flaherty's title not only posits attributes that define Nanook and his family as characters, it also asserts their existence. To be sure, the opening titles of Griffith's *True Heart Susie* likewise assert the existence of the characters central to the story. But in introducing Susie, the film's protagonist, Griffith's title also names the star who plays her (Lillian Gish), at once positing their identity (as a subject of the camera, Susie is Lillian Gish) and acknowledging their separateness (Susie has no existence apart from *True Heart Susie* (1919), but Gish exists apart from her incarnation in this film and is capable of being incarnated as any number of characters). Flaherty's title posits character and star as one, like a Rin Tin Tin or Lassie. Nanook exists, it declares; his relationship to the camera is a condition of the film's existence.

By acknowledging that the film was made through the "kindliness, faithfulness and patience" of Nanook and his family, this title's author is also declaring the reality of his acts of filming them, the reality of his own existence and that of his camera in the world of the film. The title says, in effect, "Nanook and his family exist, and thanks to their kindliness, faithfulness and patience I was able to film them." (If Nanook were really the mythical figure of Flaherty's titles—part primitive savage, part hero, part innocent child, part sage—who would the filmmaker be, mythically, to film him?)

It may be taken to be a definitive feature of documentaries that they make truth-claims about the world, claims subject to being tested not only against the testimony of the camera, as is the case with all films, but also against reality as we may know it independently of that testimony. For example, if "The hunting ground of Nanook and his followers is a little kingdom in size—nearly as large as England, yet occupied by less than three hundred souls" were a title in a conventional documentary, we would take it to be making a factual claim about the real world. (We would also take it to be implying that the other Eskimo men who are sometimes on view but never identified by name are in reality what could be called "followers" of Nanook. Throughout the film, the titles have a tendency to inflate Nanook's importance—he is the "chief," the greatest hunter in all Ungava; others are merely his followers—as if such credentials validate the camera's attention to him.) If it were a title in a fiction film, we would take it to posit a fictional premise, one we are called upon to accept for the sake of the narrative, but whose truth or falsity outside of the narrative does not matter to the film.

By this criterion, *Nanook* seems poised between documentary and fiction. When Flaherty presents this title immediately preceding his introduction of Nanook, we take it that it makes a factual claim. But we are also called upon to accept it as a premise of the film's story; whether in fact it is true or false is inconsequential. In *Nanook*, as we have suggested, the only "fact" of consequence is that Nanook and his family really participated in making the film. This fact is acknowledged by the way Flaherty effects Nanook's introduction. He follows his next title (the charmingly Griffith-like "Chief of the 'Itivimuits' and as a great hunter famous through all Ungava—Nanook, The Bear") with our first view of its star/protagonist, a medium close-up sustained for ten seconds. Within this frame, Nanook looks down, then up, without meeting the camera's gaze.

Having characterized his protagonist as a "great hunter," Flaherty might be expected to show Nanook for the first time performing some hunting-related act. Rather, when we first view Nanook he is doing nothing—nothing, that is, apart from being viewed, allowing himself to be viewed, by the camera. He does not seem to be presenting himself theatrically to the camera, but neither does he seem unaware of its presence. The frontality of the framing as well as the camera's close proximity, combined with the fact that he is engaged in no activity other than being viewed, reinforce our impression that it takes an effort for him not to look at the camera; for whatever reasons, he is avoiding the camera's gaze. And they also reinforce our impression that we do not know his reasons, that they remain private. (For all we know, Nanook avoids the camera because Flaherty, for his own private reasons, directed him to do so. But then Nanook also has private reasons for accepting Flaherty's direction.)

In his initial encounter with the camera, Nanook does not flash the "cheerful" smile we might expect of an exemplar of a "happy-go-lucky" race, but neither does he confront the camera with the threatening gaze we might expect of a "great hunter." Seeming reserved, guarded, he does not express his feelings about, or to, the camera whose scrutiny he endures. Or perhaps his evident reserve is Nanook's expression of how he feels, at this moment, about being filmed.

Contrast our first view of Nyla. The Griffith-like title "Nyla—The Smiling One" is followed by a shot of Nanook's young wife, smiling radiantly as she talks to someone offscreen. Engaged in a conversation that absorbs her, she seems not at all self-conscious in the presence of Flaherty's camera (as we have seen, Nanook is absorbed in no such activity when we first view him). The camera frames Nanook head-on, forcing him to choose between looking at it or making an effort not to. Framing Nyla obliquely, the camera assumes a less provocative position. Unthreatened by a camera from which she withholds no intimacies, Nyla appears open, warm, accepting of the condition of being filmed, in contrast to the guarded Nanook, whose relationship to the camera, when he is introduced to us, appears much more tense.

Our initial views of Nanook and Nyla make no assertions about them, do not attribute characteristics to them the way the titles that precede them do. These views simply say, in effect, "This is Nanook as the camera views him" and "This is Nyla as the camera views her." If Nanook and Nyla are nonetheless characterized by these views, as indeed they are, it is only through what these views reveal about these subjects, through what is revealed by their being placed on view, by their placing themselves on view, within these frames.

Having declared them to be real people, not fictional characters, and having acknowledged the reality of the camera in their world, Flaherty authorizes us to take these initial views of Nanook and Nyla (and by extension all our subsequent views of them) as "documenting" their encounters with a camera that was really in their presence. (This is not to deny that Flaherty may have told Nanook and Nyla how to relate to the camera, that he staged these encounters, in effect. The crucial claim is that these encounters are real, not that they are spontaneous.) By contrast, when Griffith presents us with our first view of a character, we are not authorized to take it as "documenting" a real encounter between camera and subject. As we have said, in a fiction film the prevailing fiction is that the character, not the actress, is real, hence that there is no real encounter between camera and subject, for the camera that films the actress has no reality within the character's world.

To act as if she is the character she is playing, an actress must act as if no camera is in her presence. But how is it possible for the actress to have a real relationship with the camera, a relationship through which a character is capable of being revealed? For the character to act as if no camera is present, there is no reality that must be denied. But for the actress to act as if no camera is present, she must deny the reality of the camera in her presence. To deny this camera's reality, she must acknowledge its presence in a particular way. And if the camera is to sustain the fiction that the character is real, it must relate to the actress in a particular way, must acknowledge her presence and deny her reality.

A camera is a physical object; a dog can acknowledge its presence by licking it. But when a camera is filming, it is no ordinary object. Through its presence, viewers who are "really" absent are also magically present; in the presence of a camera, what is absent is also present, what is present is also absent. What makes it possible for a maker of fiction films to use the camera in a way that acknowledges an actress's presence even as it denies her reality is the fact of human life that real people are also characters, imaginary creatures of fantasy and myth, even as they are actors capable of becoming who they are imagined to be. What makes it possible, in a fiction film, for an actress to acknowledge the presence of the camera even as she denies its reality is the equally fundamental condition of the medium of film that the reality of the camera's presence is also the reality of its absence, the absence of its reality.

Nanook's and Nyla's ways of relating to Flaherty's camera, their ways of acknowledging the reality of its presence, are also ways of acknowledging the absence that presence is capable of projecting. They, too, recognize what the camera is, in other words; their recognition is revealed to, and by, the camera. By acknowledging that his film could not have been made without their active participation, the filmmaker credits the camera's subjects with this recognition, acknowledges their acknowledgment of his acts of filming.

This is Flaherty at his most progressive. Far more disquieting is the passage that chronicles Nanook's visit to the "trade post of the white man," a passage that seems to be designed to deny that Nanook and his family are capable of participating as equals in the making of *Nanook*.

THE VISIT TO THE "TRADE POST OF THE WHITE MAN"

After effecting the introductions of Nanook and Nyla, Flaherty establishes the narrative present by the title "Nanook comes to prepare for the summer journey down river to the tradepost of the white man and to the salmon and walrus fishing grounds at sea," followed by a shot of Nanook paddling a kayak.

Now located spatially and temporally within the narrative world, Nanook is reintroduced by a title ("Nanook . . ."). Then we see Nanook pulling one family member after another out of the kayak, which seems so impossibly small to contain so many people that the effect is comic. Each emerging family member is named by a title—the child "Allee"; "Nyla," who has already been introduced to us; the baby "Cunayou"; and finally "Comock," the puppy. (This joking association between baby and puppy first sounds what will become a major theme in the film, which repeatedly associates Eskimos with animals.)

The following passage presents the family's preparations for the "long trek" to the "trade post of the white man" and then the journey itself. Consisting of such titles as "This is the way Nanook uses moss for fuel" and "The kyak's [*sic*] fragile frame must be covered with sealskins before the journey begins" paired with shots that serve as illustrations of the practices to which they refer, this is one of the film's most documentary-like passages. It is also one of the most impersonal. We view Nanook "using moss for fuel," for example, but it could be any Eskimo.

This passage culminates in a spectacular image of men carrying a huge crate across the foreground of a frame dominated by a high wall of hanging pelts, too numerous to count, framed perfectly frontally in the background, blocking out the sky. This is at once a glorious display of nature's bounty and appalling evidence of the slaughter exploited by the "white trader" (that is, the fur trade that sponsors Flaherty's film). By following this image with the title "Nanook's hunt for the year, apart from fox seal and walrus, numbered seven great polar bears, which in hand to hand encounters he killed with nothing more formidable than his harpoon," Flaherty retroactively transforms it from an illustration of the Eskimo way of life—actually, what it illustrates is the modern world's catastrophic intervention in that way of life—into a revelation of Nanook's individual prowess as a "great hunter."

But, again, Flaherty's next title implies that his larger-than-life hero is also an innocent child: "With pelts of the Arctic fox and polar bear Nanook barters for knives and beads and bright colored candy from the trader's precious store." This is followed by a shot of Nanook showing pelts to the "white trader."

In most of the shots that follow, the trader remains offscreen. Even when visible within the frame, as in this shot, he is filmed differently from Nanook. Indeed, the trader is framed in a way that identifies him less with the camera's subject than with the camera (or the filmmaker behind the camera). According to the title, Nanook is displaying this pelt to the trader, but he is really—at least he is also—displaying it to the camera. This underscores our impression that the filmmaker is employing the trader as a kind of stand-in.

The next title ("Nanook proudly displays his young 'huskies,' the finest dog flesh in all the country round") is followed by a shot of Nanook plopping a playful puppy on the ground, then by a close-up of said puppy. This is followed by the title "Nyla, not to be outdone, displays her young husky, too—one Rainbow, less than four months old," then by a shot of her baby, hugging the puppy from the previous shot.

Whether "Rainbow" is the baby's name or the puppy's is not clear, but it could not be clearer that the film is linking baby and puppy, reasserting the association between Nanook's family and animals (dogs, wolves, walruses). This analogy at once reduces Eskimos to animals and at least ironically elevates animals to the level of humans (dogs, too, are perfectly capable of showing off). In any case, this shot is followed by a longer one in which two puppies are beside the baby in the frame. The baby keeps petting the puppy on the left, but Nyla clearly wants her child to pet the other as well, perhaps to appear not to love one more than the other. In this shot, Nyla's pride in her child is evident, as is her wish to show the baby off to advantage. Obviously, Nyla is exhibiting her baby to the camera, but Flaherty's titles implicitly deny this by asserting that she is showing her baby off to the trader. It is as if Flaherty employs the trader as his own stand-in so as to bracket his original claim that Nanook and Nyla are participants in the act of filming. They are absorbed in an encounter with the trader, the titles imply, *rather than* collaborating with the filmmaker.

This strategy becomes more pointed, and more disquieting, following the condescending title "In deference to Nanook, the great hunter, the trader entertains and attempts to explain the principle of the gramophone—how the white man 'cans' his voice." In the ensuing shots, we see Nanook, bending forward, staring at the phonograph as the trader—again, the framing links him with the filmmaker behind the camera—cranks it up. Nanook half gets up, peers at the machine, and laughs, directing a big, broad grin first to the trader then to the camera. Nanook puts his ear to the phonograph as the trader cranks it again, gives the camera another look, points to the mechanism at the base of the phonograph, then looks at the trader, who has removed the record and now hands it to him. Nanook peers at it and then puts it in his mouth and bites it! He looks thoughtfully at the trader, bites the record again, looks up to communicate something to him, takes two bites, then turns to the trader yet again. They are conversing as the image fades out.

Witnessing all this, we have a strong sense that the trader and the filmmaker—two "white men"—have conspired to expose the incredible naïveté of this "great hunter" who does not even comprehend "how the white man 'cans' his voice." The clincher is when Nanook bites the record, tastes it, in an effort to determine what it is. The moment has a comical edge to it because in our culture even a man who had never seen a record would not try to figure out what it was by putting it in his mouth and biting it; only a baby would do that—or a dog. But a man in Nanook's culture cannot survive without every day making discriminations that way. Nanook's gesture really reveals a cultural difference, a difference between his culture and that of the "white man," not a difference between having and not having a culture, between being civilized and being a primitive savage bound to a natural order whose only law is "eat or be eaten," as Flaherty's title would have us believe.

If we laugh at Nanook at this moment, as Flaherty's titles invite us to do, if we assume that this gesture reveals Nanook to be more of a child,

Nanook of the North: In the trading post, Flaherty and the trader conspire to expose the naïveté of Nanook.

or more of an animal, than we are, that is a mark of our naïveté, not his. Surely when Nanook bites the record he is confirming his own provisional hypothesis that this object is not, and does not literally contain, a living thing—the "canned" voice is not "in" the record the way the seal is "in" the as-yet uncarved ivory, for example, or the way a man's soul is "in" his body (or the way Nanook-on-film is "in" the man Flaherty films). When Nanook first hears the "canned" voice, he breaks into a grin, amused that the "canned" voice is not a profound mystery but only a special effect, as it were. (Nanook has no way of knowing—has Flaherty?—the profound threat the white man's soulless technology poses to his form of life.)

Nanook's laugh, addressed to the trader and then to the camera, registers his pleasure and at the same time his impulse to share his pleasure with others. However condescending the title may have been that introduced Nanook as lovably "cheerful," through his relationship to the camera he now reveals himself to be a man of good cheer. Nanook's cheerfulness is revealed to be an expression of a winning sense of humor, which, in combination with the admirable generosity of spirit that is also revealed at this moment, makes him "lovable" indeed—worthy of Flaherty's love, and ours. What makes Flaherty seem so unlovable in this passage is that his titles seem to be betraying his subjects—and himself—by disavowing precisely what has been revealed to, and by, his own camera.

If Nanook is too naive to comprehend what a phonograph is, as Flaherty's title implies, he must be unable to comprehend what a camera is, what Flaherty is doing when he films him. This implication stands in conflict with the claim, crucial to *Nanook* as a whole, that Nanook and his family are active collaborators in the making of the film. (What gives a filmmaker the right to film the private lives of human subjects? We want to say: What is required is the subject's consent. If a subject does not comprehend what the camera is, how can that subject give consent? How can a subject ever give consent, how can anything a subject says or does count as consent, if it is a condition of the film medium that one cannot know in advance—in advance of viewing the footage that results, that is—what revelations are fated to emerge from a particular encounter with the camera?)

When he suggests that Nanook does not know what the camera is, Flaherty is not innocently revealing his own naïveté, I take it. What he is denying is something he knows, not something he simply fails to know, about his subject, about himself. This cannot be doubted, first, because Flaherty processed his footage on location and showed the dailies to Nanook; by the time he had this encounter with the phonograph, Nanook had already become quite familiar with the film image. Second, because *Nanook* acknowledges this in its introductory titles and also in the passage, late in the film, in which he carves a window for his new igloo, at the same time revealing himself to Flaherty's waiting camera, waving at it with another warm grin. Self-evidently, the business with the window was set up by Flaherty and Nanook working in tandem. They conspired to play a practical joke on the film's audience (the way, within the narrative, Flaherty and the trader earlier make Nanook the butt of a joke). When he grins at the camera through his new window, we cannot doubt that Nanook understands no less than Flaherty (but also no more than Flaherty) what a camera is. We cannot doubt that Nanook understands that a film—this film—is made to be viewed, that the camera filming him stands in not only for the filmmaker in his presence but also for viewers who are absent.

In the comic business that follows Nanook's encounter with the phonograph, Flaherty's presentation reveals a painfully evident element of exploitation. The trader "banquets" Nanook's children with sea biscuits and lard, but Allegoo "indulges to excess," and so the trader "sends for—castor—oil!" He may be justified in making the boy swallow this unpleasant medicine, but the trader is anything but innocent. He has plied the boy with sea biscuits and lard, after all. More seriously, he is the representative of the fur trade that exploits Nanook's prowess as a hunter, tempts or compels him to kill creatures whose flesh his family does not need to consume in order to survive. Flaherty, too, is anything but innocent. He conspires with the trader. And in his role as filmmaker, he exploits the boy's misfortune, which gives rise to one of the film's most magical, yet most compromised, moments. When the boy takes his medicine, he makes a face at the trader, then addresses to the camera a look so beseechingly woeful we can hardly refrain from laughing.

Almost as if caused by this memorable moment (by the boy's overindulgence of his animal appetite? by the trader's, or the filmmaker's, exploitation of the boy's innocence?), there is a change in the tone of the film, signaled by the title "Wandering ice drifts in from the sea and locks up a hundred miles of coast. Though Nanook's band, already on the thin edge of starvation, is unable to move, Nanook, great hunter that he is . . ." The boy's overeating is comical, but at another level it is not funny, as this title acknowledges. The boy and his family are "already on the thin edge of starvation," and what is at issue, it is now being made clear, is whether Nanook's prowess as a hunter will enable him to stave off the threat that looms over his family.

THE WALRUS HUNT

To acknowledge his subjects' humanity, a filmmaker must acknowledge the revelations that emerge through their encounters with the camera. Flaherty at his most progressive proves willing to do so. But *Nanook* also reveals his guilty impulse to deny his human bond with his subjects, to disavow what is revealed by, and to, his camera. Yet Flaherty's impulse to deny commonality with Nanook and his family itself reveals their commonality. For the filmmaker, no less than his "primitive" subjects, belongs to a natural order whose only law is "eat or be eaten." Flaherty's weapon is a camera, not a harpoon, but he, too, is a "great hunter." Nanook and his family are his prey, vulnerable to being exposed to his camera, exposed by his camera, in all their vulnerability. All filming has a violent aspect. This does not mean that filming is never justified, only that it always needs to be justified, that it is never innocent. Nanook is justified in hunting the walrus; his family needs to eat to survive. Is Flaherty justified in filming the hunt?

The passage that most pointedly links filming and killing, the walrus hunt, begins with the title, "For days there is no food. Then one of Nanook's look-outs comes in with news of walrus on a far off island. Excitement reigns, for walrus in their eyes spells fortune." In nine shots, we view Nanook and his "brother fishermen" gathering near a family of walruses bobbing in the sea. "With the discovery of a group asleep on shore," the next title reads, "the suspense begins." The following shots present the group of walruses, including the "sentinel" ("A 'sentinel' is always on watch," a title explains, "for, while walrus are ferocious in water, they are helpless on land"); the hunters, including Nanook; and a shot with walruses in the background and a hunter—Nanook?—creeping toward them in the foreground. Within this last frame, the sentinel suddenly rises and, followed by the other walruses, hurriedly lumbers toward the safety of the water. Nanook runs after them, followed by the other men who enter and rush through the frame. Then shots of the hunters tugging on a rope are alternated with shots of walruses bobbing in the waves, including the harpooned one.

The title "While the angered herd snorts defiance, the mate of the harpooned walrus comes to the rescue—attempts to lock horns and pull the captive free" is followed by a view purporting to show this. This shot is followed by the poignant title "Rolling the dead quarry from the undertow," then a series of shots in which Nanook and a fellow hunter flip the dead walrus over like a side of beef, culminating in a final vision of the walrus, now dead (and *alone* in death), displayed for the camera.

What follows is a frontal medium shot of Nanook sharpening his knife, his attention fixed on what he is doing, until he suddenly looks up with a grin, as if to show off his sharp blade to the camera. Nanook leans into this frame, his face now hidden from view, and places his knife blade against the base of the walrus's neck. He starts slicing the beast's flesh, his body blocking the bloody carcass from view. The title "They do not wait until the kill is transported to camp, for they cannot restrain the pangs of hunger" is followed by a shot of three hunters standing in long shot, each eating still warm flesh. Nanook is in this grouping, his knife in clear view. Then there is a cut to a medium close-up of Nanook, framed almost in profile, slicing off flesh, tearing meat with his teeth, chewing.

We feel we are glimpsing humanity shorn of its thin veneer of civilization and are repelled and fascinated by this vision. Like a cat interrupted devouring a bird, Nanook looks up. His gaze locks with the camera's. For the only time in the film, Nanook seems to view the camera as a threatening intruder—a competing hunter or, perhaps, a lowly scavenger. And his gaze, too, is threatening, as if this savage predator, his thirst for blood unsated, might next attack the camera (Flaherty, us).

When he looks up at the camera at this moment, Nanook is not sharing his pleasure, as he elsewhere does when addressing the camera. There is a fierceness to his look, as if this "great hunter" is warning that he will tolerate the camera's presence only if it keeps its distance. He is not denying his

Nanook of the North: Nanook's look suggests that the limit of his relationship to the camera has been reached.

relationship to the camera, he is declaring that it has a limit, that this limit must be respected, and that it has now been reached.

And Flaherty acknowledges this limit. When Nanook looks down, takes another bite of walrus flesh, and licks the blood off his knife blade, completely absorbed now in sating his hunger, the camera does not linger on him. Rather—I find this the most thrilling moment in the film—Flaherty cuts to a view of the sea. We can barely discern the members of the walrus family, heads still bobbing in the surf close to shore, as they wait for the father, himself a "great hunter," who is fated not to return.

Flaherty's gesture of cutting to the walrus family does not feel like a reproach to Nanook but rather an homage to this "great hunter" and to the "great hunter" he has killed. Nanook is a beast of prey, as Flaherty is; his kinship with the slain animal, and with the filmmaker, has been revealed to, and by, the camera. But the walrus family, too, is revealed to possess the "kindness, faithfulness and patience" Flaherty has recognized as attributes of Nanook's family. If there is an element of reproach in Flaherty's gesture, as surely there is, it is addressed not to Nanook but to himself insofar as he may have failed always to acknowledge his bond with his subjects, always to remember that no life is a jest, that filming is a sacred trust.

Flaherty follows the haunting shot of the forlorn walrus survivors with the title "Winter . . . ," then with two memorable views of swirling snow blowing like smoke over the desolate landscape into the unfathomable depths of the frame. These two shots, the film's most sublime visions of the "Barren Lands" in which Nanook and his family struggle against starvation, are in turn followed by a title whose language rises to the poetic level of the camera's revelations: "Long nights—the wail of the wind—short, bitter days—snow smoking fields of sea and plain—the brass ball of the sun a mockery in the sky—the mercury near bottom and staying there days and days and days." This is not the Griffith-like purple prose of so many Flaherty titles or the words of an impersonal, godlike authority who claims to stand above or outside the world of the film but words "spoken," almost confessionally, by a human being who is acknowledging that he has lived through winters like this that feel like dark nights of the soul that will never end.

This passage signals a more somber mood, as winter's arrival intensifies the threat of starvation. It is as if Nanook's killing of the walrus, or Flaherty's filming of the killing, "causes" the onset of winter (the way Lear's rage "causes" the tempest or the way Allegoo's overeating "causes" the wandering ice to drift in from the sea, occasioning the film's first invocation of the threat of starvation).

The remainder of *Nanook* is not unrelentingly somber, however. There is the aforementioned comic interlude in which Nanook and his family build an igloo. This is followed by the tenderest passage in the film, in which the family awakens the next morning, having spent the night snug and happy under one big sealskin blanket.

But even in this idyllic passage, there are reminders of the looming threat. Nanook has to make a separate igloo for the puppies to keep them "warm all night and safe from the hungry jaws of their big brothers." These puppies, cute and innocent as little Cunayou and Allegoo, have the blood of wolves in their veins; they will grow up to become beasts so savage they will eat their own kind when the "blood lust" is upon them, as Nanook's boys will grow up to be "great hunters" like their father.

When Nanook hunts " 'Ogjuk'—the big seal," the scent of flesh awakens in his "master dog" the "blood lust of the wolf—his forebear." In another Shakespearean transition, the resulting dogfight causes "a dangerous delay.... By the time the team is straightened out, a threatening 'drifter' drives in from the north.... Almost perishing from the icy blasts and unable to reach their own snowhouse, the little family is driven to take refuge in a deserted igloo.... The shrill piping of the wind, the rasp and hiss of driving snow, the mournful wolf howls of Nanook's master dog typify the melancholy spirit of the North."

Astonishingly, the film ends with a series of views of the dogs outside, hunkered down in the blizzard, alternated with intimate views of the family slipping under the sealskin blanket and drifting off to sleep. A shot of Nanook's solitary "master dog," his "blood lust" long since abated, faithfully and patiently enduring the cold, is followed by a view of the sleeping family and then a final close-up of Nanook in bed, safe for the duration of *this* night.

In a Griffith film, the machinations of villains—figures of evil incarnate—threaten dire consequences. In *Nanook,* there are no villains: the threat to Nanook's family comes from within nature. What is threatened is not a fate worse than death but death itself, a part of nature. And what saves the human community from this threat, or grants them a reprieve, is part of nature, too (the ice of the igloo that provides shelter from the storm, the sealskin blanket, the bodily warmth of huddled human animals). The dog, man's best friend, has wolf's blood in his veins; the "blood lust" in his nature is what causes the near-catastrophe. Nanook is not exempt from "blood lust"; neither is Flaherty, and neither are we. But we humans also share the dog's capacity for "kindliness, faithfulness and patience." What is noble and savage, in human nature as everywhere in nature, are aspects of the sublime and beautiful reality that is *Nanook*'s subject. But this reality—nature itself—is facing a mortal threat that cannot be said to come from within nature, although it cannot exist apart from nature. *Nanook* is torn between acknowledging and denying this threat, in which the film itself is implicated.

André Bazin believed it was the wish for the world re-created in its own image that gave rise to the emergence of film, hence that, starting with the Lumière films, a realist strand runs the length of film history (21). In *The World Viewed,* Cavell gave Bazin's idea a crucial twist by observing that it is precisely because film's material basis is the projection of reality that the medium is capable of rendering the fantastic and mythical as readily as the realistic. Reality plays an essential role in all films, but in no film does reality simply play the role of being documented. Reality is transformed or transfigured when the world reveals itself on film. Then, too, reality itself, in human experience, is already stamped by fantasy and myth.

Documentaries are not inherently more truthful than other films. Yet it does not follow that documentaries, to be truthful, must repudiate the aspiration of revealing reality. What particular films reveal (or fail to reveal) about reality, how they achieve (or fail to achieve) those revelations, and what they acknowledge (or fail to acknowledge) about the revelations they do achieve are questions best addressed by close critical readings that illuminate what separates documentaries from fiction films without denying what they have in common: the medium of film.

Works Cited

Barsam, Richard. *The Vision of Robert Flaherty: The Artist as Myth and Filmmaker.* Bloomington: Indiana University Press, 1988.

Bazin, André. "The Myth of Total Cinema." In *What Is Cinema?*, ed. and trans. Hugh Gray, 17–22. Berkeley: University of California Press, 1971.

Calder-Marshall, Arthur. *The Innocent Eye: The Life of Robert J. Flaherty.* New York: Harcourt, Brace and World, 1963.

Cavell, Stanley. *The World Viewed: Reflections on the Ontology of Film.* Cambridge, MA: Harvard University Press, 1979.

Flaherty, Robert. "How I Filmed *Nanook of the North.*" In *Film Makers on Film Making*, ed. Harry M. Geduld, 56–64. Bloomington: Indiana University Press, 1971.

Nichols, Bill. *Representing Reality: Issues and Concepts in Documentary.* Bloomington: Indiana University Press, 1991.

Renov, Michael, ed. *Theorizing Documentary.* New York: Routledge, 1993.

Rotha, Paul, and Basil Wright. *"Nanook of the North." Studies in Visual Communication* 6, no. 2 (1980): 33–60.

Winston, Brian. "The White Man's Burden: The Example of Robert Flaherty." *Sight and Sound* 54, no. 1 (1984): 58–60.

Chapter 2

"Peace between Man and Machine"

Dziga Vertov's *Man with a Movie Camera*

Seth Feldman

In 1930, when Dziga Vertov's *Man with a Movie Camera* (*Chelovek s kino-apparatom*, 1929) was the first Soviet film he saw, the young critic Jay Leyda found himself "reeling" from a New York theater, "too stunned to sit through it again" (Leyda 251). This was, one could only surmise, the desired effect. Vertov's film was, like the speeding cars, the intersecting trolleys, and spinning gears depicted in it, a high-speed machine meant to shock the viewer into empathy with the industrial age. It was a high point in early modernism's desire to wed art and the machine. It was also the product of a time when there was still hope for a totally scientific understanding of human experience. And the film was still more. For what Vertov showed us in *Man with a Movie Camera* was not just anybody's industrial age. Leyda, who was to become the English-speaking world's preeminent historian and champion of the Soviet cinema, found in the film the dynamism of the Soviet revolution itself. This was the revolution not only at work but working within the precision of Vertov's precisely edited montages.

Vertov's life had made him an embodiment of the film's concerns, an all but perfect manifestation of the three decades that preceded *Man with a Movie Camera*. He was born Denis Abramovich Kaufman on January 2, 1896, the Thursday after the Lumière brothers held cinema's first commercial screening in Paris. The Kaufman family resided in Bialystok, Poland, then part of the Russian empire. Young Denis Abramovich (he would later Russify his Jewish patronymic to "Arkadevich") studied music, an interest that was to remain with him for the rest of his career. In 1915, Vertov's family fled to Moscow and a year later to St. Petersburg. Vertov enrolled in the Psychoneurological Institute but soon gravitated toward the city's avant-garde cafés. It was there that he made the acquaintance of the young Futurist poet Vladimir Mayakovsky and one of the founders of the Russian school of formalist critics, Viktor Shklovsky.[1]

It was during this period that Denis Arkadevich Kaufman took on the Futurist pseudonym "Dziga Vertov," a term that may be roughly translated as "spinning top" or "spinning gypsy." Vertov's avant-gardism is, in itself, a significant aspect of his films and his career. Like the St. Petersburg avant-garde and the Italian Futurists who inspired them, he maintained a contempt for the classic arts. We might draw a straight line from the Italians' condemnation of the Italian legacy to Mayakovsky's call to destroy Russian museums to Vertov's "sentence of death" passed on all previous film (Vertov, "Kinoki," *Kino-Eye* 138).[2] For Vertov, the rebirth of film studios in the Soviet Union—and the consequent Soviet "Golden Age"—was a betrayal of what the cinema could have been. Vertov's avant-garde contempt for the classical expresses itself in *Man with a Movie Camera* in what was then seen as the film's most scandalous image. Toward the end of the film, Vertov uses a split screen shot to make it appear as if the Bolshoi Theatre—that icon of traditional Russian performance—collapses in upon itself.

But if one was to destroy all of classical art, what then would replace it? Inspired by the Italian Futurists and their Russian imitators, Vertov was determined to show the world seen by the movie camera *as the entire cinematic apparatus sees it* (i.e., including the editing as well as the filming process). In *Man with a Movie Camera,* images are taken from every conceivable camera angle and distance, and numerous types of camera movement are employed. We see the world in normal motion, slow motion, split frame, and freeze frame. And we see shots not only edited into seamlessly constructed sequences but also edited by theme (e.g., a shot of a movie poster for a film called *A Woman Awakens* is followed by a shot of a woman awakening). The pace of the editing ranges from the leisurely to the frenetic, from unobtrusive to dazzling sequences of one and two shots.

From the early 1920s, Vertov articulated the reasons for presenting the world this way in a series of manifestos that took his ideas well beyond those of the early Futurists. One of the most telling summaries of Vertov's intentions comes in his 1922 manifesto "We":

Because people cannot control their movements, we will until further notice not include them as subjects in our films.

Our way takes us through the poetic machine, from the corpulent gentleman to the perfect electric man.

We reveal the soul of the machine, causing the worker to love his workplace, the peasant his tractor, the engineer his engine—

We bring joy to mechanical labor,

We make peace between man and machine,

We train the new man. (Vertov, *Kino-Eye* 11)

Vertov's intent, then, is not simply to celebrate the cinema—or any other machine—in its own right. He breaks, for instance, with the Italian Futurists' glorification of speed and power for its own sake (an obsession that was to make them the official artists of Mussolini's fascism). In all of his work—and most particularly in *Man with a Movie Camera*—Vertov is looking for "peace between man and machine." We see this from the beginning of the film, when the blinking eye of a real awakened woman is intercut with

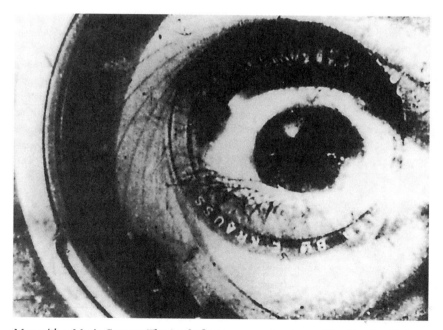

Man with a Movie Camera: The justly famous recurring logo of the film itself, the human eye superimposed on the camera lens.

the blinking Venetian blinds. We see it in the larger design of the film in the way that Vertov uses the camera in the same way to augment both the nature of the mechanical world and the human body (as with the athletes shown later in the film). And we see it in the justly famous recurring logo of the film itself, the human eye superimposed on the camera lens.

Making peace between man and machine is also the theme of Vertov's own creative biography. In 1917, he established a "Laboratory of Sound" where, working with a Pathé wax disc recorder, Vertov attempted to record sounds both inside and outside the studio and then reedit them into entirely new compositions. He was, in essence, attempting to create concrete music. The nature of the equipment mitigated against achieving satisfying results: the recorders were cumbersome, the field recordings were unsatisfactory, and the editing from one machine to another only diminished what little sound quality was obtained. Nevertheless, the use of sound in this manner was a goal that remained with Vertov. It appears in his ingenious cutting of the silent cinema orchestra in *Man with a Movie Camera*. Indeed, the film's cutting to the tempo of all manner of loud machines and human activities makes this one of the noisiest silent films ever made.

Vertov's early experiments with sound are also an indication of his formalist inclinations. He was attempting not only to record sound but to break it down into its constituent parts and put them back together—to define musical composition as a scientific or mechanical process. Vertov's formalism is, of course, central to the larger design of *Man with a Movie Camera*. This is a movie about the making of a movie. The "parts" of that movie and the assembly of those parts are continually made visible to us. The cameraman is shooting; we see the product of his shots. We also see the editor at work; she pulls clips off the shelf that suddenly fill the screen before us. Here is a clip labeled "child"; here is a child on the screen. Later we see that same child edited into a (now subverted) illusion of reality— appropriately enough, the sequence of the magician's act. In *Man with a Movie Camera*, we even see the mechanics of projecting a film as the projectionist threads the reel, creates the arc light, and switches on the projector to show us the movie within the movie.

In the context of the Soviet revolution, there is a political message to Vertov's Futurist and formalist strategies. Vertov is not only saying that "art is a machine" but also implying that we, the audience, must be made aware of this fact. We must be told that machines are made by people; and art is not magic, it is labor, the very labor we see on the screen. In a broader sense, this is the sort of thinking that lured many of the Russian formalists and Futurists to an enthusiastic support of the 1917 Bolshevik Revolution.

Man with a Movie Camera: The editor of Vertov's film at work in the film.

Vertov's contribution to the revolution coincided with his beginnings in cinema. In 1918, he joined the Moscow Cinema Committee to work on the first Soviet newsreel series, *Kinonedelia* (*Cinema Weekly*). His own description of his recruitment suggests a link between his unsuccessful sound experiments and his earliest conceptions of what the cinema could offer him. It reads almost as a shot list from *Man with a Movie Camera:*

> And once in the Spring of 1918, I was returning from a railroad station. In my ears, there remained the chugs and bursts of steam from a departing train . . . somebody cries out . . . laughter, a whistle, voices, the station bell, the clanking of a locomotive . . . whispers, shouts, farewells. . . . And walking away I thought there is a need to find a machine not only to describe but to register, to photograph these sounds. Otherwise, one cannot organize or assemble them. They fly like time. Perhaps a camera? That records the visual. But to organize the visual world and not the audible world? Is this the answer?
>
> And at this moment I met Mikhail Kol'tsov who offered me a job in cinema. (*Kino-Eye* 40)

Vertov began his work as Kol'tsov's secretary, sorting the newsreel footage coming into Moscow from across Soviet-held territory. He began editing the footage, and when Kol'tsov was drafted, Vertov became head of *Kinonedelia*. While Vertov himself admitted that the series (which withered from lack of resources in 1919) was not particularly distinguished, it did lead him to consider both the nature and potential of cinema. Sitting in the Moscow Cinema Committee's studios, he watched and edited images of the far-flung Russian civil war—one of the first people to watch the news unfold in a daily influx of moving images. Vertov was also engaged in the remarkable propaganda experiments of the early revolution: screenings in the streets and in factories, making and showing films on the agitprop trains that crisscrossed the country. He was responsible for two of the earliest historical compilation films, his *Anniversary of the Revolution* (1919) and *History of the Civil War* (1922). Ever the good Futurist-Bolshevik, he wrote the history of the revolution not on paper but with a manifestation of the hi-tech future it promised. *re-estab lishing .*

Throughout his career, Vertov insisted on the ideological link between the cinema of fact and the goals of the revolution. He often quoted what he termed "the Leninist proportion," Lenin's own declaration that Soviet filmmaking was to be largely geared toward propaganda and educational film[3]—and, for his troubles, was roundly denounced by the emerging Soviet feature film industry. This ideological battle over the proper nature of cinema is also a part of what we see in *Man with a Movie Camera*. The film is, to some extent, Vertov's 1929 declaration that the agitational-propaganda role for cinema could be best practiced as it had been ten years earlier—in the streets and with the people and things that could be found there. His goal in the film is to present a Soviet utopia, a place where almost everything and everyone works as well as the movies. Vertov tells us that the proof of this argument is that what we see before us is recognizable reality, our reality, brought to us by cinema workers who are people no different than ourselves.

Vertov's absolute belief in the power of nonfiction film was his contribution to Soviet film theory. He came to his conclusion as the result of what he saw as a scientific experiment. Arranging for a cameraman to film his descent in slow motion, Vertov jumped from a second-story balcony.

> The results. From the point of view of the ordinary eye it goes like this: the man walked to the edge of the balcony, bowed, smiled, jumped, landed on his feet and that is all. What was it in slow motion? A man walks to the edge of the balcony, vacillating. To jump or not to jump? Then it is as if his thoughts

say that everything points to the need to jump. I am entirely uncomfortable. Everyone is looking at me. Again doubt. Will I break a leg? I will. No, I won't. I must jump, I cannot just stand here. An indecisive countenance is replaced by a look of firm decision. The man slowly goes off the balcony. He is already situated in mid-air. Again, fear on his face. On the man's face are clearly seen his thoughts. (Vertov, *Kino-Eye* 123)

Vertov's experiment bridged his early exposure to the St. Petersburg avant-garde and his cinematic career. It "proved" the observational power of the medium—film, Vertov concluded, can read minds. But it could do so only if used to its full capacity—in this case, slow motion. The camera, for Vertov, would be liberated from any demand to reproduce an imitation of life as the human eye saw it. Editing must be freed from the obligation to produce a seamless narrative.

It was with these concepts in mind that Vertov embarked on the series of films that would culminate in *Man with a Movie Camera,* the fullest expression of his experiment and many manifestos. In retrospect, we begin to see *Man with a Movie Camera* emerge in 1922, when Vertov began his collaboration with his new wife and editor, Elizaveta Svilova, and his recently demobilized brother and cameraman, Mikhail Kaufman—the film's principal "cast." It was in that year that this "Council of Three" (the signature on Vertov's early manifestos) undertook the production of the *Kinopravda* newsreel series (1922–25). In the course of its twenty-three issues, *Kinopravda* moved from a conventional representation of news items to thematic studies incorporating increasingly ambitious formal experimentation (Feldman).

Kinopravda and the films that come between it and *Man with a Movie Camera* arrive at a remarkable period in Soviet history. Lenin's 1921 proclamation of the New Economic Policy (NEP), an official tolerance of a mixed economy, restored the shattered nation to the point where regular film production was once again a possibility. With this social and economic pragmatism came a significant degree of artistic tolerance. It was in this heady atmosphere that artists like Vertov could begin to dream. Vertov proposed, for instance, that Soviet films be shot by large numbers of ordinary citizens acting as film scouts, edited collectively and exchanged in a vast nationwide network. To illustrate this activity (as he would later illustrate his broader aesthetic in *Man with a Movie Camera*), Vertov made his first feature documentary, *Kinoglaz* (*Cinema Eye—Life Caught Unawares,* 1924), a film in which the Pioneers (the newly formed Soviet version of the Boy Scouts) bring the camera to the nooks and crannies of daily life. The group's next

film, *Stride, Soviet!* (1925), was a commissioned documentary made to celebrate the achievements of the Moscow city government. Vertov's *Sixth Part
of the Earth* (1926), commissioned by Gostorg, the State Import-Export
Agency, was a bold experiment in editing. It used the silent film title cards
as a poetic text to link disparate shots of life from across the Soviet Union.

The formal experimentation in *Sixth Part of the Earth* earned Vertov
a prize at the World Exposition in Paris. Gostorg was less enthusiastic.
The export agency did not appreciate a sequence at the beginning of the
film caricaturing the decadence of Western life, that is, the lives of their
potential customers. Gostorg's complaint to Vertov's studio, Sovkino, was
abetted by the general hostility Vertov had generated by his unceasing attacks on narrative filmmakers. It was one thing to condemn all narrative
filmmaking in the early 1920s, when there were very few such films being
made in the Soviet Union; but by the mid-1920s, the international success
of films like Eisenstein's *Battleship Potemkin* (1925) gave feature filmmakers new prominence. With that prominence came influence, and it was that
influence which cost Vertov his job at Sovkino in January 1927.

Without a work card, Vertov was forced to leave Moscow. He, Svilova,
and Kaufman found work at VUFKU, the Ukrainian Film Studio. Their
next film, *The Eleventh Year* (1928), was a work commissioned to celebrate
the success of the Five Year Plan in the Ukraine. While filming *The Eleventh
Year,* Vertov was making notes for *Man with a Movie Camera*—the most adamant of his many angry responses to his dismissal and the living assertion
of the nature of cinema he had "proven" in the continuing experiment of
his previous work.

It is, then, this need to reassert his principles, along with his long embrace of Futurism, formalism, and communism, that shapes Vertov's *Man
with a Movie Camera*. This is the world—and the world of cinema—as Vertov
saw it and wished it would work. Even by 1929 Vertov had reason to believe that this vision was only possible on the screen, a remembrance of
optimism past. But because he believed that, he wished his film to be as
polished an argument as he could make it.

Vertov's argument in *Man with a Movie Camera* can be summarized
by two phrases that recur throughout his manifestos and are coupled in
the title of his first feature: "Life Caught Unawares" and the "Cinema Eye."
"Life caught unawares" expressed Vertov's profound commitment to the
observational abilities of cinema. This in itself made fiction filmmaking
relatively uninteresting if not entirely pointless. The kind of film that took
full advantage of cinema's inherent observational powers, as one of the introductory titles of *Man with a Movie Camera* proclaims, was "A Film without Actors." It would have to be "A Film without a Scenario," just as it was

(after its opening credits) "A Film without Title Cards." Yet as we explore *Kinoglaz* (1924) (*Life Caught Unawares*), we are also urged in opening titles to remember its ultimate goal: the production of a completely self-enclosed cinema world. As the last of the opening titles of *Man with a Movie Camera* tells us: "This experimental work was made with the purpose of creating a true international pure language of cinema characterized by its total differentiation from the language of theatre and literature." This, in one sentence, is the Cinema Eye.

We get to the Cinema Eye through Life Caught Unawares, for one can only manipulate images by being true to their origins in the living world. In practice, the means of achieving Life Caught Unawares varies. It is more than "candid camera." We might, for instance, view the images of the woman getting dressed near the beginning of *Man with a Movie Camera* as just such an invasion of privacy. But in the larger context of the film, it is also an agreement between the director and his subject that the camera has a right to be anywhere. And ubiquitous the camera certainly is. From dawn to dusk, Mikhail Kaufman, the man with a movie camera, races about town in the back seat of a convertible. He not only visits the workplace and exhausts a long list of recreational sites but rushes to the scene of an accident and is found in the middle of a motorcycle race. He and his tripod ride a carousel and wade into the surf. The camera watches a couple fill out a marriage certificate and then, metaphorically, swings about to watch another couple file for divorce. It is present at the birth of a baby and at a funeral. In this same sequence, there is a remarkable cut between the baby emerging from its mother's womb and the cameraman superimposed upon a v-shaped convergence of buildings. This cut on form appears as a proclamation of the cameraman's own birth from the womb of the urban world.

Few people filmed in *Man with a Movie Camera* object to being the subjects of a film. As the cinema verité filmmakers of the 1960s would rediscover, the goal of observational filmmaking was not so much to hide the camera as it was to find situations in which the camera was not the principal concern of the people being filmed. When this fails in Vertov's work, it is the subject, not the camera, which is suspect. The cameraman, for instance, awakens people sleeping on park benches, some of whom are not pleased to see it. The woman filing for divorce tries to cover her face with her handbag. Later in the film, the cameraman finds his way to the inside of a beer hall, a place of relative disrepute compared to the pristine workers' club we are to see a moment later. In a superimposed image, he rises out of a beer mug placed amid the unsuspecting patrons. Like the Pioneers in *Kinoglaz* who unmask a black marketeer, the cameraman is a spy on remnants of the decadent bourgeois world.

There are other, more overt political overtones to this ubiquitously observational cinema. We are never allowed to forget that the life being caught unawares is the life of a nascent Marxist state and, moreover, the life of that state at a very particular phase of its development. Lenin's New Economic Policy had ended the year before *Man with a Movie Camera* was released. This, in turn, signaled the end of official tolerance for the Soviet middle class that profited from the mixed economy (the "NEP-men"). Hence, in Vertov's film the relationship of the subject with the ubiquitous filmmaking process must be viewed in the context of a transition to a stricter communist practice. There is, for instance, one sequence in the film in which we follow carriages home from the railroad station. A well-dressed woman in a carriage cranks her hand, imitating the cameraman shooting from the car beside her. Certainly, this is a person uncomfortable with the cinema workers going about their business. A few shots later, her driver dumps a steamer trunk out of the carriage onto her maid's shoulder. Vertov has connected her discomfort with the camera to her exploitation of a servant. And in so doing, he has isolated and exposed her, using the camera as a barometer of social involvement.

This condemnation of the NEP-woman is, of course, only possible within the context of film editing. Throughout *Man with a Movie Camera,* we are reminded that the images we are seeing are not only taken from real life but identified as images, the building blocks of montage. They are made of real material, film stock which, at one point in *Man with a Movie Camera,* even appears to break in the projector. The film clips that Svilova pulls off the shelf could have been taken anywhere (and indeed some of them do appear in Vertov's earlier work). In keeping with the spliced geography he had so brilliantly composed in *Sixth Part of the Earth,* Vertov makes no attempt to identify the city we see in *Man with a Movie Camera.* Unlike Walter Ruttmann's *Berlin: Symphony of a Great City* (1927), we are not viewing the cinematic portrait of one place.[4] Vertov shows us a city of cinema, a composite of all the observational images the editor has at her disposal.

Also unlike Ruttmann's film, we are continually reminded that the time frame of Vertov's work is not natural but cinematic: we are not working from sunrise to sunset but to the beat of the apparatus. *Man with a Movie Camera* is framed by a screening—of *Man with a Movie Camera!* When the film within the film begins, we see the Soviet equivalent of "academy leader," the number one rising, which would have been spliced to the beginning of a reel.[5] What we see next is not only a film within a film but the very film being made. The day begins the moment the cameraman starts to make his rounds. For much of the film, the cameraman and editor's activities are intercut until the "day" ends with a screening of the finished film—which now includes its audience. It is, in this way, perfect formalism, not only aware of its own structure but composed of nothing else.

In keeping with the notion of the filmmaker as worker, *Man with a Movie Camera* offers us a recurring visual metaphor for the editor, that of the traffic cop in the busy intersection. It is she who controls the flow of the film images (just as the film stock itself is compared visually to a rapidly passing railroad track seen from above). And it is also her editing that bridges the concepts of "life caught unawares" and the Cinema Eye. For while the images we see are invariably the product of the ubiquitous camera, their arrangement points to visions possible only in cinema. In, for instance, the sports sequence of *Man with a Movie Camera,* the Cinema Eye edits the image of a javelin thrower to that of a soccer goalie—making us both laugh at the incongruity and become aware of the process of editing itself. The joke would not have worked had the film not long since established the nonfiction nature of its images. But it would not exist without supplementing that observational cinema with the fuller possibilities of the medium (in this instance, editing). And it would not be a joke unless we took it for an edit of two unrelated images.

Editing is thus defined as splicing the mechanical to the human, of making "peace between man and machine." In *Man with a Movie Camera*'s climactic sequence, it is the editing between the audience watching the film and the images on the screen that links us, as viewers, with the viewers within the film. Politically (including the politics of Vertov's dispute with the Soviet cinema industry), the point of the montage is to tell us that this is our cinema too. And it is the context from which we may view all of Vertov's uses of the apparatus. In Vertov's experimental construct, the Cinema Eye's slow-motion property even seemed capable of reading a mind. *Man with a Movie Camera* augments that single employment of the apparatus with a deliberately encyclopedic vocabulary of devices. In Vertov's depiction of the hurdlers in the sports sequence, we once again see slow motion, though this time at varying speeds down to the point of freezing the frame. This is cinema used to read the body. Earlier in the film, we saw the speeding up of an image—a young woman stuffing cigarettes in boxes is made to appear as if she is working at superhuman speed. It is her reward for happily chatting to the cameraman and hence the camera's reading of her social involvement (his capturing, as per Vertov's manifesto, of the "worker's love of the workplace"). At the workers' club, the Cinema Eye reverses motion to help chess and checker players set up their pieces. In doing so, the camera, like the workers' club itself, enhances their leisure time.

Throughout *Man with a Movie Camera*, it is not just the man but also the cinematic apparatus that identifies itself as a worker in the new society.

Vertov's split screen allows the speeding trolley cars to pass impossibly close to one another. The Cinema Eye uses a dissolve to make a magician appear "magically" and to take the tarpaulin off a carousel. At the very beginning of the film, our cinema seats are made to fold down for us in stop action animation. And Vertov makes sure that the apparatus gets full credit for these and other useful gestures when the pixilated camera on its tripod takes a bow. In the very last shot of *Man with a Movie Camera*, it is the camera lens/cinema eye closing its iris that ends our cinema day.

For Vertov, *Man with a Movie Camera* was the high point of a busy career. The film was shown widely in the Soviet Union, though more in workers' clubs and other alternative venues than in movie theaters. It was exported and well received abroad. As a result, Vertov was dispatched to western Europe to prepare for the next phase in his own development and in the development of Soviet cinema as a whole: the coming of sound. He was, not surprisingly, as contemptuous of studio sound films as he had always been of studio cinema as a whole. Vertov's response was to work with Soviet engineers to invent an audio equivalent of "life caught unawares," an apparatus that would allow for the shooting of location sound. In the film produced from that shoot, *Enthusiasm: Symphony of the Don Basin* (1930), Vertov finally realized his early dream of concrete music. *Enthusiasm* might also be said to have maintained the aesthetic of the Cinema Eye, expanding it to include the Cinema Ear. Although existing prints of the film are incomplete, it is clear from surviving sequences that Vertov cut the sound with the precision and speed he had previously cut his silent images.

Vertov's next film, *Three Songs of Lenin* (1934), is a far more austere work. Its montage of folk songs about the canonized Bolshevik leader is cut with a respectfully slow cadence. Vertov's documentation of the people who generated those songs remains true to the observational commitment of his earliest work. The film—while skillful, mature, and, at times, even moving—is an example of the heavy hand of Socialist Realism methodically crushing Futurist and formalist experimentation in all of the Soviet arts. Vertov's 1937 feature-length documentary, *Lullaby*, provides yet more evidence of this progression. It is, with its highly posed subjects and staged events, little more than a dutiful propaganda piece.

During the last period of his life, Vertov, while marginalized by the mainstream of Soviet film and its foreign supporters, continued to work. He produced a last feature-length work in 1937, *Sergo Ordzhonikidze*, named for the Soviet commander in the Ukraine during the Russian civil war, and a number of short propaganda pieces during World War II. From the end of the war until his death on February 12, 1954, Vertov worked, as he had at the beginning of his film career, as a newsreel editor. He published a few articles, delivered speeches, and planned films that would never be realized (Feldman).

In the years following his death, Vertov became emblematic of changing tides in cinema theory and practice. We know him today through a series of reconceptualizations that say as much about those who created them as they do about Vertov himself. During the 1950s Khrushchev "thaw," reformers in the Soviet Union began to take an interest in Vertov as an anti-Stalinist gesture. Vertov's writings began appearing in Soviet film journals as an antidote to Socialist Realism. These writings were published in a single volume (*Stat'i, dnevniki, zamysly,* 1966) just as the Khrushchev era of tolerance was beginning to fade.

Vertov was rediscovered in the West in the early 1960s, largely through the efforts of the French film historian Georges Sadoul. Sadoul inadvertently linked the name of Vertov's early newsreel series, *Kinopravda,* to what was then a new form of documentary: he translated the Russian term into its French equivalent, *cinema verité* (Sadoul 1963). Vertov was an inspiration to those cinema verité and French New Wave filmmakers who were taking cameras into the streets and finding their stories in the lives of ordinary people (or, in the case of the New Wave, in actors acting like ordinary people).

Later in the 1960s, Jean-Luc Godard, inspired by the communist and formalist aspects of Vertov's work, formed with his collaborator, Jean-Pierre Gorin, the Dziga Vertov Group. Their project of making worker-generated political documentaries was perhaps the most apt filmic manifestation both of Vertov's original ideal of merging filmmaking with industrial labor and of the revolutionary events in France during May 1968. When the full Russian edition of Vertov's collected writings was translated into French in 1972 (*Articles, journaux, projects*), it was welcomed as a "little red book" for Godard's much-publicized and frequently imitated radical communist filmmaking.

Also during the 1960s, the American avant-garde film movement adopted Vertov as one of the forerunners of its own sensibilities. The Anthology Film Archives in New York screened his films amid those of Germaine Dulac, Man Ray, Maya Deren, Kenneth Anger, and Stan Brakhage. Vertov's *Enthusiasm* was lovingly restored by one of the founders of the Anthology Film Archives, the Austrian archivist and avant-garde filmmaker Peter Kubelka. Vertov's writings—few of which had appeared in English during his lifetime—were translated into English in a piecemeal fashion from the early 1970s. Finally, in 1984, they appeared in a version of the Russian and French collection edited by Annette Michelson (*Kino-Eye* 1984), one of the more highly regarded theorists of the American avant-garde. In 1987, the Harvard film historian Vlada Petric published his book-length shot-by-shot exegesis of *Man with a Movie Camera,* which sought to place Vertov firmly within the avant-garde tradition. Where will we find our next use of Vertov? Citing Vertov's work as archetypal of the early modernist avant-garde is an undertaking that seems to have run its course. Vertov's formalism is rather basic in the light of what it, as a movement, and later structuralism were to become.

Seeing Vertov in the context of cinema history—at the moment of this writing, in this centenary of cinema itself—is somewhat more instructive. For Vertov was the product of a time when it was still just barely possible to avoid the neat categories that now divide film practice. He began his career very shortly after the establishment of Hollywood and the kind of mainstream studio filmmaking it inspired all over the world. When he rejected this mode, there was no clear definition of an alternative, of what Hollywood was not. John Grierson's articulation of the socially conscious nonfiction film, the big "D" documentary, came after Vertov's polemics and early work and owed something to them. But the documentary tradition proper had very little influence in shaping what Vertov was doing.

By the 1920s, avant-garde filmmaking was a tiny but discernible practice. Vertov might well have been aware of the Futurist avant-garde that predated his own work. He was likely aware of the European avant-garde filmmakers of the 1920s—although here, too, this would have most likely taken place after the formulation of his own aesthetic.[6] And, unlike the European avant-garde filmmakers, Vertov had no desire to work outside the mainstream. From the beginning of his career to the end, he saw his aesthetic as the proper enterprise for all of the state's filmmaking. Indeed, that was the entire point of Vertov's work: to end the development of early cinema with a single pure practice, one that would stand as the only realization of the medium's potential as popular culture, political statement, and art. He was, not least of all in his own mind, the last gasp of cinema's invention, the most sophisticated of its primitives. As such, he provides continual incentive to explore other cinematic paths not taken and, as we are deluged with new media, to suggest a model for the exploration of new moving image technologies.

However, to begin to use Vertov in this way, we must face one last time the political context in which he worked. In the post-Soviet world, that context is more than a little suspect. *Man with a Movie Camera* is, along with everything else it is, a hymn of praise to a communist workers' paradise that was already being ridiculed in 1929 and would be a running joke inside and outside the Soviet Union for the next sixty years. The simple and horrible truth is that most of the people we see in the film would, very shortly, begin to suffer in Stalin's purges and the artificial famine he would create in Ukraine during the 1930s. Their industries would be destroyed in World War II. If what we see in *Man with a Movie Camera* appears to be a sunny day in the life of the revolution, we must view the film now with the realization that there remained very few days like it.

If there is anything redemptive in the work Vertov did for Stalin, it is perhaps that his filmmaking proved, in the end, to be antithetical to Stalin's political mission. The marginalization Vertov suffered in his later years was in some ways an inevitable vindication of his ideas. Under Stalin's reign, "life caught unawares" worked all too well. People not deliberately posed for the camera looked as desperate and distraught as they were. Nor could a highly centralized, dictatorial state encourage spontaneous mass participation in its "most important" art form: to do so would have been to subsidize not just an underground cinema but a reevaluation of all aspects of society through the images that had so faithfully recorded it. The proof of this came at last in 1991, when television news, videotapes, and other new instruments of "life caught unawares" were used as tools in the destruction of Stalin's much-corrupted heirs.

What would Vertov have made of this moment? Here was a guinea pig of mechanical perception, a man who, thirty-five years before Marshall McLuhan used the phrase, was thinking of media as "the extensions of man" (McLuhan). Vertov editing footage of the civil war at the Moscow Cinema Committee was the prototype of the net surfer downloading bits and pieces of fragmented information. Vertov the filmmaker—and advocate of mass filmmaking—could well be thought of as a pioneer in the building of a system in which millions of people reconstruct those fragments, building personalized multimedia websites that are then made available to millions of others. Vertov the manifesto writer was, like so many writers today, trying to find the words for what all this meant and how it might be used for some greater good. Certainly, were Vertov alive today he would be pleased to see that the Cinema Eye has never been more potent—or busier. And he would agree that never in human history have we so desperately needed to make peace between people and their machines.

NOTES

1. For a firsthand history of the period, see Viktor Shklovsky, *Mayakovsky and His Circle*, ed. and trans. Lily Feiler (New York: Dodd, Mead, 1972).

2. All quotations from Vertov's writings are my own translations; citations refer to corresponding passages in Vertov, *Kino-Eye*.

3. The statement was reportedly made by Lenin during a conversation with his Minister of Culture, Anatoli Lunacharsky, in 1922. It appears in a letter written by Lunacharsky in 1925.

4. Ruttmann appears to have been aware of Vertov's work prior to making *Berlin*. See Siegfried Kracauer's *From Caligari to Hitler: A Psychological History of the German Film* (Princeton: Princeton University Press, 1947), 185.

5. In the single projector venues in which the film was most often screened in the Soviet Union, this would have been the second time the audience saw the number one rising.

6. In a 1926 diary entry, for instance, Vertov discusses René Clair's 1924 film, *Paris qui dort (Kino-Eye* 163). He toured western Europe in 1929 and again in 1931. In addition, Vertov's youngest brother, Boris Kaufman, worked as Jean Vigo's cameraman from 1929 to 1933.

WORKS CITED

Feldman, Seth. *Dziga Vertov: A Guide to References and Resources.* Boston: G. K. Hall, 1979.

Gans, Alexi. "Constructivism." In *The Documents of Twentieth Century Art: The Tradition of Constructivism,* ed. Stephen Bann and trans. John Bowlt, 32–42. London: Thames and Hudson, 1974.

Leyda, Jay. *Kino: A History of the Russian and Soviet Film.* New York: Collier Books, 1960.

McLuhan, Marshall. *Understanding Media: The Extensions of Man.* New York: Signet, 1964.

Petric, Vlada. *Constructivism in Film: The Man with the Movie Camera, a Cinematic Analysis.* Cambridge: Cambridge University Press, 1987.

Sadoul, Georges. "Actualité de Dziga Vertov." *Cahiers du cinema* 144 (1963): 23, 31.

Vertov, Dziga. *Articles, journaux, projects.* Trans. Andree Robel and Sylviane Mossé. Paris: *Cahiers du cinema,* 1972.

———. *Kino-Eye: The Writings of Dziga Vertov.* Ed. Annette Michelson and trans. Kevin O'Brien. Berkeley: University of California Press, 1984.

———. *Stat'i, dnevniki, zamysly.* Ed. Sergei Drobashenko. Moscow: Iskusstvo, 1966.

Chapter 3

PARADISE REGAINED

Sergei Eisenstein's *Que viva México!* as Ethnography

Joanne Hershfield

> During my encounter with Mexico, it seemed to me to be, in all the variety of its contradictions, a sort of outward projection of all those individual lines and features which I carried and carry within me like a tangle of complexes.
>
> Sergei Eisenstein, *Immoral Memories: An Autobiography*

INTRODUCTION

There is a telling photograph of the Soviet director, Sergei Eisenstein, taken in Merida, Mexico, during the filming of his historical epic, *Que viva México!* (1932). A film cameraman stands in the foreground with his back to us, lining up a shot through his viewfinder. From the viewer's perspective, it appears that the shot will be composed along three planes extending vertically from the bottom of the film frame to the top: on the first plane, three white skulls are arranged in a horizontal row; Eisenstein sits on the ground above the skulls, and beyond him, on a third plane, stands a group of black-robed monks bearing a cross. While the shot as it appears in the film will not include the director, his presence, if not his body, permeates *Que viva México!*[1]

Previous studies of Eisenstein's attempt to compose a film based on Mexican history have focused on the film's production history, on the relation of the unfinished film to the director's larger body of work, and on his theoretical investigations into the nature of cinema. My interest here is to move away from a study of the filmmaker-as-theorist toward an examination of *Que viva México!* as ethnography. In this essay, I will suggest that Eisenstein's sojourn in Mexico, his collecting of over 170,000 feet of cinematic material, and his writings and drawings about his experiences may be considered as a form of ethnographic fieldwork. I want to point to the ideological implications of a work that, for too long, has been considered only for its part in a more narrow discourse about cinematic theories.

ETHNOGRAPHY AND FILMMAKING

Ethnographic filmmaking had not yet been recognized as a scientific endeavor when Eisenstein came to Mexico in 1931.[2] However, since the birth of the cinema, filmmakers have expressed an unwavering interest in other, "exotic" cultures. As early as 1898, an Edison cameraman filmed two Pueblo Indian ritual dances, the Eagle Dance and the Wand Dance. In 1913, geographer and explorer Robert Flaherty, often referred to as the "father" of the ethnographic film, took an old Bell and Howell into the Canadian Northwest territories and spent the next three years "documenting" the life of the Eskimo people who lived there. He edited his footage and presented to the world *Nanook of the North* (1922), which he described as a "series of ethnological moving pictures of Eskimo life, which show the primitive existence of a people in the way they lived before being brought in contact with explorers" (quoted in Barnouw 35). While there had been films about aboriginal peoples before *Nanook,*[3] this film has gone down in anthropological and film history as marking the birth of ethnographic film (Heider 20).

Film and ethnography share a number of conventional narrative and representational qualities. Historically, anthropologists have tended to write about their subjects using narrative structures derived from fictional genres. Similarly, ethnographic filmmakers organize their films based on models developed in classical narrative film. Thus it is not surprising to find that Flaherty had "mastered the grammar of film . . . as it had evolved in fiction film," anticipating "editing problems, providing crucial close-ups, reverse angles, and a few panoramic movements and tilts to yield moments of revelation" (Barnouw 39). When it was released, critics hailed *Nanook* as "more dramatic" than so-called "dramatic works of the screen" (Barnouw 42).

Working at the same time as Flaherty, anthropologists like Bronislav Malinowski used literary techniques to make their fieldwork more available to their readers. This involved narrativizing and dramatizing their field notes and experiences and providing a narrative voice to carry the reader through the text (Clifford 29).

Film and television have intensified literary and scholarly productions of other cultures by making the Other more visible. As Ella Shohat and Robert Stam note, "if the culture of empire authorized the pleasure of seizing ephemeral glimpses of its 'margins' through travel and tourism, the nineteenth century invention of the photographic and later the cinematographic camera made it possible to record such glimpses" (104). If Flaherty's *Nanook* can be seen as a fiction film staged as an ethnography, then *Que viva México!* may be regarded as ethnography staged as fiction film, enacting what Shohat and Stam define as a "historiographical and anthropological role, writing (in light) the cultures of others" (145). Moreover, as critics like James Clifford have shown us, the interpretive activity of the ethnographer (or the filmmaker) can no longer "be considered innocent" (41), for such ethnographies must be seen as "constructed domains of truth, serious fictions" that are as dependent on "strategies of writing and representation" from particular points of view as they are on scientific ethnographic practices (10).

BACKGROUND TO THE PRODUCTION
OF *QUE VIVA MÉXICO!*

In 1930, Eisenstein was invited by Paramount Pictures to make a film in Hollywood. Unable to agree on a suitable project, the relationship was terminated and the Soviet filmmaker was left stranded in the United States, without finances, looking for another project. Finally, with support from the American writer Upton Sinclair and his wife, Mary, Eisenstein left for Mexico in December with his cameraman, Eduard Tisse, and his assistant, Grigori Alexandrov, intent on making a history of that country. Promising to honor the Sinclairs' injunction to make a "non-political film," Eisenstein told his funders that *Que viva México!* would instead be "a rhythmic and musical construction and an unrolling of the Mexican spirit and character" (*Immoral Memories* 180).

Eisenstein's visit to Mexico in 1932 and his film *Que viva México!* are often credited with influencing both the style and content of the Mexican classical cinema.[4] However, there is substantial evidence that Eisenstein's Mexican film was inspired by his previous exposure to postrevolutionary Mexican theater and art. For example, while involved in a 1920 theatrical production of Jack London's story "The Mexican" (1911), Eisenstein read extensively about Mexico (Geduld and Gottesman 3–4). Six years later he met and became friendly with the Mexican painter Diego Rivera, who was visiting Moscow.

In the 1920s, Mexican artists such as Rivera and David Siqueiros were part of a postrevolutionary intellectual and political nationalist project that promoted the ideology of *indigenismo,* which argued that the roots of Mexican identity lay in Mexico's pre-Columbian Indian past. The art of Rivera, Siqueiros, José Clemente Orozco, and Frida Kahlo celebrated and borrowed from everything that was Indian: the clothing, religious rituals and iconography, as well as indigenous arts and crafts.[5]

One of Eisenstein's biographers, Marie Seton, observed the Mexican influence on *Que viva México!,* writing that one of the film's compositions "was a dynamic interpretation of David Siqueiros' unfinished and mutilated fresco, *Burial of a Worker*" (198). According to Eisenstein's own notes, a never-finished section of the film was to have been based on Orozco's fresco, *Las soldaderas.* And there are other indications that he brought these Mexican influences back to the Soviet Union. Inga Karetnikova and her coauthor Leon Steinmetz suggest, for example, that a shot from *Ivan the Terrible* (1944–46) "was influenced by the director's impressions of the endless stream of pilgrims crawling to the shrine of the Lady of Guadalupe in the immense vastness of the Mexican landscape" (30).

While Eisenstein may have been paying homage to Mexican postrevolutionary art in *Que viva México!,* the film's structure and its compositions are grounded in his evolving theories of a political and intellectual cinema evident in his last two silent films, *October* (1928) and *The Old and the New (The General Line)* (1929). Eisenstein was working out his ideas of film montage in these early films. According to montage theory, a film's meaning emerges not in the content or narrative structure of a film or through the indexical relation between the photographic image and the real object it represents, but through editing practices.

Eisenstein wrote that montage "is exactly what we do in the cinema, combining shots that are *depictive,* single in meaning, neutral in content—into *intellectual* contexts and series" ("Cinematographic Principle" 30). Eisenstein did not consider the meaning of a single shot apart from its inscription within a "phrase." According to his principles of montage, the intellectual link between the shots or "cells" of the montage phrase is produced through dialectical conflict among a series of shots. This dialectical organizing device also functions at the larger structural level of a film's narrative ("Cinematographic Principle" 38–40). As will be seen in the following discussion, *Que viva México!* is organized through such dialectical juxtapositions of shots, sequences, and chapters.

Most scholars of Eisenstein's work have focused on the formal structures of his films, examining the use of cinematic montage as a "collision" of shots within the frame involving conflicts of scales, volumes, masses, depths, distance, and light. Other critics have looked at the connection between Eisenstein's conception of historical progression and the political and ideological development of Soviet Marxism. More recently, a number of writers have noted how his quasi-historical films seem more concerned with formal and personal experimentation than with political ideology.[6] What has generally been ignored, however, is the way in which montage in Eisenstein's films surfaces as an opposition based on sexual difference.

This construction is grounded not merely in representations of gendered characters but in qualities Judith Mayne defines as abstract versus concrete and passive versus active—qualities that align themselves discursively as gendered female and male, respectively. While most histories of Soviet cinema suggest that Eisenstein, Lev Kuleshov, and Dziga Vertov developed cinematic montage as a specifically political aesthetic, Mayne argues that dialectical montage also presents a formal situation in which "the drama of opposition between the poles of activity and passivity is reenacted" (31) and that these oppositions take the form of sexual differences that are repeatedly portrayed as "natural" (31–34). For example, Mayne argues that *October* "may well celebrate the working-class solidarity of revolution, but it does so in a way that draws heavily on a sexually polarized view of the world, not to mention the revolution" (50). Mayne's larger argument is that though Soviet films were intended to "produce" socialism, it was also the case that the narratives often replicated conventional binary structures of sexual opposition. This opposition figures prominently in *Que viva México!*, a film Eisenstein himself said would "trace the theme of relationships between man and woman" (*Selected Works* 43–44).

Critics have commented on the hostile views of sexuality held by the Soviet Stalinists that resulted in censorship of sexual and erotic representation in art, literature, and cinema. Ian Christie proposes that Eisenstein's Mexican sojourn provided the director with "more personal and social freedom than he enjoyed at any other time in his life," and that Eisenstein started "drawing again with an intensity which would continue for the rest of his life" (30). These drawings were dominated by images of castration, erotically blasphemous representations of religious themes, and erotic iconography, and exemplify, according to Christie, the young director's obsessive intellectual attempt to "solve the equations of sexual difference" (22). If Stalinism demanded an intellectual response from a work of art, Peter Wollen argues generally that, for Eisenstein, "art remained a 'structure of pathos,' which produced emotional effects in the spectator," and specifically that "the primary, underlying level of thought is sensuous and imagistic . . . at the root of *Que viva México!*" (49–50).

QUE VIVA MÉXICO!

Eisenstein never completed *Que viva México!* although a number of different films were made from the considerable footage the director shipped back to the United States for processing.[7] The most recent version, released in 1979, was edited by Eisenstein's friend and collaborator, Grigori Alexandrov. Although it remains, as Laura Podalsky puts it, "a sadly incomplete document" (28), when read in relation to Eisenstein's notes and letters, his Mexican drawings and essays, Alexandrov's film does provide us with a blueprint of what could have been Eisenstein's "history" of Mexico.

In his script outline, Eisenstein envisioned four episodes dialectically bound together by three intertwined themes of life, death, and rebirth, and framed by a Prologue and an Epilogue. Writing in 1937, Eisenstein noted that he had conceived of the entire film as being "constructed like a necklace . . . [a] chain of novellas held together by a set of linking ideas" (*Selected Works* 43). According to the outline, the whole piece would "traverse the gradations of history" and would be bound together "not so much by chronological epochs as by geographical zones." Each section would also be defined by the notion of a larger historical epoch: the "Primitive" era of Mexican history; its prerevolutionary Catholicism; the revolutionary period; and, lastly, modernity. He imagined that "at every step one sees birth mingled with death" (quoted in Karetnikova and Steinmetz 19–20).

Alexandrov's translation preserves the Prologue and three of the four novels: "Sandunga," "Fiesta," and "Maguey." The footage for "Soldadera" was never shot, so that all that remains of this section are Eisenstein's notes, his drawings, and a number of still photos.

Prologue

Eisenstein intended to begin his "film-symphony" with a short piece that would introduce what he perceived to be history's direct link with the present. He writes: "In the land of Yucatan, among heathen temples, holy cities and majestic pyramids. In the realms of death, where the past still prevails over the present, there the starting-point of our film is laid" (*Que viva México!* 27).

The six-and-a-half-minute Prologue, divided into three distinct sections, is composed of eighty shots accompanied by traditional Yucatecan or Mayan music and drums. The opening montage and narration introduces the primary "characters" of the film—"stones . . . gods . . . people." While these characters may have been influenced to a certain extent by the ideology of Mexican intellectual *indigenismo*, we can also see traces of

Eisenstein's earlier film, *Battleship Potemkin* (1925), in which he tried to work out his theory of "typage." According to this theory, characters are not representations of individuals but of "types" of people, usually defined by social class, whose function in the narrative becomes apparent through dialectical montage rather than through psychological or visual coding.

After *October,* however, Eisenstein moved away from a specifically political use of typage toward what Jacques Aumont defines as "symbolic typage." According to Aumont, this use of typage is neither politically nor morally motivated but instead signifies "something much more archetypal . . . transhistorical . . . [and] precarious" (142–43). It is precisely this archetypal quality that describes the characters in *Que viva México!*[8] For example, the second section of the Prologue depicts the funeral of a young Indian who symbolizes Mexico's indigenous populations. The narration informs us that the funeral functions as "a symbol of recalling the past, as a farewell rite to the ancient Maya civilization."

The third section of the Prologue emphasizes the dialectically opposed thematic of life, announcing that "time flows slowly [in Mexico] . . . the way of life remains unchanged." Life, sexuality, and the animalistic quality of the people are emphasized through a montage of images of nature, sexuality, and procreation. This third section also introduces the theme of male and female relations with which Eisenstein intended to bind together the segments of the film and the history of Mexico, as noted above.

Sandunga

The first novel, "Sandunga," is set in the southern tropical pre-Columbian region of Tehuantepec, one of Eisenstein's "geographical zones" that is supposed to signify Mexico's "primitive" era. Eisenstein wanted to emphasize the "primitive" epoch of Mexican history through the "primitive" nature of a young girl and boy, "two creatures living almost like biological 'particles' of a carefree tropical paradise before the discoveries of Columbus and the conquests of Cortés" (*Selected Works* 43). The sequence thus centers on the courtship and marriage of a young Indian girl named Concepción and her lover, Abundio.

"Sandunga" symbolizes the end of "the romance of Tehuantepec" and the "romantic" era of Mexican history. Eisenstein again reduces a number of complex and relatively advanced societies to the realm of an isolated and rural aboriginal culture living in a mythical paradise. His representation of pre-Columbian Mexico evolved from the realm of an imaginary history that reduces the heterogeneity and complexity of pre-Columbian societies and ignores its local differences. His Indian "types," childlike, ignorant,

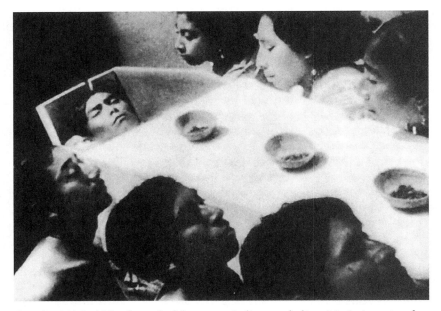

Que viva México!: The funeral of the young Indian symbolizes Mexico's past and the country's indigenous population.

and sensual, meant to symbolize the mythical indigenous Mexican proto-type, bear little relation to the diverse ethnic and linguistic groups living in Mexico in 1519 when the Spaniards arrived.

Historians of Mexico have noted the social and technical sophistication to which many pre-Columbian cultures had evolved before the invasion of the Spanish.[9] Many of these groups, such as the Aztecs, had achieved a level of complex social, cultural, and economic organization that is in no way depicted in either Alexandrov's version of *Que viva México!* or Eisenstein's own notes for the film.

Fiesta

The second novel, "Fiesta," is set during the prerevolutionary dictatorship of General Porfirio Díaz, the army commander who seized power in 1876 after the death of the Indian president Benito Juárez.[10] This section focuses on the colonial Spanish influence on Mexican culture and social practices. Eisenstein wrote that he wanted to exhibit "all the beauty that the Spaniards have brought with them into Mexican life" (*Que viva México!* 69). (Although filming for this section was never completed, Alexandrov was able to produce a coherent piece from Eisenstein's notes.) "Fiesta"'s narrative revolves around a bullfight that takes place during the annual religious celebration of the Fiesta of the Holy Virgin of Guadalupe. The film makes clear that the two rituals are divided by class: the bullfight is attended by the upper-class white *criollos* while the religious ceremony is observed by the Indians and *mestizos* who make up the lower classes.[11]

Eisenstein mistakenly marks the religious festival as an annual remembrance of the Spanish conquest of Mexico. In actuality, the ritual is enacted in devotion to Mexico's Indian Virgin and patron saint, the Virgin of Guadalupe. According to legend, a dark-skinned apparition of the Virgin Mary appeared to an Indian named Juan Diego in 1531, just ten years after the Spanish destroyed the Aztec city of Tenochtitlán. Although the Catholic Church officially recognized the validity of Juan Diego's vision and allowed a small shrine to be built on Tonantzin's hill, the "cult" of the Virgin of Guadalupe, as this dark-skinned Mary came to be known, was not immediately sanctioned.[12]

In "Fiesta," the primitiveness and purity of the Indians' penitential worship of the Indian Virgin is contrasted with the sophistication and decadence of the Spanish community. In dialectic fashion, the sequence cuts back and forth between scenes of peasants crawling on their hands and knees up the sacred hill of the Virgin in blind devotion and images of a matador preparing for the slaughtering of a bull and an adulterous embrace with a married woman. While the Indians are portrayed as engaging in what appears to be primitive and ecstatic religious rites of dancing and praying, the matador partakes of decadent bourgeois practices. The image of the "real" Mexican as pure and primal is played dialectically against the representation of the civilized and sexually corrupt European.

Maguey

While "Fiesta" takes place in the context of the upper-class Spanish colonial society, "Maguey"[13] is set in the northern arid region of Hidalgo, home to large feudal haciendas that ruled peasant life at the turn of the century. This section sets apart the indigenous populations from the landowning *criollo* elite. Eighty percent of Mexico's Indians and peasants worked in agriculture and were bound to hacienda lords through a feudal system of peonage and indentured servitude. Under the administration of General Díaz (1876–1911), most of the material wealth of Mexico was held by a small upper-class elite and by foreign investors. During this thirty-year dictatorship, real wages fell, the mortality rate among the lower classes rose, and by

1910 most of the indigenous population had lost their communal farmlands to larger domestic and foreign commercial interests (Cockcroft 10–11). The economic structure of the Porfiriato, as this historical time period is called, was nothing short of "wage-debt slavery," according to James Cockcroft (91).

"Maguey" tells the tragic story of María and Sebastian, peons in the feudal estate of the Hacienda de Tetlapayac. This area represents a Mexico that the historian Howard F. Cline situates at the "edge of the national economy and its political and social life," where the Indians of the poor area seem to exist outside of history (111–12). In the film, the Indians are visually situated within a vast and deserted landscape that was to become the visual theme of Mexican director Emilio "el Indio" Fernández and cinematographer Gabriel Figueroa. The Indians and the landscape are set apart from civilization, which is enclosed and protected within the high walls of the hacienda. María and Sebastian have no community or home outside of the inhospitable maguey deserts.

Eisenstein uses this tale to serve as an allegory of the rise to revolutionary class consciousness of the Mexican peasantry and to lay out what he sees as the basis for the Mexican revolution—the "rape" of the peasant class by the ruling class. In this historical allegory, María and Sebastian function as "types," standing in as the "mass protagonists" of Mexico's revolutionary class. María symbolizes the feminized nation of Mexico.[14] These male and female figures also function dialectically along the sexually gendered axis discussed above. María is presented as passive and pure. A commodity to be traded between men, she is given to Sebastian by her father and, in turn, Sebastian must "loan" her to the landlord of the hacienda (the narrative informs us that "every bride-to-be must be presented to the master"). In contrast, Sebastian's character is much more concrete; as male, he is depicted as the "active" protagonist, a symbol of the power of the masses.

When María is raped by the landlord's henchmen, Sebastian turns upon the landowner in revenge. The landowner's favorite daughter joins the guards as they chase Sebastian out into the desolate landscape surrounding the hacienda. She is subsequently killed in a fierce gun battle. In retaliation, Sebastian and his comrades are buried up to their necks in sand and trampled to death by the henchmen's horses.

La Soldadera *and the Epilogue*

As noted, Alexandrov used existing still photographs, documentary footage, and Eisenstein's script notes to construct a version of the final chapter of the film. The director had indicated that this story was to take place during the time of the protracted battles of the Mexican Revolution, from 1910 "until peace and the new order of Modern Mexico were established," and was to focus on the "woman who follows the soldier—the Soldadera" (*Que viva México!* 78).[15] The *soldadera* was to represent the procreative power (and duty) of women and the possibility of "New Life." He had planned on using a famous *corrida* (a Mexican form of the popular ballad) about a heroic *soldadera* named Adelita to accompany the battle scenes. In his script outline for this section, Eisenstein envisions a woman named Pancha who accompanies her soldier/husband on his revolutionary march toward freedom. When he is killed in battle, Pancha attaches herself to another soldier in order to serve him.

Eisenstein was also not able to complete the Epilogue, although he did manage to shoot important footage for this final sequence, a procession celebrating All Souls' Day, the Mexican Day of the Dead (*el dia del muerte*) in modern-day Mexico. Eisenstein dedicated this final sequence to José Guadalupe Posada, a Mexican artist known for his macabre drawings of costumed skeletons based on popular songs and ballads.

The Epilogue was to exemplify the "ways of peace, prosperity and civilization" and to reemphasize both the idea of the connection between the past and the present in Mexico and the oppositional structure of life and death threading through the whole film. For Eisenstein, this structure was emblematic of the Mexican people's "victory over death" through their "striving devotedly to achieve a single, socialist ideal of society" (*Selected Works* 44).

James Goodwin suggests that Eisenstein intended the ending to be not merely a celebration of Mexico's revolutionary classes but also a "critique of contemporary Mexico, an act of unmasking which represents the continuation of class struggle. At the end of the procession, the bourgeoisie removes masks only to reveal human skulls; workers and peasants remove mask skulls to reveal smiling faces" (136). For Goodwin, this sequence characterizes Eisenstein's belief in the revolutionary potential of Mexico's cultural heritage in the 1930s.

However, by the 1930s the indigenous populations of Mexico had dwindled to increasingly isolated pockets of small rural villages. The primary social and ethnic group in Mexico was *mestizo* and the various alliances among this group were complex. As the *mestizo* became more urbanized, connection to any Indian ancestry was often lost or ignored in the quest for social and economic assimilation.

The Indians of Mexico were neither the proletariat of Europe that Marx envisioned in his thesis of social and class revolution nor the peasants of the classic Russian serfdom in whose cause the Bolshevik revolution was waged. Eisenstein's mythical Indian, who personified for the director the

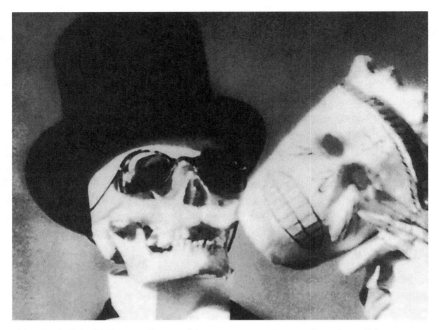

Que viva México!: The act of unmasking represents the continuation of class struggle.

hypothetical links between past, present, and future, barely even existed in Mexico in the 1930s.

CONCLUSION

I have argued that Eisenstein's *Que viva México!* is a crucial document to investigate, not merely as an example of the practice of montage theory but for the way in which it represents an encounter between Self and Other. In his autobiography, Eisenstein reveals his preoccupations with this Other, writing that "it is here in *tierra caliente* [burning earth] that I come to know the fantastic structure of prelogical, sensuous thinking—not only from the pages of anthropological investigations, but from daily communion with those descendants of the Aztecs and Toltecs, Mayas, or Huichole who have managed to carry unharmed through the ages that meandering thought" (*Immoral Memories* 211). In passages such as these, Eisenstein discloses that he, like many other travelers and artists, was temporarily seduced by what Westerners perceived as the erotic nature of non-Western peoples and cultures.

Eisenstein transformed Mexico into an erotic Other in order to play out his theories of cinema and explore the previously unconscious workings of the self. Christie asks whether Mexico "makes possible Eisenstein's fullest exploration of his hitherto repressed sexuality," noting that "Mexico's montage of the primitive, the sensual and the religious seems to have reconnected him with whatever was lost during the emotional traumas of his childhood, or repressed during adolescence and youth" (20). Whether or not Eisenstein used his experience in Mexico to come to terms with his repressed homosexuality, as some of his biographers have suggested, the fact is that Mexico became the surface through which he tried to know his self.[16] My concern in this essay has been less with the "problem" of Eisenstein's sexuality than with his use of Mexico, Mexican history, and the Mexican people in his filmmaking. Like many cinematic ethnographic encounters, the terrain of the Other became, for Eisenstein, an exotic backdrop for self-exploration.

Sergei Eisenstein's personal journey through Mexico might have been intended as a cinematic narrative depicting the Mexican people's role in the dialectic of history. However, in his search for personal meaning, Eisenstein charted a cinematic allegory of Mexican history as a single "path through modernity," collapsing the heterogeneity of indigenous and *mestizo* populations into an originary people, innocent and happy in the tropical paradise of Tehuantepec. Eisenstein's vision was not unique, however. Clifford notes that "something similar occurs whenever marginal peoples come into a historical or ethnographic space that has been defined by the Western imagination . . . their distinct histories quickly vanish" (5). If, as Karetnikova and Steinmetz profess, there were "three Mexicos" for Eisenstein—the imaginary, the real, and the remembered (4)—then *Que viva México!* is surely a documentary of the first kind.

NOTES

My thanks to Jeannette Sloniowski and Barry Keith Grant for their helpful comments on earlier drafts of this essay. The title of my essay is from a comment in Eisenstein's autobiography, *Immoral Memories*, wherein he refers to "a new return to drawing," lost, and then "found in Mexico" (44).

1. In Grigori Alexandrov's edited version, this photograph appears in the second novel, "Fiesta," as part of the celebration of the Virgin of Guadalupe and the remembrance of the Spanish Conquest.

2. It wasn't until 1950, when Gregory Bateson and Margaret Mead released six films on Balinese culture they had made in the 1930s, that "ethnography and film

were finally brought together," according to anthropologist and filmmaker Karl G. Heider (27).

3. See, for example, Edward Curtis's films about indigenous American peoples, including *In the Land of the War Canoes* (1914).

4. Eduardo de la Vega Alfaro sums up the various arguments regarding Eisenstein's influence on Mexican cinema. For some Mexican critics, his film "led to a perfectly anti-cinematic hieraticism and folkloricism," while for others, he was "the authentic 'father' of Mexican cinematic art." According to de la Vega, "Eisenstein did not invent the aesthetics of Mexican cinema . . . but he did nudge it in [inevitable] directions" (81).

5. See Charles Ramírez Berg, "Figueroa's Skies and Oblique Perspective: Notes on the Development of the Classical Mexican Style," *Spectator* 13, no. 1 (1992): 24–41. Ramírez Berg cites the painters Guadalupe Posada (1852–1913) and Gerardo Murillo (a.k.a. Dr. Atl, 1875–1964), both of whom adapted elements from popular culture as well as Mayan and Aztec art, as two of the major influences on both this nationalist project and the classical Mexican cinematic style (28).

6. For example, David Bordwell argues that the director's early aesthetic explorations in *Strike* (1924) and *October* were more aligned with processes of "mythmaking" than with "historical fidelity" (62), while Bill Nichols suggests that Eisenstein's greatest contribution lies not in his development of montage theory but in "what he contributed to a blurred border zone of fiction and nonfiction joined together for the purposes of historical representation" (xv). Finally, Jacques Aumont contends that the Soviet epoch served merely as a backdrop for most of Eisenstein's films and that within this backdrop history functioned as a "mine of metaphors" and a "convenient idea" (19–22). Aumont also argues that Eisenstein's appropriation of history "is anything but innocent" and situates the filmmaker's project as being "complicit with the Stalinist version, which fixes all individuals, groups, and concrete forces according to their place within history as a whole . . . [and] subject to revision" (23).

7. The processed dailies initially remained with the Sinclairs. After their final break with Eisenstein, they sold much of the footage to various people in an attempt to recoup their losses. With this footage Sol Lester made two films, *Thunder over Mexico* and *Death Day* (both 1933), and Marie Seton produced a short and incomplete film called *Time in the Sun* (1939). Interestingly, the French film production company Pathé made a number of ethnographic films with the footage.

8. Aumont is careful to note that symbolic typage was "never conceived of in such terms by Eisenstein" but at the same time argues that the director "would have without any doubt claimed [the definition] as his own" (143).

9. See, for example, Cockcroft, who writes that "the scientific, artistic, architectural, and state-building achievements of these pre-Columbian societies could not have occurred without the production of an economic surplus . . . a significant division of labor, a degree of political centralization . . . a growth in long-distance trade

and . . . the concentration of people into cities often more densely populated than any in Europe" (11).

10. In his outline, Eisenstein placed "Fiesta" as the third novel in the prerevolutionary period. It is unclear why Alexandrov chose to switch the sequences around.

11. The term *criollos* (those of European descent) served to designate Mexicans descended from "pure" Spanish ancestry. By the 1920s, light-skinned *criollos* and *mestizos* (Mexicans of mixed Spanish and Indian blood) comprised the economically and politically dominant classes while darker-skinned Indians occupied the lowest rung of society.

12. Not until a hundred years after Juan Diego's vision, when a Spanish bishop initiated a program to bring the straying Indians back into the fold of the Church, was the Virgin of Guadalupe officially established as Mexico's own Indian Virgin. The indigenous populations were thus persuaded to incorporate into their conceptual understanding certain "meanings" presented to them by the Catholic Church. The development of a particular form of Mexican Catholicism was thus a merging of the indigenous mystical, ritualistic religion with the new Christian one. This new version was eventually personified in the figure of the Virgin of Guadalupe.

13. The maguey is a cactus-like plant from which the Indians extract a milky, extremely intoxicating drink known as pulque.

14 Aumont notes a similar use of the female body in Eisenstein's *Old and New*, writing that the female character Martha "is not only the emblem of the Russian peasant, but also the Russian soil, and earth-mother par excellence" (94).

15. As a number of writers have noted, women were actively involved in the revolutionary struggle as *soldaderas*, or female "soldiers." See Ilene O'Malley, *The Myth of the Revolution: Hero Cults and the Institutionalization of the Mexican State, 1920–1940* (New York: Greenwood Press, 1986) and Elizabeth Salas, *Soldaderas in the Mexican Military: Myth and History* (Austin: University of Texas Press, 1990).

16. Christie writes that "we may never know how his experiences there affected what was certainly an ambiguous sexuality, but the 'unresolved' Oedipal conflict running through most of his subsequent projects is apparent" (50).

WORKS CITED

Aumont, Jacques. *Montage Eisenstein*. Trans. Lee Hildreth, Constance Penley, and Andrew Ross. Bloomington: Indiana University Press, 1987.

Barnouw, Erik. *Documentary: A History of Non-Fiction Film*. London: Oxford University Press, 1977.

Bordwell, David. *The Cinema of Eisenstein*. Cambridge, MA: Harvard University Press, 1993.

Christie, Ian. "Introduction: Rediscovering Eisenstein." In *Eisenstein Rediscovered*, ed. Ian Christie and Richard Taylor, 1–30. London: Routledge, 1993.

Clifford, James. *The Predicament of Culture: Twentieth-Century Ethnography, Literature, and Art.* Cambridge, MA: Harvard University Press, 1988.

Cline, Herbert F. *Mexico: Revolution to Evolution, 1940–1960.* New York: Oxford University Press, 1963.

Cockcroft, James D. *Mexico: Class Formation, Capital Accumulation, and the State.* New York: Monthly Review Press, 1983.

de la Vega Alfaro, Eduardo. "Origins, Development and Crisis of the Sound Cinema (1929–64)." In *Mexican Cinema,* ed. Paulo Antonio Paranaguá and trans. Ana M. López, 79–93. London: British Film Institute, 1995.

Eisenstein, Sergei. "The Cinematographic Principle and the Ideogram." In *Film Form,* trans. Jay Leyda, 28–44. New York: Meridian Books, 1957.

———. *Immoral Memories: An Autobiography.* Trans. Herbert Marshall. Boston: Houghton Mifflin, 1983.

———. *Que viva México!* New York: Amo Press/*New York Times,* 1972.

———. *S. M. Eisenstein, Selected Works: Volume II, Towards a Theory of Montage.* Trans. Michael Glenny. Ed. Michael Glenny and Richard Taylor. London: British Film Institute, 1988.

Geduld, Harry M., and Ronald Gottesman, eds. *Sergei Eisenstein and Upton Sinclair: The Making and Unmaking of* Que viva México! Bloomington: Indiana University Press, 1970.

Goodwin, James. *Eisenstein, Cinema, and History.* Urbana: University of Illinois Press, 1993.

Heider, Karl G. *Ethnographic Film.* Austin: University of Texas Press, 1976.

Karetnikova, Inga, and Leon Steinmetz. *Mexico According to Eisenstein.* Albuquerque: University of New Mexico Press, 1991.

Mayne, Judith. *Kino and the Woman Question: Feminism and Soviet Silent Film.* Columbus: Ohio State University Press, 1989.

Nichols, Bill. *Blurred Boundaries: Questions of Meaning in Contemporary Culture.* Bloomington: Indiana University Press, 1994.

Podalsky, Laura. "Patterns of the Primitive: Sergei Eisenstein's *Que viva México!* In *Mediating Two Worlds: Cinematic Encounters in the Americas,* ed. John King, Ana M. Lopez, and Manuel Alvarado, 25–39. London: British Film Institute, 1993.

Said, Edward. *Orientalism.* New York: Vintage Books, 1979.

Seton, Marie. *Sergei Eisenstein.* New York: Wyn, 1952.

Shohat, Ella, and Robert Stam. *Unthinking Eurocentrism: Multiculturalism and the Media.* London: Routledge, 1994.

Wollen, Peter. *Signs and Meaning in the Cinema.* Bloomington: Indiana University Press, 1969.

Chapter 4

SYNTHETIC VISION

The Dialectical Imperative of Luis Buñuel's *Las Hurdes*

Vivian Sobchack

Everything leads me to believe that there is a certain point in the life of the spirit at which life and death, the real and the imagined, the past and the future, the communicable and the incommunicable, the exalted and the lowly, cease to be seen as contradictory. One would search in vain in the whole spectrum of surrealist insight for anything except the exact point where one could hope to determine where these contradictions fall away.

André Breton, *Second Surrealist Manifesto*

Every concept is rational, is abstractly opposed to another, and is united in comprehension together with its opposite. This is the definition of dialectic.

G. W. F. Hegel, *The Encyclopedia of Philosophical Science*

Luis Buñuel's *Las Hurdes* (*Land without Bread/Tierra sin pan*, 1932) is a film of undeniable power. Indeed, alternately or simultaneously viewed as a bizarre surrealist film and an extraordinarily searing social documentary, this short work has often provoked and moved its critics to metaphor and poetic generalization. Octavio Paz, for example, says of *Las Hurdes:* "Reality emerges from this encounter stripped to the bone" (187). André Bazin, referring to the film, tells us that "Buñuel's surrealism is nothing more than his concern to get to the bottom of reality; what matter if we lose our breath as the diver loses his head when, in his cumbersome suit, he cannot feel the ocean floor under his foot" (191). And Ado Kyrou speaks of the film as "an image of the world in which the protective casing has been ripped off and the inner works exposed, revealing the truth" (42). It is surprising, then, given the film's affective power, its continual force and contemporaneity, that so little has been written about its structure and its methods.

What has been said about *Las Hurdes* accurately points to the film's use of contradiction as the basis of its structure. Often that use of contradiction has been emphasized as linear and progressive. Kyrou, echoed by Raymond Durgnat (Durgnat 58–59), identifies what he calls the film's "Yes, but . . ." architecture:

> That is to say, Buñuel shows an opening scene that is unbearable, then projects a ray of hope, and ends up destroying that hope. For instance, bread is unknown, *but* from time to time the schoolmaster gives a slice to the children, *but* the parents, who fear anything they don't know, throw the bread away. Again, the peasants are often bitten by snakes, *but* the poison is never fatal, *but* the peasants make the bite fatal by trying to cure it with herbs that infect the wound. Each sequence is based on these three propositions, and the progression into horror reaches extremes that can only lead to revolt. (43–45)

Kyrou's analysis is primarily horizontal and diachronic in its focus, drawing attention away from the film's equally consistent and constant articulation of disturbing vertical and synchronic relationships revealed within single shots and sequences. Another such horizontal emphasis is given by Victor Casaus, who locates the structure of *Las Hurdes* in its resemblance to a travelogue: "Such a structure turns the data over to the spectator with a seemingly naive, disinterested simplicity: the data is not even organized around related themes. But it is precisely the overwhelming sequences, the reiteration throughout the film which reveals the data to be that of a major problem" (183).

Neither of these views of the structure of *Las Hurdes* is unilluminating so far as it goes. But neither directly addresses the film's contradictions as grounded in and structured as *Hegelian dialectic* as well as by principles of *surrealist juxtaposition*. That is, both in and across shots, the viewer is confronted not merely by contradictory cinematic and semantic elements which, in their juxtaposition, become so surreal that the very notion of contradiction "falls away," but also—and perhaps more significantly—by a form of contradiction that demands another and more socially aware form of resolution. Both in and across shots, sequences, and the film in its entirety, the viewer is presented simultaneously with *thesis* and *antithesis* that can only find their resolution as a *synthesis* achieved in the *active process* of viewing the film. In terms of the structure as a whole, the thesis of *Las Hurdes* could be said to consist of the mimetic and indexical reality of the film's separate and (internally contradictory) accumulated images: the Hurdanos in all their photographic material presence. The antithesis is, of course, located in the sound track, which is symbolically complex in its simultaneous (and internally contradictory) combination of music, narration, and semantic content. At its most basic, the contradiction is between Word and Image (what we see and what is said about it). At its most complex, the contradiction is between Culture and Nature (the "culture" of the narrator and the "nature" of the Hurdanos).

In an address delivered at the University of Mexico more than twenty years after *Las Hurdes* was completed, Buñuel explains his cinematic concerns in terms that are supportive of this dialectical interpretation of the film's structure and its function:

> Do not think . . . that I am for a cinema exclusively dedicated to the expression of the fantastic and mysterious, for a cinema that flees from or despises daily reality and aspires only to plunge us into the unconscious world of dreams. A few moments ago I indicated all too briefly the capital importance I attach to the film that deals with the fundamental problems of modern man, and so I must emphasize here that I do not consider man in isolation, not as a single case, but in the context of other men. I will let Friedrich Engels speak for me. He defines the function of the novelist (and here read filmmaker) thus: "The novelist will have acquitted himself honorably of his task when, by means of an accurate portrait of authentic social relations, he will have destroyed the conventional view of the nature of those relations, shattered the optimism of the bourgeois world, and forced the reader to question the permanency of the prevailing order, and this even if the author does not offer us any solutions, even if he does not clearly take sides." ("Poetry" 112)

Starting with its very synthesis of two opposing film modes—surrealism and documentary reportage—*Las Hurdes* gives us an accurate portrait of social relations, destroys a conventional view of the nature of those relations, and forces the viewer to confront the open and synergetic dynamics that operate between social individuals, their cultures, their histories, and their conventions for understanding the world. The film shatters the complacence of prevailing tradition as it presents point-of-view as an arbitrary and transient expression of values that are questionable, which are seen less as essential verities than as the cultural blinders that must ever limit and distort clear vision.

The traditional and conventional approach to the social relations depicted in *Las Hurdes* is to see a primitive and oppressed people in relation to an irrelevant religion and an offscreen and unresponsive Spanish government. What we conventionally see *documented* by the camera is misery, poverty, illness, and death. But what the film also documents—what it shows us and unconventionally makes us aware of in its unfolding—is the *documenting* of the Hurdanos, the turning them into objects from which films are made. The accurate portrait of social relations we see and hear in *Las Hurdes* is that relationship established between the "objects" that are the Hurdanos and the "subject" who is the film's narrator. Indeed, if we are able to look at the film clearly and unconventionally—as neither "horrific" travelogue nor "liberal" documentary exposé—we must reject the narrator as our surrogate for he, as well as the Hurdanos, are alien: trapped in their lives, in their respective cultures, in their vision of the world. In this regard, *Las Hurdes* is deeply political (rather than merely partisan) in that its primary aim is to cause the viewer to question the very basis of perception itself. With no one reliable in the film to see and speak for us, we, as viewers, must learn to see and speak for ourselves. The way in which *Las Hurdes* forces this crisis of perception in the viewer is through its systemically unsynthetic presentation of thesis and antithesis, sound and image, and by demanding that the viewer provide the synthesis, the reconstruction and recombination of the whole that results in a perceptual experience transcendent to the sum of its parts. Buñuel purposefully refuses to synthesize the experience for us, to offer solutions to the crisis he provokes. And he does not clearly take sides. As Andrew Sarris notes, in all his films "Buñuel forces his audience to accept man unconditionally. When we look at the monstrous long enough and hard enough, we realize, in Truffaut's phrase, that there are no monsters" ("Interview with Kenji Kanesaka" 71). If the Hurdanos are monstrous to the narrator and the narrator monstrous to us, then we are most likely monstrous to someone or something else—to history, perhaps. If we are not monstrous objects but human subjects, then so are the narrator and the Hurdanos. There are no villains or heroes to Buñuel—only those who unquestioningly accept the vision of their culture and time, and those who try to see clearly through it even in the knowledge they are doomed to failure.

Music is the clearest cue that Buñuel gives viewers of *Las Hurdes* to be wary, to question what they will see and hear in what might be otherwise accepted as a conventional travelogue or documentary. The stately, languorous, and romantic quality of Brahms's *Fourth Symphony,* which punctuates the narration and links the images, is so antithetical to what it accompanies that it functions blatantly to announce contradiction. It is a distancing and framing device that operates in much the same manner as Kyrou suggests "a piece of royal-blue velvet would enhance the horror of a shrunken head placed upon it" (43). Given the distance, the dialectic between the regally romantic music and the gritty raw images, we are asked to begin the analytic deconstruction of what we see and hear so as finally to achieve a reconstructive and synthetic understanding of the issues before us.

This, however, is not easily accomplished. Even film critics wear the blinders of their past cinematic experience and present culture when viewing *Las Hurdes* (and this writer is no exception). While every analysis has recognized the contradictions and dissonance that exist among the film's music, imagery, and narration, there is a certain blindness and deafness to the specific method and function of those contradictions. Because of the obviously perceived contradiction between the formal music and the alien and spontaneous poverty shown in the images, because of the supposedly mediating function of the narration, it is easy to overlook the contradictions operating within the imagery and its presentation. It is easy to forget that the roughly textured images of *Las Hurdes* are *not* reality. Indeed, only one sequence in the film demonstrates—shamelessly—the manipulation at work within the "reality" we unthinkingly accept. We are told by the narrator about the goats which, of all animals, are best suited to the terrain. Supplying further information, the narrator speaks over various medium shots and medium close-ups of goats. Then we see a long shot of a goat on a ridge. The narrator says, "One eats goat meat only when one of the animals is killed accidentally. This happens sometimes when the hills are steep and there are loose stones on the footpath." During this narration, a puff of smoke rises from lower screen right and the goat falls in long shot. In this sequence, simply more blatant than others that function similarly, we are confronted with a lie, with a manipulation of reality we can see is a manipulation *for the film.* We are led not only to mistrust the narrator and regard him as unreliable and unethical (he has, after all, lied to us) but also to mistrust the reality and spontaneity of the images we see and the way in which they are offered to us for viewing.

Indeed, we need to consider the fact that the "real" images of the Hurdanos are relatively uncontextualized but for their relation to the narrator and what he chooses to tell us about them. Although, on occasion, there has been a certain equating of the narrator with Buñuel himself (perhaps because of the narrator's sometimes liberal outrage), it is extremely illuminating to compare the historical and cultural context in which the narrator locates (or dislocates) the Hurdanos and the historical and cultural context in which Buñuel himself discusses them in an interview ("Interview with Luis Buñuel" 88–89). Much of the language he uses is the same as the film's, but Buñuel provides a continuity and specificity of context that give the Hurdanos more than a fragmented and incoherent presence. Within the film itself, the Hurdanos are abstracted out of context by the stately rhythms and pauses of the editing and by the equivalencies created by the order of sequences and the equal attention given to people and buildings and terrain and mosquitoes. Ruins and toads and insects receive the same close-up scrutiny as people. Everything is given a visual equivalence, often underscored by the narration. A sequence in which the Hurdano men leave the village for work and another group returns without money or bread (about which they supposedly have no knowledge) is followed by a sequence in which the camera pans fields and shows the Hurdanos working the land. The temporal link between the sequences is made a function of a "Now" connected to a "Just Before" as well as to the reportorial impulse of the narrator that is as arbitrary as it is connective: "Now we want to report how the Hurdanos prepare the fields," he says—a phrase that not only emphasizes how every Hurdano fact of life is equally the same and reducible to the material of a report but also emphasizes the acausal, inhuman, and arbitrary temporal connections between sequences. (Here, we might remember the temporal arbitrariness of *Un chien andalou* [1928], Buñuel's collaborative work with surrealist Salvador Dali, with its intercut and nonsensically positioned titles: "Once upon a time," "Eight years later," "Sixteen years earlier.")

The spatial and temporal connective tissue of their lives missing or fragmented, the Hurdanos are further decontextualized and dehumanized by their position as mere *objects* of the camera and the narrator's scrutiny. Furthering this objective gaze is the frequency with which the Hurdanos pose for the camera. Early in the film, for example, the narrator, speaking of a local celebration, says, "Among the crowd is this child, richly decorated with silver medals." We see a close-up of a child held on its mother's lap, but the next shot deconstructs the child's body and humanity as we see only a close-up of the child's torso and the mother's hands lifting the various medals so that the camera can see them. Such submissive posing is frequent: the peasant woman who may be one of the servants of the unseen monk is shot first in low angle and then from straight on, looking exceedingly uncomfortable and static; the family group displaying their goitered condition, followed by a shot of a woman holding her child in Pieta fashion and staring at the camera; the dying child lying in the street who submits not only to the camera's gaze but also to a public examination of her mouth; the man who has been bitten by a snake and who blinks in uncertain close-up at the camera, offering his bandaged arm to the camera's stare; and, finally, the close-up in which one of the Hurdanos transporting the body of a dead child to its burial place lifts the covering from the corpse so that the camera can take a look. Indeed, the only counterpoint to the submission of the Hurdanos to the camera, to their becoming objectified by it, are those rare but compelling shots in which some schoolchildren and some reported "cretins" and "idiots" stare fiercely or smile the camera down, asserting their subjecthood, their autonomy from the film that would inspect and label them.

Even more in need of careful deconstruction and analysis than the film's visual elements is the film's narration. This has been a problematic area in the various discussions of *Las Hurdes*. Certain tacit equivalencies are often drawn—between the persona of the narrator and Buñuel himself, between the tone in which the narrator speaks and the content of what he says, and between what he tells us about the Hurdanos and what he tells us about himself as a social being. It is provocative to review some of the critical evaluation of the narration. Kyrou, for example, says the images are "underscored by the dry, factual style of the commentary, which resembles one that might accompany a documentary on the cultivation of peas in the lower Pyrenees" (43), and later adds, "The cold distant commentary . . . never takes sides and never draws conclusions" (45). Raymond Durgnat wonders, "Who can forget the dreadful images of human degradation that are accompanied by the commentary's matter-of-fact remarks" (58). Elizabeth Lyon speaks of "the travelogue-ish narrative—dry, factual, at times contemptuous" (47–48). And Victor Casaus, though fully sensitive to the film's power and effect, sees only "a narration constructed with a simple, direct text and read in a calm tone" (182) and goes on to suggest that made today, the film would not have been narrated at all: "It is a film reportage which nowadays would surely have been made with the resources of direct cinema" (184). This latter remark points to the lack of importance that has been given to the narrator as a *persona* in the film. Indeed, a direct cinema film about the Hurdanos would eliminate the narrator as mediator between the viewer and the Hurdanos, though this is precisely what gives *Las Hurdes* its force. Within the coolness, dryness, and matter-of-factness of the *tone* of the commentary is a social being who does most definitely take sides and draw conclusions, as revealed by the *content* of what he says. It is worth noting that when the film was first screened in Madrid in 1933, Buñuel read the accompanying text (written

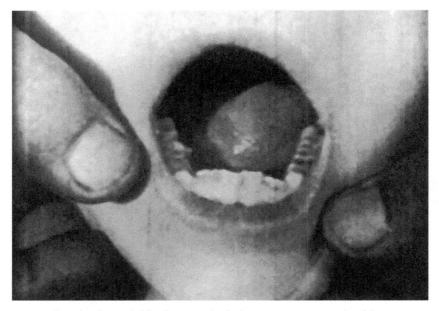

Las Hurdes: The dying child submits to both the camera's gaze and public examination.

by himself and Pierre Unik) "in a tone which combined insolent indiffer-ence and apparent objectivity" ("Interview with Luis Buñuel" 93). This was not Buñuel playing Buñuel, but Buñuel playing a "documentary" or "travel-ogue" narrator. The distinction is important.

The dialectical oppositions operating in the commentary are extremely complex. On the most obvious level, one can note the contradiction be-tween the horrifying images of human poverty and illness and the narra-tor's uninflected voice. Indeed, this is what most critics have commented upon. What the voice does in tone is to duplicate the camera's supposedly objective eye and, in both cases, the tone of the saying and the mode of the looking are an *inappropriate* response to what is said and what is seen. Thus there is a sense of discomfort when the narrator remarks flatly over the image of a man shaking with fever from the malaria brought on by a sting from the anopheles mosquito, "Here is the result of their sting: a man attacked by fever seated near his house." Or, as a head slowly rises from be-hind a ridge of ground, body following, as the entire bearded man appears looking as ordinary or extraordinary as anyone else in the film: "Here is an-other type of idiot." The very lack of human concern in the narrator's voice

Las Hurdes: "Here is another type of idiot."

and the camera's vision is in direct tension with the content of the images, which either beg for humane response or belie the factual surety imposed by the narrator's tone.

Along with this disparity between the tone of the commentary and what it addresses, a disparity that suggests the narrator lacks humanity, there is also a similar disparity within the narrator's commentary itself. Thoughts and sentences are connected by inappropriate linkage, by a concern for objects rather than subjects. Thus the narrator can say (over a medium long shot of a woman lying sick on her balcony), "This woman, lying on her balcony, does not even realize our presence. Balconies of any kind are rare in most of the villages of the Hurdes." The balcony becomes the link between his two thoughts, not the dying woman. Indeed, again and again the Hurdanos are made into objects—"scientific" anthropological objects, objects of scorn, objects of liberal sentiment, even objects of poetry (the narrator suggests that the "two skulls over the church doors seem to preside over its [the village of Alberca's] destiny," that the roofs of an Hurdano village "look like the back of a fabulous animal," and that he was welcomed at the entrance of a town "by a choir of idiots").

While one might conventionally expect a certain ethnographic emphasis by the narrator, one appropriate to the "exotic" status of his subjects, his
ethnography is culturally and personally colored by his language. His subjects are turned into objects once again as his distaste surfaces not in his
tone but in his choice of words. His is an anthropology that smacks of paternalism and imperialism. Coming into a village, he sees women "combing themselves" (rather than combing their hair, which is more humanly
descriptive) in preparation for a "strange and barbaric ceremony." The child
mentioned earlier, decorated with medals shown to the camera, prompts
the narrator to say, "Although these are Christian pendants, we cannot but
compare them to the religious charms of barbaric tribes in Africa and Oceania." Although we never see it (and there are a number of instances in the
film when the narrator tells us something that is never confirmed by the
images), he announces, "By seven in the evening, everybody in Alberca is
drunk with wine." After a description of the surrounding flora and fauna,
the narrator enters a village and tells us "we can see the inhabitants at their
daily rounds," again using an awkward phrase that reduces the subject to
object and never explains itself anyway. His discussion of the spring that
flows through the village is particularly illuminating as it describes a condition about which the villagers can do nothing both coolly and with contempt: "At some times of the year, a miserable little spring comes down
from the mountain through the center of the village. During the summer
there is no water other than this, and the inhabitants use it despite the
disgusting filth it carries. This stream is used for all purposes." He casually
describes the children going to school as "uncombed," although the shots
we see of them don't confirm the adjective. He discusses the abandoned
children cared for by the Hurdano women in exchange for welfare pay-
ments as an "industry." And his commentary on the midgets and cretins
(if, indeed, the people in the various shots we see are technically midgets
and cretins) is disturbing not only because it is not congruent with the images we actually see accompanying it but also because it exposes the strang-
est concerns and a disjointed flow of thought and attention. For example, in
part of this sequence, we watch three male figures running, then close-ups
of their smiling faces, a pan of the Hurdanos playing in some fashion with
stones, a pan of their legs, and one of them grinning, while the narrator
says: "Midgets and cretins are common in the high Hurdes. Generally, the
families use them as goatherds. Some are dangerous and will either flee
from strangers, or attack them with stones. One sees them coming back
from the mountains at sunset. We had a difficult time trying to photograph
the idiots. The degeneracy of these people is caused principally by hunger,
by lack of hygiene, and by incest."

The narrator/"anthropologist" next becomes involved with the transporting of a dead child's body from a high village to a far cemetery. He is quick to point out, over images again inappropriate to his grandiose statement, that "This cemetery shows us that despite the great misery of the Hurdanos, their moral and religious ideas are the same as in other parts of the world." What we see, however, makes the meaning of this statement ambiguous: a long pan of a badly overgrown area in which stands a single cross followed by a close-up of someone's hands parting weeds to reveal a small wooden marker. There is thus a peculiar tension generated by the lack of awareness on the part of the narrator that his statement is either false given the images of neglect we actually see or true and the images confirm its negative implication. And, finally, one has to remark on the narrator's comment that fusses over a paper and two tin pot lids on a house wall: "The cut paper and the line of pot covers on the wall indicates a certain flair for interior design." What we see has so little relevance to what he says that the narrator's choice of words is even more ridiculous than it is condescending.

The narrator, however, has a more "liberal" side, one that overtly acknowledges his role as a social being. He occasionally points to social injustice or expresses a certain "correct" shock or regret at what he sees. Right after talking about the village's "inhabitants," for example, he makes this concerned comment: "It is strange that in all the time we were in the villages of Las Hurdes we never heard a single song." After describing the schoolchildren as "uncombed," he fixes on an easy irony: "To these starving children, the teacher explains that the sum of the angles in a triangle equals two right angles." After using the word "industry" to describe the raising of others' children to get welfare money, he is offended at a picture of a woman in colonial dress: "We discover an unexpected and shocking picture on the classroom wall. Why is this absurd picture here?" Yet he makes no comment whatsoever about the absurdity in context of the maxim one of the children copies on the blackboard from a "book of morality" the narrator has opened at random: "Respect the property of others." Right before he expresses social concern about the health of the village in general and the dying little girl in particular, he has told us how he was greeted by a "choir of idiots." He is even coyly ironic when he says, "Once each year the wealthy families, if we may call them that, slaughter a pig." And, after a lengthy period in which he refrains from overt social comment about death and illness of all kinds, he finally notes, "The only luxurious thing that we saw in Las Hurdes were the churches."

The constant dialectical tension between the narrator and his various selves that surface even as they are suppressed by the matter-of-fact

intonation and the constant dialectical tension between what is reported
and what we see create a world in which everything is questioned and ne-
gated by its opposite. In more than one sense, this is liberating. The viewer's rejection of the narrator as a being unaware of his cultural bias and
narrow vision in part returns the Hurdanos to themselves. While we never
get to know them, they are, at least, realized as unknowable from the data of
a culture-laden anthropologist. They are given back their subjecthood—and
if they retain a certain status as objects of our consciousness, our caution in
regarding them so is much greater than that exercised by the film's narrator. As well, we are liberated from a conventional blind identification with
the omniscient narrator. Riddled with self-contradiction, he is after all no
better (and possibly worse) than we are. He does not see clearly. As viewers, we are finally left to our own devices; we must see and make judgment
for ourselves.

In a lengthy and moving article on Buñuel, Carlos Fuentes wrote of the
importance of sight and vision to the filmmaker and his films. Some of his
comments seem particularly relevant to the vision generated by *Las Hurdes,*
a vision that arises synthetically from the collision of opposites:

> in Buñuel sight determines content or, rather, content is a way of
> looking, content is sight at all possible levels. And this multitude
> of levels—social, political, psychological, historical, esthetic,
> philosophic—is not predetermined, but flows from vision. His
> constant tension is between obsessive opposites: pilgrimage and
> confinement, solitude and fraternity, sight and blindness, social
> rules and personal cravings, rational conduct and oneiric be-
> havior. His intimate legacies, often conflicting, are always there:
> Spain, Catholicism, surrealism, left anarchism. . . . Buñuel in-
> criminates all social orders while liberating our awareness of the
> outcast, the deformed, the maimed. . . . He never exploits this
> marginality, because he makes it central to his vision. He has set
> the highest standards for true cinematic freedom.
>
> And finally, this respect for freedom of his characters is trans-
> lated into respect for the freedom of his audience. As they end,
> his films remain open, the spectator remains free. (Fuentes 77)

It is precisely this freedom to see that is forced on the viewer of *Las
Hurdes.* The spectator is cast out of the film into freedom, into his or her
own eyes. We can see neither as an Hurdano nor as the narrator—nor
even as our once unselfconscious selves. Rather, we are led to question
our own prejudices that distort and reduce the world at every glance. Even

though we are doomed to failure, we are asked to strain and squint and peer through our own history, our own culture, to get a glimpse of some unadorned and shadowy reality—one that is not ours—which can never be made clear and visible but which will forever lurk in our peripheral vision and consciousness. Our liberty to see is confirmed as we recognize the very impossibility of freedom and clear vision. Indeed, it is this process of questioning freedom and vision that *Las Hurdes* sets in motion through its dialectical structure and method.

The Hurdanos are no longer tied to a particular historical moment—or even to a still extant culture. Looking at them today, the discomfiture they cause us is less social than ethical. The same is true of the narrator. What remains on the screen is less a specific social problem than an eternal and irreconcilable relationship between the viewer and the viewed. That relationship will remain ever vital and relevant—for it extends from within the film outward to include not only the audience but also the rest of the world beyond.

Works Cited

Bazin, André. "The Depths of Reality." In *Luis Buñuel: An Introduction*, ed. Ado Kyrou, trans. Adrienne Foulke, 189–92. New York: Simon and Schuster, 1963.

Buñuel, Luis. "Interview with Kenji Kanesaka." In *Interviews with Film Directors*, ed. Andrew Sarris, 72–74. New York: Avon Books, 1967.

———. "Interview with Luis Buñuel." Ed. André Bazin and Jacques Doniol-Valcroze, in Francisco Aranda, *Luis Buñuel: A Critical Biography*, ed. and trans. David Robinson, 87–91. New York: Da Capo, 1976.

———. "Poetry and Cinema." In *Luis Buñuel: An Introduction*, ed. Ado Kyrou, trans. Adrienne Foulke, 108–12. New York: Simon and Schuster, 1963.

Casaus, Victor. "*Las Hurdes*: Land without Bread." In *The World of Luis Buñuel: Essays in Criticism*, ed. Joan Mellen, 180–85. New York: Oxford University Press, 1978.

Durgnat, Raymond. *Luis Buñuel*. Berkeley: University of California Press, 1970. Revised 1977.

Fuentes, Carlos. "The Discreet Charm of Luis Buñuel." *New York Times Magazine*, March 11, 1973, 77.

Kyrou, Ado, ed. *Luis Buñuel: An Introduction*. Trans. Adrienne Foulke. New York: Simon and Schuster, 1963.

Lyon, Elizabeth H. "Luis Buñuel: The Process of Dissociation in Three Films." *Cinema Journal* 13, no. 1 (1973): 45–48.

Paz, Octavio. "The Tradition of a Fierce and Passional Art." In *Luis Buñuel: An Introduction*, ed. Ado Kyrou, trans. Adrienne Foulke, 186–89. New York: Simon and Schuster, 1963.

Chapter 5

THE ART OF NATIONAL PROJECTION

Basil Wright's *Song of Ceylon*

William Guynn

The Art of National Projection—this is the title of the enterprise that the British documentary movement embarked on in the 1930s. The phrase belongs to Sir Stephen Tallents, secretary of the Empire Marketing Board (EMB), who formulated the idea of a massive public relations campaign under government sponsorship designed to stimulate trade with the Commonwealth. The EMB's explicit mission was therefore propagandistic: to "project" before the mass public positive images of British industry and commerce. John Grierson, who coined the term "documentary" and dreamed of using the film medium for "putting the working class on the screen," approached Tallents in 1927. With the help of Walter Creighton, he eventually convinced the British government bureaucracy of the need for a filmmaking unit inside the EMB. In 1929 Grierson made the movement's first film, *Drifters*, which served as the unit's pilot project.

Drifters aroused general acclaim and the passionate interest of Cambridge student Basil Wright, an amateur experimental filmmaker who became Grierson's first recruit. In 1933, after several years of work within the EMB film unit, Wright was sent on assignment to shoot material in the British colony of Ceylon. In 1934, the edited footage, paired with a postsynchronized sound track, appeared as *Song of Ceylon*.

Song of Ceylon is the first great realization of the classic documentary texts of the 1930s. Exemplifying a new form of expression, it announces

a period of experimentation that would produce the movement's most interesting films. The film is extraordinarily complex, much more complex
than one could anticipate from a young filmmaker working within a newly
formed and largely amateur production unit. In 1933 Wright, by his own
admission, was still a neophyte in many respects and, like the genre itself,
open to a variety of experimental tendencies. Wright explicitly recognizes
two crucial influences: the work of American documentarist Robert Flaherty
and of Brazilian-French filmmaker Alberto Cavalcanti, both "marginal" innovators who, in the early 1930s, conserve the spirit of experimentation
apparent in their earlier silent films.

   Song of Ceylon is also complex because it embodies the political contradictions the documentary movement assumes by its position within the
British state apparatus. On the one hand, the British documentarists identified themselves as socialists with a "socially progressive outlook"; on the
other hand, they worked within a conservative state bureaucracy that demanded restraint and self-censorship. It is not surprising to find, therefore,
that *Song of Ceylon* is, in many ways, a dissonant text, the locus of conflicts
of an ideological nature. Moreover, *Song of Ceylon,* commissioned by the
EMB and the Ceylon Tea Propaganda Board, raises the colonial question:
how are British filmmakers to position themselves with regard to British
exploitation of its colonies? In the following analysis, I will attempt to disentangle some of the textual complexity of *Song of Ceylon* and uncover the
ideological dissonance that lies beneath the work's apparent coherence.

British Documentary under
"The Flaherty Spell"

John Grierson wrote his well-known article on Robert Flaherty for the peri-
odical *Artwork* in 1931. In the same year, the American filmmaker, internationally recognized for *Nanook of the North* (1922) and *Moana* (1925), worked
for a few months with the Empire Marketing Board Film Unit, giving the
British documentarists firsthand demonstrations of his shooting methods.
Grierson understood that Flaherty's approach was capable of transfiguring
"natural materials." He extols Flaherty's slow, ethnographic preparation for
filming: in Eskimo country or the South Seas, Flaherty "soaked himself in
his material, lived with it to the point of intimacy and beyond that to the
point of belief, before he gave it form" (Grierson 141). Moreover, Flaherty's
sense of form, as Grierson perceptively argues, emerges from his choice
of framing; the position of his camera, its angle and distance, gives unexpected resonance to figures and objects:

It may be some high angle of a ship, or a crane, or a chimney stack, or a statue, adding some element of the heroic by a new-found emphasis.

It may be the bright revelation of rhythms that time has worn smooth: the hand movement of a potter, the wrist move-ment of a native priest, or the muscle play of a dancer or a boxer or a runner. All of them seem to achieve a special virtue in the oblong of the screen. (Grierson 141)

As it turned out, the Empire Marketing Board had little patience with the slowness of Flaherty's methods and fired him in peremptory fashion. What he left behind was 12,000 feet of material; complemented with addi-tional footage shot by Basil Wright and Arthur Elton, the whole was edited by others and finally released as *Industrial Britain* in 1933. The film was crucial to the ideology the movement espoused in the early period. Run-ning counter to the Marxist notion of the alienation of labor in the modern era, the project for *Industrial Britain* was to humanize the British industrial landscape. Grierson, who disapproved of Flaherty's inclination to film pre-industrial cultures, realized nonetheless that Flaherty's eye could be used to transform industry and labor into proper aesthetic objects: "But how otherwise than by coming to industry, even as it is, and forcing beauty from it, and bringing people to see beauty in it, can one, in turn, inspire man to create and find well-being?" (143). Grierson enticed Flaherty to participate in the EMB mission by suggesting that industrial labor could be visual-ized as belonging to the tradition of the British craftsman. It was doubtless a challenge to the Flaherty eye to discern in the looming industrial land-scape and the monotony of the assembly line vestiges of individual human workmanship.

CAVALCANTI AND THE CONTINENTAL AVANT-GARDE

Alberto Cavalcanti came to the EMB film unit in 1933, at the moment when the British documentarists were grappling with the problems of conversion to sound, and, by all accounts, his impact on the movement's experiments in sound was crucial. Grierson disliked the "economic and ideological overhead" that sound technology brought with it. He decried the "phalanxes of experts" and hangers-on typical of studio sound produc-tion, proposing, instead, "the absolute elimination of these comic barriers between the producer and the result he wants" (quoted in Sussex 45). More-over, Grierson's writing on sound in this period suggests quite clearly the influence of Soviet theorists Eisenstein, Pudovkin, and Alexandrov, who argued for "A CONTRAPUNTAL USE of sound in relation to the visual montage" (Eisenstein 258), and the French filmmaker René Clair, who advocated the liberation of the microphone from "naturalistic" reduplication of the visual track. Grierson's polemics on the use of sound in documentary stressed the mobility of sound production equipment ("The microphone, too, can get about in the world") in a period when studio production was the norm and advocated the "creative" sound track: sound was open to all the powers of editing and, freed from its reduplicative role, could negotiate complex and shifting relationships with the image (Grierson 157–63).

Cavalcanti had been associated with the French avant-garde. His "symphonic" documentary, *Rien que les heures* (1926), made in the period of the consolidation of classic narrative codes, disrupts the conventions of linear editing. The film's opening intertitle is a categorical rejection of narrative ordering: "This film contains no story. It is just a sequence of impressions on the passage of time." Indeed, *Rien que les heures* gives us an often disconcerting montage of shots that undercuts our expectations and demands that we rethink with nearly every sequence the principles that order it and the relation between the sequence and the developing totality of the text. Grierson had seen *Rien que les heures* on a London Film Society program in 1928, and it was precisely the experimental quality of Cavalcanti's documentary work that motivated Grierson's invitation to Cavalcanti to join the EMB film unit.

Cavalcanti came as the consummate professional—in addition to his experimental films, he had worked extensively in commercial production in France—to a film unit composed of acknowledged amateurs. As filmmaker Harry Watt testifies, he had a crucial impact: "I believe fundamentally that the arrival of Cavalcanti in the GPO film unit was the turning point of British documentary. . . . Nobody had cut sound at all until Cavalcanti arrived. So he sat down, first of all, to teach us just the fundamentals, but his contribution was enormously more than that" (quoted in Sussex 49). At this time Basil Wright had just returned from filming in Ceylon—the footage for the film that would become *Song of Ceylon* had been shot silent—and he found the film unit moving into sound studios at Blackheath. Cavalcanti was there advocating a freer relationship between sound and image than the typical fiction film or documentary, with its voice-of-God commentary, had permitted. Wright observes that "all experiments in sound really started then because Cavalcanti was there. . . . His ideas about the use of sound were so liberating that they would liberate in you about a thousand other ideas" (quoted in Sussex 50).

Cavalcanti represented avant-garde tendencies in the midst of a movement committed to the political pragmatism of state-commissioned work.

Pragmatic as it was, however, the British movement was also an alternative cinema in search of alternative forms of expression, and Cavalcanti found talented disciples among the British documentarists. As a result, British documentary in this period retains some of the visual experimentation of the silent era. Moreover, it contests the logic of continuity editing in favor of more open notions of montage and liberates the sound track from a slavish reduplication of the image.

TEXTUALITY IN SONG OF CEYLON

How does the influence of Flaherty and Cavalcanti take form in the text of Song of Ceylon? It is difficult to imagine two filmmakers more different from each other in intention or in style. Flaherty has ethnographic but also strong formalist and poetic tendencies. His aesthetic centers on the act of framing: sensitivity to the camera's position and conditions of shooting produce strong formal compositions, embellished by effects of light and shadow, and a style that commentators describe as intensely lyrical. Cavalcanti's documentary work in the silent period, on the other hand, is deconstructive, ironic in tone, and socially committed. Using documentary realism, Rien que les heures mocks conventional imagery of the Parisian landscape and engages in experiments in associational editing.

However, both Flaherty's and Cavalcanti's works contain what I propose to call photogenic effects. I am referring to the notion of photogenia, first enunciated by Louis Delluc before 1920 and subsequently reformulated by other members of the French avant-garde. In the conception elaborated by Jean Epstein, photogenia evokes not just the beauty of certain film images or photographic effects but the special resonance—the transcendence—that the act of filmmaking can bring to the phenomena under observation. Founded on the photogenic powers of the camera, pure cinema is, in Epstein's poetic language, like the rediscovery of an animistic world in which all the details of filmed reality come alive: "A startling pantheism is reborn to the world and fills it to the bursting point" (134). Epstein's language fits the "transfiguration of natural materials" that the British discerned in Flaherty's work: the lyricism of the "meditative" Moana, for example, is achieved through compositional effects that often overwhelm and arrest narrative development.

Epstein's notion of photogenia is not limited to photographic and compositional effects but is also linked to the art of editing. Epstein describes montage as the search for a "cinematographic inscription of time," based on a notion of the abstract visual rhythm of shots and on systems of continuity that break with the classical model of editing (121). As Richard Abel argues, "Generally, the narrative avant-garde developed patterns of continuity that depended on a combination of graphic, rhythmic, and associative or connotative relations" (293). Liberated from the demands of linear sequencing of narrative events, Cavalcanti in *Rien que les heures* achieves photogenic effects through the unexpected and often ambiguous affinities he creates between shots.

According to the French avant-garde, photogenia plays on specific capacities of the camera—to vary its angle of vision or to move through space—photographic devices such as dissolves and superimpositions, and aspects of mise-en-scène such as lighting or composition of the frame. Moreover, photogenia appears in an editing style that responds to poetic or rhetorical as opposed to dramatic principles. Photogenic effects become observable insofar as they are departures from the norms of filmmaking, for example the norm of the eye-level camera or the norm of the dissolve as a coded mark of punctuation indicating a "jump" in time and space. It is therefore characteristic of photogenic effects that they tend to draw attention to themselves—to be "self-conscious."

It is not difficult to discern the traces of Flaherty and Cavalcanti in *Song of Ceylon;* the film is in fact full of photogenic effects that recall their work: (1) framing—the selection of position and angle—that results in special compositional effects; (2) manipulation of light and shadow for studied effects of comparison or contrast; (3) expressive use of superimpositions and dissolves; (4) camera movements that are either repeated or protracted so that they take on a self-conscious rhythm; (5) editing that brings out the poetic quality of a scene or links phenomena in unexpected, but visually coherent, associations.

Examples of photogenia abound in *Song of Ceylon.* The part titled "The Buddha" centers on a pilgrimage undertaken by the Ceylonese to the sacred mountain known to the colonialists as Adam's Peak. Basil Wright and his crew are intent upon suggesting the close relationship in the Ceylonese experience between the natural and spiritual worlds. The film's first sequence already enunciates this idea. It contains seven shots and gives us an unusual association of imagery: the first four represent exotic foliage, whose patterns are emphasized by contrasting light and shadow; the fifth shows us a reclining stone figure, overlaid with foliage patterns; the sixth a living fawn in a dark landscape; and the last, the stone image of a beast, again in contrasting light and shadow. The sequence seems to evoke a night landscape without convincing us this is a single coherent space (the foliage shots were reportedly taken in a public garden in London [Rotha 128]). However, the heterogeneity of the imagery is mitigated by two photogenic effects. (1) All the shots are linked by often protracted dissolves. This

Song of Ceylon: The natural and spiritual world of the Ceylonese rendered through photogenia.

photographic procedure moves us fluidly across the cuts and obliges us to accept the images' textual unity. (2) The camera tracks constantly across the shifting visual field. The images of foliage are all linked by the apparent continuity of a left-to-right camera movement; the reclining figure is discovered as if part of the same trajectory; the living fawn is caught in a contrasting right-to-left tracking shot before the camera returns, in the final shot, to the left-to-right movement of the first five.

It is not difficult to identify the thematic concern that emerges from this piece of photogenic continuity. The sequence of shots establishes the association between the worlds of the natural and the culturally "primitive," which Wright posits as quintessentially Ceylonese: the figure of Buddha emerges from the foliage and returns to it, the living beast is replicated in stone. The voice-over, which comes to replace the music of woodwinds and cymbals at the end of the sequence, enunciates the theme of the primordial: "In those days the primitives did prostrate themselves to the honor and service of the devil."

The first shot of the second sequence appears to give us the embodiment of devil worship. A dancer in a grotesque mask emerges in a dissolve from the shot of the stone animal, suggesting, once again, the linkage between the worlds of the natural and the human. The continuity is false, however, since the image of the dancer will be the first in a sequence of seven shots of dancing figures, most quite brief and separated by straight cuts. The sequence's frenetic rhythm contrasts with the fluidity of the first sequence. Moreover, a shift in the musical score reemphasizes the textual shift: drums and a pulsating woodwind melody replace the languorous musical theme. In this sequence, it is the stark photographic contrast between the brightly lit dancing figures and the dark background that gives the images their photogenic quality. Photographically abstracted from the background, the figures of the dancers, often seen in fragmented closer views, move through the frame in unpredictable trajectories, the flailing motions of the masked heads creating stunning visual effects. The final shot, a gradual upward frontal panning of the body of one dancer ending in a prolonged medium close-up of his torso and masked head, emphasizes the malevolent gestures of the shaking thumb and protruding tongue, and their disturbing exoticism.

The next four sequences evoke the pilgrimage itself and abound in photogenic compositions. Some images are structured so as to produce emphatic visual patterning. Take, for example, in the first of these sequences, the three shots showing the procession of pilgrims crossing a wood-planked footbridge. The first shot is taken from a low angle framing the pilgrims moving across the bridge between earth and sky. The second is an extreme low angle of the same subject in which the bridge traverses the frame in a striking diagonal composition. The third is a low angle on the bridge itself: at frame left, one of the guy ropes extends in a diagonal from background to foreground, while, at screen right, the procession of pilgrims, fragmented by framing and angle, forms a trajectory that balances and repeats the linear pattern of the rope. In addition to this self-conscious pattern of diagonals, one is struck by the "emptiness" of the center frame, only momentarily filled with a protruding umbrella or a cloth sack carried by a pilgrim. The framing is clearly "decentered" with regard to its presumed subject, the procession, in a calculated effect of compositional abstraction.

The second of these sequences is a piece of analytic editing: a group of pilgrims—we assume an extended family—seeks the shade and repose of a bench against the wall of a house. Once again, the continuity effects are stunning. The previous sequence ends with low-angle shots of pilgrims, moving at the edges of the frame against the background of a cloudless sky. The white robe of the last pilgrim floats across frame left as the bench slowly materializes in the center, and the robe of another pilgrim—this time an old man, the first of the family group—replaces it through a dissolve.

Song of Ceylon: The brightly lit dancing figures set against the dark background, an example of photogenia.

The scene is relatively static—nothing dramatic justifies the series of ten shots that compose the sequence. Rather, each reframing privileges a particular gesture: the old man removes a neck cloth with which to fan himself and, in a closer shot, the elegance of the hand gesture and the expressive sweep of the cloth take on considerable beauty of form. The manner recalls Flaherty, whose ability to anticipate his subjects' actions had such a strong impression on Basil Wright.

Song of Ceylon also recalls Cavalcanti and the symphonic documentary. The "city symphony," exemplified by Cavalcanti's *Rien que les heures,* Ruttman's *Berlin: Symphony of a Great City* (1927), or Vertov's *Man with a Movie Camera* (1929), offered alternatives to narrative ordering. It was structured with reference to a circumscribed space and time: the geographical unity of place—Paris, Berlin, a synthesized Soviet city in the above examples, respectively—and a specific measure of time—typically, a day in the life of a city. Obviously, this nebulous notion of the dramatic locus and the chronometric passage of hours are far from the classic dramatic unities of place and time. Moreover, symphonic documentaries abandon continuity of action and with it the notion of the central protagonist. There are no characters in these documentaries in the novelistic sense, since the human "actors" make episodic appearances, and, therefore, the action of specific agents cannot be traced across the unfolding of these texts. By rejecting the resources of narrative, the symphonic documentary faces problems of textual organization. On what basis are shots to be combined? How does the film move from sequence to sequence?

By its musical title, *Song of Ceylon* evokes the symphonic documentary, with which it shares several textual problems. The unity of place is even more nebulous in Wright's film than in the symphonic documentary— most of it takes place "somewhere" in Ceylon. Moreover, the linear concept of time is suspended, since one of the concerns of the film is to evoke the timelessness of traditional Ceylonese life. Finally, the film abandons the notion of the individual human agent. The "actor" may appear in a cluster of shots showing a specific action—we see several views of a young man climbing a palm to harvest coconuts, for example—but he never reappears beyond the confines of the sequence. Consequently, there is little sense of continuity of action as performed by individual human agents.

In its overall design, *Song of Ceylon* offers an alternative to narrative ordering. The film is organized thematically, each of its parts devoted to specific aspects of Ceylonese culture: Part I, "The Buddha," depicts the links between the natural and the spiritual; Part II, "The Virgin Island," concerns traditions of social existence, uncorrupted by colonial exploitation; Part III, "The Voices of Commerce," treats the effects of the colonial presence; Part IV, "Apparel of a God," returns to the imagery of ritual devotion evoked in the first part. At the level of sequences, the narrative principle is also considerably weakened. Even in Part I, which "narrates" the pilgrimage to Adam's Peak, the sequences representing the pilgrims' ascent, the moment of rest, the reading of the religious text, and the ringing of bells fail to establish a linear, causal chain of actions. We have the impression that time is at a standstill and action subjected to a dilation in space.

In *Song of Ceylon*, editing is truly an art, since it demands the conspicuous intervention of the "filmmaker" who articulates shots on the basis of paradigms that are not already given and that the text must work to establish. *Song of Ceylon*, like symphonic documentaries, makes use of a complex visual rhetoric to link the shots in figurative or conceptual relationships. Continuity is often established through the artifice of form: repetition of camera movement, repetition of motifs, repeated dissolves. To the extent that they are liberated from narrative necessity, images are opened to other principles of association and therefore to other kinds of meaning. In the closing sequence of Part I, for example, figurative comparisons between the motifs are suggested through the formal device of a consistently moving camera. We see birds taking flight, Buddhas erect and reclining, and progressively more open landscapes—images that do not suggest a coherent physical place but transcendence, an ascent toward the divine. In Part III, which describes colonial exploitation of Ceylonese labor, the visual track is structured conceptually through a series of oppositions between the traditional and the modern, represented in alternating sequences: a segment describing the harvesting of tea by manual labor, for example, is followed by three shots of industrial machinery. This conceptual dissonance also occurs within certain sequences: an ocean liner appears as an unexpected insert within a sequence showing the harvesting of coconuts; inversely, an incongruous elephant disrupts a sequence devoted to describing commercial telephone and telegraph communication.

Cavalcanti's major impact on the British documentary, however, was in the area of sound montage and the relationship between image and sound, as illustrated in such films as *Pett and Pott* (1934), *Coal Face* (1935), and *Night Mail* (1936). The proposition that the sound track is open to the resources of montage is a radical rejection of the classic film's fundamental harmony, well institutionalized in dominant production by 1934. The classic narrative film organizes the five materials of expression—the moving photographic image, written language, phonic human speech, noise, and music—so as to produce a single, coherent diegetic world. To this end, it subordinates the sound track—the elements of voice, noise, and music—to an ancillary function. Thus diegetic sound finds its source in the world evoked by the image: the voice belongs to the character, the noise and music tracks are anchored in the image and its ambient space. Extradiegetic elements are either sporadic, as in the voice-over commentary by a character, which disappears rapidly from the scene of enunciation, or they are relegated to the background of consciousness, like the musical score, which is intended to be perceived without really being noticed.

One characteristic feature of innovative documentaries from the classic period, like *Song of Ceylon*, is the exploitation of the heterogeneity of the materials of expression. Continental theorists spoke of this in terms of counterpoint between image and sound. Grierson echoes the Europeans and, we suspect, lessons he learned from Cavalcanti: "The documentary film will do pioneer work for cinema if it emancipates the microphone from the studio and demonstrates at the cutting and re-recording benches how many more dramatic uses can be made of sound than the studios realize" (163). Indeed, once liberated from its subservience to the image, the sound track assumes a new independence and new positions of enunciation.

Let's consider the example of the use of voice-over in *Song of Ceylon*. There are in fact two types of voices in *Song of Ceylon*, neither of which can be identified completely as the authoritative enunciation that speaks the truth of the images, as in the "voice-of-God" documentary. In Parts I, II, and IV, the spoken text is a "borrowed" text, identified in the opening credits as written by "Robert Knox in the year 1680." It is, therefore, "quoted" rather than enunciated. By its accent and intonation patterns, the voice that speaks the text is marked as archaic and reinforces the sense of historical enunciation. The textual gains are considerable. First, the preexisting text is perceived as "innocent." It performs the functions of the voice-of-God commentary—explicating the images, anchoring their meanings—but resists being attributed to the deliberate designs of the filmmaker. It is as if the juxtaposition of image and sound produced a critical discourse without blatant manipulation by an enunciator. Second, the commentary's historical character contributes to one of the film's overriding meanings: the "accuracy" of a 250-year-old commentary applied to images of contemporary Ceylon is textual proof of that world's timelessness.

The film's other type of voice emerges in Part III, "The Voices of Commerce." It is distinguished from the first voice in a number of ways. First, it makes little explicit reference to the images and therefore does not function in the mode of a commentary. Second, it seems to have a diegetic status of its own: the various British voices appear as a "sampling" of communication in the modern commercial world of Ceylon. The sound "shots" are fragmentary utterances: pieces of letters ("We beg to inform you that the consignment to which you refer . . ."), telephonic or telegraphic messages ("Yesterday's commodity prices. Tea."), reports on products and productivity ("The products of the coconut palm are many and varied . . ."), and so forth. Third, the montage of voices operates with apparent autonomy with regard to the images, often flowing over the demarcation between visual sequences. The voices' "indifference" to the visual track has, however, a quite specific meaning: the disembodied speech and its businesslike tones form a counterpoint to the images of the Ceylonese at work and suggest the callous nature of colonial exploitation. As if to underscore the disparity between image and sound, the voices are periodically displaced from the sound track, as music, characteristic of earlier parts of the film, returns the image-sound relationship to one of correspondence and harmony.

IDEOLOGY IN *SONG OF CEYLON*

Song of Ceylon thus produces a grand rhetorical opposition between the realm of the divine, nature, and unalienated labor on the one hand, and the crass realm of colonial exploitation on the other. Ceylonese life, as the film represents it, constitutes in this regard an admirable resistance to the debasing effects of colonial exploitation. The Ceylonese emerge, in their photogenia, as idealized beings, particularly in the film's second part, "The Virgin Island." They are in tune with the elements: a young boy's bathing takes on an ecstatic, ablutionary character; a fisherman casts his net into the sea as his son applauds from shore, his expressive hand abstracted in close-up against the sky. The motions of work produce vivid kinesthetic effects—the stages of the potter's work are sensitively observed and analytically edited. The painterly composition of the shots suggests their harmonious plenitude: fishermen repairing their nets are set out in depth against the background of their beached boat, the sea, and the sky. Moreover, this kind of aesthetic effect is meant to communicate a political dimension, for, as the voice-over informs us, labor remains a noble occupation among the Ceylonese, to whom wage-slavery is unknown: "But husbandry is the great employment of the country, and in this the best men labor. Nor is it held any disgrace for men of the greatest quality either at home or in the field if it be for themselves. But to work for hire, with them, is reckoned for a great shame, and very few are here to be found who will work so." Indeed, work is seen as a shared social activity, and, the film suggests, the Ceylonese make little distinction between work and leisure. Women wear radiant smiles as they grind the grain, children fulfill the serious social obligation of practicing traditional dance, the fisherman casts his net over his son in a playful gesture of fatherly affection.

Song of Ceylon is often cited as an example of British documentary's "socialist" tendencies overcoming the constraints of state sponsorship. As Harry Watt puts it, "Not many of us were communists, but we were all socialists and I'm sure we had dossiers" (quoted in Barnouw 91). Indeed, the film was commissioned by the EMB and the Ceylon Tea Propaganda Board, organizations that existed to promote commodities imported from the colonies, and the film's characterization of British exploitation would seem to run against the grain of those organizations' propagandistic aims. Moreover, the film's representations of harmonious life in Ceylon are surely intended to be read as inverse images of advanced industrial societies in which urbanization, widening class distinctions, and divisions of labor had become the inescapable conditions of life for the working masses. Indeed, coming on the heels of *Industrial Britain*, *Song of Ceylon* seems to quietly contest the humanized and aestheticized representation of industrial Britain that the movement aimed to produce. Grierson, whose function it was to negotiate between the filmmakers' socialist tendencies and capitalist sponsorship, is explicit in describing a policy whose aim was labor's acquiescence: "When it came to making industry not ugly for people, but a matter of beauty, so that people would accept their industrial selves, so that they would not revolt against their industrial selves, as they did in the late 19th century, who initiated the finding of beauty in industry? The British government—as a matter of policy" (quoted in Barnouw 91).

There is no record, however, in the literature of any protest on the part of the sponsors against *Song of Ceylon* for its critique of colonial exploitation or the commentary it tacitly offers on alienated social relations in Britain. Grierson was "more than delighted" with the rushes. It is perhaps also the case that the Ceylon Tea Propaganda Board was delighted by the film because its international success, as Eric Barnouw speculates, "put the Board on record as fervently admiring the Ceylonese and their culture" (93). What explains this lack of controversy?

I would like to argue that *Song of Ceylon*, through its idealization of Ceylonese life, belongs to the colonialist discourse that Edward Said calls "Orientalism." In his view, the Orient is not a geographical reality but a construction, elaborated by the Western intellectual tradition in the interest of "understanding" and ultimately subjugating the East. Orientalism is, as Said describes it, "the enormously systematic discipline by which European culture was able to manage—and even produce—the Orient politically, sociologically, militarily, ideologically, scientifically, and imaginatively during the post-Enlightenment period" (3). As Said argues, the relationship between the Occident and the Orient is based in power. Implicit in all orientalist discourse is the cultural hegemony of the European, whose "positional superiority" casts the non-European in the role of the Other. Orientalist texts therefore have much less to do with the East than they do with the hegemonic European culture.

Orientalism is at work in the great exotic art and literature of the nineteenth and early twentieth centuries, in Flaubert's *Salaambô* as in Delacroix's paintings from his sojourn in Morocco. It is not surprising that the orientalist legacy emerged in the early documentaries on foreign subjects filmed before 1920, in the Romantic travel film, or even in films with ethnographic pretensions. Patrick O'Reilly called these films, set in locations like Tahiti and New Zealand, *"documentaires romances"* (quoted in Heider 20). In *Song of Ceylon*, Basil Wright works in the tradition that sees in evocations of the East the possibility of alternative visions. Just as Joseph Conrad or André Gide sought in the Orient a model of liberated sexual experience to be pitted against the constraints of modern bourgeois manners, Wright discovered in the bodies of the Ceylonese, their relationship to the landscape, their customs, and especially their religious practice, everything he saw as lacking in contemporary British society. "Ceylon" becomes the repressed of sovereign Western consciousness—the image of everything that must be repudiated by the ideology of late capitalism in order to support the status quo.

The film's basic mechanism is therefore projection. I am borrowing the term—not from the EMB's Sir Stephen Tallents but from psychoanalytic theory: projection is a psychological "operation whereby qualities, feelings, wishes or even 'objects,' which the subject refuses to recognise or rejects in himself, are expelled from the self and located in another person or thing" (Laplanche and Pontalis 349). I am referring here not to individual human subjects but the collective social subject, whose frustrated desires seek expression in ways that do not endanger the social organism. Since in twentieth-century Britain closeness to nature, unalienated work, and spiritual transcendence must be suppressed in the interest of an increasingly urbanized, industrialized, and secularized society, the social subject can rediscover these desired objects only through a mechanism of distancing. Either the object of desire is projected back in time and enjoyed nostalgically—as in Robert Flaherty's romantic documentary *Man of Aran* (1934)—or the object is projected across geographical space and located in another, distant culture—as in Flaherty's *Moana*. This second procedure—exoticism—establishes a cultural Other, in whom we locate all that we have lost. It is even possible for this other mode of existence, a seductive combination of the real and the imaginary, to triumph, as it does in the concluding sequences of *Song of Ceylon,* which banish the cacophony of colonial voices and leave us with the mysterious images of the solitary worship of Buddha and the ritual dance. The proviso is: that we situate this ecstasy of spirit and body elsewhere than where we are.

I tend to think that anthropologist Gregory Bateson was targeting films like *Song of Ceylon* in his critique of documentary film practice. Bateson argues in *Balinese Character* for a "disinterested" methodology of ethnographic observation that considers the camera as an instrument for collecting data prior to the work of conceptualization: "We tried to use the still and the moving picture camera to get a record of Balinese behavior, and this is a very different matter from the preparation of a 'documentary' film or photographs. We tried to shoot what happened normally and spontaneously, rather than to decide upon the norms and then get the Balinese to go through these behaviors in suitable lighting" (49). The calculated effects in *Song of Ceylon* that I have referred to as *photogenia* indeed reveal an intentionality that goes well beyond observation. The film's images, with their attention to composition and photographic qualities of light and texture, their aestheticization of the Ceylonese body, the rhetorical gestures that bind the shots in sequence and that structure the relationships between image and sound, the sound track itself, with its recitative voice-over, its musical score combining "native" song and orchestral modernism, its noise track pitting the harmonious sounds of traditional culture against the stridency of colonial commerce—all resonate with the exoticism that characterizes the projective desires of the Orientalist.

The exotic is always one's own half-spoken desire. The ethical problem in documentary is that the projective desire can attach itself to images seized from another culture. The underlying assumption in Orientalism, Edward Said suggests in the epigraph to his work, is summed up by Karl Marx's proposition on representation of the East: "They cannot represent themselves; they must be represented." It is the role of the Orientalist to speak for the culture that has not sufficiently evolved from a state of nature and therefore has no access to reasoned discourse. Using the resources of photogenia and the discursive counterpoint of image and sound, the voice of Orientalism makes the mysteries of Ceylon plain for its Western spectators. Like Flaherty, Wright transfigures "natural materials" through the resources of framing, light and shadow, and camera movement. He decenters the human figures in emphatic compositional effects that stress the Ceylonese's relationship to a mystic cosmology of water, earth, and sky. *Song of Ceylon* produces images of bliss predicated on the notion of primordial innocence. Under the tutelage of Cavalcanti, Wright exploits shifting and complex relationships between image and sound that allow for new discursive forms to emerge: the historical voice-over that speaks the timelessness of the Ceylonese world, the rhetoric of antithesis that produces the dissonance between Nature/the Divine/unalienated labor, and the disembodied voices of modern commerce and exploitation.

In *Song of Ceylon* we see the Art of National Projection caught in fundamental ambivalence. Commissioned as a work of propaganda to present positive images of the British Commonwealth, the film produces instead an ecstatic evocation of a paradise nearly lost. Rather than discovering in the world of commerce and its colonial outposts new representations of humanness and beauty, *Song of Ceylon* produces a critique of the whole enterprise of National Projection, stigmatizing the British presence as callous and exploitative. However, *Song of Ceylon* also reveals another basic ambivalence, this time toward the subjects it claims to represent. In "speaking for" the Ceylonese, the film reduces them to silence. It appropriates their images and subjects them to the distortions of exoticism. They become, in effect, terms in a discourse of protest against the reality of social relations in the industrial era.

Works Cited

Abel, Richard. *French Cinema: The First Wave, 1915–1929*. Princeton: Princeton University Press, 1984.

Barnouw, Erik. *Documentary: A History of the Non Fiction Film*. Oxford: Oxford University Press, 1983.

Bateson, Gregory, and Margaret Mead. *Balinese Character: A Photographic Analysis*. New York: Academy of Sciences, 1942.

Eisenstein, Sergei. *Film Form*. Cleveland: Meridian Books, 1965.

Epstein, Jean. *Écrits sur le cinéma*. Vol. 1. Paris: Seghers, 1975.

Grierson, John. *Grierson on Documentary*. Ed. Forsyth Hardy. Berkeley: University of California Press, 1966.

Heider, Karl G. *Ethnographic Film*. Austin: University of Texas Press, 1976.

Laplanche, J., and J. B. Pontalis. *The Language of Psycho-Analysis*. Trans. Donald Michelson-Smith. New York: Norton, 1973.

Rotha, Paul. *Documentary Diary*. New York: Hill and Wang, 1973.

Said, Edward. *Orientalism*. New York: Vintage Books, 1979.

Sussex, Elizabeth. *The Rise and Fall of British Documentary*. Berkeley: University of California Press, 1975.

Chapter 6

THE MASS PSYCHOLOGY OF FASCIST CINEMA

Leni Riefenstahl's *Triumph of the Will*

Frank P. Tomasulo

Most of the scholarly literature on Leni Riefenstahl's mammoth spectacle *Triumph of the Will* (1935) deals with the hoary questions of whether or not the film's director was a Nazi, supported the National Socialists, or had an affair with Adolf Hitler. Over the past sixty years, these biographical issues have been addressed by many cinema critics, a series of postwar "denazification" boards, the filmmaker's autobiography, *Leni Riefenstahl: A Memoir*, and, most recently, in the documentary film *The Wonderful Horrible Life of Leni Riefenstahl* (1994).

The purpose of this essay is to refocus the discussion on *Triumph of the Will* by examining the *text* of the film, its cinematic imagery and "political" content, and the psychological *context* in which it was made—the 1930s historical conjuncture of the German masses with fascist ideology. Synthesizing the three modes of analysis—the ideological, psychological, and cinematic—is crucial because, as Siegfried Kracauer has said, "What films reflect are not so much explicit credos as psychological dispositions—those deep layers of collective mentality which extend more or less below the dimension of consciousness" (6). To explore the nexus between ideology, psychology, and cinematic style in *Triumph of the Will*, the ideas and writings of a contemporaneous thinker, Wilhelm Reich, will be recruited in an effort both to understand the fascinating appeal of fascism to the German *volk*

of the period and to analyze how Riefenstahl's film style, even in the documentary mode, appealed to and positioned spectators (socially and psycho-
logically), and thereby transmitted a meaning beneficial to the Nazi cause.

WILHELM REICH: *THE MASS PSYCHOLOGY OF FASCISM*

Wilhelm Reich, who combined psychological insight with sociopolitical
analysis, offers a historically contemporaneous explanation of the mesmeriz-
ing way in which *Triumph of the Will* interpellated viewers.[1] His classic study,
The Mass Psychology of Fascism, is a unique Marxo-Freudian contribution to
our understanding of fascism as a crucial phenomenon of modern life.

Reich repudiated the idea that fascism is an ideology or an action of a
single individual or nationality or of any ethnic or political group. As he put
it, "Fascism is not a political party but a specific concept of life and attitude
toward humankind, love, and work" (xxii). So, for Reich, fascism is an expression of the irrational character structure of the average human being
whose primary biological needs and impulses have been suppressed by the
authoritarian patriarchal family and the Church for thousands of years. According to Reich, "The abominable excesses of the capitalist era . . . were
possible only because the human structure of the untold masses had become totally dependent upon authority, incapable of freedom and extremely
accessible to mystification" (xxvi–xxvii). Thus Reich perceived fascism to be
more than a mere epiphenomenal "false consciousness," more than a be-
fogging or deception of the masses; instead, Reich argued, the masses were
fully accessible to the "Nazi psychosis" and hence responsible for every
social process: "Fascism is to be regarded as a problem of the masses, and
not as a problem of Hitler as a person or the politics of the National Socialist Party" (98).

Reich studied the 1932 voting statistics in Germany and learned that
"it was precisely the wretched masses (i.e., the lower middle class) who
helped to put fascism into power" (10). But why would millions of people
affirm their own suppression? The answer lies in what Reich called "complete identification with state power" (46). In short, feeling at one with the
authoritarian father figure makes a person feel at one with the fatherland.
Such emotional identification with the stern and decisive father produces
"the self-confidence that the individual derives from the 'greatness of the'
nation'" (Reich 63).[2]

How does a fascist film position its viewers, according to the Reichian
model? One has to start with the subject because "every social order produces in its masses that structure which it needs to achieve its main aims"
(Reich 23). And one must begin before the person ever sees a film because

"the structural reproduction of society takes place in the first four or five years of life and in the authoritarian family" (Reich 30).

Three other factors in Reich's teachings are significant to his analysis of fascism: the role of religion, characterological armor (what contemporary psychologists call "body language"), and the sexual symbolism of the swastika. Reich constantly referred to all religion as "organized mysticism." Based on his clinical research, Reich also developed the concept of characterological armor, represented physiologically by muscular tension and disturbances in posture. For Reich, the repressed, inhibited, and unspontaneous neurotic betrays a rigid, taut, and unrelaxed musculature, carriage, and overall affect (Rycroft 67). The unconscious social effects of the swastika help explain fascism's mass appeal and its frequent display in *Triumph of the Will*: "This symbol depicting two interlocked figures acts as a powerful stimulus . . . that proves to be that much more powerful, the more dissatisfied, the more burning with sexual desire, a person is" (Reich 103). The swastika was originally a sexual symbol, portraying the act of copulation, although it later took on connotations of a millwheel, the symbol for work. Ironically, it dates back to the Semites, to the Myrtle court of the Alhambra at Granada and to the synagogue ruins of Edd-Dikke in East Jordania (Reich 101–2).

Reich knew that it was not enough to present reasoned political platforms to the apathetic masses; an authoritative fascist leader had to strive to embody the nation's myths and thereby become "the personification of the nation" (62). By subjectifying cultural iconography into the person of one father figure and onto powerful national symbols, potent objective forces were put in place. In a nation undergoing economic and political crises, such as Germany did during the Weimar period, the longstanding myths of that culture became effective symbolic tools to promote fascism, and, in the twentieth century, those cultural myths were most forcefully conveyed on film.

TRIUMPH OF THE WILL: A TEXT IN CONTEXT

Triumph of the Will was commissioned by Chancellor Adolf Hitler, who was hailed (or *heiled*) as a charismatic leader. It was meant to be the official documentation of the annual Party Congress of September 4–10, 1934. Riefenstahl's film essentially promulgated fascism and the National Socialist Party (NSDAP) as the bases for renewed German nationalism and patriotism. As Joseph Goebbels once said, "We are convinced that films constitute one of the most modern and scientific means of influencing the masses" (quoted in Downing 21).

Although *Triumph of the Will* was made about the party convention,
it does not really articulate any specific political policy or substantive ideology. Instead, preliterate symbolic imagery and vague patriotic appeals are
used to address the emotional concerns of the populace. Indeed, Hitler
repeatedly stressed that one could not sway the masses with arguments,
logic, or knowledge, only with feelings and beliefs. True to form, the documentary establishes a "cult of personality" around its "star," a mystical aura
associated with Nature, religion, and a "folkish" family-based patriotism.
The film spectacle often connects its heroic leader with the sky, the earth,
and animals; Christian and pagan religious connotations abound; and
flags, parades, torchlight rituals, and military-national symbols dominate
the mise-en-scène. Indeed, all the signifying mechanisms of the cinema—
camera angles, editing, music, set design, lighting, and narration—are
marshaled to appeal to the irrational character structure of its malleable
mass audience.

In content, the film emphasizes upbeat and patriotic themes that
convey a renewed sense of national identity and unity following a period of economic and political instability. This is precisely the mood one
would expect in a motion picture depicting the annual rally of a partisan
political party; however, Leni Riefenstahl's insistence that "there is no
tendentious commentary for the simple reason that there is no commentary at all. It is *history—pure history*" (interview with Delahaye 460)
is too simplistic.

Susan Sontag has argued that the film "has no commentary because it
doesn't need one, for *Triumph of the Will* represents an already achieved and
radical transformation of reality: history become theater" (83). The fascist
aesthetic valorized and derived pleasure from "situations of control, submissive behavior, extravagant effort, and the endurance of pain." Furthermore, "Fascist dramaturgy centers on the orgiastic transactions between
mighty forces and their puppets, uniformly garbed and shown in ever
swelling numbers" (Sontag 91).

Although hundreds of thousands of people attended the Nuremberg
rally, Riefenstahl's telephoto lens often magnifies those numbers by compressing and welding the crowds together cinematically, thereby conveying the ideological point that the masses are closer together (united) and
solidly behind their chancellor. In fact, with the aid of 16 cameramen, 135
technicians, and a rally stage-managed by Third Reich architect Albert
Speer, she created, rather than merely documented, an event that would
not have occurred in quite the same way without the presence of cameras
and microphones. The spectacle of reality *became* reality. The film's concatenation of artificial images—its sights and sounds—created a simulacrum

of a revitalized *Zeitgeist* that appeared to be real to many viewers. It was not merely an economic revitalization that the Nazis were trumpeting but a spiritual rebirth and redemption as well.

What follows is a careful examination of *Triumph*'s design, which is usually divided into thirteen parts (Hinton 34–37).

I. Hitler's Arrival

The film begins with a specific date: September 5, 1934—the first day of the Party Congress. After that, Riefenstahl's chronology is not very strict. She positions events that occurred toward the beginning of the seven-day rally toward the middle of the film and places scenes that were filmed at the end of the proceedings near the beginning.[3] Furthermore, many of the speeches were reshot in a studio after the convention because of difficulties in recording sound at the original location.

From its very opening, *Triumph of the Will* establishes audience identification with its hero, in much the same way fictional films do. Riefenstahl's camera shows us the literal and figurative point of view of Hitler from inside his airplane as it descends upon Nuremberg from the heavens. *Der Führer*'s visual "God's eye" point of view is seen as the plane literally parts

Triumph of the Will: At the Nuremberg rally history becomes theater.

the clouds (of postwar confusion?) while soaring above the medieval city. Kracauer has compared *Triumph*'s opening sequence to "a reincarnation of All-Father Odin" (290), but these early images are also replete with Christian iconography, literalizing as they do New Testament references to "the Son of Man coming on the clouds of heaven with power and great glory" (Matthew 24:30), "a mighty angel coming down from the heavens, wrapped in a cloud" (Revelation 20:4), and "lo, a white cloud, and seated on the cloud one like a son of man, with a gold crown on his head" (Revelation 14:14). In short, *der Führer* comes out of the clouds just as the Book of Revelation predicted that the Second Coming would take place; the verbal imagery and Old German titles nail the religious point home: "Sixteen years after Germany's *crucifixion*, nineteen months after Germany's *Wiedergeburt*" (renaissance, sometimes translated as *resurrection*). Thus Hitler is cast as a veritable German Messiah who will save the nation, if only the citizenry will put its destiny in his hands.

The alliance of religion and politics in the film's imagery stems from the fact that, according to Reich, "our idea of *God* is identical with our idea of *father*" (145). Reich also contended that there was pleasure connected with "the idea of religious excitation . . . includ[ing] the excitation experienced by submissive masses when they open themselves to a beloved leader's speech" (144). He added that although "fascism is supposed to be a reversion to paganism and an archenemy of religion," it is, in fact, "the supreme expression of religious mysticism" (xv).

The musical accompaniment to this opening sequence is serene and peaceful (Herbert Windt's mix of Wagner's *Die Meistersinger* with the Nazi marching anthem, the "Horst Wessel *Lied*"). Hitler's plane is shown literally *über Alles,* so much so that it soars above and out of the frame in several shots. Its shadow is seen over the columns of marching paraders, resembling an eagle, one of the most frequently displayed symbols of the Third Reich.[4]

Once the airplane lands, anticipation is carefully built up through the montage and sound track. Repeated crosscuts between the plane taxiing to a halt and the huge crowd of enthusiastic greeters at the airport create suspense. Here, as elsewhere, telephoto shots of the overpopulated crowd make it appear that their numbers are larger than they are, while compressing the background-foreground planes of the image to suggest that the people are closely united. Their coordinated *Sieg Heil* salutes are composed along the diagonal of the frame, a powerful dynamization of screen space that visually conveys the strength of the people's devotion to their savior.

When Hitler does emerge from the plane, the assembled masses burst into a loud *Heil!* precisely as the music reaches its crescendo. Back-lighting on the leader is used to create an aura of religiosity; as the rim lighting creates a halo-like effect, clearly giving Hitler a god-like aura, it also lightens his dark hair to make his appearance better fit the fair-haired Aryan stereotype, as seen in so many close-ups of rally participants.

As the chancellor's motorcade begins to drive through the streets of Nuremberg, one shot is repeated several times: a medium shot or close-up that shows *der Führer* stable and solid, centered in the frame, arm upraised in a *Sieg Heil* posture, while the people along the route are an amorphous, out-of-focus blur. This single, reiterated image tells the whole story of *Triumph of the Will* in miniature: an unfocused and confused Germany is once again on the move, in the person of its solid, focused leader, who is the unifying frame of reference for the audience and the nation. Frequent cuts between adoring crowd members and Hitler corroborate that message.

Later, the "nation on the move" theme is strongly associated with the moving camera, which follows Hitler's motorcade through the streets, under dramatic archways, and into tunnels, often from the chancellor's point of view. The lighting in this scene is metaphorical: *der Führer*'s grand entrance from the darkness of the tunnel to the sunlight parallels the emergence of Germany from the dark shadows of Weimar into the Nazi renaissance.

The buildings along the motorcade route are festooned with huge Nazi flags and standards. The camera often glides past them, looking up in intox-icating awe at the conjuncture of the old and the new. As the camera trucks past one building, it looks up at an open window. In an eyeline match, a house cat turns its head dramatically to stare at Hitler and the passing Nazi cavalcade. Although this shot may not have been staged, its insertion into the flow of the images suggests that even nature is impressed by the sweep of the National Socialists' advance.

Next, a mother and her fair-haired daughter come up to Hitler's staff car and present him with a bouquet of flowers. The film then cuts to two other blond girls in the crowd who seem to observe this scene. Finally, the first girl, boosted up in her mother's arms, gives a cute *Sieg Heil* gesture to the chancellor. These images of maternal bliss, youthful innocence, and nature link Hitler to peace and love and thus create the impression that he is a benign and caring ruler to his flock.

Once Hitler reaches his hotel, the telephoto lens is again used to "pack" the crowd. The people's gaze up toward the second-floor balcony is mirrored in the camera's tilt up to follow their glances, culminating in a low-angle shot of *der Führer* at the window, basking in the public adulation. Here, the subtle upward camera tilt participates in and adds to the libidinal agitation of the expectant throng below.

II. Hitler's Serenade

In *Triumph*'s first night scene, torchlight is used to illuminate the area around Hitler's hotel and the pennants held aloft by the mob outside. A military marching band plays as uniformed police push back the hordes of followers trying to get a glimpse of their leader. Although all of this was no doubt part of the historical reality of the event, the director emphasizes the vastness of the congregation by filming it in deep-focus space. The pageantry of a torchlit procession, replete with huge bonfires along the route, is accentuated both by the dramatic flickering backlighting on the silhouetted marching soldiers and by the camera's motility.

III. The City Awakens

In this section, Riefenstahl creates a city symphony in miniature.[5] A window is seen opening onto a panoramic vista of Nuremberg in the early morning light. We see the city's medieval churches, its industrial smokestacks, and the rivers and bridges. In one shot, the camera slowly glides along the river, looking up at a cathedral's spires. Riefenstahl then boldly cuts to a high-angle shot, photographed from an overhead airplane, looking down on the tent city. We see young drummer and bugle boys preparing to wake the Hitlerjungen, who proceed to engage in their morning ablutions: shaving, combing each other's hair, squirting water from hoses, stoking firewood. Steamy noodle soup is prepared, and sausages are arrayed in formation like the thousands of young men and women in attendance. These images of youthful exuberance (boxing matches, foot races, shenanigans) are notable for the consistency of costume, activity, and facial reaction (smiles). A unity of national purpose is thereby established through the clothing, action, and countenances of the beaming young people. The lone exception is Adolf Hitler, who wanders through the pseudo-boot camp in his military uniform.

IV. Folk Parade

The adoring looks of the costumed Bavarian peasant women reiterate the theme of female idealization of the *Führer* established in the earlier airport and motorcade sequences. For these women and for the youngsters, the libidinal object (Hitler) has been put in the place of an ego ideal. It is just a short step to national hypnosis and subjection. Traditional folk music is played over these scenes until, eventually, an accordion player and people in matching Bavarian costumes begin to march in parade formation. After the parade, the "Horst Wessel *Lied*" emerges from the folk airs, a sonic suggestion that the Nazis materialized out of the native populace.

V. Congress Opening

After the folk parade, Deputy Chancellor Rudolf Hess officially opens the Party Congress. In an indoor meeting hall, Hess announces the death of Reich president Paul von Hindenburg.[6] As he does so, the camera tilts up to a huge swastika emblem, visually linking Hindenburg with a symbol of the Third Reich. At the precise instant that Hess calls Hindenburg the "first soldier of the Great War," there is a cut to a helmeted soldier in the auditorium, thereby visually associating the dead octogenarian with his contemporary avatar, the new Nazi warrior. Hess's verbal tribute to the fallen warrior, like the film's editing here, attempts to connect Germany's past and the present in an effort to create a historical unity of purpose that belies the fact that Hindenburg was adamantly opposed to the Nazis.

Later in his eulogy, Hess makes another linkage when, addressing Hitler, he exclaims, "You are Germany!" Riefenstahl cuts to two reaction shots: one of an older woman applauding the remark and another of a young girl who also claps loudly, thus linking the generations. Such reaction shots in a film often lead and legitimate the spectator's response by creating a diegetic "climate" for a shared reaction between spectacle and spectator. The effect on a spectator of viewing a positive reaction shot is, generally speaking, to induce the same sort of euphoria in the viewer through a process akin to "contagion."[7]

Other speakers come to the podium to tout the tyrant's virtues. Von Wagner reads from *der Führer*'s proclamation; Rosenberg expresses "our hope in the youth"; Toth extols the recent improvements in Germany; Darré emphasizes "the health of our farmers" and the improved agricultural export situation; Streicher stresses "racial purity"; and Frank, leader of the German legal profession, avers that "our Supreme *Führer* is our Supreme Judge." Finally, Goebbels closes this segment by summarizing "the creative art of modern political propaganda": "It may be good to [use guns] but it is far better to win the hearts of the people." In the context of *Triumph*'s filmic rhetoric, Goebbels's statement can be read as self-reflexive. All of the speeches given in the assembly hall are obviously designed to secure the allegiance of the populace, but the effectivity of Riefenstahl's film is similar: to influence spectators' "hearts" through cinematic means of manipulation.

VI. The Labor Corps Rally

In this sequence, Hitler addresses the 52,000-member Labor Corps—the chancellor's answer to German unemployment—who come with Nazi ensigns and their strong-lunged *Heils*. With precision timing, the drill team raises and lowers its spades, as if it were a military color guard. Rows of drummers pound out a slow, solemn beat as the crowd intones, "On with Germany to a new era." These images help to forge a common national identity. *Triumph* also shows the *Volk* working together, despite their regional differences, epitomized by the many workers who call out the names of their regions (Bavaria, Konigsberg, Dresden, Black Forest, the Saar). These individual close-ups can be considered metonymies of a splintered Germany or as celebrations of the individual spirit, but the true rhetoric of the scene is to build a sense of German unity through the accretion of such images.

Similarly, the slow montage of images that follows unites three concepts into a seamless whole. On the sound track, the masses chant, "One People, One *Führer*, One Reich," and with each phrase the film cuts, respectively, to a Labor Corpsman with a lowered flag, a huge close-up of Hitler, and an ironworks sculpture of an eagle surmounting a swastika. The solemn rhythm, edited to the cadence of the chanted words, amplifies the message of German unity under one leader and one (NSDAP) banner. Shortly thereafter, the technique is repeated when the workers, in unison, murmur, "We plant forests, we build roads . . . for Germany." Precisely at the word "Germany," there is a cut to an extreme close-up of Hitler, again making a direct visual link between the nation and *der Führer*.

Sympathy is evoked when a flag is lowered by first one, then many soldiers as they recall the martyrs of World War I and shout out the names of famous battles. When Hitler addresses this group, he reminds them of the NSDAP's accomplishments: "The Red Front and reaction are all dead." On that sentence, there is a cut on a pronounced drumbeat to swastikas being raised, thereby linking the demise of leftist parties to the rise of Nazism. Referring to the German war dead, Hitler says, "You are not dead. You live in Germany!" This oration at a memorial service for Nazi "revolutionaries" thus invokes the idea of the resurrection of martyrs, a theme that is prominent throughout the documentary.

As Hitler continues his address to the Labor Corps, he is photographed in profile, centered solidly in the frame, while the huge mob seen behind him is out of focus. Again, the leader is presented cinematically as focused, prominent, and powerful, while the masses are shown as unfocused, secondary, and powerless. When *der Führer* proclaims, "Work . . . will bind us together," Riefenstahl cuts immediately to a shot that visually binds the throng, a pan taken with a telephoto lens.

Shortly thereafter, a low-angle close-up of Hitler against a bald white sky presents a highly dramatic view of the leader at the same time as it provides a child's-eye view of the father figure. *Der Führer* then makes the patriarchal context most explicit, as he shouts to the assembled Labor Corps, "Germany proudly sees its sons in your image." The shot ends with the despot's arm in a dynamic *Heil* salute across the diagonal of the screen. That position is maintained as the image dissolves to a low-angle view looking up at hundreds of shovel-toting marchers as martial music plays on the sound track, again accentuating the strength of the growing war machine. Finally, the sequence ends as the Labor brigades, singing in staccato fashion, march directly at the camera. The military connotations of the Labor Corps' uniforms, shovels, flags, drill teams, parades, and precise regimentation are clearly in evidence.

VII. The S.A. (Sturm-Angriff)

Dramatic lighting is at the heart of the sequence in which S.A. chief Viktor Lutze addresses his stormtroopers. It opens with flags and standards blowing in the nighttime breeze. The camera moves around the Nazi symbols to reveal a blazing bonfire surrounded by singing men. At the smoke-enshrouded speaker's platform, searchlights and magnesium torches abound, creating a striking configuration on Lutze's face. In his speech, the S.A. chief stresses that "we S.A. men know only to be loyal to our *Führer* and fight for him!" Just then, the film cuts to an upward tilt shot that reveals a large swastika flag, a juxtaposition that links the S.A., Lutze, Hitler, and the symbols of the Reich in a visual mythic unity.[8] The event ends with fireworks exploding and a return to the bonfires and moving torchlights. In its entirety, this sequence—replete with its firelight, smoke, fireworks, and sensational *Sieg Heil* salutes—cultivates a milieu of ritualized male initiation and idolatry, the sort of mass mesmerization diagnosed by Wilhelm Reich.

VIII. Hitler Youth

This section begins with a giant close-up of a blaring bugle that fills the screen, followed by a cut to another circular shape, a round drum being pounded. Finally, we cut to a boy beating the drum with two sphere-headed batons. From these close-ups of rounded (cunnic) and straight (phallic) shapes, the camera pulls back to include a wide shot of the Hitlerjungen standing on their tiptoes to see their hero's arrival at the huge amphitheater, the noise level rising to build anticipation. As Hitler enters, Riefenstahl cuts to a shot of phallic trumpets bellowing. On cue, the youth *Heil Hitler* en masse. Thus the sequence builds from explicit individual sexual symbols to mass excitation that culminates with the appearance of *der Führer*. Again, Hitler is backlit in order to augment his godlike aura and lighten his hair, while the youthful crowd is out of focus.

The lectures to the Hitler Youth are permeated with messages of unity and subservience to the leader: "a youth that knows no class distinctions," "the youth of our nation is shaped in [Hitler's] image," "we want to be one people," and "we want this people to be obedient and you must practice this obedience." But beyond these verbal injunctions, *Triumph* uses cinematic means to impart the same ideas. In one particular long shot, the enormous assemblage stands and shouts, "*Heil.*" In the foreground several people salute and cheer Hitler, while the deep-focus space of the background is filled with thousands of closely packed youngsters.

Later, a high-angle image shows the grandiose crowd arranged in box-shaped patterns, imparting the sort of symmetry the Nazis were trying to impose on the chaotic German nation. This image of disciplined, rectangular order is followed by the chancellor's pronouncement, "We want to be one people," thereby linking the visual and verbal themes. A series of reaction shots of beaming, fair-haired boys reiterates that message, while adding a subtle Aryan dimension to the idea of national unity.

Even when Hitler is stationary in the frame, as he is when he speaks to the packed stadium, the camera dollies around him, imparting an intoxicating kinesthetic quality to an otherwise static image. The cut—to an extreme long shot showing thousands of closely crammed-together youngsters *Heiling* their leader—bolsters the relationship between Hitler and his youth movement, especially since the arm salutes are composed across the diagonal of the frame. Thus the juxtaposition of the moving camera shot that circumnavigates *der Führer* with the static long shot of the *Heiling* masses of young people establishes a wished-for paternal nexus between this "father" and his "children" that belies the fact that six to ten years later he ordered these same young men into battle as cannon fodder for the imagined glory of the Third Reich. Ironically, Hitler's speech includes a line—"In Germany, you will *live!*"—that is followed by a reaction shot of a grinning face in the crowd. At the end of his oration, Hitler reinvokes the religious connotations that have been just below the surface of the entire party rally. Lecturing the young people, he declares, "You are flesh from our flesh and blood from our blood," a formulation that conjoins Eucharistic ("This is my body; this is my blood") and Aryan undertones.

The final image of the sequence is an elaborate tracking shot that travels around the entire circumference of the massive stadium, focusing on the enormous line of youths on the stadium floor. Although the swirling image may suggest destabilization, the triumphant music on the sound track in fact underscores the physical movement and psychological captivation of the entire "Hitler Youth" scene.

IX. *Review of the Army*

When Hitler reviews the army, the film's rhetoric becomes divided. For internal German consumption, Riefenstahl shows the army's maneuvers—a nationalistic and militaristic display of flags, precision horsemen galloping in review, mini-tanks driving in formation, and cannons being drawn along by horses. As such, the film cannily portrays the economic, military, and spiritual recovery of the German nation. When exported, however, these images suggested to the world that Germany's army was a less-than-mighty force with outdated technology, ostensibly in compliance with the demilitarization provisions of the Treaty of Versailles.

X. *The Evening Rally*

The sequence begins with a view of storm clouds, but the camera gradually tilts down to reveal a sculpted eagle grasping a swastika. Here, through a shrewd camera movement, Riefenstahl ties a portentous scene of nature with the force of the Reich. We then see masses of party bureaucrats hoisting swastika flags to the beat of triumphant music. Telephoto lenses capture the held-aloft standards on the move, squeezing them together to evince the "tightness" of the Party's supporters, and an extreme long shot documents the sheer number of disciples who attended the rally. (Hitler observes that 200,000 people are assembled.)

In his speech, *der Führer* says, "The State does not order us [to attend]! We order the State! We created the State!" He adds, "Our movement stands like a rock!" Both these verbal assertions are aided by the cinematography. Hitler is photographed as erect and ramrod straight, firmly centralized in the mise-en-scène, his *Sieg Heil* salute acknowledging the plaudits of the roaring mob.

Another torchlight procession commences, shot as a montage of marching feet, solemn faces, and upraised pennants, all to the incessant rhythm of martial music. At one point, Riefenstahl cuts from a high-angle view down on the gigantic crowd to a low-angle shot looking up at Hitler, underscoring his power, authority, and superiority to the masses.

XI. Hitler and the S.A.

The segment begins with a shot of a giant stone statue of an eagle astride a swastika. Then Riefenstahl cuts to one of the most famous images in *Triumph of the Will*, an extreme long shot showing three men (Hitler, Lutze, and S.S. chief Heinrich Himmler), tiny in the frame, marching up an imposing aisle in a vast outdoor stadium, the War Memorial, surrounded on both sides by a sea of humanity.[9] The three men walk slowly toward three mammoth swastika banners unfurled at a tall granite platform at the top of the screen. The camera glides majestically as funereal music marks the solemnity of the event—the laying of a wreath at the eternal flame dedicated to Nazi martyrs.

Again, Riefenstahl uses aggressive framing on the marchers walking directly toward the camera, along with bird's-eye views looking down on

Triumph of the Will: Hitler, Lutze, and Himmler at the War Memorial.

the organized masses. These contradictory viewpoints suggest that the German people are both active and passive, on the move, but only as followers. The telephoto lens is used again from a high angle to show hundreds of Nazi banners approaching the camera, seeming to have a life of their own. In another montage, the director cuts from a long shot of men marching in formation to a close shot of Hermann Göring, then to an extreme long shot of the rally, followed by close-ups of a swastika and an eagle. These juxtaposed images link the military, Nazi leaders, the masses, and the symbols of the Reich in a mystical bond of unity and obeisance. Reich has noted that "the sexual effect of a uniform, the erotically provocative effect of rhythmically executed goosestepping, [and] the exhibitionistic nature of militaristic procedures" are often exploited by fascism (32). The segment concludes as one of the military leaders declaims, "We comrades know only to obey."

In Hitler's address to the S.A. and S.S., photographed against a threatening, cloud-filled sky, he attempts to quell any internal fears about dissension in the ranks or the "blood purge" of disloyal Nazis. He avers that there is no split in the Party, adding that "our Party stands like a rock!" This remark, delivered from a massive stone platform, is the second such invocation of a rock analogy in the film, a metaphor that may derive from Christ's founding of the apostolic church on the pun "Thou art Peter [stone], and on this rock I found my church." But the Nazi "rock" comes with a sword, not an olive branch: after Hitler's fiery speech, artillery is fired and the flags of the regiment are consecrated in a paganlike rite.[10]

XII. The Parade

The parade scene begins with an extravagantly theatrical shot: the camera glides under an immense swastika flag to reveal the arrival of *der Führer*. This perspective approximates the raising of a theater curtain and sets the stage for an exalted entrance. Huge throngs are seen hanging out of windows to catch a glimpse of Hitler's motorcade. Drummers and marchers in military apparel parade through town, along with goose-steppers, who lead the way with Nazi standards and *Heil Hitler* salutes.

In a composition reminiscent of earlier shots, Hitler is situated in the foreground as a legion of out-of-focus troops file past in the background. Even the army is presented as unfocused, needing the solid hub of *der Führer* for guidance and direction. This shot is followed by a cut to a metonymic close-up that shows only the dictator's extended right arm in the foreground (the marchers remain blurred) until the camera pans across his arm to reveal his face. His willful and emphatic gesture—emphasized by Riefenstahl's camera angle—tells us more about the NSDAP policies than all the perorations in *Triumph of the Will* because, at its base, the Third Reich was about the exercise of brutal force over a country seeking direction. Fascism did not promulgate a rational political discourse or policy; instead, Hitler revived the concepts of the German philosopher Hegel concerning the exultation of the Will.[11] But in the end, *Triumph of the Will* is not really about the will at all; as Sontag observed, the film is "about the triumph of power" (87).

Constantly moving shots of Nuremberg are used in this sequence—of cathedrals, medieval architecture, porticos, bridges, the city hall, the river, and packed reviewing stands—to the accompaniment of radiant music, all in an effort to demonstrate how the city has turned out for the rally. One shot from on high shows the entire metropolis decked out in fascist regalia, permeated with saluting citizens. Hundreds of marchers file across the screen along the diagonal or as seen from above, looking like a meticulously orchestrated ant colony. One image of thousands of paraders is shot from directly overhead, highlighting the rigid geometric configuration of the people.

This section provides evidence that the rally's chronology was altered substantially in the editing room. In particular, footage of *der Führer* wearing a light-colored outfit (with light shirt and tie) was intermixed throughout the parade sequence with footage from another day on which he wore a darker jacket with a wide belt. The reason for combining footage from two separate occasions was probably to extend the screen time of the final parade. The sequence ends with the appearance of a goose-stepping color guard bearing the Party flags through the streets.

XIII. The Closing—Entry of the Party Standards

The closing scene begins with the ubiquitous Nazi emblem, featuring an eagle surmounting a swastika, but Riefenstahl quickly cuts to a shot of Hitler entering the Kongresshalle with dozens of Party officials. The camera tilts up slowly to reveal the enormity of the spacious auditorium and the immense swastika insignia draped over the podium. Loud shouts of the faithful are initially mixed with soft music, but the tune segues to a more martial melody once the standards are brought in. Everyone *Heils* the hundreds of banners, which seem to march straight at the camera without the aid of any human agency. The low camera angle foregrounds and imparts life to the standards over the human beings who display them. This optical rhetoric is perfectly appropriate to the spirit of fascism, which favors devotion to the autocrat and his symbols over individualism.

Nonetheless, individuals *are* singled out in *Triumph of the Will*. At the beginning of *der Führer's* final address at the rally, for instance, he refers to "the old fighters" of the NSDAP. At that moment, Göring, Himmler, Goebbels, and other longtime allies are shown, listening intently. One line sums up the content of Hitler's closing address; remembering the early days of the Party, he proclaims, "We wanted to be the one and only power in Germany." The next cut—to the eagle-over-swastika standard—brings home the message. Hitler's parting words are "Long live National Socialism! Long live Germany!" thereby equating his movement with the state.

His concluding speech shows how Adolf Hitler was able to capitalize on both his oratorical style and the cinematic depiction of that style in *Triumph of the Will*. Throughout the film, *der Führer* evinces stiff and rigid postures. For rhetorical flourishes, he frequently folds his arms over his chest, the classic body armor of the unreceptive, unemotional individual. His gestures are limited to the ever-present *Sieg Heil* salute, another stilted physiological movement. As he himself says, "The German people are happy to know that this fleeting image [the troubled past] has been replaced by a fixed pole." He posits himself as the national phallus and acts the part physiologically by maintaining ramrod poses for the camera. In Wilhelm Reich's schema, neurotic individual traits are also present on a collective (i.e., national) scale (Cattier 48).

In his final harangue, however, Hitler's body language is decidedly different than in his previous sermons, in which he evinced symptoms of the "characterological armor" and "biologic rigidity" Reich felt were at the basis of both personal neurosis and national fascism (342). It is only in his last speech that the dictator manifests any kinesthetic passion, moving about on the platform, gesticulating dramatically, and raising his voice. As a fitting conclusion to a motion picture that emphasized duty, submission, and a rein on one's emotions, *der Führer's* "star power"—his uninhibited surrender to the flow of biological energy and his ability to discharge pent-up sexual passion through animated facial reactions—allows the audience to experience national catharsis and orgastic release at the climax. In Reichian terms, a nation composed of frustrated individuals who repress their hostility behaves in a pathological manner, leaving them inaccessible to logical proof; such a people easily fall victim to the demagogic propaganda of mystical fascism.

All that is left is for Hess to reappear and affirm that "the Party is Hitler, and Hitler is Germany, just as Germany is Hitler." This irrational "syllogism" leads to the entire assembly breaking into the "Horst-Wessel-*Lied*" as the camera pans around the hall. The "documentary" ends on a dissolve from that singing mob to a huge swastika, then to a striking low-angle shot of hundreds of men marching against a background of clouds.

CONCLUSION:
THE MASS PSYCHOLOGY OF FASCIST CINEMA

Through the *emotional* appeal of *Triumph of the Will*, viewers are positioned in a very accustomed place—their own psyches. The myth, story, and spectacle created by this "nonfiction" film found receptive homes in the hearts and minds of their German viewers because the imaginary discourse it established was preconstructed in the German "national character" (Kracauer 8). The epic film succeeded because its emotional program resembled that of the vast cross-section of the public known collectively as the nation. Propaganda films such as *Triumph of the Will* not only promote the mythic rebirth of their nations, they also celebrate the rebirth of myth itself. There is only one role for the individual or collective spectator of these spectacles: as acceptor of the foreordained meanings of their cultural myths. Viewers are hailed (or *Heiled*) into "participation," but only if political, racial, gender, and class differences are elided in favor of an acceptance of an all-encompassing "we." As Kracauer indicated, "The technique, the story content, and the evolution of the films of a nation are fully understandable only in relation to the psychological pattern of that nation" (5).

That may be true because, as Karl Marx postulated, "In every epoch, the ideas of the ruling class are the ruling ideas. . . . The class that has the means of material production at its disposal also has the means of ideological 'production' at its disposal" (89). In what Walter Benjamin called "the age of mechanical reproduction" (i.e., the film epoch), Marx's famous formulation has a special relevance. Not only those who control the means of production but also those who control *the means of production of meaning-production* have power over both the material facts and the ideological spirit of an era.

Reich understood that in the twentieth century, the classic Marxist model—according to which the economic relations of production *determine* the artistic and philosophical trends of a given era—needed modification. In the modern world, propaganda artifacts like *Triumph of the Will* mingle historical realities and cultural expression to such an extent that the film has a tangible material and historical effect on society and social consciousness (Tomasulo 341). As Reich stated, "Social ideology not only reproduces itself in man but [it] has become an active force, a material power" because "the ideology of every social formation has the function not only of reflecting the economic process of the society, but also . . . of embedding the economic process in the *psychic structures of the people*" (17–18).

Triumph of the Will: Hitler's
rigid "body armor" is
contrasted with the masses
in the background.

The phenomenon of mass domination is hardly a recent development, but Reich added a new wrinkle to the scrutiny of an ancient political practice. The "bread and circuses" doled out to the Roman masses of
yore at least had one nutritious ingredient, bread, in a two-course menu for
promoting ideology and manipulating political hegemony; *Triumph of the
Will* provided only mindless spectacle and empty optimism for its passive
public, but it achieved the same results because "the films of a nation reflect its mentality . . . [because] films address themselves and appeal to the
anonymous multitude. Popular screen motifs can therefore be supposed to
satisfy existing mass desires" (Kracauer 5).

As Joanne Morreale noted in reference to more recent propaganda
cinema, "There is increasing difficulty reading from 'outside' the dominant ideology when psychological, political, cultural, and technological
apparatus[es] work to keep the reader/viewer inside" (90). Wilhelm Reich's
ideas can therefore be used to illuminate how material, historical, psychoanalytical, and mythic determinants in spectators' lives, *long before they are*

subject to a given film text, influence their comprehension of the content and style of a fascist text like *Triumph of the Will*—and the larger texts of life and society. No one is ever interpellated by a single text; we come to every film with the accumulated baggage of a lifetime of moviegoing—and living. Cinema scholars tend to analyze only the epiphenomenal symptoms of society—the individual films and the institution of cinema—rather than those complex and overdetermined extra-cinematic subjective factors of history that play such a vital role in positioning viewers long before they ever enter a movie theater.

Critics can "deconstruct" and perform oppositional readings of fascist propaganda films, but the hard work of raising consciousness entails much more. Rereading Hitler and *Triumph of the Will* necessitates reframing our entire experience of history, the world, and the cinema. The *subject in history,* not just the subject of a given motion picture text, must be analyzed if we ever expect to understand the complex mechanisms of film spectatorship and the mass psychology of fascist cinema.

Notes

1. An early member of the Vienna Psychoanalytic Society and Freud's assistant at the Polyclinic (1920–27), Reich was also a member of the Austrian and German Communist parties (1927–1933). During the early Fascist period (1933–34), however, Reich was expelled from both the International Psychoanalytic Association and the Communist Party. His expulsion from the former was due to theoretical differences regarding the social implications of psychoanalysis. In particular, the German Psychoanalytical Society felt it could not survive the rise of Nazism if it was associated with communism. Ironically, Reich was barred from the Communist Party because he was perceived to be diverting energies into mental health and sexual hygiene campaigns (Rycroft 5–7).

2. In this regard, Reich anticipated Louis Althusser's notion of the Ideological State Apparatuses. See Althusser's *Lenin and Philosophy,* trans. Ben Brewster (New York: Monthly Review Press, 1971), 127–86.

3. For a complete chronology of the events as they appear in the film, as well as their actual dates, see Hinton 37.

4. Indeed, the first image of the film is a fade-in to a stone eagle perched on a swastika. The camera then tilts down to the title, *Triumph des Willens,* in bold, severe, block letters.

5. The "city symphony" is a genre of documentary film, popular in the 1920s and 1930s, that creates impressionistic portraits of various international cities through rhythmic editing and lyrical musical scores. Examples include *Berlin: Symphony of a Great City* (1927), directed by Walter Ruttmann, who also designed the titles for

Triumph of the Will; Alberto Cavalcanti's *Rien que les heures* (1927); Dziga Vertov's *Man with a Movie Camera* (1929); and Jean Vigo's *À Propos de Nice* (1930).

6. Hindenburg died on August 2, 1934, a scant month before the Nuremberg rally. Hindenburg's demise allowed Hitler to consolidate the office of president, held by Hindenburg, with that of chancellor. As such, Hitler became both the head of state and the leader of the government (Hinton 132).

7. Sigmund Freud speaks of contagion as one of the major factors involved in the formation of the "group mind." See Freud, *Group Psychology and the Analysis of the Ego*, trans. James Strachey (New York: Bantam, 1960), 6–18.

8. This apparent show of solidarity masks the story of how Lutze came to be named S.A. chief. Former S.A. commander Ernst Rohm and his chief supporters were assassinated in the "blood purge" of June 30, 1934—just two months before the Nuremberg rally. The tension was so intense that extra Gestapo security was put in place to prevent an assassination attempt on Hitler *by his own Brownshirts*. See William L. Shirer, *Berlin Diary* (New York: Popular Library, 1940), 20–21. The film shows none of this acrimony. As Richard Meran Barsam implies, "*Triumph* transforms the reality of 1934 party disunity and chaos into a massive spectacle of regimentation, unity, and fidelity under the Führer." See Barsam, "Leni Riefenstahl: Artifice and Truth in a World Apart," *Film Comment* 9, no. 6 (1973): 34.

9. This shot is so ubiquitous in film history books that it was even copied in the final scene of George Lucas's *Star Wars* (1977), in which Luke Skywalker, Han Solo, and the Wookie Chewbacca walk up an aisle to receive their awards for saving the galaxy.

10. Hitler consecrates the flags by pressing the Nazi "blood flag" against other flags held by the stormtroopers. The "blood flag" was the banner carried during the 1923 Munich Beer Hall Putsch, in which fourteen Nazis were killed and Göring wounded. See Alex de Jonge, *The Weimar Chronicle: Prelude to Hitler* (New York: New American Library, 1978), 111–20.

11. The exultation of the Will is loosely based on the tradition of German Idealism. Schopenhauer emphasized the Will as a metaphysical concept, while Nietzsche decried the "slave morality" of Judaism and democracy and valorized the *Ubermann*, developed in harsh regimen and striving for global rule as "Lords of the Earth." Wagner's anti-Semitic writings and operas stressed the pagan blood feuds and tribal codes of German antiquity.

WORKS CITED

Benjamin, Walter. "The Work of Art in the Age of Mechanical Reproduction." In *Illuminations*, trans. Harry Zohn, 217–51. New York: Schocken Books, 1969.

Cattier, Michel. *The Life and Work of Wilhelm Reich*. New York: Avon, 1971.

Downing, Taylor. *Olympia*. London: British Film Institute, 1992.

Hinton, David B. *The Films of Leni Riefenstahl.* 2nd ed. Metuchen, NJ: Scarecrow Press, 1991.

Kracauer, Siegfried. *From Caligari to Hitler: A Psychological History of the German Film.* Princeton: Princeton University Press, 1947.

Marx, Karl. *The German Ideology.* New York: International Publishers, 1947.

Morreale, Joanne. *"A New Beginning": A Textual Frame Analysis of the Political Campaign Film.* Albany: State University of New York Press, 1991.

Reich, Wilhelm. *The Mass Psychology of Fascism.* Trans. Vincent R. Carrfagno. New York: Noonday, 1970.

Riefenstahl, Leni. "Interview with Michele Delahaye." In *Interviews with Film Directors,* ed. Andrew Sarris, 453–73. New York: Avon, 1967.

———. *Leni Riefenstahl: A Memoir.* New York: St. Martin's Press, 1993.

Rycroft, Charles. *Wilhelm Reich.* New York: Viking Press, 1971.

Sontag, Susan. "Fascinating Fascism." In *Under the Sign of Saturn,* 73–105. New York: Farrar, Straus and Giroux, 1980.

Tomasulo, Frank P. "Propaganda Films." In *Schirmer Encyclopedia of Film,* ed. Barry Keith Grant, 3:339–48. New York: Schirmer, 2007.

AMERICAN DOCUMENTARY FINDS ITS VOICE

Persuasion and Expression in *The Plow That Broke the Plains* and *The City*

Charlie Keil

> I left still photography because it could not provide the things that I knew films could provide. I was excited and interested in film as a pure medium of expression, but I was more interested in using it for a social end.
>
> Willard Van Dyke, "Thirty Years of Social Inquiry"

> During the [1930s], the idea that documentary filmmaking was a poetic activity emerged as a recurring critical theme: the force of cinematic composition, of patterns of light and movement, and of montage rhythms and juxtapositions was widely recognized as central to documentary forms.
>
> Charles Wolfe, "Poetics and Politics"

If we accept that documentary filmmaking has gravitated toward a limited number of broad functions—identified by Michael Renov as preservation, analysis, persuasion, and expression (21)—then independent American nonfiction films of the 1930s demonstrably embraced the latter two tendencies. And as Willard Van Dyke's statement reveals, documentary filmmakers during this period understood the medium of film to

suited to both. Arguably, the very formulation of the term
ary," which occurred in the United States during the 1930s, was
ted upon the meaningful convergence of the poetical and the po-
al.[1] For most of these filmmakers, discovery of the expressive potential
of the medium occurred in concert with an awakening to its role as an
instrument of progressive social change. The recollections of Leo Hurwitz,
a central figure in the Film and Photo League, Nykino, and Frontier Films,
all American-based leftist film organizations of the 1930s, testify to the assumed interdependence of these two aspects of documentary film practice
during this period; Hurwitz charts his political coming-of-age as coincid-
ing with his awareness of film's potential for artistry. His appreciation of
Eisenstein, Pudovkin, and Dovzhenko derives as much from their political
engagement as their poetic expressiveness. He sees his work as an attempt
to fuse these two tendencies while representing "real experience": "We
thought of films as a medium of conveying experience and insight. We
proposed, in the process, to enlarge and deepen the expressive values and
techniques of the art. . . . Our underlying belief was that the penetration
of real experience and a substratum of real feelings were prime energies
for art" (Hurwitz 13–14).

If, as Bill Nichols has argued, the defining conventions of documentary are negotiated through the interaction of a community of practitioners and a constituency of viewers via a corpus of texts (*Reality* 12–31), the
situation in the United States during the 1930s provides one such moment when the term "documentary" came to "mean" a particular type of
film practice. Though by no means the only kind of nonfiction film produced during this time, independent works such as *The Plow That Broke
the Plains* (1936), *The River* (1937), *People of the Cumberland* (1938), *The
City* (1939), *Valley Town* (1940), and *Native Land* (1942) are indicative of
a politically committed and aesthetically ambitious branch of American
filmmaking that both dominated documentary discourse and helped define the terms by which documentary was understood in the United States
up until World War II.

Certainly U.S. documentaries of the 1930s were not unique in mixing
poetic expressiveness and social progressiveness; figures such as Dziga
Vertov and Joris Ivens served as obvious forerunners of this tendency, while
John Grierson's various efforts in Great Britain slightly predate American developments. Nonetheless, the institutional forces operating within
the United States, particularly the prohibitive distribution/exhibition
structure, militated against nonstudio productions and all but ensured
their marginalization; this intensified American documentary filmmakers' notions of being "independent," even if aligned with the government

or corporate sponsors. Moreover, as some critics have noted, the confluence of economic deprivation and political turmoil marked the 1930s as a decade of crisis in the United States (Stott). This, in turn, facilitated the emergence of a trend toward "documentary expression," which involved other media in addition to film and actively encouraged the contributions of other artists to film projects of a documentary nature. The influx of a great number of artists from diverse fields into documentary film production elevated its artistic stature while confirming the importance of its activist mandate.

William Stott has also argued that experience was the essential "criterion of authenticity in expression at the time" (36). This finds an echo in Hurwitz's earlier quoted claim that the role of art is "the penetration of real experience." The notion that authentic expression is predicated on experience may help explain not only why cinema became the preferred medium for realizing the documentary impulse during this era but also how the aims of expression and persuasion could be yoked together. With the recent acquisition of sound recording techniques, cinema became the preeminent forum for aspiring documentarians: the expressive capacity of film outstripped that of its two chief competitors in the realm of reproductive technology by virtue of combining the experiential qualities of photography's visual testimony with those of radio's aural record. Building on the ontological link photography and radio could promote between experiential reality and their recordings of it, cinema could also borrow and expand upon these media's formal strategies, whether compositional or commentative.

Ideally, then, the experiential qualities of cinema would effect the successful merger of expression and persuasion, art and politics. Such a synthesis would necessarily occur on the level of style, as efforts to achieve artistry and social effectivity converged in the systematic deployment of cinematic techniques. Similarly, any attendant tensions resulting from this attempted synthesis would also manifest themselves in the films' stylistic systems. Nichols has argued that emerging from a documentary's style is the "sense of a text's social point of view" ("Voice" 18); he originally labeled the procedures by which a nonfiction film orchestrates its perspective the documentary "voice."[2] While the term is not meant to be restricted to the aural components of a film's style, the choice of language is revealing nonetheless. A documentary's "voice" should not be confused with its literal voice, which in the case of 1930s American documentary is inevitably some form of voice-over narration. But the tensions informing the integration of expression and persuasion during this period do arise most noticeably in the contested use of sound as a stylistic device.

In both senses of the word, then, the emergence of documentary in the United States during the 1930s manifests itself in a struggle to find its proper "voice."

It would be tempting to map out the apparent oppositions between creative representation and social argumentation in these films in terms of a schematic division separating sound and image. In such a reading, image-based properties would be aligned with artistry, with elements typified by those Wolfe mentions in this essay's epigraph (notably excluding sound) signaling a commitment to poetic expression; conversely, sound would inevitably emerge as the agent of persuasion, articulating social positions in equal mixtures of didacticism and authority. Yet such a schema would overlook a number of important complicating factors: sound in these films is never restricted to voice-over narration, as music and sound effects also occur throughout; the films' stylistic systems depend upon an oscillating relation between sound and other techniques, which can vary from absolute correspondence to deliberate and ironic counterpoint; and other aspects apart from sound can be enlisted for the purposes of persuasion, just as sound can function in an evidently expressive capacity. Analyzing the style of two representative documentaries from this period, *The Plow That Broke the Plains* and *The City*, we shall find that the respective articulation of each film's "voice" entails a considerably more complicated interplay of sound and image than the dichotomous model proposed above allows. Instead, the ideal of fusion constantly gives way to a more embattled separation of impulses, resulting in films whose integration of sound and image exists in a state of ongoing negotiation. The tensions of the films' style embody the struggles of the period, wherein filmmakers worked toward realization of a distinct, and viable, model of film practice.

I have chosen *The Plow That Broke the Plains* and *The City* as examples of this period's documentary practice because both bear the marks of such struggles quite literally: production rows erupted in each instance, resulting in either a change in personnel or amendment of the films' scripts. Most dramatically, during the making of *The Plow*, director Pare Lorentz eventually fired his camera team of Ralph Steiner, Leo Hurwitz, and Paul Strand, all Nykino regulars. When Steiner and Willard Van Dyke secured the contract for *The City*, a commissioned film, it formally severed their ties with Frontier Films.[3] At stake in these battles was the selection of the preferred means to effect social change, a contestatory process determining the final contours of each film's voice. Played out in terms of sound and image, the struggle resists categorization as either purely aesthetic or political—as the filmmakers themselves came to realize, expression and persuasion could not be separated so easily.

Perhaps most telling is how divisive the incorporation of sound proved to be. Lorentz's stormy relationship with his cameramen on *The Plow That Broke the Plains* centered on the script, which the Nykino-trained personnel wanted rewritten to emphasize potential political activism, But tension also stemmed in part from differing perceptions regarding the centrality of the image. The visually oriented photographers perceived Lorentz as lacking a sense of how to exploit the imagery the camera could capture. Van Dyke, who worked with Lorentz on *The River,* once complained to the director that "a lot of his ideas were literary, not translatable into visual terms" ("Letters" 44). Lorentz's involvement in the filming became most pronounced in the postproduction stages, during which he supervised editing (correlated to the development of the musical score) and wrote the narration. When critics took note of Lorentz's style, they invariably made mention of the poetic recitative nature of its commentary and the evocative use of music, written by well-known American composer Virgil Thomson (Wolfe 369).

When it came time to make *The City,* its co-directors (in collaboration with Henwar Rodakiewicz) consciously avoided the Lorentz style of extensive lyrical narration and agreed to eliminate commentary whenever possible. According to Rodakiewicz's proposal, "An absolute minimum of spoken words is desirable, and the film is so planned, since the story is told both directly and by inference mainly through picture continuity. Totaled— but, at the most, one third of the final cut length of the film will follow voice continuity" (279). Opposition from *The City*'s sponsors blocked some of the attempts in that direction and led to the Lewis Mumford–composed commentary the film employs. Yet the aversion of the makers to a reliance on voice-over narration demonstrates how contentious this aspect of sound was for documentary at this time. Certain filmmakers may have sensed that voice-over commentary might mitigate the experiential dimension of documentary even while they valued its potential for persuasion. As Pascal Bonitzer has indicated, the disembodied status of this technique, unmoored from any spatial or temporal frame, exercises an indisputable power (324). Building on Bonitzer's claims, Mary Ann Doane has observed, "It is precisely because the voice is not localizable, because it cannot be yoked to a body, that it is capable of interpreting the image, producing its truth" (42). As we shall see, how voice-over commentary is deployed in each of the films speaks to an awareness—and wariness—of its potential to disrupt the balancing of persuasion and expression.

This potentially disruptive power of voice-over commentary could be offset in two principal ways: by investing other components of a documentary's style with an immediacy and strength that would signal their own claims to authority and experience; and by rendering the commentary itself as lyrical, impassioned, contributing to the film's style rather than overwhelming it.[4] Referring to Lorentz's scripted voice-over for *The River*, Van Dyke has described his notions of the "perfect commentary": "It was poetic. It fitted the film perfectly. It didn't insult your intelligence by telling you what you were seeing on the screen, and it extended the dimensions of the visual images and the music" ("Documentaries" 45). The establishment of the ideal documentary voice, then, entailed maintaining close control over its literal voice so that the latter did not eclipse the former.

One way to minimize control of documentaries through voice-over narration was to supply structuring principles that lent the films an internal organization. That Rodakiewicz would speak of *The City* in terms of "story" and "continuity" indicates that such principles could derive from the classical narration dominant in narrative models of the period. As Paul Arthur has indicated, these films employ "stylistic fragmentation and multiplicity, a concatenation of discrete segments containing disparate visual and aural cues yet bracketed by a unifying theme and narrational logic" (110). Both *The Plow That Broke the Plains* and *The City* rely on a discernible overall structure to enhance this sense of narrational logic and to contain what might otherwise appear as a collection of random images.

The Plow That Broke the Plains, for example, uses a pattern of discrete yet interrelated segments, characterized by advancing chronology, cause and effect, and a tonal variation determined by alternating positive and negative events. This pattern, successfully adopted for *The River* as well, is further characterized by a succession of dominant movements which, unlike the singular flow of water in the later film, vary from segment to segment. In the full version of *The Plow That Broke the Plains* there are eight distinct sections, excluding the prologue; all but one are punctuated by a fade-out. In each of these eight segments, one can discern a dominant movement, often literalized through the deployment of a force of nature or technology defined by its mobility. Moreover, in each segment, the presence or absence of some form of stasis contributes to the general tone; if present, such stasis operates to modify the effect of the movement depicted.

The following chart outlines the structure of the film, while also demonstrating how tone and movement/stasis are interdependent:

	Movement	Tone
Prologue		
Segment One (Initial Settlement)	cattle	+
Segment Two (Continued Development)*	settlers/plows	+
Segment Three (Development)	thrashers	+
Segment Four (Desolation/Return to Activity)	tractors/tanks	- +
Segment Five (The Golden Harvest)*	thrashers/presses	+ -
Segment Six (Return to Desolation)~/*	dust storm	-
Segment Seven (Aftermath)~/*	exodus	-
Segment Eight (Reconstruction)		"+"

* = ends in stasis
~ = begins in stasis

Segment One, detailing the earliest use of the Great Plains region, is defined by the lateral movement of the grazing cattle, underscored by the repeated use of panning. The buoyant music and narration confirm the generally positive tenor of the section, which gives way (via a dissolve) to the arrival of the settlers in the second segment, whose horizontal progress across the screen is mirrored by the traversals of plowshares in later shots of the same section. However, the slightly disruptive vertical movements of the driven posts, which emphasize the rending of the ground (a violation compounded by subsequent shots of plowing), intimate the impending negative consequences, made evident in the spoken warning, "settler, plow at your peril." The shots of an immobile farmer leaning against his plow effectively halt the previous movements and foreshadow the eventual end to prosperity toward which the film inexorably moves.

Though Segment Three still centers on activity by way of the lateral movement of the thrashers, an ominous tone comes to overshadow the expansion as the narration hints at the natural limitations to growth: "Two hundred miles from water . . . two hundred miles from town." The cumulative effect of the agrarian development chronicled in the first three segments is revealed at the opening of the fourth, as activity has given way to complete stasis: a wagon wheel, a definably American icon of pioneer progress, the spirit of which has been conveyed previously by the film's citation of indigenous folk music, lies covered in dust. A vertical bomb blast, which presages World War I and a renewed lateral movement, disrupts this momentary stasis, however; Segment Four features both tractors and tanks moving across the screen, equated through juxtaposition. The next segment (Five) features unbridled activity, as more developed farm machinery continues the harvest unabated, while printing presses (in opposing vertical movement) push out enticements for increased land purchases. All activity halts with the smashing of a stock ticker machine at the end of the segment, a metonymic representation of the economic crash that destroyed the market for wheat.

Segments Six and Seven, in which desolation succeeds depression, constitute the film's emotional low point, from which the final segment will act as deliverance. (This tactic is also repeated in *The River*.) Both segments begin and end with stasis, thus compounding their negativity, but are still characterized by movement, the former by the winds of the dust storm, the latter by the western exodus of poverty-stricken landowners. Throughout Segments One through Seven, each dominant movement has been either replaced or stilled: both Segments Four and Six open with shots of once active farm machinery abandoned in the dust; Segment Seven concludes with the farmers themselves having been *moved off*, leaving only ravaged nature. The billowing grass from the opening shots of Segment One offers a pointed contrast to the toppled and gnarled trees from the close of Segment Seven. The eighth and final segment marks a return to the map of the prologue, followed by a movement of government action into the area.[5] The film qualifies optimism with a warning to heed the lessons of the past and suggests restoration through a return to a closing shot of grass blowing in the wind.

The Plow invokes history as a means of authorizing its narrative while also asserting the inevitability of the solution it proposes. History is enlisted as demonstration of the ill-advised nature of the actions of the past. The film suggests that history has already passed judgment on the follies depicted; discrediting past activities implicitly sanctions present government intervention. But the film's progressive chronology also posits government action as the natural outgrowth of the events that preceded the current situation. Its incessant forward movement works both spatially and temporally, pointing the viewer toward the federal policies the film advocates. Balancing this progression is a parallelism, which builds "a sense of repetition in the history of the Midwest" (Alexander 103). This, in turn, fortifies the film's pattern of cause and effect, which draws a neat line through history, so that, as Richard Dyer MacCann has pointed out, the "crash produces not only falling prices, but drought" (80). History seems to control the sequence of events in the film, but history is itself controlled by the film, which organizes and comments upon history. Moreover, history ends in the present, at the moment the film supplies the solution that

The Plow That Broke the Plains: The wagon wheel, icon of American progress, lies covered in dust.

arrests the decline it charts as a function of history. In its organization of history, the film (and, by extension, the government that produced it) has the knowledge to show in totality what can only have been understood in fragments.

The omniscient character of this controlling knowledge registers itself most obviously at the level of the sound track. The narration slips effortlessly from third person to first person plural, implying detached observation while advocating mutual responsibility. The film's/government's ability to employ retrospection assumes a similar capacity for foresight. Established thus, it can both comfort and advise, as knowledge of the past *and* the future seems to rest in its ability to bridge time.

The music shares the narration's temporal flexibility and variable voice. It recalls the past by utilizing strains of established folk tunes and hence links itself to the experience of the times recalled, while also operating as commentary on the visuals. Thus the music colors seemingly neutral images through a "darkening" of tone, working to foreshadow the negative events those images precipitate. In this way, the music both expresses and "possesses" the same degree of knowledge as the narrator, one that extends beyond the temporally limited information exhibited within the images themselves. Music and narration are also aligned through repetition: as certain phrases are repeated ("high winds and sun"), so, too, are certain musical passages; their recurrence again reinforces their mutual atemporality.

While the images thus seem more obviously rooted in the time they represent, dependent upon aural embellishment for an expansion of meaning, certain exceptions exist. The manipulation of the imagery through editing creates commentary itself, as when juxtaposition equates tractors and tanks in the "wheat will win the war" sequence, and montage produces the dubious cause-and-effect relationship linking 1920s jazz, excessive wheat production, and the stock market crash. Other techniques employed by the film include expressive lighting effects (as when shots of combines, in ominous silhouette, produce clouds of dust and chaff); optical effects (such as the fade-out of Segment Six, which leaves the blazing sun as the final visible image); and framing, which self-consciously evokes sectors of offscreen space (the settler's legs seen shuffling across the dusty ground in Segment Six; the "disembodied" shovel entering and leaving the frame in the digging-out sequence following the dust storm).

The film thus fuses persuasion and expression through a variety of stylistic means but often locates its voice primarily within the atemporal qualities of the voice-over commentary. Ironically, the evident temporal progression of the film promotes a reliance on a voice rooted in a perspective beyond the time frame employed. A comparison with *The City* reveals that the later film attempts to lessen the claims to authority of the commentative voice by altering its arrangement of temporal order and intensifying the relationship among patterns of imagery.

The City, probably because it is based on an outline by Lorentz, does share the same problem-solution format employed in *The Plow That Broke the Plains* and *The River*. However, *The City*'s tripartite structure of reverie, problem, and solution is both less elaborate and more fully integrated than the pattern of steady progression found in the other two films. *The City* develops a complex interrelationship between the past, present, and future by recalling (or inverting) earlier images and sequences in different contexts. The film's first section, set in a timeless New England town, establishes a paradigm of harmonious existence against which the remainder of the film will operate. Again, an outline of the film's structure can indicate how the sections interrelate:

      Section One (New England)
        narrative
        narration (First Voice)
        narrative

Section Two (The City—Part One: Industry)
    industry/narration (Second Voice)
    slums/narration (First Voice)
    smoke
        (The City—Part Two: The Metropolis)
    the office/narration (Second Voice)
    the street
    the diner
    the street
        (Part Three: The Highway)
Section Three (The Greenbelt)
    Introduction/narration (Third Voice)
    A Day, First Part/narrative
    A Day, Second Part/narration (Third Voice)
    Comparison (Third Voice)

The City's very structure posits an essential difference between the communities of the first and third sections and that of the second: while the former two share a unified space, the latter exists in several different locales, embodied by disparate segments. Thus the segmentation of the middle section echoes the fragmented nature of contemporary urban life. An accelerated style of editing also marks the second section, which exacerbates the sensation of fragmentation while also emphasizing a basic lack of continuity in the images. The notion of community comes to define life in the first and third sections; various visual similarities between the two sections further consolidate their connectedness.

Just as the film depends upon associative imagery to equate the New England town of Section One and the Greenbelt city of Section Three, so it absents or perverts such images in Section Two. Thus notions of community implied in the collective act of watching (at the blacksmith's in the first section; at the baseball game and at the pond in the third) are undercut in Section Two by the spectacle of a crowd gathered to gawk at an accident and the solitary shot of a mother watching her children cross the railroad tracks near their home. The institutions that encourage community interaction (the town hall of Section One; the community centers and schools of Section Three) are either omitted or dwarfed by surrounding architecture in Section Two. Hence the tolling bell at the end of Part Two of the second section (which recalls the advent of the town meeting in Section One) greets an empty street, vacated by city dwellers who will "commune" in Part Three of the same section by further isolating themselves in their automobiles. The bumper-to-bumper congestion is itself a perversion of the leisurely modes of transportation envisaged in the first section's wagon ride and the bicycles and horses of the third; these forms of conveyance seem perfectly natural, propelled as they are by either man or animal.

The film's chief signifiers of nature—water and vegetation—operate in abundance throughout Sections One and Three: images of a waterwheel and a dam figure prominently in the New England town and the Greenbelt, respectively; the leisure activities of both communities necessarily involve central bodies of water; the harvest and consumption of fruits and vegetables receive similar emphasis. Section Two stresses the absence/perversion of natural imagery: no trees are ever seen, and the only water is the dirty river near the docks, where youths must furtively steal dives before being chased away by a dock foreman. In the city, even leisure is a forced activity (as will be reiterated in the highway segment). Moreover, such activity is shorn of its innocence by the fact that the unselfconscious skinny-dippers of the first and third sections are replaced by older, swimsuit-clad boys in the second. In the urban nightmare of Section Two, nature has been forced out of sight, a fact reinforced by the various shots of slum dwellers pumping water: the people are now cut off from easy access to resources so plentiful in the other communities. The film later links the strain of perverted natural imagery to the degradations of technology in the automat sequence, where food itself has become mechanized. The third part of Section Two offers a variation on the connection between food and mechanization: fruit is advertised as a commodity for sale on roadside signs but never shown growing in its natural state.

Fire and smoke, by-products of industry, define the degraded city while remaining noticeably absent in depictions of the other two communities. The film intimates that fire and smoke have effectively eliminated and replaced water and vegetation, both as a source of energy (coal versus hydroelectrical power) and a salient characteristic of the environment: the molten steel from the factories literally burns up the countryside; smoke continually obscures the sky throughout Section Two's first part. The film expresses the complete invasion of industry into the domestic sphere in two ways: by the former's spatial proximity to the latter and the equation, through editing, of smoke emitting from a slum with that from a factory stack and a locomotive.

The sanctity of home and community that Section Two violates so insistently is reinforced in the surrounding sections by a concomitant attention to the individual. Links between the individual, the home, and the community are especially discernible in Section Three, wherein a young boy's house serves as a microcosm for the community itself. Thus the three rooms shown—bedroom, kitchen, study—correlate directly to the activities provided on an expanded scale by the Greenbelt community: rest/leisure, nourishment, and learning. Later the narration will make such links explicit: "The human market is just an annex to the kitchen"; "The public world is just as human as the private." Characteristic of the attention to the individual is the construction of a narrative involving a little boy in each of these two sections; the narratives devised serve to reveal the benefits of the respective environments, while the film also employs the boys' journeys as guided tours.

In Section Two, however, such narrative strategies are abandoned, as the film features an anonymous rush of humanity in a variety of causally unrelated sequences. Pace rather than purpose defines the lives depicted, with the pressure of time communicated stylistically by the increased tempo of the background music, the general rapidity of the editing, and the increase of directionally inflected graphic motifs. *The City* builds to climaxes through the escalation in emphatically directional action, which often prepares for a transition to a new sequence. Accordingly, the film effects a transition from the first section to the second through a jarring montage of hot metal being hammered, the violent action compounded by shifts in camera angle for each successive shot; the diner sequence ends with a repeated and accelerated thrusting of objects diagonally into the frame;

The City: Factories dominate urban space.

a similarly repeated series of directionally related movements in Section
Two's third part climaxes in the unimpeded descent of a car over a cliff,
which crashes at the bottom of the frame. Further, this downward motion
is opposed by the ascent of the construction worker in the first shot of Section Three, graphically emphasizing the quality of renascence embodied by
the new plan enacted.

This analysis has generally emphasized the visual means by which *The
City* communicates its ideas. In effect, the film's deployment of commentary promotes such an emphasis, as the voice-over narration is relegated to
particular isolated sequences in the film and is typically avoided throughout nearly all of the second and third parts of Section Two. What operates in
its place in these sections is a variety of diegetically motivated noises, which
often act in concert with the previously described actions to effect structural
climaxes. Hence both the office and the diner sequences culminate in a
cacophony of overlaid voices, aurally echoing the frenzy of the accelerated
montage; various sirens and alarms act as sonic perversions of the placid
chiming bell of Section One; and an uncontrollable air horn continues to
blare until silenced by the final crash at the end of the second section's Part
Three. Thus though most of Section Two lacks narration, it is by far the
noisiest section of the film.

When the film employs narration, it is conveyed through two distinct
voices, distinguished by differences in cadence, speed of delivery, and attitude.[6] The Second Voice is used only twice, to introduce the first and second
parts of Section Two. Its application is ironic, as its overheated advocacy of
increased industrialization is belied by the effects of such efforts demonstrated in the images. The employment of narration in this manner undercuts its traditional status as reliable and superior to the image; rather, it
acts as a counterpoint to the visuals, which constitute the primary source of
information. The other voice appears four times, though its implementa-
tion in Section Three is radically different from that in its previous manifestations. During its first two appearances (labeled as First Voice in the
chart), the voice consistently employs the first person plural; the "we" of the
New England town becoming the "we" of the urban slums thus represents
a marked degradation. The retention of the same voice serves to reinforce
connections between the two communities, demonstrating to what degree
the latter is a perversion of the former. However, the voice in Section Three
(labeled as Third Voice) represents a departure, a break from the past. The
film signals the distinctiveness of the third section by the form of transition
employed to introduce it: whereas the movement from Section One to Section Two occurs through a match cut transition, the second section ends
on a note of destruction, irrevocable and definite, and is punctuated by a

fade-out. The palpable change in the function of the narration in Section Three (particularly given its restricted use in the second section) manifests itself more clearly in the degree to which the narration acts to control the images depicted. No longer a voice of experience, this narrator adopts an organizational role, fitting the images into a catalogue of community benefits.

The only rupture of the narration's control throughout Section Three comes with the emergence of the narrative involving the young boy (which echoes a similar sequence in Section One). Significantly, the patterning supplied by voice-over narration is supplanted by the narrative logic of the boys' stories. Whenever these narratives give way to the voice-over narration, the images no longer connect in an indisputably causal manner. As was the case in *The Plow That Broke the Plains,* the voice-over narration becomes most dominant when its temporality is least specified. Such is the power of narration at these moments that it can draw together images seemingly unrelated in space and time, as when the narration lends coherence to otherwise disconnected shots of handicraft in Section One. The ascendance of the visuals during the narrative sequence in Section Three is marked by a commensurate return to prominence of the musical score, which plays a far less active role during the moments devoted to narration. (Whenever the voice-over narration appears, the music either subsides or loses all shades of variation; rarely do the two "compete," as in *The Plow That Broke the Plains.*) The rupture produced by the introduction of this narrative passage seems to affect the narration, which temporarily returns to a first person plural voice but thereafter fluctuates among various modes (first, second, and third person). By its conclusion, *The City* appears to have opted for a more conventional (i.e., omniscient) type of narration, largely characteristic of *The Plow That Broke the Plains,* but in its overall approach to the use of voice-over the film comes much closer to attaining the goal of sustained stylistic diversity advocated at the time as a defining feature of documentary.

In its rather adventurous employment of contrasting voices in the first part of Section Two, *The City* approaches a dialectic of address; in this respect, it most resembles radio news broadcasts of the day, which often synthesized the direct and vicarious modes of aural persuasion (Stott 80–91). Similarly, both films' varying concern with the central issue of sound-image relationships aligns them with the documentary book, which sought to balance the competing claims of photo and text.[7] It was the express goal of these documentary books to allow "the photographs to assert their independence. They are not illustrations. They carry the message with the text" (Newhall 183). Again, experience operated as the chief criterion for determining the persuasive capacities of the selected mode of expression.

In those terms, probably the "purest" (and most persuasive) example of documentary expression within the two films is Part One of *The City*'s second section, which employs an experiential narrational voice in conjunction with its Lange-influenced portraits of individuals, their unfocused gazes dominating the sequence's depiction of slum life. Abstract yet "real," ostensibly unmediated while unquestionably stylized, such a passage abandons any sense of omniscience by granting the experiential dimension the primacy 1930s documentary prized.

If the attempt by documentary films of this era to achieve such experientiality inevitably led to a (qualified) abrogation of narrational tendencies, this only demonstrates the ultimate difficulty inherent in fusing image and voice, in persuading through expression. The introduction of sound increased cinema's potential for authenticity, and its status as an authentically expressive medium, but it also challenged the filmmaker to avoid relying on sound to carry the role of persuasion too obviously. The eventual solution (abetted by another technological development, in the form of direct sound recording) was to substitute the interview for narration as a means of providing a more authentic "voice" (cf. Nichols, "Voice"). But with this shift came a reconceptualization of the function of the image track as well, wherein the spatial anchoring of the interview subject (source of the sound) limited the image track's expressive potential in other ways.

The struggle of the documentary form to maintain a balance between sound and image, wherein experience and authenticity would prevail, parallels the problems of fiction film after the advent of sound. The adjustment to sound caused a rethinking of the roles of montage and mobile framing, as the expressive tendencies of silent cinema were reconfigured to suit the demands of (classical) sound filmmaking. What resulted was a greater degree of verisimilitude at the expense of the narrationally obtrusive deployment of style (most evident in certain movements within national cinemas—German Expressionism, Soviet Montage, the French avant-garde). Similarly, as documentary filmmaking absorbed the changes to sound technology, its realist mandate signaled a move not only away from omniscient voice-over narration but also away from the types of visually oriented strategies that mark *The Plow That Broke the Plains* and *The City*. Ironically, though the effort to maintain documentary's expressive and persuasive potential in mutuality manifested itself most obviously in the struggle to prevent sound from overpowering the image, the ultimate solutions devised relegated the latter to a function divorced from the aesthetic realm. Perhaps the stylistic dilemmas of American 1930s documentaries demonstrate most powerfully what was entailed once the struggle abated: "the historical fact of a repression of the formal or expressive domain within tradition" (Renov 33).

NOTES

1. Wolfe argues persuasively how the term "documentary" came to be understood in relation to film during this decade. Wolfe's work did not appear until after I had already completed an initial draft of this essay, but I am in agreement with much of what he says concerning the films in question and their historical context. I recommend his essay to anyone interested in an illuminating overview of the period.

2. Later Nichols reconsiders his employment of this term, preferring to substitute "argument." According to him, "Argument (carried by commentary and perspective) allows for a wider range of strategies than voice and retains the basic idea that argumentation is a property of the documentary text regardless of its own claims of objectivity" (*Representing* 281). Nonetheless, I have chosen to retain the term "voice" because it ties the notion of argument more directly to stylistic properties, a particular concern in the period under discussion here.

3. Such were the conditions of production at this time that both films feature some of the same talent, though operating in different capacities. Accordingly, while *The City*'s co-directors, Steiner and Van Dyke, both had strong ties to Nykino, each also worked with Lorentz, the director of *The Plow*, on separate New Deal documentaries. Lorentz, in turn, provided the scenario for *The City*, even though his primary association was with the federal government, culminating in his brief role as production chief of the U.S. Film Service. *The City*'s backers, the American Institute of Planners, originally offered the project to Lorentz; he came back to the production when Steiner enlisted his onetime employer to write the film's outline.

4. Jeffrey Youdelman provides an incisive assessment of this quality in 1930s documentaries, while also arguing that such a use of voice-over contributes immeasurably to what Nichols identifies as the documentary "voice." Youdelman, "Narration, Invention, and History: A Documentary Dilemma," *Cineaste* 12, no. 2 (1983): 8–15.

5. Even so, these shots lack the dynamic quality of the comparable "solution segment" of *The River*. Many prints of *The Plow That Broke the Plains* still lack this final section, dropped sometime soon after the film's initial release. This excision might have been motivated by fears concerning the film's advocacy of government intervention (Snyder 37; Alexander 140).

6. Though there are only two actual voices employed, the function of one of them (which initially occurs on the sound track in Section One as the "First Voice") is split among the sections in which it is used. During the third section, its role changes sufficiently such that I have designated it as the "Third Voice" at that point to signify

‿ distinctions between its use there and in the previous two sections, where it is labeled "First Voice."

7. The documentary book is an important example of the popularity of the documentary "approach" prevalent in American culture during the 1930s. Combining photographs and texts, these books were a precursor of the methods popularized by such magazines as *Life* and *Look* in the same decade. In the documentary book, photographs by such noted still photographers as Dorothea Lange and Walker Evans would be tied to the often deliberately poeticized prose of famous writers like Archibald MacLeish and James Agee. The documentary book of the 1930s, much like the documentary film, often attempted a fusion of expression and persuasion, as exemplified by, for example, *An American Exodus* (1939), *You Have Seen Their Faces* (1937), and *Land of the Free*. The most famous of these is the Agee/Evans collaboration, *Let Us Now Praise Famous Men* (1941).

Works Cited

Alexander, William. *Film on the Left: American Documentary Film from 1931 to 1942.* Princeton: Princeton University Press, 1981.

Arthur, Paul. "Jargons of Authenticity (Three American Moments)." In *Theorizing Documentary*, ed. Michael Renov, 108–34. New York: Routledge, 1993.

Bonitzer, Pascal. "The Silences of the Voice." Trans. Philip Rosen and Marcia Butzel. In *Narrative, Apparatus, Ideology*, ed. Philip Rosen, 319–34. New York: Columbia University Press, 1986.

Doane, Mary Ann. "The Voice in the Cinema: The Articulation of Body and Space." *Yale French Studies* 60 (1980): 33–50.

Hurwitz, Leo. "One Man's Voyage: Ideas and Films in the 1930s." *Cinema Journal* 15, no. 1 (1975): 1–15.

MacCann, Richard Dyer. *The People's Films: A Political History of U.S. Government Motion Pictures.* New York: Hastings House, 1973.

Newhall, Beaumont. *The History of Photography from 1839 to the Present Day.* New York: Museum of Modern Art, 1949.

Nichols, Bill. *Representing Reality: Issues and Concepts in Documentary.* Bloomington: Indiana University Press, 1990.

———. "The Voice of Documentary." *Film Quarterly* 36, no. 3 (1983): 17–30.

Renov, Michael. "Towards a Poetics of Documentary." In *Theorizing Documentary*, ed. Michael Renov, 12–36. New York: Routledge, 1993.

Rodakiewicz, Henwar. "Treatment of Sound in *The City*." In *The Movies as Medium*, ed. Lewis Jacobs, 278–88. New York: Farrar, Straus and Giroux, 1970.

Snyder, Robert L. *Pare Lorentz and the Documentary Film.* Norman: University of Oklahoma Press, 1968.

Stott, William. *Documentary Expression and Thirties America.* New York: Oxford University Press, 1973.

Van Dyke, Willard. "Documentaries of the Thirties." *Journal of the University Film Association* 25, no. 3 (1973): 45–46.

———. "Letters from *The River.*" *Film Comment* 3, no. 2 (1965): 38–56.

———. "Thirty Years of Social Inquiry: An Interview with Willard Van Dyke." Interview by Harrison Engle. In *Nonfiction Film: Theory and Criticism,* ed. Richard Meran Barsam, 271–95. New York: Dutton, 1976.

Wolfe, Charles. "The Poetics and Politics of Nonfiction: Documentary Film." In *Grand Design: Hollywood as a Modern Business,* ed. Tino Balio, 351–86. New York: Charles Scribner's Sons, 1993.

Chapter 8

"Men Cannot Act before the Camera in the Presence of Death"

Joris Ivens's *The Spanish Earth*

Thomas Waugh

In July 1936, when General Franco launched his revolt against the Spanish Republic, Joris Ivens, the thirty-eight-year-old avant-gardist-turned-militant, was in Hollywood showing his films to industry progressives. One year later, Ivens was in Hollywood again, this time officiating at the glittering world premiere of *The Spanish Earth*. A hasty, spontaneous response to the Spanish plight, directed by a Dutchman who had spent only a few months in the United States, *The Spanish Earth* was also the prototypical cultural product of the Popular Front, a moment that brought the left closer to the American mainstream than at any other time previously or since.

The Spanish Earth represents also the convergence of two basic traditions of radical filmmaking in the West, of which Ivens was the standard-bearer throughout his sixty-year career. It is the definitive model for the "international solidarity" genre, in which militants from the First and Second Worlds have used film to champion each new front of revolutionary armed struggle. It is also the model for the more utopian genre in which the construction of each new revolutionary society, as it emerges, is celebrated and offered as inspiration.

For filmmakers engaged in the less romantic dynamics of domestic struggles, with documentary continuing to be the first recourse of radical artists on every continent, *The Spanish Earth* remains a film of utmost pertinence. A special Ivens issue of *Cinéma politique*, a French review of militant cinema, listed in 1978 the major issues of contemporary radical cinema and declared Ivens's relevance to each one: "the relationship of form and content; collective work; the use of reenactment in documentary reportage; the role of the party, political direction, and the commissioned film; the opposition between amateur and professional (here one might add the increasingly important intermediate category of 'artisanal'); the marginalization of militant cinema in relation to traditional film distribution; exoticism, the romanticism of the distant valiant struggle, opposed to everyday struggles, and traversed by the complex notions of cultural neocolonialism" (*Cinéma politique* 10). What is striking about this list is that, aside from a few overtones of 1970s jargon, it could just as easily have been written during the period of *The Spanish Earth*, so little had the "issues" changed in the intervening years.[1]

The Spanish Earth, finally, has a central place within the evolution of the documentary form. It defines prototypically the formal and technical challenges of the thirty-year heyday of the classical sound documentary, 1930 to 1960, in particular its first decade. It confronts, with still exemplary resourcefulness, the problems of sound and narration; the temptation to imitate the model of Hollywood fiction with mise-en-scène, individual characterization, and narrative line; the catch-22s of distribution, accessibility, and ideology; the possibilities of compilation and historical reconstruction, and of improvisation and spontaneity. Once again this list sounds surprisingly contemporary.

Joris Ivens disembarked in February 1936 in New York for what was to become a decade of work in the United States. He was entering a political context strikingly different from the familiar ones of western Europe and the Soviet Union where his output had included avant-garde film poems (such as *Rain*, 1929), epics of collective labor in both Holland (*Zuiderzee*, 1933) and the Soviet Union (*Komsomol*, 1932), industrial commissions (such as *Philips-Radio*, 1931), and militant denunciations of the capitalist system (*Borinage*, 1933, and *The New Earth*, 1934).

The left intellectual milieu to which Ivens and his partner/coworker/editor Helen Van Dongen attached themselves upon their arrival was deeply concerned by the buildup to war already evident in Ethiopia, China, Germany, and, soon, in Spain. Ivens had made his previous political films during a period when the international socialist movement had been oriented toward militant class struggle. The militant era was coming to an end at the time of Ivens's arrival in New York. The main reason for the about-face of mid-decade was an official change of policy promulgated by the Communist International at its 1935 World Congress and obediently followed by all the national parties. The crucial political struggle of the day was to be not socialism versus capitalism but democracy versus fascism. Communists were to participate in joint action within popular fronts with the socialist parties, civil libertarians, and liberal intellectuals. American communists thus allied themselves enthusiastically with Roosevelt and the social programs of the New Deal.

Leftist cultural strategy inevitably followed suit. The militant vanguardism symbolized by the U.S. Film and Photo League (FPL) was replaced by efforts by left cultural workers to express themselves within the mainstream of American culture. They were largely successful: the last half of the decade saw the left achieve a close interaction between popular culture and progressive politics. The influx of leftist intellectuals and artists from Europe, most of whom were political refugees from fascism, stimulated this interaction, and the active involvement of the state in the cultural domain sustained it. The New Deal would expand into motion pictures in 1936 and enlist the talents of hundreds of leftist artists, including Ivens himself.

The documentary movement was another dominant influence on Ivens's American cultural context. This movement shaped not only all the arts during this period, even modern dance, but also the humanities, the social sciences, journalism, education, and, yes, advertising. At the center of this current was the work of still photographers such as Dorothea Lange and Walker Evans, who began photographing the economic crisis in the first years of the decade. The infusion of state sponsorship into the documentary movement after 1935 ensured that the photographs of the Depression would become its most recognizable artistic legacy, but they do not represent its full scope. Photographers and filmmakers, especially those on the left, spread out from providing local evidence of hunger, unemployment, and police repression, to shape encyclopedic manifestos in which the entire politico-economic and cultural system would be analyzed, challenged, and sometimes celebrated.

At first, the left documentary constituency thrived mostly on imports. Soviet documentaries, for example, were continuously on view in New York and other large centers throughout the 1930s; Dziga Vertov's *Three Songs of Lenin* was a hit in 1934. British films were also prestigious and popular, beginning with Grierson's *Drifters* (1929), which appeared in New York in 1930. The first documentaries by American directors to play theatrically in New York, outside of the FPL agitprop milieu, appeared in 1934. The appearance of Time-Life's *The March of Time* in 1935, however, injecting dramatized elements into the traditional newsreel, precipitated a floodtide of new documentary work in the United States. The nontheatrical showing of Ivens's films in the spring of 1936 caught the momentum. Interest in documentary was so high that the work of the obscure Dutchman was praised rapturously, not only in leftist periodicals but in the liberal media as well. The Rockefeller Foundation and Museum of Modern Art were important institutional props to the growing movement. The latter sponsored the official Washington premiere of Pare Lorentz's New Deal–funded *The Plow That Broke the Plains* in May 1936, presenting a program that also included five European documentaries. The White House staff, diplomats, and members of the Supreme Court all showed up. *Plow* went on to 16,000 first-run showings and raves in every newspaper. The World's Fair in 1939 became the showcase for this first phase of the documentary movement, with Ivens's work much in evidence.

The strong popular foundation of documentary culture was essential to Ivens and other leftist filmmakers. Unquestionably a mass phenomenon, its artifacts ranged from *Life* magazine to the Hollywood feature *I Am a Fugitive from a Chain Gang* (1932). For socialists in the era of the Popular Front, mandated to enter the mainstream after years of marginality, and to combat fascism on a mass footing, here was a vehicle for their aims. For socialist filmmakers still too distrustful of monopoly capitalism and the entertainment industry to take on Hollywood, the independent documentary clearly offered an appealing cultural strategy.

What was less clear at mid-decade was the direction that the socialist documentary of the future would take. Members of the Film and Photo League were sharply divided as to whether they should take advantage of the gathering steam of the documentary movement, as shown by the box-office success of *The March of Time,* or stick to their original "workers' newsreel" mission, with its marginal base and confrontational aesthetics.

Leo Hurwitz, a chief ideologue of the movement, as early as 1934 established three priorities for radical filmmakers, which ultimately became part of a new consensus during Ivens's first years in the United States:

(1) Mass access for radical film work through commercial or theatrical distribution. Leftists were greatly encouraged by the work of their colleagues in Hollywood who had contributed to such "progressive" films as Fritz Lang's *Fury* (1936) and the Warner Bros. biopics. Ivens praised such films on his tour and stressed the importance of "combining our work with the mass movement" and of, as he would put it a few years later, "break[ing] into commercial distribution [in order to] recover the social function of documentary."[2] Significantly, Van Dongen stayed behind in Hollywood to study

narrative editing. Where an earlier generation of documentarists, including both Ivens and the FPL, had assimilated the strategies of the European and Soviet avant-gardes, the Popular Front generation was looking west.

(2) The development of new "synthetic" film forms. Hurwitz argued that the form of the earlier newsreels had simply been an economic and technical necessity, not an ideological or aesthetic choice per se, and that these forms must now give way to hybrid forms including "recreative analysis and reconstruction of an internally related visual event" or, in other words, mise-en-scène (92). He stressed the professionalism of the required new filmmakers who would replace the earlier amateur and artisanal cadres. Ivens's films, screened repeatedly for the New York radicals upon his arrival, unambiguously bolstered the Hurwitz side with their rich mix of actuality, compilation, mise-en-scène, narrative, and even scripting (in his Soviet film *Komsomol* [1932]). "We must learn," he argued in a manifesto of the early 1940s, "to think of documentary as requiring a wide variety of styles—all for the purpose of maximum expressiveness and conviction" ("Making" 21).

(3) More profound political analysis. For Hurwitz the early FPL newsreels of strikes and demonstrations had been too "fractional, atomic, and incomplete" for adequate political analysis. The new "synthetic" forms would facilitate more "inclusive and implicative comment," and could "reveal best the meaning of the event" (Hurwitz 91). This "meaning" was to be a deeper, materialist analysis of the class struggle within capitalist society, in both world-historic and individual terms, not just in the local and collective terms that the workers' agitprop newsreels had stressed. Once again, Ivens found himself on Hurwitz's side of the debate. Earlier films, he stated in a lecture on his tour, including his own, were "just seeing things, not understanding." Art must have a "definite point of view" and must express this without "aestheticism" or sentimentality. "The difference between newsreel and the documentary film," he later explained, is that "the newsreel tells us where-when-what; the documentary film tells us *why,* and the relationships between events . . . and provides historic perspective" (*Camera* 209). The new "deeper approach," in particular the tactic of introducing identifiable characters into nonfiction filmmaking (which Ivens began calling "personalization"), is capable of "penetrating the facts . . . achieving a real interrelation between the particular and the general" (*Camera* 215).

The debate among leftist filmmakers was accompanied by organizational changes. Nykino, a new film production outfit, had been formed by Hurwitz and his allies as early as the fall of 1934, in order to put into practice the new priorities. The East Coast radicals were thus already set on a path closely parallel to that traced by the films Ivens showed in New York in 1936, that is, the evolution from agitational newsreel work to more systematic and ambitious explorations of new outlets, new forms, and deeper analysis. Ivens's effect, then, was one of reinforcement of directions already chosen and tentatively tested. Ivens's Soviet credentials—he was fresh from almost two years within the Soviet film industry—added in no small way to the impact of this encouragement.

Ivens officially cemented his affiliation with the Nykino tendency in the spring of 1937 when that group inaugurated yet another production company, fully professional this time: Frontier Films. Though in Spain at the time, Ivens joined the dazzling array of American artists and intellectuals who signed up as founding members of Frontier Films, from liberals to fellow travelers to party members. In fact, Ivens had anticipated this approach the previous fall when he had enlisted many of the same luminaries to support his first American film, *The Spanish Earth*.

As soon as it became apparent that the Franco rebellion posed a serious threat, Ivens assembled the group of leftist artists and intellectuals who were to become the producing body for a Spanish film. Their idea was to bolster American support for the Republican cause by means of a short, quickly made compilation of newsreel material. This would explain the issues to the American public and counter the already skillful Franquist propaganda. They called themselves Contemporary Historians, Inc., and had as their spokespeople the Pulitzer Prize–winning poet Archibald MacLeish and the novelist John Dos Passos, both well-known fellow-travelers (Lillian Hellman and Dorothy Parker were other pillars of the group). Van Dongen was to put together the film. It soon became clear, however, that not enough good footage was available and that even the shots at hand were of limited use since they were taken from the Franco side—burning churches and the like—as well as expensive and difficult to pry out of the notoriously reactionary newsreel companies. The group then decided to finish the project as quickly and cheaply as possible, which Van Dongen did using a Dos Passos commentary and relying on Soviet footage on the front. This feature-length work, called *Spain in Flames*, was hurriedly released in February 1937. Meanwhile, the producers put most of their hopes on a film of greater scope that Ivens would shoot from scratch on Spanish soil, personally underwriting a budget of $18,000.

As the autumn progressed, the project became more and more urgent: the left press began denouncing the German and Italian interventions and the "democracies" began nervously discussing neutrality. By the time Ivens arrived in the first bitter January of the war, a tentative scenario in his pocket, he had already been preceded by the first of the International Brigades and by a stream of Western artists, intellectuals, and activists, including filmmakers from the Soviet Union and England.

In Valencia, the new Republican capital because of the expected fall of Madrid, Ivens and John Ferno, his cinematographer from the Dutch days, joined up with Dos Passos and got right to work. They soon concluded, however, that their script was unworkable in the worsening situation. It emphasized the background to the war and revolution, calling for considerable dramatization. The Republicans they consulted urged them instead to head straight for Madrid to find their subject on the frontline. As the film's commentary would later make clear, "Men cannot act before the camera in the presence of death."

The final version of *The Spanish Earth* turned out to be much more complex than the original outline called for, an improvised hybrid of many filmic modes, but certain elements remained. The most important of these was the notion of a village as a microcosm of the Spanish revolution. The chosen village, Fuenteduena, was ideal in this and every other respect. Its stunning riverbank location on the Madrid-Valencia lifeline was symbolically apt, a link between village revolution and war effort. The community had reclaimed a former hunting preserve of aristocrats and had begun irrigating their new land. The filmmakers could thus keep their original theme of agrarian reform and hints of conflict between landowners and peasantry.

As for an original cloak-and-dagger plot about the young villager, Ivens and his collaborators attempted to telescope it into a simple narrative idea involving Julian, a peasant in the Republican army. Even this scaled-down idea was only partly realized since Julian disappeared on the front after his village sequences had been filmed. Julian appeared in only four scenes of the final film, stretched out by the editor to the maximum: a brief moment on the Madrid front where he is seen writing a letter home, the text provided in an insert and read by the commentator; a scene where he is seen hitching a ride back home on leave to Fuenteduena; next, his reunion first with his mother and then with his whole family; and finally, a sequence where he drills the village boys in an open space. The footage was insufficient even for these scenes, so that the commentator must repeat his name and flesh out the story. The reunion scene would be the biggest challenge to editor Van Dongen. Using close-ups of villagers apparently shot for other uses, she ingeniously fabricated a fictional mini-scene from unrelated material, where Julian's small brother runs to fetch their father from the fields upon his arrival. The family thus shown in this sentimental but effective scene would be largely synthetic. After Julian's disappearance, a symbolic close-up of an anonymous soldier was taken for the defiant finale of the film.

But this forced postponement of Ivens's dream of "personalization" did not stand in the way of other efforts to heighten the personal quality of the film. At every point in *The Spanish Earth,* the filmmakers would intervene in the postproduction to make individual figures come alive dramatically: through the commentary, as when a briefly seen Republican officer is identified by name and then laconically eulogized when it is disclosed that he was killed after the filming; or through complex editing, as when a miniature story of two boys killed in the bombing of Madrid is chillingly wrought out of noncontinuous shots and a synthetic flash-frame detonation; or through lingering close-ups of anonymous onlookers, some of whom are even dramatized through first-person commentary. Several years later, Ivens would conclude that such vignettes, "hasty and attempted identities now and then walking through a documentary," had fallen short of his goal of continuous "personalization" (*Camera* 212). It would not be until Ivens's third American film, *Power and the Land* (1940), that the relative luxury of peacetime filmmaking would allow him to experiment with fixed characters developed consistently throughout an entire film—in this case, a wholesome American farm family.

"Personalization" was not the only aspect of the Fuenteduena shooting that imitated Hollywood narrative. Using their heavy tripod-based Debrie camera, Ivens and Ferno developed a kind of documentary mise-en-scène, a collaborative shooting style staging "real" actors in "real" settings, eventually constituting about two-fifths of the film. Ivens matter-of-factly used the vocabulary of studio filmmaking such as "retake" and "covering shot"; on location, he set up shot-countershot constructions with his peasant subjects that aimed at the spatio-temporal continuity of studio fiction of the period. This approach enabled not only a clear chronological summary of the Fuenteduena irrigation work as it progressed before the camera, Ivens's emblem of the Spanish revolution, but also framings and movements that idealized the workers and their relationship to the Spanish earth.

Ivens was of course not alone in "setting up" his subjects: the other major documentarists of the period, from Basil Wright to Pare Lorentz, all used variations of the same method. Filmmakers and critics of the late 1930s agreed on the need for a dramatization of the factual, its "vivification," as some put it. This trend was partly in reaction to the impersonality of the newsreels and the other journalistic media. Was Ivens making a film or just newsreel shots, he would later wonder in his public lectures. Truth was not a function of ontological scruple but of political principle. Truth was not to be found on the surface of reality but in deeper social, economic, and historical structures. The generation of filmmakers who developed mise-en-scène as a documentary mode believed, like their cousins the Socialist Realists, that their work had the vocation not only to reflect the world but also to act upon it, to change it. This was true even for liberals like Lorentz and Grierson, who did not subscribe to Marxist ideals. Ivens's primary question was not whether he had shown the "truth" but whether "the truth has been made convincing enough to make people want to change or emulate the situation shown to them on the screen" ("Making" 299).

This is not to say that documentary mise-en-scène would have looked like fiction to 1930s spectators. An overwhelming system of "documentary" codes prevented it from doing so, from nonsynchronous sound, to unmade-up faces, to specific marketing approaches, to the use of "social" typing.

Mise-en-scène, a luxury affordable in the calm of Fuenteduena, was rarely possible on the frontlines, however. In Madrid, the filmmakers attached themselves to the communist-affiliated Fifth Regiment. Here they shot the siege of the city from the point of view of both its defenders in the frontline suburbs and the air raid shelters within the city itself. By the time of the key battle of Brihuega (Guadalajara) in March, Ernest Hemingway, a recent convert to the Republican cause, became the production's guide and literary mentor. At Brihuega, buoyed by the International Brigades, the Republicans won a major victory against a twelve-to-one firepower disadvantage and prevented the capital from being cut off. The battle's additional political significance was the proof it offered that organized Italian units were taking part—Italian casualties and their letters home are shown in a particularly moving scene of *The Spanish Earth* (a scene that would lead to a fruitless screening of the film at the League of Nations). The battle material, from both Madrid and Brihuega, as well as from one other village that the filmmakers shot under bombardment, has a style whose spontaneity contrasts with the orderly, lyrical mise-en-scène of Fuenteduena.

The "spontaneous" mode, relying primarily on the crew's two small hand-cameras, is notable for the unrehearsed flexibility and mobility required to cover the soldiers and civilian victims who could not "act before the camera." This mode, as Ivens had not foreseen while scriptwriting in New York, would make up more than half of the finished film. With this style, the camera operator, rather than rearranging an event in front of the lens, follows it spontaneously—the storming of a building, a run for cover during an air raid, the evacuation of children, panic in the streets of the bombed-out village. The principles of spatio-temporal continuity were left for the editor to find in the cans: it was too dangerous for the operator to think about retakes and reverse shots. "Spontaneous" shooting provided spectators with its own distinctive documentary codes: unmotivated and random detail of behavior or atmosphere, the flouting of

The Spanish Earth: The spontaneous panic in the streets.

taboos on out-of-focus material, looking at the camera, illegibility, and so on. The mystique of "life caught unawares" (Vertov 41) was still an essential element of the documentary sensibility despite the universal acceptance of mise-en-scène. "Spontaneous" elements thus often had the greatest impact on spectators: the reviews of the day never failed to mention a woman seen wiping her eye amid the rubble of her village. The great sensitivity of "spontaneous" material such as this in *The Spanish Earth* confirms Ivens as the heir of Vertov and a precursor of direct cinema.

It was in Madrid also that Ivens shot some material in a third cinematic mode that constitutes only a fraction of the finished film but deserves brief mention nonetheless. These static, controlled images of public events, taken with a heavy, stationary camera, I call the "newsreel" mode—ceremonious long shots of files of dignitaries, cheering crowds, military parades, or beauty contests. Though Ivens and his friends avoided "newsreel" shooting as much out of distaste for clichés and superficiality as from any ideological scruple, the opportunity to use a borrowed newsreel sound truck to record a People's Army rally could not be refused. Newsreel-style cinematography was the only means by which 1930s documentaries could attempt synchronous sound on location—twenty years would pass before technology would catch up, in the television age, with the aspiration to hear as well as to see "life caught

The Spanish Earth: An example of the newsreel mode.

unawares." The rally scene of *The Spanish Earth* featured the stirring oratory of La Pasionaria and other Republican leaders (some dubbed in New York because of technical problems) and, for this reason, would avoid the pitfalls of the mode.

The Spanish Earth, then, unexpectedly became a cinematic hybrid in the uncontrollable laboratory of war and revolution. In this, as a compendium of different filmic modes, it was typical of most documentaries of the late 1930s. The general trend, however, was toward greater and greater use of mise-en-scène. Wherever circumstances and resources permitted, Ivens and most other documentarists built up the mise-en-scène components of their hybrid works, experimenting more and more with characterization, narrative vocabulary, and even scripting. Writers became standard crew members, not only for commentaries but also to provide plots, continuity, and dialogue. During the 1940s, this mode became the basic component of most documentary (rivaled only by the compilation mode for which the war had created a special market), and "mise-en-scène" would continue to dominate right up until the advent of direct cinema around 1960.

Meanwhile Helen Van Dongen had begun assembling the consignments of rushes in New York as they arrived from Spain, wiring the filmmakers whenever she thought that a given topic was now well covered or that another was weak. When the shooting wound up in May, she began shaping material in each of the three modes according to the methods of narrative continuity that she had perfected in Hollywood. Individual sequences began emerging—the Fuenteduena irrigation project, civilians under bombardment, the Madrid and Brihuega fronts—each built strictly with the sequential and temporal logic of short fictional units. Obviously, the "spontaneous" rushes presented the most challenge since they had not been shot "for the editor." But she responded with ingenuity, building up to each split-second bomb impact with systematic precision and then having the clearing smoke reveal the rubble and the panic, or following each Republican artillery shot with an image denoting an on-target hit. Part of her skill was in picking out visual motifs to assure a narrative fluidity; images of children in a bombed-out street, for example, would underline an implied continuity. Seldom before had the principles of fictional narrative editing been so skillfully and unobtrusively adapted for the purposes of nonfiction. The abandonment of the modernist-derived editing strategies of the young Ivens in his avant-garde days—for example, unsettling contrasts in scale, angle, and movement direction, or ironic or dialectical idea-cutting, often Soviet-inspired—was a price that the couple were willing to pay to achieve the Popular Front goal of speaking the narrative film language of the people.

Within the emerging film as a whole, Van Dongen alternated short scenes of the military struggle and the social revolution. Two stunning scenes depicting the bombardment of civilians were placed at a climactic point about two-thirds of the way through the fifty-two-minute film, so that the concluding movement, the victorious battle interpolated with the completion of the irrigation system, seems like a defiant riposte of the people against their oppressors. A coda alternates single shots of water rushing through the new irrigation trough and images of a lone rifleman firing, so that the two themes, defense and revolution, are fused, two dimensions of a single struggle.

The alternating pattern of civilian and military struggles was therefore not just an effective editing device but also a crucial ideological statement. *The Spanish Earth* articulates a worldview that sees people as agents of history, not its casualties. The final word is given not to the mercenaries and their bombs but to the people rooted in the central symbol of the film, the earth. In alternating the military resistance with the civilian struggle, *The Spanish Earth* equates them, merges them into the ideological concept of the people's war. Ivens would often return to this construct as he continued to chronicle the people's struggles of our era, from China and the Soviet Union

to Cuba and Vietnam, each time echoing *The Spanish Earth*'s equation of
peasants and soldiers, of hoes and guns.

Ivens and Van Dongen brought to the sound track of *The Spanish Earth*
the same embrace of popular narrative film language as was evident in the
shooting and editing, and the same creative resourcefulness in integrating it to their political task. The modernist virtuosity and clamorous experimentation of Ivens's early sound documentaries yielded to the subdued
purposefulness of the Popular Front. The sound effects were innovative to
the extent that Van Dongen experimented with more convincing laboratory synthesis (on-location sound effects were still primitive) and varied the
newsreel cliché of wall-to-wall noise with moments of well-chosen silence
and subtle transitions. The sound effects functioned essentially as textural
support for the narrative thrust of the film, however, heightening the especially powerful scenes such as the bombardment episodes, injecting dramatic and informational energy into scenes that were less interesting visually, such as the long shot Brihuega ones. Continuing the Popular Front
practice of lining up prestigious contributors, Ivens recruited two well-
known composers to handle the music: Marc Blitzstein, the in-house composer of the New York left, and Virgil Thomson, who had been acclaimed
for his brilliant folk score for *The Plow That Broke the Plains*. Blitzstein and
Thomson, pressed by the filmmakers' tight schedule, compiled Spanish
folk music, both instrumental and choral, for the score, reflecting the influence of the documentary movement on musical taste of the late 1930s.

It was the commentary, however, that attracted more attention than any of
the other sound tracks, and not only because of its star author. Hemingway's
text is a high point in the benighted history of the documentary commentary and unusually prophetic of future developments in documentary
sound. What was most striking to contemporary spectators was its personal
quality. Ivens, Van Dongen, and Hellman made a last-minute decision to
replace Orson Welles's slick reading with a less professional recording by
Hemingway himself. This voice, with its frank, low-key roughness, added
to the text's aura of personal involvement. It was a stark contrast to the oily,
authoritarian voice-of-God for which *The March of Time* was famous and
which most documentaries imitated. Instead of an anonymous voice, the
commentator became a vivid character on his own terms, a subjective witness of the events of the film, a participant. Though this was already common in Popular Front print journalism, Hemingway's contribution set off
a trend in documentary film that would last throughout World War II, an
effective substitute for the still impossible ideal of direct on-location voices.

Hemingway's text had other innovative aspects, too—its obliqueness, its variations in tone, its detail and immediacy, its multiplicity of postures toward the spectator, its ability to be at times dramatic and at times lyrical or reflective. Most remarkable of all, perhaps, was its restraint. Ivens and Hemingway concentrated on "let[ting] the film speak for itself," on avoiding words that would duplicate the image-continuity, on providing "sharp little guiding arrows" of text, "springboards," often at the beginning of a scene, to invite the audience's involvement (Ivens, *Camera* 127–28). The commentary's role as information and exposition was secondary. Not surprisingly, it is in the narrative passages set in Fuenteduena that the commentary intervenes least, and in the extreme long shot accounts of combat where it is, of necessity, most effective.

A careful look at the commentary in *The Spanish Earth,* as well as in most films by the "art" documentarists of the day, undermines a still current myth of how sound operated in the classical documentary. This myth depicts the classical sound documentary as an "illustrated lecture," a film dominated by a direct address commentary to which images played a mere supporting role. Trained within the silent avant-garde cinema, Ivens and Van Dongen had nothing but contempt for this "illustration" approach and usually succeeded in avoiding it, commissioning commentaries only after an autonomous image-continuity had been established and then reducing them ferociously. Most of the British directors in the Grierson stable did the same, as did Flaherty, Lorentz, and Vertov. Humphrey Jennings and Leni Riefenstahl did away with the commentary almost completely. Van Dongen had her own simple test of silencing the sound track to test the visual sufficiency of a given film. *The Spanish Earth* must be seen as a highlight of a whole tradition of experiments in sound-image structures that fought against the voice-of-God tedium of the newsreels (and the later wartime compilation films) in search of creative alternatives for the still new audiovisual art form.

Postproduction now completed, a massive publicity campaign got underway. In July, a White House preview led to a plug in Eleanor Roosevelt's column, the impossible dream of all Popular Front filmmakers. Immediately thereafter, Ivens and Hemingway arrived in Los Angeles for huge sellout premieres and private fund-raisers, where $20,000 was collected for medical relief. The publicity photos with Joan Crawford were not for the sake of vanity. The West Coast connections were deemed essential to the filmmakers' hopes for commercial distribution. Political documentaries had never received distribution by the "majors" up to this point, but the overwhelming feeling was that a breakthrough was imminent, thanks to Lorentz's obstinate and successful campaign the previous year to distribute *Plow* through independent exhibitors. But the fanfare was deceptive. *Variety*'s Scully summed up Ivens's predicament in this way: "This can make money where any picture can make money but it won't make it there. It won't make it there because it won't get in there. It will have to depend as it did here in its world premiere, on lecture halls which are wired for sound and can gross enough in one performance to justify a week's buildup."

Nothing is new under the sun. The filmmakers resigned themselves to the traditional marginalized distribution that political, documentary, and Soviet films had always relied on. The film opened August 20 at a Manhattan art house, one level above the usual purgatory for Soviet films, but Ivens's disappointment was profound, and record-breaking crowds scarcely consoled him. The film's small leftist distributor, Garrison Films, tried to repeat *Plow*'s success. The ads played up the Hemingway name so much that *The Spanish Earth* was often called a Hemingway film, a prestige-oriented tactic that was buoyed by the film's inclusion in the National Board of Review's "ten best" list for 1937. Audiences more interested in entertainment were assured by the film's original 1937 advertising campaign how undocumentary the film was: it was "The Picture with a Punch," and a "Dramatic Story of Life and People in a War-torn Village in Spain." Further publicity resulted from short-lived censorship squabbles in Rhode Island and Pennsylvania. A review in *The Nation*, while acknowledging the bind of independent distribution, optimistically reported that Ivens was making progress and that more than eight hundred theaters across the United States had been signed up (Belitt 142). The real figure was closer to three hundred. In other words, the film made an enviable splash in the art house/political circuit but a mere ripple in the commercial sea.

Looking back at his most famous film for *Cinéma politique* from the vantage point of the late 1970s, Ivens felt that he could identify a certain impact that *The Spanish Earth* had exerted on its own period:

> Of course you must not think that you are going to change the world with a film; all the same, there have been examples in history of films that have helped the revolution, like the Soviet films at the beginning of the October Revolution. In my own life, I saw the influence of *The Spanish Earth* also. . . .
>
>   . . . it really provided information about a problem that spectators were not very familiar with, and it helped the antifascist movement enormously . . . directly even. People gave money

for the International Brigades. There are militant films that have enormous power, and that is linked to the moment at which they are shown. (Ivens, "Entretien" 20)

As part of this moment and movement, *The Spanish Earth* reflected cultural and ideological tactics that were not directly related to the Spanish subject. The agrarian theme, for example, with its basic icons of bread, earth, and water, was central to the Depression imagination. Ivens's climactic image of water rushing through a new irrigation trough had already appeared in King Vidor's *Our Daily Bread* and Vertov's *Three Songs of Lenin* (both 1934), and impoverished migrant workers and sharecroppers had been the focus of countless photographic essays and books, as well as Lorentz's first two films. The Fuenteduena peasants were thus recognizable, universal, as were Hemingway's vague references to the "they" who "held us back." Yet Ivens's Socialist Realist-tinted vision of the cheerful collective work of his villagers lacks the plaintive, almost defeatist feeling of most American or western European agrarian imagery. The primitive irrigation project of *The Spanish Earth* will seemingly feed an entire besieged capital. What is more, the collective, nonhierarchical initiative of the peasants is behind this success, not the expertise of Lorentz's New Deal agronomists who dispense their advice on crop rotation from on high.

All the same, Ivens's refusal of a certain Socialist Realist dogmatism in his vision of collective work has a Popular Front ring to it. There is clear division of responsibilities among the workers and Ivens carefully avoids innuendoes of collectivization, forced or otherwise; authority springs, spontaneously, out of an implied tradition of folk common sense. Though the Fuenteduena scenes delineate the material terms of the village collective, with impeccable Marxist attention to the forces of production, they do so in a way that lets the signals of tradition, exoticism, and patience, conventionally attached to the peasant icon in Western culture, overshadow the signals of revolution. Discretion is the better part of this vision of the agrarian revolution in the Spanish countryside.

Meanwhile, another theme emerges in *The Spanish Earth* for virtually the first time in Ivens's career—the family. This theme revolves primarily around Julian's homecoming, but it is also notable elsewhere: in the images of two distraught mothers, one trying to load her children on a Madrid evacuation truck, the other in the bombed village bewailing her slaughtered children, and in a young soldier's good-bye to his wife and child before the final battle, elevated by Hemingway into a symbol of the courage and tragedy of the family unit at war: "they say the old good-byes that sound the same in any language. She says she'll wait. He says that he'll come back.

Take care of the kid, he says. I will, she says, but knows she can't. They both know that when they move you out in trucks, it's to a battle." The family accent in *The Spanish Earth* clearly points to the Popular Front strategy of recuperating the values of mainstream culture.

The Spanish Earth, the first of the major antifascist films with widespread distribution, initiated a preoccupation with military imagery that would dominate the screens of the next decade, and it did so in a specifically Popular Front manner. Beyond Ivens's respectful treatment of soldiering as work is his emphasis on the humanity of the Republican troops. The soldiers are presented as little men, nonprofessionals. Shots showing "unsoldierly" signals are present throughout—untidiness, awkward drilling, grins at the camera. In one sequence about life in camp, the emphasis is on everyday nonmilitary activities such as getting haircuts, eating, reading newspapers, with the implication that the stake of the war is the quality of everyday life. The parade scenes show the rawness of recruits eagerly joining up rather than seasoned troops, and seem more interested in small irregular groups than in the symmetrical formations of Riefenstahl. Nazi ballets of banners and boots have nothing in common with the human scale and detail of Ivens's People's Army.

At the same time, Ivens's attitude toward the Communist Party, its participation in the Republican government, and its leadership of the People's Army follows the usual Popular Front practice of "self-censorship." A film courting mass distribution and Eleanor Roosevelt, as well as following the CPUSA line, declined of necessity to identify the lineup of communist speakers during the rally scene: for example, La Pasionaria and others appear as "the wife of a poor miner in Asturias," a "member of Parliament," and so on. Explicit political labels for subjects and artists complicated the broad-based popular coalitions that were the mainstay of the Popular Front, as well as the effectiveness of Republican propaganda. The existence of the International Brigades, composed primarily of Western leftists, passes unmentioned. Other important gaps in Ivens's coverage of the war are conspicuous: Soviet aid to the Republicans; the question of the Church, a major focus of pro-Franquist propaganda; the identification of the enemy (the Italians and the Moroccan mercenaries are discussed in surprisingly respectful or pitying terms, but the Spanish classes who supported Franco's insurrection are omitted, as is Franco's name and even, with the exception of one excerpted speech, the very word "fascist"); and, finally, the political struggle within the Republican camp, which would later come to a head in the Communist-Anarchist showdown in Barcelona near the end of the war. Of course, all of these elisions can be justified in terms of dodging domestic red-baiters, religious groups, and censors (who had the habit of cutting hostile references to "friendly" powers such as Italy), but they are also part of a systematic depiction of a simple nonideological struggle of "little people" against "rebels" and invaders. The stakes of the war came across as loosely "democratic" rather than involving class struggle. Ivens was perfectly consistent with CPUSA policy, which preferred in the late 1930s to call its ideology "Americanism," stressing "democracy" and "civil liberties" rather than class allegiance and soliciting the support of nonleft unions, the middle classes, elected officials, intellectuals, and even the clergy.

Ivens's carefully constructed image of the Spanish war and civil revolution succeeded on that level without a doubt. The *New York Times* was persuaded after seeing the film that the "Spanish people are fighting, not for broad principles of Muscovite Marxism, but for the right to the productivity of a land denied them through years of absentee landlordship" (McManus). Of course, the price Ivens and his contemporaries paid for this achievement— the soft-pedaling of specific radical programs and identity, the adoption of popular filmic forms—is still fiercely debated even to this day. But it was a price that the filmmakers of the Popular Front paid in full conscience.

And what of Spain? How successful were the filmmakers in their short-term pragmatic objectives? The commercial success of their film in its art house/political circuit accumulated eighteen ambulances for Madrid. Late in the war, when the situation was hopeless (for ambulances save lives, not revolutions), Hemingway gave a special presentation of *The Spanish Earth* in Barcelona when a real air raid interrupted Van Dongen's synthetic ones. The film was revived in New York in February 1939, just in time for the final triumph of Franco. Its next revival came upon the death of Franco in 1975, nowhere more eagerly than in Spain, a monument to the struggles two generations earlier of the Popular Fronts of both the Old World and the New, inspiration and instruction for coming struggles.

NOTES

1. The most detailed and reliable account of the ideological context of the films of the American Popular Front is Russell Campbell's *Radical Cinema in the United States, 1930–1942: The Work of the Film and Photo League, Nykino, and Frontier Films* (Ann Arbor: UMI Research Press, 1981), to which I must acknowledge my indebtedness. William Alexander's *Film on the Left: American Documentary Film from 1931 to 1942* (Princeton: Princeton University Press, 1981) is a less comprehensive, more easily available treatment of the same subject.

2. Quotations from Ivens's writings and speeches of the period are from his lecture notes for his American tour, preserved in the Nederlands Filmmuseum,

Amsterdam, or from his well-known 1969 autobiography, *The Camera and I*, in its final or early versions, for which some parts, also available in Amsterdam, began appearing as early as 1938.

Works Cited

Belitt, Ben. "The Camera Reconnoiters." *The Nation*, November 20, 1937. Reprinted in *The Documentary Tradition*, rev. ed., ed. Lewis Jacobs, 141–45. New York: Norton, 1979.

Campbell, Russell. *Cinema Strikes Back: Radical Filmmaking in the United States, 1930–1942*. Ann Arbor: UMI Research Press, 1982.

Cinéma politique. "Joris Ivens et le cinéma militant." *Cinéma politique* (Paris) special unnumbered issue (November 1978): 9–15.

Delmar, Rosalind. *Joris Ivens: 50 Years of Film-Making*. London: British Film Institute, 1979.

Hurwitz, Leo T. "Revolutionary Film—Next Step." In *The Documentary Tradition*, rev. ed., ed. Lewis Jacobs, 91–93. New York: Norton, 1979.

Ivens, Joris. *The Camera and I*. New York: International Publishers, 1969.

———. "Entretien avec Joris Ivens." *Cinéma politique* (Paris): 14.

———. "Making Documentary Films to Meet Today's Needs." *American Cinematographer* 23, no. 7 (1942): 298–99, 332–33.

McManus, John. "*The Spanish Earth* at the 55th St. Playhouse, Is a Plea for Democracy." *New York Times*, August 21, 1937, 7.

Scully, Frank. "Hemingway's War Film on Coast Grosses $15,000 from Audience of 15." *Variety*, July 21, 1937.

Vertov, Dziga. "The Birth of Kino-Eye." In *Kino-Eye: The Writings of Dziga Vertov*, ed. Annette Michelson and trans. Kevin O'Brien, 40–42. Berkeley: University of California Press, 1984.

Chapter 9

THE POETICS OF PROPAGANDA

Humphrey Jennings and *Listen to Britain*

Jim Leach

The films made by Humphrey Jennings during World War II are widely regarded as the peak of his achievement as a filmmaker. In particular, *Listen to Britain* (1942), *Fires Were Started* (1943), and *A Diary for Timothy* (1945) have been recognized as key examples of a "poetic" style whose beautiful images and striking montage effects seem to challenge John Grierson's emphasis on the social purpose of documentary. When *Listen to Britain* was released, it was dismissed by Edgar Anstey, one of Jennings's colleagues at the Crown Film Unit, as a work of great beauty that "will not encourage anyone to do anything at all" (quoted in Sussex 144). After the war, however, it was this "poetic" approach that appealed to a group of young critics opposed to the Grierson tradition. In an influential article published in *Sight and Sound* in 1954, Lindsay Anderson not only celebrated Jennings's "poetic style" but also argued that he was "the only real poet the British cinema has yet produced" (53).[1]

Even though Anstey and Anderson arrived at opposing conclusions with regard to the value of the films, they shared the assumption that poetry and propaganda are incompatible. Yet the depiction of the war effort in these films is closely associated with the enduring myth of the "people's war," and Andrew Britton has argued that Jennings was creating propaganda for "the British Imperial Myth," which is "still incorrigibly there to this day" and "emphasizes . . . the homogeneity, the unambiguous political unity, of British wartime society" (38). Jennings is thus seen to be complicit with a myth that created the illusion that the British class system had been swept away and sought to dupe the people into believing that no further social change would be required once the war had been won.[2]

While Britton does show how both the films and the myth were appropriated by the conservative ideology of the Thatcher years, I believe that he misrepresents how the films work as poetic documentaries and, in so doing, tends to downplay the complexity and contradictions in their relationship to the myth that they reflect and help to construct. In this essay, I will offer a close reading of *Listen to Britain* to suggest how its poetic style and propaganda purposes unsettle and enrich each other, and I will outline some general principles regarding the relationship of poetry and propaganda within the documentary mode.

Although the opening credits assign joint responsibility for the direction and editing of *Listen to Britain* to Jennings and Stewart McAllister, I will continue to refer to Jennings as the film's author, partly for the sake of convenience but also because the film clearly anticipates the two later films with which it forms an informal trilogy documenting the progress of the war effort in Britain. Jennings received sole credit for directing both films; McAllister edited *Fires Were Started* but not *A Diary for Timothy*. The joint credit on *Listen to Britain* acknowledges the difficulty of separating direction from editing in a film which, as we will see, depends so heavily on montage effects. Clearly others also contributed significantly to these Crown Film Unit productions, but they are all centrally informed by a sensibility that derives from Jennings. In any case, my concern here is not with questions of authorship but with how this sensibility has been defined through the categories of "poetry" and "propaganda."

POETRY IN MOTION

Recent historians and theorists of documentary continue to place Jennings in what Stuart Legg once called "the poetic line" (quoted in Sussex 159). Thus Paul Swann refers to "a uniquely poetic element" in Jennings's films and Bill Nichols identifies "a poetic form of exposition" in *Listen to Britain* (Swann 163; Nichols 179). Although Swann's wording suggests that Jennings's work stands apart, it is clear that, by the 1940s, the "poetic line" already encompassed a wide range of films, including the city symphonies, the films of Leni Riefenstahl and Robert Flaherty, and even a few British documentaries such as Harry Watt and Basil Wright's *Night Mail* (1936), which incorporated verse by W. H. Auden and music by Benjamin Britten. My analysis of *Listen to Britain* will, therefore, not offer a comprehensive account of the possibilities of the poetic documentary but rather will try to pin down exactly what it means to call this particular film "poetic."[3]

While the usual implied opposite of poetry is prose, the literary analogy is rarely rigorously employed and is often blurred by equally vague allusions to painting and music. Jennings was called an "unrepentant impressionist," and *Listen to Britain* has been described as "a 'symphony' of the sounds of Britain at war" (Hardy 171; Barsam 172). In Jennings's case, such analogies were especially plausible because of his work in other media, as a poet and a painter and as an organizer of the London surrealist exhibition of 1936. He had already spoken out in "defence of the poet" and against a general tendency in the arts of the 1930s toward an emphasis on the "social and useful" (Hillier 70–71).

There are clearly problems involved in transferring the literary category of "poetry" to an audio-visual medium, and it is certainly not clear that propaganda needs to be associated with prose. A more pertinent opposition might be that suggested by Claude Lévi-Strauss between poetry and myth: the density and complexity of poetic speech means that it can be translated only "at the cost of serious distortions," while the substance of myth lies not "in its style, its original music, or its syntax, but in the *story* which it tells" (Lévi-Strauss 210). It may seem to make little sense to ask whether *Listen to Britain* could be translated, but this formulation does suggest the way in which its "poetic style" works with and against what Roland Barthes, building on the ideas of Lévi-Strauss, has called the "frozen" speech of myth that sets out to "immobilize the world" (129, 155).[4]

Before looking at specific examples of how this "poetic style" functions in *Listen to Britain,* I will briefly review three criteria for identifying the "poetry effect" that emerges from the discourse surrounding Jennings's films. According to Anderson, there is no doubt that the primary criterion should be the filmmaker's ability to develop a personal vision. While admitting that Jennings's films were "official, sponsored propaganda," Anderson valued them because the "manner of expression was always individual" (53). This idea was taken up by Jim Hillier, who compared Jennings to John Ford, another director whom Anderson greatly admired, arguing that each director develops a "personal vision" within the constraints of "the propaganda documentary" and the Hollywood genre system, respectively (Hillier 70). More recently, Kevin Jackson has reiterated this argument, claiming that Jennings "used the most seemingly anonymous of all film forms to work out an unmistakable personal language" (x).

Anderson's allusion to Ford underlines the links between this line of argument and Andrew Sarris's use of personal vision as one of the criteria in his version of the auteur theory. Indeed, in Hillier's account, Jennings emerges as "the British cinema's one undoubted *auteur*" (Hillier 62). Since the auteur theory has subsequently been widely attacked as a vestige of a Romantic investment in the notion of individual creativity that ignores not only the industrial basis of film as a medium but also the extent to which the meanings generated by any work of art are produced by its cultural context, its application to Jennings might seem to confirm the doubts of those who rejected his work as anachronistic and socially irrelevant. The criterion of personal vision would thus seem to be quite consonant with Edgar Anstey's judgment that a poetic documentary like *Listen to Britain* is "a figment of the romantic imagination" (quoted in Sussex 144).

Without denying that Jennings's films do exhibit recurring motifs and preoccupations that reflect the sensibility of their prime author, I want to suggest that this criterion is of limited value in distinguishing a poetic documentary. What is the point of stressing the "personal vision" in *Listen to Britain* when the film itself goes to great lengths to conceal the presence of the filmmakers, developing what might even be called an "impersonal" style in order to suggest that the "personality" it documents is that of the British people? This impersonality certainly has ideological implications, which will be examined later, but there seems to be nothing intrinsically "poetic" about it.

I do not want to reject the category of the "personal" out of hand, how-ever, since it emerges in a new form from a consideration of the other two criteria that have been most often used for identifying the poetic style in these documentaries. For many critics the most telling sign was a negative one: the lack of an omniscient voice-over commentary. In the Griersonian tradition, the "voice" of the documentary is identified with that of the male voice-of-God commentator, whose claim to authority and omniscience de-pends on the denial of a personal viewpoint.[5] The film's argument is con-veyed through the commentary, and the images are subordinate to its de-mands. Although the commentary claims to explain the images, it actually determines their structure, just as the narrative does in popular fiction films.

Jennings consistently resisted the dominance of the voice-of-God com-mentator in his major work. After eliminating commentary completely from *Listen to Britain,* he moved toward the indirect address of classical nar-rative cinema in *Fires Were Started* (following the lead of Robert Flaherty) and used second-person address (ostensibly to a baby born at the end of the war) to complicate the spectator-commentator relationship in *A Diary for Timothy.* The absence of a commentator in *Listen to Britain* leads to a sense of "ambiguity," often seen as one of the hallmarks of poetic language.[6] Since the relationships between the images are no longer determined by a verbal discourse, the editing must create its own continuity which, however, is at least partially open to interpretation. Thus Hillier refers to the "rich ambiguity" of Jennings's style in which "the meanings of an image, or more frequently the connections between images, are left to the audience's emotions for interpretation" (Hillier 87). This refusal to impose meanings implies both a respect for the personal freedom of the spectator and an awareness that meanings are always complex and plural.

From this perspective, the poetic activity involves encouraging new ways of seeing, as suggested by Mick Eaton's claim that the use of "montage both within and between shots" in Jennings's films works to "transform the familiar iconography of British life through the revelation of the bizarre in the everyday" (81). I would suggest that what is revealed is more often incongruous than bizarre, but Eaton's formulation does suggestively link the surrealist influence on Jennings to his involvement with Mass Observation, an organization dedicated to the anthropological investigation of everyday life and culture in Britain. In a radio talk broadcast in 1938, Jennings expressed his concern that modern poetry and everyday life "have got out of touch with each other," and his wartime practice as a filmmaker can be seen as an attempt to reunite them (quoted in Jackson 255).

In the absence of a commentary, the spectator must seek meanings in the images and sounds and in the linkages established between them. To some extent, this effect recalls Sergei Eisenstein's famous definition of montage: "from the collision of two given factors *arises* a concept" (37). In discussing the implications of this idea for Jennings's films, Eaton argues that this "concept" can never be "completely circumscribed in advance" and that "it must always oscillate between the personal and the social" (82). If the poetic discourse of *Listen to Britain* is, as I have suggested, impersonal, it is because the style is supposed to emanate not from the director's personal vision but from the "power of poetry," which Jennings attributed to the English people and that thus encompasses both the director and the spectator.[7]

The implication of the spectator in this "contamination" of the social with the personal is closely related to the third criterion that has been used to define the poetic documentary. According to Andrew Higson, documentary is normally confined to the "public gaze," unlike fiction films, which can use point-of-view shots to encourage identification with characters (77). The poetic effect of Jennings's wartime films is associated with what might be called the introduction of a "private eye."

Anderson argued that Jennings developed a "style based on a peculiar intimacy of observation" in which the "commonplace" is made significant (54). In *Listen to Britain,* the war has created a context within which everyday life gains a new significance because its patterns can no longer be taken for granted. What is at stake is what Bill Nichols has called "the social sub-jectivity of viewing, or listening," to which the film draws attention through a style that "fractures the time and space of its scenes from the visible world of wartime Britain into a large number of dissociated impressions" (179–80). If we couple Nichols's description with Gavin Lambert's much earlier claim that "the technique of *Listen to Britain* is based completely on the power of association" (25), the film's "intimate" address can be seen to disturb the ideological continuity of the public sphere and to generate a psychological tension around the competing forces of association and dissociation, continuity editing and montage.

"Only Connect"

Although it is only about eighteen minutes long, *Listen to Britain* is made up of over two hundred shots, organized into seventeen sequences of vary-ing lengths whose boundaries are, however, often obscured by ambiguous transition shots and overlapping sound. The frequent shifts—from country to city, from work to leisure activities, from noise to music—promote an alertness to the possibility for unusual and ambiguous linkages between shots, even when the editing within sequences seems to conform to more conventional continuity rules, an alertness that also extends to juxtaposi-tions within single shots. While the spectator is caught up in the flow of images and sounds, however, the film does intermittently draw attention to the act of looking through the use of point-of-view editing that works both to focus the spectator's viewing and to draw this viewing into the "so-cial subjectivity" that supposedly grows out of the experience of living in wartime Britain.

The film opens with two images of the countryside, the first of trees with leaves blowing in the wind, the second of wheat rippling in a field. While this second image introduces the idea of cultivated nature, both carry connotations of a traditional image of rural Britain as a "garden." However, these connotations are disturbed by the noise of planes on the sound track, and the third shot duly shows planes flying across the sky. The human presence and the look are then introduced into the film as we see three land workers looking at something outside the frame and then two shots of men at an anti-aircraft installation peering up into the sky. Another shot of planes is followed by a shot of a tractor working close to the anti-aircraft gun, and the noise of the tractor drowns out that of the planes. The se-quence ends with a closer shot of the tractor and a shot of the sky with planes at high altitude.

This opening sequence, which consists of eleven shots and lasts a little more than one minute, quickly establishes the kind of spectatorship that the film will invite. The contrast between rural peace and intimations of war is fairly obvious, but the meaning of the contrast depends on whether we emphasize the visual and aural dissonance or the harmony implied by the war effort. If the land workers and gunners contribute to this effort in their different ways, their unified purpose is expressed through their looks at the sky, implying the need for alertness against an enemy who will remain unseen and unmentioned throughout the film. Rather than instigating a paranoid search for an enemy, however, this sequence prepares for a film that will encourage a similar alertness in the spectator, who is asked to reflect on the experience of unity within difference.

The next sequence is anticipated by a beep heard over the end of the last shot of planes and then, as we see a house framed by trees and a fence, a radio announcer introduces the news. However, instead of news, his voice is followed by lively dance music, which is soon located in a dance hall where the floor is filled with couples dancing to "Roll out the Barrel." Shots of the dancers are intercut with shots of civil defense crews looking out to sea, silhouetted in the moonlight, and of a young woman showing a photograph (which we do not see) to a soldier as they sit beside the dance floor. The communal activity of dancing in couples mediates between intimate (and private) looks and the social need for continued watchfulness.

The following sequences alternate between work necessary for the war effort and leisure activities that provide temporary relief from this effort. After shots of coal miners at work, a train stops at a signal, and Canadian soldiers pass the time by playing cards and singing "Home on the Range." As the train pulls away, a sound overlap bridges the transition to an aircraft factory where three shots of a plane being assembled are followed by one of a plane taking off. The camera then pans to a sign identifying "Ambulance Station 76" while a woman's voice is heard singing to a piano accompaniment. A middle-aged woman in uniform is then shown performing for a group of younger women who tentatively join in as she sings the traditional song "The Ash Grove." The ambulance station is located in what seems to be a museum, with a large statue looming over the women, but a cutaway to a close-up of hard hats hanging on the wall places both folk music and classical art in the urgent context of the war effort to preserve these traditions.[8]

Tradition is also invoked by the next shot of Big Ben and by the synchronous sound of its chimes. But this sound is then relocated to a radio broadcast as an announcer declares, "This is London calling," and the theme music of "The British Grenadiers" is heard. A rapid montage sequence then illustrates the work of the BBC World Service by presenting snatches of foreign-language programs over shots of radio equipment, an effect that evokes both Britain's traditional role as a world power and the role of modern technology in maintaining it.

Having broadened its perspective to include the international scope of the war effort, the film then includes a sequence in which the "private eye" comes into its own. The montage of radio equipment is followed by a shot of the countryside at sunset while a woman's voice reads a message for the armed forces overseas. A fade leads into shots of the country at dawn, with the sound of birds singing on the sound track. These sounds then merge into the noise of horses' hooves, and a man is shown leading a horse past a factory, which workers are entering. The motif of "morning" continues as the camera pans over a city, recalling similar imagery in "city symphony" films such as Ruttman's *Berlin: Symphony of a Great City* (1927) and Vertov's *Man with a Movie Camera* (1929). A male voice calls out instructions for physical exercise to the rhythmic accompaniment of a piano, while the camera follows another man walking briskly along a city street wearing a bowler hat and carrying a hard hat as well as a briefcase.

Three shots of industrial buildings accompanied by factory noises are followed by a shot of a tree in sunlight as a piano begins to play. The next shot shows a woman preparing tea in a domestic interior. Her look out of the window cues a reverse-shot of children dancing in a school playground from which (presumably) the sound of the piano is coming. Just before a cut back to a close-up of the woman looking out of the window, a girl's voice calls out "Mummy!" Another shot of the children dancing is followed by a cut back to the woman, who now looks away from the window, cueing a second reverse-shot of a framed photograph of a man in uniform. By inviting identification with the woman's private experience through the use of point-of-view shots, the film temporarily adopts the strategies of fiction cinema and implies that both empathy and detachment, private eye and public gaze, are required to adequately comprehend the impact of war as a public event on people's lives.

While the child's cry anchors the sequence firmly within the emotional and ideological framework of the "family," its meanings are immediately opened out again. The framed image of the "father" is not followed by a cut back to the "mother" but by a closer shot of the children in the playground. This shot is bound to the next shot of armored vehicles moving through the streets by the continuation of the piano music, which only gradually gives way to the noise of the vehicles. Once again, the present reality of war impinges on a space associated with peace and tradition, the latter here represented by several shots of a building of Tudor design that a sign reveals to be a "Guest House and Tea Room." Just before this sequence ends, a close-up of a young girl watching the troops pass by links its meanings to the "family" motif of the previous sequence.

IDEOLOGY AND UTOPIA

At this point, just before the film's concluding and most famous sequences, I want to break off my analysis to address the issues of propaganda and ideology that have so far remained largely implicit. To some extent, the film's "poetic" address masks its propaganda function; but *Listen to Britain* was clearly made as a contribution to the war effort, and we now need to examine the implications of the interaction of poetry and propaganda.

As we have seen, Edgar Anstey felt that the film's poetic style was incompatible with its intended use as propaganda. He argued that "it will be a disaster if this film is sent overseas" because "our Allies" would be appalled to "learn that an official British film-making unit can find time these days to contemplate the current sights and sounds of Britain as if the country were some curious kind of museum exhibit" (quoted in Sussex 144). When the film was released in the United States, its ambiguity was reduced by a strident verbal introduction, apparently added by "a nervous civil servant" (Hodgkinson and Sheratsky 59), and Anstey later admitted that it "had enormous influence overseas" (quoted in Sussex 145).

The apparent success of *Listen to Britain* in influencing public opinion suggests both that propaganda should not be too narrowly defined and that the boundary lines in the debate over social utility and aesthetic pleasure are not as distinct as they might seem. Grierson seems to have assumed that documentary could combine propaganda with social responsibility because of its close ties to actuality, but there is no doubt that documentaries can reflect and construct myths as much as fiction films do. In most fiction films, and in many documentaries, these myths function ideologically as hidden assumptions, but propaganda normally makes its intentions apparent. In a sense, then, propaganda is more open and honest about its ideological workings than films that disclaim any social or political purpose, although the process of selecting evidence for use in propaganda films may be governed by ideological assumptions or assumptions about the ideological framework the spectator will bring to bear.

In assessing the implications of *Listen to Britain* as propaganda, then, we need to attend both to the myths circulated in the film and to the ways in which it envisages the spectator's relations to these myths. There can be little doubt that the most pertinent myth to which *Listen to Britain* contributes is that of the "people's war." Leonard Quart situates the film in relation

Listen to Britain: The woman's look from children to photograph expresses the private eye.

to this myth when he describes it as "a portrait of a nation where all classes (despite the existence of clear class divisions), sounds, and images act as one against a common enemy" (63).⁹

Andrew Britton adopts a similar view but argues that this vision of national unity serves the interests of "the dominant class culture" (44). He refers to "the imperialist content of the war myth" as "Churchillian" and links it to Thatcherist rhetoric during the Falklands crisis (38–39). By simply eliding the "people's war" with the conservative ideology that dominated Britain in the 1980s, however, Britton ignores the contradictions the myth was struggling to contain. While he does admit that the Labour Party's victory in the 1945 General Election and the establishment of the Welfare State testify to "the material content of the popular aspirations which secured the united British nation," Britton does not allow that these aspirations may have been incorporated into what he calls "the *ideology* of war unity" and, in fact, may be a major factor in its effectiveness and endurance (38).

As my analysis of the film has already suggested, the social and cinematic unity is less assured than Quart and Britton suggest. The attempt to read the film as a simple expression of the myth misses the fragility of the connections made through montage in *Listen to Britain*. Questions about the extent to which similarity overrides difference and about the permanence of the social bonds forged by the war effort are central to the experience of the film and even to its ideological meanings, since it implies that such an uncertainty could be resolved only through the imposition of an authority like that against which the war is being fought. Thus Geoffrey Nowell-Smith suggests that the film's vision is "consonant with Churchillian rhetoric, but by no means equivalent to it" since "it both holds more together and shows more awareness of its own instability" (330).

Clearly this "instability" is related to the "ambiguity" of the film's poetic effect. What this suggests is that the ideological implications of a film cannot be separated from its formal strategies. Thus in Leni Riefenstahl's *Triumph of the Will* (1935), for example, the film's rhetoric becomes an extension of the documented event (most visibly apparent in shots that show cameras moving up and down on elevators in the walls of the stadium). While this film has also been regarded as a poetic documentary and also has no commentary, there is little room for ambiguity in its style, which draws on and extends the monumentality of an event staged by Hitler as a propaganda statement glorifying his authority.

While Riefenstahl's aerial shots and panoramic views of the Nuremberg spectacle evoke what Michel de Certeau has called the "totalizing eye," *Listen to Britain* offers instead the view from "'down below,' below the thresholds at which visibility begins" (92–93). The camera observes, poised between involvement and detachment, activities that the shifting flow of the editing designates as parts of a larger reality, setting up a tension between the fragmentation of the representation and the implied unity of the whole, between what can be seen and what can be imagined. Of course, the title of the film directs us to "listen," and the pull between sight and sound adds to the fragility of the film's discourse. The result is something very like what Raymond Williams has called the "subjunctive mode," a mode that tries to identify the utopian possibilities that cannot be detected by works in the "indicative" mode that simply "state that this is what reality is like" (218).

POETRY, PROPAGANDA, AND MYTH

Listen to Britain does have its blind spots, some of which it shares with the myth of the "people's war." Yet this myth was so successful because it did address an important aspect of many people's experience of the war: it tried to reconcile the contradiction between the need for social change, if only to gain support for the war effort, and the forces resistant to such change. What I am suggesting is that *Listen to Britain* activates the tensions involved in the very construction of the myth and builds them into the spectator's experience of the film. Its ideological limitations thus need to be assessed in the context of its refusal to settle for either reality or myth or to elide the differences between them.

One of the blind spots seems to emerge in the sequence involving the woman's look at child and husband that I had just reached in my analysis of the film. While many women are depicted in uniform or at work, the representation of this woman as housewife and mother seems to anticipate the ideological pressures for a return to more traditional gender roles once the war was over. That there is an element of strain in the film's discourse is indicated by the rather artificial device of adding the cry of "Mummy" to the sound track to reinforce the effect of the point-of-view editing that situates the woman clearly within the framework of the family unit. The elimination of the possibility of ambiguity here is out of keeping with the general tendencies of the film's style. But, as we have seen, this is also the sequence in which the tension between public and private is most fully resolved in favor of the latter. By adopting the strategies of classical narrative at the moment of its most conservative representation of gender relations, the film implicitly points to the ideological limitations of the private eye. Yet this sequence does invite identification with the way the war was actually experienced by many women without denying other possibilities, some of which the film also represents.

The complexities of the subjunctive mode become most apparent in the film's next movement, which includes its most celebrated effect, the sound bridge that merges the conclusion of a song by the music hall team of Flanagan and Allen into the introduction of a Mozart piano concerto played by Myra Hess. These concerts make up the two longest sequences in the film, but music is also prominent in the sequence that introduces them. Over a shot of an armored vehicle passing a group of people watching from a doorstep, a fanfare is heard and lively music begins. A dissolve leads into an aerial shot of the countryside (one of the film's few views from above), and a radio announcer is heard, "Calling all workers." As if in response to this call, the film bursts into a flurry of movement: a truck passes under a freight train crossing a bridge, the camera moves rapidly past terraced houses, and a close-up of a wheel spinning on a machine takes us into a factory. Women working and singing are then intercut with the loudspeakers from which the music is supposedly coming. Appropriately, in view of the "family" sequence that has just ended, the song is "Yes, My Darling Daughter."

This sequence is built out of a cluster of meanings related to music, gender, and technology, all of which refer back to earlier moments in the film and gain new resonance through their present juxtaposition. Then, as the camera once again moves rapidly past rows of houses, the music fades out and is replaced by station noises that cue four brief shots of men and women in uniform waiting at a train station, another aspect of wartime experience. This brief lull leads into a performance by Flanagan and Allen of one of their most popular songs, "Underneath the Arches," for an enthusiastic audience of workers on their lunch break. This concert is linked, via the famous shared chord, to one of Myra Hess's lunchtime performances at the National Gallery in which she is accompanied by an orchestra of musicians from the Royal Air Force.

The juxtaposition of these two concerts, one decidedly "popular" and the other the product of "high" culture, has been seen as the climactic point in the film's drive to forge links between all elements of British society. As David Thomson puts it, the effect is "a way of saying all people, all classes, have their music" (58). Although the sound overlap does reveal a basic affinity at the level of musical language, the unity created in the editing does not eliminate the need to notice the differences as well as the similarities the film finds in its representation of the two concerts as musical and social events. Geoffrey Nowell-Smith captures the complexity of the sequence when he argues that its meaning is "left open" so that "the union of popular and high culture and their possible divergence" can be "held in the balance" (331).

The lunchtime concerts by Myra Hess did become part of the myth of the "people's war" because they attracted many people who had not attended concerts of classical music before. Another concert is featured in *A Diary for Timothy* where Hess's performance of music by Beethoven prompts the commentator to remind "Tim" that this is "German music" and that he will have to think about this apparent contradiction when he grows up. The Mozart piano concerto heard in *Listen to Britain* is not quite "German music" (given Mozart's Austrian origins), but it is close enough to raise similar issues, especially since it follows the evocation of familiar London sites in "Underneath the Arches" (although the only arches that the film actually shows are those in front of the National Gallery). The power of music to transcend class and national boundaries is affirmed, but significant differences remain.

These differences emerge precisely because of the similarities in the way that the two concerts are represented. Both are introduced by signs that appear shortly after the music has begun, and both intercut shots of the performers on stage with shots of the audience. Yet parallels also reveal differences: thus a menu chalked on a blackboard at the first concert finds its equivalent at the second in a program listing the order in which the music will be played. Both audiences obviously enjoy the music, but the workers sit at tables and sing along as they eat while at the National Gallery some people eat discreetly on the margins of the audience but most concentrate on the performance. Two shots reveal the queen as a member of this audience, suggesting the closeness to the people of the British royal family and/ or the cultural distinctions that make the National Gallery rather than a workers' canteen an appropriate site for the queen to visit.

This last distinction may well have been qualified for the original audience who would know that, under the right circumstances, members of the royal family would attend performances by popular entertainers. Of course, these would then tend to become more formal occasions, but formality is not completely absent even in the workers' canteen. After Flanagan and Allen have appeared in medium shot, singing in a gently relaxed manner, a long shot from the audience reveals them on stage in front of a grand piano and orchestra. Such details suggest influences flowing both ways across the divide between popular and high culture, and their effect could be complemented by the specific extra-textual knowledge that a spectator might bring to the film, as suggested by Nowell-Smith's comment on the Jewish backgrounds that link Bud Flanagan and Myra Hess (331).

The symmetry between the representations of the two concerts is disrupted when the camera's attention wanders away from the Mozart performance (which continues on the sound track) and follows a sign to a War

Artists' Exhibition where a sailor is seen examining a painting of a ship in harbor. After a brief return to the concert, we are shown sandbags and the empty frames of paintings that have been removed to protect them from bomb damage, both digressions extending the concern with the impact of the war on art. The exhibition suggests the need for painters (and filmmakers like Jennings) to record the experience of war, while the empty frames attest to the threat to the cultural heritage. In a sense, the persistence of music-making compensates for the removal of the paintings, but if the cultural and economic value of the originals has led to their absence, they return in the form of reproductions (presumably) that decorate the concert area and (at least to the camera eye) are indistinguishable from the originals.

As the concert sequence comes to an end, the camera moves outside the National Gallery, and we see two shots of the statue of Nelson atop the column in Trafalgar Square, reminding us of an earlier war. The music continues even into the next sequence, which shows men and women building tanks, and is only gradually drowned out by the factory noises. A single shot of a military band leading a parade through city streets cues the return of music to the sound track, but even before the shot ends, industrial noises once again fade in, cueing a sequence in a blast furnace that includes shots of a molten ingot from the point of view of the workers. The interaction of music and noise, the slight disjunctions between sight and sound, the move from public gaze to private eye all work to stress the range of experiences tenuously held together by the war effort.

Over the final shots of the blast furnace, music again returns as the voices of a choir emerge from the industrial noise. The music swells up over shots of factory chimneys, wheat rippling in the wind (a reprise of the second shot), and cooling towers at a power station, and the film ends with an aerial view of the countryside. Some clouds pass in front of the camera, rhyming with the smoke and steam of the chimneys and cooling towers, but move away to leave an unimpeded view of land and sky, with no sign of the planes of the opening sequence (their noise replaced by the triumphal music). The effect is a rather rapid but powerful movement toward closure: Hillier points out that the music here is "the only sound whose source is not identified in the film" so that "it seems to well out from *all* the elements of the film" (89).

However, this ending does seem to violate the rule of ambiguity that operates throughout the rest of the film, especially since the powerful concluding music is a performance of "Rule Britannia!" David Thomson thus questions the effect of the ending because "there's no sight of the choir, and too little thought of what 'Rule' means" (58). It is not quite true that this is the only sound whose source is not identified, since the voice of the fitness instructor also comes from nowhere, although we are clearly meant to assume that the source is a radio broadcast. However, the use of one of Britain's unofficial national anthems in the ending, even if it may also emanate from a radio broadcast featuring one of the country's many amateur choirs, does carry imperialist connotations that have not been emphasized in the rest of the film.

The final shot, too, seems to verge on a "totalizing" view, although the cuts back and forth from city to country imply that the whole still cannot be encompassed by a single shot. Perhaps it also makes a difference that the only "waves" we see are in a wheat field and that the music may be broadcast over the airwaves that have earlier been shown to be an important part of the war effort. Even if propaganda wins out at the end of *Listen to Britain*, the rather abrupt closure and the "poetic" openness of all that has gone before make this victory itself somewhat ambiguous. The film documents a historical moment in which the claims of poetry and propaganda come together in the evolving myth of the "people's war," and this unstable partnership signals a challenge both to the nation and to the documentary form.

NOTES

1. The critics, including Gavin Lambert and Lindsay Anderson, who defended Jennings were paving the way for a new approach to documentary that would eventually become known as Free Cinema. Since Jennings died in an accident in 1950 and his postwar films disappointed even his admirers, his influence on the Free Cinema filmmakers was almost entirely confined to his wartime films.

2. For a thorough treatment of the historical and cultural contexts of the myth of the "people's war," see Angus Calder, *The People's War: Britain 1939–1945* (London: Jonathan Cape, 1969).

3. One of the most suggestive treatments of the "poetic" in cinema is still Pier Paolo Pasolini's "The 'Cinema of Poetry,'" in Pasolini, *Heretical Empiricism*, trans. Louise K. Barnett (Bloomington: Indiana University Press, 1988), 167–86. Jennings's films might be usefully discussed in relation to Pasolini's argument that people "'read' reality visually" through their encounters with "objects and things that appear charged with multiple meanings and thus 'speak' brutally with their very presence" (168); but, as Pasolini made clear in a later essay, he was interested only in "narrative poetry" and opposed to "a cinema of lyric poetry obtained through editing and the intensification of technique" (251–52). The "poetic" style of Jennings's wartime documentaries is approached through the linguistic theory of Juri Lotman in Bjorn Sorenssen, "The Documentary Aesthetics of Humphrey Jennings," in *Documentary and the Mass Media*, ed. John Comer (London: Edward Arnold, 1986), 47–63.

4. The issue is far from simple, however, because there is a clear parallel between Jennings's "poetic style" and Lévi-Strauss's argument that meaning "cannot reside in the isolated elements which enter into the composition of a myth, but only in the way those elements are combined" (Lévi-Strauss 210). The relationship of poetry and myth is approached in a rather different way in Barry K. Grant, "Tradition and the Individual Talent: Poetry in the Genre Film," in *Narrative Strategies: Original Essays in Film and Prose Fiction,* ed. Syndy M. Conger and Janice R. Welsch (Macomb: Western Illinois University Press, 1981), 93–103.

5. Bill Nichols defines the "voice" of a documentary as "that which conveys to us a sense of a text's social point of view, of how it is speaking to us and how it is organizing the materials it is presenting to us." "The Voice of Documentary," *Film Quarterly* 36, no. 3 (1983): 18.

6. Hillier notes that "Jennings was a product of the I. A. Richards school of criticism that produced Empson's conception of the ambiguity or multiplicity of poetic statements" (87). William Empson's influential *Seven Types of Ambiguity* was first published in 1930.

7. The reference is to a 1947 review by Jennings of a book on the "English character" in Jackson, *Reader,* 238; Jennings takes his lead from the book in referring to the "English," but as the title of *Listen to Britain* suggests, he normally sought to invoke the national unity of the "British" people.

8. This sequence was apparently shot in the basement of the Old Bailey (Hodgkinson and Sheratsky 58).

9. Quart's formulation here suggests the need to compare the apparent unifying effect of the war in Jennings's films with the depiction of male groups, in British and Hollywood war films of the postwar period, who overcome social and/or racial differences for the sake of their struggle against a common enemy.

WORKS CITED

Anderson, Lindsay. "Only Connect: Some Aspects of the Work of Humphrey Jennings." In *Humphrey Jennings: Film-maker, Painter, Poet,* ed. Mary-Lou Jennings, 53–59. London: British Film Institute, 1982.

Barr, Charles, ed. *All Our Yesterdays: 90 Years of British Cinema.* London: British Film Institute, 1986.

Barsam, Richard Meram. *Nonfiction Film: A Critical History.* Rev. ed. Bloomington: Indiana University Press, 1992.

Barthes, Roland. *Mythologies.* Trans. Annette Lavers. London: Jonathan Cape, 1972.

Britton, Andrew. "Their Finest Hour: Humphrey Jennings and the British Imperial Myth of World War II." *CineAction* 18 (1989): 37–44. Reprinted in *Britton on Film: The Complete Film Criticism of Andrew Britton,* ed. Barry Keith Grant, 302–13. Detroit: Wayne State University Press, 2009.

de Certeau, Michel. *The Practice of Everyday Life*. Trans. Steven Rendall. Berkeley: University of California Press, 1984.

Eaton, Mick. "In the Land of the Good Image." *Screen* 23, no. 1 (1982): 79–84.

Eisenstein, Sergei. *Film Form: Essays in Film Theory*. Trans. Jay Leyda. New York: Harcourt, Brace and World, 1949.

Hardy, H. Forsyth. "British Documentaries in the War." In *Nonfiction Film: Theory and Criticism*, ed. Richard Meram Barsam, 167–72. New York: E. P. Dutton, 1976.

Higson, Andrew. 1986. "'Britain's Outstanding Contribution to the Film': The Documentary-Realist Tradition." In *All Our Yesterdays: 90 Years of British Cinema*, ed. Charles Barr, 72–97. London: British Film Institute, 1986.

Hillier, Jim. "Humphrey Jennings." In Alan Lovell and Jim Hillier, *Studies in Documentary*, 62–132. London: Seeker and Warburg, 1972.

Hodgkinson, Anthony W., and Rodney E. Sheratsky. *Humphrey Jennings: More Than a Maker of Films*. Hanover, NH: University Press of New England, 1982.

Jackson, Kevin, ed. *The Humphrey Jennings Film Reader*. Manchester: Carcanet Press, 1993.

Jennings, Mary-Lou, ed. *Humphrey Jennings: Film-maker, Painter, Poet*. London: British Film Institute, 1982.

Lambert, Gavin. "Jennings' Britain." *Sight and Sound* 20, no. 3 (1951): 24–26.

Lévi-Strauss, Claude. *Structural Anthropology*. Vol. 1. Trans. Claire Jacobson and Grundfest Schoepf. New York: Basic Books, 1963.

Nichols, Bill. *Representing Reality: Issues and Concepts in Documentary*. Bloomington: Indiana University Press, 1991.

Nowell-Smith, Geoffrey. "Humphrey Jennings: Surrealist Observer." In *All Our Yesterdays: 90 Years of British Cinema*, ed. Charles Barr, 321–33. London: British Film Institute, 1986.

Quart, Leonard. "Wartime Memories." *Cineaste* 20, no. 3 (1994): 63–64.

Sussex, Elizabeth. *The Rise and Fall of British Documentary*. Berkeley: University of California Press, 1975.

Swann, Paul. *The British Documentary Film Movement, 1926–1946*. Cambridge: Cambridge University Press, 1989.

Thomson, David. "A Sight for Sore Eyes." *Film Comment* 29, no. 2 (1993): 54–59.

Williams, Raymond. *Politics and Letters*. London: New Left Books, 1979.

Chapter 10

"It Was an Atrocious Film"

Georges Franju's *Blood of the Beasts*

Jeannette Sloniowski

Blood of the Beasts (*Le sang des bêtes*) (1949) is one of several controversial documentaries that use exceedingly cruel and violent images to assault the spectator.[1] Certainly it is one of the most emotionally grueling films imaginable. Made just after World War II, it is part of a documentary triptych that also includes *En passant par la Lorraine* (1950) and *Hôtel des Invalides* (1951). It consists of nine sequences, four of which document the slaughter of animals for the markets of Paris, and five (including the introduction) that show the suburbs that surround the slaughterhouses. The slaughterhouse sequences are shockingly graphic and have often been regarded as among the cruelest in the history of documentary.

As a political/aesthetic strategy, cruelty has a long history in European society, beginning (insofar as such beginnings can be known) with early Greek tragedy. Cruelty has been used variously as an assault on the spectator to chastise, morally improve, politically outrage, and, more ambiguously, to provide pleasure and sexual arousal. The most outspoken and well-known of the spokespeople for cruelty in art is Antonin Artaud, creator of the "Theater of Cruelty." A surrealist, like Franju himself, Artaud proposed "a theatre in which violent physical images crush and hypnotize the sensibility of the spectator" ("Masterpieces" 83). For Artaud, Franju, and others practicing the aesthetics of cruelty, art was to be so intense and so painful, and the spectator so engaged by it, that subjectivity itself would be temporarily (and masochistically, as I shall later explain) lost during a performance. Although Artaud pays lip service to the moral improvement that might result from such chastisement, his cruelty, like Franju's, remains ambivalent and distressing.

The problem of a documentary like *Blood of the Beasts* is that it resists easy classification as a moral statement about cruelty to animals, or humankind's survival at the price of the deaths of its fellow creatures, or even as an allegory about the Holocaust; the film may be all of these things, but it is not obviously any of them. Unlike *Nuit et brouillard* (*Night and Fog*) (1955), to which it will be compared later in this essay, Franju's film resolutely resists easy categorization. It would be far more comfortable for spectators to suffer the pain of *Blood of the Beasts* if moral reassurance or a lesson learned was a clear and comfortable position when the film had run its course. But because Franju, like Artaud and Luis Buñuel, plays between the spaces of pleasure and pain, the film sounds no morally reassuring note. Indeed, in a manner not dissimilar from Buñuel, Franju's play at informing, in the usual bland, didactic documentary manner, is rendered ludicrously incongruous by the intense and painful emotions generated by the film. One need think only of the lecture about anopheles mosquitoes in *Las Hurdes* (*Land without Bread*, 1932) or the killing equipment in *Blood of the Beasts* to see the critical, ambivalent, black humor of these filmmakers.

While cruelty as an aesthetic device is exceedingly powerful, it also engages many in an ethical dilemma, particularly, as in the case of *Blood of the Beasts*, when the moral position is not clear and also because documentary films are, generally speaking, associated with useful knowledge, ethics, and moral improvement. Peter Brook, who attempted to re-create Artaud's Theater of Cruelty in *Marat/Sade* (1967), finally questioned the morality of the aesthetics of cruelty: "How passive does it make the spectator? Is this contact with our own repressions creative, therapeutic? Is there even a fascist smell in the cult of unreason? Is it a denial of the mind?" (60).

Roland Barthes has also noted the ambivalence of "traumatic" images, claiming that "the traumatic photograph . . . is the photograph about which there is nothing to say; one could imagine a kind of law: the more direct the trauma, the more difficult is connotation; or again, the 'mythological' effect of a photograph is inversely proportional to its traumatic effect" (30–31). Barthes concludes by noting that both pro- and antiwar newspapers used shock photographs with impunity during the Vietnam War despite what one might think about the powerful, negative sentiments that should be generated by photographs of napalmed children. But as one of Artaud's philosophical predecessors, Friedrich Nietzsche, noted, terrible cruelty can overwhelm and lead to "apathy and hostility to any political action, and eventually to a totally Buddhistic withdrawal from the public world in pursuit of mystical self-abnegation" (quoted in Silk and Stern 84). Clearly, if it is documentary film's mission to inform but nothing can be learned from traumatic images (especially if those images are not clearly contextualized in moral frameworks), then *Blood of the Beasts* exists, with the Theater of Cruelty, in an ambivalent moral universe.

Indeed, *Blood of the Beasts* can perhaps be seen as the purest application of Artaud's theory on film. Coming, as it does, at the end of the Second World War, it is especially potent. Franju's view of cruelty may be judged by the following story:

> The other day I met my old projectionist from the Musée de l'Homme. "M. Franju," he said, "we haven't seen each other for nineteen years. Do you remember that surgical film which had twenty people flat out on the floor?" Nineteen years later, he still remembered that one! And he'd got used to some grueling films there. The film was Dr. Thierry de Martel's *Trépannation pour crise d'épilepsie bravais jacksonienne*. That was an authentic horror film, twenty people out flat, I've never seen anything so drastic. It was an atrocious film, but a beautiful and poetic one—because it was so realistic. (Quoted in Durgnat 28)

Of significance in Franju's words, apart from their humorous perversity, is the idea that film can have "drastic" effects upon spectators and that years after exposure to such works these effects still stick in the mind. It is doubtful that anyone who has seen *Un chien andalou* (1928), for example, does not remember the infamous image of the eyeball being sliced. Noël Burch, one of the few commentators to discuss "structures of aggression" in films, argues that this shot never loses its disturbing power: "The shot is just as shocking after several viewings of the film, and during a second or subsequent viewing the traumatic power inherent in it sends out a shock wave that reaches right back to the beginning of the film, so that the 'flat' opening sequence takes on the most bizarre sort of emotional shading in anticipation" (125).

What, then, is one to make of *Blood of the Beasts*? Is it a moral tale, an allegory about the Holocaust, or a chastisement about our brutal treatment of animals? Is it a cautionary tale about blind obedience to authority? Perhaps it is just a cruel joke perpetrated on the audience, or a beautiful, painful, but ultimately ambivalent critique of documentary as a form of knowledge. In the end, is the only point Franju makes that one learns nothing useful from documentary? These are the issues that must be considered in an analysis of Franju's difficult and demanding text.

Mercifully, it is a short film, only about twenty minutes long, but it would be difficult to conceive of a more taxing workout. A poetic, surrealistic documentary about slaughterhouses, this film was shot on the outskirts of Paris, and in three different abattoirs. The beginning of *Blood of the Beasts* is similar to the beginning of Buñuel and Dali's *Un chien andalou,* although there are also some marked differences that critics tend to overlook. Both films open with reasonably innocuous footage that renders the sudden eruption of extraordinary violence all the more unexpected and wrenching. But Buñuel's footage is of much shorter duration and is more "romantic" and less peculiar than the opening of Franju's film. The spectator is truly unprepared for Buñuel's slitting of the eyeball, although this act of violence is foreshadowed by the clouds that cut across the moon before the slashing. But in truth the slashing has the effect of coming from nowhere. It is an extraordinarily violent act that the film renders with almost medical realism.

The first sequence of the Franju film, however, is not as innocuous as that of *Un chien andalou.* To begin with, the film opens with a title sequence that contains "sentimental" music of the travelogue type. Behind the opening credits the image shows a statue of a bull, a powerful, noble beast of mythology, taken from a low angle so that its power and dignity are emphasized. This shot is accompanied for a time by a trumpet fanfare that sounds like clichéd bullfighting music. All of this is rather ironic in light of what develops later, but it does have the effect of pushing the viewer toward a certain incorrect view of what is about to happen. The "myth" of the bull is a harsh contrast to the way in which the animals are treated in the main body of the film, and indeed, the film documents the cruel treatment as opposed to the way animals are ordinarily represented. This is certainly a rather bizarre, ironic beginning to a film of such great violence.

The next shots are of what Raymond Durgnat has called "a wasteland" (32), but this is in fact only partially true. After shots of the bull the film continues with shots of particularly bleak Paris suburbs—this is hardly Paris as the "city of light." The lack of leaves on the trees adds to the bleakness. Much of this footage is accompanied by pleasant extradiegetic Muzak reminiscent of the uninspired music common in travelogues. A young woman then enters the frame from the lower right; a large, leafless tree dominates the upper left. These shots are photographed in high-contrast black and white to make them seem all the more stark and the suburbs even more barren. Also, the aestheticism of the high contrast is rather too "arty" for this documentary, and the use of beautiful photography set against the horrendous content of many of the later images is one of the film's most unsettling effects. Franju claims that he waited until November to shoot *Blood of the Beasts* to capture the striking quality of light in Paris in the late fall. He wanted the depiction of the violent deaths to be aesthetically pleasing: "The choice of the month of November for shooting the interiors was dictated by the fact that at this season of the year the animals are slaughtered by electric light, and the blood streaming in the glacial cold of the scalding bays allowed us, despite all the technical problems, to compose our images" (Franju quoted in Durgnat 34).

This first sequence, however, consists of far more than a high-contrast view of a suburban wasteland. Like *Night and Fog*, Franju's film is a more complex experience than an easy juxtaposition of the banal with the extraordinary: its basic structural principle is a highly affective, wrenching juxtaposition of unsettling contrasts, not merely a contrast of the everyday with the outrageous. *Blood of the Beasts* begins to unsettle the spectator in this first sequence by depicting the suburbs of Paris as rather odd—not really distressing but a little inexplicable. There are a number of shots of what appears to be a flea market. Shots of rubbish and rows of radios are followed by an extraordinary structure built of billowing, translucent white material in the midst of the rubbish-filled fields. This is followed by what can only be described as a typically strange surrealist image of an armless female mannequin standing in a field beside a busy road with an antique gramophone beside her.

This is followed by a long shot of a small, ornately framed painting of two Victorian girls, one playing the piano, the other leaning over her shoulder. Beside this is an open umbrella, another of Franju's odd surrealistic touches. The camera moves in for a close-up of the two girls. The music sounds childlike, in harmony with the youth of the two girls, and anticipates the next image, a low angle shot of a group of children playing "ring-around-a-rosie" taken against the sky and barren trees. Next is a low angle shot of a plain metal chandelier hanging from the branch of a tree, swinging in the breeze, followed by a shot of a man seated at an old table in the midst of a barren, rubbish-filled field surrounded by anonymous high-rises in the background. At this point a jeweled fan unfolds across the screen, filling it completely. The sequence ends with a close-up of a beautiful blond girl, who proceeds to kiss a young man leaning into the frame from the left. The opening sequence ends here, and what follows (the entrance into the slaughterhouses) is quite different.

A number of significant ideas are presented in this first sequence. Suburban Paris is depicted as a rubbish-filled wasteland. But this suburb is not merely a shabby, depressing part of a big city; it is also bizarre, full of odd bits of junk and strange juxtapositions. The inexplicable juxtapositions are fantastic, completely unexpected by the spectator and unexplained by the narrator. This first sequence is a mixture of ordinarily incompatible objects

Blood of the Beasts: The image of the mannequin and the gramophone is one of several surrealistic landscapes in the film.

which, combined with the absence of a clear exposition (what is this documentary going to be about?), creates a lack of stability and clear orientation for the spectator.

Ian Cameron has argued that Franju does not indulge in any rhetorical heightening of the images in the film. Reviewing *Eyes without a Face* (1959), one of Franju's fiction films, Cameron writes: "In the treatment of the physically unpleasant details, Franju shows only what is necessary. His work has true restraint—there is no gratuitous horror nor any heightening of the horror by its presentation. The same was true of *Le Sang des bêtes*" (*Les yeux sans visage*) (23). Despite the fact that Cameron is writing about fiction here, this view is rather typical of much writing about documentary. It is generally said that in documentary film extreme angles and pushy rhetorical devices—in Cameron's terms, "heightening"—are to be avoided because they interfere with the supposed objectivity sought after by documentarians. These devices are said to be manipulative rhetorical figures that produce propaganda or fiction, not documentary proper. This documentary mythology is a totally inaccurate description of most documentaries, including the Franju film, which takes no pains at all to hide its poetic construction. Franju is forthcoming about his view of documentary, declaring that "The documentary is a biased and unreserved form of cinema. An equivocal documentary is insignificant and there is no place for it. One can be ambiguous in one's sentiments, but not in the expression one gives them. In the depiction of one's sentiments one must be clear, direct" (quoted in Armes 28).

The obvious manipulations of the angles, high-contrast black and white photography, and the addition of inserts like the unfolding fan (to say nothing of the strange shots of mannequins and gramophones) underscore the constructed nature of the film because unmotivated inserts draw attention to an authorial presence behind the "reality" of the image. Generally speaking, attention is not drawn to either the provenance of documentary footage or its constructed nature. A great deal of documentary filmmaking relies upon the spectator's belief in the objectivity of the reporting, of "life caught unawares" (Vertov 41). Carl Plantinga observes that in the United States and countries accustomed to the Griersonian documentary tradition, the reception of clearly subjective documentaries, such as *Blood of the Beasts,* has been problematic. He further contends that when critics fix objectivity as a prime criterion for documentary, they "set an unreachable standard for the genre, and limit our understanding of the ways in which actual documentary films function" (41). Documentaries like *Blood of the Beasts* blur the distinction between "fact" and "fiction" by freely adding obviously "poetic" touches.

For the popular audience the obviously manipulated and composed images of *Blood of the Beasts* undermine the naive view of documentary objectivity and truth. The text denies the spectator the comforting, secure position of documentary knowledge and mythical objectivity. One might add to this the prevalence of low angle shots in this first sequence. Almost half of the shots are taken from an angle well below eye level, which tends to position spectators in a vulnerable low position and further undermines their conventionally privileged position. If anything, the Franju film might be read as an assault on safe, aesthetic spectatorship and the Griersonian school of moral improvement.

Following the opening sequence are dark, low angle shots of electric wires and railroad yards—a rather abrupt transition from the kiss. This is quite unexpected and tends to draw attention to itself because it appears structurally disconnected from what comes before. This is in part the effect of the first sequence as a whole, particularly of the abrupt cut between the kiss and the trains. There is also a change in narration at this point. The narrator in the first sequence is female. For reasons that are never explained, the narrator becomes male as the killing tools are described. This alternation occurs throughout the film: the street sequences are narrated by the woman, the abattoir sequences by the man. Throughout, the narration is sporadic, as is the music; lengthy periods pass with neither music nor narration. Because these are heard abruptly now and again, they draw attention to the existence of the sound track itself. The text makes its "authorship" apparent—uncomfortably so in a genre that tends to eschew notions of authorship in favor of the idea that in documentary the real world speaks for itself.

The second sequence continues by showing the gates of an abattoir that are disturbingly similar to the gates of Auschwitz. As in *Night and Fog,* the exterior gives no clue to the events inside. It is innocuous enough to be unremarkable. The male narrator then introduces shots of various killing devices, naming and describing them. The next shot is of a white horse being led through an alley to a group of workers. There is a cut to a device being placed against the horse's head, a close-up of the head, a loud report, and finally a long shot of the horse collapsing gracefully. It is extremely difficult to describe both the shock and the horror of this killing. The violence erupts very suddenly into the film and thus comes as a profound and painful surprise.

Despite Cameron's denial of a rhetorical design, there is a clear attempt here to increase affect through the close-up and the long shot of the horse's collapse. The suddenness of the violence and the depiction of "real" death onscreen are part of this design. Also, the choice of a beautiful white horse as first victim is shocking in and of itself. It is an apparently healthy animal, and, of course, white horses have a mythic stature. The real death of any animal is highly charged, but the choice of the white horse seems to intensify the brutality of the killing. Thus the textual rhetoric is intended to work on the viewer. The close-up of the device on the horse's head and its discharge, with the sound, then the cut to the horse's collapse make the death scene more intense than if it had been shown in one lengthy shot.

Further, the cool efficiency of the butchers is in sharp contrast to the affect produced in the spectator. They go about their business efficiently, without any apparent feeling. Even the revelation that one of the butchers has lost a leg because of an accident while butchering an animal seems rather banal, despite being a comment on the danger and difficulty of the work. (Blandly giving this kind of information is dear to the hearts of the surrealists and recalls the peculiar lectures given by the narrators in both *Land without Bread* and *L'Age d'or* [1930].) The feelings that this sequence attempts to generate are very intense and tend to block recognition of the text's rhetorical devices. Viewers are offered horror and shock. Durgnat expresses surprise that few people remember the structure of films in general, and of this film in particular. He theorizes that this is a kind of blocking out, arguing that "perhaps this forgetting is a sort of fainting"; he also notes that

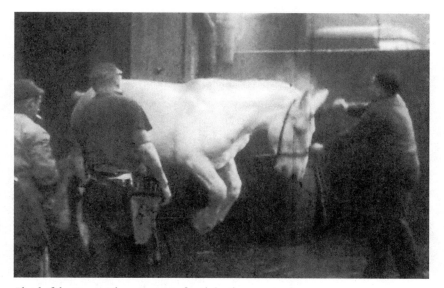

Blood of the Beasts: The moment of real death onscreen.

spectators tend to remember the film "emotionally rather than visually" (34). "Fainting" here may be equated with a masochistic loss of subjectivity suffered by the viewer—that is, as Roy Baumeister argues about masochistic experience, "the sensation of pain removes one's broader awareness of the self in symbolic terms—self enmeshed in the world by means of interpersonal commitments and relationships, personal values and opinions, and so forth. Pain shrinks awareness to the here and now. It deconstructs the self and the world" (71). Sudden and assaultive cruelty can traumatize and disable the intellect: a much-desired condition in the cinema of cruelty. As Artaud argues, the cruel work of art must make the audience "gasp with anguish" ("Plague" 29).

The film then proceeds to document the further butchery of the animal, in graphic detail and frequent close-up, sparing us nothing of the process. The narrator describes it all very coldly, documenting each step as the butchers work. One of the most emotionally difficult moments of this sequence is the close-up slitting of the horse's throat and the collection of the blood—made more "aesthetically pleasing" through the depiction of the steam that rises from the warm blood. The horrible is aestheticized, resulting in a subversive assault on spectatorship itself. This sequence ends with an insert of the leather covers of a book closing and being locked with a clasp—another obvious "poetic" touch.

The next sequence marks a return to the city, including some brood-
ing, expressionist shots of a river and a canal, apparently at sunset. The
female narrator returns, although there is little narration in this section.
She does not perform the usual voice-of-authority duties of a conventional
narrator, and there is no comfort in her words. She speaks rather sadly
and appears to have little authority over the images beyond a notification
of place-names, unlike her male counterpart, who briefly describes the activities in the abattoirs with more aplomb than the woman can muster.
Although this comes as a relief after the violent abattoir footage, it is only a
brief respite, for the next sequence begins with a shot of the exterior architecture of another slaughterhouse, described by the female narrator, while
a row of cattle cross an overhead bridge into it.

As the male narrator takes over, a group of workers herd the cows into
the abattoir. The narrator extols the skill and strength of the butchers, describing one as a former boxing champion, another as the firm's "best ax-
man." In a clearly "heightened" series of shots the text shows the killing of
a cow. The first shot is taken from a low angle where the camera has been
placed directly below and to the left of the ax-man. The ax-man towers over
the camera position and the spectator, ax held ready to strike. The next shot
is a close-up of the ax striking the cow in the middle of the forehead. The
low angle shot of the ax-man was clearly set up for the camera and serves
the function of placing the spectator in the position of the victim, about to
be struck with the ax—a graphic assault analogous to the text's assault on
the process of spectatorship. Once again the text details the butchering of
the carcass, many of the shots close-ups of the unappetizing details. The
film also shows the reflex twitching of the body after death. Although the
narrator is careful to say that the animal is in fact dead and the twitching is
just reflex, the butchery is rendered more violent by these jerky, involuntary
movements.

Franju's cruelty is not only visual in *Blood of the Beasts* but also thematic. His anticlericalism is well-known, and he indulges in some crude,
and cruel, black humor at the expense of the Sisters of Charity. In two
rather scatological moments he implies that the Sisters are scavengers. In
the first, a workman drags a huge cow's stomach toward the camera, slits
it, and allows its noisome contents to spill out toward the viewer; the narrator says that the Sisters of Charity will come to the abattoir to collect the
scraps of fat from the slaughtered animals. Durgnat comments that "the
commentary is talking about nuns while the image shows the excrements
of a cow. Franju's humor has its peasant flavour" (36). At the beginning of
the next sequence the narrator remarks, rather blandly, that St. John the
Baptist is the patron saint of butchers, conjuring up images of St. John's

Blood of the Beasts: The spectator is put in the place of the victim.

head on a plate. In the last sequence, while the butcher sings "La Mer," crooning about seagulls and "white birds soaring to the earth," the image shows two nuns with very tall white headpieces leaving the abattoir. The text invites us to compare the nuns with gulls swooping down on what is left of the kills. The fact that the kills have been a large number of lambs makes the nuns' appearance doubly ironic. The film is marked by such sardonic black humor.

The second slaughterhouse sequence continues with a close-up of a fetal cow removed during the butchering process. This foreshadows the next violent sequence, which deals with veal. But before the veal comes Henri Fournel, who, the male narrator says, can split an ox during the twelve chimes of noon. The film cuts back and forth between exterior shots of the suburbs with bells ringing and shots of Fournel hacking away at a carcass. One shot is taken from in front of the butcher as he hacks. The knife cuts through the carcass, toward the viewer. The viewer is again threatened by the film's rhetoric and also asked to be amused at something rather bizarre. (This absurd fact may also be another of Franju's jabs at the quality of documentary information.)

The shots of the suburbs while Fournel splits the ox are the only respite granted the viewer between the slaughter of the cow and the slaughter of the calves. But it is only a short respite, as the pace of the film picks up here. Along with the killing of the horse, this is the most difficult part of the film. The calves are young, dappled, very handsome animals but very roughly treated. We see the calves, their rear legs off the ground, being shoved along by the butchers. They are caught up, thrown down on bed-like racks, and their throats cut, while the narrator explains that the blood must be drained in order for the meat to be called veal. The decapitation, of course, is shot in close-up. Unlike the killing in the first sequence, which erupts into the text quite suddenly, here one knows what is coming, and this produces a state of painful anticipation, which is not disappointed by what follows. The process is rendered even more affective by the close-up shot of the eyes of a calf, tied and awaiting execution. The text resists the temptation to anthropomorphize the animal, but by showing the whites of its eyes, terror is clearly suggested. There is no sentimentality, no music, nothing but the depiction of a cold-blooded process efficiently performed. No emotion is wasted in pathos and there is no catharsis. The butchers merely toss the calves' heads into a corner, while their bodies remain neatly laid out on the killing tables. Once again the text indulges in some black humor as the music track plays the kind of typical "French-sounding" accordion music used in travelogues to connote "gay Paree" while the image shows the results of much carnage.

Again, there is a brief respite where the image shows the exterior of another abattoir, this one looking churchlike. The image immediately following is of a herd of sheep being led down an alley. The narrator discusses the "Judas goat" that leads its fellows to the slaughter, while being spared itself; he describes the sheep as being "like condemned men," leading Durgnat to compare explicitly the slaughter of the sheep to the Holocaust (36–40). The killing begins abruptly here, with little preamble. A sheep is hoisted onto a conveyor belt and its throat promptly cut, in close-up. Another is killed in the same way, and there is a cut to an extraordinarily grotesque shot of ten or twelve rapidly twitching carcasses on the belt. The sight of the row of madly twitching, headless bodies is appalling—it is no surprise that this sequence often induces a response of defensive, ambivalent laughter from viewers. The sight of the bodies is both strangely humorous and unbearable, and the laughter does little to resolve the tension created by the brutality of the events.

The narrator now informs the viewer that this kind of assembly-line killing is very hard on the butchers. The image shows a shot of a swollen hand, and he explains that sheep killers often develop cysts because of the high number of sheep that they slaughter. The narrator is so matter-of-fact that his statement appears superfluous in this context, like a parody of the industrial documentary. This is followed by the introduction of a poem by Baudelaire, as the narrator repeats, " 'I will strike thee without anger or hatred, like a butcher' said Baudelaire." This is a fair description of the activities of the workers as far as we can see. There is only efficiency and dispatch, no emotion expressed. The viewer might expect disgust or some display of feeling, but it is all perfectly cold. The only feelings are on the spectator's side of the screen.

The last sequence details the cleaning up at the end of the day and is an occasion for another display of black humor resulting from a number of ironic juxtapositions. While one of the workers hoses down the blood-soaked floors, he sings Charles Trenet's "La Mer." While the camera looks from a high angle upon the gory floor, the viewer hears "Dancing white caps on the sea / silver gleaming, joyous free." Clearly the lyrical words of the song are incompatible with the images. Specifically, images show sheep being held in pens awaiting the slaughter in the morning while the singer croons, "fleecy clouds like white sheep" and "shepherd of the azure sky." Fleecy clouds are the sheep of romance, not the sheep of the slaughterhouses. Ironically, the "azure sky" is black and white. The juxtaposition of the romantic song and the brutal images is, as in *Land without Bread,* a grotesque combination of incompatibles that is at once awful and laughable.

After the song the female narrator returns and closes the film with an ironic narration that both speaks about and shows the "troubled" sheep in the "pastoral" night awaiting the morning and their execution. The images show various dark shots of the suburbs at dusk. Finally, the travelogue music returns and the gates of the slaughterhouse are closed. Franju has commented about the unusual nature of one of the final shots of the film, an image of a barge which, although moving along a canal, appears to be moving through land instead. He claims that he waited weeks after the rest of the film was shot to get this piece of surreal footage (interview with Levin). It is certainly a disconcerting shot and in harmony with the earlier fantastic shots of the flea market. The result is that the spectator is not returned to "normalcy" after the bloody events but retained in a strange world of which the slaughterhouse is a part.

In the end, *Blood of the Beasts* is an extraordinary film. Many consider it one of Franju's best achievements, even a masterpiece (Durgnat, Burch). It is an extremely taxing, emotional experience for the spectator. Not only is it at once brutally violent and grotesquely humorous, but it also strains the conventions of the documentary to the breaking point—especially for an anglophone spectator accustomed to Griersonian expository documentary, which has generally been so careful to preserve a pretense to objectivity and to keep a lower emotional temperature than the more experimental European tradition. Perhaps the greatest difficulty the film presents is its tendency to overwhelm the spectator with pain. It takes a number of viewings of *Blood of the Beasts* to be able to attain emotional distance. As in most justifications for masochistic subject positions, Franju's view is that the violence in the film is ultimately helpful for the viewer. He argues that "violence will always be violence, but violence is not an end, it's a weapon which sensitizes the spectator and which lets him see what's lyric or poetic beyond or above the violence, or what's tender in reality. Violence, for me, is a means, like blasphemy for Buñuel" (interview with Levin 124).

But if this film is painful, it is also pleasurable and, in a way, extremely beautiful since the photography and the composition of the images are aesthetically pleasing. Noël Burch comments that some of the film's sequences reach a "fioritura of an astonishing beauty that nonetheless seems to emit the very smell of death" (126). The extraordinary affect of the film depends upon this juxtaposition as well as upon the suddenness of the killings. As in *Night and Fog*, the knowledge given is not knowledge that is of any comfort to the spectator. Durgnat's view of *Blood of the Beasts* as removing the spectator's "cataracts" (9) has a surgical, Artaudian ring to it. Franju, at least, found this kind of experience desirable, if not pleasurable. He once argued:

> Also there's a question of conditioning, not so much to condition the audience, but to condition oneself. I've noticed that all the documents—and I'm speaking precisely of documentaries—that I've done have a relationship to subjects I'm afraid of. If I made *Le Sang des bêtes*, it's because I never saw that; . . . if I made *la Lorraine*, it's because I'm afraid of fire, and I condition myself and stay in the fire. Since I'm afraid, then that makes others afraid, obviously. It's a way of sensitizing oneself by violence, and in doing violence. (Interview with Levin 120)

As in any grotesque or masochistic experience, pain or discomfort is used to focus attention. Experiences of this nature are profoundly unsettling, and they are intensified by the use of the documentary mode. Real death replaces aesthetic death, and complex and ambiguous emotional reactions often result. Films like *Blood of the Beasts* are both pleasurable and painful at the same time. Of all of the films that use cruelty, Franju's is the most ambivalent. It never clearly ties itself to a political project; it heightens reality surrealistically and offers despair and pleasure in suffering. It is perhaps the visual proof that beauty need not be tied to morality, despite both Durgnat's and Roy Armes's suggestion that Franju was a maker of socially conscious films. It is clear that Franju, at least, took pleasure in this kind of experience and expected his audience to do the same, and like Artaud he repeatedly subjects himself, and his audience, to the most painful of aesthetic pleasures.

Durgnat, one of the few critics to have paid serious attention to Franju outside of France, claims there is a temptation to compare *Blood of the Beasts* to the better-known *Night and Fog.* As suggested above, there are a number of visual similarities between the two films, made about six years apart. The gates of the death camps are very similar in design to the gates of the abattoirs; the carcasses of dead sheep, so neatly arranged in a row, are repeated in the stacked rows of dead bodies in *Night and Fog;* and the tossing of the calves' heads into a heap in a corner in *Blood of the Beasts* is reminiscent of the pail of human heads in Resnais's film. But more than this, the atmosphere of slaughter and cruelty, especially the cold, methodical cruelty of the butchers and of the SS, seems to echo back and forth. Both are beautiful, and it has been disturbingly suggested in *The Architecture of Doom* (1989), a documentary about fascist aesthetics, that murder was thought to be an "aesthetic" event by the Nazis.

But perhaps the single most significant similarity between the two films is their structure. Both are based upon an alternation between two kinds of sequences: first something peaceful (in *Night and Fog* the sequences shot in color, in 1955; in *Blood of the Beasts* the suburban street scenes), then scenes of incredible violence and cruelty (in *Night and Fog* the black and white archival footage shot in the camps; in *Blood of the Beasts* the footage shot in the abattoirs). Both films shuttle the spectator between the two kinds of footage, developing a highly charged affective experience; both plunge the spectator into a nightmare world of shocking cruelty (Franju's film more precipitously than Resnais's).

Durgnat argues that "If Franju intersperses the paroxysmic sequences with asides of an elegiac and/or ironic nature it is to resensitize the spectator, and therefore his response to violence; it is with his finer fibres that he bears the shock. The cutaways repoeticize, they reintellectualize, and they reassert that the slaughterhouse and the city are an entity" (33). This is not the only way to view the affective charge of this footage, although it has something to recommend it. The footage outside of the slaughterhouses at first appears as a relief from the cruelty. A pattern of pain and relief from pain is evident early on in the film. But because both films keep plunging the spectator back into the nightmare, what are in themselves often quite beautiful sequences become objects of dread. They precede the horrors to come and are an all-too-brief respite from the more difficult parts; in short, they come before pain and foreshadow suffering.

Burch argues that in *Blood of the Beasts* this is a rhythmic construction, but we might more precisely call it an affective rhythm.[3] *Blood of the Beasts* is more cruel than *Night and Fog* if only because it shows the moment of real, violent death. Its shocks explode upon the spectator in a far more intense way than the cooler and more elegiac and politically situated Resnais film. Few spectators are likely to see this film more than once since it is such a masochistic experience—all shocks and insufficient distance for the spectator to get at whatever point the director is trying to make. As John Berger has observed, there comes a point where violent images are so overwhelming that they fill the viewer with despair, thus disabling the intellect (37–40).

Indeed, after an experience of this nature one might well ask what point is being made. Whatever it may be, it is quite possible to see the brutality of the film as excessive. Yet upon sober reflection, *Blood of the Beasts* is a highly structured, grotesque, and sardonic depiction of a society that lives on death but chooses to deny it. Durgnat humorously refers to those who have implied that the film intends to convert its audience to vegetarianism, and he also has drawn attention to certain connections that the film might have to the Holocaust. Indeed, it is tempting to read the film as a parable about the slaughter of the innocent, since it was made a scant three years after the war had ended and, as suggested above, there is some justification in the text for this. Such a reading is encouraged by the fact that many of the unforgettable photographs of stacked bodies published at the end of the war resonate in the film's imagery. The slaughterhouse is an apt metaphor for Europe from 1939 to 1946, and Franju would have had ample experience from which to draw his material. But the film makes no direct reference to the war or the camps, so it is problematic to read it in this way.[4]

Durgnat also argues, along with Roy Armes, that "Franju's parable is a warning about the folly of all blind habitual obedience to those set in authority over us, for our own good, of course" (Durgnat 36). This, too, is a tempting argument, but again the text resists this kind of interpretation. The butchers are not the authorities but just workers who, as the film is careful to point out, do a difficult, dangerous, and unpleasant job. This is part of the problem raised by the text: it does not give away too much, and because critics always seem to look for some justification for films of this kind, they tend to fall back upon the idea of the moral or political parable.

Other cruel documentaries like *Night and Fog* and Buñuel's *Las Hurdes* have more accessible political views, and in the end one is in no doubt that both texts have strong points to make about historical events and even the medium itself. But *Blood of the Beasts* is another matter. The suffering put upon the spectator may seem excessive, and the ethical point is never entirely clear. This is often one of the ambiguous aspects of the aesthetics of cruelty. What exactly is being offered to the audience—moral improvement, masochistic pleasure in suffering, or just an ugly, brutalizing experience? The Franju text, like Stan Brakhage's *The Act of Seeing with One's Own Eyes* (1971), offers few enough textual clues as to what the spectator's ethical response, if any, should be—and in fact these films might be construed as an attack upon the audience and the comfortable pigeonholes with which they habitually classify films. Hence the strain that critics undergo, trying to justify taking pleasure in *Blood of the Beasts*. The ambiguity of the pleasures offered to the spectator is unsettling, to say the least. It completely defies simple classification and, indeed, it precipitates a paradigm crisis for the spectator who might ask "what kind of film is this, what kind of response is asked for?" It might also be thought, because its ethical position is so tenuous, to create guilt or at least discomfort in a spectator who enjoys the film. Pleasure here is mixed with pain and guilt, and thus problematized.

Both Durgnat and Tom Milne argue that the film makes an existential point about the nature of life and death. This is a much easier position to maintain. It merely appears to be saying, like Brakhage's film, that death is real, that it is both gruesome and violent, but also that it can be aesthetically beautiful at the same time. In the Franju film death is necessary if people are going to eat meat. The film says no more and no less than this. As Durgnat convincingly argues about *Blood of the Beasts*, "it's a reminder that what is inevitable may also be spiritually unendurable, that what is justifiable may be atrocious, that the best we can do will always be an organized butchery" (43). This is clearly a cruel point to make to audiences reared in cultures that like to pretend that death does not exist, or to poeticize or aestheticize it. Like Buñuel, Franju does not romanticize death and suffering. He never attempts to anthropomorphize the animals. Rather, the cruelty in the film is cold and unmelodramatic. No emotional energy is wasted in the pursuit of pathos or romance. One butcher sips a cup of something while skinning an animal; another sings "La Mer" while hosing down blood-drenched floors. There is no call here for hand-wringing. The film merely encourages an acceptance of life as it exists in the slaughterhouses. On one side the spectator has the Paris of myth, "the city of light"; on the other, there is this film with its bizarre suburbs and the slaughterhouses that feed the city.

NOTES

1. Other documentaries in this category include *Las Hurdes* (1932), *Night and Fog* (1955), *The Act of Seeing with One's Own Eyes* (1971), and *Mourir à tue-tête* (*Scream from Silence*) (1979), among others.

2. As Annette Kuhn argues, in documentary, and indeed in discussion of documentary, style is "disavowed and subject to a work of effacement: the image 'speaks for itself'" (72).

3. Franju once said, "The trouble with [Henri-Georges] Clouzot is that he tries to knock the audience's head off. That's wrong; you should twist it off" (quoted in Durgnat 16–17). The affective rhythm in *Blood of the Beasts* effectively accomplishes this twisting!

4. Given the problems in representing the Holocaust in France, one might argue that Franju's film is indeed allegorical. Representations of the Holocaust have been politically difficult for a French government and populace, many of whom were collaborators. See Marcel Ophuls's *Hotel Terminus* (1988) for a painful, and sarcastic, documentary look at the continuing guilt and fear that surround the French involvement with the Nazis.

WORKS CITED

Armes, Roy. *French Cinema since 1946*. Vol. 2, *The Personal Style*. London: Zwemmer and Barnes, 1970.

Artaud, Antonin. "No More Masterpieces." In *The Theatre and Its Double*, trans. Mary Caroline Richards, 74–83. New York: Grove Press, 1958.

———. "The Theatre and the Plague." In *The Theatre and Its Double*, trans. Mary Caroline Richards, 15–32. New York: Grove Press, 1958.

Barthes, Roland. "The Photographic Message." In *Image-Music-Text*, trans. Stephen Heath, 15–31. New York: Hill and Wang, 1977.

Baumeister, Roy. *Masochism and the Self*. Hillsdale, NJ: Lawrence Erlbaum Associates, 1989.

Berger, John. "Photographs of Agony." In *About Looking*, 37–40. New York: Pantheon Books, 1980.

Brook, Peter. *The Empty Space*. New York: Penguin, 1968.

Burch, Noël. *Theory of Film Practice*. Princeton: Princeton University Press, 1981.

Cameron, Ian. Review of *Eyes without a Face*. Film 26 (1960): 23–25.

Durgnat, Raymond. *Franju*. Berkeley: University of California Press, 1967.

Kuhn, Annette. "The Camera I: Observations on Documentary." *Screen* 19, no. 2 (1978): 71–128.

Levin, G. Roy. *Documentary Explorations: 15 Interviews with Film-Makers*, 117–29. Garden City, NY: Anchor Press, 1971.

Milne, Tom. "George Franju." In *Cinema: A Critical Dictionary: The Major Film-makers,* ed. Richard Roud, 387–93. New York: Viking Press, 1980.

Plantinga, Carl. "The Mirror Framed: A Case for Expression in Documentary." *Wide Angle* 13, no. 2 (1991): 40–53.

Silk, M. S., and J. P. Stern. *Nietzsche on Tragedy.* Cambridge: Cambridge University Press, 1981.

Vertov, Dziga. "The Birth of Kino-Eye." In *Kino-Eye: The Writings of Dziga Vertov,* ed. Annette Michelson, trans. Kevin O'Brien, 40–42. Berkeley: University of California Press, 1984.

Chapter 11

The "Dialogic Imagination" of Jean Rouch

Covert Conversations in *Les maîtres fous*

Diane Scheinman

In recent decades much attention has been devoted to the issue of the production of ethnographic texts, both literary and filmic. Anthropologists have had to confront the ideological problems inherent in the ethnographic enterprise—namely, the power relations inscribed in their construction of "self" and "Other," the representational frames and discourses utilized, and the locating of "authority" within Western academic traditions. The question has been raised by James Clifford (1986) and others as to how to open up the "closed authority" of such texts—so that monologic stylistics privileging the researcher's point of view would give way to greater participation by Others, whose roles as authors of much of the text have often been unacknowledged.

What follows is a Bakhtinian analysis of Jean Rouch's most controversial film, *Les maîtres fous* (The Mad Masters, 1954), that seeks to reveal the complex chorus of voices embedded in the film, beneath the narration provided by Rouch himself. What appears to be a monologic representation—Rouch's voice-over inquiry into the Hauka cult and the possibly therapeutic function of the rite of spirit possession performed by migrant workers in Accra in the 1950s—is shown to be a more complex, multicultural, and polyphonous text, one that allows the "dialogic imagination" of the culturally distinct conversants to be expressed in idioms not restricted to the verbal. I suggest that the film may be a useful model for future ethnographic filmmaking endeavoring to present a more politically engaged cinema, containing more "open" spaces for the expression of ethnic dialogism, and political and cultural critique.

Though the Russian literary critic Mikhail Bakhtin never wrote about cinema, it is instructive to apply his theories of the analysis of literary forms to the study of film—particularly ethnographic film—as he emphasizes the complexly dialogic nature of human communication, which subverts the monologic authority of any text. Bakhtin's concept of "dialogism" was developed via his study of literary theory, most notably his interest in the novels of Dostoyevsky. In contrast to literary forms such as poetry and the epic, which he characterized as "monologic"—reflecting the singular voice of the author—Bakhtin discovered in Dostoyevsky's approach to his characters a "dialogic" world in which multiple voices and diverse speech types were to be found. "A plurality of independent and unmerged voices and consciousnesses, a genuine polyphony of fully valid voices is in fact the chief characteristic of Dostoevsky's novels," Bakhtin avers (*Problems* 6). Dostoyevsky's contribution to the genre of the novel, Bakhtin suggests, includes his innovative presentation of characters' inner lives, or "inner speech," in which they muse to themselves about events and personalities around them.

This, Bakhtin claims, constituted a new style of writing, one that appeared to present a plurality of "voices" in the text not subordinated solely to the author's (Bakhtin's "polyphony"), voices that negotiate meaning in response to the "utterances" of others. According to Bakhtin, "A word, discourse, language or culture undergoes 'dialogization' when it becomes relativized, de-privileged, aware of *competing definitions* for the *same* things" (*Dialogic* 427, emphasis added). Dialogism thus refers to the relationship between a speaker and a listener, to all conversation—literary or verbal— that involves the negotiation of meaning via the personal, social, historical, and political context of its occurrence. "Everything means, is understood, as a part of a greater whole—there is a constant interaction between meanings, all of which have the potential of conditioning others" (*Dialogic* 426). For Bakhtin there really is never a monologue, or "neutral" speakers, as a "responsive listener" is always present, reacting to any given text.

In Bakhtin's view, the "word" is an arena of struggle, a site of ideological battle, a matrix for simultaneous and contending "voices" expressing their versions of events. Each speaker is multivocal, daily employing numerous intracultural "languages" of class, gender, occupation, religion. Further, this chorus of languages is not limited to the merely verbal, as verbal communication is "always accompanied by social acts of a nonverbal character (the performance of labor, the symbolic acts of a ritual, a ceremony, etc.)," and "is often only an accessory to these acts, merely carrying out an auxiliary role" (Volosinov 95).[1] Therefore, the "word" may include gesture, choreography, and music, as well as internal monologue ("inner speech") and written and filmed texts. Bakhtin stresses the importance of this range of social voices operating within not only one culture but one speaking community. It is to the borders of the verbal and the nonverbal, the speaker and the listener, that Bakhtin points our attention, as he believes the multiple meanings of "discourse" ("language in its concrete living total- ity") can be understood only within the social matrix of daily, shared usage (*Problems* 181). Any study of discourse that removes it from the social milieu and from consideration of the historical moment, Bakhtin claims, denudes it of its "intonation," that complex series of associations (socially inflected and evaluative elements) brought to the text by the speaker and listener. Thus it is the continual interpenetration of text, context, and intertext that concerns Bakhtin.

Robert Stam suggests that "The task of the Bakhtinian critic . . . is to call attention to the voices at play in a text, not only those heard in 'aural close-up,' but also those voices dominated, distorted, or drowned out by the text" (19). My analysis of *Les maîtres fous* engages with this task, as I seek to make apparent those voices not heard in "aural close-up" yet very much "there" in this film. I wish to draw attention to these insufficiently theo- rized voices—particularly the nonverbal ones such as music, choreography, gesture—that exceed and escape Rouch's dominating voice-over and may not initially be apparent to or aimed at a Western audience.

Though not an unproblematic film (both European and African audi- ences objected to their representations as too "savage"), *Les maîtres fous* is expressive of the inescapably dialogic nature of human life, of cultural con- tact. Attention to the message-carrying potential of the diverse film tracks (music, "wild" sound, visual), which enable the Hauka to "speak" through the film to audiences not limited to Western viewers, reveals potentially subversive spaces of dissent and challenge to dominant ideology and power that coexist with Rouch's commanding voice-over. The film can be seen as a forerunner of Rouch's subsequent anthropological filmmaking objec- tives, to create films that allow dialogue and dissent to be expressed "across societal lines" (Rouch interview with Taylor 97).

Shot in 1954 in Accra (then the capital of the colonial Gold Coast, pres- ently the Republic of Ghana) and its environs, *Les maîtres fous* is ostensibly a film of inquiry into the Hauka cult, recording a ritual event of spirit pos- session and questioning the possibly therapeutic functions of this rite per- formed by migrant workers. In structure, the film presents a view of three days in the lives of selected members of the cult. Day one is shot entirely in the city, where the cult members are shown working at their menial jobs.

Rouch's voice-over, in English, explains they are "Hygiene boys—mosquito killers," "Tin boys who sell empty petrol drums," and "Gold mine boys who work underground." Later they are seen at the Salt Market, where they meet nightly after work. Day two records their trip to the countryside to reach the compound of Mountyeba, the high priest; there the spirit possession ceremony occurs. Rouch observes that the initiates and penitents "violently" go into trance, as they are entered by the spirits of their gods, "the gods of the city, the gods of technology, the gods of power, the Hauka." Modeled on the colonial administrators, the Hauka's presence is signaled by the symbolic and parodic use of objects, costuming, and behaviors that imitate, and comment on, the Europeans (for example, in the performance of a "round table conference," the "Governor" insults the "General"). The ceremony culminates in the sacrifice and eating of a dog, an action that signifies the breaking of a strict taboo to demonstrate that the Hauka are "stronger" than other men, "black or white." Day three presents the adepts back in Accra. Contrasting images of them at work (in the marginalized roles they perform daily) with images of them in trance on the preceding day (in the personae of the powerful Hauka spirits), Rouch explores his thesis that the curative power of the violent trance experience may be its function as a "panacea against mental disorders." He wonders whether the practitioners "may have found a way to absorb our inimical society."

The study of "our inimical society" becomes interwoven with Rouch's inquiry into the phenomenon of the Hauka cult. Colonialism is the cult's intertext. The ruptures and dislocations caused by cultures confronting one another and the adaptive and creative responses this mingling of cultures requires are of particular concern and interest to Rouch. Thus the release from the pressures of colonialism sought by members of the apparently bizarre and violent trance cult appears an eminently sane reaction to the violence and madness of Western society. Through the double entendre of Rouch's title, madness comes to be associated as closely with the colonial administration ("the mad masters") as with the unusual behavior exhibited by the members of the cult it engendered ("the masters of madness").[2] This dialogic relationship, the meeting, mingling, and "refusals" of culture contact, is central to Rouch's inquiry.

One of the most significant figures in the development of ethnographic cinema, Jean Rouch, in a career spanning fifty years, has made more than seventy films, nearly fifty of which have dealt with possession. As his technological, theoretical, and stylistic innovations have had a considerable impact on the cinematic representation of the Other, it is important to discuss his career at some length and to situate *Les maîtres fous* within this larger body of work. As space does not allow in-depth assessment of Rouch's oeuvre,[3] the following focuses on selected films illustrative of the evolution of his anthropological and cinematic concerns.

Originally trained as a civil engineer, Rouch fled the German occupation of France, accepting a job building roads in the French colony of Niger. There, in 1942, his interest in ethnology originated when the construction site he was supervising was struck by lightning and ten African laborers were killed. In response to this unusual event, a local Sorko priestess led a possession ritual of "desacralization" to "cure" the bodies of the dead. Fascinated by the "extraordinary" ritual, Rouch realized he was witnessing an event "about which I understood nothing," a moment in which, entering a possessed state, people were "able to transform themselves simply through bodily techniques that we have altogether lost" (Rouch, "Totemic" 230). After attending further possession rituals, he decided to study the phenomenon of possession; after the war, he began to study anthropology in Paris under Marcel Griaule and Marcel Mauss.

Returning to West Africa several years later to make a trip down the river Niger, Rouch was advised by Griaule and Mauss to take a movie camera to document his journey. With a secondhand 16mm Bell and Howell camera he shot his first silent film, *Au pays des mages noir* (In the Land of the Black Magi), in 1947. Rouch claims he discovered the technique of handheld camera-work as the result of losing his tripod overboard while canoeing through the Niger's rapids; he discerned the value of creating his own sound tracks when he sold this first footage to Actualités Françaises, which added music and narration that he felt shamefully exoticized the film's subject.

In 1948–49, Rouch shot his first ethnographic films—Les *magiciens de Wanzerbe* (The Magicians of Wanzerbe), *La circoncision* (Circumcision), and *Initiation à la danse des possédés* (Initiation into the Dance of the Possessed)—this time employing a portable tape recorder to record location sound. Armed with his camera and tape recorder, he then returned to refilm the hippopotamus hunt conducted by the fishermen who had appeared in his 1947 film; in *Bataille sur le grandfleuve* (Battle on the Great River, 1951–52), Rouch reports that "I used for the first time the technique of the 'participating camera' developed by [Robert] Flaherty, showing the hippopotamus hunters their own images" (interview with Fulchignoni 278). This concern to involve the subjects of his films in the filmmaking and anthropological process by showing them their own images, attending to their reactions, and incorporating their commentary was to become a hallmark of Rouch's ensuing film work.

Rouch had been encountering Hauka spirits since 1942, when he began his studies of the Songhay religion. As these divinities accompanied the migratory movements of the young Nigerians who sought work during the dry season in the cities of the Gold Coast, Rouch's fieldwork focused increasingly on both the seasonal migrations of the Songhay and the nature of their Hauka possession rituals. Along with his three African friends, Damouré Zika, Lam Ibrahim Dia, and Illo Gaoudel, Rouch left Niger for Accra, where he would shoot *Les maîtres fous* with their assistance. As in his subsequent films, in *Les maîtres fous* Rouch is concerned with the psychological impact of colonialism on indigenous populations and with the adaptive responses such cultural contact occasions. Mick Eaton observes that unlike the majority of ethnographic films, "*Les maîtres fous* does not construct African culture as somehow occupying a sphere discrete in itself and unaffected by Western contact" (7). Already in the 1950s Rouch was addressing an issue of particular concern to anthropologists today, that of greater participation by the ethnographic Other. In *Les maîtres fous* he not only calls for the participation of his African subjects in the creation of the film (the Songhay priest interprets trancers' use of glossolalia, while viewing footage in the editing room, thus educating Rouch and informing the narration) but also begins to provide film training (Damoure became a sound man).

In 1954, Rouch also began to shoot *Jaguar* and to utilize fiction to deal with the complex event of Songhay seasonal migration. *Jaguar*, Rouch's first feature-length film, is a picaresque tale of three travelers' adventures during their migration from country to city and back again. Rouch has said that the film is "pure fiction," a "postcard in the service of the imaginary" (quoted in Eaton 22). The three principals (Damouré, Lam, and Illo) worked out the action at the time of shooting, later improvising the commentary in the editing room while responding to their own images. Like Flaherty's famous dictum, "Sometimes you have to lie to tell the truth," Rouch saw fiction as "the only way to penetrate reality" (quoted in Eaton 8), a penetration enabling him to shoot a story and emphasize those aspects he thought important, in contrast to ethnographic documentary in which "one is obliged to show almost everything" (quoted in Eaton 7).

His second feature-length film, *Moi, un noir* (*Me, a Black Man*, 1957), shot in the Abidjan slum of Treichville, is another attempt to mix reality with fiction. The characters, three young Nigerian migrant laborers who cope with their city existences by adopting the pseudonyms of famous Western movie stars, were asked to play out their lives in front of the camera. The improvised commentary was recorded in the editing room as each principal nonprofessional cast member reacted to his image. "This bizarre dialogue with truth, this autobiography on film," as Rouch characterized it, was notable because it was "the first real feedback on the character who recounts his own story," the first time an African spoke on film about his own life (quoted in Fulchignoni 281). Jean-Andre Fieschi has observed that from *Moi, un noir* onward, for Rouch "the camera assumes an entirely new function: no longer simply a recording device, it becomes a *provoca-teur*, a stimulant, precipitating situations, conflicts, expeditions that would otherwise never have taken place" (quoted in Eaton 74).

Such "cine provocations," using the camera as a catalyst of events and personal revelations, are critical to the effects produced in subsequent Rouch films such as *Chronique d'un été* (*Chronicle of a Summer*, 1960), a feature-length film experiment focusing on Parisians, Rouch's "own tribe." *Chronique*, one of his most significant films, represents the birth of cinema verité, a practice that relied for its effect on an entirely new technique of synchronous sound, made possible by cinematic technology Rouch helped develop (light, portable cameras; the first use of lavalier mikes in cinema, enabling speakers in the film to wander the streets of Paris, interviewing others or revealing their own inner thoughts). In *Chronique*, Rouch and French sociologist Edgar Morin provoke responses to questions about po-litical and personal attitudes and experiences from a "cast" of nonprofes-sional actors (Europeans and African students who, in a sort of reverse eth-nography, comment on the strange behavior of the white French people). Members of the cast interview one another, have adventures in the city and on vacation, and, toward the end of the film, share a reflexive moment, re-acting in the screening room to the movie—about themselves—they have just witnessed. The final sequence finds Rouch and Morin wandering the halls of the Musée de l'Homme, reflecting on the outcome of their experi-ment. Cinema verité, Rouch's novel technique, acknowledges the effect of the camera on the film's subjects; the camera is never a neutral pres-ence but one that prompts constructions of "reality" by those on whom it is turned. Stylistically, the film was inspired by the ideas of Russian film-maker Dziga Vertov who, in the 1920s, wrote about *kino pravda* (film truth), suggesting that the camera recorded life and therefore led to a "cinema of truth." Rouch, in contrast, felt the camera provoked the behavior of those in front of the lens, resulting in a "truth of cinema."

In subsequent films such as *Petit à petit* (Little by Little, 1969), a fable about African businessmen who come to Paris seeking a European model for their own proposed African skyscraper, Rouch developed his concept of "shared anthropology," his goal of creating "an anthropological dialogue between people belonging to different cultures, which for me represents the discipline of human sciences for the future" (quoted in Eaton 26). Through his film innovations, Rouch hoped "to transform anthropology, the eldest daughter of colonialism, a discipline reserved to those with power interrogating people without it" (quoted in Eaton 26). His concept of "shared anthropology" may be said to represent Rouch's attempt in his own developing film work to replace his monologic voice of authority (such as that heard in his early ethnographic documentaries) with more dispersed voices of authority, offering their versions of the social world around them. *Les maîtres fous* is a good example of this, for it is a film in which contestation with the institutionalized discourses of colonialism—including that of anthropology—is given such expression.

A contextualizing passage, written in French, precedes the film's opening credits. Presenting itself as a "warning" to the public of "the violence and cruelty of certain scenes,"[4] the passage establishes the filmmaker's desire to make the audience "participate completely" in a ritual that is at once both "a particular solution to the problem of readjustment" and an event that "shows indirectly how certain Africans portray our Western civilization." Further, the text states that these "documents" are presented "without concession or concealment." However, this is a disingenuous claim, as a great deal is in fact concealed in Rouch's film—in particular, the problematic history of the cult vis-à-vis the colonial administration and the priests' political agenda in requesting the making of the film. Directing his audience's attention toward the shocking scenes of men in trance and the ritual's role as an African reflection of, and on, our culture, Rouch diverts attention from his own role as critic of the colonial power structure. Only fleetingly, in a passage that follows the opening credits, does Rouch acknowledge that the film was made at the request of the Hauka priests themselves: "This film was shot at the request of the priests, Mountyeba and Moukayla, proud of their art." A final passage states that scenes are not "prohibited or secret" but "open to those who are willing to play the game," this "violent game" that is "only the reflection of our civilization."

In fact, the cult first appeared among the Songhay people in Niger about 1927, in the context of traditional possession rituals. New "gods" began to possess individuals ("horses") who, Rouch explains, announced that "We are Europeans, we are strength/power" ("nous sommes la force") (Rouch, "Migration" 175). These new gods, "the crazed masters," modeled on the colonial power structure and technology, appeared through the possessed dancers in personae named "the General," "the Governor," "Madame Locotaro, the doctor's wife," "the Engineer," "the Truck Driver," and so on. Speaking pidgin French and aping European behavior, they were novel responses to the pressures of modern African life under the French administrators.

At first these new Hauka spirits were not welcomed by the priests of the traditional religion, who could not control them. Nor were they welcomed or tolerated by the French colonial administrators, who considered them an insult to French culture and authority. The French, and later, in 1935, the British administrators of the Gold Coast, jailed cult members in order to discourage their practices. This religious persecution strengthened the cult and led to the outbreak of civil disobedience while practitioners were held in jail. An agreement was eventually reached between the priests and the government that the ceremonies would be held only on weekends and in designated areas. The continuing practice of the cult (which was eventually expelled from French colonial Niger but traveled to, and thrived in, the British-held Gold Coast, among migrant Nigerian laborers) represented ongoing resistance to the assault on traditional Songhay culture. Anthropologist Paul Stoller observes that "In the ruins of the old order, the *Hauka* symbolically resisted the cultural invasion of the French and protected the last vestige of Songhay cultural identity—their links to their ancestors" ("Horrific Comedy" 169). F. Fugelstad notes that the Hauka were openly dissident and suggests the "most original aspect" of their movement was "their total refusal of the system put into place by the French" (quoted in Stoller, *Cinematic Griot* 155).

The Hauka priests had seen a film Rouch shot among the Sorko, which included footage of a trance possession. They cabled him, inviting him to come to Accra to film their annual ceremony. The priests had two goals for the film: first, to document the ceremony; second, more subversively, to project the film to audiences, including Hauka cult members, who would be triggered, by the film's music and images of the possessed, to go into trance. Rouch has commented that the priests had hoped

> to go beyond what had been done before. You see, when they first decided to eat a dog it was really breaking a very strong taboo. They were doing something very bad, and maybe if they used the film there would have been a fantastic emergence of all the Hauka power at the same time. Well, they were ready to try a kind of experiment because they felt they could command any aspect of European-based technology, including cameras and film, and so it would have been a challenge. (Interview with Marshall and Adams 1009)

It is noteworthy that the Hauka, as early as 1954, intended to utilize the potential of cinema, its ability to reach and mobilize a mass audience, for indigenous political purposes. Their recognition that making a film—like the Hauka possession ceremony itself—is inherently a political activity and that projecting it can induce a strong physical and ideological response in the viewer predates by several decades other indigenous groups' commission and use of cinema to draw attention to and seek support for their own political causes.

Aware of the priests' desire to challenge the colonial masters and attuned to the Europeans' hostility toward the cult, Rouch uses his own speaking voice to provide the film's commentary. The film appears solely to represent Rouch's anthropological investigation of the possession ritual and his meditation upon the nature of "the great adventure of African cities." However, the nature of the music track, ambient sound, and the visuals of the possessed provide Rouch and the Hauka additional space to "voice" their critiques of the colonial experience and to speak through the film to audiences other than Western viewers. Subverting his apparently monologic control of the film, subversive spaces are thus allotted to a series of "speakers" who, in a Bakhtinian sense, call upon a "responsive listener" to react to, and participate in, the developing and dialogic "text."

Working within the confines of his equipment's limited field recording capabilities (a hand-cranked tape recorder and a camera that allowed a shot length of only twenty to twenty-five seconds; no sync sound or low-light film stock), Rouch constructed sound tracks that capitalize on the juxtapositions of music, city noise, and speech. His voice-over commentary was recorded in the editing studio, where he worked with Moukayla, the "quiet priest" of the Hauka cult, who interpreted for him the trancers' use of glossolalia ("the narration was made from a language that does not exist," Rouch stated at a 1988 New York University seminar on his work). He improvised the remaining narration while viewing the footage in the editing room.

Rouch utilizes music and ambient sound as metaphors for the dissonance in the political and social spheres of contact his film examines. Western military marches and popular tunes are set against "wild" sound (recorded sound that is not synchronous with the image track) of traffic, city noise, and indigenous music, underscoring his thesis that the points of contact (dialogue) between African and Western culture are usually "violent." As the opening credits roll, a band playing a Western march is heard. This martial music continues under the opening text: "Coming from the bush to the cities of Black Africa, young men collide with machine-made civilization. Thus conflicts and new religions are born. Thus the Hauka sect was formed, about 1927." As the text proceeds, explaining that the film shows an episode in the Hauka's life in the city of Accra, the sounds of car horns and voices join the march music. While the voice-over comments on "the violent game" that is "only the reflection of our civilization," the volume of the march music fades while that of honking horns rises.

Following an opening sequence of shots introducing the migrant laborers at work, Rouch continues his voice-over narration: "And, by day and
by night, in the bars—'Weekend in California,' 'Weekend in Havana'—you
can hear the calypso from the West Indies." Elements drawn from international musical currents are thus shown entering the African domain.
"Every Saturday and Sunday there are processions in the streets," Rouch
intones, as marchers and street musicians dance by, carrying gourd rattles
and drums. "These are Yoruba, celebrating a wedding. These are Rausa
prostitutes, protesting against lower wages. These are Daughters of Jesus,
singing their faith in the streets." Music, a political idiom of the streets, announces the marchers' economic protests and religious celebrations; carrying culturally coded associations and meanings, it acts, in Bakhtin's view,
as an authentic "voice" of the people.

The ensuing commentary becomes Rouch's bridge into the next major
segment of the film, the record of the spirit possession ceremony. A series
of close-ups of African musicians playing Western instruments (trumpets,
French horns, trombones) is followed by a series of shots of the possessed.
Rouch explains: "All this noise, all this [sic] brass bands, forces the men
that come from the north, from silent savannah, to seek some peace in the
suburb of a city and there, every Sunday night, they go through ceremonies
not yet known to us. They call the new gods—the gods of the city, the gods
of technology, the gods of power, the Hauka." These first images of men in
trance are shocking, not only because of the physical manifestations of the
effects of possession but also because of Rouch's camera style. The only
images in the film that were shot at night, they are extremely dark. The first
shows men, almost in silhouette, performing a circle dance. Next a light,
apparently from a flashlight held off-camera, illuminates the faces of the
possessed, making the close-ups garish. These entranced men foam at the
mouth, their noses running with heavy mucus, as they stare wide-eyed and
dazedly into the camera. A "wild" sound track of men's voices and music
accompanies the images and is heard beneath Rouch's voice-over. Rouch
does not explain that the musical motifs accompanying the trance, which
we hear played on the monochord violin, are used to "call down" the Hauka
spirits to enter their "horses"; for a Hauka viewer, this sequence would
be the first encounter with aural and visual stimuli capable of inducing a
trance reaction.

Music is only one of the idioms of trance the film's sound track
presents to the viewer. This track also carries the priests' chants, trance-
associated glossolalia, and the community's comments as they watch and
participate in the event. Another key idiom of trance is dance, a form of religious "text" that conveys a choreographed message. Anthropologist Sheila

Les maîtres fous: Rouch's camera captures the physical manifestations of the trance ritual.

Walker comments that through dance in African spirit possession, "a man first becomes the god, then dons the appropriate costuming." Not only clothing but also the dancer's body becomes costuming: "his physiognomy changes to simulate that of the god" as the transformation of identity occurs (122). The image track carries these postural "messages," documenting the physical metamorphoses of the trancers. The priests hoped that the film, providing both the sight of those possessed and the Hauka's special music played on the monochord violin, might induce mass response, possessing spectators, thereby bringing about a massive emergence of Hauka power. (This hypothesis, however, was never tested on a general audience, as the colonial authorities banned the film.)

As Rouch's camera records it, the ceremony proceeds from the nomination of new members, to the public confession of guilty doings by the initiated, to the onset of trance and the appearance of the "mad" Hauka gods. Deconstructing the symbolism of the ritual objects and behavior associated with the ceremony, Rouch explicates its extreme modeling on, and parody of, colonial life: "Colored rags flutter in the sky. They are the Union Jacks. Just below is a statue of the Governor with his moustache,

his sword, his guns and his horses." To remind the Hauka of the real colonial governor, an egg, representing the white plume on the governor's
helmet, is cracked over the wooden statue's head. Here Rouch intercuts
footage of the actual governor and his troops at the opening of the Assembly in Accra and observes, "Amid the crowd there are Hauka dancers looking for their model. If the order is different here, from there, the
protocol remains the same." Hauka protocol includes convening, while in
trance, frenetic "round table" discussions and arguments involving "the
Governor," "the Lieutenant," "the Wicked Major," "Madame Salma," and
others. Burlesquing European behavior and dress, the possessed don red
sashes and pith helmets (aping British military dress), carry wooden guns
with which they "threaten" and control the penitents, salute and insult one
another, do the British army parade march, and act "coy." As Europeans
were thought to be afraid of nothing, their Hauka counterparts prove their
fearlessness and superior power by burning themselves with torches and,
finally, by sacrificing and eating a dog. While still deeply in trance, the cult
members share this carnivalesque feast of nearly raw dog meat, placing
their bare hands in the boiling pot of dog soup to extricate their portions.
As evening nears, the trance is brought to a close and the community
returns to the city.

Bakhtin's model of medieval carnival has obvious parallels in the
Hauka possession ceremony, which can be seen as a carnivalesque, community rite of political resistance and cultural renewal, a struggle for empowerment. Bakhtin posits the European carnival as an arena of subversive
pleasures, a participatory, "second life" of the people. A sacred time set
apart from everyday life, characterized by a logic of inversions of status
and meaning, carnival enabled the "low" to comment on, satirize, and
burlesque the "high." Cultural conflicts were worked through via parodic
comment, costuming, and impersonations.

> The suspension of all hierarchical precedence during carni-
> val time was of particular significance. . . . Here, in the town
> square, a special form of free and familiar contact reigned
> among people who were usually divided by the barriers of caste,
> property, profession, and age.
>
> . . . a special idiom of forms and symbols was evolved—an
> extremely rich idiom that expressed the unique yet complex
> carnival experience of the people. This experience, opposed to
> all that was readymade and completed, to all pretense at im-
> mutability, sought a dynamic expression; it demanded ever

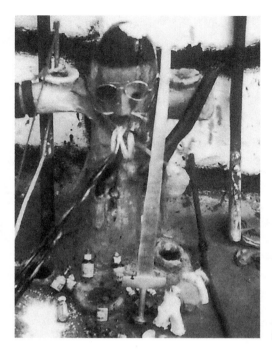

Les maîtres fous: The statue of
the colonial governor-general.

changing, playful, undefined forms. . . . We find here a characteristic logic, the peculiar logic of the "inside out" (*à l'envers*),
of the "turnabout," of a continual shifting from top to bottom,
from front to rear, of numerous parodies and travesties, hu-
miliations, profanations, comic crownings and uncrownings.
(*Rabelais* 10–11)

Walker has observed that "Both possession and carnival can be likened
to rituals of rebellion, in that behavior forbidden under normal circumstances is the norm during these periods" (99). Ritual possession, she
avers, provides a periodic catharsis, enabling the individual to act out suppressed facets in a culturally approved manner and setting. Such events
provide public, collective arenas in which to utilize supernatural sanctions
to punish individuals for antisocial behavior. Men must cooperate in these
possession rituals in order "to bring on the presence of the gods and when
the gods come, the men incarnating them interact and dialogue with each
other within the sacred frame of reference created by the ritual" (Walker 5).

In the possession ceremony, Rouch captures the Hauka adepts in sacred dialogue with their gods and the earthly Hauka community; the film places the spectator in cinematic and cultural dialogue with them as well.

The concluding section of the film shows the possessed penitents returned to the profane life of the city. Under dialoguing shots of the penitents, shown first in trance and then working at their quotidian jobs, Rouch observes, " 'Madame Locotoro, the doctor's wife,' is a rather effeminate boy who uses a lot of hair vaseline but, as a shop clerk, is excellent"; " 'The General' in real life is just a private." In his final voice-over, he muses about the Hauka's possible "panacea against mental disorders" and absorption of "our inimical society," while the "General Staff" of the possession ceremony are shown standing in front of the colonial mental hospital.[5]

When Rouch first showed *Les maîtres fous* in Paris, prior to its release, improvising his voice-over while the silent footage was projected for the Musée de l'Homme audience, the reaction of the spectators was overwhelmingly negative. African intellectuals felt they were exoticized, due to the scenes of blood sacrifice, the ingestion of dog meat, and lurid close-ups of men foaming at the mouth. Europeans objected to the ugly reflection of themselves enacted in the possession ritual. But Rouch felt he had documented something important and powerful and, though disturbed by such reactions, released the film in 1955. He was, however, unable to show it in the Gold Coast because of British censorship—it was felt that the film was an insult to the Queen and British authority and that it showed cruelty to animals. French administrators believed it insulted French culture. The African viewers of the film who were triggered to go into trance did so in such an uncontrollable manner that Rouch was unable to screen it for the Hauka themselves. In the 1960s, African intellectuals reacting to the film accused Rouch of perpetrating racist stereotypes, decontextualizing their lives, and studying them like insects. Today, however, according to Rouch, they no longer ban his film in black African cinemas but screen it as a "rare audiovisual document" that gives "a very precise image of what British and French colonialism was" and that reflects the Hauka's understanding of "the concept of colonial power" ("Totemic" 232).

Filmmaking, like the creation of written ethnography, is a discursive practice penetrated by relations of power. Bill Nichols, borrowing from Bakhtin, calls for new alternatives to the old "regimes" of ethnographic representation, suggesting that "dialogue, heteroglossia, political reflexivity, and the subversion of ethnocentrism" are employed to disrupt the power relations inherent in these texts. He argues that such stylistics "dissolve the oppositions of Them/Us, Self/Other, male/female that mask hierarchy as difference. These alternatives arise as voices from 'the other side' that insist on being heard" (227). Rouch's *Les maîtres fous* contains such insistent voices from "the other side" that seek to disrupt the power relations inherent in the institution of colonialism. Though this powerful and "cruel" film (to use Rouch's word) is problematic and controversial—admittedly, there is a gap between the Hauka priests' avowedly political agenda to challenge the colonial system and Rouch's overtly Eurocentric meditation on our "inimical" Western society; and the behavior of the possession cultists may be misread by viewers, appearing to be more bizarre and "mad" than that of the colonial authorities it mirrors and critiques—I would nevertheless suggest that it points the way toward a more multivocal form, like that of Rouch's ensuing films.

The challenge for the European novel, as Bakhtin saw it, was to free itself from the monologic control of the author. Ethnographic film confronts a similar challenge: to free itself from the extreme privilege accorded the framer of a text who is empowered to speak for Others. Its task, like that of Dostoyevsky, may be said to be the construction and expression of a polyphonic world, a world of multiple speakers overtly voicing their contending versions of the events of human interaction in "a dialogue where no voice is done the 'slightest violence'" (Emerson xxxvii). *Les maîtres fous* raises questions as to how the variety of voices embedded in the cross-cultural dialogues always "there" in anthropological texts can best be mobilized, so that repressed voices seeking their own constituencies are attended to and the power and diversity of the "dialogic imaginations" of the cultural conversants are accorded equal textual value. The film may be considered a useful model for future ethnographic filmmaking as it suggests possible ways to creatively employ the potential inherent in cinema, via the utilization of its diverse film tracks, to create texts that are more "open" spaces for cultural critique, more multivocal accounts of encounters between two cultures.

NOTES

1. Among Bakhtin scholars there is considerable debate concerning the authorship of the text *Marxism and the Philosophy of Language*, attributed to Volosinov. Some suggest that Bakhtin is, in fact, the sole author, while others claim that he coauthored considerable amounts of the text. I cite Volosinov here as a synecdoche for Bakhtin.

2. *Hauka*, in the Hausa language, means "crazy," according to Stoller (*Cinematic Griot* 145). It should be made clear that the crazy Hauka spirits were understood by cult members to be not only grotesque but also quite humorous, as in their parodies

of European behavior and dress. Considering themselves to be the "masters of madness," the Hauka adepts' behavior and bravado signaled their political resistance to the institution of colonialism.

3. For a good overview of Rouch's career, see Eaton and Stoller, *The Cinematic Griot*.

4. All translations from the film are my own.

5. Paul Stoller reports that Rouch was later to retract this idea of possession as a "panacea" for the mental traumas of colonialism. See his "Jean Rouch's Ethnographic Path," *Visual Anthropology* 2, nos. 3–4 (1989): 249–63.

WORKS CITED

Bakhtin, Mikhail. *The Dialogic Imagination*. Ed. Michael Holquist, trans. Caryl Emerson and Michael Holquist. Austin: University of Texas Press, 1981.

———. *Problems of Dostoevsky's Poetics*. Ed. and trans. Caryl Emerson. Minneapolis: University of Minnesota Press, 1984.

———. *Rabelais and His World*. Trans. Helene Iswolsky. Bloomington: Indiana University Press, 1984.

Clifford, James. "Introduction: Partial Truths." In *Writing Culture: The Poetics and Politics of Ethnography*, ed. James Clifford and George E. Marcus, 1–26. Berkeley: University of California Press, 1986.

Eaton, Mick, ed. *Anthropology-Reality-Cinema: The Films of Jean Rouch*. London: British Film Institute, 1979.

Emerson, Caryl. Preface to Mikhail Bakhtin, *Problems of Dostoevsky's Poetics*. Minneapolis: University of Minnesota Press, 1984.

Nichols, Bill. *Representing Reality: Issues and Concepts in Documentary*. Bloomington: Indiana University Press, 1991.

Rouch, Jean. "Conversation between Jean Rouch and Professor Enrico Fulchignoni." *Visual Anthropology* 2, nos. 3–4 (1989): 265–301.

———. "A Conversation with Jean Rouch." Interview by Lucien Taylor. *Visual Anthropology Review* 7, no. 1 (1991): 92–102.

———. "Jean Rouch Talks about His Films to John Marshall and John W. Adams." *American Anthropologist* 80, no. 4 (1978): 1005–22.

———. "Migration au Ghana (Gold Coast) (Enquete 1953–1955)." *Journal de la Société des Africanistes* 26 (1956): 33–196.

———. "Our Totemic Ancestors and Crazed Masters." *Senri Ethnological Studies* 24 (1988): 225–38.

Stam, Robert. *Subversive Pleasures: Bakhtin, Cultural Criticism, and Film*. Baltimore: Johns Hopkins University Press, 1989.

Stoller, Paul. *The Cinematic Griot: The Ethnography of Jean Rouch*. Chicago: University of Chicago Press, 1992.

————. "Horrific Comedy: Cultural Resistance and the Hauka Movement in Niger." *Ethos* 12, no. 2 (1984): 165–88.

Vertov, Dziga. *Kino-Eye: The Writings of Dziga Vertov*, ed. Annette Michelson and trans. Kevin O'Brien. Berkeley: University of California Press.

Volosinov, V. N. *Marxism and the Philosophy of Language*. Trans. Ladislav Matejka and I. R. Titunik. Cambridge, MA: Harvard University Press, 1973.

Walker, Sheila S. *Ceremonial Spirit Possession in Africa and Afro-America: Forms, Meanings, and Functional Significance for Individuals and Social Groups*. Leiden: E. J. Brill, 1972.

Chapter 12

DOCUMENTING THE INEFFABLE

Terror and Memory in Alain Resnais's *Night and Fog*

Sandy Flitterman-Lewis

> If one does not forget, one can neither live nor function. The problem arose for me when I made *Nuit et brouillard*. It was not a question of making yet another war memorial, but of thinking of the present and the future. Forgetting ought to be constructive.
>
> Alain Resnais, 1966

The common assumption about documentary film is that it confers on its subject the authority of history. Documentary commits its actors and events to the historical record—assertive, inviolable, and impervious to the distortions of perception, passion, or psyche. But it is precisely these "distortions" that have concerned Alain Resnais throughout his career. Whatever stories his films tell, they always provide a reflection on time, memory, history, and their relation to both personal and social identity. With *Nuit et brouillard* (*Night and Fog*, 1955), a 32-minute documentary made before his first feature fiction films, Resnais uses this complex relation between mind and material as the framework for an analysis of the Holocaust's systematic extermination of millions. In spite of the unimaginable brutality and suffering associated with the Holocaust, this proves to be the ideal subject for Resnais, in part because histories of the Holocaust are almost always filtered through recollections, what survivors tell us. This works against any single unified account, with its foregone conclusions, predetermined impact, and anticipated effects.

Every present rendering of some moment of this past evokes the future in a temporal continuum whose constant is social responsibility. Because of this, *Night and Fog* achieves Resnais's objective; it avoids the limitations of the war monument, whose finality, unproblematic meaning, and instant significance are the result of its capacity to surround history and keep it safely distanced in the past. Instead, the film's open structure and unresolved tensions create a space for the viewer that invites contemplation. In so doing, *Night and Fog* becomes not only a powerful document of the past but a film about "forgetting and not forgetting," posing a dialectical relation to history that produces true healing and social consciousness while unrelentingly narrating the horror of past events.

Still, the project of a documentary about the Holocaust poses several problems, not the least of which is the possible neutralizing effect of excessive footage of atrocities. The newsreel images are so horrible, so viscerally disturbing, that defense and denial are unavoidably invoked. Yet how does one document inconceivable horrors and incalculable pain? How does one maintain the image's power to shock without evoking either total disbelief or incapacitating grief? Resnais's concept of "constructive forgetting" provides an answer by tempering forgetfulness with a call to action: "It is absolutely necessary to act. Inaction and withdrawal into oneself lead only to despair. The real danger is in passivity, in stopping the struggle, in giving up" (50). While Resnais's emphasis on consciousness and memory might seem to contradict the objectivity associated with documentary, it is this very strategy that allows him to represent the unrepresentable, to image an unspeakable terror, and to simultaneously produce both anxiety and reflection on the part of the viewer, precisely the combination that turns documentary evidence into living history and social action.

Night and Fog begins and ends with a fluid, contemplative camera that glides across the austere landscapes of deserted barracks, barbed wire, and weed-choked railroad tracks of the concentration camps in 1955. Within this symmetrical frame, Resnais experiments with multiple temporalities, moving back and forth between the muted colors and abandoned sites of these tracking shots and black-and-white archival footage of every stage of the Final Solution, the efficient liquidation of the Jewish people (including still photographs and newsreels, documentation, shots from other films, including some from Leni Riefenstahl's 1935 *Triumph of the Will,* the state-sanctioned document of Nazi political power). This movement between present and past works in counterpoint to the painstaking linear chronology that details the bureaucratized genocide that was the cornerstone of Nazi policy.

The title "1933—The machine gets underway" introduces the spectacle of German military parades.[1] The construction of the death camps, deportations, cattle cars, and the processing of prisoners all comprise this first section of the film. In the second "movement," the specter of death haunts the scenes of daily life in the world of the concentration camp ("another planet"). The continuous tally of the dead, the slave labor system, starvation, dysentery, the class hierarchy, the hospital with its experiments and mutilations: against this background of horror the inmates survive in small creative ways. They dream, they write, they make toys, they debate, they remember. Even the social organization of this ersatz world has its function in the process of systematic mass annihilation.

Acceleration marks the third part of the film as schemes designed to increase the number and efficiency of the killings are put into action, the result of Himmler's 1942 visit to Auschwitz.[2] The special mobile killing units of the SS and the machine-gun massacres precede the gas chambers, with their Zyklon cylinders and their ceilings gouged by scratching hands. "1945—Full production," the fourth section, the final stage in the extermination process, illustrates the demonic logic of Nazi technology in extremis: bodies are incinerated in ovens and crematoria; eyeglasses, clothing, and shoes are recycled back into German society; every bit of "waste" is used, as ashes become fertilizer, bodies become soap, hair becomes textiles, and skin becomes paper for drawing. Section five juxtaposes extremes by pairing liberation with atrocity, as the Allied forces deal with masses of corpses, piles of severed heads, and living skeletons. Images of bulldozers shoving rubbery corpses into mass graves conjure a terrifying yet absurd vision of hell. War crimes tribunals evince impassive protestations of innocence.

But since *Night and Fog* must leave us in the present, Resnais gives us a coda, bringing us back from the safe distance of past time to our own responsibility. We are told that the potential for such evil is all around us, that we must be vigilant in our own lives and compassionate regarding others. Against a background that returns us to the film's beginning (but with a difference—the same landscape, the same barbed wire, but now these crumbling relics of crematoria and watchtowers signify the horror we, too, have experienced), the narrator intones:

> Who among us is on the lookout from this strange tower to warn us of new executioners? Are their faces really different from our own? Somewhere among us, there are lucky Kapos, reinstated officers, and unknown informers. There are those of us who refused to believe this, or believed it only from time to time. And here we are, with all good intentions, looking at the

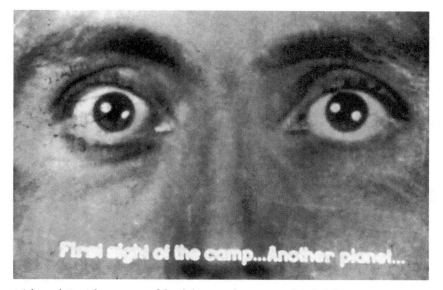

First sight of the camp...Another planet...

Night and Fog: The specter of death haunts the scenes of daily life in the concentration camp world.

ruins today as if the old concentration camp monster were dead and buried beneath the debris; and we pretend to take hope as the image recedes, as though one could be cured of the concentration camp plague; we pretend to believe that all this happened only once, at a certain time and in a certain place, and we refuse to look around us, we who do not hear the endless cry.[3]

Made in 1955, a scant ten years after the war, *Night and Fog* is one of the earliest documentary films about the Holocaust; it is also one of the first films to devise cinematic strategies for representing it.[4] Thus Resnais is able to accomplish the paradoxical task of turning a horrific reality into an aesthetic object while still maintaining a social perspective. By answering social and ethical questions with a work of art and, conversely, by making aesthetic concerns raise issues of history and morality, Resnais succeeds in integrating art and politics. Jean Cayrol, author of the haunting, contemplative poetry of the film's voice-over, adds a note of urgency: the film "is not only an example on which to reflect, but an appeal, an alarm, a warning siren." This is why, in his words, it "is a film of recollections, but also of a great anxiety" (132–33).

The film was commissioned by the Comité d'Histoire de la Seconde Guerre Mondiale to memorialize the concentration camps. The group chose Resnais to make a newsreel compilation film of Nazi atrocities, but Resnais had other ideas: "The short-subject documentaries made about the camps in '45 and '46 did not really reach the public. With *Night and Fog* I wanted to make a film that a great number of people would see. I thought if it was beautiful, it couldn't help but be effective" (quoted in Oms 14). Resnais was also concerned with the authenticity of experience, something he felt would affect the integrity of the film's impact on the viewer: "I did not dare make this film myself: I was never deported myself. Then I met Jean Cayrol who had been, and he agreed to make it with me" (quoted in Armes 48).[5] The film's authorship is often seen as dual (even by Resnais); the resulting counterpoint of spoken text and visual imagery organizes the film and provides its hauntingly powerful effect.

It is from Cayrol's book of poetry that the film's exquisitely evocative title comes. But the origin of the phrase "night and fog" has nothing beautiful about it: it is deeply rooted in the material circumstances of the Final Solution. In 1946, Cayrol, a Catholic who had been a political prisoner in Matthausen and had seen his brother perish at Oranienburg, published a volume of poetry titled *Poems of Night and Fog* (*Poèmes de la nuit et du brouillard*) together with a series of lamentations, *Public Tears* (*Larmes publiques*). The book contains extraordinarily haunting and lyrical texts that evoke an atmospheric sense of loss as they search for meaning and identity among the shards of a horrific past. Cayrol's title is a reappropriation of the language of the Holocaust: Hitler's 1941 Night and Fog Decree (*Nacht und Nebel Erlass*).[6] But just as certainly as the Germans had twisted a common phrase, so do Resnais and Cayrol (himself a "night and fog" prisoner) reinfuse it with a new meaning. And this new significance appropriately suggests one of the film's primary strategies, a movement from the accustomed meaning of a relatively "obvious" term to its subjective (and renewed) significance, a new meaning that valorizes human possibility in the face of what clearly seems to deny it. The darkness of "night" suggests despair, hopelessness, and demoralized inaction; "fog," by contrast, suggests the subjective uncertainty of multiple meanings, a blurring of sense that threatens to turn into either a confusion of meanings or no meaning at all. It is only when the terms are combined in the transforming catalyst of the film that the *salutary* meaning emerges, just as in the seeming paradox of Resnais's "constructive forgetting." Memory of the past is positively combined with responsibility for the future (that is, human agency, the sense of self that makes us capable of compassion and understanding). With *Night and Fog* one survives the desperation of the night, sees through the confusion of the fog, and emerges as a social being with a commitment to that human connection fundamental to life—a sense of shared responsibility to (and for) oneself and others.

The double authorship of Resnais and Cayrol also structures the film by providing a dual optic formed by each artist's life experience and personal relation to the Holocaust. Before the camera has shot a single image, then, the filters of perception and memory are engaged. As Ilan Avisar notes, "The collaboration . . . achieves a special effect: the viewer becomes aware of the simultaneous presence and the double perspective of the former inmate and the visitor, the actual witness and the curious spectator, the encumbered survivor and the meditative artist" (7). For the viewer, this creates a complex position of spectatorship somewhere between detachment and absorption. "Somewhere" is the operative term: the spectator of *Night and Fog* is situated between two points of viewing, two kinds of emotional involvement, and this dynamic creates the viewing space most productive of critical thought. Nevertheless, there is a certain direction to this critical thinking. As *Night and Fog* proceeds, the viewer changes from an observer of documented events to a witness with the capacity for moral judgment. It is this transformation that anchors the film's hopeful message.

The shift from observer to witness invokes a central metaphor of the film, one that hinges on two different conceptions of "looking" and two different relations to what is seen. With the *observer,* the camera documents; with the *witness,* the camera testifies, renders an account. The observer takes a detached stance toward the seen; the image becomes the visual equivalent of that staple of the newsreel, "fact." By contrast, the witness has a subjective relation to the image (the ability to see oneself *in* the scene), transforming what is seen through the prism of human feeling by means of communication. Requiring an "other," the human connection inherent in communication adds moral responsibility to the act of seeing. While observation suggests the self in isolation (or denies the self altogether in its objective form), witnessing is defined as a question of conscience, a relay between self and others through language. *Night and Fog* accomplishes this transition from detached observation to socially inscribed witnessing by transforming the function of spectatorship at the same time that it documents historical events.

Even still, with the unimaginable horror of the Holocaust, the problem of expression remains. Author Elie Wiesel, one of the best-known survivors of Auschwitz, asks, "How can one recount when—by the scale and weight of its horror—the event defies language? A problem of expression? Of perception, rather. . . . The essential will remain unsaid, eradicated, buried in the ash that covers this story. . . . The question inexorably asserts itself:

Does there exist another way, another language, to say what is unsayable?"
(quoted in Insdorf xi). Yet by the example of his prolific writing career,
Wiesel asserts, "I have always felt that words mean responsibility."[7] Resnais
takes on this responsibility when he documents the history of the death
camps through another kind of language, that of cinema. Against the silence and indifference that made the Holocaust possible, the film conveys
a message of hope and conviction without in any way diminishing the
suffering and horror of the Holocaust itself.

In search of a cinematic form capable of expressing the inexpressible,
Resnais and Cayrol employ a strategy of indirection: a horror too great to
be encompassed must be approached obliquely, even metaphorically. According to Marcel Oms, "A tone between revulsion and complacency had
to be found, a tone that made no compromise but still engaged the viewer"
(67). Oms points out that Resnais felt some traditional documentaries had
a desensitizing effect because of their straightforward style. To remedy this,
as Cayrol explains, "From an ungraspable, unreasonable, intransmittable
experience we chose major images which permitted the viewer . . . to participate in this enormous slaughter—people today, or those born after that
time, or those who never tried to understand to what lengths men will go
when they hate freedom and have contempt for everyone" (quoted in Bounoure 132). The dialectic between the peaceful landscapes and the devastating newsreel documents is one of the means by which Resnais and Cayrol
make the viewer both experience and contemplate this massacre. When
all the world had distanced itself (whether by design or honest ignorance)
from these images of inconceivable horror, Resnais found the cinematic
way to bring the audience into the center of the experience itself.[8]

Resnais accomplishes this by creatively redefining the documentary
form in three general areas. Concepts of the *film-text* (and the cinematic
language that forms it), the *viewer* (spectatorial modes of address), and *history* (subjective recording of the past) are reformulated as *Night and Fog*
both documents and invites reflection on the human tragedy of the concentration camps. First, images and sounds are put into new relations in
order to comment on, rather than homogenize, meaning. The image track
is composed of varied materials such as archival footage from a variety of
sources, newsreels, photographs, films of the period, personal footage shot
by Allied soldiers, and other documentaries. And to this diversity is added
the famous contemplative camera-tracking, gliding, flowing in incessant
movement across the deserted space of the present, filmed in color. The
dimensions of time and space are reconfigured to better approximate the
flow of human thought, thereby enabling viewers to experience *subjectively* the objective horror of the camps. The sound track, too, is a complex

orchestration of words, silence, and music (specially written by the Marxist composer Hanns Eisler).[9]

As for the spectator, that crucial transition from observer to witness is accomplished, in part, by a transformation in the mode of address. At first the viewer is the impartial observer of fact, a position traditionally associated with the documentary in general. But as the film progresses, the impersonal third person of narrated history becomes the intimate participant in direct address (between first and second person), the "I-You" relationship of dialogue and conversation. And by the end of the film this intimacy is so profound that the "I-You" of speaker and listener becomes the inviolable "We" of moral consciousness.

Finally, the reformulation of historical discourse is achieved through shifting ambiguities and contradictions, adding a subjective dimension to the enumeration of historical facts. Resnais, along with many of the artists of modernism, continually emphasizes the presence of unconscious desire in all aspects of everyday life. Intimate questions of the self, racial identity, family history, and personal memories thus become the broader issues of culture itself. As the French philosopher Youssef Ishagpour asserts, " 'Image-time' is, for Alain Resnais, not a mirror of reality, but an 'image-thought.' . . . This historical conscience becomes, like memory itself, Resnais' central theme and, like time, the structuring principle of his films" (75).

Recognizing that the "truth" of an event always exceeds the documented fact, Resnais attempts to locate those other tributaries of meaning and association (social, personal, ideological, emotional, philosophical, ethical/moral, national/cultural) through a metaphoric play of contrasts and oppositions that includes the viewer in the very definition of meaning itself. In its purest form, the ambiguity produced by this dialectic is what structures all modernist art; in *Night and Fog,* this structuring ambiguity is rendered in temporal terms that have moral consequences. Most pointedly, the haunting sense of absence produced by the camera's relentless track across deserted space is continually put into relation with the finite temporality of the documentary shots, providing the viewer with a space in which to consider the enduring effects of the specific historical moment.

In *Night and Fog* this constant interplay of permanence and instability, of the enduring and the contingent, creates the feeling of anxiety invoked earlier by Cayrol. Uncertainty, ambiguity, an anxious tension—all are experienced by the viewer, who is unsettled by this haunting blend of actuality and subjective vision. A disturbing sense of strangeness results from the juxtaposition of the visibly horrifying documentary material and the impassive calm of the vacant landscapes. Thus the nightmare images of attested

events (the documentation) have a phantom quality, not because the Holocaust is denied but because that inevitable feeling, halfway between belief
and disbelief, is so intensely invoked. This is why some critiques of *Night
and Fog* that invoke a value hierarchy between documentary material and
formalist experimentation are based on a misunderstanding of the film's
strategies. For it is precisely because the two are not separated, but rather
interrelated in an approximation of the structure of thought itself, that an
engaged and critical spectator is produced. As Resnais himself says, "The
idea that stimulated us in our work was 'Do we have the right to do formalist
research with such a subject?' But maybe with this element, it would have
more of an audience. For me, formalism is the only way to communicate"
(quoted in Insdorf 213).

If we understand formalism to mean "work on cinematic language,"
Resnais's strategy becomes clear. Finding a way to viscerally and materially
evoke—rather than simply describe—the brutal realities of the concentration camps means reinventing the function of the image and the process by
which the viewer engages with it. As has often been claimed, *Night and Fog*
is not so much about the camps themselves as it is about the *experience* of
the camps. According to James Monaco, "*Nuit et brouillard* deals more with
our [public] memory of the camps, our mental images of them, than with
the camps as they actually existed, for the memories are real and present,
as are the physical remains" (20). Yet as soon as the neat division of past
(archival footage) and present (the camps today) is posed, our experience of
the film contradicts this. Historical memory becomes our present collective
memory as a culture; temporalities and definitions become interchange-
able. In fact, *Night and Fog* is a concrete demonstration of Cayrol's later
statement about the film: "Memory of the past is only permanent when
illuminated by the present" (quoted in Bounoure 133).

On the most literal level, the wartime footage is narrated in the *present
tense,* while the tracking shots of the camps today are matched by narration that uses the *past tense* (with one important exception to which I shall
return). The film thus works by inscribing the past within the present (our
present viewing shapes how we see historical events), just as it does the reverse (the present-day tracking shots evoke the memory of camps long since
abandoned). The same is true of spatial relations: the vacant spaces of the
camps today are gradually filled with icons of the terrible past, as enigmatic
emptiness becomes full with meaning. Five shots of "the camps today" open
the film, as barbed wire and cryptic buildings impinge on peaceful landscapes; five shots of "the camps today" close the film, as memories of the
deportations, the concentration camp universe, the systematic genocide,
the diabolical efficiency, the disbelieving liberation, and the expressionless

denials float between the tangle of wire fences, cement debris, upended roads, and rusty structures, with just a glimpse of pale blue horizon prefacing the final shot of a black screen. The music's last chords continue as this screen invites contemplation of the images that preceded it.

Thus, while the film's structure can be described as an alternation of present and past, there is a specific direction to its flow of meaning that depends on a blurring and blending of those (and other) categories. The accelerating tempo of both what is heard and what is seen is paralleled by another kind of movement from dispersed fragmentation to cohesion. The spoken text of the sound track opens the film with a languid repetition: "Even a peaceful landscape . . . even an open field . . . even an ordinary road . . . even a resort town with a steeple and a marketplace . . . can lead to a concentration camp."[10] Its closing call for moral conscience is prefaced by the staccato triple repetition of the Nazi soldiers' claims (" 'I am not responsible,' says the Kapo / 'I am not responsible,' says the officer / 'I am not responsible. . . .' "), the culmination of a surprisingly rapid depiction of the war's end and its aftermath. The accelerating rhythm of the editing moves from a number of relatively long sequences of the roundups, deportations, and arrivals at the concentration camp to the short, jagged evidentiary shots of the Allied cleanup. In contrast, the content of the spoken text moves

Night and Fog: The tracking camera shows the camps at the time of filming, ten years after the end of the war.

from the geographical diversity of the deportation sites to the circumscribed ruins of the concentration camp—a single "receding image," the perimeter of "a diseased site," the lie of a "unique time and place"—augmented by the fluid, paragraph-long single sentence whose cohesive repetitions work to reinforce the film's message of personal and social responsibility.

Where the empty spaces first intrigue us with the promise of meaning ("Going slowly along the tracks, looking for what?"), then tease us with mere facts, the film finally leaves us not with answers but with questions of social and moral obligation to which the facts can only partially reply. The documentary facts address the fundamental journalistic questions: Who? What? Where? and When? But by the end of *Night and Fog* we are left asking the one question that is never answered—that never can be answered—but must always be asked: Why? The mute eloquence of the empty spaces leaves us, finally, with our questions unanswered, but through the film we learn that it is in the vigilant *process of asking itself* that moral conviction and human commitment lie. Resnais wanted the public "to be shaken by what is not seen" (quoted in Krantz 13),[11] hence the many vacant spaces of his film. But we also learn that the terms "empty/full," "present/past," "presence/absence" are relative and reversible. The camera's first visit to Auschwitz is already a return, the absences of the present image denoting a past "scene of the crime." And conversely, the camera's farewell to the ruined camp is a call to look around us today.

The tracking camera that glides over the present-day camps is restless and probing. These tracking shots have a dual function: they provide the viewer with the time and space to reflect on the preceding documentary images; and they reinforce the power of "the look" (the camera's, the viewer's) in the production and reception of the film's meaning. They act as a kind of formal punctuation, creating a particular type of critical spectator. Resnais is explicit: "My goal is to put the spectator in such a frame of mind that, when confronting some new problem, one week, six months, even a year later, having seen my film will allow him to assess things honestly, without any deceptions or preconceptions. . . . I want to address the viewer in a *critical state*, and one way to do so is to 'denaturalize' the cinema, cultivate the unexpected in order to make the viewer break out of habitual ways of seeing" (quoted in Samson 104). This appeal to the spectator's critical consciousness brings with it sociopolitical concerns, for self-reflection entails awareness of one's own position in history.

As for the centrality of "the look" in *Night and Fog,* cameraman Ghislain Cloquet formulates it best: "*Night and Fog* . . . was about a space traversed by a particular kind of look [*un espace parcouru par un certain regard*]. Resnais, like all truly great directors, is someone who creates . . . a veritable mental universe . . . *Night and Fog* is a devotional prayer, a hymn of praise, a *Te Deum*—there's no better way to say it" (58–60).[12] Cloquet's concept of "mental world" (*univers mental*) and Resnais's version of spectatorship return us to the observer/witness dyad, this time at the level of form. The viewer of archival footage is like the observer of historical facts (emaciated prisoners stand at roll call, Himmler studies models for extermination chambers). The meaning of each documentary image comes from the content of the shot; what is seen can be described in precise, factual detail. In contrast, the punctuating tracking shots are much harder to describe and require more sustained contemplation on the viewer's part. Because their focus is on the moving camera, vision is foregrounded, suggesting the subjectivity of witnessing. The camera seems to survey not objects but representative visual synecdoches—buildings, a field, barbed wire, bunks, latrines, ceilings, ovens—necessarily engaging the viewer's associative and conceptual capacities.

But it is in the final portion of the narrated text that the most radical transformation in spectatorship occurs (the impact is a bit less for English-subtitle readers). After the triple denial of responsibility by the German soldiers, a question is addressed in voice-over to no one in particular, which is to say, to everyone: "Who, then, is responsible?" (*Alors, qui est responsable?*) This question, which accompanies the final four archival shots (a woman with shaved head and three shots of bodies in random piles), emphatically marks this shift in spectatorial address. For the viewer is about to be invoked *explicitly* by the film, and this question—the question of responsibility—paves the way.

All of a sudden the narrator's tone changes, becoming more direct: "*At this very moment, just as I am speaking to you* [*Au moment où je vous parle . . .*], the icy waters of bog and wreckage fill the hollows of this scene of devastation." Time coalesces into a single instant (the present time of the viewing, the film-time of the narration, and the historic-time of the depicted events) at the very moment that the viewer is explicitly addressed (*vous*) by a voice that now belongs to someone (*je*). This voice introduces both social and subjective dimensions while it designates a single instance: *now.* But this is not a moment fixed for all time, for the meaning of the word varies according to each screening of the film ("now" in 1956 is very different from "now" as I write this in 1996, as it will be from "now" at any other moment in the future). In every case it is memory that turns past history into a palpable presence.

In addition, presence is reinforced by a shift in verb tense. Throughout the film, as already noted, the archival footage is narrated in the historic present tense of documentary film ("The deportation extends throughout the whole of Europe"); by contrast, the present-day interludes are narrated in the past imperfect, signifying continuous duration or habitual repetition ("They closed the doors. They watched. . . . Even the concrete ceiling was shredded.") The coda inverts this pattern, uniting present images with present-tense narration, as in "Nine million dead haunt this landscape," over a desolate image of upended reinforced concrete. Finally, in a stunning demonstration of the inescapable social and historical consequences of filmmaking and viewing, the very end of the coda replaces the interlocutory structure of "I-You" with the all-encompassing "We": "And here we are, with all good intentions, looking at the ruins today. . . . And we refuse to look around us, we who do not hear the endless cry."[13] Thus presence, responsibility, and active engagement make both viewer and filmmaker witnesses to history (and to historical representation), projecting the film's implications beyond the theater and into the future, binding them in the social processes and moral obligations of human culture.

Resnais's interest in bringing the unconscious into the historical process dovetails with his defining concerns about structures of the mind and the movement of thought. His concept of "constructive forgetting," like William Faulkner's remark that "memory believes before knowing remembers" (119), distinguishes between two types of mental activity regarding the past: *remembering* as a recollection of specific historical facts and *memory* as a deeper, constantly changing process. Mental time has unconscious effects that destabilize the certainty of objective fact. Given that, how does one get viewers to experience—as a collective social memory—a history in which they have not participated? Resnais's answer involves focusing on the "memory believes" part of Faulkner's statement, for the collective memory of a culture often works at an unconscious level. Knowledge, on the other hand, remains conscious, as specific facts are recalled. In commonsense terms, one observes and records with the head, one believes and understands with the heart. A shared cultural history can only come about if both perspectives are equally engaged. Within this context, memory becomes a living process, at once part of the individual whose memory it is and the culture to which the person belongs.

Forever in the past, remembering is tied to a specific event, date, or time. Its monument can exist without the individual; its meaning is self-contained. Memory, on the other hand, cannot exist without a subject and is shifting. Remembering can involve preconceived ideas, the fitting of the past into familiar assumptions; memory, however, involves variable and contradictory ideas that emerge from a subjective relation to the past. "Constructive forgetting" always engages the interface between the two— between public, official memory and its private, subjective counterpart.

From this perspective, language does not simply transmit a ready-made meaning but is a process of human connection. This transforming feature, that "something else" or "in between" of the human dimension—call it faith, spirituality, belief—is the very thing that Resnais tries to capture as he renders the specific history of the concentration camps.

Prescription for Survival: A Found Poem
Train the memory
    with dreams
write   dispute
Look after
    friends
        worse off
When the body
    is worn
        out
with fatigue
The Mind
    works
        on[14]

The strands of language in this poem (taken from Cayrol's subtitled narration) emerge from and indicate the way to the very heart of the film. The poem illuminates the film's quiet celebration of the capacities of the human mind, spirit, and sense of social connection that are antidotes to the horrors of the camp. But we must look more closely to understand how the very process of communication is an affirmation and a demonstration of the film's hopeful message. As long as there is language, there is the tiniest spark of humanity; a work of the imagination, an address to another, a new meaning given to an old idea, a sign of an active intelligence, an act of compassion, a capacity to dream—all of these affirm the sacred inviolability of human life.

The structure of *Night and Fog* carefully embeds this gentle celebration of humanity deep within the texture of the concentration camp world. Its location is not arbitrary; in fact, the film is almost perfectly symmetrical, making this reverential sequence appear very close to both its structural and temporal core. *Night and Fog* begins and ends in the same ambiguously featureless location, the deserted ruins of the abandoned concentration camp. The mirroring constituted by the prelude and coda provides a frame within which other parallel or contrasting sequences similarly mirror and respond. As the film moves toward (and away from) its emotional center, the comparison between humanity and inhumanity intensifies. What is best in the human spirit confronts the absence of humanity; respect for others and for oneself contrasts with a brutal lack of respect; imagination and human feeling throw into relief diabolical calculation and lifeless technology-worship; language confronts silence; and conscience confronts immorality.

The meditative tracking shots intersect the archival material, creating a complex pattern; within the symmetry of the responding tracking shots, the documentary footage accelerates in pace. Thus while the "story" of the Nazi genocide machine follows the inevitable sequence of a narrative, the human core of the film—the brief, understated sequence of hope—is centrally positioned, "surrounded" by six pairs of tracking shot sequences. Rather than call attention to itself, it fits into the sequence of events, thereby achieving both the linear movement of the documentary and the associative logic of poetry. After the fields and barbed wire of the prelude, three separate present-day sequences depict weed-choked train tracks, the gateway to the camp, abandoned brick buildings, wooden bunks, and latrines. The corresponding three interludes that precede the desolate rubble of the coda reveal the exterior of the crematoria, the terror-engraved interior of the gas chambers, the gaping ovens in rows. The remaining four interludes (combined with their alternating archival sections) make up the central six minutes of the film. The countryside seen from a guard-tower whose windows divide the landscape into frames has its parallel in the tracking shots of the brothel and the prison, whose vented cells, we are told, could not muffle the screams within. And finally, surrounding an archival sequence depicting barely breathing living corpses, two tracking shots, one on either side, depict the brick ruins of the camp hospital.

The sequence of hope begins with a statement in the narrator's voice-over that condenses all of the film's hopeful, healing, reverential meaning in a single six-word phrase (not in the subtitles): "Man has a remarkable capacity for resistance." In terms of historical images, nothing really distinguishes this sequence from the other archival documents. Twelve shots depict an aspect of ordinary daily life in the death camp: an upward pan reveals a handmade marionette; seven close-up photos show us a toy monster, a box, handwritten notes on a scrap of paper, a recipe for "*Écrivisses a la basquaise*" (Basquestyle crayfish), a makeshift scroll, a prisoner in conversation, and some numbers; finally, four photos show weakened prisoners being helped by other prisoners. On the sound track, a descriptive catalogue follows the assertion of human resistance (the word suggests resilience, tenacity, and strength): "The body worn out with fatigue, the mind and spirit work on, bandaged hands work on. . . . One might think of God. They even manage to organize politically, to debate common law, to set up rules regulating camp life, to care for the sickest among them, to help one another. As a last resort, with anguish, they take those most in danger to the hospital."

This last sentence, of course, initiates the first of the two parallel tracking shots of the abandoned hospital that surround the archival sequence of bedridden, emaciated souls at death's door. At the center of the film's symmetrical design, and preceding the answering color tracking shot of the hospital ruins, this six-image sequence has a powerful, haunting impact, an effect negotiated through the most subtle of means. At first the prisoners appear to be in still photographs, but gradually, almost imperceptibly, eyes blink, a body shudders, troubled breathing barely moves the chest. Soft as a sigh, these movements convey the absolute tenuousness of life, life rendered all the more precious because its termination is so calculated and cruel. It would be natural to consider this sequence as the epicenter of the film, but that would contradict the film's strategies of indirection. For although the sequence itself is rendered with subtlety, its central textual position gives it a surprising emphasis, just as its content and conclusions are far from unexpected.

It is Resnais's structure of responding pairs that provides us with a way to read the crucial connotative meanings, those that bear the burden of interpretive significance beyond the more evident denotations of documentary footage. Our interpretation of the importance of the "sequence of hope" must be understood in the context of its match, for an implicit contrast is suggested by the "medical sequence" that counters it. Immediately following the single tracking shot that takes us away from the dead and dying, this archival sequence of the hospital depicts vacant operating rooms, surgical equipment, contraptions for unknown purposes, toxic drugs, experiments on human flesh, human guinea pigs, and a photo of emaciated legs that serves as closure to this voyage through hell. The brute monstrosity of the activities of this "hospital" is indictment enough, but Resnais makes these images work toward a comparison instead; meaning derives from juxtaposition. When the stark terror of the Nazis' scientific obsession depicted here is considered in relation to the "hope sequence," we are offered stunning evidence of what it takes to survive. The actions are small but the significance great, for each project taken on in the desperate world of the camp is evidence of a life-affirming belief in human connection and social discourse. The fabrication of a puppet becomes a reverential act when seen in the context of operating rooms whose professional-looking setting masks "useless operations, amputations, experimental mutilations," where "anyone, kapo or surgeon, can take part." While prisoners remember recipes, imagine problems of philosophy, and write stories to exercise their minds, Nazis invent "scientific" theorems to be tested on living beings.

In the concentration camp, prisoners organize their "community" even as in the hospital "chemical companies try out their toxic drugs on an ever-replenished stock of human subjects."

But the most devastating contrast to emerge from this pairing—or, rather, the most hopeful and redemptive—involves an unexpected reference to language as the moral connective in the human bond. The last part of the hospital sequence involves a catalogue of victims ("Among these guinea pigs, a few will survive; castrated, burned with phosphorous. There are those whose flesh will be marked for life, despite their return"). Two of the accompanying images have a barely perceptible but crucial distinction: the victims are seen speaking to offscreen interlocutors. One castrated man is apparently answering a question; a woman rolls up her prisoner's sleeve and speaks about her arm. These images are the film's only evidence of prisoners' speech in the concentration camp world. Ironically, these speaking subjects fail to be seen as human beings by their torturers; so brutal and inhumane is the Final Solution that even language's assertion of humanity fails to invoke morality or compassion.

In contrast, the corresponding portion of the "hope sequence" demonstrates the value of communication as a means of social connection. The images continue to be still photographs (of prisoners helping their weaker comrades), so communication is only implied. But these photos depict scenes of kindness and concern in which the language of compassion is revealed through gesture and stance. The voice-over reminds us that these prisoners are "anguished" as they help those in the worst condition; in the midst of this agonizing silence, the human connection cannot be denied. Here, in the most inhuman of circumstances, the possibility of true humanity emerges all the more.

However, this is far from a simple metaphor devised for a film. If an actuality-based example is needed, history readily provides it. One has only to compare the infamous experiments of the Nazi doctor Josef Mengele with the actions of one Warsaw Ghetto martyr, Dr. Emmanuel Ringelblum, whose efforts to document and preserve the memory of ghetto life resulted in an archive—hidden in milk cans and metal boxes, buried beneath the Warsaw streets. As one historian notes, "There were many acts of quiet heroism. . . . Gestures of friendship bridged the loneliness and sorrow. Moral dignity was preserved by some even to the end" (Berenbaum 91).[15] The very act of collecting, preserving, and documenting, quite apart from what the material reveals, superbly demonstrates the living process of memory. The act itself, the will to inscribe that present moment, which is now history, for the benefit of future generations, exemplifies an active concept of history, Resnais's "constructive forgetting."

Returning to that small glimpse of humanity found in community, one is reminded of the words of theologian Abraham Joshua Heschel, who sees the human capacity for communication as salvation and redemption: "Remember that there is meaning beyond absurdity. . . . Be sure that every little deed counts, that every word has power, and that we can, everyone, do our share to redeem the world. . . . Build a life as if it was a work of art . . . and remember that life is a celebration" (412).[16] *Night and Fog,* to use Ghislain Cloquet's words, certainly is a celebratory hymn, a *Te Deum,* for within the horror of the concentration camps it is still possible, even if only tenuously, to see, along with Resnais and Cayrol, the fundamental beauty of humanity.

NOTES

This article is written in honor of my father-in-law, Morton Lewis, a Holocaust survivor. I also wish to thank Wesley Brown, Eric Aranoff, Joel Rosenberg, Pat Narcisco, and especially my sister, Dr. Sharon Flitterman-King, without whom this article would never have been written. And, as ever, thanks go to my husband, Joel Lewis, for his insight, his sense of humor, and his prodigious knowledge.

1. My division of the film into five parts (plus prelude and coda) does not appear in the film, which flows easily from section to section with no divisions. The dates I have included (1933, 1942, 1945) do appear in both the written text and the voice-over narration.

2. Auschwitz was a collection of three major death camps and more than forty-five subcamps in southern Poland. Most of the prisoners were gassed; the others worked as slave laborers at the camps and in nearby farms, mines, and factories. Most of the 1.5 million Auschwitz victims (10 percent of the total Holocaust deaths) were Jews. After the Liberation in 1945, Auschwitz (the German name for the Polish town of Oswiecim) became a kind of universal shorthand for evil.

3. This is translated from the script printed in *L'Avant-scène du cinema* 1 (February 15, 1961). All translations are my own. Though the subtitles are inadequate, they do give the general idea. But most critical writing on the film works from either the English subtitles or incorrect translations of the written text. They leave out the "we" in favor of "they" or the impersonal. One translation (by R. Hughes and Merle Worth) of Jean Cayrol's narrated text can be found in Robert Hughes, ed., *Film: Book 2—Films of Peace and War* (New York: Grove Press, 1962). Some subtitles on DVD releases have corrected this as well.

4. When *Night and Fog* was released, most accounts of the concentration camps were in book form. For example, see *Tràgedie de la déportation, 1940–1945* (Paris: Hachette, 1954), by Olga Wormser and Henri Michel, who acted as advisors to Resnais. Elie Wiesel's memoir, *Night,* was published first in Yiddish in Buenos Aires in

1956; revised and significantly abridged, it appeared in French in 1958 and then in English in 1960. A good overview of the Holocaust is provided by Martin Gilbert in *The Holocaust* (New York: Holt, Rinehart and Winston, 1986).

5. Cayrol is a prolific poet, novelist, literary theorist, and editor whose entire work has been marked by his concentration camp experience. Haunted by his memories and plagued by the unanswered question, "Why have I been allowed to return from the dead?" his theory of "Lazarean fiction" answers questions about identity, community, family, and meaning with an affirmation of language. Language thus becomes a means of both integrating the fragmented self and escaping the emotional isolation engendered by that fragmentation. But this resolution comes only after a profound struggle with self-imposed demons born of impossible life circumstances. At the center of French literary culture for over half a century, Cayrol has authored nearly sixty books and six screenplays.

6. According to film historian Ilan Avisar, "The Nazis adapted the common German idiom *'bei Nacht und Nebel davon gehen,'* meaning to get away or escape under cover of darkness or the night, to designate one of their rules of terror" (14). Avisar goes on to cite Holocaust historian William Shirer: "This grotesque order, reserved for the unfortunate inhabitants of the conquered territories in the West . . . was to seize persons 'endangering German security' who were not to be immediately executed and make them vanish without a trace into the night and fog of the unknown in Germany. No information was to be given their families as to their fate even when, as invariably occurred, it was merely a question of the place of burial in the Reich." Avisar adds that "Nazi usage has poisoned this neutral linguistic expression" (14–15). The Shirer quote is from *The Rise and Fall of the Third Reich* (Greenwich, CT: Fawcett, 1960), 1247–48.

7. This is quoted in Jack Kolbert, "Elie Wiesel," in the *Dictionary of Literary Biography*, vol. 83, *French Novelists since 1860,* ed. Catharine Savage Brosman (Detroit: Gale Research, 1989), 323.

8. For purposes of discussion I am returning to Resnais (in the singular) as author of this film. Resnais often works with authors—Marguerite Duras for *Hiroshima, mon amour* (1959), Alain Robbe-Grillet for *Last Year at Marienbad* (1961), Jorge Semprun for *La guerre est fini* (1966), and Cayrol again for his most significant film, *Muriel (Ou le temps d'un retour),* 1963. In all cases, Resnais has devised cinematic solutions to problems of representation and thus has earned the status of author of his films.

9. Henri Colpi, who edited both sound and image of *Night and Fog* with his wife, Jasmine Chasney, says that Eisler's music opens with a long melodic phrase over the credits that is left in suspense. The theme reappears only at the very end of the film, where it is resolved.

10. In French the problem of verb tense (past-tense narration with present images) is avoided through the use of the subjunctive necessitated by the term "even" (*même*).

11. It was in the course of a 1984 interview that Resnais made the (now legendary) claim that "The whole point [of *Night and Fog*] was Algeria," leading to countless interpretations of the film as a parable of the Algerian War (quoted in Krantz 14). But nothing could be further from Resnais's consistent method of making films that refuse to provide simple, fixed meanings to works whose entire process evokes the contradictory and mutable play of human consciousness. Resnais's refusal in *Night and Fog* to make "yet another war memorial" emphatically resists the attribution of an absolute, authoritative, singular meaning that denies the productive work of the spectator. This, it seems to me, is the whole point.

12. Cloquet and Sasha Vierny both worked as cameramen on *Night and Fog*. Both went on to have highly regarded careers in cinematography.

13. *"Et il y a nous qui regardons sincèrement ces mines . . . nous . . . qui ne pensons à regarder autour de nous et qui n'entendons pas qu'on erie sans fin."* The English subtitles on the film read, "There are those who look at these ruins today . . . those who refuse to look around them, deaf to the endless cry." The deliberate inclusivity of the French text is lost.

14. Sharon Flitterman-King, April 27, 1993, from *Night and Fog*.

15. A historian and social activist, Ringelblum remained in the Warsaw Ghetto until its liquidation in 1943; he was later shot to death by Nazis in Aryan Warsaw. As for the archive, two milk cans have been recovered; one is in Warsaw, and the other occupies a place of honor in the U.S. Holocaust Memorial Museum in Washington, D.C.

16. Dr. Abraham Joshua Heschel (1907–72), one of the foremost Jewish thinkers of modern time, was internationally known as a scholar, author, activist, and theologian.

WORKS CITED

Armes, Roy. *The Cinema of Alain Resnais*. London: Zwemmer, 1968.

Avisar, Ilan. *Screening the Holocaust: Cinema's Images of the Unimaginable*. Bloomington: Indiana University Press, 1988.

Berenbaum, Michael. *The World Must Know: The History of the Holocaust as Told in the U.S. Holocaust Memorial Museum*. Boston: Little, Brown, 1993.

Bounoure, Gaston, ed. *Alain Resnais*. Paris: Editions Seghers, 1962.

Cayrol, Jean. "Nuit et brouillard." In *Alain Resnais*, ed. Gaston Bounoure, 132–34. Paris: Editions Seghers, 1962.

Cloquet, Ghislain. "Le Tournage." *L'Arc* 31. *Alain Resnais, ou la création au cinéma*. (1967): 60.

Faulkner, William. *Light in August*. New York: Random House, 1932.

Heschel, Abraham Joshua. *Moral Grandeur and Spiritual Audacity*, ed. Susannah Heschel. New York: Farrar, Straus and Giroux, 1996.

Insdorf, Annette. *Indelible Shadows: Film and the Holocaust.* Cambridge: Cambridge
    University Press, 1989.
Ishagpour, Youssef. *Le Cinema.* Paris: Flammarion, 1996.
Krantz, Charles. "Teaching *Night and Fog:* History and Historiography." *Film and
    History* 15, no. 1 (1985): 2–15.
Monaco, James. *Alain Resnais.* New York: Oxford University Press, 1978.
Oms, Marcel. *Alain Resnais.* Paris: Editions Rivages, 1988.
Resnais, Alain. "Entretien." *L'Avant-Scène du Cinéma* 61/62 (1966): 49–52.
Samson, Pierre. "Le Lyrisme critique d'Alain Resnais." *L'Arc* 31 (1967): 103–11.

Chapter 13

MAKING THE PAST PRESENT

Peter Watkins's *Culloden*

John R. Cook

Tuesday, December 15, 1964. Time: 8:05 PM. *Culloden*—Peter Watkins's groundbreaking documentary reconstruction of the last land battle to be fought on British soil—was first broadcast on British television. Many who saw it for the first time that night never forgot the power of its images. Its influence over subsequent film and television has been immense. Directed by Watkins for BBC TV, it has been screened in cinemas and on television all around the world and hailed as one of the most remarkable professional film debuts ever, bringing a new realism and authenticity to film depictions of war. Meticulously researched as a documentary, it also pioneered, within a dramatic performance context, the handheld verité style of filmmaking that has come to be so ubiquitous in contemporary film and television fiction-making as a signature of gritty authenticity. From the work of social realist directors like Ken Loach to contemporary war films, "mock-docs" (mock documentaries), and even Hollywood movies such as the Jason Bourne trilogy, all owe a debt to *Culloden*. The contemporary form of the hybridized genre we recognize today as docudrama began with this film.

Culloden is no conventional production. It is important to realize it is an amateur film and the work of an amateur director. This is not meant in any derogatory, negative way but in the sense that the roots of *Culloden* lay in the burgeoning amateur film movement in Britain of the late 1950s and early 1960s, from which Watkins emerged. In many ways, the amateur film movement functioned as Britain's true underground cinema during

this period and, certainly, it provided Watkins with the opportunity to experiment with techniques he would bring to fruition with *Culloden*. Examining
these early roots provides us with important clues in terms of understanding how *Culloden* works as a film and how its key theme of war arose from
the formative experiences of its director.

Born in Norbiton, Surrey in 1935, Watkins, during the mid-1950s,
joined a local amateur dramatic group in Canterbury, Kent, while stationed
there on two years compulsory national service with the British army. The
strong feelings of solidarity, communality, and friendship he enjoyed while
acting with members of the Playcraft amateur theater group formed a stark
contrast to his experiences of the hierarchical regimentation of army life
and is crucial to his subsequent film work (Watkins interview). His consistent preference throughout his films, including *Culloden*, for casting amateur (or, as he prefers to call them, "nonprofessional") actors has its origins
in his work for Playcraft, as does his perception that nonprofessional actors often bring something more of themselves to a role, something more
"natural" and "spontaneous" than the sometimes theatrical, declamatory
style of the professionally trained performer. Properly cast, the nonprofessional can literally embody the part he or she is playing. Watkins's subsequent film career, beginning with his *Culloden* debut, became almost an
attempt to recapture the spirit of those amateur Playcraft years. His consistent casting of nonprofessional actors, as well as his bringing together
of performers and crew for an intense communal experience that becomes
the process of shooting the film, owe a tremendous debt to his early work
with the Playcraft group.

Watkins began to make short films in his spare time using members of
the Playcraft group as actors. Two of these, *The Diary of an Unknown Soldier*
(1959) and *The Forgotten Faces* (1961), would go on to win him amateur film
awards in the form of the "Ten Best" film competition run each year by
Amateur Ciné-World magazine. Watkins became established as one of the
leading creative figures within Britain's growing amateur film movement
of the period, and it was in this way that he first came to the attention of the
BBC, gaining his chance to direct *Culloden* for national television.

The Forgotten Faces is especially important for understanding how
Culloden works as a film text. This earlier amateur film experimented with
faux-newsreel techniques, offering a meticulous documentary-style reconstruction of the events that occurred in Hungary in late October 1956 when
Hungarians rebelled against Communist rule, winning for themselves a
brief moment of freedom before being brutally crushed by the arrival of
Soviet tanks a few days later. Watkins shot *The Forgotten Faces* in this style

to make it appear as if cameras had captured the events spontaneously as they were unfolding.

So meticulously reconstructed was *The Forgotten Faces* that many who saw it on first viewing assumed it must have been astonishing footage of the events of the time somehow smuggled out of Soviet-controlled Hungary (Shulman 240). In fact, Watkins had shot the film in the backstreets of Canterbury, using actors from the local Playcraft group to play the Hungarians, meticulously matching his faces and locations to hundreds of still photographs of the Hungarian Uprising drawn from the pages of *Paris Match* and *Life* magazines (Welsh 4). Alongside his actuality-style footage, Watkins also deployed, at the editing stage, a newsreel-style "voice-of-God" narrator (Frank Hickey) who details the facts and contexts behind what we are seeing in a hard, clipped, seemingly detached tone. Both this newsreel-style reconstructive technique and the "voice-of-God" narration would become key features of *Culloden*.

As a consequence of the success of *The Forgotten Faces*, Watkins was invited to join the BBC, working as a program assistant from April 1963 (Shaw 1357) for the Television Documentary and Music Department. All during this period, however, he was impatient and chomping at the bit to be allowed to make his own films. He had come to the BBC, via the amateur route, as an already established filmmaker and now he wanted the space and the freedom to produce his own work. In a long internal memo to his Head of Department, Huw Wheldon, in February 1964, Watkins spilled out a whole series of ideas for films he could make for the broadcaster if only he were given the chance. Examining this memo is very important for understanding Watkins's overall conception behind *Culloden*.

"All the internal discussions about the new 'camera liberty,'" Watkins wrote to Wheldon, "seem to have been dealing with the attempts to capture the passing moment as it is actually happening and the problems that this incurs" (memo, February 24, 1964, 2). Here Watkins was acknowledging the influence of Robert Drew's "Direct Cinema" in the United States as well as Jean Rouch's cinema verité in France—new candid styles of documentary filmmaking where the "camera liberties" included the use of lighter-weight, more portable 16-mm filming equipment plus the development of synchronized sound recording, both of which facilitated greater, more continuous location shooting. This seemed to bring an ostensibly rawer and more truthful feel to the representation of documentary subjects of the type we recognize today as "fly-on-the-wall." As Jamie Sexton has shown, 16-mm film cameras had found their way into the BBC in the late 1950s and early 1960s, first through newsgathering and then later, into the

1960s, in documentary productions, where some of the more cutting-edge styles had begun to mirror the aforementioned developments in the United States, France, and other parts of the world. In his 1964 memo, Watkins, however, was arguing for a direction completely opposite to the apparent uncontrolled "spontaneity" of the new documentary shooting techniques. Instead, he said that "My idea is to have, by re-staging, every second under *total organised and pre-planned control,* and yet still give it the appearance of *actually happening at that moment*" (2, emphasis in original). He went on to declare that "The linking of this technique to the as yet untapped sources of nonprofessional faces and personalities, and the tremendous range of subjects open to this form of cinema, I find tremendously exciting. I am convinced this can open up a totally new path and direction in documentary television film" (2).

From the dawn of documentary, restaging and reconstruction of events has often been a fundamental production necessity on account of the technical limitations of the early equipment and the consequent constraints this has imposed upon the extent of actual location shooting. For example, *Night Mail* (1936), directed by Harry Watt and Basil Wright for the GPO (General Post Office) Film Unit, famously had to resort to restaging some scenes in the studio because of the difficulty of filming postal workers in situ on a moving night mail train (Izod and Kilborn 427). Even more famously, the head of the GPO Film Unit, John Grierson, had helped elevate such techniques into an intrinsic part of the form itself when he defined documentary as the "creative treatment of actuality" (1). Following World War II, the "creative" legacy of the British Documentary Film Movement continued into British television with scripted "story documentaries" (Sydney-Smith 20). Often these focused on issues of law and order and policing, such as writer-producer Robert Barr's *War on Crime* (BBC TV, 1950) and his subsequent *Pilgrim Street* series (BBC TV, 1952) about life in a London police station. In the mid- to late 1950s, a number of dramatized documentaries on social issues were written for the BBC by Colin Morris and directed by Gilchrist Calder, including *The Unloved* (1955), about juvenile delinquency, and *A Woman Alone* (1956), which concerned the plight of unmarried mothers (Sydney-Smith 127). These productions were all based on documentary research but because of the sensitive subject matter and the difficulties of shooting real subjects on location with the bulky camera equipment of the time had been re-created and scripted by a professional writer. That is to say, information elicited through research was subsequently dramatized and then reenacted in the television studio, employing professional actors and using conventional TV drama direction techniques of the period.

In setting out his own ideas for a form of "dramatized documentary" in which everything would be equally preplanned and controlled in advance, Watkins, in one sense, was working out of this older BBC tradition of "controlled" documentary production. But it was a tradition that was waning owing to the arrival of newer lighter-weight, sync-sound equipment. In professional documentary terms, Watkins's innovation with *Culloden* was to marry these modes—the older restaging with the newer verité styles—using nonprofessional rather than professional actors in a manner that gave the production more of the feel of a contemporary documentary than a drama. In essence, though, the work defied both categories. Its strong performative element meant it was not quite "pure" documentary, but the documentary meticulousness of its reconstruction of the events of the battle of Culloden, together with its involvement of nonprofessional participants, meant neither could it be dismissed as fictionalized drama. Watkins's own purpose was a radical one since his particular approach toward restaging (verité-type documentary style using nonprofessional actors) not only posed a challenge to conventional production boundaries but also eschewed the notion of professionalism in film and TV production, particularly through the involvement of members of the public as actors.

Watkins was trying to bring to television the reconstruction techniques in a newsreel style he had innovated as an amateur with *The Forgotten Faces* and with which he had felt most comfortable as a director. Looking down the long list of film projects Watkins would like to make, Wheldon gave him the go-ahead for a film about the battle of Culloden that "tore apart forever the clan system of the Scottish Highlands" (Watkins, memo, February 24, 1964, 2). On April 16, 1746, the Jacobite rebellion, which had been attempting to restore the Catholic Stuarts to the English monarchy, was finally crushed by British government forces on the field of Culloden, near Inverness in Scotland. Fatally misled by Charles Edward Stuart ("Bonnie Prince Charlie"), the rebellion and its disastrous outcome precipitated the "Highland Clearances," a ruthless form of ethnic cleansing whereby over the next hundred years the Scottish Highlands were systematically cleared to make way for cattle and sheep and the Scottish Highland clan system and its traditional way of life were destroyed forever (Watkins, "Peter Watkins").

Watkins elaborated on his film idea to Wheldon: "The film will be shot entirely out on the rough locations where these events happened. The cameras will live with the fleeing clansmen amidst the swirling mists and damp heathered mountains and tell, in a vividly personal way, the story of an event that altered forever Scottish history" (Watkins, memo, February 24, 1964, 2). As with Watkins's production style, so too did the idea for a film about the battle of Culloden stem from his amateur roots. Stan and

Phyllis Mercer, two friends from the Playcraft group, had recommended Watkins read the 1961 book *Culloden* by popular Scottish historian John Prebble (Welsh 5), thinking that its subject matter (another uprising brutally crushed, whose losing participants were effectively "disappeared" from history) might make a suitable amateur follow-up to *The Forgotten Faces*. Watkins responded to Prebble's novelistic eye and his subjective empathy for ordinary people, particularly for the Highlanders who had found themselves caught up in the machinations of larger political events not of their own making that had led to their bloody defeat and in turn helped usher in the subsequent Highland Clearances. In its depiction of the brutality of the British army and of how the British state effectively was built upon the blood of the suppression of dissident groups, the book clearly spoke to Watkins, not least in light of his own army experiences. He realized, however, that to restage events from the eighteenth century and to do the subject matter justice would cost far too much for an amateur. It was only with the financial support of the BBC that Watkins was finally able to make the film in the way that he wanted.

Commencing production, one of his first acts was to recruit John Prebble as his historical advisor. Writing to Prebble in July 1964, just prior to beginning shooting that August, Watkins revealed a key facet of his approach to making the film, one that marked a distinct development from the newsreel technique he had pioneered with *The Forgotten Faces*: "Every single foot of the film, be it violent action or someone uttering forth to camera, is going to be filmed with bumpy journalistic grain and realism, exactly as though it *is* happening there and then, and is being recorded by a sort of *World in Action* team" (Watkins, memo, July 10, 1964). *World in Action* was a long-running current affairs program on British television that had started a year earlier, in 1963 (it would run until 1998). Made for the BBC's rival, ITV, then the sole independent commercial channel on British television, *World in Action* was famous for its distinctive hard-hitting, almost tabloid style of journalistic presentation, particularly in its early days under its founding editor, a pugnacious Australian journalist named Tim Hewat. This distinctiveness was not only a function of its investigative journalism but also the style of its presentation. Instead of an onscreen presenter, the series used a voice-over narrator who relayed facts in a punchy news headline style that consisted of short, declarative statements designed to arrest the attention of the viewing audience and complement the often gritty visuals. *World in Action* also was an early pioneer on British television of the direct cinema approach of location filming using 16-mm handheld cameras and of direct synchronized sound recording, the aim being always, as the program's title made clear, to capture a changing "world in action."

As an amateur, Watkins, too, had used voice-over narration in his attempt to emulate the style of the cinema newsreels. For him, this had been a production necessity: the constraints of filmmaking on an amateur budget had prevented the use of location sound recording. Hence a voice-over was important in helping to explain the visuals and to bind the film together. Now, with *Culloden,* Watkins had the resources of BBC TV behind him and location sound recording became a possibility. If *The Forgotten Faces* had deconstructed the style of cinema newsreels through close simulation, *Culloden* aimed to do the same with the reporting styles of television. In Watkins's TV film, it is as if a *World in Action* team is filming the events leading up to and during the Scottish battle, interviewing participants who present their testimony straight to the camera rather than to an onscreen interviewer.

It is a technique that is a little different than the format of the earlier *You Are There* program (CBS, 1953–57) on U.S. television to which *Culloden* might at first appear similar. *You Are There,* an educational series hosted by CBS news anchor Walter Cronkite, was an attempt to bring history to life for 1950s TV audiences through imagining what it would have been like if news reporters had been around to cover famous events of the past. Key events from U.S. and world history were portrayed in dramatic re-creations and reporters appeared onscreen in contemporary suits interviewing historical protagonists, just as if it were a modern TV news report (Auster). With *Culloden,* however, there is no contemporary onscreen interviewer, only a voice-over narrator (voiced by Watkins himself in post-production) who details facts and events in a hard, clipped, declarative style very much in the mode of *World in Action.* Here, though, the camera *is* the reporter and, by extension, the audience becomes the reporter. In *Culloden,* there is a voice (played by Tony Cosgrove) who interviews the various participants on the battlefield, but he is always an unseen presence behind the camera. In that sense, he functions as the audience's representative, asking the kind of questions we, from our present-day vantage point, might like to know the answers to. The characters who are interviewed always give their responses by looking directly into the camera, as if they are looking at us and answering questions we ourselves have asked. In this way, there is much more direct immediacy to Watkins's film than in the *You Are There* format.

The French New Wave director François Truffaut—whose debut film, *Les quatre cents coups* (*The 400 Blows,* 1959), was a big early influence on Watkins (Brownlow)—asserted that when a character turns straight to the camera and looks directly at the audience, an almost instant identification between character and audience is established: "The camera becomes subjective when the actor's gaze meets that of the audience" (Truffaut 161). In

the famous ending of *Les quatre cents coups,* Truffaut had his fictional alter-
ego character, the young boy Antoine Doinel (played by Jean-Pierre Léaud),
look briefly toward the camera. Then, in perhaps the most famous freeze-
frame in film history, the image of Doinel's gaze to the camera ends the
film, encouraging identification on the part of the audience with the boy
and the uncertain future he faces. In *Culloden,* Watkins acknowledges his
debt to the subjective, empathetic cinema of Truffaut when, toward the end
of the battle scene of his own professional film debut, he freezes the image
of the death of Walter Stapleton, the commander of the Irish pickets who
fought with the Jacobites on the field of Culloden. This freeze on Stapleton's
face-slashing by a sword at the end of the battle scene is a forceful way of
summing up the depth of the slaughter that took place on Culloden moor.

The influence of *Les quatre cents coups* on Watkins goes much further
than the use of a freeze-frame, however. In *The Forgotten Faces* the director experimented with actors looking directly to camera. At the end of the
1961 amateur film, as the voice-over narrator dispassionately outlines the
fates of the Hungarian rebels we have just seen fighting and whose rebellion has now been crushed by the arrival of Soviet tanks in Budapest,
Watkins employs a final series of tableau shots of his freedom fighters.
As the voice-over grimly intones each of their fates ("Refugee. Executed.
Deported. Missing. Killed."), each of his amateur actors moves their eyes
from the side and turns their gaze to look directly into the camera. We
have been looking at them, but suddenly they are now looking at us and
the effect is disconcerting. The cold, penetrating gaze of the camera has
been turned back on us, as we become the ones in the spotlight whose
actions and attitudes are being examined and interrogated. These are the
"Forgotten Faces" of Hungary, silenced and disappeared when Soviet tanks
invaded. Their gaze at us becomes a rebuke that the West, for its own politically expedient reasons, turned away from their plight in October 1956 and
allowed Soviet domination to take place unimpeded. Watkins now forces
us to look the Hungarians in the eye. Their gaze becomes a challenge to
us not to forget them and a plea for us to finally come to their aid in their
continuing struggle for freedom.

Breaking the cardinal rule of dramatic filmmaking that actors must
never look into the camera allowed Watkins to give the impression that
a newsreel camera had captured the actual events and that these characters were real people. Bringing this technique to television with *Culloden,*
Watkins consciously deploys a non-Hollywood framing device in order to force
the audience to look into the eyes of his staring Highland clansmen with the
similar aim of confronting the audience with his subjects' gaze. Going against
what is often referred to as the standard "Warner Bros. close-up," in which

the whole head is seen, Watkins frequently crops his close-up shots at the hairline so that only the face fills the screen. As the director has stated of this technique: "Normally the weight of most camera and most television shots is down-loaded. You always see the air over the heads [in Hollywood films] . . . I close the air off over the head to stop the strength of the scene going out. You can see more of the body. The whole thing is very much solid, and you are forced to look at the person—into their eyes" (Quoted in Gomez 23).

This technique provides other opportunities as well: it allows, for example, the subversion of the television convention of who is normally allowed to look directly into the camera lens. Looking directly at the viewing audience through the television camera lens commands an authority that traditionally has been delegated only to the professional broadcaster and, less commonly, the elected politician (for example, in the case of a political broadcast). By convention, interviewed subjects normally have not been allowed to do so, instead having to look to the side at a reporter or presenter who is interviewing them. With *Culloden,* the tables are turned on the professional broadcasters and the participants of the historical "news" events have the chance to put their own testimonies directly to camera. This is particularly important in the case of the disenfranchised and lowly members of the Highland clan system, who were pressed into fighting a conflict they barely understood and whose stories, the film argues, have been effectively marginalized or downgraded in conventional historical accounts. *Culloden* thus becomes an alternative "people's history": made by the people for the people insofar as Watkins, an amateur filmmaker at heart, has used his new-found position within the BBC to bypass the professional mediators through involving members of the public as nonprofessional actors and mounting a kind of community reenactment of events that had affected their ancestors.

This sense of an alternative "people's history" as set against official accounts is dramatized within the film through the inclusion of the historical figure of Andrew Henderson. Henderson was the official historian of the battle and claimed to have witnessed it, watching it from a distance using his telescope. However, he was a historian working for the British government, and in the film he is depicted as observing the battle from a position firmly behind the government lines, peering through his eyeglass over the stone walls at the oncoming charge of the Highlanders prior to turning to the camera to relay to us what he sees, for all the world like a TV reporter providing on-the-spot updates on the progress of a sports match.

Including Henderson in the film allows Watkins to draw attention to the mediation of history, of how historical events are mediated to us and of how history, in that well-known phrase, is always written from the side of the winners. Henderson represents the "official" historical point of view from the winning side, which Watkins's film challenges. Viewing at a distance with his telescope from the government lines, Henderson only sees one point of view, that of the Highlanders as savage "others" charging toward his lines, thus posing a threat and needing to be suppressed. But while Henderson can relay only one perspective, Watkins's camera in the film is constantly shifting around to look at events from other points of view, including that of the "ordinary" Redcoat soldiers who bore the brunt of the actual fighting on the ground at Culloden. Above all, Watkins gives us the perspective of the poor Highland clansmen, whom the film portrays as downtrodden victims of a ruthless feudal system that had forced them, ill-equipped, ill-led, exhausted, and starving, into fighting for a Jacobite cause that could only lead to certain defeat on the battlefield of Culloden, death, and lasting despair. Watkins is asking his audience to identify, for a change, with the point of view of the "enemy": the Highlanders crushed at Culloden who were effectively marginalized and demonized by events and their aftermath so that a unitary nation-state—its power firmly residing in and emanating from London—could be successfully forged across the length and breadth of the British Isles. This is Watkins's challenge with this film: the history of Britain has largely been told from only one side, those who gained by these events, and now he is going to tell it from the side of those who lost deeply as a result of them. What is history ultimately depends upon where you come from and, like Henderson, from which side you are choosing to look. It is an approach Watkins would also develop in his later work, including *La Commune (Paris 1871)* (2000), in which historical events of the 1871 Paris Commune are depicted from the perspective of two rival (and anachronistic) TV channels: TV Nationale, representing the establishment and bourgeoisie, versus TV Communale, which operates much closer to the point of view of the workers, the Communards.

With such an approach to revising and retelling history, casting became particularly crucial. While individuals to play the Redcoat army in *Culloden* came from a variety of sources, including many from amateur theater groups in southeast England with which Watkins had worked in the past, the Highlanders were cast from members of the local community from the Inverness, Ballachulish, and Kinlochleven areas in Scotland (Walker 8). During preproduction for the film in May 1964, Watkins went on reconnaissance to Scotland, holding meetings for interested townspeople and outlining the kind of film he wanted to make. He was particularly looking for individuals with interesting or striking faces who could pass for Highlanders of the period or who might have a special affinity with the events the film was going to depict. According to the director, "In any town or village I made a beeline for the organizers of the local drama or operatic group, and soon the whole thing snowballed. I got half a dozen excellent Highlanders from the aluminum works at Kinlochleven. They had never been in front of a camera before, but they were terrific" (Quoted in Walker). For the key part of Bonnie Prince Charlie, Watkins cast Olivier Espitalier-Noel, an Anglo-French student from Mauritius whom he recruited from a French amateur drama club in London because of his striking resemblance to portraits of the prince ("Driven by Furies"). Prince Charles Edward Stuart is depicted in the film not as the noble prince of romanticized history but that "cowardly Italian," as the narrator describes him, who fled his loyal Highlanders at the end of the battle when he realized they had been defeated.

In all, 142 nonprofessional actors were cast for the production. Filming for *Culloden* took place for three weeks during the summer holiday period of August 1964. This helped facilitate the availability of the actors, particularly the English Redcoat performers who had come up from the south to take part. Looking back on filming, Watkins admitted the pace had been exhausting, "But the rewards are wonderful. I have got some totally unselfconscious performances from town clerks, firemen, makers of bagpipes" (Quoted in Rose, "Faces" 834). Both he and many of his Scottish Highland participants recognized the living connection between past and present, of how the events of Culloden still resonated within the Scottish Highlands: "We had people coming on the moor where we were filming and we would take them away, stain their bodies with iodine, put wigs and bonnets on them and suddenly they took on a roughness . . . they became their ancestors" (Quoted in Rose, "Faces" 835).

This feeling of retelling an important part of their own history to a wider audience generated a fierce loyalty, enthusiasm, and respect toward Watkins among his cast. Coupled with Watkins's skilled direction of non-professionals, this in large part accounts for the quality and the intensity of the performances we see in the film. Tony Rose, an early champion of Watkins during his days as an amateur filmmaker, summed up this aspect well in a 1967 article that looked back on *Culloden:*

> Butchers and bakers and local government officers donned the kilts and bonnets of the '45 and went out on the moors, there to do battle with the chill wind and the driving rain. Peter, no doubt, led them a merry dance and they followed him with just as much loyalty as ever their ancestors had shown to Bonnie Prince Charlie. They were not out to make money or even to make names for themselves; they were simply out to help young Peter Watkins show the world what a hell the battle of Culloden had been for the Scots. And show the world he did. ("Running" 263)

Culloden: Nonprofessional actors playing the Highlanders experienced the difficult environment of the moors.

The wholesale casting of nonprofessionals in key parts incurred the wrath of Equity, the British professional actors' union, which subsequently raised a formal complaint with the BBC, protesting that professionals should have been used for the speaking parts (Turnell 1). Using professionals, however, would have gone against Watkins's purpose of avoiding theatrical modes of dramatic performance. His aim, instead, was to create "an overall framework of film-style . . . a style of using nonprofessionals, quite ordinary people, to capture the inside heart-beat of other people and events, past and present" (Watkins, memo, February 24, 1964, 2). The faces of "ordinary people" stare out at us through the camera and the events of the past are suddenly made to seem vividly present. This form of living history avoids what critic Maurice Richardson, in a contemporary review of the film, labeled the "dim fuzz of unreality" that can sometimes afflict more conventional costume-drama productions. Characters looking out to us through the camera, answering questions to it and generally acknowledging its presence, force us to recognize our relationship to the events of long ago and to realize that the past is not something dead and gone, irrelevant for us today, but instead has a direct effect upon the present. The past in that sense is running alongside our present and is informing it. We cannot easily disentangle ourselves from it because we are in fact its product and its outcome. This is particularly well illustrated by the very end of the film, in which the camera pans in close-up across a line of faces of some of the bedraggled Highlanders following their defeat at Culloden. Watkins's voice-over attempts to draw the ongoing lesson for the present: "Thus within a century from Culloden, the English and the Scottish lowlanders had made secure forever their religion, their commerce, their culture, their ruling dynasty . . . and in so doing, had destroyed a race of people." The film ends on a close-up of the face of the last in the line of Highlanders.

In an echo of the similar technique Watkins had used at the close of *The Forgotten Faces*, the clansman raises his eyes to stare out at us, hauntingly and accusingly, just at the very moment Watkins's voice-over ends with the word "peace" in the following quotation: "They have created a desert and called it peace." The quotation is from the first-century Roman historian Tacitus, who was writing in his *Agricola* an account of his father-in-law, the Roman general Gnaeus Julius Agricola (AD 40–AD 93). Agricola was responsible for much of the conquest and subjugation of Britain in the first century AD, particularly the troublesome lands of Caledonia to the north, in what is now Scotland. In the summer of AD 84, Agricola confronted the massed tribes of the Caledonians at the Battle of Mons Graupius in northeast Scotland and, using battle strategies reminiscent of the tactics later used by the government army at Culloden, routed the native tribes. Many of the defeated Caledonians subsequently had to flee for their lives into "the trackless wilds" (Tacitus 870) of the Scottish Highlands, just as the defeated clansmen had to flee almost seventeen hundred years later after the battle of Culloden. Tacitus attributes the "desert" quotation to Calgacus, who led the Caledonians into battle at Mons Graupius; before the battle, Calgacus is supposed to have rallied his troops with the following condemnation of imperial Rome: "To ravage, to slaughter, to usurp under false titles, they call empire; and where they make a desert they call it peace" (Tacitus 872).

"Peace given to the world" was frequently inscribed on many Roman medals, and Julius Caesar famously described the brutal and bloody conquest of Gaul (France) as a "pacification" (Caesar 195). Watkins's voice commentary in *Culloden* echoes this when, over the depiction of events following the defeat of the Highlanders in battle, as government troops go on the rampage and brutalize the local population in retaliation, the director states: "The Duke of Cumberland mounts what he terms 'the pacification of the Highlands'" (Watkins, Post-Production Script 51). With these references to Imperial Rome, Watkins makes uncomfortable links for the audience between the Roman and British empires, the latter supposedly more "peaceful" and "benign" yet, Watkins is arguing, sharing the same tendency of all imperial powers to conquer and crush any indigenous peoples that threaten its hegemony, including those within its own borders. Britain's elevation of itself into an imperial power, the film argues, was based on the subjugation and genocide of elements of its own populace, such that far from being the heroes of dominant Empire myth, British troops are portrayed here as villainous plunderers, behaving, as Watkins's commentary puts it, quoting an eyewitness to the battle's aftermath, "less like Christian men than so many butchers."

These were radical themes for a BBC documentary production of 1964 premiering on television to a native British audience, much of which had been brought up to believe in the inherent rightness of Britain and its empire. Several reviewers of the initial broadcast picked up on the twentieth-century parallels. For example, Mary Crozier of *The Guardian* commented on the "Congo-like brutality" of the rout of the Highlanders.[1] To the twentieth-century catalogue of imperialist brutality could be added the British crushing of the nationalist Mau Mau rebellion in Kenya in the 1950s (a campaign Watkins narrowly missed serving in) and, perhaps most significantly for the 1960s, the ongoing conflict in Indochina that would escalate throughout the decade to become the Vietnam War. When *Culloden* began to be aired on U.S. public television in the late 1960s (*National Educational Television Playhouse* screened it in May 1967),[2] many U.S. commentators read it as an allegory specifically critical of U.S. policy in Vietnam and its own "pacification" of the Vietnamese Highlands (Welsh 103). It is a parallel that Watkins continues to push on his personal website.

More recently, subsequent generations have drawn parallels between *Culloden* and the situation in Iraq (Jeffries 260). In August 2009, for example, the actress Tilda Swinton and the filmmaker Mark Cousins screened the film at Culloden moor itself as part of a summer mobile roadshow of film screenings around the towns and villages of the Scottish Highlands. However, their aim was not only to commemorate a Scottish battle but to show how relevant both it and Watkins's film depiction still were to the ongoing

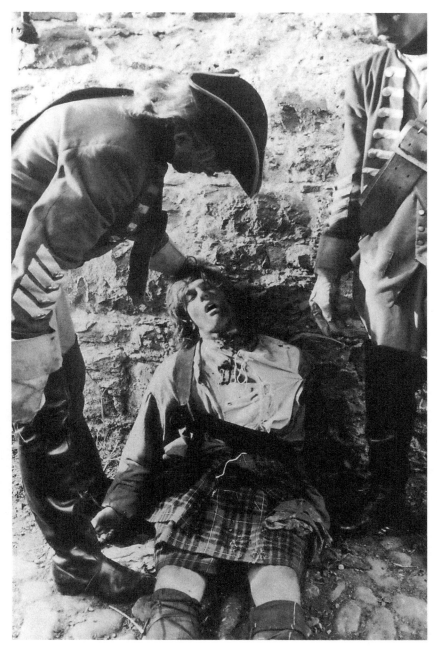

Culloden: The British army engages in the "pacification" of the Highlanders.

problems of the present. Cousins asked filmgoers to dress somberly in tribute to those who fell in this and more recent conflicts. He said:

> We are asking people to dress in tartan or black if they wish because the film is an angry work of art that says to the dead "you have not been forgotten," and to the audience "look how military f***-ups cost lives," and so we want to make a visual statement of respect for those who died. (Horne 2009)

If this is a striking example of the ongoing relevance of *Culloden* to audiences today, it illustrates how much the film continues to make the past seem vividly present for us, largely because it draws upon the techniques of TV reportage in a manner and style we still readily recognize and to which we therefore readily respond. There is, however, a complex dynamic at work. The film's audience is confronted with a distinct representational dilemma: a meticulously researched documentary-style evocation of the 1746 battle that brings a new identificatory realism to the depiction of war. But it is one achieved through the anachronistic device of having a television documentary crew supposedly following and interviewing historical characters on the battlefield almost two hundred years before the invention of television. This textual strategy implicitly raises critical questions about the documentary and current affairs coverage we see on TV and in film generally. If it is possible to achieve the effect of documentary simply through clever handheld camerawork and the use of nonprofessional actors, then what does this tell us about the documentary form itself? Are the greater truth-claims made by documentary, particularly the new verité techniques of the 1960s, as much a function of the style as of the content? Watkins's film, in this way, becomes as much a critique of the media as it is about achieving more "authentic" media representations. Ultimately *Culloden* invites the audience to ask critical questions about the ways in which war and other events are mediated to us today through television and film. Made just as the "fly-on-the-wall" style was coming into vogue, *Culloden* was one of the first films to open up questions about how the apparent truthfulness of documentary may be merely the product of a visual style which the audience has simply come to recognize as true. With *Culloden*, Watkins showed that documentary was a form with an inherent capacity to be faked. In its self-reflexivity, his film was way ahead of its time, anticipating today's more sophisticated understanding of the active role the media play in shaping events, influencing what is recorded as history and, crucially, what is not.

Given this implicit, radical critique of the professional media within which he was working, the immediate critical acclaim *Culloden* earned among contemporary opinion-formers may seem surprising. After viewing a rough cut of the film, Huw Wheldon, Watkins's patron at the BBC, declared it the best first assembly he had ever seen. Word began to spread around the BBC that Watkins had a natural gift "to make films in the same sort of way that Mozart could compose music when he was four" (Ferris 182). A primetime place in the BBC TV schedule was found for the debut of a filmmaker of whom few had heard, and Wheldon himself penned the introduction to the film in the BBC program guide, the *Radio Times*, declaring *Culloden* "a definite moment of originality" in the development of documentary (Wheldon 31). The vast majority of TV reviewers agreed: "A Time-Machine Triumph," declared Maurice Richardson of *The Observer*, while Philip Purser in the *Sunday Telegraph* stated "no reservations at all about the instant stardom of Peter Watkins. This young *auteur* leaps straight from nowhere to the first rank." The film went on to win Watkins a British Screenwriters' Award of Merit the following year and was recognized by the Society of Film and Television Arts at its annual awards ceremony (Welsh 49).

A year later, however, Watkins, the golden boy with *Culloden*, was the reviled outcast with *The War Game* (1965), his follow-up film that ended up being banned by the BBC from TV screens around the world for twenty years on account of its harrowing depiction, using the same verité techniques Watkins had successfully deployed in *Culloden*, of the likely effects of a nuclear bomb falling on Kent, England. This censorship provoked Watkins's resignation from the BBC in protest and created a 1960s cause célèbre that still resonates to this day.[3] Looking back on *Culloden* nearly ten years later, at a point when, having quit Britain angrily for self-imposed "exile" overseas, he was now in a long-term struggle to find financing for his films, Watkins pointed to a possible reason why this particular production should have been so successful compared to the others that were to follow within his highly radical oeuvre. *Culloden*, he asserted:

> can be responded to on the level of armchair, white liberal discomfort at a historical event. It was not intended to be taken on this level, but I know that a lot of people accept it this way; that, I think, is the reason for its popularity. People can say, *Culloden*, oh yes, that's a fantastic film, look what they did in those times, isn't war bad! But although the film does affect us all—and I think all of us can see ourselves in the faces of those people at that time—I think there is a mental loophole so that you can say that you don't. It just sits at that edge of the definition where a white, middle-class liberal—and in fact a broader area even than that—can sort of indulge in the cathartic exercise of

looking at something, getting a kick out of it, washing his guilt
off, and then getting on with the dishes afterwards. (Gomez 35)

This was why thirty-five years after *Culloden,* when Watkins came to
make *La Commune (Paris 1871),* his first professionally funded film since
1976, he had learned the lessons from his past.[4] *La Commune* was another major historical reconstruction of a failed popular uprising that was
brutally crushed: in this case the 1871 Paris Commune, when citizens of
Paris rebelled against the Versailles government in the aftermath of the
Franco-Prussian War, only to be slaughtered en masse by government
troops over the course of a week in May 1871 that came to be known as *La
semaine sanglante* ("Bloody Week"). His most recent major production to
date, *La Commune* neatly bookends Watkins's professional career because,
as with his debut *Culloden,* it involved the participation of the community
in telling a hitherto repressed part of their history. In this case, over two
hundred Parisian citizens from all walks of life came together to reenact the story of the Paris Commune for an intensive shoot over three hot
weeks in July 1999, recalling the earlier short summer shoot for *Culloden.*
Watkins screened *Culloden* to his French cast in advance of filming as an
indication of the kind of "non-Hollywood" effects he was attempting to
achieve with this new film. During shooting (at which I was present for
research purposes at the invitation of Watkins), I watched *Culloden* past
become *La Commune* present as Watkins's nonprofessional actors donned
their costumes and "became" the French Communards, just as in 1964
his Inverness citizens had "become" their Highland ancestors. There was
one important difference, however. Employing his characteristic newsreel
technique, in which historical characters spoke to TV news crew interviewers, Watkins this time encouraged his French cast to step out of character
and to respond to the camera from their present-day vantage point on the
historical events they were reconstructing. He asked them to speculate on
whether they would go "on the barricades" today like their Parisian ancestors, and he invited them to discuss the role they felt that the media—TV,
radio, and the Internet—played in the political situation of their present.
Watkins was back, and this time he was determined no one was going to
take this film simply on the level of "armchair, white liberal discomfort" at
a bygone historical event.

Notes

1. This Belgian colony had seen effective genocide of its indigenous African
population in the early twentieth century.

2. National Educational Television was a forerunner in the United States of PBS (Public Broadcasting Service).

3. See, for example, Shaw. In a supreme irony, *The War Game* would go on to win an Academy Award for Best Documentary in 1967.

4. In the intervening ten years since the production of *La Commune* and its critical success, many of Watkins's films, once very difficult to find, have now been successfully rereleased on DVD. Both *Culloden* and *La Commune,* together with a range of his other films, are available on Region 1 DVD as part of *The Cinema of Peter Watkins* collection (Project X/New Yorker Films). Though Watkins has made no other major film since *La Commune,* he continues to campaign for change in the contemporary media. He has an extensive personal website *(http://pwatkins.mnsi. net)* that contains copies of his most recent statements on the media, as well as updated information on the availability of his films across different parts of the world.

Works Cited

Auster, Albert. "Walter Cronkite." Museum of Broadcast Communications, *http://www.museum.tv/eotvsection.php?entrycode=cronkitewal.*

Brownlow, K. Interview by the author. April 13, 2002, London.

Caesar, Julius. *The Gallic War.* Trans. Carolyn Hammond. New York: Oxford University Press, 1998.

Crozier, Mary. *"Culloden* on BBC-1." *The Guardian,* December 16, 1964, 18.

"Driven by Furies." *The Observer,* January 24, 1965, 24.

Ferris, Paul. *Sir Huge: The Life of Huw Wheldon.* London: Penguin, 1990.

Gomez, Joseph. *Peter Watkins.* Boston: Twayne, 1979.

Grierson, John. *Grierson on Documentary.* Ed. Forsyth Hardy. London: Faber and Faber, 1979.

Horne, Marc. "Tilda Brings *Culloden* Classic Home." *The Scotsman,* July 26, 2009, http://news.scotsman.com/scotland/Tilda-brings-Culloden-classic-home.549 4236.jp.

Izod, John, and Richard Kilborn. "The Documentary Film." In *The Oxford Guide to Film Studies,* ed. John Hill and Pamela Church Gibson, 426–32. New York: Oxford University Press, 1998.

Jeffries, Stuart. *Mrs Slocombe's Pussy: Growing Up in Front of the Telly.* London: Flamingo, 2000.

Purser, Philip. *"Culloden* Reconstructed." *Sunday Telegraph,* December 20, 1964, 18.

Richardson, Maurice. "A Time-Machine Triumph." *The Observer,* Weekend Review, December 20, 1964, 15.

Rose, Tony. "Faces of the '45." *Amateur Ciné World* (December 1964): 834–37, 839.

———. "Running, Jumping, and Never Standing Still." *Movie Maker* (June 1967): 260–63.

Sexton, Jamie. "'Televérité Hits Britain': Documentary, Drama, and the Growth of 16mm Filmmaking in British Television." *Screen* 24, no. 4 (2003): 429–44.

Shaw, Tony. "The BBC, the State and Cold War Culture: The Case of Television's *The War Game* (1965)." *English Historical Review* 121, no. 494 (2006): 1351–84.

Shulman, Milton. *Marilyn, Hitler and Me*. London: André Deutsch, 1998.

Sydney-Smith, Susan. *Beyond Dixon of Dock Green: Early British Police Series*. London: I. B. Tauris, 2002.

Tacitus Cornelius. *The Works of Tacitus: The Oxford Translation*. Vol. 2. New York: Oxford University Press, 2008.

Truffaut, François. *The Early Film Criticism of François Truffaut*. Ed. Wheeler Winston Dixon. Bloomington: Indiana University Press, 1993.

Turnell, George M. Note of a Meeting with Equity at Broadcasting House on July 19, 1965. July 30, 1-2, BBC WAC, T32/515/17.

Walker, Frank. "Slaughter of the Clans, and How the Locals Did It." *Daily Mail*, December 18, 1964, 8.

Watkins, Peter. *Culloden* Post-Production Script. BBC WAC, Project no.: 51/1/4/2307, 1964.

———. Interview by the author. July 10, 2001, Vilnius, Lithuania.

———. Memo to Huw Wheldon, February 24, 1964, 1–4, BBC WAC, T32/515/1.

———. Memo to Huw Wheldon, March 17, 1964, 1–3, BBC WAC, T32/515/4.

———. Memo to John Prebble, July 10, 1964, BBC WAC, T32/515/8.

———. "Peter Watkins: Filmmaker/Media Critic." http://pwatkins.mnsi.net, 2009.

Welsh, James. *Peter Watkins: A Guide to References and Resources*. Boston: G. K. Hall, 1986.

Wheldon, Huw. "*Culloden*." *Radio Times*, December 10, 1964, 31.

Chapter 14

"Don't You Ever Just Watch?"

American Cinema Verité and *Dont Look Back*

Jeanne Hall

Introduction

In the early 1960s, members of the Drew Associates recorded the exploits of American politicians, diplomats, musicians, and movie stars in "crisis moments," treating them all "equally" (if not "objectively") as celebrities, and finally subordinating them to the *real* star—a documentary movement known as cinema verité.[1] *Dont Look Back* (1967), directed by D. A. Pennebaker and co-produced by Richard Leacock, both Drew Associates expatriates, is an important part of that body of works. *Dont Look Back* chronicles Bob Dylan's triumphant 1965 tour of England on the heels of his third album, *The Times They Are A-Changin'* (1964). It captures, as Janet Maslin writes, a moment "of perfect energy, perfect efficiency, a man using all his resources to come brilliantly alive and work at the edge of his power"; Dylan "was at his most despotic then, a gaunt silhouette with stovepipe legs and a fabulous corona of unkempt hair" ("Dylan" 224). And the film, as John L. Wasserman puts it, "is pure cinema verité. Pennebaker lugs his 16-mm camera into any available cubbyhole, lurks still until he blends into the background, waits for a moment of verité, then rolls" (10).

Dont Look Back follows in the tradition of Robert Drew's *Primary* (1960), a documentary heralded as "a revolutionary step and a breaking point in the recording of reality in cinema" ("Third Independent") and widely regarded as "a landmark film in the aesthetic development of cinema verité"

(Allen and Gomery 224). *Primary* is generally considered to be the work that first captured John Kennedy's impact and charisma on film, marking a cultural shift in the United States to a political system dominated by media influence. The stylistic elements of the film—the restless, wandering movements of lightweight, handheld cameras; the blurred, grainy images of fast, monochrome film; the preference for (even unintelligible) synchronous sound over authoritative voice-over narration; and the impromptu performances of apparently preoccupied social actors—epitomize early American cinema verité.

Primary won the *Film Culture* award for best independent film, the Flaherty award for best documentary, and a blue ribbon at the American Film Festival. In Europe, according to Drew, "*Primary* was received as a kind of documentary second-coming" (396). And in the decade that followed, cinema verité emerged "as a full-fledged avant-garde aesthetic movement: not only a body of works with common stylistic characteristics, but also, as David Bordwell puts it, 'polemics, theories, and activities which constitute both internally coherent positions and explicit challenges to already existing styles'" (Allen and Gomery 217).

Dont Look Back treated Dylan much as *Primary* treated Kennedy, and in this sense contributed to the conventionalization of many of the innovations of early American cinema verité. In *Dont Look Back,* for example, Pennebaker tracks Dylan just as Al Maysles tracked Kennedy from the street onto the stage in *Primary:* the camera follows the singer as he strolls out of the shadows and onto the stage, into a burst of light and an avalanche of sound. At least one review of the film suggests that this device remained fresh in 1967: "Rather than show Dylan in the dressing room, then on stage, Pennebaker starts in the dressing room, joggles through a doorway, weaves down a dark passageway and *then* arrives on stage" (Wasserman). But such shots would become de rigueur in the years to come and, indeed, would be parodied in Rob Reiner's "rockumentary" *This Is Spinal Tap* (1984), in which the camera follows members of a heavy metal band as they make their winding journey through the corridors of an auditorium only to end up in the boiler room. And they would remain fodder for tongue-in-cheek imitation in "mockumentaries" such as *Bob Roberts* (1990), in which a handheld camera trails a singer/politician through the interior of a theater.

Actually, as Robert Sklar notes, *Bob Roberts* links itself with early American cinema verité in other, more significant ways. Most notably, it "foreground[s] the role of the journalist, the investigator—the 'media' more generally—in contemporary politics" (78). In this essay, I want to examine how *Dont Look Back,* like other early cinema verité films, mounts a critique of the dominant media informed by a liberal view of the role of the press in contemporary democracy. One of the primary philosophical underpinnings of cinema verité is American liberalism (Allen and Gomery 233), and central to modern American liberalism is the belief in an "enquiring and critical press":

> The press is viewed as a sort of social watchdog, calling to the attention of citizens and their government tears and holes in the social fabric that required mending. . . . The very style of cinema verité documentary made it the perfect form for an "enquiring and critical press." Its technology (mobile and versatile cameras and synchronous-sound recorders) not only enabled the filmmaker to capture on film social problems hidden from public view, but it also allowed the subjects of the films to speak for themselves. The refusal of the filmmaker to inject himself or herself into the subject matter of the film heightened the perceived truthfulness of the images captured on film. . . . The implicit assumption here is that if right-thinking people become aware of the way things "really are," they will take steps to correct injustices and inequities. The advocacy of a specific program of change is not the filmmaker's task; it is enough to reveal the "truth" of a social situation to the viewer. (Allen and Gomery 234)

Pennebaker's philosophy of filmmaking, much like Drew's and Leacock's, can be seen to grow out of a liberal concern for the proper role of the press in democratic societies. "It's possible to go to a situation and simply film what you see there, what happens there, what goes on, and let everybody decide whether it tells them about any of these things," he has said. "But you don't have to label them, you don't have to have the narration to instruct you so you can be sure and understand that it's good for you to learn. You don't need any of that shit" (325). Pennebaker thus finds the perfect cinema verité subject in Bob Dylan, who is quite willing and able to "speak for himself"—and by extension, as I will argue, for the filmmaker as well.

DON'T LOOK BACK

I know more about what you do—and you don't even have to ask me how or why or anything—just by looking, than you'll ever know about me. Ever.

Bob Dylan

The above quotation is excerpted from a lengthy diatribe spewed at a reporter for *Time* magazine by a twenty-four-year-old Bob Dylan very near
the end of the film. To describe Dylan's attack on this particular reviewer as
devastating is indeed an understatement; it culminates in the poet challenging the journalist to take his job and his very existence seriously, knowing
that he will someday disappear from the face of the earth, "and it could be
tomorrow." The sheer savagery of the attack remains shocking today; one is
torn between a sometimes grudging admiration for Dylan's canny insights
about the press and the eloquence and arrogance with which he articulates
them and an instinctive pity for the hapless representative of the Fourth
Estate who serves as his straw man. Certainly, the scene illustrates what
Janet Maslin has described as Dylan's "ability to magnify any squabble into
a struggle of heroic proportions, an ability that attested to both his genius
as a poseur and his enormous reserves of free-floating fury" ("Dylan" 223).

But its very inclusion in the film and privileged placement so near the
end surely serve other functions as well. The scene is, in fact (merely), the
most explicit and sustained example of a recurrent motif that forms the dominant structural pattern of the film: a systematic critique of traditional newsgathering and reporting practices. And it serves as least as much to "reveal"
or "reflect" Dylan's own affectations and attitudes toward the popular press
as it does to validate and celebrate Pennebaker's "alternative" documentary
aesthetic. The notion that we might have greater access to the truth "just by
looking"—or, as Dylan asks another reporter, "Don't you ever just be quiet?
Keep silent? Just watch?"—was central to that aesthetic.

I have argued elsewhere that part of the project of early American
cinema verité films like *Primary* was to celebrate this new "observational"
form of documentary as a unique source of heretofore privileged information, and that the perceived realism of the style depended in part upon
its implicit investigation and covert criticism of more conventional documentary forms—still photography, television news, radio interviews and
newspaper reports (Hall). The unproductive interviews and forced photo
sessions scattered throughout many early Drew films (for example, *Primary; On the Pole,* 1960; and *Crisis: Behind a Presidential Commitment,* 1961)
become the raison d'être of *Dont Look Back;* Pennebaker's camera looks on
with bemusement as Dylan savages reporters and Joan Baez, "apparently
along for the ride" (Wasserman), mugs for photographers.

It is worth noting that Pennebaker himself does not privilege such a
reading of *Dont Look Back,* nor would it be in his interest to do so. As
a cinema verité filmmaker, Pennebaker cannot advertise, explicate, or
even admit to having any "hidden agenda." Critical debates surrounding
the film are thus cast in the rhetoric of the cinema verité movement, and

"the issue" becomes whether or not and to what extent Pennebaker captures, "just by watching," some essence of Dylan "the man" on film. And here Pennebaker is characteristically and sometimes maddeningly equivocal, echoing his elusive subject with contradictions, answering questions with questions.

On the one hand, he alludes to the theatricality of his subject's performance and to the constructed nature of the filmmaker's craft. For example, he describes Dylan as "a guy acting out his life" and notes with delight that someone in fact performed part of *Dont Look Back* onstage. "He learned all the lines and just did it as a play. Does it matter?" (241). He stresses the artifice of the filmmaker's craft: "The trouble with documentary is it really requires a lot of artfulness, and most people making documentaries, for one reason or another, feel embarrassed at being artful" (243). On the other hand, he insists that "You couldn't fake it in a hundred years" and stresses "It's Dylan that breaks through, not me. . . . I haven't brought any great truth about Dylan to the stage, I just haven't done it—Dylan does that. So if there's any artistry in what I do, it is deciding who to turn this fearsome machinery on" (261).

If it is not in Pennebaker's interest to expose his film as an argument, neither is it in the interest of popular press reviewers to interpret the film as an indictment of their very enterprise. Hence most reviewers stressed a "contradiction" between Dylan's onstage and offstage personae as the central conceit of the film. For example:

> Because Dylan is kept constantly under the camera's surveillance, certain salient features of his personality emerge clearly—a taut, in-drawn quality even when he is among friends, his tension as he prepares for a performance, a pseudo-intellectual arrogance (as in his interview with a hapless *Time* reporter), and a subcutaneous hostility toward friend and fan alike. All this in fascinating contradiction to his onstage personality, in which he gives every appearance of trying desperately to connect with his audience. ("I want to be with yeew!" he beseeches in one of his songs.) (Knight)

This interpretation has endured for thirty years and, indeed, has attained the status of "received wisdom" about the film: a recent entry on the World Wide Web echoes original reviews in reporting that *Dont Look Back* covers "[Dylan's] touring in London and demonstrating that he can be even nastier to dumb fans and dull reporters than anyone would have imagined. At the same time he's performing extraordinarily sensitive and literary acoustic

material on stage. Director Pennebaker emphasizes this contradiction, allowing it to become the center of the film" (Asher).

But I would argue that this "contradiction" is more a product of the
imaginations of reporters and reviewers—influenced, undoubtedly, by interviews with Pennebaker specifically and the rhetoric of the cinema verité
movement in general—than an accurate description of the Dylan constructed by the film itself. In fact, in *Dont Look Back* Dylan is neither "hostile" nor "nasty" to fans whether onstage or off. Indeed, he is consistently
patient and polite to them—even in situations where one might well grant
him the right to be testy.

For example, he signs autographs for a group of giggling schoolgirls,
and responds to their echoes of popular press critiques of his move to electric guitar with a smiling "But you know better, right?" He talks shop with
a band of admiring young boys, and reacts to the news that they do "twenty
or thirty of [his] numbers," giving them all "a big band sound," with a quiet
"Thank you." Even the "High Sheriff's Lady" (!) who invades Dylan's suite
with her three teenage sons like the Welcome Wagon, extolling the virtues
of the city and inviting Dylan and his friends to pay a visit to "the man-
sion house," is treated with respect and given a souvenir harmonica. (This
scene, "in which Dylan seems to have fallen into a polite coma" [Gilliatt
116], is one of several scenes in the film specifically parodied in *Bob Roberts*.)
Moreover, the "sweet onstage and sour offstage" equation drawn by so
many reviewers of *Dont Look Back* is rendered patently false when one
listens to the music Dylan performs on this tour. *The Times They Are A-
Changin'* has been seen as Dylan's "most fervent and emphatic" album,
and "With God on Our Side" and "The Lonesome Death of Hattie Carroll"
among his "most outraged songs about pacifism and racism, respectively"
(Maslin, "Dylan" 223).

Dylan is, on the other hand, consistently condescending to and contemptuous of reporters, perhaps most notably those who underestimate
the intelligence, integrity, or loyalty of his fans. Popular press reviewers
reported this in a rather cheerful "he doesn't mean us" fashion. But they
attribute the critique solely to Dylan as the film's subject rather than to its
maker, Pennebaker, or to the film itself. The *New York Times,* for example,
noted that "Mr. Dylan parries and thrusts with interviewers (some of them
impossibly square, of course, and therefore perfect targets for the put-on);
he doggedly and sullenly resists attempts to probe his psyche" (Henahan).
And *Variety* reported that "There is Dylan, faintly hostile, 'putting on' the
press. In one scene destined to become a classic, he tells a *Time* magazine
reporter exactly where *Time* and its readership are at" (Rick).

I have found only one review that recognizes a critique of the press as a central conceit and organizing principle of the film, rather than merely a portrait of Dylan's own hostile attitudes and opinions: "*Dont Look Back* is really about fame and how it menaces art, about the press and how it categorizes, bowdlerizes, sterilizes, universalizes, or conventionalizes an original like Dylan into something it can dimly understand" (Morgenstern). (And it is perhaps no accident that this report comes from *Newsweek,* which can more comfortably celebrate the critique since its rival, *Time,* bears the brunt of the singer's most vicious attack.)

It is striking just how much of *Dont Look Back* is in fact comprised of Dylan's dealings with the news media. The opening performance (and a brief transitional scene in which Dylan and his entourage arrive at Heathrow) is followed by a press conference, which *Newsweek's* Joseph Morgenstern captures in spirit (if not to the letter):

> "What is your attitude toward life?" asks an idiot reporter, leering into the camera at an inane press conference. "Are you angry?" asks another, making him angry. "Do you love people?" burbles a third. "Well," mumbles the evasive sage, the cornered philosopher . . . trying to save a shard of self-respect and doing a bum job of it, "well . . . it all depends on how you define terms like Love and People." Nervous Laughter. Baffled titters. If he sings so well, why ain't he Socrates?

The press conference is followed by a photo shoot during which a photographer snaps a photo of Joan Baez and, upon learning who she is, exclaims, "Truth? I didn't recognize you, I'm sorry. I've been looking for you all day!" He instructs her to "Put your hands up to your face," and she responds, "I can't pose," and makes faces. "No, you don't have to pose—but just do it." In both the press conference and the photo shoot, *Dont Look Back* exposes and delights in the constructed nature of popular press images and words—and, crucially, effaces its own. A close analysis of *Dont Look Back* reveals a number of specific, often more subtle strategies the film employs to mount its critique of the media. Here I would like to outline and illustrate four of these strategies.

1. Let Dylan Do It Directly

This is the most "convenient" device for Pennebaker, since the cinema verité filmmaker purports not to interview, argue, or editorialize but simply to look and to listen, himself silent and invisible. And, as Dylan's vitriolic encounter with the *Time* reporter suggests, he is only too willing and able to do so. The exchange (if one can call it that, since the interjections of the reporter are barely audible, attesting to the subjective nature of cinema verité sound recording) is worth excerpting here at some length:

> Are you gonna see the concert tonight? You gonna hear it? Ok. You're gonna hear it and see it. And it's gonna happen fast, and you're not gonna get it all. And you might even hear the wrong words, you know. And then afterwards—I won't be able to talk to you afterwards. I've got nothing to say about these things I write, I just write them. I'm not going to say anything about them. I don't write them for any reason. There's no great message.
>
> If you want to tell other people that, go ahead. But I'm not going to have to answer to it. And they're just going to think, "What's this *Time* magazine telling us?" But you couldn't care less about that either. You don't know the people that read you. Because I've never been in *Time* magazine, and yet this hall's filled twice. And I've never been in *Time* magazine. I don't need *Time* magazine.
>
> And I don't think I'm a folk singer. You'll probably call me a folk singer, but you know, the other people will know better. Because the people that buy my records, listen to me, they don't necessarily read *Time* magazine. The audience that subscribes to *Time* magazine, the people that want to know what's happening in the world week by week. The people that work during the day and can read it small, right, and it's concise. And there's pictures in it. I mean, it's a certain class of people that take the magazine seriously. I mean, sure, I could read it. I read it on the airplanes. But I don't take it seriously. If I want to find out anything, I'm not going to read *Time* magazine, I'm not going to read *Newsweek*. I'm not going to read any of these magazines. I mean, because they've just got too much to lose by printing the truth. You know that.

REPORTER: What kind of truth?

> On anything, even on a worldwide basis. They'd just blow off the stands in a day if they printed really the truth.

REPORTER: What's really the truth?

> Really the truth is just a plain picture. A plain picture of, let's say, a tramp vomiting in the sewer. You know, and next door to the picture Mr. Rockefeller or Mr. C. W. Jones on the subway going to work. You know, any kind of picture. Just make a collage of pictures. Which they don't

do. They don't do that. There's no ideas in *Time* magazine, there's just these facts.

Even this article you're doing—don't you see? It can't be a good article. Because the guy that's writing the article is just sitting at a desk in New York City. He's not ever going out of his office. He's gonna get these fifteen reporters and they're gonna send him a quota. And he's gonna put himself on, he's gonna put all his readers on, and in another week we'll have some space in the magazine. But that's all. It means nothing to anybody else. I'm not putting that down, because people gotta eat and live, you know, but let's at least be honest about it.

I know more about what you do, and you don't have to ask me how or why or anything, just by looking, than you'll ever know about me. Ever.

The scene is striking for several reasons, most obviously, perhaps, because of its sheer length: a full seven minutes in a ninety-minute film compiled from twenty hours of footage shot over a period of several days and weeks. It should not be surprising, then, that most popular press reviews of the film mentioned it specifically—or, perhaps, that the only one that actually complains about it is *Life:*

> In several long interviews which Pennebaker filmed, Dylan is both elusive and cruel. "What do you mean, 'care'?" he barks. "What do you mean, 'people'? Can't you ever stop wondering 'why'?" The seeker squirms. The obeisant entourage smiles. Dylan's reasoning is enlightening; his method of expressing it too often is ruthless and arrogant.
>
> Questions are answered with questions. His thin, bony, tight-skinned face is unsmiling or mocking. "I don't believe in anything," he says, and then, "I am not a cynic." And, "I have nothing to say about the things I write, I just write them." Which is all very well. But nobody asks the obvious question: "Why did you grant the interview?" (Wasserman)

Another pointed question is why Pennebaker included it. For one thing, Dylan's critique of the press is remarkably sophisticated (as *Variety* puts it, "if his outburst lacks tact, it seems to the point" [Rick]). Indeed, it corresponds quite closely to what Denis McQuail years later would identify as three fundamental levels of media analysis: individual, organizational, and institutional.

The *individual* level of analysis focuses on the human agent who carries out media work and is subject to certain requirements of the organization but also has some freedom to define his or her place within it (McQuail 189). On this level, Dylan questions the motivations of the reporter, suggesting that he neither cares about his readership nor understands his subject. He also notes the potential for human error or ineptitude in newsgathering ("you might hear the wrong words," and later, "you have to weed it out—I can't teach you to weed it out"). Finally, though, he acknowledges the subordinate position of media workers in the corporate system ("I'm not putting that down, because people gotta eat and live").

This leads him to the *organizational* level of analysis, which focuses on specific news organizations (especially newspapers but also multipurpose media corporations such as Time-Life). Here Dylan refers to *Time* magazine specifically, to its well-known mode of production characterized by a strict division of labor (reporters send a "quota" of words to an editor in New York City), as well as the simplified format of the finished product ("it's concise" and "there's pictures in it"). He alludes to the magazine's pretense to objectivity ("there's no ideas in *Time* magazine, there's just these facts"). Finally, he denigrates *Time's* particular readership as "a certain class of people that take the magazine seriously."

Although reviewers for many publications took delight in the attack on *Time,* it's clear that Dylan is ultimately working at an *institutional* level of analysis, one that implicates and indicts the media in general. This level of analysis concerns itself with news organizations in relation to society as a whole—the unwritten social and cultural guidelines they follow and implicit ideological assumptions they make. And although the *Time* reporter undoubtedly felt less personally vulnerable at this level, it is here that Dylan makes his most devastating blow: "They've just got too much to lose by printing the truth."

Of course, Dylan's notion of the truth as "just a plain picture" is deceptively simple—note, for example, that he further suggests juxtaposing one picture with another, much as filmmakers—including, of course, the practitioners of cinema verité—edit strips of film together to "make meaning." But his critique of the mainstream press in this scene, as well as in several others ("You just read those interviews the first few days I was here? Lies, all lies and rubbish, you know that") surely serves Pennebaker's overall purpose in *Dont Look Back* very well.

2. Let Dylan Do It Indirectly

This device involves Dylan and/or members of his inner circle reading newspaper stories and responding to them with laughter, anger, or simple disbelief. In one scene, for example, Dylan reads aloud: " 'Puffing heavily on a cigarette—he smokes eighty a day,'" then exclaims, "I'm glad I'm not me!" In another, a companion quotes, "'Bob Dylan sat scowling,'" and grins with delight at the description. (And here, the viewer is reminded of an earlier scene in which Dylan responds to the question "Are you angry?" with a glib "I'm not angry. I'm a delightful sort of person.")

This is perhaps the weakest of the four strategies in terms of critiquing the popular press and staking cinema verité's claim to privileged access to the Truth, since it essentially involves Dylan's word against theirs—and he sometimes comes across as more self-absorbed than self-aware. So the digs are made, but viewers may not necessarily be convinced of their validity. We rarely see him not smoking a cigarette, after all, and his demeanor is often decidedly less than delightful.

3. Show the Opposite of What Dylan Says (and/or What the Press Reports about Him)

This device is more compelling because it offers "visible evidence" of Dylan not telling the truth or the press not telling it like it is. For example, in one scene Dylan tells a reporter that he doesn't compose music or write lyrics while he is on the road. "This is the part where I don't write. Anything that happens now, I'll just remember." Later, however, Pennebaker includes extended scenes of the bard tapping away at a typewriter in his hotel room while Joan Baez sings in the background. This is not "proof positive" that Dylan has misled the reporter—he could, after all, be writing letters or answering fan mail—but the scene at least informs us that he uses a typewriter on tour, suggesting that the interviewer who trusts what Drew would call "word logic" might get it wrong, while Pennebaker, relying on "picture logic," gets it right.

Another example of this strategy concerns a running joke in *Dont Look Back:* Dylan and his friends making fun of rival pop star Donovan. In one scene, Dylan refers to Donovan as "a loser"; in another, he rebuts Donovan's decidedly saccharine performance of "I'll Sing a Song for You" with a biting rendition of "It's All Over Now, Baby Blue." Popular press reviewers once again cast this device in terms of the alleged "tension" at the center of the film—whether Pennebaker "captures" the real Dylan or only reflects his posturing: in terms of his treatment of Donovan, the question is "Is it petty jealousy or artistic criticism?" (Knight). But this running joke becomes part of the film's overarching critique of the press when Dylan derides the tabloid headline "Dylan Digs Donovan." The conflict, finally, is between the Dylan *Dont Look Back* represents and the one represented in the mainstream press.

Dont Look Back: Bob Dylan's demeanor is often less than delightful.

4. Abort (or Omit) Potentially Productive Interviews

The best example of this strategy is Dylan's radio interview with a reporter from the African Service of the BBC. The scene is interesting in large part because of, rather than despite, its brevity. It is one of very few interview scenes in the film in which Dylan is not openly condescending to or contemptuous of a reporter. And it becomes even more significant in light of the hostile, confrontational meetings that come later. Perhaps because the interviewer is black; perhaps because he tells Dylan that they share an old acquaintance; perhaps because his questions are actually more thoughtful than most (the singer is not asked to impart his "real message" or to explain his "whole attitude toward life" but rather to say a few words about how he got started and to comment on the extent to which his "deeply humanitarian [i.e., antiracist] attitudes" have presented problems for him in the United States); or perhaps Dylan was simply not in the mood for a fight— whatever the reason, he sits quietly and nods agreeably as the interviewer previews four questions "for your approval before we ask them."

Then, on tape, the interview begins: "How did it all begin for you, Bob? How did you get started?" "Um . . . ," Dylan begins to reply. Just then

Dont Look Back: The intercut footage of the young Dylan.

something striking occurs. Pennebaker abruptly cuts to a snippet of footage of (an even younger) Dylan singing and playing his acoustic guitar for a group of black men, apparently farm workers, in a rural setting. Here the film implicitly suggests, as Dylan later explicitly declares to the *Time* reporter, that the interview "can't be any good."

Pennebaker seems to be referring to this scene when he remarks that *Dont Look Back* is "not a documentary at all by my standards. It throws away almost all its information and becomes purposely kind of abstract and tries to be musical rather than informational" (243). Pennebaker thus explains what his intent may have been, but the effect of the aborted interview in the film is to suggest that a bit of cinema verité film footage of Dylan's "beginnings" is ultimately more truthful, more revealing, than hearing him talk about them. One is reminded here of Janet Maslin's pithy observation that Dylan's own accounts of his roots are not necessarily reliable: "He was apparently not, as he would later claim, the descendant of a Sioux Indian, or a runaway, or a hobo, or a carnival roustabout, or Bobby Vee. He was a babyfaced boy whose parents didn't like him to stay up late and who, when he began making trips to Minneapolis to meet the black musicians there, would sometimes borrow the family car for the occasion" ("Dylan" 219).

Pennebaker's abrupt interruption of what might actually have been a productive (i.e., informative) interview is telling and perfectly in keeping with *Dont Look Back*'s systematic critique of the value of conventional reporting methods. This strategy is perhaps the most remarkable and unusual of the four, precisely because it flaunts itself most flagrantly and self-consciously as a directorial/editorial choice. So why, one might ask, is the pre-interview scene included at all? I would suggest that it functions in part to show the "falseness" or constructed nature of the very endeavor, in which the subject is informed in advance of the questions he will be asked, suggesting the opportunity to censor ("for your approval") and to prepare, however quickly, a reply. (In this sense, the scene is reminiscent of one in *Primary* in which a quote from John Kennedy is apparently subject to both verification and censorship by the candidate before finding its way into print; cf. Hall 43.)

Finally, all four of these strategies function to mount *Dont Look Back*'s systematic critique of the documentary strategies of the mainstream media and to validate Pennebaker's alternative, cinema verité approach. And the deceptive simplicity of Dylan's notion of the truth as "just a plain picture" is mirrored in Pennebaker's quiet reserve, "the born filmmaker's quality of attentiveness, and the repose that allows things to occur before the camera as they can in life" (Gilliatt 116).

CONCLUSION

In the final scene of *Dont Look Back,* Pennebaker takes his last, quiet dig at the media. As "the vanishing American" escapes from his last performance, he presses his face up to the limousine window, pounds on it with his palm, and waves to ecstatic fans (again, in stark contrast to descriptions of him as indifferent or hostile to them). "God! I feel like I've been through some kind of thing!" he exclaims. "You have," a member of his omnipresent entourage replies. "No, but I mean there's something special about it," Dylan insists, acknowledging, strikingly, his emotions as well as his momentary inability to articulate them.

It is one of those almost embarrassingly intimate moments, a hallmark of cinema verité, in which a subject seems to be caught with his defenses down. But as Pennebaker undoubtedly knew all too well, such moments take on their significance, their status as Truth, only in juxtaposition with and in contrast to other, more obviously guarded ones. "They've started calling you an anarchist," his manager Albert Grossman announces abruptly, dispelling the magic of the moment and giving Dylan an opportunity to regain his cynical cool. "Just because you don't offer any solutions." "You're kidding!" Dylan responds in disbelief. "An anarchist. Gimme a cigarette." And, almost immediately, the posturing begins again: "Give the 'anarchist' a cigarette. A singer such as I. It probably took them a while to think of that name."

On one level, the scene punctuates a recurrent motif in the film: the media's propensity to label (Dylan is a folk singer, a pop singer, a communist, an anarchist). Dylan's aversion to such tactics is shared by Pennebaker, who repeatedly claims he doesn't make documentary films and refers to his works variously as "records of moments," "half soap operas," and "semimusical reality things" (234, 239–240). But on another, more profound level, the scene serves to underscore both the singer's and the filmmaker's political underpinnings, which are decidedly less anarchistic than liberal. "By exposing social problems without explicitly commenting upon them, verité documentaries leave solutions to problems outside the film," writes Allen. "The advocacy of a specific program of change is not the filmmaker's task; he or she merely reveals the 'truth' of a social situation to the viewer in as unbiased a way as possible. . . . The verité filmmaker has no specific alternative programmatic to present" (Allen and Gomery 237). Nor, apparently, does the pop star.

D. A. Pennebaker once taunted an overenthusiastic critic with the suggestion that his nonfiction film might have been staged: "Would you care if I told you it was all fake? What if I told you it was only a script?" (240). I have argued that *Dont Look Back* has an agenda, if not a script, and that it mounts a systematic critique of the dominant media informed by a liberal view of the role of the press in contemporary democracy. But as a cinema verité documentarist, Pennebaker is compelled to mask his artistry, to let his subject "speak for himself." Finally, Pennebaker's notion of "the truth" is as deceptively simple as Dylan's: "If I just watch what is happening, it will happen right in front of me" (Gilliatt 116).

Notes

1. The term "cinema verité" was used by early film critics to denote both the French and North American schools of the movement. See, for example, "Special Feature on Cinema-Verité: Three Views," *Film Quarterly* 17, no. 4 (1964), 26–40. Thus, although Erik Barnouw refers to the French school as "cinema verité" and the North American as "direct cinema" in his widely used textbook, most contemporary documentary scholars (e.g., Robert C. Allen, A. William Bluem, Noel Carroll, Stephen Mamber, Bill Nichols, Thomas Waugh) use the former term for both. The

term appears in a baffling array of forms in the literature, including not only italics and various combinations and quantities of diacritical marks, but also hyphens, capitals, and inverted commas. The editors have assumed the phrase has entered the English language and requires the final accent for purposes of pronunciation.

WORKS CITED

Allen, Robert C., and Douglas Gomery. *Film History: Theory and Practice*. New York: Knopf, 1985.

Ansen, David. "The Man of the Moment: Tout Cannes Is Abuzz about Star Tim Robbins." *Newsweek*, May 25, 1992, 92.

Asher, Levi. "Literary Kicks." Brooklyn@netcom.com.

Belton, John. *American Cinema/American Culture*. New York: McGraw-Hill, 1994.

Bernard, Jami. Review of *Dont Look Back. New York Post*, September 4, 1992, 92.

Drew, Robert. "An Independent with the Networks." In *New Challenges for Documentary*, ed. Alan Rosenthal, 389–401. Berkeley: University of California Press, 1988.

Gilliatt, Penelope. "The Current Cinema: Under Thirty." *New Yorker*, September 9, 1967, 109–16.

Hall, Jeanne. "Realism as a Style in Cinema Verité: A Critical Analysis of *Primary*." *Cinema Journal* 30, no. 4 (1991): 38–45.

Henahan, Donald J. "The Screen: Bob Dylan and Company." *New York Times*, September 7, 1967, 50.

Knight, Arthur. "Cinema Verité and Film Truth." *Saturday Review*, September 9, 1967, 44.

Maslin, Janet. "Bob Dylan." In *The Rolling Stone Illustrated History of Rock and Roll*, ed. Jim Miller, 219–27. New York: Random House/Rolling Stone Press, 1980.

———. "At Cannes, Tim Robbins Proves a Double Threat." *New York Times*, May 13, 1992, Cl3.

McQuail, Denis. *Mass Communication Theory*. London: Sage, 1994.

Morgenstern, Joseph. "Face in the Crowd." *Newsweek*, August 21, 1967, 65.

Pennebaker, D. A. "Interview with Donn Alan Pennebaker by G. Roy Levin." In *Documentary Explorations: 15 Interviews with Film-makers*, 221–70. Garden City, NY: Doubleday, 1971.

Rick. Review of *Dont Look Back. Variety*, June 14, 1967, 7.

Sklar, Robert. Review of *Bob Roberts. Cineaste* 19, no. 4 (1993): 77–79.

"Third Independent Film Award." *Film Culture* 22–23 (1961): 11.

Wasserman, John L. "Bob Dylan through a Lens Darkly." *Life* 63, no. 6 (August 11, 1967): 10.

Chapter 15

"Ethnography in the First Person"

Frederick Wiseman's *Titicut Follies*

Barry Keith Grant

Titicut Follies (1967) is a powerful documentary that exposes the appalling conditions at Bridgewater, a state institution for the criminally insane in Bridgewater, Massachusetts. The first in a series of documentaries about American institutional life by Frederick Wiseman, it has also been one of his most controversial. Testifying to its power is the tangled history of litigation it engendered.[1] Wiseman began making films in the 1960s, working contemporaneously with such filmmakers as Richard Leacock, D. A. Pennebaker, and David and Albert Maysles during the great period of American direct cinema. But he has developed his own distinctive style and vision, one already evident in *Titicut Follies*. Like his subsequent films, *Titicut Follies* not only explores the situation at Bridgewater but deftly uses its subject metaphorically to explore broad social issues as well as the ethical implications of its own approach to documentary.

Observational Cinema and Personal Expression

Wiseman sees his films as a series of works that presents "a natural history of the way we live" (quoted in Eames 97), and, in a sense, his work constitutes a form of ethnographic cinema that looks at the filmmaker's own culture rather than another.[2] Each of his films focuses on a different

American institution. In the twenty-seven feature-length documentaries Wiseman has made in as many years, he has ranged from examining institutions concentrated within individual buildings (*High School*, 1968) to those international in scope (*Sinai Field Mission*, 1978), from specific government institutions of social service (*Juvenile Court*, 1973; *Welfare*, 1975) to those less tangible ones organized by principles of ideology and culture (*Canal Zone*, 1977; *Model*, 1980). He has broadly defined an institution as "a series of activities that take place in a limited geographical area with a more or less consistent group of people being involved" (quoted in Rosenthal 69). Unlike the rich and famous individuals chronicled in the films of Leacock, Pennebaker, and the Maysles, Wiseman claims to want to make documentaries in which "The institutions will be the star" (Rosenthal 69).

Two successive five-year contracts with WNET, New York's PBS station, allowed Wiseman to make one film a year, from 1971 to 1981, beginning with *Essene* (1972), without constraint as to subject matter or running time.[3] Generally, the WNET showings have been followed by national PBS broadcasts and, with the exception of *Titicut Follies*, all of Wiseman's documentaries have been broadcast on PBS stations. As well, they have been shown on television in numerous European countries.

In all these films, Wiseman combines detached observation and expressive manipulation, merging observational cinema's aesthetic of the seemingly "uninvolved bystander" (Barnouw 254–55) with an expressive use of mise-en-scène and montage. The result is what Jean Rouch has called "ethnographic cinema in the first person" (quoted in Eaton 23). This unique approach has garnered consistent praise from appreciative critics, who have called him "the most sophisticated intelligence in documentary" (Kael 204) and even "the most interesting of American directors" (Bromwich 508).

Titicut Follies was shot by ethnographic filmmaker John Marshall (*The Hunters*, 1958), a choice that suggests Wiseman's approach to Bridgewater is that of a detached observer. Yet the film is also carefully structured to advance its maker's personal sense of moral outrage. Wiseman says he began making films out of an urge for social reform, and *Titicut Follies*, his first film, is in fact his most overtly didactic. Before becoming a filmmaker, he taught courses in criminal law, family law, legal medicine, and psychiatry and the law at Boston and Brandeis universities beginning in 1958. Wiseman got the idea for *Titicut Follies* from visits he made with his students to Bridgewater, feeling that they should know where they might be sending convicted criminals later on when they became district attorneys and judges. He says that "the idea of the movie came out of the absolute sense of shock about what Bridgewater was about" (quoted in Robb 29), and the film works to evoke a similar response in most viewers.

In *Titicut Follies,* as always, Wiseman uses lightweight, portable 16-mm cameras and sync-sound equipment, filming with a handheld camera rather than a tripod, and capturing events as they happen, without a script. The style implies a belief that life captured on film spontaneously—"life caught unawares," as Dziga Vertov put it (41)—is more revealing, more truthful, to the complexities of experience than either fiction or documentary reconstruction. It requires the filmmaker to be particularly attentive to the nuances of profilmic events in order to catch material that "works" as cinema.

Wiseman operates the tape recorder and not the camera during shooting, but he determines where the camera goes through a series of hand signals worked out with his cameraman in advance or by leading the cameraman with the microphone. He claims this method gives him greater freedom to see what is around him than if he were looking at profilmic events through the viewfinder of the camera (cf. interviews with Halberstadt 19, and Levin 318). He tends to work consistently with the same camera operator—William Brayne for ten films, from *Law and Order* (1969) through *Sinai Field Mission;* John Davey since *Manoeuvre* (1979)—thus allowing for the communication between the two crew members to become well established. Certainly one of Wiseman's great skills as an observational filmmaker—a talent to which his first film, *Titicut Follies,* amply testifies—is that he knows where to look and how to capture images on film that resonate with meaning despite the uncontrolled circumstances in which he shoots.

Yet editing is also a crucial feature of Wiseman's cinema, both within individual sequences and in the structural relations between them. Wiseman edits his films himself, devoting a considerable amount of time to the task. For each film, he spends four to six weeks shooting on location but as many months or more in the editing room sifting through and giving shape to his footage. It is in the process of editing, this "thinking through the material," that Wiseman engages in a kind of second order looking. Wiseman readily admits the creative manipulation in his films in his own description of them as "reality dreams" or "reality fictions" (interview with Graham 35, Rosenthal 72). The individual shots themselves originate in the real world, but, says Wiseman, in terms of cinema they "really they have no meaning except insofar as you impose a form on them" (interview with Graham 35). In this editing process elements of profilmic reality are compressed, reordered, and omitted, creating what Vertov called a "film-object" ("On *Kinopravda*" 45), an aesthetic construction that, like an essay, advances a rhetorical argument.

In all his films, while it is true that the profilmic events are always real, never staged, re-created, or rehearsed for the camera, the footage remains for Wiseman only a record of the events, textually meaningless until he structures it at the editing table. He claims that he enters an institution with some inevitable preconceptions or stereotypes about it, but the first-hand experience reveals to him a greater complexity there (interview with Westin 48); in the editing he works out a "theory" about the events, which is then reflected in the film's structure. He sees the process as a "voyage of discovery" and the end result as "a report on what I've found" (interview with Graham 34).

By contrast, most of the practitioners of direct cinema have insisted that their work must be organized chronologically in order to remain as faithful as possible to the profilmic events. Leacock, for example, claims that the documentary filmmaker should avoid nonchronological editing "like the plague" (17), while Al Maysles has declared, "In the long run what works best—and we find ourselves coming back to it—is having it happen just the way it happened" (Maysles and Maysles 27). When chronology is violated, as Stephen Mamber has pointed out regarding the work of the Drew Associates, it is for the purpose of grafting onto the material conventional narrative structures, such as protagonists overcoming obstacles to achieve goals (140).

Wiseman's films clearly are structured according to principles other than chronology and narrative. Rather, they are designed in a manner that Bill Nichols describes as a distinctive "mosaic" structure (*Ideology* 208–36). For expressive purposes, the chronology of profilmic events is shuffled in his work, sometimes drastically. As Nichols notes, while in each film the individual sequences, the facets or "tesserae" of the mosaic, are organized by narrative codes of construction, aiming for a smooth flow of time and space, the relations *between* these facets are organized by principles that are more rhetorical. Sequences in Wiseman's films may relate, for example, in terms of comparison, contrast, parallelism, inversion, irony, evidence, summation, and so on.

At the same time, Wiseman says he never pushes his point of view on the audience, for he abhors didacticism. Indeed, it is at this level of overall structure that the viewer must work to grasp the films' logic. Wiseman's cinema is therefore a dialectical one, always involving the viewer in teasing out meaning rather than documenting absolute truths. In *Titicut Follies,* as always in Wiseman's work, there is no narrator, either within the profilmic events or as voice-over. Neither are there markers of temporal relations between sequences—wipes, dissolves, titles. Thus in a sense the viewer is forced to repeat Wiseman's own process by discovering the structural logic of the film's parts and exploring their implications. In Wiseman's words, viewers "have to fight the film, they have to say, 'What the hell's he trying to say with this?' . . . And they have to think through their own relationship to what they're seeing" (interview with Graham 37).

THE "TITICUT FOLLIES"

In *Titicut Follies* this engagement is taken a step further, for the viewer is not allowed to maintain the comfortable invisibility of the unacknowledged "fly on the wall." The film challenges our usual physical position as voyeurs as well as our moral position as possessors of knowledge. This striking use of the observational approach is presented immediately in the film's opening sequence, part of the annual musical show performed by the inmates at Bridgewater. It begins by showing some darkened, at first indistinct faces; the camera pans from one to the next, momentarily bringing each face out of the engulfing darkness into the light, only to disappear into darkness again outside the frame. The light itself seems ghastly, its source harsh footlights emanating from below, as in the conventional lighting design of horror films. Wilfred Sheed's description of the production as "a travesty of the latest Ziegfeld, as interpreted by Trappist monks" (55) only begins to capture its eerie quality. These sickly faces sing the Gershwins' strident "Strike up the Band," announcing their presence with ironic pomp and circumstance.

In retrospect, it is also a call, asking us to pay heed to the social problems the film goes on to chronicle. This opening sequence reflexively expresses the filmmaker's awareness of the ethical issues surrounding observational cinema.[4] Because it depicts a performance, and one that is excessively marked as such, the sequence also addresses the debate about how the camera affects the profilmic event and to what extent the people being photographed inevitably perform for it. For some people, the presence of the camera either makes them self-conscious and inhibited or, conversely, allows them an opportunity to perform, but in neither case are people acting naturally. For Wiseman, though, as for Rouch, the camera is more an accelerator than a brake. Wiseman believes that people do not significantly alter their behavior for the camera, that if they are made self-conscious by its presence they will tend to fall back on behavior that is comfortable "rather than increase the discomfort by trying out new roles."[5] Thus one of the implications of the opening sequence of *Titicut Follies* is that people may, and sometimes do, perform, but this does not necessarily invalidate the observational method. Indeed, the postmodern view would have it that the nature of our being in the world, our very identity, is more performance than essence.

The camera views the show from the physical position of the audience at the show, suturing our point of view into the space of the event as
if the performance is put on *for* the viewer. We are even thanked at film's
end, in the lyrics of the "finale," for being a spectator. But any sense of voyeuristic invisibility is methodically undercut in the film. Surveillance cameras appear periodically in the background, mirroring our own act of watching. Further, the film prevents us from maintaining a unified point of view
when the television competes for our attention in the frame, pitting foreground against background, as one inmate attempts to sing "Chinatown,
My Chinatown" while Nana Mouskouri sings on TV behind him. Also,
Wiseman occasionally allows his camera's look to be returned by inmates.
The most powerful instance occurs when the camera follows the naked
ex-schoolteacher Jim, who goes into his cell and huddles in a corner trying to cover his genitals with his hands. Jim's futile attempt at modesty
signals his awareness of the camera's presence, as does his look, a direct
return of the camera's gaze. The shot maintaining the lock of gazes between Jim and the camera is held for several excruciating seconds. Inevitably, we become painfully aware of the camera's (and of our) intrusive
presence. One is reminded of Norman Bates's verbal attack on Marian
Crane in Hitchcock's *Psycho* (1960) when she euphemistically suggests
he send his ailing mother to "someplace." His acknowledgment of her
tactful avoidance suddenly makes us, along with Marion, feel ashamed,
and we are made to respond similarly in *Titicut Follies*. The film's implication of us is wholly appropriate: because Bridgewater is our institution,
created by us and our tax dollars, the film, as Richard Barsam notes, "exposes more about us than it does about Bridgewater" (274). And, more
generally, Jim's discomforting return of our look acknowledges the inevitable politics of documentary, wherein power belongs to the bearer of the
look (Rabinowitz).

Titicut Follies ends, as it begins, by showing parts of the same musical
show. This framing device serves several functions simultaneously. First,
the concluding performance is a departing gesture (blackly humorous,
with its lyrics "We've had our show / The best that we could do / To make
your hearts aglow"), reminding us that the film we have been watching is
a constructed representation. As well, because of its emphasis on musical
performance, we are invited to consider the film in the context of the fictional genre of the musical. But where the classical musical's vision, largely
articulated through its performances, is of a harmonious, utopian community,[6] *Titicut Follies* presents a dystopian collection of alienated individuals. Finally, the film's structural symmetry, with performances at both the
beginning and end, underscores the sense of entrapment that it elsewhere

documents: the fact that the performance at the end "reprises" the one at the beginning—that it is, in fact, the same performance broken up with other footage in between—further suggests the timelessness, the infinite sense of alienation, that for Wiseman characterizes Bridgewater.

The concluding performance, moreover, structurally sums up the motif of performance that is manifest throughout *Titicut Follies*. The film suggests that the inmates are forever "onstage," as they are always under observation by the staff. As Michel Foucault has argued, in the mental institution (aptly described by Norman Bates as a place "with cruel eyes studying you") the behavior of people labeled insane is always being observed and judged by those in control, "a sort of invisible tribunal in permanent session" (265). This is made explicit in Vladimir's unsuccessful meeting with the staff. He argues (on good empirical evidence, it would seem) that he came to Bridgewater "for observation" but has been there for a year and a half and that the institution's environment is harming rather than helping him. Much of his argument cannot help but appear sensible to viewers, given what we've seen to this point, but everything Vladimir says, even his talk of possible rehabilitation, is interpreted as a sign of deepening mental illness to be dealt with by increased dosages of medication.

Elsewhere we see inmates in a variety of performances, some overt, others more subtle. Inmates declaim from soapboxes, play trombones, and sing; Albert, having his bath, seems to relate to his guards with playful teasing. Vladimir, trying too hard to convince the staff that he is sane and should be sent back to prison, ultimately overplays his role, with the result that his request is denied. Even Eddie, one of the guards, seems to define himself more as a performer than a guard, acting as host of the Follies revue and singing in several other scenes. After his song in the party sequence, he does an encore like a seasoned vaudevillian and then exits with a theatrical flourish.

The film's title, virtually alone among Wiseman's documentaries, gives us no indication of its subject, and its significance (it is the name of the inmates' annual revue) is never explained. Even if we happen to possess this information in advance, the opening performance is still confusing because it is impossible to know with any degree of certainty the status of some of the people we are shown: are these all inmates, or are some of the men guards? We do not discover that Eddie is in fact a guard until shortly thereafter, when in a later sequence he is glimpsed walking by the camera in his uniform. In his review of the film, Robert Hatch complained about the film's ineptitude because it raises but fails to answer so many questions: "is the show a part of their therapy, how does the audience respond (there is not a single shot into the house), is this a regular feature of the hospital

Titicut Follies: Eddie the guard
performing.

life?" (446). But, of course, this is quite to the point, for the sequence attacks our comfortable position as spectators from several flanks at once.

After Vladimir is taken from the staff meeting, a social worker states
their common view that "He argues in a perfect paranoid pattern. If you
accept his basic premise the rest of it is logical but the basic premise is
untrue." (Might not the same be said of the film itself?) When we hear
the staff's interpretation and response, we are likely to wonder who, in
fact, is paranoid. After the finale, Eddie, as MC, with unintentional irony
asks, "Weren't they terrific?" These are the film's last words, leaving us with
the question of determining the nature of our response to, and judgment
about, the inmates and the conditions they endure.

INSTITUTIONS AND INTERTEXTUALITY

At the same time as the film forcefully confronts us with these particular
people in this specific institution, we are also invited by the text to view
Bridgewater metaphorically, as a social microcosm, what Wiseman calls
"a cultural spoor." Wiseman says he is "interested in how institutions reflect the larger cultural hues" and that he is "trying to see if you can pick

up reflections of the larger issues of society in the institutions" (quoted in Mamber 217). One patient delivers a delirious monologue that explicitly makes an analogy between Bridgewater and America itself. The country's military aggression is, he says, a result of frustration, of being "sex crazy"— the same opinion Dr. Ross holds of the sex offender Mitch. The courtyard debate between two inmates about American intervention in Vietnam is a crazy mirror of the "hawks and doves" arguments that at the time the film was made were dividing Americans everywhere.

The film also suggests its larger implications through intertextual references. Several writers have compared *Titicut Follies* to Peter Weiss's play *Marat/Sade* (1963), which had been made into a successful film by Peter Brook the year before Wiseman's and was shot in a pseudo-direct cinema style (Armstrong 29–30, Barsam 274, Gill). Both Wiseman's film and Weiss's play are set in a mental institution, both feature aspects of performance within the text, and both explore the nature of madness in the context of politics and the state. But an equally resonant comparison might be made to Ken Kesey's novel *One Flew over the Cuckoo's Nest* (1962), as it shares with Wiseman's film a view of the mental institution as a metaphor for the "larger cultural hues" of contemporary America. Thomas Benson and Carolyn Anderson report that, according to Wiseman, the cast and crew of Milos Forman's 1975 film adaptation of Kesey's novel watched *Titicut Follies* repeatedly before beginning production (331).

The book's self-conscious "American theme" is suggested by Kesey's narrator, a mute Native American, just as Wiseman refers to Native America in his film's title—"Titicut" being the Native American name for the Bridgewater area. Both texts focus on issues of emasculation through medication—in *Titicut Follies*, one patient imagines that the doctors are going to remove his testicles—and other severe forms of treatment as a way of maintaining social control. Both works, finally, question our very definition of madness and sanity. During their discussion in the yard, Dr. Ross startlingly declares that if he is wrong in predicting that if released Vladimir will return to Bridgewater immediately, then "you can spit on my face." Vladimir responds with the sensible question, "Why should I do that?" as taken aback as the viewer is likely to be. At this moment the doctor, like Kesey's Nurse Ratched, seems the mad one. At other times, the behavior of some of the guards, like the staff discussing Vladimir, also seems nothing short of "crazy."

In *Titicut Follies*, however, insanity is less the seething, controlled hostility of a Big Nurse than the banality of common callousness, as in the taunting of Jim about his dirty room and the teasing of Albert in the bathtub. Vladimir, like the novel's Billy Bibbitt, can mount only a weak protest,

Titicut Follies: Vladimir arguing his sanity with Dr. Ross in the yard.

the inevitable response to which is increased medication. His inescapable position is poignantly suggested by the brick wall behind him when he tries to reason with Dr. Ross (and for much of the shot, they are graphically divided in the frame by a dark drainpipe between them). In Kesey's book, McMurphy's lobotomy serves as a sacrificial act that redeems the Chief from his muteness; in the end, Bromden escapes the institution to return to his land—"I been away a long time," he says in the novel's last line (311). But the vision of *Titicut Follies* is considerably darker, for it seems that the only way out here is through death. Vladimir wants to leave but cannot, while, as far as we are shown, only a corpse is allowed to depart; the funeral in a graveyard, just before the finale, is the only time the camera leaves the grounds. In Wiseman's vision of the American "snake pit" there is no bois-terously physical embodiment of the life principle to equal Kesey's robust Randall Patrick McMurphy.

Nor is spiritual solace offered by religious belief. The film's two scenes of Christian ritual are of last rites and a funeral service—presumably for Malinowski, the dying inmate who refuses to eat, although again, the am-biguity is richly suggestive. Wiseman introduces Christian elements rather sardonically, cutting from a physically dysfunctional inmate picking his nose to the hand of the priest, Father Mulligan, performing the last rite. Toward the end, one inmate stands on his head in the yard, singing of sacred glory; the upside-down close-up of the man's face suggests that the world—the world of *Titicut Follies*—is topsy-turvy, for it is a world where moral and spiritual values are inverted.

MORAL INDIGNATION AND EXPRESSIVE EDITING

The dark vision of *Titicut Follies* is clearly signaled from the outset by the word "Follies" in the film's title. Indeed, Wiseman criticizes the conditions at Bridgewater with a use of editing that is far from subtle. Immediately after the opening performance, there is a quick shot of a guard ordering an inmate to get his clothes. This is followed by Mitch's interview with Dr. Ross, who questions him in a blunt way that seems unduly callous. As the interview proceeds, Wiseman cuts suddenly to some guards strip-searching newly arrived inmates. The film then returns to the interview, where Dr. Ross's questions become more aggressive, perhaps even tinged with cruelty. Viewer sympathy here is more likely to align itself with the patient, who willingly admits his problems and seeks help, than with the doctor, who says weakly, perhaps even begrudgingly, "You'll get it here, I guess." Tellingly, in his review of the film Arthur Knight described him as "a German-accented doctor who licks his lips over every sex question," while Amos Vogel called him a "Dr. Strangelove psychiatrist" (187). The inserted shot of the physical stripping of the inmates offers an obvious comparison between the two procedures: Dr. Ross's interview with Mitch, that is to say, is a psychological stripping down of the inmate, an impersonal, cold prodding that offers little compassion or comfort. As Foucault says of the science of mental disease as it developed in the institution of the asylum, it would always be observation and classification, never a dialogue (250).

Similar in tone to the treatment of the inmates in the strip-search sequence is Wiseman's presentation of Malinowski, the inmate who is force-fed because he has refused to eat. Like them, the man is naked, a sign of his vulnerability and powerlessness. As the tube is lubricated and pushed through one of Malinowski's nostrils (on a wall behind the doctor hangs a calendar with an advertisement for "Perfection Oil"!) and he is force-fed, Wiseman inserts six quick shots of the same man being prepared for his funeral at a later date. The shaving of the corpse connects the treatment of Malinowski to the earlier rough shaving of Jim's face, which caused blood to trickle down his chin and, as Stephen Mamber notes, ironically suggests that Malinowski receives more attention in death than he did when alive

(219). Several of these shots draw precise ironic parallels between the two procedures: when the tube is put into his nose, there is an inserted shot of the dead Malinowski being shaved; when Wiseman's camera pans to the watching eyes of the guards holding him down, there is a shot of the dead man's eyes being stuffed with cotton; when Dr. Ross removes the tube from Malinowski's nose, there is a shot of the shaving process completed, both procedures concluding with a towel daubing; and when Malinowski is led away, there is a shot of the body being placed in storage in the morgue. Finally, while force-feeding the inmate, Dr. Ross smokes a cigarette, its long ash captured by the camera in close-up hanging precipitously over the funnel through which the patient is receiving his food. Like the cigarette and ruler in the hand of the coroner at the end of Stan Brakhage's *The Act of Seeing with One's Own Eyes* (1971), the image is a powerful objective correlative of institutional detachment.

Wiseman further underscores the contrast here by his editing of the sound track, for the feeding procedure is accompanied by a clutter of ambient noise and voices while each of the embalming shots is starkly silent. Indeed, Wiseman always pays careful attention to his sound track, and *Titicut Follies* is no exception. Consider again, for example, the opening of the film. The first images are accompanied by an off-key performance of "Strike up the Band," its out-of-tune quality an indication that something is amiss. Later, when a guard talks about how they used to gas patients, making his eyes tear, a few notes of what sounds like Erroll Garner's "Misty" are heard coming from the radio in the room! Such instances, however, are often more significant than simply ironic. The lyrics to "Chicago Town," for instance, sung by Eddie and Willie, express the wish to be a child ("Oh, what a joy / to be only a boy") who delights in amusements ("I want to ride on the shoot-de-shoot / And the merry-go-round") of the big city ("That's where I long to be"). Unfortunately, according to Vladimir, all that is available to the inmates of Bridgewater (and we see nothing to contradict this view) is "a ball and a glove." While the inmates are in fact frequently treated like children (cf. Armstrong), it is also significant that the wish of the song contrasts sharply with the stultifying reality of the institution. Most of the musical numbers feature lyrics about "elsewhere": like the irony of "Chicago Town," the trombone rendition of, for instance, "My Blue Heaven" in the yard contrasts pointedly with its purgatorial reality of people aimlessly milling about.

LAW, ETHICS, AND POLITICS

The stark, unsettling power of *Titicut Follies* embroiled Wiseman in a lengthy legal battle that severely limited its accessibility. Before the court's decision, however, *Titicut Follies* was screened as part of the "Social Change in America" program of the New York Film Festival in the fall of 1967 and then had a six-day commercial run. But generally the film received poor reviews. One critic saw the film as exploiting the inmates ("offering a vulture's-eye view," Sheed 52), while another thought it violated "common decency" and even falsely accused Wiseman of shooting with hidden cameras (Knight). Yet a third claimed it "was a sickening film from start to finish" and that it "has no justification for existing except to the extent that it is intended to have legislative and other non-aesthetic consequences" (Gill 166).

Such response is not surprising, for *Titicut Follies* is perhaps the clearest example of what Nichols has called Wiseman's "tactlessness," his disregard for "the ideological constraints of politeness, respect for privacy, queasiness in the face of the grotesque or taboo" (*Ideology* 209). The force-feeding of Malinowski and the insistent filming of the naked Jim are particularly vivid instances of this "tactlessness," so pronounced in *Titicut Follies* that the presiding judge in the initial case against the film, Harry Kalus, called the film "a nightmare of ghoulish obscenities" (quoted in Wiseman interview with Westin 63). The result of the extended legal battle was that the film itself became the focus of attention rather than the conditions at Bridgewater. The much-publicized litigation may have gained Wiseman some notoriety early in his career, but it did little to improve conditions at the institution. It was reported by the press in the spring of 1987, twenty years after Wiseman's film, that five inmates had died that year alone at Bridgewater, three of them by suicide, and later that summer (August 25) the institution was the subject on ABC-TV's *Nightline*, with Wiseman as one of the guests.

Wiseman's distinctive institutional emphasis in *Titicut Follies*, as in all his documentaries, reflects a social concern that follows in the tradition of John Grierson. Like Grierson, Wiseman conceives of the documentary within the context of social reform and sees it as a potential source of information for the purpose of creating an informed and responsible citizenship. One of the primary functions of documentary, for Wiseman, is to provide public education and awareness. He has discussed documentary as analogous to the news and considers his films as similarly protected by the First Amendment (interviews with Westin 60, and Levin 319). As he pointedly explained when asked by Ted Koppel on *Nightline* why he was opposed to a public screening of a censored version of *Titicut Follies*, "The censoring of *Titicut Follies* or any other film prevents people in a democracy from access to information which they might like to have in order to make up their minds about what kind of society they'd like to live in—it's as simple as that."

But if Wiseman's documentaries are news, they are also styled as editorials, as arguments about the institutions on which he is reporting. And it is at this level that his films work politically, for they democratically allow the spectator considerable "space" as textual readers. Wiseman's distinctive mosaic structure discourages empathy or identification with specific individuals, asking us instead to consider the logic of both institutional organization and cinematic construction. Even in those brief moments when we empathize with someone, as we are likely to with Jim, for example, the focus remains diffuse enough so that the possibility of sustained identification is thwarted. The absence of voice-over narration further obliges us to watch *Titicut Follies*, like Wiseman's other films, in this way. In short, we are offered no overtly obvious spectatorial position but must instead be attentive to the text.

So, even without a robust McMurphy figure, *Titicut Follies* is not really as bleak as it might seem to be. For if it is significant, as suggested above, that while the camera does not leave the Bridgewater grounds (except in the case of death), the viewer of *Titicut Follies* does. Our perspective, as a result of the multiple points of view generated by the mosaic structure, is wider than that of any individual within the film. We are left to contemplate the film and its implications.

For Nichols, this aspect of observational cinema is a potential problem, for it "appears to leave the driving to us" and, therefore, one can respond to it as to a Rorschach test (Nichols, "Voice" 20, 21). Some critics have dismissed Wiseman's films because, they contend, their structural subtleties allow him to avoid taking a clear position, leaving it to viewers to interpret the films as they wish (Wiseman interview with Westin 49–50). But a close examination of most of them would show, as has this analysis of *Titicut Follies*, that they do have a definite point of view.

Wiseman's films have been seen as politically suspect in large part because they seem not to acknowledge their involvement or complicity in the act of documentation and so maintain the viewer's "imaginary" relationship to the images (Nichols, *Ideology* 235). Interestingly, in Thomas Waugh's important anthology on the "committed" documentary, *Show Us Life* (1984), Wiseman is treated only in passing and disparagingly—which is curious, given that his work fulfills all of the requirements the book's contributors put forth as necessary for progressive political documentary filmmaking, including the absence of an authoritative narrator and dominant individual "stars," a sense of structure reflecting the complexity of events, and their use value as a catalyst for discussion. Certainly Wiseman does not endear himself to leftist critics with remarks that his politics are Marxist, but more Groucho than Karl. Yet I would argue that Wiseman's style in fact constitutes a profoundly political cinema because of the "open" way it engages viewers.

It is true that *Titicut Follies* typically shows us disillusioned and shattered people treated impersonally and disdainfully. In Wiseman's films, the culmination of institutional logic is to constrain individuality and to rationalize difference, as in the dismissive diagnosis of Vladimir ("They call that the Ganser syndrome"). The image of Jim being forcibly shaved metaphorically suggests the conforming pressures of institutional processing. Tellingly, variations on this image appear in such later Wiseman films as *Hospital* (1970), *Basic Training* (1971), *Primate* (1974), and *Meat* (1976). (*Welfare,* it is worth noting, was made between *Primate* and *Meat:* the films' chronological order is a further example of the larger mosaic structure of the series, as these films together chronicle the way institutions treat people as less than human—that is, like meat.) In a letter submitted as testimony in the *Titicut Follies* litigation, Wiseman said the film is "about various forms of madness" (quoted in Anderson 18). America, Wiseman's films suggest, is itself in some ways a social bedlam, no longer a dream of opportunity but a nightmare of conformity.

Yet despite the bleakness of the institution as presented in *Titicut Follies* and in some of his other films, Wiseman encourages democratic participation from viewers through his "open" style. If anything, his films have grown increasingly more subtle, showing even greater respect for viewers. (Significantly, *Primate* is the only other Wiseman documentary to have raised any substantial controversy; it, too, is tactless in its broaching of the sensitive issue of medical research on animals.) For Wiseman, "The true film lies halfway between the screen and the mind of the viewer" (quoted in "Talk of the Town" 32), and so he refuses to dictate to the viewer by assuming an authorial superiority. In the end, the film constitutes one person's "report"—no less than Vladimir's claims and the staff's diagnosis, it is an argument based on a perceptual premise. While it may be true that his tactlessness may invite misplaced controversy or voyeuristic pleasure (Nichols, *Ideology* 209), *Titicut Follies* does not allow us to innocently enjoy that pleasure—if indeed that is the right word, given the harrowing events Wiseman's camera shows—for it forces us to think about that "someplace" of which we are all aware but may prefer not to acknowledge.

NOTES

1. For a detailed account of the film's legal history, see Carolyn Anderson, *Documentary Dilemmas: Frederick Wiseman's Titicut Follies* (Carbondale: Southern Illinois University Press, 1991). A transcript of the film appears in *Five Films by Frederick Wiseman,* ed. Barry Keith Grant (Berkeley: University of California Press, 2006.)

2. David MacDougall includes *Titicut Follies* in his list of ethnographic films about industrialized societies. "Prospects of the Ethnographic Film," *Film Quarterly* 23, no. 2 (1969/70): 16. For a discussion of all of Wiseman's films through *Central Park* (1990), see Barry Keith Grant, *Voyages of Discovery: The Cinema of Frederick Wiseman* (Urbana: University of Illinois Press, 1992).

3. However, according to Wiseman's own account he had to battle with network executives over sequences in both *Law and Order* (1969) and *Hospital* (1970), and was forced to make cuts for the telecast of *Basic Training* (Benson and Anderson 351–52).

4. Dan Armstrong also discusses this aspect of the film in his essay, "Wiseman's Realm of Transgression."

5. Interview with the author, January 1989.

6. See, for example, Richard Dyer, "Entertainment and Utopia," *Movie* 24 (spring 1977): 2–13.

7. See especially the essays by Chuck Kleinhans, "Forms, Politics, Makers and Contexts: Basic Issues for a Theory of Radical Political Documentary," and Julianne Burton, "Democratizing Documentary: Modes of Address in the Latin American Cinema, 1858–72," in *"Show Us Life": Toward a History and Aesthetics of the Committed Documentary*, ed. Thomas Waugh (Metuchen, NJ: Scarecrow Press, 1984), 318–42, 344–83.

WORKS CITED

Anderson, Carolyn. "The Conundrum of Competing Rights in *Titicut Follies*." *Journal of the University Film Association* 33, no. 1 (1981): 15–22.

Armstrong, Dan. "Wiseman's Realm of Transgression: *Titicut Follies*, the Symbolic Father, and the Spectacle of Confinement." *Cinema Journal* 29, no. 1 (1989): 20–35.

Barnouw, Erik. *Documentary: A History of the Non-fiction Film*. New York: Oxford University Press, 1974.

Barsam, Richard Meran. *Nonfiction Film: A Critical History*. New York: Dutton, 1973.

Benson, Thomas W., and Carolyn Anderson. *Reality Fictions: The Films of Frederick Wiseman*. Carbondale: Southern Illinois University Press, 1989.

Bromwich, David. "Documentary Now." *Dissent* (October 1971): 507–12.

Eames, David. "Watching Wiseman Watch." *New York Times Magazine*, October 2, 1977, 96–102, 104, 108.

Eaton, Mick, ed. *Anthropology—Reality—Cinema: The Films of Jean Rouch*. London: British Film Institute, 1979.

Foucault, Michel. *Madness and Civilization: A History of Insanity in the Age of Reason*. Trans. Richard Howard. New York: Pantheon Books, 1965.

Gill, Brendan. "The Current Cinema." *New Yorker* 43 (October 28, 1967): 166–67.

Hatch, Robert. Review of *Titicut Follies. The Nation* 205 (October 30, 1967): 445–46.

Kael, Pauline. Review of *High School.* In *Frederick Wiseman,* ed. Thomas R. Atkins, 95–101. New York: Monarch Press, 1976.

Kesey, Ken. *One Flew over the Cuckoo's Nest.* Ed. John Clark Pratt. New York: Penguin, 1973.

Knight, Arthur. "Cinema Verité and Film Truth." *Saturday Review* 50 (September 9, 1967): 44.

Leacock, Richard. "One Man's Truth: An Interview with Richard Leacock." Interview by James Blue. *Film Comment* 3, no. 2 (1965): 15–22.

Mamber, Stephen. *Cinema Verite in America: Studies in Uncontrolled Documentary.* Cambridge, MA: MIT Press, 1974.

Maysles, David, and Albert Maysles. "Thoughts on Cinema Verité and a Discussion with the Maysles Brothers." Interview by James Blue. *Film Comment* 2, no. 4 (1964): 22–30.

Nichols, Bill. *Ideology and the Image.* Bloomington: Indiana University Press, 1981.

———. "The Voice of Documentary." *Film Quarterly* 36, no. 3 (1983): 17–30. Reprinted in *Movies and Methods,* vol. 2, ed. Bill Nichols, 258–73. Berkeley: University of California Press, 1988.

Rabinowitz, Paula. *They Must Be Represented: The Politics of Documentary.* New York: Verso, 1994.

Robb, Christina. "Focus on Life." *Boston Globe Magazine,* January 23, 1983, 15–17, 26–34.

Rosenthal, Alan, ed. *The New Documentary in Action: A Casebook in Film Making.* Berkeley: University of California Press, 1972.

Sheed, Wilfred. Review of *Titicut Follies. Esquire* 69, no. 3 (1968): 52, 55.

"The Talk of the Town." *New Yorker,* October 24, 1988, 31–32.

Vertov, Dziga. "The Birth of the Kino-Eye." In *Kino-Eye: The Writings of Dziga Vertov,* ed. Annette Michelson, trans. Kevin O'Brien, 40–42. Berkeley: University of California Press, 1984.

———. "On *Kinopravda.*" In *Kino-Eye: The Writings of Dziga Vertov,* ed. Annette Michelson, trans. Kevin O'Brien, 42–47. Berkeley: University of California Press, 1984.

Vogel, Amos. *Film as a Subversive Art.* New York: Random House, 1974.

Wiseman, Frederick. "Frederick Wiseman." Interview by G. Roy Levin, 313–28. In *Documentary Explorations: 15 Interviews with Film-Makers.* Garden City, NY: Doubleday, 1971.

———. *"High School."* Interview with Alan Rosenthal. In *The New Documentary in Action: A Casebook in Film Making,* ed. Rosenthal. Berkeley: University of California Press, 1972.

———. "An Interview with Fred Wiseman." Interview by Ira Halberstadt. *Film-maker's Newsletter* 7, no. 4 (1974): 19–25.

———. "There Are No Simple Solutions: Wiseman on Film Making and Film Viewing." Interview by John Graham. In *Frederick Wiseman,* ed. Thomas R. Atkins, 33–45. New York: Simon and Schuster, 1976.

———. "'You Start Off with a Bromide': Conversation with Film Maker Frederick Wiseman." Interview by Alan Westin. In *Frederick Wiseman,* ed. Thomas R. Atkins, 47–66. New York: Simon and Schuster, 1976.

Chapter 16

THE TWO AVANT-GARDES

Solanas and Getino's
The Hour of the Furnaces

Robert Stam

The struggle to seize power from the enemy is the meeting-ground of the political and artistic vanguards engaged in a common task which is enriching to both.

Fernando Solanas and Octavio Getino,
"Towards a Third Cinema"

If there are two avant-gardes—the formal and the theoretico-political—then *La hora de los hornos* (*The Hour of the Furnaces,* 1968) surely marks one of the high points of their convergence. Fusing Third World radicalism with artistic innovation, the Solanas-Getino film revives the historical sense of avant-garde as connoting political as well as cultural militancy. It teases to the surface the military metaphor submerged in the very expression "avant-garde"—the image of an advanced contingent reconnoitering unexplored and dangerous territory. It resuscitates the venerable analogy (at least as old as Marey's *fusil photographique*) of camera and gun, charging it with a precise revolutionary signification. Art becomes, as Walter Benjamin said of the dadaists, "an instrument of ballistics" (165). At the same time, *The Hour of the Furnace*'s experimental language is indissolubly wedded to its political project; the articulation of one with the other generates the film's meaning and secures its relevance.

It is in this exemplary two-fronted struggle, rather than in the historical specificity of its politics, that *The Hour of the Furnaces* retains vitality
as a model for cinematic practice. Events subsequent to 1968 have if not
wholly discredited at least relativized the film's analysis. Unmoored and set
adrift on the currents of history, the film has been severed from its original
context, as its authors have been exiled from their country. The late 1960s
were, virtually everywhere, the hour of the furnaces, and *The Hour of the
Furnaces,* quintessential product of the period, forged the incandescent expression of their glow. Tricontinental revolution, under the symbolic aegis
of Frantz Fanon, Che Guevara, and Ho Chi Minh, was deemed imminent,
waiting to surprise us around the next bend of the dialectic. But despite
salient victories (Vietnam, Mozambique, Nicaragua), many flames have
dwindled into embers, as some of the Third World has settled into the era
of diminished expectations. In most of South America, the CIA, multina-
tional corporations, and native ruling elites conspired to install "subfascist"
regimes, that is, regimes whose politics and practices are fascist but lack
any popular base. In Argentina, class struggle in a relatively liberal context
gave way to virtual civil war. Perón—the last hope of the revolutionaries
and the bourgeoisie—returned, but only to die. His political heirs veered
rightward, defying the hopes of those who returned him to power until
a putsch installed a quasi-fascist regime. Rather than being surprised by
revolution, Argentina, and *The Hour of the Furnaces* with it, was ambushed
by a historical equivocation.

The Hour of the Furnaces is structured as a tripartite political essay. The
first section, "Neocolonialism and Violence," situates Argentina internationally, revealing it as a palimpsest of European influences: "British gold, Italian hands, French books." A series of "Notes"—"The Daily Violence," "The
Oligarchy," "Dependency"—explores the variegated forms of neocolonial
oppression. The second section, "An Act for Liberation," is subdivided into a
"Chronicle of Perónism," covering Perón's rule from 1945 through his depo-
sition by coup in 1955, and "Chronicle of Resistance," detailing the opposition struggle during the period of Perón's exile. The third section, "Violence
and Liberation," consists of an open-ended series of interviews, documents,
and testimonials concerning the best path to a revolutionary future for Latin
America. Much of this section is taken up by two interviews, one with an
octogenarian, oral archivist of the national memory of resistance who recounts past combats and predicts imminent socialist revolution, the other
with labor organizer Julio Troxler, then living and working underground,
who describes mass executions and vows struggle until victory.

While reawakening the military metaphor dormant in "avant-garde,"
The Hour of the Furnaces also literalizes the notion of the "underground."

Filmed clandestinely in conjunction with militant cadres, it was made in the interstices of the system and against the system. It situates itself on the periphery of the periphery—a kind of off-off-Hollywood—and brashly disputes the hegemony of both the dominant model ("First Cinema") and auteurism ("Second Cinema"), proposing instead a "Third Cinema," independent in production, militant in politics, and experimental in language.[1] As a poetic celebration of the Argentine nation, it is "epic" in the classical as well as the Brechtian sense, weaving disparate materials—newsreels, eyewitness reports, TV commercials, photographs—into a splendid historical tapestry. A cinematic summa, with strategies ranging from straightforward didacticism to operatic stylization, borrowing from avant-garde and mainstream, fiction and documentary, cinema verité and advertising, it inherits and prolongs the work of Eisenstein, Vertov, Ivens, Glauber Rocha, Fernando Birri, Resnais, Buñuel, and Godard.

The most striking feature of *The Hour of the Furnaces* is its openness. But whereas "openness" in art usually evokes plurisignification, polysemy, the authorization of a plurality of equally legitimate readings, the Solanas-Getino film is not open in this sense: its messages are stridently unequivocal; its ambiguities, such as they are, derive more from the vicissitudes of history than from the intentions of its authors. The film's openness lies elsewhere, and first of all in its process of production. Coming from the traditional Europeanized left, Solanas and Getino set out to make a socially minded short documentary about the working class in Argentina. Through the filmmaking experience, however, they evolved toward a left Perónist position. The production process, in other words, inflected their own ideological trajectory in ways that they themselves could not have fully predicted. (One need not endorse the specific nature of this inflection to appreciate the *fact* of the inflection.) Once aware of the tenuous nature of their initial "certainties," they opened their project to the criticisms and suggestions of the working class. As a result, the film underwent a process of constant mutation, not because of authorial whims (à la Fellini's *8½*, 1963) but under the pressure of proletarian critique. Rather than performing the mise-enscène of preconceived opinions, the film's making entailed inquiry and search. The reformist short became a revolutionary manifesto.

The Hour of the Furnaces is open, secondly, in its very structure as a text, operating by what might be called tendentiously aleatory procedures.[2] At key points, the film raises questions—"Why did Perón fall without a struggle? Should he have armed the people?"—and proposes that the audience debate them, interrupting the projection to allow for discussion. Elsewhere, the authors appeal for supplementary material on the theme of violence and liberation, soliciting collaboration in the film's writing. The "end" of the film refuses closure by inviting the audience to prolong the text: "Now it is up to you to draw conclusions to continue the film. You have the floor." This challenge, more than rhetorical, was concretely taken up by Argentine audiences, at least until the experiment was cut short by military rule.

Cine-semiologists define the cinema as a system of signification rather than communication, arguing that the gap between the production of the message and its reception, doubled by the gap between the reception and the production of an answering message, allows only for *deferred* communications. *The Hour of the Furnaces,* by opening itself up to person-to-person debate, tests and "stretches" this definition to its very limits. In a provocative amalgam of cinema/theater/political rally, it joins the space of representation to the space of the spectator, thus making "real" and immediate communication possible. The passive cinematic experience, that *rendezvous manqué* between exhibitionist and voyeur, is transformed into a "theatrical" encounter between human beings present in the flesh. The two-dimensional space of the screen gives way to the three-dimensional space of theater and politics. The film mobilizes, fostering motor and mental activity rather than self-indulgent fantasy. Rather than vibrate to the sensibility of an auteur, the spectators become the authors of their own destiny. Rather than a mass hero *on the screen,* the protagonists of history are *in the audience.* Rather than a womb to regress in, the cinema becomes a political stage on which to act.

Bertolt Brecht contrasted artistic innovation easily absorbed by the apparatus with the kind that threatens its very existence. *The Hour of the Furnaces* wards off co-optation by a stance of radical interventionism. Rather than being hermetically sealed off from life, the text is permeable to history and praxis, calling for accomplices rather than consumers. The three major sections begin with *ouvertures*—orchestrated quotations, slogans, rallying cries—that suggest that the spectators have come not to enjoy a show but to participate in an action. Each screening is meant to create what the authors call a "liberated space, a decolonized territory." Because of this activist stance, *The Hour of the Furnaces* was dangerous to make, to distribute, and, not infrequently, to see. When a repressive situation makes filmgoing a clandestine activity punishable by prison or torture, the mere act of viewing comes to entail political commitment. Cinephilia, at times a surrogate for political action in the United States and Europe, became in Argentina a life-endangering form of praxis, placing the spectator in a booby-trapped space of political commitment. Instead of the mere firecrackers under the seats of the dadaists, the spectator was faced with the distant possibility of machine-gun fire in the cinema. All the celebrated "attacks on the voyeurism of the spectator" pale in violence next to this threatened initiation into political brutality.

In its frontal assault on passivity, *The Hour of the Furnaces* deploys a number of textual strategies. The spoken and written commentary, addressed directly to the spectator, fosters a discursive relationship, the I-you of the *discours* rather than the he-she voyeurism of *histoire*.[3] The language, furthermore, is unabashedly partisan, eschewing all factitious "objectivity." Diverse classes, the film reminds us, speak divergent languages. The 1955 putsch, for the elite, is a "liberating revolution," for the people, "the gorilla coup." Everything in the film, from the initial dedication to Che Guevara through the final exhortation to action, obeys the Brechtian injunction to "divide the audience," forcing the audience to "take sides." The Argentine intellectual must decide to be with the Perónist masses or against them. The American must reject the phrase "Yankee imperialism" or acknowledge that it corresponds, on some level, to the truth. At times, the call for commitment reaches discomfiting extremes for the spectator hoping for a warm bath of escapism. Quoting Frantz Fanon's "All spectators are cowards or traitors" (neither option flatters), the film calls at times for virtual readiness for martyrdom—"To choose one's death is to choose one's life"— at which point the lukewarm entertainment-seeker might feel that the demands for commitment have escalated unacceptably.

The Hour of the Furnaces also short-circuits passivity by making intense intellectual demands. The written titles and spoken commentary taken together form a more or less continuous essay, one that ranks in rhetorical power with those of the authors it cites—Fanon, Césaire, Sartre. At once broadly discursive and vividly imagistic, abstract and concrete, this essay-text, rather than simply commenting on the images, organizes them and provides their principle of coherence. The essay constitutes the film's control center, its brain. The images take on meaning in relation to it rather than the reverse. During prolonged periods, the screen becomes an audio-visual blackboard and the spectator a reader of text. The staccato intercutting of black frames and incendiary titles generates a dynamic *cine-écriture;* the film writes itself. Vertovian titles explode around the screen, rushing toward and retreating from the spectator, their graphic presentation often mimicking their signification. The word "liberation," for example, proliferates and multiplies, in a striking visual and kinetic reminiscence of Che's call for "two, three, many Vietnams." At other times, in a rude challenge to the sacrosanct "primacy of the visual," the screen remains blank while a disembodied voice addresses us in the darkness.

The commentary participates mightily in the film's work of demystification. As the caption "for Walter Benjamin" could tear photography away from fashionable clichés and grant it "revolutionary use value," so the commentary shatters the official image of events. An idealized painting celebrating Argentine political independence is undercut by the offscreen account of the financial deals that betrayed *economic* independence. Formal sovereignty is exposed as the facade masking the realities of material subjugation. Shots of the bustling, prosperous port of Buenos Aires, similarly, are accompanied by an analysis of a general systemic poverty: "What characterizes Latin American countries is, first of all, their dependence—economic dependence, political dependence, cultural dependence." The spectator is taught to distrust images or, better, to see through them to their underlying structures. The film strives to enable the spectator to penetrate the veil of appearances, to dispel the mists of ideology through an act of revolutionary decoding.

Much of the persuasive power of *The Hour of the Furnaces* derives from its ability to render ideas visual. Abstract concepts are given clear and accessible form. The sociological abstraction "oligarchy" is concretized by shots of the "fifty families" that monopolize much of Argentina's wealth. "Here they are . . . ," says the text; the "oligarchy" comes into focus as the actual faces of real people, recognizable and accountable. "Class society" becomes the image ("quoted" by Birri's *Tire dié/Throw Me a Dime*, 1958) of desperate child beggars running alongside trains in hopes of a few pennies from blasé passengers. "Systemic violence" is rendered by images of the state's apparatus of repression—prisons, armored trucks, bombers. The title "No Social Order Commits Suicide" yields to four quick-cut shots of the military. Cesaire's depiction of the colonized—"Dispossessed, Marginalized, Condemned"—gives way to shots of workers, up against the wall, undergoing police interrogation. Thus *The Hour of the Furnaces* engraves ideas on the mind of the spectator. The images do not explode harmlessly, dissipating their energy. They fuse with ideas in order to detonate in the minds of the audience.

Parody and satire form part of the strategic arsenal of *The Hour of the Furnaces*. One sequence, a sightseeing excursion through Buenos Aires, compares in irreverence to Buñuel's sardonic tour of Rome in *L'Age d'or* (1930). The images are those customary in travelogues—government buildings, monuments, busy thoroughfares—but the accompanying text is dipped in acid. Rather than exalt the cosmopolitan charm or the bustling energy of Buenos Aires, the commentary disengages its class structure: the highly placed *comprador* bourgeoisie, the middle class ("eternal in-betweens, both protected and used by the oligarchy") and the petite bourgeoisie ("eternal crybabies, for whom change is necessary, but impossible"). Monuments, symbols of national pride, are treated as petrified emblems

The Hour of the Furnaces: The state apparatus of repression at work.

of servility. As the camera zooms out from an equestrian statue of one of Argentina's founding fathers (Carlos de Alvear), an offscreen voice ironizes: "Here monuments are erected to the man who said: 'These provinces want to belong to Great Britain, to accept its laws, obey its government, live under its powerful influence.'"

Satiric vignettes pinpoint the reactionary nostalgia of the Argentine ruling class. We see them in an antique car acting out their fantasy of *la belle époque.* We see "La Recoleta," their cemetery, baroque testimonial to an atrophied way of life, where the oligarchy tries to "freeze time" and "crystallize history." Just as Vertov destroys (via split screen) the Bolshoi Theatre in *Man with a Movie Camera* (1929), Solanas-Getino annihilate the cemetery with superimposed lightning bolts and thunderous sound effects. Using techniques reminiscent of Resnais's art documentaries, they animate the cemetery's neoclassical statues, creating a completely artificial time and space. The statues "dialogue" in shot/reaction shot to the music of an Argentinian opera whose words ("I shall bring down the rebel flag in blood") remind us of the aristocracy's historical capacity for savage repression. Still another vignette pictures the oligarchy at its annual cattle show in Buenos Aires. The sequence interweaves shots of the crowned heads of the prize bulls with the faces of the aristocracy. The bulls—inert, sluggish, well pedigreed—present a perfect analogue to the oligarchs who breed them.

Metonymic contiguity coincides with metaphoric transfer as the auction-
eer's phrases describing the bulls ("admire the expression, the bone structure") are yoked, in a stunning cinematic zeugma, to the looks of bovine
self-satisfaction on the faces of their owners.

On occasion, Solanas-Getino enlist the unwitting cooperation of their
satiric targets by having ruling-class figures condemn themselves by their
own discourse. Newsreel footage shows an Argentine writer, surrounded
by jewelry-laden dowagers, at an official reception, as a parodic offscreen
voice sets the tone: "And now let's go to the Pepsi Cola Salon, where Manuel
Mujica Lainez, member of the Argentine Academy of Letters, is presenting
his latest book, *Royal Chronicles.*" Lainez then boasts, in nonsynchronous
sound, of his international prizes, his European formation, his "deep sympathy for the Elizabethan spirit." No professional actor could better incarnate the intellectual bankruptcy of the elite, with its fossilized attitudes, its
nostalgia for Europe, its hand-me-down culture, and its snide ingratitude
toward the country and people that made possible its privileges.

Recorded noises and music also play a discursive and demystifica-
tory role. The sound of a time clock punctuates shots of workers hurry-
ing to their jobs, an aural reminder of the daily violence of "wage slavery."
Godardian frontal shots of office buildings with their abstract geometrical-
ity are superimposed with sirens; innocuous images take on overtones of
urban anxiety. A veritable compendium of musical styles—tango, opera,
pop—makes mordant comment on the image. A segment on cultural colonialism has Ray Charles singing "I don't need no doctor" as a pop-music
junkie nods his head in rhythm in a Buenos Aires record store. A med-
ley of national and party anthems ("La Marseillaise," "The International")
lampoons the European allegiances of the traditional left parties. And one
of the most poignantly telling sequences shows a small-town prostitute,
pubic hair exposed, eating lunch while sad-looking men wait in line for her
favors. The musical accompaniment (the patriotic "flag-raising" song) suggests that Argentina has been reduced to exactly this—a hungry prostitute
with her joyless clientele.

Solanas-Getino prolong and critically reelaborate the avant-garde heritage. One sequence fuses Eisenstein with Warhol by intercutting scenes
from a slaughterhouse with pop-culture advertising icons. The sequence
obviously quotes Eisenstein's celebrated nondiegetic metaphor in *Strike*
(1924) but also invests it with specifically Argentinian resonances. In Argentina, where livestock is a basic industry, the same workers who can
barely afford the meat that they themselves produce are simultaneously
encouraged by advertising to consume the useless products of the mul-
tinational companies. The livestock metaphor, anticipated in the earlier

prize-bull sequence, is subsequently "diegeticized" when a shot of the exterior of a slaughterhouse coincides with an account of the police repression of its striking workers. The advertising/slaughter juxtaposition, meanwhile, evokes advertising itself as a kind of slaughter whose numbing effect is imaged by the mallet striking the ox unconscious. The vapid accompanying music by the Swingle Singers (Bach grotesquely metamorphosed into Ray Conniff) counterpoints the brutality of the images, while underlining the shallowly plastic good cheer of the ads.

In *The Hour of the Furnaces*, minimalism—the avant-garde aesthetic most appropriate to the exigencies of film production in the Third World—reflects practical necessity as well as artistic strategy. Time and again one is struck by the contrast between the poverty of the original materials and the power of the final result. Unpromising footage is transmogrified into art, as the alchemy of montage transforms the base metals of titles, blank frames, and percussive sounds into the gold and silver of rhythmic virtuosity. Static two-dimensional images (photos, posters, ads, engravings) are dynamized by editing and camera movement. Still photos and moving images sweep by at such velocity that we lose track of where movement stops and stasis begins. The most striking minimalist image—a close-up of Che Guevara's

The Hour of the Furnaces: The famous photo of Che Guevara in death's repose.

face in death—is held for a full five minutes. The effect of this inspirational death mask is paradoxical. Through the having-been-there of photography, Che Guevara returns our glance from beyond the grave. His face even in death seems mesmerizingly present, his expression one of defiant undefeat. At the same time, the photo gradually assumes the look of a cracked revolutionary icon. The long contemplation of the photograph demystifies and unmasks: we become conscious of the frame, the technical imperfections, the filmic material itself.[4]

The most iconoclastic sequence, titled "Models," begins by citing Fanon's call for an authentically Third World culture: "Let us not pay tribute to Europe by creating states, institutions and societies in its mould. Humanity expects more from us than this caricatural and generally obscene imitation." As the commentary derides Europe's "racist humanism," the image track parades the most highly prized artifacts of European high culture: the Parthenon, *Dejeuner sur l'herbe,* Roman frescoes, portraits of Byron and Voltaire. In an attack on the ideological hierarchies of the spectator, haloed art works are inexorably lap-dissolved into meaninglessness. As in the postcard sequence of Godard's *Les Carabiniers* (1963), that locus classicus of anti–high art semioclasm, the most cherished monuments of Western culture are implicitly equated with the commercialized fetishes of consumer society. Classical painting and toothpaste are leveled as two kinds of imperial export. The pretended "universality" of European culture is exposed as a myth masking the fact of domination.

This demolition job on Western culture is not without its ambiguities, however; for Solanas and Getino, like Fanon before them, are imbued with the very culture they so vehemently denigrate. *The Hour of the Furnaces* betrays a cultivated familiarity with Flemish painting, Italian opera, French cinema; it alludes to the entire spectrum of highbrow culture. Their attack is also an exorcism, the product of a love-hate relationship to the European parent culture. The same lap dissolves that obliterate classical art also highlight its beauty. The film's scorn for "culture," furthermore, finds ample precedent within the antitraditionalist modernism of Europe itself. Mayakovsky asked, even before the revolution, that the Russian classics be "thrown overboard from the steamer" of modernity (quoted in Woroszylski 47). The dismissal of all antecedent art as simply a waste of time recalls the *antepassatismo* of the futurists. "One must spit daily at the *Altar of art,"* said Marinetti (quoted in Woroszylski 261). And both Mayakovsky and Godard have evoked the symbolic destruction of the shrines of high culture. "Make bombardment echo on the museum walls," shouted Mayakovsky, and Godard, in *La Chinoise* (1967), has Veronique call for the bombing of the Louvre and the Comédie-Française.

While drawing on a certain avant-garde, *The Hour of the Furnaces* critiques what it sees as the apolitical avant-garde. Revolutionary films, in this view, must be aesthetically avant-garde—revolutionary art must first of all be revolutionary *as art* (Benjamin)—but avant-garde films are not necessarily revolutionary. *The Hour of the Furnaces* eludes what it sees as the vacuity of a certain avant-garde by politicizing what might have been purely formalistic exercises. The ironic pageant of high art images in the "Models" sequence, for example, is accompanied by discourses on the colonization of Third World culture. Another sequence, superimposing shots of Argentinians lounging at poolside with vapid cocktail dialogue about the prestige value of being familiar with op art and pop art, abstract art and concrete art, highlights the bourgeois fondness for a politically innocuous avant-garde that is as much the product of fashion and commodity fetishism as styles in shirts and jeans. In Argentina, its promotion formed part of a pattern of United States cultural intervention in which organizations such as the U.S.I.S. exhibited modernist painting as part of a larger imperialist strategy.

An apolitical avant-garde risks becoming an institutionalized loyal opposition, the progressive wing of establishment art. Supplying a daily dose of novelty to a satiated society, it generates surface turmoil while leaving the deep structures intact. The artists, as Godard once pointed out, are inmates who bang their dishes against the bars of their prison. Rather than destroy the prison, they merely make a noise which, ultimately, reassures the warden. The noise is then co-opted by a mechanism of repressive desublimation and cited as proof of the system's liberality. *The Hour of the Furnaces* has nothing to do with such an avant-garde, and to treat it as such would be to trivialize it by detaching it from the revolutionary impulse that drives and informs it.

Embracing elements of this critique of an apolitical avant-garde does not entail endorsing all features of the film's global politics. Without diminishing the directors' achievement or disrespecting the sacrifice of thousands of Argentinians, one feels obliged to point out political ambiguities in the film. *The Hour of the Furnaces* shares with what one might call the heroic-masochistic avant-garde a vision of itself as engaged in a kind of apocalyptic self-sacrifice in the name of future generations. The artistic avant-garde, as Renato Poggioli has suggested, often cultivates the image, and symbolically suffers the fate, of military avant-gardes: they serve as advanced cadres "slaughtered" (if only by the critics) to prepare the way for the regular army or the new society (Poggioli). The spirit of self-immolation on the altar of the future (*"Pitié pour nous qui combattons toujours aux frontiéres / De l'illimité et de l'avenir"* [Pity us who struggle always at the edge of boundlessness and the future]) merges in *The Hour of the Furnaces* with a quasi-religious subtext that draws on the language and imagery of martyrdom, death, and resurrection. One might even posit a subliminal Danteesque structuring that ascends from the *inferno* of neocolonial oppression through the *purgatorio* of revolutionary violence to the *paradiso* of national liberation. Without reviving the facile caricature of Marxism as "secular religion," one can regret the film's occasional confusion of political categories with moral-religious ones. The subsurface millenarianism of the film, while it partially explains the film's power (and its appeal even for some bourgeois critics), in some ways undermines its political integrity.

Equipped with the luxury of retrospective lucidity, one can also better discern the deficiencies of the Fanonian and Guevarist ideas informing the film. It is deeply imbued with Fanon's faith in the therapeutic value of violence. But while it is true to say that violence is an effective political language, the key to resistance or the taking of power, it is quite another to value it as therapy for the oppressed. *The Hour of the Furnaces* misapplies a theory associated with a specific point in Frantz Fanon's ideological trajectory during the period of *The Wretched of the Earth* (first published in 1961, the point of maximum disenchantment with the European left) and with a precise historical situation (French settler colonialism in Algeria). Solanas and Getino also pay rightful tribute to Che Guevara as model revolutionary. Subsequent events, however, have made it obvious that certain of Che's policies were mistaken. Guevarism in Latin America gave impetus to an ultravoluntarist strategy that often turned out to be ineffective or even suicidal. One might even link the vestigial machismo of the film's language ("El Hombre": Man) to this ideal of the heroic warrior who personally exposes himself to combat.[5] Guerrilla strategists often underestimated the repressive power of the governments in place and overestimated the objective and subjective readiness of the local populations for revolution.

As a left Perónist film, *The Hour of the Furnaces* also partakes of the historical strengths and weaknesses of that movement.[6] Solanas-Getino rightly identify Perón as a Third World nationalist *avant la lettre* rather than the "fascist dictator" of Eurocentric mythology.[7] ("Perón was a fascist and a dictator detested by all good men . . . except Argentinians," said Dean Acheson, slyly insinuating that Argentinians are not good men.) While the film does score the failures of Perónism—its refusal to attack the power bases of the oligarchy, its failure to arm the people against right-wing coups, its constant oscillation between "democracy of the people" and the "dictatorship of bureaucracy"—the filmmakers see Perón as the man through whom the Argentine working class became gropingly aware of its collective destiny. Perónism, for them, was "objectively revolutionary" because it embodied this proletarian movement. By breaking the imperial stranglehold on Argentina's economy, Perónism would prepare the way for authentic socialist revolution. The film fails most crucially, however, in not placing Perónism in its most appropriate context—Latin American populism. In this version, populism represents a style of political representation by which certain progressive and nationalist elements of the bourgeoisie enlist the support of the people in order to advance their own interests. Latin American populists, like populists everywhere, flirt with the right with one hand and caress the left with the other, making pacts with God and the devil. Like the inhabitants of Alphaville, they manage to say yes and no at the same time. As a tactical alliance, Perónism constituted a labyrinthine tangle of contradictions, a fragile mosaic that shattered, not surprisingly, with its leader's disappearance.

Perónism was plagued by at least two major contradictions, both of which are inscribed, to a certain extent, in the film. Wholeheartedly anti-imperialist, Perónism was only halfheartedly antimonopolist, since the industrial bourgeoisie allied with it was more frightened of the working class than it was of imperialism. Although Solanas-Getino at one point explicitly call for socialist revolution, there is ambiguity in the film and in the concept of "Third Cinema." The "third," while obviously referring to the "Third World," also echoes Perón's call for a "third way," for an intermediate path between socialism and capitalism. That *The Hour of the Furnaces* seems more radical than it in fact is largely derives from its skillful orchestration of what one might call the revolutionary intertext, that is, its aural and visual evocation of tricontinental revolution. The strategically placed allusions to Che Guevara, Fanon, Ho Chi Minh, and Stokely Carmichael create a kind of "*effet de radicalité*" rather like the "*effet de reel*" cited by Roland Barthes in connection with the strategic details of classical realist fiction.

Perónism's second major contradiction has to do with its constant swing between democracy and authoritarianism, participation and manipulation. With populism, a plebeian style and personal charisma often mask a deep scorn for the masses. Egalitarian manners create an apparent equality between the representative of the elite and the people who are the object of manipulation. The film, at once manipulative and participatory, strong-armed and egalitarian, shares in this ambiguity. It speaks the language of popular expression ("Your ideas are as important as ours") but also resorts to hyperbolic language and sledgehammer persuasion.

The Hour of the Furnaces is brilliant in its critique. And history has not shown its authors to be totally failed prophets. It is facile for us, equipped with hindsight and protected by distance, to point up mistaken predictions or failed strategies. The film's indictment of neocolonialism remains shatteringly relevant. The critique of the traditional left, and especially of the Argentine Communist party, was borne out when the PCA offered its critical support to a right-wing regime, largely because it concentrated its repression on the non-Stalinist left and made grain deals with the Soviet Union. The film also accurately points up the ruling class potentiality for violent repression. The regime in power when this essay was first published, with its horrendous human rights record, its *desaparecidos* and its anti-Semitism, merely reaffirms the capacity for violence of an elite that has "more than once bathed the country in blood."

Despite its occasional ambiguities, *The Hour of the Furnaces* remains a seminal contribution to revolutionary cinema. Transcending the narcissistic self-expression of auteurism, it voices the concerns of a mass movement. By allying itself with a concrete movement, which however "impure" has at least the virtue of being real, it practices a cinematic politics of "dirty hands." If its politics are at times populist, its filmic strategies are not. It assumes that the mass of people are quite capable of grasping the exact meaning of an association of images or of a sound montage; that it is ready, in short, for linguistic experimentation. It respects the people by offering quality, proposing a cinema that is simultaneously a tool for consciousness-raising, an instrument for analysis, and a catalyst for action. The film provides a model for avant-garde political filmmaking and a treasury of formalist strategies. It is an advanced seminar in the politics of art and the art of politics, a four-hour launching pad for experimentation, an underground guide to revolutionary cinematic praxis.

The Hour of the Furnaces is also a key piece in the ongoing debate concerning the two avant-gardes. It would be naive and sentimental to see the two avant-gardes as "naturally" allied. (The mere mention of Ezra Pound or Marinetti refutes such an idea.) The alliance of the two avant-gardes is not natural; it must be forced. The two avant-gardes, yoked by a common impulse of rebellion, concretely need each other. While revolutionary aesthetics without revolutionary politics is often futile, revolutionary politics without revolutionary aesthetics is equally retrograde, pouring the new wine of revolution into the old bottles of conventional forms, reducing art to a crude instrumentality in the service of a preformed message. *The Hour of the Furnaces,* by avoiding the twin traps of an empty iconoclasm on the one hand and a "correct" but formally nostalgic militancy on the other, constitutes a major step toward the realization of that scandalously utopian and only apparently paradoxical idea—that of a majoritarian avant-garde.

NOTES

1. The idea of "Third Cinema" is fully developed in an essay by Solanas and Getino titled "Towards a Third Cinema." This highly influential essay, translated into at least a dozen languages, appears in both *Afterimage* 3 (summer 1971): 16–35, and *Cineaste* 4, no. 3 (1970–71): 1–10, and is anthologized in *Movies and Methods*, ed. Bill Nichols (Berkeley: University of California Press, 1976), 44–64.

2. Aleatory procedures are, of course, typical of art in the 1960s. One need think only of "process art" in which chemical, biological, or seasonal forces affect the original materials, or of environmental art, or happenings, mixed media, human-machine interaction systems, street theater, and the like. The film formed part of a general tendency to erase the boundaries between art and life, but rarely did this erasure take such a highly politicized form.

3. Christian Metz explores this distinction, drawn from Emile Benveniste, in "Story/Discourse (A Note on Two Kinds of Voyeurism)," in *The Imaginary Signifier: Psychoanalysis and the Cinema*, ed. Celia Britton, Annwyl Williams, Ben Brewster, and Alfred Guzzetti (Bloomington: Indiana University Press, 1982), 91–98.

4. The Argentinian junta paid inadvertent tribute to the revolutionary potential of photography when they arrested Che Guevara's mother in 1962, accusing her of having in her possession a "subversive" photograph. The photograph was of her son Che.

5. Gérard Chaliand, in *Mythes révolutionnaires du tiers- monde* (New York: Viking Press, 1976), criticizes what he calls the "macho" attitudes of Latin American guerrillas that led them to expose themselves to combat even when their presence was not required, thus resulting in the death of most of the guerrilla leaders. He contrasts this attitude with the more prudent procedure of the Vietnamese. During fifteen years of war, not one of the fifty members of the central committee of the South Vietnamese National Liberation Front fell into the hands of the enemy.

6. Should there be any doubt about the Perónist allegiances of the film, one need only remember the frequent quotations of Perón, the interviews with Perónist militants, and the critiques of the non-Perónist left. In 1971, Solanas and Getino made a propaganda film for Perón: *Perón: La revolucion justicialista* (*Perón: The Just Revolution*). The Cine-Liberacion group that made the film, according to Solanas, served as the cinematic arm of General Perón. During the (pro-Perónist) Campora administration, Getino accepted a post on the national film board. Upon Perón's death, Solanas and Getino made a public declaration supporting the succession of his wife, Isabel. Ironically, the repression unleashed after her ouster was leveled as much against Solanas and Getino as against those who had been more consistently on the left.

7. The simplistic view of Perón as a fascist has been revived in many of the reviews of the Broadway production of *Evita*, with a number of critics comparing the play to the kind of spectacle parodied in Mel Brooks's *The Producers* (1967).

Works Cited

Barthes, Roland. *Image/Music/Text*. Ed. and trans. Stephen Heath. New York: Hill and Wang, 1977.

Benjamin, Walter. "The Work of Art in the Age of Mechanical Reproduction." In *Illuminations,* ed. Hannah Arendt, trans. Harry Zohn, 219–53. New York: Schocken, 1969.

Poggioli, Renato. *The Theory of the Avant-garde*. New York: Harper and Row, 1971.

Woroszylski, Wiktor. *The Life of Mayakovsky.* Trans. Boleslaw Taborski. New York: Orion Press, 1970.

Chapter 17

SEEING WITH EXPERIMENTAL EYES

Stan Brakhage's
The Act of Seeing with One's Own Eyes

Bart Testa

Stan Brakhage's Pittsburgh Trilogy, three films each approximately one half hour long, are regarded by many as exceptional in his large and brilliant oeuvre, which virtually defines the American experimental cinema in its lyrical, subjective dimension. The reason these films stand strikingly apart in Brakhage's oeuvre is that they are documentaries. *Eyes* (1970) focuses on the city's police; *Deux Ex* (1971) on a hospital; and *The Act of Seeing with One's Own Eyes* (1971), the last and most notorious of the films, depicts with uncompromising directness several autopsies performed in Pittsburgh's city morgue. The most salient feature of *The Act of Seeing* is the film's unadorned and troubling directness. No viewing position like we gain in a conventional documentary (or fiction film, for that matter) is available in this film.

Brakhage's handheld camera closely and intently observes coroners perform autopsies on six or seven bodies. The camera has little interest in the coroners themselves, less in their "findings" regarding the causes of death. Although there are a couple of shots showing them speaking into microphones, these merely underscore what we do not hear in this soundless film. There are no voice-over explanations, no interviews, no music, no intertitles. Nor does the montage of images develop a systematic exposition of autopsy procedure. The camera remains fixed on the bodies in medium or close-up shots, as hands and tools go about their work of measurement and then of dismemberment. No overall narrative evolves.

The Act of Seeing is therefore a very difficult film to watch. For, in addition to its inherently gruesome subject matter and unflinching directness, it seems to offer nowhere to hide from its raw literalness. We can readily imagine watching another equally explicit movie of autopsies; but very likely we will also imagine that such a film would allow us to slip behind verbal explanations of the pathologists' procedures, analyses of the cause of death, or perhaps some moral argument that necessitates showing such images. However, as Bill Nichols notes, none of these familiar viewing strategies is on offer here: "We witness what exceeds our sight and grasp. The camera gazes. It presents evidence destined to disturb. The evidence cries out for argument, some interpretive frame within which to comprehend it. Nowhere is this need more acutely felt than in a film that refuses to provide any explanatory commentary whatsoever" (81).

But if images seem to demand explanation or interpretation to be comprehended, it is conversely true that an "interpretive frame" requires images to serve the explanatory purpose of that frame. To give substance to the conventional claim made for documentaries—that they make a literal representation of a truth (even if the claim is made only by the label "documentary," "direct cinema," or "nonfiction")—documentary films need images to be evidential. But evidence of what? Of the films' arguments, Nichols says. Critics often claim that documentary film images present viewers with images of "*the* world." This distinguishes them from fiction films, which show aspects of "*a* world," one built up by the fiction. "The literalism of documentary centers around the look of things in the world as an index of meaning" (Nichols 27). When the documentarian places images into a structure of exposition, explanation, or argument, the images become evidence of certain facts of *the* world. This is achieved by the use of voice-overs, printed titles, and/or "quasiverbal" montage constructions, any and all of which offer an interpretation or make an argument about *the* world witnessed by the images. "Every cut or edit," says Nichols, "is a step forward in an argument" (29).

Such submission of filmed images to argument causes the images to "speak" on behalf of that argument. Yet this subordination is a vital part of showing the world "as an index of meaning," and it engenders comprehension of what images depict. The evidential function images assume by being both visibly of *the* world and subordinated to argument sustains a whole film as *meaningful*. In turn, that subordinate function of the images also allows the meaning of each image to come forth as a significant and understandable, if also partial, statement about *the* world. Ideally, in a wellmade documentary there is a symmetry in the exchange of signifying relations between images and "interpretive frames," and this exchange makes showing and explanation a unity. This is the case whether the images are made to illustrate the steps of a technical process (as in, say, a medical or industrial education film) or to provide forceful evidence for a moral or political argument. The uses of images in documentary filmmaking hold in common the role of performing what, in simple summary terms, could be called *acts of showing*.

In any of the types of documentary just enumerated, the difficulty of watching bodies under autopsy—images that are of themselves undeniably "traumatic"—is mitigated by the process of subsuming them. To illustrate a procedure that needs to be explained, for example, or to support a moral argument, provides a ready-made position from which to comprehend what is shown. By creating such a position, which is what structures of understanding do, even traumatic images are softened by making them significant evidence within an interpretive frame. The *act of showing* implants images within a wider and controlling function of meaning. This implantation subordinates *seeing* images as literal presentations to the higher-order process of argumentation. Witnessing and seeing recede, to a greater or lesser degree, behind signification and showing.

By way of illustration, consider another piece, a video that concerns a morgue but is entirely different in style from Brakhage's film. Peter Greenaway's *Death in the Seine* (1990) can even be taken to be an inverse of *The Act of Seeing with One's Own Eyes*. Its documentary source is a mortuary archive of written reports compiled between 1795 and 1801 in Paris. It deals with a sample of twenty-three reports (out of 306 extant records) composed about bodies pulled from the River Seine by two "mortuary attendants" (ancestors of modern coroners). A voice-over recites, in careful paraphrase, minute particulars from entries made for each corpse while the images display the following in strict series, repeated twenty-three times: first, a fictional tableaux of actors playing the attendants drawing the bodies (also played by actors) from the river; second, stripping and washing the bodies and taking depositions from witnesses; and, last, a slowly traveling close-up tracking over the naked bodies as the voice-over sums up the findings. Even though the images are fictional constructs, they serve, in the manner common to documentaries, to substantiate the detailed paraphrases of actual historical texts in acts of showing. The matches between written descriptions and the images of bodies are quite rigorously maintained. At any rate, the actor-bodies' still nakedness possesses a strong enough semblance of witnessing for the work to have its intended effect. Naturally, viewers know, and the video frankly acknowledges, that showing literally real images is in this case impossible.

The intended *argument* of *Death in the Seine* is that the lives that ended in the river also ended inconclusively for us, the living. Our historical record cannot really—or rather, cannot fully—remember. The Parisian mortuary archive is the slenderest of records and even it has many gaps and enigmas, as the voice-over gently admits. Yet these records are all we have since no other trace of these obscure, ordinary people exists and, over the six generations since 1801, no living relation of these dead could possibly have even a faint recollection of them. These are the shards of *the* world of the past. The detailing of death's circumstances through a few words can explain neither a life nor its finish, but it does offer some slight remembrance of these persons, some comprehension of who they were.

Death in the Seine is a reflexive pseudo-documentary. Its images are fictions and its structure is conspicuous. Like many works of the pseudo-documentary type, Greenaway's video engages in scrupulous reconstruction of irrecuperable realities in order to reveal paradoxes surrounding truth claims about *the* world when one tries to capture them in literal images. It offers the viewer an elaborate interpretative framework cobbled from a written literalism, but it also reflects back on its own processes. Indeed, *Death in the Seine* is, one could say, all interpretative framework but one made of literal verbal means and tightly matched (i.e., subordinated) fictional images. The images, it follows, are purely *acts of showing*, but by showing what can never be really shown, Greenaway pursues the paradox of representation when death is itself at stake.[1]

In contrast to Greenaway's reflexively exaggerated strategies of "interpretive framing," Brakhage radically reduces the interpretive resources of his film. *The Act of Seeing with One's Own Eyes* bluntly states its rather different and direct strategy in its very title. This is a film that completely dispenses with any verbal explanation. It is not a film about showing but about bringing us very close to actual bodies in a morgue; in other words, it is a film rigorously about *seeing*. It remains at a literal level of confrontation with a truth, which is why Nichols says it "exceeds our sight and grasp": Brakhage's film restricts its means to an act of seeing, and seeing *this,* as the direct witness to bodies under autopsy. However, from this seeming simplicity and directness, interpretive possibilities arise, if only because Brakhage's film does not interpret its images for us. Although neither expository nor argumentative, this film *is* composed, and it is rich in implications.

Hollis Frampton has suggested that since seeing is made the pointed issue of this film, Brakhage's camera must be taken as the compassionate surrogate of us all in its role as "staring" witness of death's body. Frampton writes: "All of us, in the person of the coroner, must see that, with our own eyes. It is a room full of appealing particular intimacies, the last ditch of individuation. Here our vague nightmare of mortality acquires the names and faces of *others*."

This last is a process that requires a *witness;* and what "idea" may finally have inserted itself into the sensible world we can still scarcely guess, for the *camera* would seem the perfect eidetic witness, staring with perfect compassion where we can scarcely bear to glance.

This is a strong and sensitive interpretation. Yet to understand *The Act of Seeing with One's Own Eyes,* which really means to grapple with how a filmmaker composes such a document of acts of seeing seriously, and to grasp its highly reflexive and implicatory form, we are obliged first to consider the fact that the film is not only a documentary but also an avant-garde documentary.

On first sight, the expression "avant-garde documentary" may seem an oxymoron. In many important respects, documentary and avant-garde filmmaking are polar opposites. But, in a sense, they share a space in the "cinema institution" by dint of *not* being fiction feature-film cinema; they cohabit the margins of film culture, which is dominated by fiction films. There are some important affiliations and differences that bind documentary and the avant-garde as cinematic practices. These are borne out—both theoretically and historically—and sometimes powerfully manifested through single films that are in fact avant-garde documentaries. *The Act of Seeing with One's Own Eyes* is one of these films that offers insight into the cinematic bonds which tie the two modes. Most important, both avant-garde and documentary filmmaking are founded on a deep commitment to pursuing the truth of the film image. This allies them and fundamentally distinguishes them from fiction filmmakers. In fiction films, claims to truth (when they are made at all) reside in the true *story,* and its true telling, not in the truth of the image.

But affiliation is not the same thing here as agreement, and in this case it marks a place of difference. I have already suggested one limited but sharp difference between Brakhage's film and documentary practice: it arises out of the distinction between a documentary's *acts of showing* and Brakhage's (antithetical) *acts of seeing.* Further, Nichols has isolated a significant positive structural feature that allows us to distinguish the efforts of documentarians from the exertions of experimental filmmakers. Documentarians are committed to exposition, explanation, and arguments of a kind that are shared by the socially defined "discourses of sobriety," those recognized as serious explanations of truth, such as science, politics, and religion (Nichols 3). Documentary's "interpretive frames" are homologies of socially recognized, knowable, and understood meanings. Avant-garde cinema, in contrast, often pursues less socially recognized sorts of meaning; artists are drawn to subject matter that goes unaccounted by, or seems incomprehensible, mysterious, and/or forbidden to "sober discourse." Arguments and interpretations of the sober type are very often ignored by experimentalists in favor of exploratory and hence unfamiliar aesthetic, philosophical, and poetic structures of expression, many of which are not actually assimilable to "discursive" forms at all. This is true of Brakhage's film. It completely abandons verbal argument and other ready "interpretive frames" and deliberately focuses on what seems, in principle, to be unknowable and mysterious—the spectacle of death.

A reason why works like *The Act of Seeing*—in which an experimental filmmaker enters the domain of the "literal" film image—are of uncommon critical interest is that they expose the affinities and differences between documentary and avant-garde film. What formal tactics can redeem such a film to meaning? In light of this question, we need to consider the question of why Brakhage made such a film. Frampton's suggestion that Brakhage's camera in the morgue is our collective eye is amplified by P. Adams Sitney, perhaps Brakhage's most insightful critic. Sitney suggests that after a dozen years of intensely subjective filmmaking Brakhage was responding to a felt danger of solipsism and that making the Pittsburgh Trilogy allowed him the relief of turning his lens on what we hold in common (421). Most of Brakhage's films do turn on an extremely private vision and concentrate on natural, domestic, erotic, and childhood themes. In taking up distinctly urban and public material—the police, a hospital, a morgue—Brakhage embraced a distinct and realistic style because it was suited to the casting of his film-eye upon shared dimensions of experience. Indeed, all three films of the Pittsburgh Trilogy do concern "public seeing": *Eyes* casts city police as the means we use to watch over our public lives; *Deus Ex* depicts the hospital as the house of the protective and curing medical gaze; and the coroner's look, as Frampton suggests, is the last collective gaze we cast upon ourselves, our bodies in death.

However, Brakhage himself entertains no deep distinction between subjective, expressionist modes and realist, public modes of filmmaking. Quite the contrary, he insists that all films are, at least ideally, documents of vision and so all films are really documentaries, albeit in a much expanded sense. All his filmmaking has been devoted to realizing this ideal. Like certain philosophers of perception, notably the French phenomenologist Maurice Merleau-Ponty, Brakhage conceives vision to be a whole-body experience, or the experience of "the body in the world" (see Sobchack 89–92).[2] Emotions, imaginings, dreams, the pulse of the heart, and the "sparking of the synapses" are all registered in acts of vision.

The connection of vision to the body, Brakhage explains, is why he uses a handheld, often shaking or trembling camera, unusual lenses, painted-on-film footage, complex superimpositions, eccentric exposures and focusing, disjunctive cutting rhythms—and why he usually makes silent (and emphatically wordless) films. All these techniques manifest his attempt to come closer to a mimesis of holistic-corporeal acts of seeing. Even when they may appear abstract (for example, as in his painted films, such as *The Dante Quartet*, 1987), Brakhage still takes his films to be reportage of acts of seeing. "Pictures"—clear, recognizable film images—are just a special case of vision and not its definitive form. The different stylistic moments in his filmmaking are, therefore, to be accounted for by the themes that attracted him and the states of emotion or mind that gave rise to his films.[3] The idea of a public seeing can and should remain highly pertinent, but *The Act of Seeing with One's Own Eyes* should not be taken as thematically anomalous within his filmmaking, even though the style of the film and its affinity with documentary cinema must still be regarded as exceptional in his oeuvre.

If we reach back further into his career, we uncover another such seemingly anomalous work, one through which Brakhage actually discovered the lineaments of his mature style. As a young filmmaker in the 1950s, he was commissioned by Joseph Cornell, the American surrealist, to make a film document of New York's Third Avenue "EL" (elevated train) just prior to its demolition. The resulting *The Wonder Ring* (1955) is the film in which Brakhage decisively shifted from the black and white psychodramas (acted films involving hermetic subjective states played out in front of the camera) that had previously dominated his filmmaking to a cinema of "direct seeing" characterized by rapid handheld camera movement, vivid color, and rhythmically assertive, disjunctive editing. Although associated with subjectivism, that style's inspiration was the desire to capture the peculiar light, movement, and vibration of an elevated part of a quintessential public and urban subject, the New York subway. In a fascinating paradox, *The Wonder Ring* is a city documentary that drew Brakhage outside himself (the realm of psychodrama) and led him into his mature style.

Cornell was not alone at the time in being an American artist with a surrealist lineage involved in making urban avant-garde documentary work. Indeed, Brakhage's emergent style owed much to New York painter-filmmaker Marie Menken's wordless silent films of the 1940s and 1950s, an influence he has enthusiastically acknowledged (Brakhage, "Menken"). These likewise involve a handheld moving camera, intense color, and a strong emphasis on acts of seeing. Menken also made several stunning avant-garde city documentaries in this mode, notably *Go, Go, Go* (1964). But her signal work, and the historic connector between the history of avant-garde documentaries and *The Act of Seeing,* is her collaboration with her husband, Willard Maas, and poet George Barker, *Geography of the Body* (1943), one of the most famous of all American experimental films.

Menken shot this film, which moves about and probes several naked bodies in extreme close-up, through a magnifying glass that so enlarges the images that they are barely recognizable. The transforming effect of magnification on the body (and of the voice-over text on the images) in *Geography of the Body* is a strong cinematic instance of surrealist "seeing as" in which the literal and the imaginative become combined into a sort of hallucination (Krauss 60). The human body in this film is also surrealist in another, transgressive way. By entering the most secret spaces of the body, the camera crosses into a culturally forbidden, literal intimacy with the flesh. Considered as a whole, *Geography of the Body* is not precisely an avant-garde documentary. However, Menken's close-up literalism of the body connects the film to other features of surrealist documentary films such as Luis Buñuel's *Las Hurdes* (*Land without Bread,* 1932) and Georges Franju's *Le sang des bêtes* (*Blood of the Beasts,* 1949) in overturning the humanism and optimism of the documentary mainstream—that is, the prevailing "sober discourse"—and in making us see what is forbidden to sight. It is this entrance into forbidden realms of seeing—especially seeing the flesh—that joins *Geography of the Body* to surrealist documentary.

Geography virtually invented the avant-garde "body film," which later drew a number of important filmmakers (see Elder). *Blood of the Beasts* invented the "abattoir film," in which documentary abattoir passages (or whole films) serve to augment (or make) moral arguments.[4] Another direction taken by "body films" is less rhetorically metaphoric than either mode and leads to films that dwell, contemplatively, on the flesh under duress. There are many examples, but Brakhage's *The Act of Seeing* is the major work in this lineage.

Both the "body film" and the "abattoir film" arise from surrealism. Despite its reputation for fantastic imagery, surrealism was no less drawn to literal documentary images and, we might say, to acts of looking for the shock, disturbance, and imaginative effects literal images can have. This tendency developed strongly in the period of surrealism's geographical dispersion during and after World War II and then developed further in the American and European avant-gardes of the 1950s and 1960s. But we need to distinguish *The Act of Seeing with One's Own Eyes* from both the abattoir and the body film, as well as from surrealism. These are pertinent, orienting "sources"— historical antecedents of the film—but they do not explain the film itself any more than the departures from conventional documentary films I discussed earlier can explain it, although some contrasts can be drawn.

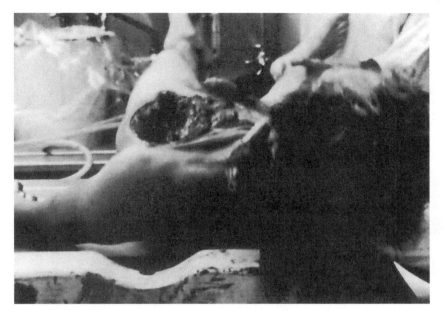

The Act of Seeing with One's Own Eyes: The flesh under duress.

The abattoir film is driven by a moral purpose, and it is this purpose that leads it to forbidden imagery. The intention is to liberate a repressed pathos, to expose what is taken for granted but usually ignored: the fact that animals are meat. Its moral purpose is to tear the veil from this ignored knowledge, and abattoir imagery passes through an outrage that cannot but make the viewer uncomfortable. The moral end is to sensitize us to a hidden inhumanity that is actually commonplace. Now, such a meeting of the viewer and the appalling image cannot be undertaken by a filmmaker lightly. Morality here is a solemn obligation, and it also serves as the means to comprehension, for the danger such strong imagery presents is callous sensationalism.

The solemnity of *The Act of Seeing* is the first formal feature that impresses a viewer. But it is a solemnity without the familiar moralism of a film like Franju's or other documentaries that show flesh under duress. The reason is soon apparent. This is not a film about how human, or animal, bodies are abused or disrespected under autopsy; on the contrary, the dismemberment by the coroners is treated in this film as a serious and respectful, if also mysterious, ritual. Nonetheless, when the film also strips the viewer of the type of moral comprehension we may find in Franju, one faces traumatic imagery unarmed interpretively.

The Act of Seeing also has a moral purpose, however, and Brakhage insists that we travel toward it through a series of very disturbing images. Brakhage times and paces the shots, and frames sequences, so none remains long enough or repeats often enough to desensitize the viewer. We are never allowed to get used to the film's imagery, to watch it as part of a procedural routine, and so *not* see it. The act of seeing, its shock and troubling power, is constantly renewed. Indeed, the images are so relentlessly literal and, in the main, so clearly shot that all there seem to be in this film are successive acts of seeing, and seeing *this*. And this seeing is itself, Brakhage seems to imply, the film's moral end.

There are three basic compositional devices (with combinations and variants of these at work) the film uses to produce this effect I have called solemnity: veiling, juxtaposition, and camera movement. In my analysis each of them is set within an opposition and signified through difference and frequency: unveiling/veiling; like imagery/unlike imagery (in juxtaposition); static camera/moving camera, respectively.

Veiling is the most consistent, isolatable, and readily explicable device and provides *The Act of Seeing* with its most obvious structural accents. Veiling further involves the film's important color patterns, which develop into a red/white antinomy and a seen/not seen opposition that is critical to the renewed acts of seeing the film maintains. Unveiling is weighted by permitting us to see, veiling preventing us. The veiling device arises from two types of "found" images: the covering of bodies with white cloths and the blockage of screen space by parts of the coroners' white lab coats. Brakhage usually shoots both cloths and coats in tight close-up, so that white often fills all of the image field. Bodies are seldom shown being uncovered, but sustained shots are devoted to the coroners covering bodies with white sheets. When this white fills the screen, it marks the transition from seen to not-seen.

My analysis divides the film into ten sections, taking the major breaks as marked by long veiling or withdrawals of the camera. These ten sections are:

1. Prelude: measuring and moving bodies

2. Measuring; outside the body; the gestural close-ups

3. Blood samples, stripping the bodies, moving bodies

4. The skull/eye sockets; the first opened torso

5. The face; the second opened torso

6. Torsos; the dimmed light; water and blood

7. The short body-parts montage; the man with the mop

8. Cutting open the thorax

9. The long body-parts montage; the old man's face

10. Coda: the coroner and the tape recorder

The opening shot shows fabric in close-up, then cuts to a series of shots showing hands testing parts of the body for flexibility and taking measurements of exterior parts with a small white plastic ruler. Brakhage then cuts to a (belated) establishing long shot of a whole body (from slightly above and behind the head) and then a medium shot including the body and the hips of a coroner. This latter composition sets the manner of shooting the morgue workers: they are represented by synecdoche—their hands, arms, and hips—almost never their faces. The series of shots of measurement then resume, followed by another long shot; then a covering of the body, ending with white cloths that fill the screen. A short transitional montage follows: medium shots of bodies being moved on gurneys, and from them onto tables; more measuring; then a series of close-ups of an eye, a hand, a toe. A pattern of visual repetition, in effect a doubling back bracketed by major accentual interruptions—most emphatically cuts to white cloths (veiling)—is established early in the film. Camera movement thus far has been used only for some very slight reframing. However, movement within the frame and medium long shots serve as variations and rhythmic markers within usually static images. This same pattern is repeated in the next two expanded sections, which also concern measurement and again include shots of hands (including hands wrapped in plastic bags), feet, a toe, an eye.

The film, then, has opened with a double-panel of similar segments ("Prelude" and "Measuring and Moving Bodies") where the static camera stays on the outside of the body and extremities, especially hands, feet, and eyes—body features associated with the personal. Because the images of these bodily features have long been culturally coded, through painting especially, as "gestural" icons expressive of personality, even when stilled in death they suggest a person, a subject. They are, however, juxtaposed with shots of measurement and moving bodies that show them to be inert, lifeless, and, in several shots, in rigor mortis. These signs of human gesture, or the personal, will not return until the penultimate segment of the film.

The pattern of veiling becomes more emphatic as the film progresses into the third section. Now, the coroners penetrate the bodies for the first time, first to extract blood samples; then follows the removal of clothing, and there are a few shots of opened bodies, although these are largely veiled from view by lab coats and are seen at the rear of the frame. Camera

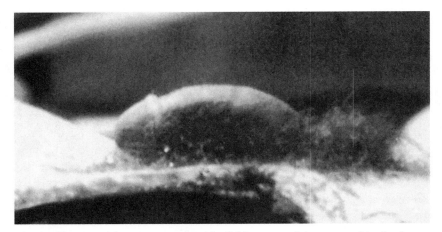

The Act of Seeing with One's Own Eyes: The lifelessness of the personal in death.

movement (panning shots) comes into play now in a short series of moving the bodies, seen in medium long shot. Then the section ends as a veiling of the whole image—white lab coats closing most of the frame—which slides into a split frame, when we briefly see cut-open bodies in part of the image, the white coats filling the rest.

But the first major collision (juxtaposition) of imagery occurs between the third and fourth sections. The latter begins in medium close-up, revealing a chrome circular surgical saw cutting into a skull. In a series of long-take static close-ups, the brain is removed and the camera then moves slowly to enter the skull cavity and briefly look through the eye sockets from behind. Brakhage then veils the scene with a series of shots of cloths and coats, but returns to renewed work on the open skull followed by an extreme close-up of scissors cutting what is soon recognizable as a rib cage. He cuts to a shot showing the internal organs exposed and beginning to be removed—all in extreme close-up. Then the camera withdraws.

The first emphatic camera movement of the film is that of the camera's entrance into the skull cavity; the second is the withdrawal ending the section. Since Brakhage is shooting with a handheld camera, there are frequent slight movements, and he reframes slightly or pans to follow the gurneys. But generally the shots are uniformly steady and brief, the cutting carrying the rhythm, so that these two moving-camera shots gain notable expressive force as a strong response to the most traumatic sights. In this section, these two camera movements occur at points of penetration of the body: the first, involving the skull, uses forward movement answered by white-veiling shots; the second, the exposed and evacuated torso, is answered by the camera's emphatic withdrawal.

This concluding withdrawal is, in turn, juxtaposed with a repeat of the head procedure in the next section, the fifth. This time the procedure is taken from its start: the coroner's hand forcibly peels the back of the entire scalp over the face to expose the naked skull. Then comes a series of quick, extreme close-ups of cutting, followed by a medium shot of the body entirely opened, the organs already removed, and the flesh peeled all the way back. This in turn is followed by a series of white cloths and coats, and the covering of the body. The alternations/oppositions in the three registers proposed here—veiling, juxtaposition, and camera movement—generate the formal pattern of the rest of the film, although, as I shall explain, the patterning undergoes variations. But we have already entered far enough into the fabric of the film so that the differences between it and surrealism, the abattoir film, and the body film can be made evident.

As I suggested earlier in connection with surrealist aesthetics, the abattoir film shows us the unseeable because of a cultural forbiddenness, a gruesomeness that transgresses codes of decorum that concern animal bodies. But the abattoir film is often redeemed from simple outrage, as is Franju's, by a moral purpose that converts disturbing surrealist "seeing as" into humane allegory. By pointing up our everyday inhumanity as carnivores, the documentary spectacle of animal slaughter readily becomes an allegory of human slaughter. Whatever the provocations films like *Blood of the Beasts* initially produced, their absorption into the "sober discourses" was swift. The body film is similarly given to allegorization, the body in such films being given over to either positive or negative mythification.[5]

The collision of the body and abattoir film in *The Act of Seeing* transforms each, turning them away from allegory, for a reason exemplified by the skull segment. In this sequence we are involved in the act of seeing that with which we see—the eyes and the brain, whose cavity, always a hidden place, the camera now penetrates. This is a supremely strange, literal confrontation between our act of seeing and the body's means of seeing. For Brakhage, for whom vision is so importantly corporeal, the image he has taken here is the literal image of his artistic imagining: the seat within the body of vision itself.

Why Brakhage chose to place this most disturbing sequence near the start of the film is apparent. For it is here that he inscribes in the toughest and most cruelly intimate way one could imagine the common fact of our common seeing and makes it literally public. Our shock here when the camera approaches the eyes from behind is the shock of a horrible recognition. It is especially emphatic when in the act of watching any film that we do literally see (or, even more richly, imagine ourselves to see) from that mysteriously infinite and imaginary zone *behind* our eyes. Brakhage's film makes us visit that very place, in an act of seeing now become a literal, unimaginable vacancy. Many critics have said there is no way to "show death" in a film (see, for example, Russell), but *The Act of Seeing with One's Own Eyes* compels us, through this penetration into the physical site of vision, to confront this universal and final vacuity of death. "Showing death" in the sense the critics mean scarcely matters anymore when there is no seeing. And what we see here is death of the means of seeing.

When Brakhage returns to the skull procedure, now witnessed from the start, the effect is compounded: pulling the face over the skull radically denies the face. It is a final negation of personality that comes *before* the skull is penetrated. But we see it here later, and, in a sense, it is the image of Frampton's "last stand of individuation," the face. What we saw moments before in the skull was death's end of the paradox of what is at once common to us all and ours alone, the contents of our skulls. What we see now is something else over and done with—for we see the end of a unique personality's sign, the face literally effaced in death. This supremely gruesome long take of the face peeling is followed by rapid shots of cutting into the lower body and the proleptic shot of the evacuated torso.

The next section continues with work on the torso of a woman, beginning with a cut of the skin and then, elliptically, shots of the inner cavity exposed. The dimming of light as Brakhage closes the lens aperture of his camera shifts color values, slowly pulses, and picks up the dark blood reds. Brakhage then cuts to the whites of coats and cloths. This segment develops the accentual juxtaposition between white and red, as the body now emphatically becomes flesh. Another body is now opened up, more quickly, followed by a segment of water being pumped into the corpse, and then shots of a draining pump outlet, pulsing red and white liquid. It is followed by white coats and cloths again, as the bodies are moved out. In this sixth section, the literal assumes some aspect of the liturgical. The effect is not symbolic but a sign of respect and a softening underscored by the gentle pulsing rhythm of the segment. This effect is then amplified in the next passage when the camera, in a series of shots, moves emphatically among the covered and exposed bodies in a reddish light, as if this were the film's ending. However, like the withdrawal of the camera noted above, this moving-camera passage, although longer, is another segment-marker. It is followed by an extended passage of preparing another body, a reprise of the earlier measuring segment. Instead of ending, the film seems to be beginning again.

Brakhage then, in section seven, develops a montage of body parts and open bodies, using the first extended rapid cutting pattern of the film. He intercuts shots of covering, bodies being moved and lifted, coroners talking into microphones, viscera, and cutting. There are then more shots of body parts and the coroners' hands taking samples of organs, slicing and weighing them. This long montage ends with a cut to a medium shot of an attendant dressed in luminous white with a mop, one of the few shots in which we see a living person's face. This montage is remarkable for the use of static-camera close-ups that show the liquidity of body organs, how they quiver and reflect the light, their reddish colors. Brakhage brings his cutting into a strangely intimate relation with these visual aspects, and it is tempting (and appropriate) to call the section an awestruck song to the inner flesh.

The next, eighth, section begins with a long-expected (and dreaded) shot that Brakhage has withheld, a major vertical incision into the torso opening the whole thorax. This shot is a prelude to the last major section of the film, an accelerating montage that juxtaposes shots of an open body: very red, extreme close-up shots of cutting inside the torso; organs; shots of an old man's fingers, ears, eye, all seeming pale gray to the point of whiteness. There follows a quick interruption of a blank white shot, then a montage of the same elements begins again and speeds up—until suddenly the camera careens toward the floor. This is the last major camera movement of the film, and a conspicuous physical response on the part of the filmmaker.

The next shot begins a series of fast zooms—the only ones in the film, and a strong variation of the opposition between moving and static camera that otherwise informs the film. These shots show the body's removed parts, figured almost like a landscape (*Geography of the Body* radically revised) with liquids making the flesh glisten with light. The camera comes so close here that the body no longer appears as a recognizable human form but merely as a series of enigmatic shapes. Then there is a cut to a held shot of an old man's face and, finally, to a door closing. But for a brief coda, the film is over.

This last montage, the longest single segment, and the film's most stylistically assertive, is also a recapitulation, accelerating most of the stylistic motifs discussed earlier. But it drops veiling. In its place appear the near-white shots of the old man who recuperates the personal-gestural pathos of the dead from the start of the film and the filmmaker's own literal fall almost to the floor with his camera. When we return to the old man, we see his gray-white face, and the last veiling in white. It is the final memorial of personality amid this montage of the flesh itself.

Recapitulating the idea of veiling, the door closes emphatically, solemnly, on this space. The morgue we see in this film is not coextensive with life. That is, it does not extend outward to the everyday but folds inward; analogously, the film is not an allegory that reaches beyond itself, but is about *this*. Part of the solemnity of *The Act of Seeing with One's Own Eyes* is that this is a special space of transformation: universal, for we all die, but also a space with a decided threshold. The film has transformed that space by seeing it—in the most literal, documentary fashion—from a secret, forbidden zone into a space where the body at once ceases to be human in our usual sense yet remains compellingly human in ways that cannot be escaped or destroyed.

The last segment consists of shots showing a coroner speaking into a microphone. There are no bodies around him; we have passed to *our* side, the living side, of the threshold. Brakhage begins with a medium long shot, then follows with close-ups of his face, hand, chin, hips. Then the man goes to turn off the tape recorder and the film ends. We have no notion of his words, of course, since this segment is also silent, but by now the troubling refusal of the film to speak, as a documentary "should," to explain its images, no longer bothers us. Viewers are relieved to have arrived here. Is the coroner a stand-in for Brakhage, another recorder of the dead? Probably he is that, but he is also an ideal stand-in for everyone, as Frampton's interpretation avows; the readily imagined precision of what he is saying, his professional seriousness, and his bent stance all make him the embodiment of Nichols's and Frampton's figure of the witness in this film. In fact, as a coroner, that is exactly what he is—every day he goes to work, pure collective witness to death.

NOTES

1. For a full theorization on this issue, see Vivian Sobchack, "Inscribing Ethical Space: Ten Propositions on Death, Representation, and Documentary," *Quarterly Review of Film Studies* 9, no. 4 (1984): 283–300.

2. Brakhage's position has often been considered eccentric. However, in addition to Sobchack's study, recent histories of "visuality" in modern culture have also emphasized what Martin Jay terms "the return of the body" in *Downcast Eyes: The Denigration of Vision in Twentieth-Century Thought* (Berkeley: University of California Press, 1994), 152.

3. Nichols poses experimental filmmakers negatively—i.e., that they *refuse* the "referentiality" of the film image—and he applies this to Brakhage, implying that his films should be approached as purely formal constructs (81). However, Brakhage's could also be construed as the uncompromised pursuit of the film image as "indexical

sign," to use one of Nichols's (and other film theorists') favorite terms, and one that they mistakenly use as a synonym for images that are directly referential or "realistic." In the philosopher C. S. Pierce's semiotics, from where the term comes, indexical signs prescribe nothing necessary about "realistic" pictures but only the direct effect of the referent's registration. Examples include a bullet hole in a wall or a medical symptom registered on the surface of the body. Brakhage's whole-body account of filmmaking and vision conforms more closely to Piercean indexes than does the more familiar realistic "picture"-image. Cinema verité's hand-and-eye stylistics, dependent upon the immediate responsiveness of the filmmaker to events as they unfold, partake of indexicality in Brakhage's sense as much as they do referentiality in Nichols's sense—as in the case where the film powerfully registers a death with the camera's violent fall when its operator was shot down in a famous sequence of Pablo Guzman's *The Battle of Chile* (1974–79), to use Nichols's own example (Nichols 84). Brakhage's style of filmmaking is a radical pursuit of the further implications of this indexicality.

4. Further examples might include the fiction films of Dusan Makavejev and Rainer Werner Fassbinder, the late-surrealist work of Arrabal, and many documentary films, especially those made in protest against violence and environmental degradation. In addition, a whole exploitation documentary genre of "forbidden footage" arose with *Mondo Cane* (1963). This genre is possessed of uncommon amoral sensationalism that continues today. Mikita Brottman, in "Carnivalizing the Taboo: The Mondo Film and the Opened Body," *CineAction* 38 (1995): 25–37, discusses this genre at length, emphasizing the most recent manifestations.

5. Once the allegorization of the abattoir and the body film is achieved, by cultural appropriation and/or further filmmaking, the surrealist force of shock or outrage is dissipated. The films in question more or less comfortably assume a place in the "sober discourses" though not always without retaining some of their original poetic idiosyncrasy. Bruce Elder's schema amply describes the allegorization in most "body films," which he terms mythification. As an example of an actual conjuncture, the appropriation of Franju's film doubtless prepared for the possibility that Alain Resnais could marry Holocaust footage and a "sober discourse" (indeed a powerful one by a Holocaust survivor) with his *Nuit et brouillard* (*Night and Fog*, 1955). The political and aesthetic importance of Resnais's film to documentary cinema in this respect can never be overestimated.

WORKS CITED

Brakhage, Stan. *Film at Wit's End: Eight Avant-Garde Filmmakers*. Kingston, NY: Documentext/McPherson, 1989.

———. "Stan Brakhage on Marie Menken." *Film Culture* 78 (1994): 1–9.

Elder, R. Bruce. *The Body in Film*. Toronto: Art Gallery of Ontario, 1989.

Frampton, Hollis. *"The Act of Seeing with One's Own Eyes." Film-Makers' Cooperative Catalogue No. 7* (1989): 48.

Krauss, Rosalind. "Corpus Delecti." In *L'Amour fou: Photography and Surrealism,* ed. Rosalind Krauss and Jane Livingston, 57–114. New York: Abbeville Press, 1985.

Nichols, Bill. *Representing Reality: Issues and Concepts in Documentary.* Bloomington: Indiana University Press, 1991.

Russell, Catherine. *Narrative Mortality: Death, Closure, and New Wave Cinemas.* Minneapolis: University of Minnesota Press, 1995.

Sobchack, Vivian. *The Address of the Eye: A Phenomenology of Film Experience.* Princeton: Princeton University Press, 1992.

Sitney, P. Adams. *Visionary Film: The American Avant-Garde, 1943–1978.* 2nd ed. New York: Oxford University Press, 1979.

Chapter 18

"A Bastard Union
of Several Forms"

Style and Narrative in *An American Family*

Jeffrey K. Ruoff

> Our story begins in the Loud home at 35 Wooddale Lane. . . .
>
> Craig Gilbert, *An American Family*

An American Family (1973) bridges the stylistic conventions of independent documentary film and broadcast television, marrying the innovations of American cinema verité to the narrative traditions of TV. The twelve-episode series chronicles seven months in the lives of the Loud family of Santa Barbara, California, including the divorce proceedings of the parents. Producer Craig Gilbert deliberately chose an upper-middle-class family whose lifestyle approximated that of families seen on situation comedies such as *Make Room for Daddy* (1953–65). Under his supervision, Susan and Alan Raymond filmed the everyday lives of Pat and William Loud and their children, Lance, Kevin, Grant, Delilah, and Michele. The completed documentary captured the imagination of the American public when it was first aired by the Public Broadcasting Service in the winter of 1973. Ten million viewers followed the Louds' unfolding marital problems in a controversial weekly show that some critics called a real-life soap opera.[1]

Like all cultural artifacts, films and television programs cannot be fully understood outside their historical contexts of production and reception. *An American Family* would never have been made by the commercial networks

(ABC, NBC, or CBS), which, by the early 1970s, had scaled back documentary productions in the race for audience ratings (Brown 198). Even for educational and public TV, the form and content of the series were radical innovations, for Gilbert's use of dramatic storytelling techniques in a nonfictional account of family life blurred conventions of different media forms.

As Robert Allen notes, fictional television programs usually employ a "narrative mode" of viewer address, adopted from classical Hollywood cinema, while nonfiction shows generally rely upon a "rhetorical mode" of viewer address adapted from radio ("Criticism" 90–91). A distinctly hybrid work, *An American Family* confounds this typology; it represents, in the words of Yale drama professor Richard Gilman, a "bastard union of several forms" (quoted in Carlin 25). Though widely known as an example of observational cinema, the series mixes the narrative traditions of the film and television industries. Furthermore, it struggles against its own interpretive tendencies, striving to show "life as it is" while simultaneously criticizing American society in the early 1970s. As such, like the Loud family it depicts, *An American Family* is a text at war with itself.

The documentary consists of twelve hour-long episodes. The first show introduces the family members and the central story line, while the next eleven programs follow their activities in the summer and fall of 1971. Individual shows emphasize certain events and characters over others as, for example, hour seven explores Grant's attitude toward his summer job. With one crucial exception, the series proceeds in a loose chronological order. Though it often falls short, *An American Family*, like many works of observational cinema, strives for the clarity and comprehensibility of Hollywood cinema and American commercial television.[2] Observational documentaries typically depict actual events in dramatic form, using continuity techniques conventionally associated with mainstream fiction film. Whereas most nonfiction programming, particularly TV news, speaks directly to the audience, Gilbert's series addresses the viewer only indirectly through the telling of a story.

As a style, observational cinema tends more toward the "open" textual pole of Jean-Luc Godard and Roberto Rossellini than the "closed" pole of Alfred Hitchcock and Alain Resnais (Allen, *Soap Operas* 81–84). Vis-à-vis traditional documentaries, observational films are polysemic because they lack the devices of voice-over, interviews, and nondiegetic music through which point of view may be unequivocally expressed. A comparatively open text, *An American Family* ends on a decisively ambiguous note. Discussing her anticipated alimony arrangement, Pat Loud mentions that she may never marry again. As she concludes that "these things happen," the final episode freezes on her smiling face in medium close-up. Thus, in an ending reminiscent of François Truffaut's *Les quatre cents coups* (*The 400 Blows*, 1959), producer Gilbert opts for an open-ended conclusion.

Throughout the series, narrative omniscience remains the order of the day. In episode three, the coverage of the annual recital of the Rudenko School of Dance presents sequential and simultaneous actions occurring backstage, onstage, and in the audience, shown from a panoply of different angles. Numerous performances by Delilah and Michele Loud are featured. Music bridges the movement from the stage to the dressing room, maintaining continuous spatial and temporal relations. This sequence, and the episode with it, ends with a freeze frame on Bill and Pat Loud applauding from their seats in the Lobero Theater.

The pronounced story emphasis of the actuality material calls to mind the strong continuity of classical Hollywood narration. For example, a tarot-card reader in episode two accurately hints at Pat Loud's coming separation from her husband. The scene forecasts later plot developments, as the card reader suggests to Pat that "This year is a year of changes. You'll have a choice to make which you are building up to. Something is ending now." For some critics, use of such continuity editing techniques, suspense, and foreshadowing partially undermines the reality effect of the series (Gaines 48). In other words, the narrative drive of *An American Family* grates against the realism of the handheld camera and direct sound. In *The Classical Hollywood Cinema*, David Bordwell suggests that "the strongest illusion of reality comes from tight causal motivation" (Bordwell, Staiger, and Thompson 19). Just the opposite appears to be the case with nonfiction: if things fit together too neatly, viewers distrust the narration and question the realism.

An American Family, then, blurs generic categories. The twelve-part program violates viewer expectations about what documentaries are supposed to do. Normally genres restrain the range of possible interpretations. The innovative style of *An American Family*, coupled with the absence of clearly articulated standards for nonfiction, challenges conventional forms of representation. A roundtable discussion broadcast by WNET on April 5, 1973, in the same weekly time slot as the series, aired the opinions of Margaret Mead and five experts in literature, drama, history, psychiatry, and anthropology on the series. The sheer variety of disciplines represented on the panel demonstrates the difficulty contemporary critics had fitting this documentary series to established genres and forms.

Its "neither fish nor fowl" generic instability remains one of its most defining features. Though shot on film, in a style associated with observational cinema, Gilbert's hybrid show adopts some of television's characteristic modes of narration. Five years before *Dallas* (1978–91), *An American*

Family blurred the distinctions between daytime serials and prime-time programs. To paraphrase Robert C. Allen's description of the codes of soap opera, Gilbert's work, to a greater extent than any other documentary, walks the line between a program that "spills over into the experiential world of the viewer" and a program that may be "read as fiction" (*Soap Operas* 91). As such, *An American Family* announces the breakdown of fixed distinctions between reality and spectacle, public and private, serial narrative and nonfiction, film and television.

MULTIPLE-FOCUS NARRATIVE

An American Family capitalizes on one of the historically dominant characteristics of American television—namely, serial narrative. Scene changes in the twelve-part program are facilitated by the large cast of principal characters and the ability to shift focus from one family member to another. Story lines are temporarily abandoned only to be picked up later in the documentary. This multiple-focus narrative results in several ongoing plots. For example, Grant and Kevin's band practices in the garage in episode one, discusses recording contracts in episode three, performs at a high school pep rally in episode ten, and auditions for a club gig in episode twelve. *An American Family* presents not the strict linear causal chain of classical Hollywood cinema, with its goal-oriented protagonists and question-and-answer story structure, but rather the slow pace of serial narrative, confirming John Ellis's intuition that, on television, "The normal movement between segments is one of vague simultaneity (meanwhile . . . meanwhile . . . a bit later . . .)" (150).

While there are multiple stories in *An American Family,* the dominant plot line involves the marital problems of Mr. and Mrs. Loud, which culminate in their separation and preparation for divorce. Other developments explored include the affairs of Bill's business, the relations between the Louds and their children, Lance's activities in New York City and his travels in Europe, Delilah's dance performance and her budding relationship with boyfriend Brad (one of the underdeveloped plot lines), Pat's visit to her mother in Eugene and her vacation in Taos, Kevin's business trip to Southeast Asia (another story more absent than present), Grant's summer job as a construction worker, and the evolution of the garage band. The documentary rarely veers from the characters' immediate concerns with interpersonal relationships. Of a filmed discussion about the Vietnam War between Bill Loud and striking longshoremen in San Francisco, coordinating producer Jacqueline Donnet said, "You could have made an hour show on that discussion alone. But there was just no way to fit it in. It didn't move forward the story of the family" (quoted in Ruoff, "Family Programming" 85). As a result, the so-called great events of contemporary history are wholly absent from *An American Family*. As in daytime TV serials, the stories focus on the personal problems of the characters.

In *Speaking of Soap Operas*, Robert C. Allen describes the characteristics that distinguish daytime serials from other narrative forms: a continuous format that indefinitely postpones closure in favor of process; multiple characters and multiple narrative plot lines; and a focus on the intimate daily lives of the characters. As such, soaps rely on consistent viewer involvement over weeks, months, and years. Similarly, *An American Family* encourages viewers to think about the Louds as if they were their next-door neighbors. The open-ended episodic structure of the program accentuates similarities with everyday life and promotes strong identification with the Louds, powerfully combining the reality effect of soap operas with documentary conventions of authenticity. Many scenes simply give insight into the family members and their relationships without creating any suspense. Pat's visit to her mother in episode four focuses on their shared history, not on any future event. In fact, in terms of narrative development, Mrs. Loud's trip to Eugene *delays* the main plot line of her deteriorating relationship with her husband.

The episodic story structure employs greater redundancy than classical Hollywood narrative. Soaps reiterate plot developments extensively to keep irregular viewers up-to-date (Allen, *Soap Operas* 70). In *An American Family*, although most scenes occur only once, there are interesting exceptions. At the end of episode eight, having returned from his cross-country trip, Bill asks Grant, "How's everything on the home front?" After a brief, but revealing, conversation, a freeze frame sets father and son off against the darkness of the Santa Barbara airport parking lot. Hour nine begins by repeating the airport exchange between Bill and Grant in its entirety, including Mr. Loud's uncanny concluding remark, "Walk right into the lion's den, huh?" While offering background information, the repetition also signals the scene's importance, further building suspense for Bill's return to 35 Wooddale Lane for the pivotal exchange in which his wife asks him to move out of the house.

MULTIPLE CHARACTERS

Like soap operas, *An American Family* leaves room for active involvement of spectators through multiple stories drawn out through multiple episodes. In between shows, viewers have time to speculate with friends about future character developments. For many, the interest of *An American Family* comes from watching the intimate life of an actual family in serial form: "You find yourself sticking with the Louds with the same compulsion that draws you back day after day to your favorite soap opera. The tension is heightened by the realization that you are identifying, not with a fictitious character, but a flesh and blood person who is responding to personal problems of the kind you yourself might face" (Harrington 5).

Like most multiple-focus narrative television shows, *An American Family* offers viewers choices for sympathetic identification among different characters, their values, and behaviors (Allen, *Soap Operas* 171). Most consistently, the series contrasts Mr. and Mrs. Loud's conflicting attitudes toward marriage and parenting, implicitly suggesting a "battle of the sexes" drama typical of situation comedies. For example, the twelve-hour documentary ends with a scene of Bill at lunch with a friend talking about marriage and its discontents followed by a similar scene of Pat at dinner with friends discussing her likely divorce settlement.

Nevertheless, on the basis of time devoted to her, Pat Loud emerges as the lead character in the series. At the beginning of episode three, after she inspects a shipment of materials in Baltimore for her husband's business, the company representative gives her the backhanded compliment, "Well, I think that you did a very good job for a housewife." Over the course of the twelve shows, Pat gradually changes from a married homemaker to a single mother looking for work. Episode four focuses almost exclusively on Mrs. Loud, detailing her memories through such exceptional techniques as first-person voice-over narration, home movies, and snapshots. Five subjective flashbacks introduce incidents from her childhood and young adult years. Even so, the narration never restricts itself to her point of view, combining omniscient and subjective perspectives for this nostalgic journey home.

In addition to the "battle of the sexes" dynamic, the family members represent different normative systems: Bill's work ethic and, to a lesser extent, Pat's; the children's pleasure principle (especially Grant's); and Lance's avant-garde, *épater le bourgeois* attitude. Though occasionally blatantly articulated, these contrasts often remain implicit within the documentary. Having seen *Vain Victory,* the drag queen parody of the American musical at La Mama Theater in Greenwich Village, in hour two, audience members cannot avoid making comparisons with Delilah and Michele Loud's amateur dance performances in the following episode. While the sequencing favors the transvestite variety review, either can appear ridiculous. Sitting at Ratner's Deli afterward in episode two, Pat Loud expresses her view that *Vain Victory* was "pretty gross."

Hour five explores the main characters' attitudes toward work. An independent businessman, Bill Loud embodies a conservative entrepreneurial mentality that his children, and the series itself, ridicule. After arranging a business trip to Southeast Asia for Kevin, he tries to find work for his other son still living at home. Unaware of his father's plans, Grant listens to The Who sing "We Don't Get Fooled Again." Suggesting utopian desires unfulfilled, Roger Daltry exhorts his young admirer to "take a bow for the new revolution." Meanwhile Mr. Loud secures a job for Grant with the "curb king of southern California." Offered work pouring cement, the seventeen-year-old refers to his father's machinations as "the concrete caper." Subsequently, at the airport with Kevin, Bill describes the beauty of strip-mining: "When that great big Marion 5600 shovel throws that bucket out there and sucks that dirt back up there, and it's cold, you know, and you see more metal roll off that thing, I mean, you're on Broadway, you know. You're really at the top of the heap." The program then juxtaposes Bill's euphoric remarks with a scene of Grant at work under the searing Santa Barbara sun—he's definitely not on Broadway. Although the sun sets during their ride to the airport, the episode cuts to a daytime sequence of Grant and then back to Kevin again at the departure gate, a subtle manipulation of story order for contrast.

Hour seven picks up this ideological argument between the generations, as Grant complains to his father about a lack of support for his career interests in music: "I'm not even going to go into it with you, because you'll just give me all this jazz about, well, 'You gotta go to college and take some economics, and a banking course, and you'll be set for the rest of your life.'" Laughing, Bill remains true to form in his response: "Well, don't you think you would be?" In episode eight, Mr. Loud jokingly tells some mine workers that his teenage son is "the forerunner of the three-day week." Meanwhile, Lance, traveling abroad in hour six, invents a story about having his money stolen so that his parents will send more. In the final show, Bill refers to his eldest son as the "greatest con artist you ever saw." The use of overlapping stories and numerous characters offers a more supple range of viewing positions than is usually seen in classical Hollywood films. The multiple-focus narrative style leaves room for audiences, as one reviewer noted, "to root for" their favorite Loud (Rosenblatt 21).

Nevertheless, the documentary itself often favors Lance's perspective for the critique he extends of his family and life in Southern California. Lance is the only family member other than Pat to be the focus of an individual show. Purchasing a ticket at Kennedy Airport for his return to the West Coast in episode eleven, Lance dryly tells the reservations clerk that Santa Barbara is "more than just a home, it's a way of life." The documentary, however, does not limit itself to his point of view; editorial perspective circulates freely among the different characters. In the final hour,

Mr. Loud's friend Robert sums up the pessimistic point of view of *An American Family* during a lunch date with Bill: "The family as we knew it in our youth is a thing of the past and you see all the signs of it coming to an end."

THE STRUCTURE OF EPISODE ONE

At the outset of *An American Family,* producer Craig Gilbert provides an on-camera introduction that recalls the standard direct address of nonfictional TV (Ruoff, "Conventions" 229–31). After this prologue, and at the beginning of each subsequent episode, a split-screen montage sequence and musical theme song introduce the family members one by one. Nothing in Gilbert's series smacks of television situation comedies such as *The Adventures of Ozzie and Harriet* (1952–66) so much as this title sequence. Even more than the episodic structure, the suburban setting, and the family focus, the series title sequence sets up television representations of family life as the primary intertext. For this reason, Gilbert's series functions at least as much as a critique of the representation of family life on fictional TV programs as a statement about contemporary society.

The first twelve scenes feature New Year's Eve preparations and celebrations on December 31, 1971. As Pat arranges flowers in a vase at home, Gilbert announces in voice-over, "Pat Loud and her husband, Bill, separated four months ago after twenty years of marriage." Introduced alone in his apartment, Mr. Loud mechanically sifts through a large pile of commercial Christmas cards, chuckling laconically in response to one of them. The parallel editing structure implies simultaneity of time, and indeed, later, the program includes a terse phone conversation between Bill and Pat. Another phone call, between the Louds' fifteen-year-old daughter and her boyfriend, immediately follows this exchange. Delilah and Brad's awkward tenderness toward each other contrasts vividly with the tired cynicism of her parents' discussion.

Pat Loud is the only adult present at the New Year's festivities at 35 Wooddale Lane. The camera lingers on her isolation as she reads, pets the dog, and watches her children dance to the Andrews Sisters' "Boogie Woogie Bugle Boy." Continuing the earlier crosscutting paradigm, strictly parallel scenes compare her evening with her husband's. A close-up on Pat's face slowly dissolves to a similar shot of Bill dancing with another woman, suggesting the source of Pat's discontent. The strains of Carole King's "You've Got a Friend," sung by a piano man in the back of the restaurant, fill in the details. The poignant symbolism of the new year, with its retrospective glance toward the past and resolutions for the future, underlines this segment.

When the story of the Louds then jumps back to the spring of 1971, viewers scan for the signs of the future in the status quo. Having shown the effects—the Louds' separation—the documentary returns to explore the causes. The flashback structure strongly enforces a cause-and-effect chain of narrative associations. Pat's irritation as she prepares breakfast reads as her dissatisfaction with her husband. Bill appears and asks if she has seen his keys. "No, sir," she replies curtly, "I'll look for them."

Producer Gilbert uses this flashback structure to rein in the inherent polysemic quality, the openness, of the observational footage. Thanks to this teleological structure, audience members know the trajectory and outcome of *An American Family* from the opening episode. The flashback puts viewers in a position of superiority in relation to the characters. This hierarchy of knowledge, and the omniscient narration, may have contributed to the tone of moral superiority TV critics exhibited toward the family in 1973 (Ruoff, "Real Life").

Despite the emphasis placed on the Louds' separation in hour one, their marriage only indirectly surfaces as an issue in the next five hours of *An American Family*. Bill does not appear at all during episode two; in hour four, he figures in only one scene, a telephone conversation with Lance. Indirect references to marital problems in the early shows become comprehensible only in light of Gilbert's announcement that the Louds have separated. The state of their relationship must be inferred by its relative *absence* in the narrative. For example, Pat and Bill take separate vacations in programs four and five. In this way, the central dilemma of the documentary remains tantalizingly offscreen, indefinitely postponed through story techniques that delay the split until episode nine.

Having effectively raised the marital question during the "late spring morning," the first episode cuts thirty-five hundred miles to New York City to introduce the one family member not present at the breakfast meal. Lance delivers a long tirade about his family, entirely in voice-over, as he sorts his clothes alone in a room at the Chelsea Hotel. Through this veiled interview technique, *An American Family* implicitly endorses Lance's outsider point of view.

Although the multiple-focus narrative allows for abrupt shifts from story line to story line, or character to character, a degree of continuity carries one sequence into another. For example, Lance's concluding comment about his younger brother—"I think that of all of us Grant will probably succeed most"—sets up the next scene. In a social studies class at Santa Barbara High School, Grant gives a report on the Reconstruction period in American history. The teacher tries to get him to elaborate on his description of it as a "tragic era." Grant's lackluster performance in class amusingly contradicts Lance's prediction. After much clowning, he remarks that Reconstruction was an attempt to give blacks "equal social status with the whites," so that they, too, could achieve "the American dream."

The following shot shows Mrs. Loud pushing an overflowing cart at a supermarket; she can barely put in another bottle of salad dressing. Buying goods for six people, Pat clearly has no time or interest in comparison shopping. Grant's reference to the "American dream" carries over explicitly as a commentary on the family's upper-middle-class way of life, consisting primarily of taken-for-granted material abundance. The reference to "the American dream," a crucial one for the program, stands out thanks to the juxtaposition of otherwise unrelated scenes. Like other social critics of the period, Craig Gilbert wanted to say that the American dream had become, in Charles Reich's words, "a rags-to-riches type of narrow materialism" (22). In the next sequence, viewers learn where the money comes from that supports the family's comfortable lifestyle. Mr. Loud stands beneath an enormous forklift in a strip-mining field. As he discusses the sale of industrial tools with another man in a hard hat, they watch a hill in the distance explode. Having provided a glimpse of

An American Family: Grant and classmate clowning around in school.

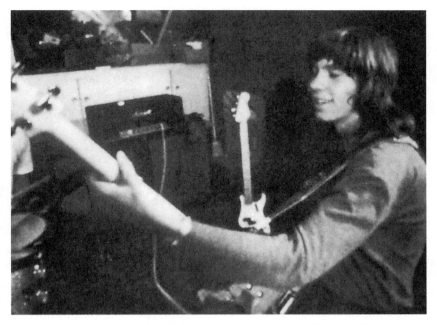

An American Family: Kevin Loud joins in a rousing version of "Summertime Blues."

Bill at work, the episode cuts to Delilah and her class rehearsing a dance routine to "In the Mood."

Delilah's segment segues into an afternoon cocktail party. The careless party chatter, the sunshine, the liquor, the leathered faces, the Hawaiian T-shirts, and the suggestion of extramarital affairs all combine to create an atmosphere of upper-middle-class suburban decadence, California-style. (In episode five, Pat jokes with friends in Taos about her adopted home state, "The theory is that all of California is like Sodom and Gomorrah; it's all going to drop into the sea—God's wrath and all.") The cocktail party ends dramatically on Pat's riposte to Bill's question about another woman, "Well, for the record, she's just passing through."

In the next scene, Michele grooms her horse, a gentle moment rendered all the more tranquil by the preceding noisy party. The peacefulness of Michele's ride through the Santa Barbara hills is interrupted by a cut to a raucous rehearsal of "Jumping Jack Flash" by the garage band. Meanwhile, in the living room, Pat, Bill, Delilah, and Michele take turns talking long-distance to Lance on the telephone. Back in the garage, the band gives a rous-ing performance of "Summertime Blues." The lyrics, energetically belted out by Grant, introduce the themes of teenage alienation and economic dependency that will be explored in detail in hours five and seven. Episode one ends with a freeze frame of the group over which the credits roll.

REPRESENTATIVE SCENE CONSTRUCTION

Thirty minutes into episode one, as the New Year's celebrations conclude, the voice-over states, "Our story begins seven months earlier at six-thirty on a late spring morning." This scene of the Louds at breakfast fulfills the stated goals of observational cinema inasmuch as there are no interviews, nondiegetic music, or voice-over narration. Similarly, the family members never explicitly address the camera. The scene consists of thirty-four shots and lasts seven and a half minutes; the average shot runs approximately thirteen seconds. A different shot shows each family member's "entrance" to the dining room, allowing the viewer to identify each person clearly. In addition, whenever possible, characters exit the frame before the program cuts to another shot, smoothing the transitions. All the action takes place in the kitchen and the dining room. Although some of the images are taken from the same camera angle, the framing varies significantly to allow the scene to flow smoothly. The handheld camera remains steady through-out as it refocuses to follow the action. Sounds flow across image cuts to maintain continuous spatial and temporal relations.

The breakfast provides a host of information about the Louds. Pat and her daughters are the only family members working in the kitchen, suggesting a traditional division of labor in the home. The tone of Mrs. Loud's voice suggests thinly repressed discontent. Over the course of the twelve episodes, her anger grows and bursts into view, culminating in her demands for a divorce. Mr. Loud, however, avoids direct conflict and chooses instead to joke with his kids about their neglect of the backyard. Bill's jocular attitude, even in the face of adversity, remains his most no-table personality trait in the documentary. When Kevin asks for lunch money, Mr. Loud complains—as he does on several occasions—about his son's laziness.

When Bill addresses his youngest child, he looks screen right in the direction of the kitchen. In the following shot, Michele, in the kitchen, looks screen left, acknowledging his words. The sounds and images rein-force one another; after Bill and Pat refer to Michele's health, a shot shows their daughter gently touching her throat. The editing maintains continuity through eyeline matches, overlapping sound cuts, point-of-view shots, and cutting-on-action, techniques all common to fiction film. There are some jump cuts, however, such as consecutive shots of Grant, and the transitions are not as smooth as those of classical Hollywood movies. Furthermore, the production values, especially the lighting, remain those of verité documentary rather than conventional fiction with its polished look. The continuity techniques condense time and space without calling attention to the ellipses. An event that lasts up to an hour in real time takes only seven and a half minutes of screen time, yet nothing significant has been left out. The family sets the table, cooks breakfast, eats, cleans up, and leaves. As Pat casually glances out the kitchen window, a point-of-view shot from her perspective shows the children leaving for school. Their departure in a pickup truck ends the sequence; the episode cuts to an establishing shot of the Chelsea Hotel in New York, and a new scene begins.

While *An American Family* may be the most famous example of observational cinema, it deviates from the prescriptive rules of that style in, for example, the use of both first-person and third-person voice-over narration (Ruoff, "Conventions" 229–34). Nevertheless, with the exception of occasional stylistic detours, Gilbert's series constructs stories, episodes, and individual scenes by employing techniques from fictional film and television. The multiple-focus narrative intersperses story developments among many different characters. The teleological structure sets up an eleven-and-a-half-hour flashback—the longest in the history of moving images—while it simultaneously forges a stronger narrative chain of causes and effects than simple chronology. Within this structure, transitions between otherwise unrelated scenes remain key moments for expressing editorial point of view. Although the observational sequences seemingly represent life as it occurs, the documentary exhibits a fascinating and subtle narrative sophistication.

REFLEXIVITY AND OBSERVATIONAL CINEMA

Like fiction films, observational documentaries generally employ an impersonal narration that does not explicitly address the viewer. Nevertheless, anyone who actually watches *An American Family*, even just a single episode, witnesses numerous references to the audience. Although these may seem more incidental than deliberate, the narration does not systematically mask or disguise its tracks. Too many to catalogue, these are not the first elements viewers notice or the last. Thus Gilbert's style falls in between the pronounced reflexivity of ethnographic filmmaker Jean Rouch and the mostly transparent approach of Frederick Wiseman.

In episode four, for example, an amusing discussion takes place about the proper way to display mayonnaise on the table at 35 Wooddale Lane.

Pat invokes standards proper for entertaining guests: "You're supposed to put it in a dish and not put the jar on the table." Her good-humored children refuse to participate in this charade and ignore her remonstrations, implicitly welcoming the filmmakers as members of the household. Alone in Bill's office in hour eleven, Lance finds a letter he wrote to his father and reads it aloud to the camera: "There are two things you can count on in life as the world turns. They are that at the end of the summer Lance always returns from an unsuccessful take-off on life's big runway, limping home on a path of wired money. And Ma and Pa Loud plummet head first from their Olympian heights of love and matrimony." Lance acknowledges the melodramatic associations of the documentary through his comparison of his family's experiences to the long-running soap opera *As the World Turns* (1956–2010). Only Bill's sudden return to his workplace interrupts this remarkable frame-breaking soliloquy.

In hour eight, Bill confesses his worries about Lance traveling in Europe to his colleagues in strip-mining, but his fears are dispelled by the fact that, as he remarks, "They have the camera crew with them over there, following them around." In episode ten, when Pat criticizes Grant's lack of interest in his classes, he turns to the camera to appeal to the audience for support, saying, "Nothing like a sympathetic mother!" Such ubiquitous references to the filmmaking process go beyond those of other observational works from the same period, predating similar instances in, for example, Albert and David Maysles's *Grey Gardens* (1975). Critics who denounce observational documentaries as transparent forms that disguise the work of mediation, such as E. Ann Kaplan, would do well to look closely at *An American Family* (80).

The single most reflexive element of *An American Family* is Lance Loud, who relentlessly breaks the frame, acknowledging the presence of the camera throughout the twelve-hour series. Unlike the more naturalistic performances of his siblings and parents, Lance acts like a character from an Andy Warhol movie let loose in a film by Frederick Wiseman. A fan of Warhol's work, Lance gives one of the great camp performances in the history of the medium. Indeed, American television came out of the closet through *An American Family*. In *Heavenly Bodies*, Richard Dyer defines camp as a "characteristically gay way of handling the values, images and products of the dominant culture through irony, exaggeration, trivialization, theatricalisation, and an ambivalent making fun of and out of the serious and respectable" (178). Shooting footage in super-8 on a Santa Barbara beach in episode twelve, Lance tells his cast of friends, "Realism is our aim for this film; it's going to be like a documentary," but his directions verge on camp horror: "Okay, now a close-up of you looking like a hungry sex-devil." Probably the first openly gay character ever seen on American TV, Lance consistently makes fun of the serious pretensions of the documentary, parodying the codes of observational cinema.

CONCLUSION: THE CHILDREN OF *AN AMERICAN FAMILY*

While some may read Gilbert's program as the harbinger of the "society of the spectacle"—and it is a precursor of reality programming such as MTV's *The Real World* (1992–present)—its greater merit lies in opening up the institution of the family, and issues of gender, sexuality, and interpersonal relations, to nonfiction film and video. Though experimental filmmakers such as Stan Brakhage had explored autobiographical themes in the previous decades, by the mid-1970s these topics were moving to the center of independent documentary through the efforts of such filmmakers as Joyce Chopra, Amalie Rothschild, and Ed Pincus. Pincus commenced work on his autobiographical epic *Diaries, 1971–76* (1981) at the same time that Gilbert proposed his nonfiction television series. Arguing that the personal is political, these filmmakers chose to make movies about themselves, their families, and their friends. *An American Family* accelerated and validated this tendency.

For the coming generation of documentary filmmakers, Gilbert's twelve-hour program was a revelation. Mark Rance—whose own works, including *Mom* (1978) and *Death and the Singing Telegram* (1981), are clearly influenced by *An American Family*—recalled watching the broadcast as a high school student, discovering in the process that "family life is the great subject of drama and the movies" (96). Other filmmakers—like Rance, students of Pincus and Richard Leacock at the Massachusetts Institute of Technology in the 1970s—continued to push nonfiction into increasingly private subject matter: Joel DeMott (*Demon Lover Diary,* 1979), Ann Schaetzel (*Breaking and Entering,* 1980), David Parry (*Premature,* 1981), Ross McElwee (*Backyard,* 1981; *Sherman's March,* 1985). Similarly, later first-person video diaries—such as those by Tom Joslin and Peter Friedman (*Silverlake Life: The View from Here,* 1992) and Marlon Riggs (*Tongues Untied,* 1989)—descend directly from the new terrain opened by Craig Gilbert's documentary in 1973. As more intimate life comes under the gaze of independent producers, the once scandalous revelations about the Louds may pale by comparison. But as its influence implies, *An American Family* marks a new stage in the filming of the everyday lives of ordinary individuals, a landmark in the history of nonfiction film. In its aftermath, the American documentary would never be the same.

NOTES

For general comments on my work on *An American Family*, I am grateful to Lauren Rabinovitz. I would also like to thank Jeannette Sloniowski and Barry Keith Grant for their close readings of successive versions of this essay.

1. Readers interested in the making of *An American Family* and the responses it engendered should see *Pat Loud: A Woman's Story* (New York: Coward, McCann, and Geoghegan, 1974); Craig Gilbert, "Reflections on *An American Family*," *Studies in Visual Communication* 8, no. 1 (1982): 24–54, reprinted in *New Challenges for Documentary*, ed. Alan Rosenthal (Berkeley: University of California Press, 1988), 191–209, 288–307; and Ruoff, "Real Life."

2. For a more extensive discussion of the narrative intelligibility of Hollywood cinema in comparison to observational cinema, see Ruoff, "Conventions," 221–26.

WORKS CITED

Allen, Robert C. "Reader-Oriented Criticism and Television." In *Channels of Discourse: Television and Contemporary Criticism*, ed. Robert C. Allen, 74–112. Chapel Hill: University of North Carolina Press, 1987.

———. *Speaking of Soap Operas*. Chapel Hill: University of North Carolina Press, 1985.

Bordwell, David, Janet Staiger, and Kristin Thompson. *The Classical Hollywood Cinema: Film Style and Mode of Production to 1960*. New York: Columbia University Press, 1985.

Brown, Les. *Television: The Business behind the Box*. New York: Harcourt Brace Jovanovich, 1971.

Carlin, Sybil. "Bye, Patty. Bye, Bill. Bye, Margaret." *Village Voice*, April 12, 1973, 25.

Dyer, Richard. *Heavenly Bodies: Film Stars and Society*. New York: St. Martin's Press, 1986.

Ellis, John. *Visible Fictions: Cinema, Television, Video*. London: Routledge and Kegan Paul, 1982.

Gaines, Jim. "TV: The Decline and Fall of an American Family." *Saturday Review of the Arts*, January 1973, 47–48.

Harrington, Stephanie. "*An American Family* Lives Its Life on TV." *New York Times*, January 7, 1973, 5.

Kaplan, E. Ann. "Theories and Strategies of Feminist Documentary." In *New Challenges for Documentary*, ed. Alan Rosenthal, 78–102. Berkeley: University of California Press, 1988.

Rance, Mark. "Home Movies and *Cinema Verité.*" *Journal of Film and Video* 38, nos. 3–4 (1986): 95–98.

Reich, Charles. *The Greening of America.* New York: Bantam Books, 1971.

Rosenblatt, Roger. "Residuals on *An American Family.*" *New Republic,* November 23, 1974, 20–24.

Ruoff, Jeffrey. "Can a Documentary Be Made of Real Life?: The Reception of *An American Family.*" In *The Construction of the Viewer: Media Ethnography and the Anthropology of Audiences,* ed. Peter Ian Crawford and Sigurjón Baldur Hafsteinsson, 270–96. Aarhus, Denmark: Intervention Press, 1996.

———. "Conventions of Sound in Documentary." In *Sound Theory/Sound Practice,* ed. Rick Altman, 217–34. New York: Routledge, Chapman, and Hall, 1992.

———. "Family Programming, Television, and American Culture: A Case Study of *An American Family.*" Ph.D. thesis. University of Iowa, Department of Communication Studies, 1995.

Chapter 19

The Documentary of Displaced Persona

Michael Rubbo's
Daisy: The Story of a Facelift

Joan Nicks

I think every documentary is a product of one's personality and approach—intuitive, objective, or conscious.

Michael Rubbo (August 1980)

My critical framework for analyzing Michael Rubbo's *Daisy: The Story of a Facelift* (1982) concerns the documentary processes that foreground Rubbo's onscreen interventions into a woman's personal narrative and addresses the implications of the facelift in late twentieth-century culture. Rubbo troubled documentary cinema with his onscreen presence, opening up the institution of the National Film Board of Canada to the documentary of directorial persona. Making himself not only a presence and a problem onscreen, Rubbo takes up the behaviors of patriarchal privilege to enter a feminine space afforded by Daisy and her facelift. The cultural preoccupations underlying the facelift unfold in the surgical and screen "operations" that displace Daisy as subject and Rubbo as filmmaker-friend. The film assumes the character of a parody of male voyeurism in Rubbo's obsession with what drives Daisy's pursuit of a more youthful face to recapture a romantic past. Not only do Rubbo and Daisy's perspectives conflict, but the documentary ideology of their home institution, the middle-aged National Film Board, is destabilized through the film's strategic shifts involving private and public domains. Such an argument needs to be anchored historically in prior institutional slippages within the National Film Board of Canada.

RUBBO'S NFB ROOTS

John Grierson's belief in the expository documentary (cf. Morris 183–84; Nichols 34–38) became institutionalized in the wartime propaganda and the cultural films of the National Film Board (NFB) of Canada, the federal government agency he founded in 1939 and headed until 1945.[1] Grierson's left-of-center politics and benevolent paternalism shaped the NFB documentary, conventionalized in the Board's nation-building thesis films to promote unity during the wartime period. The necessary but essentialist ideology of a universally wholesome state was endemic to Grierson's pan-Canadian, nationalist vision for the NFB as "the eyes of Canada."[2]

Between the mid-1950s and mid-1960s, a period discussed widely in the critical literature on documentary for the changes effected by the new portable equipment (cf. Elder; Harcourt; Nichols), the evolving strategies and aesthetics that came to be known as direct cinema/*le cinema direct* developed in the Film Board, as elsewhere (France, Great Britain, the United States). The concept of a transparent "window on life" became embedded aesthetically within the NFB's direct cinema/*le cinema direct* style. In practice, the camera's flexibility prevailed and appeared to be motivated by found subjects and events rather than by the filmmaker's close engagement with people, though Michel Euvrard and Pierre Veronneau summarize the practice this way: "Legitimately, the direct is only a technique, a method, offering new possibilities which alter the shooting, and only the shooting, of films, but which cannot replace investigation and analysis. It is a discovery, a progression, but it is not, in itself, another type of cinema" (92). Bruce Elder distinguishes the early English Canadian, Candid-Eye cinema from the American cinema verité approach (e.g., the Drew Associates): the chief characteristic of the latter is the "use of the dramatic form" (87), whereas the former "can in part be written as a history of the rejection of the dramatic forms" (89). Elder further argues that historically the Canadian practice anticipates the American one. Rubbo inherited these documentary contexts and employed strategies that capitalize on time constraints. He fuses them in the shooting with his interventions before the camera, pursuing human subjects who possess an instinct for the dramatic and for performing. His films are informed by his research and ultimately by his eye for prevailing patterns by which to shape the work.

Rubbo's particular struggle to foreground the filmmaker as a persona and voice operating *within* the NFB documentary also owed much to the independence afforded by the Film Board's evolving production systems (units, pools, studios).[3] Even more telling, he came to the Board during the experimental ferment of the mid-1960s, spearheaded by such Québécois filmmakers as Gilles Groulx, Claude Jutra, and Denys Arcand, and English Canadians Don Owen and Allan King. These filmmakers were skilled practitioners of direct cinema but dissatisfied with the Board and the limits of this more open documentary style on their personal visions. They began to explore autobiographical and documentary-inflected fictional forms, notably in Jutra's *A tout prendre* (1963), Groulx's *Le chat dans le sac* (1964), and Owen's *Nobody Waved Good-bye* (1964). Such auteur films would usher in what Roger Daudelin has described as "this marriage of the direct and fiction":

> As with any discovery, any pause in the history of an art or technology, the direct method was the product of a combination of circumstances (television, mass communications, popular photography, publicity, etc. etc.), which more or less affected everyone at the same time. Certain factors were responsible for the fact that this type of cinema developed to a greater extent in Canada than elsewhere, and that even our fiction films derived most of their originality from it. (106)

An Australian, Rubbo arrived at the NFB in 1964 from the United States where he had been studying. Hired on the merits of his accomplished master's thesis film, Rubbo unexpectedly began his career at the NFB making short films for and about children. These were mostly dramas, a vital experience in light of his later documentary films, which present human dramas catalyzed by his signature practice of onscreen interventions between the camera and his cultural players,[4] who increasingly act as go-betweens in his work. On the heels of direct cinema and its legacy, and before reflexivity became a common device of contemporary documentaries in both film and television, Rubbo's onscreen interventions in his key documentaries visibly acknowledged the filmmaker's inescapable participation in the documentary dynamic. Rubbo showed himself prompting situations and people as part of the shooting process, instigating social narratives that displaced his official (NFB) documentary topics and purpose.

Here I take a different critical emphasis than Bill Nichols, who finds in Rubbo's assumed screen roles a restriction of "our knowledge" to Rubbo's own understanding or exploration (119). One might entertain the theory that Rubbo and the NFB have shared the notion of self-interest but with divergent interpretations of documentary purpose: Rubbo's persona-driven indulgence in the human folly of his documentary subjects is at historical odds with the Board's initial expository tradition of voice-of-God narrations manipulating idealized images of Canada and its citizens. Rubbo's onscreen persona foregrounds the inexpert "self," the out-of-place NFB filmmaker acting and improvising his way through the shooting. His numerous documentary projects between 1970 and 1975 in foreign countries such as Australia (*The Man Who Can't Stop,* 1973), England (*Bate's Car: Sweet as a Nut,* 1974), Vietnam (*Sad Song of Yellow Skin,* 1970), Java (*Wet Earth and Warm People,* 1971), Cuba (*Waiting for Fidel,* 1974), and France (*Solzhenitsyn's Children . . . Are Making a Lot of Noise in Paris,* 1978) allowed him to test the full implications of his interventions. Far from his institutional base and before the camera, Rubbo could assert his subjective stake in the interests of those people, places, and events he engaged, notably in the films concerned with colonized subjects. Onscreen, Rubbo appeared to be a struggling auteur, often an ego at odds with the documentary he was supposed to be making as an NFB filmmaker. The impulse that propelled Rubbo to "dig in" culturally as an inexpert persona, in the guise of a footloose documentary filmmaker displaced from the Board and Canada (and his native Australia), ultimately mocks the imperialist bias of most Western documentaries about exotic others.

Rubbo's displaced-filmmaker persona breached the fundamental notion that documentary processes ought to behave according to generic or institutional rules, subverting the Griersonian legacy of benevolent paternalism and the notion that NFB films ought to teach Canadians something about the common good. Rubbo's interventions in fact made the inexpert documentary filmmaker his very subject, whatever the particular documentary's more obvious topic. This tack pricked the male center of documentary authority and, in most of Rubbo's documentaries, revealed patriarchal conditioning. Rubbo was well aware of white male privilege, for he had come of age in the era of the modern women's movement and had participated in the political event addressed in his master's thesis film, *The True Source of Knowledge* (1965), featuring Stanford University's elite, white student population. In the film, sobered football players, displaced from institutional comfort and class privilege, testify confessionally before Rubbo's camera about how they had ventured into the American South to act as democracy's volunteers during the black voter-registration project, only to be beaten up by white racists.[5]

Persistent and Finagling (1971) is the linchpin of Rubbo's mature work at the Film Board. The film works to open a documentary space for a group of environmentally active women in Montreal, as well as for Rubbo's found strategies. As he says, "I developed in this film an interest in unity of time and space. We stay with them for three weeks and see the story through to its climax. From this point on, I was instinctively looking for three-week events as film subjects. Because of this time limit, the filmmaker . . . starts to force the pace and have an overt influence on the course of events." Rubbo's intervention into the women's activities in *Persistent and Finagling* functions as both a bridging and a distancing device. He draws close to these members of STOP (Society to Overcome Pollution) to encourage a political goal (clean air) that he cannot hope to achieve either as a sympathetic male among other patriarchal males or as a more detached Board filmmaker tracking their specific project of orchestrating an anti-tourist bus tour of bleak industrial sites. Rubbo's sometimes childish goading, in cahoots with the husband of Sheila, one of the most adept women of STOP, makes him a calculating antagonist critical of the women's missteps; through this improvised persona, he teases out the gender tensions underlying the women's environmental crusade to stop industrial pollution in Montreal.

While the film's environmental topic represents the activism of the 1970s as one consequence of the 1960s phase of the women's movement, it also befits the Board's tradition of the Griersonian documentary of social purpose. But it is the miniature human dramas in *Persistent and Finagling* that crack the patriarchal intrigues besetting gender relations and thereby hindering the potential for social, and documentary, action. Rubbo edges onto the women's activities and their concerns about the local environment in the very city that houses the NFB's main production plant. He appears displaced, treading a line between supporting the women's project and upholding steadfast patriarchal traditions. That Rubbo does so while James Cross, the British High Commissioner, was being held hostage in 1970 in Montreal by a radical cell of the FLQ (Front de libération du Québec) seems apolitical. The only allusion to the Québécois separatist event known as "the FLQ crisis" is a quick shot of a newspaper headline. The obvious sharp pan away from the headline signals the film's detour from journalism's official story of national politics into the realm of gender politics,[6] as the camera is led by the personal crises of the STOP women, who routinely are thwarted by patronizing male experts. Just as persistent negotiation becomes the women's tool, ultimately Rubbo's organizing principle for the film's structure is the shifting male interventions amid the women's steady activism.

DEFINING THE DOCUMENTARY OF PERSONA

The documentary of persona might be called a documentary subgenre that takes off from auteurist flights into how reflexivity and personality merge to alter the preconceptions, conventions, shooting processes, and ideological collisions between competing subjectivities, directorial manipulation, and the seeming validity of found events. It is a process that entails risk, based on the filmmaker's interventions, which can as easily fail as succeed. The postproduction structuring of the work tends to be based on the filmmaker's negotiations, problems, or blunders with subjects, as well as the more general constraints at work within documentary filmmaking. All of these factors make up the Rubbo documentary of displaced persona, instigated within the NFB in a period of creative producers like Tom Daly, where Rubbo's tactics were alternately supported, ignored, and stalled at the postproduction, promotional, or exhibition stage. (Initially, for example, *Waiting for Fidel* was promoted outside the Film Board largely through Rubbo's own perseverance.)

In retrospect, Rubbo might be viewed as a filmmaker who fell into experimenting with documentary's potential within the Film Board, treating the NFB as his "lab" in assuming a license to test the boundaries of personal intervention. While his filmmaking is not "radical" (whatever this term might mean), it is not mainstream. Rubbo established his documentary of displaced persona as a filmmaking trajectory within nonfiction cinema by insistently asserting his own practice. Rubbo's screen ego (the Board's "man with a movie crew") becomes a central means of problematizing the documentary filmmaker's lack of control in the shooting processes. Intuitive and self-indulgent, like the classical dramatic fool, he obscures his knowledge and engages with others, thereby evoking intriguing patterns of human behavior ("always searching for that kinship thing"). Rubbo's documentary of displaced persona is informed by his anthropological interests (the focus of his undergraduate studies).[7] But at the same time, as he says, "I profit from the little moments, even the private moments, when they come my way. But I am less and less averse to setting things up in order to create a special vision."

Rubbo's visible interventions are an active signifier of his male perception, a paternalistic type that he plays parodically. Onscreen, central to the privilege of this male type is the evident technology (the NFB cameras and crew) at his disposal. When Rubbo visibly partakes of contradictory role playing, he sometimes confronts the status quo and suggests alternatives in cultural and documentary behavior. His "friendly imperialist" visiting with "smaller people" (from children to Third World citizens) mocks the pretensions of the colonizing persona he enacts as a Western white man of 1960s liberal sensibilities. His tourist-turned-traveler delving into disparate territories ferrets out cultural characters who act as his local "go-betweens." These local go-betweens themselves teeter in their roles, at once Rubbo's agents and ambiguous figures within their own cultures.

PERSONA AND IDENTITY IN *DAISY*

Daisy: The Story of a Facelift follows a woman's personal odyssey into the culture and drama of the facelift. Coming near the end of Rubbo's work at the Board,[8] it is his most intimate problematization of the individual's uncertain status within contemporary Western culture. Daisy is a woman whose imagination is colonized by her past and invested in a sentimental future based on her body's surface. In the film, the facelift represents a desire for a physical image that can be grafted onto a nostalgic narrative promising romance. Though Rubbo includes scenes of Daisy performing competently in her executive office (as an administrator at the NFB), he permits her the romantic narrative space she seeks. He integrates a restaurant scene in which Daisy confides to a male companion (Canadian director Paul Almond, who has a past in the NFB and a toe-hold in Hollywood) some of her adventures with men. Though Rubbo's Daisy is not constructed as a dupe merely serving his film's special concern with "facial language," her personal narrative is reminiscent of the domesticated female characters of Hollywood melodrama (*A Woman's Face*, 1941; *Now Voyager*, 1942) as she fluctuates between self-knowledge and delusion about being an older woman without a man.

The film locates a Daisy of contradictions, providing insights into the cultural devolution of the late twentieth-century face and the cultural weight it carries—from personal fears through romantic quests to public success. The tradition in feature films has been to mystify the screen face and to *fix* it in screen time and space as a luminous, untouchable surface, as with Greta Garbo and Marlene Dietrich (a tradition defamiliarized in Ingmar Bergman's 1966 *Persona*). Rubbo seems to have absorbed something of Bergman, given his definition of the contemporary face as our most "mobile" body part, central to our personality and social status, yet plastic in the "functional" manipulation to which it is subjected. Rubbo packs *Daisy* with documentary conventions, including personal research, experts' reflections on the industrialized preoccupation with the face, and personal testimonials. This web of conventions invokes the topic-driven documentary, yet this very conformity "insists" that Rubbo insinuate himself in Daisy's life to provoke a gender drama in documentary form. In this drama, an expert woman puts herself in the hands of expert men, Rubbo included, who possess the technology and position to manage her face as an image. Thus Daisy represents a decorative object and a problematic femininity. In looking romantically forward she glances backward to a colonial past. Narratively, Daisy is at a personal crossroads, with doubts about her feminine capital. She declares herself a career woman with a girlish yen for perpetual romance, having internalized the couple as her destiny. She is talkative, but her vocal chords seem to be giving out—as if, with slippage into middle age, her voice will betray her reconstituted visage.

In the first shots, Rubbo establishes Daisy's face as the film's central image—a physical mask that projects her desires. Rubbo's judgment of Daisy lies in his scrutiny of her private desires through the events surrounding her facelift. Because Rubbo knows Daisy, he enjoys her confidence when she laments her lack of romance. At first, his voice "hangs around" the screen, neither narration nor interview. Unseen but present in her apartment, he might be a neighborhood gossip or a potential lover on reconnaissance while she brews coffee. He is in fact neither, although as watcher Rubbo implicitly fulfills Daisy's constant need for male approval. At her bedside, he is a comforting friend in her presurgical lethargy; but as a detached filmmaker, he observes Daisy's habit of playing to the male gaze with her physician's husband and the poolside man for whom Daisy parades her figure.

Daisy's dependence upon a persona determined by appearance discloses a culturally induced anxiety involving women's romantic competence. She undertakes the facelift because she bases her personal identity on visual acceptance, an acceptance that must provide a pleasing femininity within male codes of spectatorship. Daisy harbors a specific male code within herself, schooled in a convention she recalls with clarity from a World War II Royal Canadian Air Force poster, to "serve under the man who flies." This slogan speaks to the tradition of the male expert with cultural license to soar, perhaps to play judge from above. For viewers familiar with the NFB's wartime recruitment documentaries (such as *Wings on Her Shoulder*, 1943), Daisy's memory of the slogan puts a sober perspective on a myth that hangs over from the patronizing imagery and nostalgic ideals of the Griersonian-era Film Board.

At the end of *Daisy*, Rubbo visualizes the Board's patriarchal past still present in Daisy, as she surrenders herself wholly to romantic myth on her departure for Europe. A glamorous figure riding to the airport in a limousine, then waving farewell to Rubbo at the departure gate, Daisy achieves narrative closure with her facelift. Rubbo's camera keeps a polite distance, treating Daisy as a remote figure of dubious glamor. This visual distance

Daisy: The Story of a Facelift:
Wearing the NFB logo on
her necklace, Daisy comes to
represent the history of the
National Film Board.

from the film's key figure formalizes Rubbo's withdrawal from the stock
feminine role that Daisy has assumed. The film's final image, an airplane
lifting off with Daisy aboard, is an ironic echo of her submission to "the
man who flies." On the sound track, Willie Nelson's melancholic version of
"September Song" fleshes out Daisy's sentimental afterglow and Rubbo's
detachment from her illusions. The Board's wartime female recruit seems
to disappear into a classical Hollywood fantasy.

Though feisty and accomplished, the quirky-voiced Daisy is a victim
of enduring myths, tied to an ideology of femininity that valorizes the pic-
turesque female body (a "package," as she calls it). Daisy questions female
roles, but her preoccupation with men persists in her conversations. Before
her surgery, Daisy meets with her daughter, who remarks that she accepts
"screwed up" men without altering them, while her mother tries to change
them. Together this mother and daughter connote the culturally embedded
notion that *women* carry the responsibility for emotional failure, particularly in romance.

Since these two generations of women are united by uncertainty about
their relations with men, we cannot assume that Daisy's impending facelift simply betokens a middle-aged woman's fear of aging and mortality.

Somehow, women are not seen as capable of dealing with the males they encounter, marry, or trust. In the latter part of a century where self-doubt feeds consumer and cosmetic industries, women are not usually represented as being expert enough to dismantle male expertise. In one revelation, Daisy jokes about being good at the beginning and the end of her marriages but that the middle—marriage itself—gives her trouble. Daisy may be seen as another of Rubbo's ambivalent go-betweens determined by larger cultural forces. When her hair is being tinted, she confesses to Rubbo, "I don't know how to behave anymore." Throughout, her petite stature underscores her reduced ego, particularly evident in the shot where she enters the clinic pulling her suitcase behind her. In long shot, Daisy appears childlike, overwhelmed by baggage, both material and ideological.

In the poolside scene, Daisy's impulse to display her body as physically becoming for an apparent male stranger is both poignant and painful to view. Her physical and metaphoric smallness as she parades in her bathing suit before this man is established by her easy agreement to his presumptuous patriarchal scrutiny of her body. The camera's downward angle encourages this male purview of Daisy: she is a feminine specimen for male judgment. The scene is more troubling because of Rubbo's seeming complicity with the scrutinizing male gaze and his consequent betrayal of Daisy as trusted go-between. The same strategy informs Rubbo's collusion with Sheila's husband in *Persistent and Finagling*. But this duplicity is made meaningful within the texts of Rubbo's films. That the collusion in *Persistent and Finagling* emanates from Sheila's kitchen as the film begins indicates something of Rubbo's tentative desire to enter conventionally female spaces. With *Daisy*, Rubbo establishes the kitchen as a feminine space but does not enter it, remaining at the doorway. His camera's collusion with the privileged male observer in the poolside scene indicates that all public spaces are male-determined or monitored and that "femininity" is the toll the woman pays to access them.

RITUALS OF GROOMING AND SUTURING

Some ten years after *Persistent and Finagling* Rubbo came to *Daisy*, carrying forward the experience of his documentary excursions in Third World cultures and his continuing fascination with personal rituals and spaces in areas struggling with the remnants of colonialism. With Daisy as conduit into rituals of the hair salon, Rubbo plays male inquisitor in the "foreign land" of a colonized femininity. He puns on his male curiosity and condescension by inserting a close-up of himself performing a self-conscious double take for the camera. Rubbo wants to watch women and what they do, and so must conspicuously mock his male documentary gaze if he is to be credibly self-effacing in tilting against patriarchal expertise through the coy persona he brings to gender politics. The public salon affords him the opportunity to perform this double play.

Though he weaves public and private rituals concerning appearance around the crucial example of Daisy and implicates himself, it is industrialized grooming rituals themselves that Rubbo perceives to be pernicious, regardless of age or gender. The facelift is an extreme rite of industrialized grooming conducted in a theater run by male technical experts. Here the person risks becoming both a product and a victim, with suturing, the bloody marker of the facelift, obscured by the surgeon's initial description of Daisy's potential transformation at his hands. Rubbo implicates documentary in the management of Daisy's surgical imagery and thus depends upon our ambiguous relation to the screen as voyeurs. He intercuts a facial massage so seamlessly with shots of Daisy's surgery that the two activities seem continuous and identical.

In the movement from the image industry to the wounding aftermath of cosmetic surgery, we are led to a distant sympathy for Daisy's physical condition and fate as patient/victim. Still groggy from the anesthetic, in her moment of truth Daisy utters an instinctive rejection of her folly: "How could I have done that!" This is likely the very thought we share. Daisy's face, grossly distorted, swollen, and wounded, shows cosmetic ritual gone too far, expertise seemingly gone awry. This is hardly a conventional female image of fiction film, except in the horror genre's graphic expression of the "monstrous-feminine" (cf. Creed).

Codes of masculine spectatorship, engineered by the male expertise behind technology, drive Rubbo's Daisy culturally and physically. In the prologue, Daisy's face is presented as an alterable image for public inspection. The surgeon alludes to her mirror image and speaks of it as if speaking to the woman herself. Within the mirror's frame, Daisy's humanity seems absent, displaced from the discussion of procedures despite the doctor's soothing words. This is how hairdressers reassuringly discuss hairdos, rarely connecting the projected style to the person before the mirror. All attention is on the mirror image, which is the way we see and envision our own faces. Here proof of existence is the Lacanian "mirage" reflected in the mirror (Lapsley and Westlake 68–71). The image of the reflected face becomes a mode of presentation, technically adjustable and tailored to an "ideal" ego. Rubbo's camera closes in on the mirror couple, male expertise and female compliance posed together but hardly equal. A series of shots frame and reframe Daisy and her surgeon, implicating the camera in an ideological suturing "operation" wherein Daisy accepts the surgeon and a refashioned femininity. Just as Rubbo can adjust his camera at will, the female image can be modified. But the quick intercuts of Daisy's actual surgery, showing the physical penetration of the scalpel, belie the doctor's assurance that his repair will transform Daisy "without distorting" her. Rubbo's own structuring overrides this rhetoric of medical comfort to show the slippages between the word, the image, and the deed, between the female object and male direction.

In another scene, one that appears conventional to direct cinema and a throwback to the Grierson documentary, Rubbo's camera eavesdrops in the NFB cafeteria to extol the unnamed faces that register ordinary humanity. One female's squint lines show the sunny disposition of her ready smiles; a man explains that he has had his "pouches" since he was thirteen. These are personalities attached to the facial "faults" (the persistent "pouches" and sharp "angles") that have shaped these people physically and culturally. If we read this scene as a sampling of the NFB's contemporary persona in 1982, it remains a place of uncredited cultural workers given to unspectacular imagery, naturalized discourse, and the ideal of Canadian wholesomeness institutionalized in the Griersonian period (1939–45). Though Rubbo's Daisy has been "feminized" by the Board's patriarchal past, in a sense her reflections about her cultural worth tilt against this legacy even as she acts otherwise.

PROFESSING FEMININITY

With the industrial and ideological influences that have made the face a consumer commodity, Rubbo sees a reduction of human value to the lowest common denominator of surface style. Culturally, he perceives that North Americans have grown indistinguishable, aiming for straight noses or enlarged breasts. In part, *Daisy* provides a peepshow glimpse into an industry immersed in physical engineering, and Rubbo adopts an appropriate tabloid manner in one sequence to demonstrate the constructed need within this industrial model. A bride-to-be in an American cosmetic surgery clinic testifies to the role her reshaped nose promises as an image: "I'm getting married on Sunday and I'm all ready for action, all ready for the pictures." This linkage of an enhanced femininity and marital bliss parallels the myth Daisy chases when she flies abroad, "starting a new chapter" in her quest for romance. Rubbo concludes his narration with the coda, "Later I would get a card—from Salzburg, I think it was—'having a wonderful time.'" The rhetoric of tourist romance summarizes the culture of fantasy, uniform image, and female compliance, for which the body is abandoned to expertise for excision or implantation.

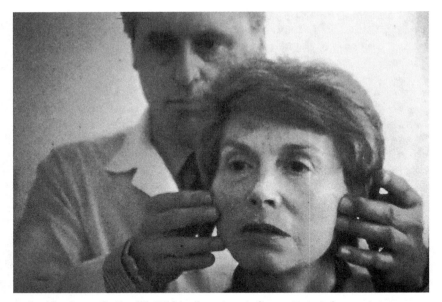

Daisy: The Story of a Facelift: Within the mirror's frame, Daisy's humanity seems
displaced by the discussion of surgical procedures.

Through this excessively processed femininity, Rubbo achieves his
documentary intention, which, as he has said, is to "catalogue" the cultural person as "a moving image" in a "snapshot of changing attitudes."
The myth that appearance stands for stable identity is anthropologically
anchored in Rubbo's initial rhetorical voice-over: "Are we as a species more
or less obsessed than in times past?" Rubbo's question informs his structuring of *Daisy* as a documentary narrative of testimony, scrutiny, intervention, and research. Whether Daisy simply fingers *Vogue* magazine while
waiting to see her surgeon or confides her fading past to Rubbo, she is a
feminine embodiment of consumer culture's obsession with appearance.

In this context, though cosmetics traditionally have been allocated to
women to shore up the colonizing ideology of "the feminine," Rubbo's
graphic imagery of an actual facelift concentrates on the surgical facelift
of a man named Peter. Rubbo's witty narration works in conjunction with
Willie Nelson's nostalgic rendition of "Georgia," which overdetermines the
prevailing male discourse in its "operation" on our viewpoint, as he warns,
"close your eyes, take a quick peek now." With his elaboration of spectatorial pleasure, instruction, and caution, Rubbo charts a viewing course that
pushes us to understand this contemporary ritual as imbricated within the

larger contexts of popular culture. "See, our faces are really masks," Rubbo exudes, aligning himself with the surgeon's spectacle on our behalf as Peter's thin facial skin is lifted inches away from his head.

We might discern that Rubbo is working well within the shock tactics of the surrealist *Un chien andalou* (1928) or the experimental *The Act of Seeing with One's Own Eyes* (1971). We might be stunned at how abstracted human character can become before medical technology and expertise. Or we might find irony in this collision of delight, the grotesque, and male colonizing of the body's surface to conform to cultural codes (Hutcheon 134). If we take the ironic implication of Rubbo's intervening documentary rhetoric, the parodic narration along with the Hollywood-style theme song (Willie Nelson's "Georgia") can be read as a critique of a complicitous male spectatorship revealed as discourse.

Rubbo draws a subtle parallel between surgical manipulation of the body and the function of fragmented images in the black and white photographs of patients' eyes and mouths lining an operating room wall. In the photos, facial fragments are but blueprints for enhanced iconography—precisely the operation of classical cinema. Given the possibility of medical "mistakes," other photos elsewhere in *Daisy* document for the surgeon, as for us, the horrific results of failures in expertise.

RUBBO'S "ABOUT FACE"

With *Daisy*, Rubbo's literal and figurative "about face" stretches the narrative, drama, and popular pleasures of the documentary topic ("the story of a facelift"). He even gives Daisy the mythic closure she desires, but it is a closure befitting a femininity defined by patriarchy and fantasy. In its excessiveness, it opens the film for wider critical speculation by Rubbo and by us as spectators.

In my analysis of *Daisy*, I have considered Rubbo's own decentering of the documentary process as a meditation on both the cultural significance of the facelift and the very concept of "beauty," as well as a metaphor of the contemporary state of the NFB as an institution. Daisy is both a Film Board expert and an unstable documentary subject, an insider and an outsider, who carries the NFB's contemporary insecurity about its self-image in an era of forced redefinition. Such redefinition has been common to the Board (periodically from the late 1950s to the recent years of severe funding cutbacks) as the institution has pondered its continuing mandate and plotted its survival as a Canadian cultural agency rooted in documentary. By circling back to the Film Board in the last phase of his work there, in the 1980s, Rubbo reenters the institution through a gendered "space" permitted by Daisy, a feminine subject whose personal preoccupation with a facelift can be read as a symptom and a sign of the NFB's drifting position and fading impact.

By inscribing personal intervention into his documentary filmmaking, at a historical juncture in the 1970s when the documentary was becoming a more contested and hybrid form, Rubbo troubled the NFB film with post-colonial interests in individuals marginalized by traditional documentary topics and practices, even when his subjects did not perceive their own colo-nized imaginations. Rubbo's persona of intervening filmmaker displaced at the cultural margins, with go-betweens acting doubly and ambivalently as both agents and subjects, is an important precursor of such later filmmak-ers as Ross McElwee (*Sherman's March*, 1985) and Michael Moore (*Roger & Me*, 1989). Following in Rubbo's documentary footsteps, McElwee and Moore circle back to known territories—respectively, a feminized Ameri-can South and an industrially masculinized Flint, Michigan. McElwee and Moore inflate and deflate their egos in places freighted with image, gender, and cultural contradictions too entrenched for the individual docu-mentary filmmaker to "correct" or alter. In the subtle colonization of the patriarchal traditions that still inform these otherwise different corners of American society, McElwee and Moore share with their ordinary citizens and screen "familiars" instabilities similar to those of Rubbo and his go-betweens. McElwee and Moore's onscreen interventions appear to bring the documentary no further than Rubbo could, to thresholds that open per-sonal documentary spaces in the very act of "visiting" cultures ambiguously invested in nostalgic imagery of their pasts.

Such work remains at the edges of the mainstream, even as nonfic-tion and hybrid documentary/fictional forms are gaining wider audiences. It may be an even more necessary documentary approach today, an era of computerization, given its true engagement of the viewer in contrast to mere user "surfing." Rubbo addresses the fragmentation of our humanness and the individual's insecurities within culture, evident in the postmodern traces of nostalgia (reminiscences, photos) that sidetrack Daisy in middle age. His documentary of displaced persona installs itself in the disjunctions and links of Daisy's colonized memory and desire, anticipating the para-doxes Linda Hutcheon sees at work in postcolonialism and postmodernism: "The postcolonial is as implicated in that which it challenges [colonialism] as is the *postmodern* [with modernism]" (134). Fredric Jameson's claim for "the figure of homeopathic medicine" might be merged with Hutcheon's observa-tion and help us theorize further Rubbo's documentary of displaced persona, with its onscreen interventions central to his practice. According to Jameson, this metaphoric figure, often only accepted in medical communities as an unofficial expert, undoes "postmodernism homeopathically by the methods of postmodernism: to work at dissolving the pastiche by using all the instruments of pastiche itself, to reconquer some genuine historical sense by using the instruments of what I have called substitutes for history" (59). Thus, if Daisy is absorbed by romantic myth, Rubbo immerses himself in his own documentary instruments in his attempt to make sense of the cultural contradictions embodied in his subjects.

Notes

Quotations by Michael Rubbo are from an interview I conducted with him at the NFB in Montreal in August 1980 and from a talk at the Canadian Images Film Festival in Peterborough, Ontario, in March 1983.

1. Through an act of Parliament in 1939, the National Film Board of Canada was institutionalized as Canada's official filmmaking agency. The Board's legislative mandate reads that it is "to produce and distribute and to promote the production and distribution of films designed to interpret Canada to Canadians and to other nations."

2. My varied references to "the NFB," "the Film Board," and "the Board" reflect fifty-nine years of popular usage in Canada's cultural vocabulary.

3. Two of the most celebrated units were ("the English") Unit B and ("the French") Unit A. The unit system was inaugurated in 1948 and replaced with a pool system in 1964 (and later, studios, e.g., the Women's Studio D). See Gary Evans, *In the National Interest: A Chronicle of the National Film Board of Canada from 1949 to 1989* (Toronto: University of Toronto Press, 1991), 68–90.

4. Bill Nichols has used the term "social actors" to define documentary's various uses of human subjects. In Rubbo's case, I prefer the term "cultural players" to define his go-betweens' engagements in cultural processes as well as the filmmaker's interventions.

5. Rubbo was invited to the Board in the mid-1960s, following his strong M.A. thesis film at Stanford University in California. *The True Source of Knowledge* compares the tranquil, lush life at Stanford with the beginnings of student activism on the Berkeley campus. Officials at Stanford were impressed by it as a record of the period's campus activism and chose it to replace the university's public relations film. Given the current marketing of university programs and campuses in Canada and the United States, this official recognition by Stanford is remarkable in relation to the consciousness-raising of the 1960s.

6. Rubbo alluded to journalistic methods and problematized them in such other films as *Sad Song of Yellow Skin*, *Waiting for Fidel*, and *Solzhenitsyn's Children*.

7. Margaret Mead argues that "anthropology, as a conglomerate of disciplines, has both implicitly and explicitly accepted the responsibility of making and preserving

records of the vanishing customs and human beings of this earth" because "The recognition that forms of human behavior still extant will inevitably disappear has been part of our whole scientific and humanistic heritage." Mead, "Visual Anthropology in a Discipline of Words," in *Principles of Visual Anthropology* (The Netherlands: Mouton, 1975), 3.

8. A few years after *Daisy*, Rubbo left the Board to make fiction features for independent Montreal producer Roch Demers's series of children's films. He has also been head of documentary at ABC, the Australian Broadcasting Corporation.

WORKS CITED

Creed, Barbara. *The Monstrous-Feminine: Film, Feminism, Psychoanalysis.* London: Routledge, 1993.

Elder, Bruce. "On the Candid-Eye Movement." In *Canadian Film Reader,* ed. Seth Feldman and Joyce Nelson, 86–94. Toronto: Peter Martin Associates, 1977.

Euvrard, Michel, and Pierre Veronneau. "Direct Cinema." In *Self Portrait: Essays on the Canadian and Quebec Cinemas,* ed. Piers Handling, 77–93. Ottawa: Canadian Film Institute, 1980.

Daudelin, Robert. "The Encounter between Fiction and the Direct Cinema." In *Self Portrait: Essays on the Canadian and Quebec Cinemas,* ed. Piers Handling, 94–106. Ottawa: Canadian Film Institute, 1980.

Harcourt, Peter. "The Innocent Eye: An Aspect of the Work of the National Film Board of Canada." In *Canadian Film Reader,* ed. Seth Feldman and Joyce Nelson, 67–77. Toronto: Peter Martin Associates, 1977.

Hutcheon, Linda. "Circling the Downspout of Empire." In *The Post-Colonial Studies Reader,* ed. Bill Ashcroft, Gareth Griffiths, and Helen Tiffin, 130–35. London: Routledge, 1995.

Jameson, Fredric. Interview by Anders Stephanson. In *Postmodernism/Jameson/Critique,* ed. Douglas Kellner, 43–74. Washington: Maisonneuve Press, 1989.

Lapsley, Robert, and Michael Westlake. *Film Theory: An Introduction.* Manchester: Manchester University Press, 1988.

Morris, Peter. "After Grierson: The National Film Board, 1945–1953." In *Take Two: A Tribute to Film in Canada,* ed. Seth Feldman, 182–94. Toronto: Irwin, 1984.

Nichols, Bill. *Representing Reality: Issues and Concepts in Documentary.* Bloomington: Indiana University Press, 1991.

Chapter 20

GENDER, POWER, AND A CUCUMBER

Satirizing Masculinity in *This Is Spinal Tap*

Carl Plantinga

As a military term in the nineteenth century, "heavy metal" signified "large guns, carrying balls of a large size" (Walser 1); today "heavy metal" refers to a kind of rock music practiced by bands such as Metallica, Black Sabbath, and Mötley Crüe. The two meanings are not unrelated, as the satiric *This Is Spinal Tap* (1984) implies. During a concert tour of North America, a member of the fictional band Spinal Tap has trouble clearing an airport security checkpoint. With each pass through the metal detector, bass player Derek Smalls (Harry Shearer) trips the alarm. After several unsuccessful attempts, and having now become the object of many stares, Derek sheepishly reaches into his spandex tights and removes the item that tripped the alarm—an oversized cucumber wrapped in aluminum foil.

This moment succinctly embodies a chief satiric target of *This Is Spinal Tap*—the hypermasculinity of Spinal Tap and heavy metal culture, taking its most exaggerated form in Derek's phallic cucumber. Spinal Tap's masculinity is expressed through flashy displays of technical virtuosity, a choreography of sexual display and male bonding, the "power chords" of the music itself, and phallic guitars and microphones. The band promotes what one (fictional) reviewer calls a "retarded" sexuality stripped of all romanticism or spirituality. Moreover, it is significant that the security guards at the airport checkpoint are women. Heavy metal's emphasis on male power is sometimes manifested in celebrations of the domination of females and defines femininity as passive and erotically available. That it is two *women* who force Derek to publicly reveal his pretensions thus doubles the embarrassment.

The promotion of stereotypical gender roles is the province not merely of heavy metal but of rock music generally. Simon Frith and Angela McRobbie claim that rock music solidifies gender stereotypes and that hard rock, or what they call "cock rock," is a "male form" (373). "Both in its presentation and in its use," they write, "rock has confirmed traditional definitions of what constitutes masculinity and femininity" (387). The music video has also been scrutinized for its gender implications (Kaplan, Lewis). Lisa Lewis argues that rock videos draw on ideologies of adolescence and masculinity, creating a "male preferred address" that supports "a social system of male privilege" (35). In this regard, heavy metal is not qualitatively different than mainstream rock music; it is simply more extreme.

Heavy metal has diverse critics, ranging from the religious right to Tipper Gore to rock critics on the progressive left. Yet even sympathetic commentators describe heavy metal as a discourse of power and masculinity that defines masculinity in traditional terms as the binary opposite of femininity (Weinstein 102–6; Walser 108–36). The audience for heavy metal, as Deena Weinstein notes, "is more than just male; it is masculinist" (104). Recent developments in heavy metal culture include "lite" or "glam" metal (with bands such as Poison and Bon Jovi), forms that attract more female audiences. At the time of *This Is Spinal Tap*'s 1984 release, however, heavy metal culture was, when not overtly misogynist, unwelcoming to females, excluding women from the rank of equals, and emphasizing male bonding. Yet like Derek's cucumber, heavy metal's image of masculinity is a fabrication and an exaggeration. And like the security guards at the airport, *This Is Spinal Tap* displays the pretensions of this hypermasculinist discourse for all to see.

This Is Spinal Tap was director Rob Reiner's first feature film, though previous experience included his role as Meathead on television's *All in the Family* (1971–79).[1] Spinal Tap, the band, consists of Nigel Tufnel (Christopher Guest) on lead guitar, David St. Hubbins (Michael McKean) as lead vocalist, Derek Smalls (Shearer) on bass, Viv Savage (David Kaff) on keyboards, and Mick Shrimpton (R. S. Parnell) on drums. Reiner, Guest, McKean, and Shearer share the writing credits, and the latter three wrote and performed all the music. Guest had long been toying with the character of grimacing lead guitarist Nigel, and in 1979, he, McKean, and Shearer appeared on a television show spoofing "Midnight Special," with Reiner playing Wolfman Jack. Out of this experience grew Spinal Tap. Later, on the strength of a twenty-minute demonstration reel, Avco Embassy agreed to finance the feature film, which eventually cost $2.2 million to produce.

This Is Spinal Tap: The problem with cucumbers—Derek is forced to reveal his pretensions in public.

This Is Spinal Tap played well in the large urban markets generally thought to be "sophisticated"—New York, Chicago, Los Angeles, Toronto. Reiner notes that his previews of the film in a Dallas shopping mall proved less successful: "A small section of the audience laughed. The rest asked why we would make a serious documentary about a terrible band they had never heard of" (quoted in Harmetz 20). But the film's overall success resulted in Spinal Tap's appearance on *Saturday Night Live* (1975–present), commercial album sales, a music video, and a tour. The group even re-formed in 1992, with their new album, *Break Like the Wind*.

Clearly an appreciation for *This Is Spinal Tap* depends on taking it not as a "serious documentary" about an obscure and untalented band but as a *pseudo-documentary*, a fiction film which, like *Zelig* (1983) and *Bob Roberts* (1992), parodies the forms of documentary.[2] An appreciation of the acting, writing, and filmmaking—the art of the film—depends on our reflexive understanding of its parody and satire, as I discuss below. *This Is Spinal Tap* mimics rock documentaries such as *Woodstock* (1970), *Gimme Shelter* (1970), and *The Last Waltz* (1978). Reiner contracted documentary producer Karen Murphy to give the film a surface authenticity and hired cinematographer Peter Smokier, who had worked on *Gimme Shelter*, as director of photography. *This Is Spinal Tap* was largely improvised during production; the group improvised scenes around a loose outline, giving the film a stronger documentary feel than the tightly controlled films of mainstream Hollywood.

I have referred to *This Is Spinal Tap* as a *satire* of the heavy metal discourse on masculinity and a *parody* of rock documentaries. The terms "satire" and "parody" are often used as synonyms but have slightly different meanings. Both involve the imitation of and ironic commentary on another discourse. Yet satire implies ridicule of its target, while a parody need not devalue its object but may range from an ethos of condemnation to one of homage and celebration (cf. Hutcheon 30–49).

This Is Spinal Tap parodies the rock documentary in part through an imitation of its methods. The film employs familiar cinema verité techniques in its "coverage" of Spinal Tap's tour—handheld cameras, zooms and reverse zooms, rack and follow focusing, and swish pans. In this case, however, all scenes consist of actors performing loosely scripted actions. The film also depends heavily on the filmed interview. *This Is Spinal Tap* successfully imitates this documentary technique, staging individual and group interviews that appear throughout the film. Unlike the documentary, however, both interviewer and interviewee play the scripted roles of fictional characters. The structure of the film alternates between "cinema verité" scenes that follow the band on tour and the interviews that provide biographical and historical "information." The film also parodies rock documentary by making oblique references to earlier such films. For example, Reiner appears in the film's exposition to introduce himself as filmmaker Marti Di Bergi, a reference to Martin Scorsese, director of *The Last Waltz*, a documentary about the farewell concert of The Band. (Like The Band in *The Last Waltz*, Spinal Tap is portrayed as a veteran group, having been around for seventeen years and having made fifteen albums.)

Although *This Is Spinal Tap* parodies the rock documentary, it reserves its satire and ridicule for Spinal Tap and its hypermasculinity. Both parody and satire depend on the sophistication of the viewer and on some familiarity with the satiric or parodic target. *This Is Spinal Tap* tempts us to approach it as a "serious" documentary but introduces comic markers—typically ironic incongruities or exaggerations—to disrupt our "serious" viewing (Jenkins 40). Irony is essential to both parody and satire and is the "main rhetorical mechanism" for expressing textual interpretations and evaluations (Hutcheon 31). Comedy presents ironies for the sake of laughter, as when various characters continually mangle the band's name.

The limousine driver meets Spinal Tap at the airport with a cardboard sign reading "Spinal Pap" and, later, Lt. Bill Hogstraat refers to the band as "Spinal Tarp." Satire typically has a more critical bent, often with a social or political point. The band's stage antics and relationships with women, a point to which I shall return later, are satirical. In this way *This Is Spinal Tap* represents heavy metal music and culture, exaggerates it or highlights incongruities, and critiques it through satire.

Central to heavy metal culture is the concert performance—an expression of power, intensity, energy, freedom, and virtuosity. In a context in which power is construed as essentially male, the heavy metal performer marshals every technique possible to express potency and power—through music, costume, staging, choreography, and displays of skill with voice and instrument. The music features a heavy beat with a deep bass "bottom rhythm," together with power chords and distorted voices, both produced literally by excessive power, as the performers intentionally exceed the capacities of guitar amplifiers and vocal chords. One of the running gags of *This Is Spinal Tap*—the bizarre deaths of the band's drummers, both past and present—plays on this emphasis on manic energy. Like some actual rock drummers (Keith Moon of The Who comes to mind), those in Spinal Tap live crazed, intense lives and meet premature ends. The first drummer, Stuffy Peeps, died in a freak gardening accident, while the next, Stumpy Joe, expired while choking on someone else's vomit. As Derek remarks, "They can't prove whose vomit it was." Mick Shrimpton survives until close to film's end when during a manic performance he spontaneously combusts, a victim of ever-increasing levels of intensity and distorted sound.

Much of the visual humor of the film occurs during the tour and performances. Heavy metal, Walser writes, "often stages fantasies of masculine virtuosity and control" (108), in which "spectacular gladiators compete to register and affect ideas of masculinity, sexuality, and gender relations" (111). Spinal Tap's pathetic reality contrasts with these delusions of mastery and grandiosity. Coverage of the tour begins with an optimistic, energetic montage as Spinal Tap arrives in New York, with the requisite shots of the band members moving purposefully through the airport, roadies unloading equipment, excited fans wildly cheering in a packed concert hall, and the band itself in the film's first concert footage. However, the tour soon leads Spinal Tap on a downward spiral of failure and humiliation. And though the concert performances are designed to convey grandeur, power, and virtuosic skill, various mishaps create an opposite sense. One of the film's best visual gags occurs at "Shank Hall" in Milwaukee, where during the performance the band is supposed to emerge, in a choreographed "birth," from three egglike pods.[3] Unfortunately Derek's pod malfunctions and does not

This Is Spinal Tap: The concert performance is an expression of masculine virtuosity in heavy metal culture.

open, and while he tries to retain his composure, a roadie hacks at the pod with a hammer and then burns it with a blowtorch. Finally it opens and the relieved Derek bursts free, but at just the wrong moment—immediately after David and Nigel have returned to their pods for the end of the number. What is intended as a skilled display of choreographed movement turns into travesty and farce.

In Chicago, the band checks into the Holiday Inn, where on the familiar company sign we read "Welcome National Company of the Wiz and Spinal Tap," a juxtaposition that belies the grandiose image Spinal Tap strives to create. Promo man Artie Fufkin (Paul Shaeffer) has set up an autograph session at a Chicago record store, but as the band sits glumly, dressed as "metal gods" to receive the adulation of their fans, no customers show up. Cleveland finds the band wandering in mazelike passageways beneath the stage, unable to find its way to the waiting audience. A band that cannot find the stage hardly conveys skill and power. Heavy metal bands often turn to images and themes of the occult or of Satan that supposedly carry implications of mystery and power. The occult theme backfires for Spinal Tap, however. The Stonehenge debacle, during which, after a breakdown in communication, a diminutive 18-inch (rather than 18-foot) Stonehenge sculpture descends from the rafters and is almost trampled by two dancing dwarves, leads to audience peals of laughter and to the departure of manager Ian Faith (Tony Hedra). But more important, it serves again to contrast pretensions of grandeur with actuality.

David's partner, Jeanine Pettibone (June Chadwick), takes over as manager, but she is unable to reverse the band's downward trend. In Seattle, their regular gig is canceled so they find themselves playing for the "monthly at ease weekend" at Lindbergh Air Force Base, where the audience expects easy-listening music. (Black Sabbath—then called "Earth"— once found itself in a similar predicament: a booking mistake found them at a party where the audience expected waltzes (Weinstein 32–33). At the base Lt. Bob Hogstraat allows the band thirty minutes to set up so they can "get it over with." After transmissions from a control tower interfere with the guitars, Nigel, who decides he has had enough, walks offstage, and quits the band. Near the bottom of Spinal Tap's steady downward trajectory, the band appears at Themeland Amusement Park, where the billboard reads "Puppet Show and Spinal Tap." Jeanine tries to put an optimistic face on events, noting that at least they've got a large dressing room. David sarcastically replies, "Oh, we've got a bigger dressing room than the puppets!" In all of these cases, the satire foregrounds the incongruity between the music and its presentation, which are intended to signify extreme vitality and power, and the pathetic situations in which the band finds itself.

Heavy metal performance celebrates maleness specifically through sexual and virtuosic display. Performance in what Frith and McRobbie call "cock rock" "is an explicit, crude, and often aggressive expression of male sexuality" (374). For example, Van Halen lead singer David Lee Roth sometimes performed while wearing tight leather pants with the cloth around the buttocks cut out. On the cover of the band's first album, *Van Halen* (1978), Roth appears with a naked chest and a microphone jutting from his crotch. His running, jumping, and gymnastic moves onstage all were meant to signify physical prowess and sexual vitality. Such individualistic display is often allowed only to the lead singer and lead guitarist, although the drummer sometimes gets his solo as well.

It is thus fitting that Derek, the bass player, is the quiet man of Spinal Tap, content to allow David and Nigel center stage. With his measured demeanor, thick beard, and meerschaum pipe, he initially seems older and wiser than Nigel and David, carrying an air of dignity and intelligence. All such pretensions disappear when he speaks, however. During one interview he calls Nigel and David the visionaries of the band, rather like English poets Shelley and Byron. (The band regularly equates itself with canonized writers and composers.) If Nigel and David are like fire and ice,

Derek says, he stands somewhere in between, like "lukewarm water." Lead singer David St. Hubbins, who says he is named after "the patron saint of quality footwear," is the group's intellectual "force" (such as it is) and the "straight man" of the group. The lead singer of a heavy metal band often "fronts" the group, acting as spokesperson in interviews. So David is more articulate than Derek and Nigel, with fewer comic quirks and eccentricities. He is the only band member who apparently remains separate from the groupies populating the film and is the only member to have a steady partner. (At the Recording Industry Convention, however, Derek, Nigel, *and* David have prominent herpes sores on their lips.) David's chief function is to serve as leader and stabilizing figure, until his weaknesses allow Jeanine's "female intrusions" into the male enclave and result in the film's chief dramatic conflict.

Through Nigel, Spinal Tap's lead guitarist and the film's lead player, the film most pointedly satirizes the hypermasculine theater of heavy metal performers—especially guitarists. Onstage, Nigel's strutting gyrations, facial contortions, and tongue-wagging exaggerate what every wannabe rocker recognizes as the conventions of heavy metal's "cult of the lead guitarist." The performances of Nigel and the band reduce sexual relations to animal drives and strutting sexual display. While the music keeps time to a throbbing, erotic rhythm, the lyrics to songs such as "Sex Farm" and "Big Bottom" ("I just can't leave her behind") equate sexuality with expressions of aggression and lust. Moreover, the stage show becomes a display of erotic gymnastics. Spandex was introduced to heavy metal around 1980. As Weinstein notes, "Pants made of this material allow greater freedom of movement onstage and better display of the athletic bodies of the performers, thereby promoting an image of vital power" (30). Moreover, for Spinal Tap, the skin-tight Spandex outfits feed their obsession with penis size (also echoed by Derek's airport incident). Nigel imagines that the band's impressive bodies and bulging genitalia cause "terror" in many of their fans. His guitar-playing epitomizes the band's sexual display; his instrument metaphorically becomes a giant phallus, as he holds it against his crotch and swings it toward the crowd, while grimacing and suggestively wagging his tongue. In short, the art this band practices is a none-too-subtle celebration of animal masculinity.

Heavy metal emphasizes the guitar solo as much as any subgenre of rock; nearly every heavy metal song features at least one such solo, and few other instruments are allowed solos. The guitar solo is a primary means through which the heavy metal performer expresses *virtuosity;* it is a forum for the display not only of musical skill and technical wizardry but of a more diffuse masculine quality. As Walser writes, "Virtuosity—ultimately derived from the Latin root *vir* [man]—has always been concerned with demonstrating and enacting a particular kind of power and freedom that might be called 'potency'" (76). Thus Eddie Van Halen's extended guitar solo on *Van Halen* is called "Eruption," a metaphor for male ejaculation.

In *This Is Spinal Tap*, all displays of what the band considers virtuosity become ironic implications of its lack. Nigel has meager talents at best, as is clear from a dismal guitar solo during which, after the requisite riff of repeated high notes, he grates his tennis shoe and then a violin against the guitar strings, creating a deafening cacophony. During another solo, he is so overcome by the sublimity of his playing that he descends—in orgasmic bliss, it seems—to the stage floor, where a roadie tries to pick him up without disturbing his performance. (The mediocrity of Nigel's playing stands in contrast to the guitar skills of the best *actual* metal guitarists—e.g., Eddie Van Halen, Randy Rhoads—whose obvious technical skill belies the contention that just anyone could play heavy metal guitar.)

Nigel's pretensions and fastidious nature—both privileges of rock stardom—become one of the film's motifs. Spoiled fussiness is apparent at Vandermint Auditorium in North Carolina, where Nigel becomes infuriated at the miniature bread (which confuses him because the meat slices are full-size) and at the fact that some of the Spanish olives are missing their little red pimentos. Later Nigel plays piano and ruminates about his music with Di Bergi. As he plinks on the keyboard, Nigel speaks of the key of B-minor, which "makes people weep instantly." "I'm really influenced by Mozart and Bach," he says, in a transparent attempt to link his virtuosity and musical genius with theirs. The tune he plays, "a Mach piece really," he calls "Lick My Love Pump." The neologism he creates—"Mach"—not only suggests the heavy metal guitarist's emphasis on speed but also refers to Ringo's joke in *A Hard Day's Night* (1964), where after a question about whether he's a mod or a rocker, he answers that he's a "mocker."

Another memorable scene has Nigel walking Di Bergi through the room that houses Nigel's collection of electric guitars. One might expect a skilled guitarist, as a requirement of virtuosity, to have expert knowledge of his instrument. Unlike Eddie Van Halen, who constructed some of his guitars himself, Nigel seems to know little about the instruments. At each guitar or piece of equipment, Nigel displays either capriciousness or ignorance. As they stop at the first guitar, Nigel asks Di Bergi to listen to the "sustain." When Di Bergi protests that he doesn't hear anything, Nigel thinks for a moment, then replies, "You would if it were playing." Nigel has difficulty describing a guitar with special equipment allowing him to freely roam the stage, and Di Bergi tells the uninformed collector that it's called a "wireless." An heroic fantasy requires sacred idols, and for Nigel this is his "virginal" guitar, which has never been played. Nigel tells Di Bergi not to touch it, then not to point at it. Di Bergi asks if he can look at it. Loudness contributes to an ethos of power and intensity, and *This Is Spinal Tap* pokes fun at the mentality that valorizes sheer volume. As Nigel and Di Bergi move on to an amplifier with volume controls that reach "11" rather than "10," Nigel impresses on Di Bergi the importance of being able to play one notch louder. Di Bergi tries to explain that an "11" rather than "10" on the volume control doesn't guarantee a louder amplifier.

Heavy metal's theater of hypermasculinity doesn't simply relate to men; it has implications for women as well. Weinstein notes that "Women are aliens in the heavy metal subculture because of their otherness" and that heavy metal culture is "an enormous male bonding group" (135). Walser describes what he calls the "exscription," or exclusion, of women from heavy metal culture and its misogyny. Heavy metal, he writes, is "a world of action, excess, transgression . . . , one in which men are the only actors, and in which male bonding among members of the 'hero team' is the only important social relationship" (114–15). Women are also seen as a threat because their attractiveness "threatens to disrupt both male self-control and the collective strength of male bonding" (Walser 118). This in part accounts for the misogynistic lyrics of bands such as W.A.S.P., Guns N' Roses, and Mötley Crüe and the prevalence of the femme fatale figure in the songs of Dokken and Whitesnake, for example.

Essential to the theme of misogyny and exclusion, as developed in *This Is Spinal Tap*, is the arrival of Jeanine Pettibone. After the Memphis show is canceled, David is heartened because Jeanine has announced that she is coming from England to accompany David and the band. Other than Jeanine and the relatively positive character of Bobbi Flekman (Fran Drescher), who articulately castigates Ian for the band's sexist album cover, the women who populate *This Is Spinal Tap* are groupies whose main function is to adore the band members and reinforce their masculine identities. Jeanine hearkens to media caricatures of well-known rock 'n' roll wives such as Yoko Ono and Linda McCartney. She represents a threat to Spinal Tap's unity, not only because she is a female who demands power in this boys' club but because she is secretive, scheming, and utterly humorless. She eventually usurps Ian's role as manager and controls David, and thus the band. The film takes care to emphasize the lifelong friendship of Nigel and David with pictures of their boyhood life in "Squatney" to set up Jeanine, in the eyes of Nigel, as an intruder in this world of "legitimate" male relationships.

Jeanine is controlling and a bit dotty, charting the band's travel plans according to horoscopes. Her hold on David, and through him her influence on the band, is significant. David needs the "direction" she gives, saying that she "sorted out his life for him." On the telephone before she arrives, she tells David she can determine by his voice that he's been eating too much sugar. Jeanine becomes a kind of nuclear threat to the male culture of *This Is Spinal Tap*. She monopolizes and influences David and associates little with other band members. In the band's bus, David and Jeanine sit in front, and Jeanine refuses David's mumbling requests for permission to join the other band members at the rear. During an interview David says that Jeanine influences the band's music through the criticisms she reveals only to David: "She gives me the brutally frank version and I sort of tart it up for [the rest of the band]." She sometimes whispers into David's ear, and he obediently acts. Despite David's claim that Jeanine and Nigel love each other (though admittedly their "communication is blocked"), their mutual antipathy is obvious in their competition for David's attentions. During a recording session, Nigel loudly criticizes David's playing, saying that Jeanine has been distracting him. The real issue is that Jeanine violates the masculine code of the band because she usurps the power usually reserved for men.

As Jeanine assumes greater control, both Nigel and Ian (the manager) become increasingly alienated. During a restaurant meeting, Jeanine suggests that their latest album has been mixed poorly, but her references to "Dobly" (rather than "Dolby") give Nigel cause to make fun of her. She then unveils her ideas for a new production design for the band, featuring masks for the three band leaders that not-too-subtly reveal her sympathies. While Nigel is to wear a Capricorn mask that resembles a devilish goat and Derek a scorpion-face derived from Scorpio, David's Leo mask would be a handsome lion. Nigel quickly rejects Jeanine's plans and hastily draws the Stonehenge sketch on a napkin, which becomes the ill-fated idea for their newest prop.

The conflict comes to a head after the Stonehenge concert, when David and Jeanine suggest that Ian share managing duties with Jeanine. Ian sees this as a demotion and an insult, especially since his would-be partner, as he notes, is "a woman." Lugging his cricket bat as a totem of phallic power, and after the requisite round of insults (cruelty is the surest sign of power over others), he quits the band and storms out. Later Nigel walks off the stage mid-concert at Lindbergh Air Force Base when his electric guitar picks up control tower transmissions. Of his departed partner, David later says, "We shan't work together again." At their lowest point, the short-handed band plays freeform "jazz" to a jeering audience at Themeland Amusement Park. Having successfully replaced both Ian and Nigel, Jeanine joins the band onstage with a tambourine, her presence breaking the unwritten rule that the heavy metal stage be a site of masculine theater and male bonding.

Neither the band members nor their manager accepts women as equals; for them women are either complacent sex kittens or monstrous manipulators. The band's sexism is "retarded," or juvenile, because it is completely unselfconscious. The album cover for their release, *Smell the Glove,* alludes to the ties between heavy metal and sadomasochism, and features a greased, naked woman on all fours, wearing a dog collar and leash, supine before a black glove, pushed to her face. When Bobbi Flekman denounces the cover to Ian, he tells her she "should have seen the cover they wanted to do. It wasn't a glove, believe me." When the band is told that the album will not be released due to its sexist cover, Nigel naively asks, "What's wrong with being sexy?" Ian is a well-drawn character, and an important means by which the film satirizes a masculinity that can barely control aggression. Ian percolates with the threat of both verbal and physical violence (he carries the phallic cricket bat with him wherever he goes). Weinstein notes that heavy metal culture is homophobic, tending toward "an attitude of extreme intolerance toward male homosexuality" (106). Although this aspect of heavy metal culture is mostly ignored in *This Is Spinal Tap,* it is apparent in the insults Ian hurls at other adult men, featuring derogatory terms for homosexuals. Sir Denis Eton-Hogg (Patrick MacNee) is the overstuffed president of Polymer Records (the pun on "Polydor" denoting the plastic or ersatz nature of his enterprise). When Sir Denis cancels plans for the album cover, Ian covers the telephone mouthpiece and mutters, "fucking old poofter." Later Ian abuses a thickly lensed hotel clerk, calling him a "twisted old fruit."[4]

Although *This Is Spinal Tap* satirizes the hypermasculine theater of Spinal Tap and heavy metal, the film transcends mean-spirited ridicule. Thomas Hobbes, one of many thinkers who have mused on the psychology of humor, explained laughter as a sudden rush of self-esteem occurring when we imagine our superiority over the situation or state of others (quoted in Munro 91). At first glance, the humor of *This Is Spinal Tap* would seem to fit this formula, as we guffaw at the naive antics of this untalented band on their descent from stardom. Yet humor is not necessarily grounded in sneering contempt (though it sometimes is) but often stems from a more democratic view in which we all look pretty much alike in our weaknesses, pretenses, and fundamental lovableness. *This Is Spinal Tap* makes its major characters (Nigel, David, and Derek) into likable fools, quite boyish and gentle despite their macho posing and tough lyrics. Though we feel confident they would find some way to blithely rationalize total failure, we nonetheless cheer for what may be their final triumph when, at film's end, they reunite for a road trip to Japan.

The North American tour temporarily sends the band on a downward trend of canceled gigs and interpersonal conflict. This move toward defeat and disintegration, characteristic of ironic narrative structure, culminates at the "End of Tour Party" in Los Angeles. The scene begins with a reverse zoom from two old women lying on lawn chairs by the pool, an image expressing the opposite of energy and power, and suggesting that the band has lost its adolescent male audience. Nigel and Ian have quit the band and are absent, and the small number of guests makes the party seem lonely. One interviewer, in a reference to the Scorsese film, asks David if this is Spinal Tap's "Last Waltz." David feebly philosophizes about what "the end" really means, in an attempt to avoid the implications of the question. Derek and Nigel then engage in a classic example of rationalization. Derek asks, "Who wants to be a forty-five-year-old rock 'n roller farting around for people less than half our age, cranking out some mediocre head-banging bullshit? . . . It's beneath us." They begin to talk about future projects—for example, a rock musical based on the life of Jack the Ripper ("You're a naughty one, saucy Jack")—that suggest a continued naive promotion of "retarded sexuality." They conclude that they are "lucky." "People should be envying us," Derek says optimistically. "*I* envy us."

The film's ironic ending is essential to its project. Backstage, before their planned last show, Nigel returns unexpectedly to "deliver a message" from Ian. "Sex Farm" is on the charts in Japan, and Ian wonders whether the band would be interested in re-forming to tour there. David at first acts outraged at the suggestion but later asks Nigel to join the band onstage, and Spinal Tap is reunited. The traditional male bond is reestablished, and Jeanine, the feminine "intruder," is no longer seen on the stage. The film's narrative ends with a return to former "glory," as the energized band plays to wildly cheering crowds in Tokyo. Jeanine and Ian give each other cold glances, enduring an uneasy truce.

This is both a comic and an ironic ending. However much it seems "tacked on" or "throwaway," it softens the hard edge—the bleakness—of irony by ending with the comedy of social integration.[5] *This Is Spinal Tap* encourages allegiance with the band members, and especially with Nigel, David, and Derek. Thus when the band reunites and their fortunes take a wildly fortuitous turn, the audience may be relieved. However, the ending cannot be taken at face value, for this social integration also signifies moral defeat. It ironically suggests that the band has learned nothing from its trials, that its newfound fortunes are undeserved and temporary, and that an audience can be found for just about any music, as long as it's for sale. Moreover, the ending furthers the film's critique of gender discourse in rock culture; this return to the status quo also reconfirms Spinal Tap's hypermasculine posturing.

The ending also raises problematic issues for the film's cultural critique, suggesting ideological contradictions in its thematic project. Portraying Jeanine as a stereotyped "bitch" encourages us to take pleasure in her final exclusion and the re-formation of the original male group and to justify such pleasure by appealing to her personal shortcomings—her controlling nature, lack of humor, inability to manage the band, and so on. The critique of gender relations in *This Is Spinal Tap* would have been far stronger had Jeanine been made a more likable, well-rounded character, with negative *and* positive qualities like those of Nigel, David, and Derek. Had she been portrayed more sympathetically, *This Is Spinal Tap* would more clearly highlight the cultural practices leading to her exclusion.

Among the handful of pseudo-documentaries and documentary parodies, *This Is Spinal Tap* is most similar to *Zelig* and *Bob Roberts*. While *This Is Spinal Tap* may in fact have deceived some spectators, its status as parody and satire depends on the spectator's recognition of its numerous comic markers. The audience must recognize the film as a "false" documentary to fully appreciate its art. The same is true for *Zelig* and *Bob Roberts*, during which the viewer recognizes that despite textual markers indexing the films as "documentary," Woody Allen and Tim Robbins play fictional characters in fiction films.

Films that satirize the documentary, such as *Mondo Cane* (1963) and Chris Marker's *Letter from Siberia* (1957), target the "serious" or "classical" documentary by pointing to silly, incongruous, or shocking subjects, while ironically wearing the mantle of serious investigation. In contrast to these films, the purpose of *This Is Spinal Tap* is not primarily to mock or investigate the sober informational function of the conventional documentary but, like *Zelig* and *Bob Roberts*, to mimic the documentary for other ends. Thus *Bob Roberts* explores the relationships between popular culture and the American electoral process, and *Zelig* examines the possibility of finding personal identity in a world where illusion and reality seem confused, and where the self is defined from the outside.

The effect of *This Is Spinal Tap*, then, is not so much to explore the nature of documentary as to focus outward, onto another kind of representation—what we might call the social representation of the self. *Bob Roberts*, *Zelig*, and *This Is Spinal Tap* all explore social representation—the representation of the self as political figure (*Bob Roberts*) or masculine ideal (*This Is Spinal Tap*) or the social construction of personal identity generally

(*Zelig*). As Hutcheon notes, satire is a means "of bringing the 'world' into art" (104); both satire and parody are useful to contest and/or examine social codes or practices. In this way *This Is Spinal Tap* uses satire to examine and critique heavy metal generally and, in particular, its promotion of a "hypermasculine" mythology, an ethos that reduces sexuality to animal instincts, devalues feminine qualities, and excludes women.

NOTES

Thanks to the editors for their insightful comments on an earlier draft of this essay.

1. Reiner has since become successful as a director and, to a lesser extent, actor, with *The Princess Bride* (1987), *When Harry Met Sally* (1989), *Misery* (1990), and *A Few Good Men* (1992) among his directorial credits.

2. I assume here that *This Is Spinal Tap* is a fiction film—with a loose script and actors playing roles—that mimics the forms of nonfiction. Some might object that this division is too neat. Some deny a distinction between fiction and nonfiction altogether, pointing out that all (so-called) nonfictions must make use of imaginative form and various manipulations, and thus resemble fictions. See Jacques Aumont, Alain Bergala, Michel Marie, and Marc Vernet, *Aesthetics of Film,* trans. Richard Neupert (Austin: University of Texas Press, 1992), 77–79. This observation, while accurate, is somewhat beside the point. A film is nonfiction not because it lacks imagination or the manipulation of its materials (as though a nonfiction should be a perfect copy or replica of "the real") but because it is socially marked or indexed, because through it the filmmakers make direct assertions about the actual world, and because when audiences recognize a film as nonfiction, they mobilize different viewing strategies than they do in the case of fiction. See my *Rhetoric and Representation in Nonfiction Film* (Cambridge: Cambridge University Press, 1997), especially chapters 1 and 2.

The ontological status of the band is more difficult to gauge; after the success of the film, Spinal Tap first played at clubs in Los Angeles and New York, next on *Saturday Night Live,* and then on a full-fledged concert tour. Spinal Tap at that point had become an actual band, but were Guest, McKean, and Shearer members of the band or simply playing the roles of band members who are fictional characters?

3. An actual heavy metal band would more likely incorporate death than birth imagery into its stage show. This is one respect in which Spinal Tap misses the mark in its imitation of heavy metal.

4. One significant development in heavy metal has been androgynous bands such as Poison and Mötley Crüe, and the adoption by male performers of makeup, costumes, and elaborate hairstyles that have traditionally been associated with female display. While some commentators see such bands as progressive in their

deliberate confusion of traditional gender boundaries (Walser 131–33), I prefer a less sanguine explanation for their popularity. "Glam" metal, with its stage flamboyance, is calculated to appeal to young women, with whom it finds its largest audience. (Male heavy metal fans are often disdainful of the subgenre.) Through the performers, who are "made-up" in traditionally feminine ways, females gain identificatory entry into a "masculine" world of aggressive power, without threatening traditional feminine identity. *This Is Spinal Tap* was released just as such bands were gaining popularity. Although during concert performances the band occasionally wears stage makeup, the film deals little with the phenomenon of androgyny.

5. I use the terms "irony" and "comedy" here much as Northrop Frye uses them in *The Anatomy of Criticism: Four Essays* (Princeton: Princeton University Press, 1957). Although romance, tragedy, comedy, and irony are usually discussed in reference to the narrative structure of fiction, they are applicable to *This Is Spinal Tap* for two reasons. First, I have argued that *This Is Spinal Tap* is fiction. Second, even were this not the case, Hayden White, in his *Metahistory: The Historical Imagination in Nineteenth-Century Europe* (Baltimore: Johns Hopkins University Press, 1973), has made a convincing argument that nonfiction texts, and specifically narrative histories, make use of the kind of narrative structures Frye describes. Various scholars have extended White's claims beyond written histories to nonfiction films (e.g., Nichols 60, 143, 244; Plantinga). Frye notes that narrative forms are often mixed, as *This Is Spinal Tap* blends comic and ironic narrative structure to become an ironic comedy. It features the social integration characteristic of comedy but one that signifies the moral disintegration of irony.

WORKS CITED

Frith, Simon, and Angela McRobbie. "Rock and Sexuality." *Screen Education* 29 (78/79): 3–19. Reprinted in *On Record: Rock, Pop, and the Written Word*, ed. Simon Frith and Andrew Goodwin, 371–89. New York: Pantheon Books, 1990.

Harmetz, Aljean. "Reiner Has Last Laugh with His Rock Spoof." *New York Times*, April 25, 1984, sec. C, 20.

Hutcheon, Linda. *A Theory of Parody.* New York: Methuen, 1985.

Jenkins, Henry III. "The Amazing Push-Me/Pull-You Text: Cognitive Processing and Narrational Play in the Comic Film." *Wide Angle* 8, nos. 3–4 (1986): 35–44.

Kaplan, E. Ann. *Rocking around the Clock: Music Television, Postmodernism, and Consumer Culture.* New York: Methuen, 1987.

Lewis, Lisa A. *Gender Politics and MTV: Voicing the Difference.* Philadelphia: Temple University Press, 1990.

Munro, D. H. "Humor." In *The Encyclopedia of Philosophy*, ed. Paul Edwards, 3:90–93. New York: Macmillan, 1967.

Nichols, Bill. *Representing Reality: Issues and Concepts in Documentary.* Bloomington: Indiana University Press, 1991.

Plantinga, Carl. *Rhetoric and Representation in Nonfiction Film.* Cambridge: Cambridge University Press, 1997.

Walser, Robert. *Running with the Devil: Power, Gender, and Madness in Heavy Metal Music.* Hanover, NH: Wesleyan University Press, 1993.

Weinstein, Deena. *Heavy Metal: A Cultural Sociology.* New York: Lexington Books, 1991.

Chapter 21

Documentary Film and the Discourse of Hysterical/ Historical Narrative

Ross McElwee's *Sherman's March*

Lucy Fischer

The film *Sherman's March* (1985) takes its name from the events of 1864–65 when Civil War general William Tecumseh Sherman trekked through the South, crossing many geographical and political borders along the way. The opening of Ross McElwee's film, with its momentary assumption of standard documentary conventions, presents us with a map of the region and the animated trajectory of Sherman's infamous march to the sea. On this level, we might imagine the text as an historical epic in nonfiction form—and its initial voice-of-God narration, its display of archival photographs and its recitation of the "facts" do nothing to disappoint us.

But within short order this grandiose prologue begins to unravel. McElwee is heard offscreen inquiring whether the sequence should be re-shot (revealing its synthetic status), and the filmmaker is caught in a demeaning visual pose—sweeping the floor of a New York City loft. He then describes (in voice-over) how he had just begun to make a film about General Sherman when he stopped in New York to visit a girlfriend who proceeded to dump him. Devastated, he headed south "to see [his] family and try to begin [his] film."

With these revelations, *Sherman's March* crosses the first of its own fluid borders—from the realm of *historical* into *hysterical* narrative. As we shall see, this "traversal" is only one of many, as the film skirts the boundaries of biography versus autobiography, fiction versus nonfiction, objectivity versus subjectivity, public versus private, classicism versus postmodernism, and cinema verité versus drama. Hence *Sherman's March* is a highly self-reflexive documentary that consciously inscribes within its discourse an interrogation of the documentary form itself. In a confusion of self and other, the film almost immediately superimposes the life story of Ross McElwee (the ostensible man *behind* the movie camera) upon its profile of General Sherman (the hallowed figure *upon* the movie screen).

Clearly we are to find the opposition of Sherman and McElwee one of droll incommensurability. Sherman is a Northern Civil War conqueror, a soldier who brought General Lee to his knees. He is a figure whose troops "raped and plundered" as he carved a "path of destruction" upon the military and civilian populations of the South. In other words, he is a "hero"—in the Western sense of the term. McElwee, by contrast, is a (then) unknown Southern artist who, pathetically, becomes derailed from his epic project through the humiliating pain of unrequited love. For the rest of the film, he stumbles around Sherman's historic landscape—no longer documenting or dramatizing the general's monumental journey so much as using it as a shameless alibi to pick up women. Though he received grant money to make a film about American history, it rapidly becomes a work about "Ladies of the South."

Ultimately, in McElwee's eyes, the projects of love and war are not entirely unrelated. The subtitle of *Sherman's March* is "A Meditation on the Possibility of Romantic Love in the South during the Era of Nuclear Weapons Proliferation"—a phrase that reminds us of the subtitle to *Dr. Strangelove* (1964): "How I Learned to Stop Worrying and Love the Bomb." He informs us that when his love life wanes, his war dreams wax. Hence we are not surprised to find a continual intercutting between sites of historic military battle and scenes of personal romantic strife—their routes hopelessly entangled. After he is rejected by Karen, he visits Sherman's final battlefield and evokes symbolic castration by commenting on the soldiers' amputated limbs. Similarly, when he visits a monument dedicated to the Confederate dead, an elderly matron reminds him that many of the fallen were so young that they had not yet had their first sweethearts.

Ironically, *Sherman's March* soon levels the differences between the war-torn Sherman and the lovelorn McElwee. In a postmodern gesture, the film fractures secure notions of the humanist subject—by merging identities and confusing biography and autobiography. Historian Robin Winks has noted that "The one person the historian cannot afford to have missing is himself" (61), but, clearly, McElwee takes this principle to dizzying

heights. He tells us that Sherman (like himself) had a red beard and suffered a love-hate relation with the South. (McElwee left his North Carolina
home to teach film up North but no longer feels rooted in any part of the
country.) The filmmaker also empathizes with Sherman's anxiety, insomnia, and melancholy, as well as with his artistic bent. (Evidently Sherman
painted a series of portraits of his friends, a project not unlike McElwee's in
Sherman's March.) Both men confronted failure in their careers: McElwee
as a filmmaker and Sherman as a politician. Finally, Sherman's death on
Valentine's Day 1891 endears him to McElwee, who imagines them both as
casualties of love. As evidence of the two men's doubling, McElwee, at one
point, dons a Civil War uniform for a costume party—becoming a Sherman
stand-in, like the Burt Reynolds lookalike he later meets.

But aside from McElwee's resemblance to an historical hero, his cinematic replay of Sherman's March also likens him to the classic protagonist
of Western fiction. For Teresa de Lauretis, such a figure is always male and
motivated by Oedipal desire. The archetypal narrative involves his journey
to "manhood, wisdom and power." Within this scenario, women may be
"obstacles man encounters on the path of life." As such, "they must be

Sherman's March: Ross McElwee is both a social actor within the film and the
film's director.

slain or defeated" (110). When they are not snares, women (at least within the standard heterosexual scenario) are objects of the male hero's quest. De Lauretis also makes clear how women serve a *psycho-spatial* function within the dramatic terrain—which equates "the womb, the earth, the grave, the woman" (121).

As though to introduce the Oedipal theme into his work (and scramble notions of family and national history), McElwee's first stop is to visit his dad and stepmother at their North Carolina home. (Later there is poignant talk of his birth mother's death.) This is also the site of Lee's surrender to Sherman. But McElwee refuses such defeat. Though his parents want him to marry a "nice Southern girl," he has "no desire to meet or talk to any of the young women [he's] been introduced to." (Hence, ironically, *Sherman's March* is initiated by the *lack* of desire.)

However, a conversation with his sister soon provides the key to McElwee's future (and to his cinematic enterprise). She remarks that although his luck with women in ordinary situations is lackluster, he has an "instant rapport with people" from behind the camera. He takes her advice to heart, and the next sequence commences the format that the rest of the film will follow. From offscreen, he interviews Mary, a divorcée and childhood playmate who is visiting home. When she leaves town precipitously, McElwee is despondent and reverts to a "listless contemplation of [his] single status." Before long, he finds another female subject who sparks his interest—Pat, a would-be actress who roller skates and does cellulite exercises before the camera. He admits to feeling a "strong primal attraction to her." When she leaves for an audition in Atlanta, he travels with her, filming along the way.

These scenes establish a prototype for future sequences. McElwee is repeatedly attracted to a female subject whom he films as the two become acquainted. Though he develops a crush on her (and is often, admittedly, "lust-ridden"), she rebuffs him, and his romantic hopes are dashed. His itinerary (originally consonant with Sherman's) is detoured by his pursuit of miscellaneous women and their random, peripatetic paths. (Eventually he is also diverted by a bizarre search for Burt Reynolds, who, he learns, is filming in the South.) If McElwee visits the war sites he has intended, it is often serendipitously. Only because he is enamored with Pat, for example, does he end up in Atlanta, the scene of Sherman's notorious attack.

In filming his series of women, McElwee borrows from the techniques of cinema verité (interview format, handheld 16-mm camera, portable sound gear, location shooting). Significantly, the narrative voice heard in the first moments of the film belongs to Richard Leacock—McElwee's former film teacher and one of the fathers of the movement (*Primary*, 1960;

Sherman's March: Pat, the aspiring actress.

Quint City, U.S.A., 1963; *Monterey Pop,* 1967; *Chiefs,* 1969). Valorizing film "truth," the cinema verité school attempts to capture life spontane-ously and unawares, without manipulation through scripting. As Peter Graham notes, such filmmakers "follow their subjects almost anywhere, and because of their unobtrusiveness . . . people soon forget the presence of the camera and attain surprising naturalness" (34). Verité documenta-ries shun prefabricated scenarios, reenacted vignettes, voice-over narra-tion, and theme music—"theatrical" touches seen as inappropriate to the nonfiction mode. Clearly these prohibitions obtain for *Sherman's March* and for McElwee's filming of his cast of female characters.

From a certain perspective, McElwee's journey might be said to follow de Lauretis's paradigm for the Western fictional hero. His narrative pivots on the traversal of space. Like Odysseus returning from the Trojan War, his itinerary derives from military events—at least through the mediating figure of Sherman. (David Ansen of *Newsweek* calls the film an "Ameri-can *Odyssey"* [my italics].) For McElwee, women function as stops along the way—Pat in North Carolina, Joy in South Carolina, Winnie on the Georgia coast. At points, he cavalierly abandons his women. After romancing Win-nie, he takes an editing job in Boston, without any thought to the devastat-ing effect of his absence on their budding affair. The film also evinces other associations between topos and femininity. When he and Charleen walk through an overgrown tunnel at a defunct military site, he compares it to a grave, reminding us of the masculine womb/tomb equation. Alternately, she likens the space to "pubic hair" and orders him to "part the bushes and go into it." Though McElwee imagines the women he encounters as erotic prizes, they frequently function as obstacles. Thus he finds himself struggling to convince Karen that she should love him, a stance that is particularly farcical given her status as a trial lawyer.

It is also obvious how McElwee's film plays on issues of voyeurism and sadism, so central to the classic cinematic narrative. According to Margaret Atwood, scopophilia is crucial to historical discourse since "historians are the quintessential voyeurs, noses pressed to Time's glass window" (123). McElwee's only means of engaging women is through the camera eye, which, in true verité fashion, often catches them at private moments (undressing or putting on makeup). For critic Pat Graham, McElwee trains "his lens with phallic resolve." Perhaps this is why he anticipated a "feminist onslaught that never came" (McElwee interview with Lucia 34). That attack was certainly marshaled against Ugly George, the crude and infamous New York City cable host of the 1980s who roamed the urban streets trying to convince women to disrobe before his camera. Unlike lascivious George, McElwee is a consummate Southern gentleman whose carnal impulses are overlaid with an air of gentility. In a gesture of patrician discretion, he refuses to show us explicitly any of the sexual trysts he may have had along the way. Furthermore, McElwee has a sense of humor about his masculine position. For example, while he visits Karen (and chastises her for rejecting him), they attend a feminist demonstration; he jokes about the prudence of arguing with her in the midst of "ten thousand angry women." Similarly, in one of the film's final images, he mocks his own voyeuristic tendencies. While describing his crush on Pat, he directs the audience to locate her in an extreme long shot of a chorus singing onstage. It is a little like finding Waldo in a picture puzzle.

Charleen ultimately accuses McElwee of "hiding" behind the lens, reminding us of the voyeur's secretive stance. (McElwee claims that he is "camera shy in reverse.") By the end of the movie he confesses that he films his life in order to *have* a life—thus highlighting connections between looking and living. As for sadism (an accusation leveled at Sherman), Karen entreats McElwee to cease shooting when the conversation gets too disturbing; when he refuses, she calls him "cruel."

But, clearly, *Sherman's March* means more to subvert patriarchal male identity than to enshrine it. If the real Sherman was near-heroic, his cinematic alter ego is mock-heroic. If McElwee's project is tainted with sadism, it is also saturated with masochism, as he makes a spectacle of his unreciprocated affections. (Somehow it seems appropriate that Joy jokes of singing "Mean to Me" in her lounge act.) While McElwee bounds through space, his itinerary is dictated by women (whom he follows unabashedly, like a heartsick puppy). Furthermore, his car (that icon of male action) constantly breaks down. Periodically he must "jump-start" his vehicle and his narrative by reminding himself that his original goal was to retrace Sherman's steps.

McElwee is also frequently depressed—an emotional state with cultural associations to women. He talks of "psychosexual despair," holes up in a motel watching *The Love Boat* (1977–87), has bouts of insomnia, and suffers nightmares of thermonuclear war. Significantly, it is mostly at these "hysterical" moments that he allows himself to appear onscreen—talking to the camera in a whispered, confessional mode, as though to wallow in his pain. (As Linda Williams has noted, many recent documentaries focus on "trauma" and relate it to "an inaccessible [historic] past" [12].) If Freud testily inquired, "What do women want?" McElwee pitifully whimpers, "What do women want of *me?*"

Finally, McElwee is acutely aware of his failure to fill the shoes of the classic male hero. Pat jokes of their childhood Superman games and implies that she prefers Christopher Reeve. Pat wants a man who is Tarzan to her Jane. And when she confesses her awe of certain male movie greats, McElwee muses, "I'm disconcerted to find myself in competition with the likes of Burt Reynolds and Stanley Kubrick." The former is, of course, a macho screen star (with a dinner theater in Florida) who is associated with such action film series as *Smokey and the Bandit* (1977, 1980, 1983)—car chase/road movies set in a Southern terrain. In truth, the Civil War locales of *Sherman's March* also link it to *Gone with the Wind* (1939), leading us to measure McElwee against no one less than Clark Gable or Rhett Butler. While the latter is a strong, virile character who brashly tells Scarlett O'Hara that he does not "give a damn," McElwee is an unassuming and entreating presence, whom Charleen declares "insufficient" to the heroic "quest." Even Sherman does not escape disparagement. When McElwee reads Sherman's diary entry on the war dead to Winnie, she asks, homophobically, if Sherman's bravura was an attempt to prove that "he wasn't a faggot."

If McElwee is weak, the women he encounters are incredibly strong. Winnie is a pioneer woman, milking cows, baking bread, keeping bees; Jackie is an ecology activist; Karen is an ardent women's rights proponent; Charleen just bosses him around. When McElwee's car fails in a Georgia hamlet and he spends the night in jail, he overhears a radio broadcast about four prisoners escaped from the Women's Correctional Institute. He fantasizes that he is held hostage by them.

It is no accident that, to describe McElwee's documentary stance, I choose the phrase "mock-heroic," a term that usually attaches to fictional works. For Hayden White has underscored the similarities between imaginary and factual narratives. As he notes, "history is a mixture of science and art" and the process of writing it "an essentially poetic act" (*Metahistory* x). If the fiction writer fabricates his tales, the historian "finds" them in reality. For White, "This conception of the historian's task, however, obscures the extent to which 'invention' also plays a part in the historian's operations" (*Metahistory* 6–7). As though to emphasize this point, McElwee films a ludicrous reenactment of a Civil War battle performed at some tourist site. One of the ways in which the historian imposes meaning is by choosing a mode of "emplotment"—"identifying the *kind of story* that has been told" (7). For White, the options reflect the paradigms established by Northrop Frye in *The Anatomy of Criticism:* tragedy, comedy, satire, or romance.

Once more, like the march of General Sherman, the path of McElwee's film crosses many formal borders. On the one hand, it promises to deliver a tale of romance—of two brave heroes' idealistic searches: Sherman's for military glory, McElwee's for amorous ecstasy. But both quests are marked by ruin. Sherman's political ambivalence leaves him "reviled" by the South and "rebuked" by the North. McElwee's psychic conflicts leave him rejected by some and rejecting of others. It is on the boundary of comedy and satire that *Sherman's March* truly hovers. Like the former, its focus is on the pairing of a heterosexual couple. But, unlike traditional comedy, the film ends without a marital resolution. (In truth, one could argue that McElwee's next work and companion piece, *Time Indefinite* [1993], fulfills that function by documenting his eventual wedding.)

But comedy is a utopian form that imagines a superior society emerging around the youthful couple. *Sherman's March* offers no such hope. McElwee's romantic optimism is continually tinged by social pessimism—a pose encapsulated in the image of him sleeping alone in a South Carolina tree house, bitten by bloodsucking cone-nosed insects, while Winnie sleeps nearby with someone else. But the tone of nihilism enters primarily through the film's historical and political agenda, so at odds with its private bourgeois melodrama. It comes not only in McElwee's visitation of the locales of Civil War carnage but in his encounter with present-day militarists. While following Claudia around the South, he meets a group of "survivalists" who are preparing for the Apocalypse by arming themselves in the woods. Unlike McElwee, these are "real" Southern men of the working class, who chew tobacco and tote guns. Later McElwee encounters a Mormon woman who stockpiles provisions in preparation for World War III. In voice-over meditations soliloquized to the camera (accompanied by vistas of the evening sky), a sleep-deprived McElwee returns to the theme of nuclear holocaust and to the childhood memories that plague his consciousness (a missile launch on television, a hydrogen bomb detonation during a Hawaiian vacation). The bomb shelter becomes a synecdoche for contemporary existence—simultaneously representing the retreat from society, the impossibility of human contact, the ravaged state of the self.

Likewise, the Civil War becomes a multivalent metaphor not only for McElwee's divided self but for American political discord. Clearly one conflict the film interrogates is the "battle of the sexes," but another is the continuing tension between North and South. As McElwee explains, *Sherman's March* is "a film about a region, [and] to some degree about a way of life" (interview with MacDonald 22). But the work's focus on regional antagonism also invokes the fissure of race, both in contemporary and historic contexts. This topic enters only peripherally in the film, as McElwee encounters black people who play "bit parts" in his autobiographical narrative: a car mechanic who knew his family, a domestic in the home of a friend, a blues musician who plays in Joy's band. At one point, the subject of slavery slips into the dialogue as a reactionary woman states that it should be a "right." But it is largely through the *absence* of a black woman on McElwee's list of potential lovers that the issue of race is registered—her very lack suggesting the taboo of miscegenation and its legacy in private life. (As Williams has noted, in many contemporary documentaries, "We . . . see the power of the past not simply by dramatizing it, or reenacting it . . . but . . . by finding its traces . . . in the present" [15].) A black woman does eventually enter McElwee's discourse but, as it were, through the "back door." When he hears that Burt Reynolds is in Charlotte, he tracks him down at a film shoot and encounters some female "groupies" waiting to get his autograph and embrace. After Reynolds kisses a black woman and her infant daughter, the former exuberantly recounts her experience and openly voices her passion. She talks of how she had to "take herself a kiss" from Reynolds, of how his kiss "knocked her baby out," of being ready to trample other women to reach the star. Her friend confesses that she, too, could not "control" herself. The black women's rapturous discourse is so much bolder than McElwee's that it makes his seem, retrospectively, repressed. It also flaunts the interdiction against interracial desire, making McElwee seem constrained.

Kobena Mercer has noted that "the real challenge in the new cultural politics of difference . . . is to make 'whiteness' visible for the first time." He feels that "the identity of the hegemonic white male subject is an enigma in contemporary cultural politics" (20). Almost unconsciously, McElwee engages that "mystery" in this lighthearted moment of the film. While at first glance the sequence seems "trivial," on second glance it is resonant. Such occasions are precisely those that Toni Morrison finds fascinating in mainstream literature. She is interested "in the way black people ignite critical moments of discovery or change or emphasis in literature not written by them" (viii). For Morrison, this is part of a broader project of investigating "the impact of racism on those who perpetuate it" (11). Significantly, we recall that the very signature of General Sherman bears its own mark of racial stress: his middle name, Tecumseh, ostensibly alludes to a Shawnee Indian who fought against the European settlers.

But it is in *Time Indefinite* that the issue of race plays a larger part. During a period of despondency following his father's death, McElwee returns to his North Carolina home. Though both of his parents are deceased, the black couple employed by his family for some thirty years is still there, putting the household in order. McElwee finds special comfort in reminiscing with Lucille about his childhood. The couple asks him to film their fiftieth wedding anniversary party and, in so doing, he reverses the pattern of Southern race relations, becoming part of *their* family instead of they becoming part of his. He also implicitly acknowledges their function as parent-surrogates, then and throughout his growing up.

Not only does *Sherman's March* cross the boundaries of comedy and satire, it confuses the borders between diverse nonfiction forms. It begins as a traditional documentary (of the "biopic" variety), then adopts a cinema verité mode. Beyond that, it draws on the ethic and aesthetic of the home movie, as well as the personal diary film. As McElwee has stated, "I try to create an almost literary voice-over" (interview with MacDonald 23).

Hayden White has noted how the historian (like the creative writer) selects a particular trope with which to chronicle events (*Metahistory* 29). For McElwee (who started his career as a writer), that tool is irony. When he finds himself attracted to Winnie (a language scholar), he confesses (with aural deadpan), "My interest in linguistics continues to grow." In an absurd scene worthy of Ionesco, he films Karen's lover hauling around a life-sized statue of a rhinoceros, for no apparent reason. When he films Pat exercising, he claims to have accidentally forgotten to record the sound. Watching her in silence emphasizes her suggestive, gyrating movements—making them look almost pornographic.

Clearly it is McElwee's wry tone that makes his amorous disasters palatable to us, that saves them from being maudlin. In fact one might argue (against the grain of my previous claims) that his irony serves to seduce the viewer (as it does the women), impressing us all with his rapier wit (as sharp as Sherman's sword), if not his animal magnetism. Ultimately it causes us to question our belief that we are confronting an authentically poignant Ross McElwee rather than a distanced, sardonic artist, whose presence is as crafted as that of Woody Allen. As McElwee confesses, "I'm creating a persona for the film that's based upon who I am, but it isn't exactly me" (interview with MacDonald 23).

If McElwee's version of history employs figurative language, it also foregrounds the question of desire in a manner normally associated with fictive discourse. McElwee's wants are omnipresent in the film—be they artistic, erotic, or romantic; be they fulfilled or (more characteristically) thwarted. What is not so apparent is how historical narratives (like fiction) themselves tap human desire. According to White, history "makes the real desirable" by "its imposition, upon events that are represented as real, of the formal coherency that stories possess" (*Content* 21). For White, this wish has "its origin in . . . daydreams, [and] reveries" (*Content* 24).

While revealing the desire inherent in the documentary project (through its displacement onto McElwee's ubiquitous aspirations), *Sherman's March* uncovers a repressed aspect of the historian's stance—a penchant for fiction. But as McElwee's romantic desires remain unfulfilled, so do ours for narrative resolution. While the film comes full circle geographically, with McElwee passing back through New York (another site of Sherman's travels), it overshoots its mark and ends with our hero in Boston, developing yet another crush on a new woman. Hence desire is, ultimately, obsessive in the film, and history (both personal and public) is doomed (as the maxim warns) to repeat itself. The only auspicious sign at the conclusion of *Sherman's March* is that McElwee plans to ask his new love out to a movie. Perhaps that is better than putting her *in* one.

White remarks that "Insofar as historical stories can be completed, can be given narrative closure," they become "an embarrassment" to the historian (*Content* 21). Perhaps this is the *only* embarrassment that McElwee spares himself and us in *Sherman's March*.

WORKS CITED

Ansen, David. "One Man's March through Georgia." *Newsweek* 108, no. 12 (September 22, 1986): 84.

Atwood, Margaret. *The Robber Bride*. New York: Bantam, 1995.

de Lauretis, Teresa. *Alice Doesn't: Feminism, Semiotics, Cinema*. Bloomington: Indiana University Press, 1984.

Frye, Northrop. *The Anatomy of Criticism: Four Essays*. Princeton: Princeton University Press, 1973.

Graham, Pat. Quoted on video jacket for *Sherman's March*, from *Chicago Reader's Circle*.

Graham, Peter. "Cinema Verité in France." *Film Quarterly* 17, no. 4 (1964): 30–36.

McElwee, Ross. "Southern Exposure: An Interview with Ross McElwee." Interview by Scott MacDonald. *Film Quarterly* 41, no. 4 (1988): 13–23.

———. "When the Personal Becomes Political: An Interview with Ross McElwee." Interview by Cynthia Lucia. *Cineaste* 20, no. 2 (1994): 32–37.

Mercer, Kobena. "Skin Head Sex Thing: Racial Difference and the Homoerotic Imagination." *New Formations* 24 (1992): 1–23.

Morrison, Toni. *Playing in the Dark: Whiteness and the Literary Imagination.* Cambridge, MA: Harvard University Press, 1990.

White, Hayden. *The Content of the Form: Narrative Discourse and Historical Representation.* Baltimore: Johns Hopkins University Press, 1987.

———. *Metahistory: The Historical Imagination in Nineteenth-Century Europe.* Baltimore: Johns Hopkins University Press, 1973.

Williams, Linda. "Mirrors without Memories: Truth, History, and the New Documentary." *Film Quarterly* 46, no. 3 (1993): 9–21. Reprinted in this volume as "Mirrors without Memories: Truth, History, and *The Thin Blue Line*" (chapter 23).

Winks, Robin W., ed. *The Historian as Detective.* New York: Harper and Row, 1969.

Chapter 22

SUBJECTIVITY LOST AND FOUND

Bill Viola's *I Do Not Know What It Is I Am Like*

Catherine Russell

> To take up the Vertovian terminology, he [the ethnologist] is "cine-ethnowatching," he "cine-ethno-observes," he "cine-ethno-thinks." Those who confront him modify themselves similarly, once they have placed their confidence in this strange habitual visitor. They "ethno-show" and "ethno-talk," and at best, they "ethno-think," or better yet, they have "ethno-rituals." . . . Knowledge is no longer a stolen secret, later to be consumed in the Western temples of knowledge.
>
> Jean Rouch, "Vicissitudes of the Self"

In his description of filming possession rituals, Jean Rouch reveals the ultimate goal of participatory ethnography: to transcend the divide between observer and observed. Through the possession ritual, culture is performed, and in the display empirical knowledge is seemingly displaced by a more spiritual understanding of the Other. Bill Viola articulates this desire in his videotape *I Do Not Know What It Is I Am Like* (1986), but he does not figure as a "participant" in the ethnographic encounter. He represents himself as another Other.

The medium of video enables Viola to come closer to transcending the divide than Rouch's cinema, but only by transforming culture into an effect of representation. The tape imagines a utopian breakdown between

observer and observed, technology and nature, and spectator and performer. Paradoxically, this desire is articulated through an elaborate demonstration of the impossibility of transcending the barriers between subjectivities. This failure in turn is linked to the terms of power within colonial
culture, terms that Viola has not yet transcended.

The title of Viola's tape, *I Do Not Know What It Is I Am Like,* halts the
quest for knowledge before it even begins, announcing a kind of failure of
knowledge and a quest for identity. Viola forces the question of subjectivity into the foreground of documentary representation through a gamut
of technological and aesthetic devices. The tape has become a canoni-
cal example of video art, drawing not only on the ethnographic genre of
documentary but equally on the structural experiments of the avant-garde
film. At ninety minutes, it also borrows the narrative time of feature filmmaking. It is structured as a movement from subterranean life-forms to
transcendental consciousness, a union of the cycle of life with ritual and
electronic transmission.

Video potentially brings to documentary an increased sense of intimacy, immediacy, and access, and thus a higher degree of participatory,
non-hierarchical observation (cf. Burnett). Certainly it makes the process of
documentation cheaper, faster, and potentially less intrusive, thus increasing its activist potential. Yet the "essence" of video is elusive, as its aesthetic
nature varies according to its many applications—from music videos to
medical technologies. Furthermore, it is important not to idealize the cam-
corder aesthetic as "more real" than other forms of documentation. Bill
Viola's high production values place his work at the high end of the eco-
nomic-aesthetic spectrum. His videos are anything but cheap or accessible,
and his work is rarely considered within a documentary frame of reference,
belonging much more obviously to the art gallery.

Nevertheless, the video signal in *I Do Not Know* is figured as having
a particular indexical quality, an access to the real that is specific to video,
which may be partially due to Viola's consistent use of ambient sync sound
that links audio and video signals in an existential fusion to place. The
tape addresses the physical presence of the experimental artist at the source
of the documentary gaze. The gaze is at once human—attached to a body
in the world—and dehumanized, becoming an appendage of technology.
Video may extend the operator's body into the world seen, but it is also the
instrument of surveillance. The transcendental gesture of the tape, the desire to overcome the division of representation, can be accomplished only
through a critique of the power relations of the gaze.

In significant ways, Viola is on the cusp of a new aesthetic and a
new cultural practice we might call postmodernist and postcolonialist,

respectively. But he is not quite there yet: his posthumanism is produced through a modernist interrogation of the specificity of his medium. Of all the definitions and explanations of video aesthetics, it is Hollis Frampton's that seems most appropriate to Viola's reflexivity:

> And as the feedback mandala confirms the covert circularity, the centripetal nature, of the video image, it offers also an obscure suggestion. If the spiral implies a copulative interaction between the image and the seeing mind, it also may become, when love is gone, a navel . . . the video field is continuous, incessantly growing and decaying before our eyes. Strictly speaking, there is no instant of time during which the video image may properly be said to "exist." (168)

Viola shares with Frampton and his contemporaries an ambition that Frampton describes as "nothing less than the mimesis, incarnation, bodying forth of the movement of consciousness itself" (164). With Viola, consciousness moves into the world and encounters other consciousnesses grounded in other bodies.

The tape has five segments, which Viola says correspond to "different consciousness[es] representing the world." Or more specifically, different models of "inner and outer consciousness, observer and observed" (interview with Nash 63). In an introductory passage the camera plunges into a lake and descends to underwater coral structures that drip in a dark silence and look almost like the inside of the human body. In the first section, "Il Corpo Scuro" (The Dark Body), buffalo graze slowly, lazily, peeing and dying in a perfect pastoral landscape. In "The Language of the Birds," birds and fish are observed in close-ups that allow us to study their remarkable features. As with the buffalo, Viola privileges the eyes as the windows on impenetrable souls. In "The Night of Sense," Viola himself works in his study (or a studio representation thereof). A German shepherd attacks the camera to initiate the short fourth section, "Stunned by the Drum," a rapidly edited sequence of flash-frame imagery. "The Living Flame," the fifth and last section, consists of fragments of a firewalking ritual performed in Fiji and to some extent constitutes the narrative climax of the tape, suddenly turning to ethnographic imagery in pursuit of what? Self-knowledge? It is this sequence that most graphically pushes Viola out of the art gallery and into the contested sphere of identity politics. Answering the opening imagery, the tape concludes with the camera rising out of the lake, "flying" over a mountain landscape, and descending into the woods to finally settle on the slow sight of decomposition until the grain of the video image itself dissolves to darkness.[1]

As representations of consciousness, the different parts of the tape involve looking at various things, species, and people with an intensity that can only be described as "staring." J. Hoberman describes it as a series of "zoological observations" (71). Throughout most of the tape, Viola employs a static camera and very long takes that draw attention to their occasional movements and zooms, techniques of getting a better look. In Fiji, however, the camera is in medias res, picking out and following individual participants in the ritual, pulling back for longer shots and cutting into close-ups with fairly invisible editing. In contrast to much of the tape, the Fijian section has a strong documentary feel to it. The images of animals, birds, and fish are studied images, aestheticized within the conventions of landscape and portraiture. Despite the shift in style in Fiji, Viola and the viewer of the tape are, of course, still staring.

SENSE AND NON-SENSE

Sean Cubitt has argued that *I Do Not Know* exemplifies what he calls "the final stage of colonialism," that of withdrawal (68). He points out that "Viola's eye is still that of the ethnographer. Yet much of the work involves a self-scrutiny, under the eye of the bird, which is specifically in the realm of the visible" (73). The most explicit self-scrutiny takes place in the "Night of Sense" segment, which is highly ironic and self-deprecating. In his sterile environment, Viola performs the discourse of reason in all its scientific, colonial, and religious forms. It is a discourse with which Viola clearly identifies, by virtue of his education and ethnicity, but struggles against. Viola's study contains a model pirate ship and a book opened to a page on which a male figure crouching over a fire is labeled "stimulus and response."

On Viola's desk in "The Night of Sense" is a small monitor in which images of birds from the preceding section are juxtaposed with imagery from the forthcoming Fijian section. Viola works on this material, which is rendered exotic and small in his study. At the same time, the body of the artist becomes in its turn material, mortal, and strange. He eats a fish and drinks wine in a ritualistic meal that is so closely miked that the sounds of chewing, swallowing, and the clinking of expensive cutlery are excessively amplified. The Christian myth of transubstantiation may be literalized, but the sequence also has a distinct sense of magic as the wealth and power of privilege are transformed into material processes.

I Do Not Know What It Is I Am Like: In his study Viola performs the discourse of reason.

This section is also the point in the tape where a surrealist discourse is most overt. Tricks with perception, the entry of an elephant, the passing of a cat, the movement of a snail from a golden shell, and the hatching of a chick transform the artist's study into a dreamscape where the familiar is made strange and the strange made familiar. If the surrealists brought to ethnography a sense of the Other as transforming, here Viola embraces that transformation as an effect of the video medium. The electronic circuitry of video is endowed with the mystical power of reincarnation in the redemption of the alienated postmodern subject.

"The Night of Sense" ends abruptly with the dog's attack on the camera. The passive quietude that has thus far pervaded the tape erupts in a violent stroboscopic assault on the spectator. Fragmentary images juxtapose landscape, lightning, rituals, fire, domestic activities, accidents, live animals, dead animals, and other "found" images. One of the more protracted series of shots, interrupted by a constantly darkening screen, is a photo shoot of a zebra. The domestication of the exotic becomes a discourse on the violence of photography and the cruelty of representation, and a descent into "the frenzy of the visible."[2] The brevity of the shots, the stroboscopic flashes, and the pulsing audio-video signal send the imagery back onto the retina of the viewer, as dream-images or fragments of a consciousness riddled with reason.

The strobe rhythm transforms the montage into an effect of the medium, as if the imagery belonged to a memory of the television monitor itself. The electronic impulse registered on the sound track's pulsating beat eventually fuses with the drums of the firewalking ritual. Medium specificity, in this tape, refers to the sound track as the indice of presence located in the electronic medium itself. Even in the crucial passages of silence—the shots of the birds and fish, for example—the sound track constitutes the tape's most intimate form of address. In the "Stunned by the Drum" sequence the regime of the visible becomes a nightmare of aggressive technology, while the sound track pulses electronically, almost like a dance-club beat. Gradually fused into the drumming of the Hindu ritual, its rigor is transformed into the seductive beat of the trance.

In the following sequence set in Fiji, the camera lingers on the faces of men punctured by skewers. The radical juxtaposition of imagery and the discourse of the grotesque point to Viola's fundamental debt to surrealism. James Clifford valorizes ethnographic surrealism for its utopian possibilities (119), noting that before ethnography became fixed as a human science, and before surrealism became fossilized as an aesthetic, both ethnography and surrealism were "cultural dispositions" or "attitudes" toward reality in which otherness served to unfix and destabilize the familiar: "The surrealist moment in ethnography is that moment in which the possibility of comparison exists in unmediated tension with sheer incongruity. . . . Ethnography cut with surrealism emerges as the theory and practice of juxtaposition. It studies, and is part of the invention and interruption of meaningful wholes in works of cultural import-export" (Clifford 146–47).

Viola's return to this moment goes against the grain of contemporary cultural politics. The "I" of the title is the artist and not the "social actor" in Fiji. The non-identity of the "I" given twice in the title may position the other as a kind of mirror, but the question posed by the title is not "Who am I?" but "What am I?" in an apparent denial of subjectivity. We, in turn, need to ask, "What is that I?" The gaze in this tape is not an abstract representation of consciousness but refers specifically to Viola's consciousness, the artist's gaze, with which the spectator may or may not identify. In this sense the real cruelty of the tape is not the masochism of the exotic ritual but the rapid-fire assault of the imagery in the "Stunned by the Drum" section of the tape. The regime of the visible is torn asunder, making any psychological or political relation to the imagery very difficult. It is made doubly "Other" in its relation to his, Viola's, identity, not mine or yours. The category of "Man" is reduced in this tape to the identity of one (white North American) man, who is the artist with the machine.

POSSESSION

The firewalking sequence emerges from the flashing lights and images in a series of unfocused dissolves, anticipated by its sound track of drumming. One interviewer asked Viola whether this imagery was the "resolution," answering the "problem of the tape," to which Viola responded that "The firewalkers become the resolution in the sense that they represent the power of the mind and the will, but they represent it through action. You can think you can walk on fire and eat fire. You can read 20 different books about it and become an expert about people who do it, but doing it is another story" (interview with Nash 63). The action is of course performed by others, and Viola's comments imply that the division of representation is still in place. The ability to walk on fire, eat fire, and sustain flagellation and skin piercing are feats available only as images, not as experience. Viola tests the limits of the visible by filming people who are not only other than and other to the filmmaker but whose consciousness transcends the discourse of reason that gives rise to the desire to know.

The firewalkers never return the gaze of the camera. They are completely involved with their own activity; their attention is turned entirely inward, not only to themselves as individuals but to each other as a community. If we can agree that Viola's depiction of "consciousness" is also a discourse of power, a contest over the gaze, the men in Fiji resist the inquisition with a refusal to be known. The public context of the ritual further deflects the penetration of secrecy, as they literally perform their interiority. Insofar as the ceremony is observed by tourists on bleachers and the performers are clearly neither "primitives" nor "natives," the "authenticity" of the ritual is not implied by the usual ethnographic stereotypes. The firewalkers have urban haircuts, pot bellies, and familiar Western clothing mixed with their saffron-colored robes.

Viola offers no indication in the tape of the geographical, cultural, or ethnic setting of the performance.[3] Demystification of the ritual may contravene Viola's intention, but it is instructive to compare his version of this ritual with that of the anthropologist. Carolyn Henning Brown has offered some intriguing insights into this ceremony. She argues that this particular *puja*, performed by Hindu descendants of the Southern Indian indentured laborers brought to Fiji by the British in the 1870s, is a demonstration of a disenfranchised ethnic minority. Although few British remain in Fiji, people of Indian descent now comprise about 50 percent of the Fijian population but are marginalized economically and culturally by the indigenous nationals. Firewalking is a major tourist attraction and, since the 1930s, has become an important means of preserving South Indian identity.[4]

Firewalking originally enabled the South Indian community to distinguish themselves from Northern Indians in Fiji, although it has begun to function as a demonstration of Indian cultural autonomy with which both Southern and Northern Indians can identify (Brown 241). Within the diasporic Fijian context, where Indians are economically marginalized, firewalking is a display of spiritual empowerment. The devotees are not Brahmin or religious professionals but working men who want to commune with the goddess in gratitude for some gift of providence or simply in order to accumulate good karma (Mayer 93). They spend ten days in the temple before the ceremony begins, purifying themselves through abstinence and meditation. Firewalking is only the climax of a complex series of ordeals that the men undergo in one afternoon, including the flagellation and skin piercing that are depicted in Viola's tape. The resistance to fire and pain, the supernatural ability to withstand heat, is proof of the participants' faith and proof of the goddess Maariama's presence in their bodies.

I Do Not Know What It Is I Am Like: The Fijian firewalkers resist the inquisition with a refusal to be known.

The anthropological discourse actually confirms that this is a ritual of cultural power and resistance. It attracts not only tourists but large numbers of local Indian and Fijian residents, most of whom watch the ceremony from outside the temple compound, behind a chain-link fence on the surrounding hills (Brown 223–25). (Both ranks of spectators can be seen in the background of some of Viola's footage.) Brown argues that the tourists validate the firewalking ritual by representing the gaze of the world outside the islands. They are "simply used by their hosts in the only game that matters, the game of interethnic competition" (243). It may be that Viola is "being used" in the same way, except that he quite radically decontextualizes the interethnic contest. The new framework for the firewalking strips the participants of their historical identities and isolates the spiritual essence of the ritual within a strictly audio-visual economy. We do not know what the anthropologist knows.

The authenticity of the ritual is never doubted by Brown, although she does suggest, rather obliquely, that the coals might not be as hot as one might think (240). If "the idea of danger must be protected" by the community, as Brown suggests (240), Viola eliminates any sense of danger from his depiction. The facial expressions and body movements of the participants convey only intense concentration. Although the mediated version has even more potential for duplicity, we cannot doubt our perception because we don't know what to doubt. With no terms of reference, the behavior is mystified rather than psychologized, perhaps even more so than in the circus-type arena in which it was originally performed.

Throughout the tape the frame signifies the gaze, but in Fiji the frame disappears and the viewer not only has no explanation for the ritual but has no point of view either. The sequence moves from the dark temple interior to the oceanside procession outside the temple grounds to the fire-pit without warning. This refusal to contain, to orient or offer a point of view, together with the retardation of sound and image make the imagery very dreamlike. The camera is very much in medias res, yet the viewer has no idea what is going on. Technology effectively becomes a representation of the limits of knowledge and vision, limits beyond which an excess of the profilmic can be apprehended without being known. In Fiji we can see only the outward appearances of men who are "possessed," whose subjective experience is unknowable and perhaps even unimaginable.

The possession ritual is an important point of contact between artistic praxis and anthropology, which is perhaps why it is a plum of ethnographic cinema.[5] Filming a possession ritual dramatizes the ethnographic relationship because it is a performance in which a great deal is still hidden. The entranced dancers are oblivious to those around them, while the real drama is radically invisible, taking place in their minds. The possession ritual naturalizes the performer-spectator apparatus because it is an exhibition, but it also registers its limits.

Bill Nichols suggests that the trance, with its hypnotic drumming and fascinating spectacle, poses a real threat to ethnographic objectivity and scientism (221). But pushed to its extreme by Rouch in *Les maîtres fous* (1954) and *Tourou et Bitti* (1971) and by Viola in *I Do Not Know,* this detachment is not really ever jeopardized. It remains guaranteed by the cinematic apparatus, which limits participation to phenomenological observation. The Fijian ritual, in its touristic context, is a good example of how the outsider's gaze in fact authenticates the possession of the dancer.

In trying to penetrate the enforced detachment, the other culture in *I Do Not Know* becomes, in a sense, a fantasy, a blend of illusion and reality enhanced by Viola's slow motion. In a video trance, the cultural landscape is superseded by a purely audio-visual landscape, and it is the video medium that becomes possessed by the bodies of the dancers. It is at this point that Viola makes the most significant break with traditional anthropology, ethnography, and Rouch's participatory cinema. Under the auspices of the human sciences, these practices assume an ontological bond between cultures which it is their ambition to resurrect. Differences between observed and observing cultures form the ideological support for a discourse of humanism, a colonial construct that works to deny the threat of cultural difference. The Fijian Hindus, however, performing for huge crowds, appear oblivious to any reality beyond the most spiritual and subvert any premise of humanism. Moreover, it is precisely when Viola's camera is turned onto the human "Other" that it becomes both inquisitive and invisible, inscribing a certain voyeurism and desire for knowledge and vision that are only frustrated by the inaccessibility of the subjectivity of the Other.

Viola's recourse to ethnography is instructive because of the film's lack of ethnological detail. The visual economy is reduced to its purist voyeuristic structure within the context of a crisis of bourgeois subjectivity. For Viola, violence is implicit in the technologized gaze, but its redemptive power rests in the splitting of subjectivities for which he uses the metaphor of lightning ("Selected" 23). The conjunction of video and ritual performance in *I Do Not Know* produces a discourse on history that is the inverse of nostalgia. The ethnographic other, represented as a subjective presence in a visual economy, does not belong to a lost past but enters into a utopian desire for a discourse of intercultural knowledge. Unlike the ethnographic pattern of the salvage paradigm, in which the Other represents a premodern ideal of authentic humanity (Clifford 228), this tape discovers the Other fully immersed in modernity and the society of the spectacle. By bringing his high-tech electronic apparatus, the state of the art in imaging technology, into the ethnographic dynamic, the power relation is necessarily tipped toward the observer. In Fiji Viola finally encounters a power equal to his own.

Zoos

Viola's fusion of technology and spirituality veers toward another form of humanism that can only be described as a "New Age" aesthetic of holistic spirituality that transcends cultural differences. The representation of nature and the theme of decay, death, and rebirth further suggest an existential conception of "mankind" bound up, through contemplation and beauty, in a grand aesthetic gesture. In comparison to the surrealists, Viola does not challenge the category of art but remakes it in a new technology. It is significant that this is accomplished by way of a detour through documentary, because where Viola's work departs from all forms of humanism is through its commentary on the gaze, interrogating not only human subjectivity but also the question of the consciousness of other species.

The limits of vision are most strongly implied in the footage shot in the San Diego Zoo, in which the video frame replaces the cage. Although the signs of "the zoo" are absent, the effect of containment and restriction is reduced to an effect of vision and the technological apparatus of the gaze. "The Language of the Birds" is that of cultural marginalization. The electronically reproduced silence echoes the profound failure of communication that is intimately bound to the exotic character of endangered species. John Berger has argued that "The animal has secrets which, unlike the secrets of caves, mountains, seas, are specifically addressed to man" (3).

Most striking about the birds and fish in *I Do Not Know* is the failure of the animals to return the gaze. They look without seeing. Berger has pointed out that "Nowhere in a zoo can a stranger encounter the look of an animal. At most, the animal's gaze flickers and passes on. They look sideways. They look blindly beyond. They scan mechanically. They have been immunized to encounter, because nothing can any more occupy a *central* place in their attention" (26). Viola may catch his own reflection in the eye of the owl, but it is true that nothing and no one looks back at him with any interest. A buffalo may catch sight of the camera but pisses lazily while looking. This disinterested decenteredness extends to the firewalkers, who reflect the gaze without seeing, without knowing. When Viola offers himself up to the viewer's gaze in his study, as another animal in a zoo, his body seems to be in excess, a supplement or appendage to the workings of consciousness. The self-consciousness of his performance is precisely what is transcended in the spectacle of the trance and in the subjectivity of animals.

Berger's point is that zoos constitute the living monument to the disappearance of animals from daily life. The alienation of humans from nature is fetishized in the animal imagery that plays such a large role in visual culture. He claims that anthropology begins with the question of the similarities and differences between men and animals (4), although he questions neither the category of "man" nor the historical consequences of such an anthropology. Certainly there are numerous disturbing parallels between zoology and ethnography that point doubly at the colonial subject in whose perspective (and in the institutions governed by that perspective) the trajectory from nature to culture is traced. The historical alignment of zoology and ethnography incorporates the multiple praxes of collecting and exhibiting. Viola's invocation of these techniques attempts to transform them into effects of representation by which otherness might be redeemed as subjectivity.

Viola wants to circumvent those institutions of the gaze and pose the question of the alienation of humans from nature anew. If the cinema has been a crucial instrument in the institutionalization of the colonial gaze, video offers an opportunity to rearticulate that look and frame the Other differently. In this videotape the otherness of animals, along with the otherness of a mystical, spiritual consciousness, serves to place the identity of the viewer in question. "Man" is effectively reduced to the clumsy individual in the red sweater (Viola). If Viola is the last modernist, he is also the last man to claim to be "Man," and lurking within the tape's anxiety of identity is a waning of that capital "M," a withdrawal of its sovereignty.

THE ALLEGORICAL LANDSCAPE

Viola's technologized gaze enables him to rejoin the natural world in the form of electricity, after the fall from humanism. In the transcendent finale of *I Do Not Know,* video itself becomes magically superhuman and supernatural, flying through the sky (on a crane) over the spectacular scenery of western Canada. A fish is mounted across the bottom of the frame, creating a two-tiered perspective of close-up and long shot. The camera then drops down through the pines to the forest floor where, in a series of dissolves, the fish disintegrates. Visited by birds and animals, the decaying fish acts as a kind of bait, or visual trap. When it finally disappears, the frame of the image becomes redundant and the forest becomes an empty stage. The

I Do Not Know What It Is I Am Like: The fish superimposed on the spectacular scenery of northwest Canada.

music from the previous Fijian segment continues over the magnificent 360-degree pans but fades out when the fish comes down to earth. The sound of flies buzzing while the fish decays takes over the sound track, eventually fading out to silence.

In this coda Viola deploys the most extravagant special effects for an allegorical representation that stands in stark contrast to the embodied depiction of transcendence in Fiji. If the landscape is distinctly North American, the production values are coded as expensive. The contrast between the ritual drumming and chanting and the cold North American wilderness is a means of articulating difference within the transcendental gesture. Likewise, the delimitation of the frame through the placement of the fish qualifies the triumphant sweep of the landscape as the sign of such a camera movement, an allegory of transcendence.

This coda, like "The Language of the Birds" segment of the tape, might be seen in terms of Viola's debt to "structural film," the experimental film form labeled as such by P. Adams Sitney in 1969. Like the work of Michael Snow, Hollis Frampton, Ernie Gehr, and David Rimmer, Viola foregrounds the materiality of the medium and deploys the frame as a metaphor for consciousness. If "content" in Sitney's version of structural film "is minimal and subsidiary to the outline [form]" (Sitney 370), Viola privileges the pro-filmic equally with the act of perception. The structure of the gaze is rendered as a relation of power that was invisible in the earlier films. Within Viola's postcolonial milieu, the apparatus of vision is no longer innocent, and it is this knowledge with which the tape struggles to come to terms.

The video signal, furthermore, extends the metaphor of consciousness onto a more material plane, which may account for its documentary impulse. Viola's camera renders the means of perception, the form of vision, as a natural process that mimics the natural flow of nature in order to allegorically circumvent representation. Lightning, the spectacle of natural electricity, is seen with the buffalo and also within the rapid-fire montage of the fourth section. Along with the audible sound of flies on a buffalo carcass, and later on the decaying fish, the nature of electricity refers back to the technology of representation and the perceiving "self" who desires to find himself in the sight of landscape.

Viola's transcendental gesture of contemplation is more Zenlike than Bazinian, completely immersed as it is in the transience of life. If Bazin envisioned the cinema as a means of overcoming mortality,[6] Viola envisions video as a means of overcoming immortality. He embraces mortality, violence, and decay as the means of transcending the existential divide between consciousness and nature. In the Fijian ritual, Viola finds the Bazinian desire to transcend the material world actually realized in the pro-filmic. The power of reincarnation is the power of nature, and while this cyclical power cannot be represented as an image, it is implied in the very process of representation: in the video apparatus itself as a form of energy.

THE LESSON

The epic structure of the tape implies that something has been learned, that the threat of technology has been overcome and, in the process, so has the desire for what Bazin refers to as "total cinema." In *I Do Not Know* Viola brings the discourses of video technology and tourism to bear on a cultural ritual without, however, jeopardizing the surreal depiction of an unconscious reality. Viola identifies himself as an artist, invoking an aesthetic discourse that enables him to transcend the scientism of ethnographic representation to which Rouch and the verité documentarians remain committed.

Surrealist ethnography (as represented, for example, in the journal *Documents* of 1929–30) challenged aesthetic conventions by bringing cultural phenomena, non-art artifacts, imagery, and objects, into the avant-garde domain. Viola likewise deposits imagery of grotesque cultural practices within this tape, which in many ways has epitomized an aesthetic ideal of "video art." Fully cognizant of the ideological dangers of Orientalism and exoticism, Viola goes to Fiji anyway and takes the people's images for his own art under the banner of his own anxiety. He does so precisely because his subjectivity is hopelessly bourgeois, Western, and technologized. The psychic realm of the Hindu *puja*, steeped in a mythology of purification, becomes a language of subjectivity that remains outside his art, at the limits of artistic practice.

And this is where the artist "finds himself," fused with technology, identified with representation. In the "withdrawal" from colonialism, new forms of subjectivity need to be recognized and reconfigured within institutions of representation such as the art gallery and the documentary film. Viola's conceit of placing his own identity in question is in fact a narrative strategy of neutralizing technology. The power of nature is not only mystified, but in the spectacle of landscape, the eyes of animals and the spirituality of Fijian Hindus, that power becomes an empowerment of the Other in representation.

The address to the viewer, oscillating between contemplation and repulsion, is precisely the means of articulating subjectivity as unfixed but desired. By registering this desire within a utopian framework of transcendence, Viola significantly overcomes the anthropological idealization of loss. Neither category of authenticity nor primitivism enters into the equation when the other is encountered as an effect of representation. Straddling the break between the modern and the postmodern, the colonial and the postcolonial, Viola demonstrates that there are lessons yet to be learned from the avant-garde. Experimenting with documentary conventions in a medium that may not be new, *I Do Not Know* nevertheless renews the debate about subjectivity as the link between art and documentary representation.

Notes

1. The five segments of the tape are only named in the end credits and are not actually as distinct as this description might imply. It is not at all obvious, because of the transitional material and diversity of imagery within sections, where Viola's five subtitles might fall. Unlike the first three sections, which are clearly demarcated by fade-outs, the Fijian section is dissolved at both its beginning and its end. The prologue and epilogue, both set in the Canadian Rockies, are not named in Viola's five-segment postscriptural outline.

2. "The frenzy of the visible" is a term introduced by Linda Williams to refer to the pleasure invested in technologies of the visible. She uses it in the subtitle of

her book on pornography, *Hard Core: Power, Pleasure, and the "Frenzy of the Visible"* (Berkeley: University of California Press, 1989), but it is equally applicable to other audio-visual imbrications of power and pleasure, including ethnography and compilation films.

3. In the end credits the Mahi Devi temple in Suva, Fiji, and the name of the chief priest are mentioned.

4. The money collected from tourists goes to the maintenance of the temple, and although it does not seem to be a major commercial venture in itself, it does make a significant contribution to the tourist economy of the islands (Brown 224).

5. Bill Nichols points out that the ethnographer usually explains away the magic of possession rituals with authoritative voice-over narration (224). This is certainly true of Margaret Mead and Gregory Bateson's *Trance and Dance in Bali* (1952), Rouch's *Tourou et Bitti,* and Maya Deren's *Divine Horsemen* (1985), as it was edited after her death.

6. One of the central tenets of André Bazin's film aesthetics is the potential of cinema to "preserve life by the representation of life." "The creation of an ideal world in the likeness of the real" is the guiding aim of all developments in film aesthetics and technology (Bazin 9–22). "The myth of total cinema" is, I would argue, the human desire for immortality. See my *Narrative Mortality: Death, Closure, and New Wave Cinemas* (Minneapolis: University of Minnesota Press, 1995), 75–77, as well as Philip Rosen, "History of Image, Image of History: Subject and Ontology in Bazin," *Wide Angle* 9, no. 4 (1987): 7–34.

Works Cited

Bazin, André. *What Is Cinema?* Vol. 1, trans. Hugh Gray. Berkeley: University of California Press, 1967.

Berger, John. "Why Look at Animals?" In *About Looking,* 1–26. New York: Pantheon Books, 1980.

Brown, Carolyn Henning. "Tourism and Ethnic Competition in a Ritual Form." *Oceania* 54, no. 3 (1984): 223–44.

Burnett, Ron. "Video Space/Video Time: The Electronic Image and Portable Video." In *Mirror Machine: Video and Identity,* ed. Janine Marchessault, 142–83. Toronto: YYZ Books, 1995.

Clifford, James. *The Predicament of Culture: Twentieth-Century Ethnography, Literature, and Art.* Cambridge, MA: Harvard University Press, 1988.

Cubitt, Sean. "Video Art and Colonialism: An Other and Its Others." *Screen* 30, no. 3 (1989): 66–79.

Frampton, Hollis. "The Withering Away of the State of the Art." In *Circles of Confusion: Film, Photography, Video Texts, 1968–1980,* 161–70. Rochester, NY: Visual Studies Workshop, 1983.

Hoberman, J. "The Reflecting Pool: Bill Viola and the Visionary Company." In *Bill Viola*, ed. Barbara London, 63–72. New York: Museum of Modern Art, 1987.

Mayer, Adrian C. *Peasants in the Pacific: A Study of Fiji Indian Ritual Society.* London: Routledge and Kegan Paul, 1961.

Nichols, Bill. *Representing Reality: Issues and Concepts in Documentary.* Bloomington: Indiana University Press, 1991.

Sitney, P. Adams. *Visionary Film: The American Avant-garde, 1943–1978.* New York: Oxford University Press, 1979.

Viola, Bill. "Bill Viola's Re-visions of Mortality." Interview by Michael Nash. *High Performance* 37 (1987): 60–65.

———. "Selected Works and Writings." In *Bill Viola*, ed. Barbara London, 23–62. New York: Museum of Modern Art, 1987.

Chapter 23

MIRRORS WITHOUT MEMORIES

Truth, History, and *The Thin Blue Line*

Linda Williams

The August 12, 1990, Arts and Leisure section of the *New York Times* carried a lead article with a rather arresting photograph of Franklin Roosevelt flanked by Winston Churchill and Groucho Marx. Standing behind them was a taut-faced Sylvester Stallone in his Rambo garb. The photo illustrated the major point of the accompanying article by Andy Grundberg: that the photograph—and by implication the moving picture as well—is no longer, as Oliver Wendell Holmes once put it, a "mirror with a memory" illustrating the visual truth of objects, persons, and events but a manipulated construction. In an era of electronic and computer-generated images, the camera, the article sensationally proclaims, "can lie."

In this photo, the anachronistic flattening out of historical referents, the trivialization of history itself, with the popular culture icons of Groucho and Rambo rubbing up against Roosevelt and Churchill, serves almost as a caricature of the state of representation some critics have chosen to call postmodern. In a key statement, Fredric Jameson has described the "cultural logic of postmodernism" as a "new depthlessness, which finds its prolongation both in contemporary 'theory' and in a whole new culture of the image or the simulacrum" ("Postmodernism" 58). To Jameson, the effect of this image culture is a weakening of historicity. Lamenting the loss of the grand narratives of modernity, which he believes once made possible the political actions of individuals representing the interests of social classes, Jameson argues that it no longer seems possible to represent the "real" interests of a people or a class against the ultimate ground of social and economic determinations.

While not all theorists of postmodernity are as disturbed as Jameson by the apparent loss of the referent, by the undecidabilities of representation accompanied by an apparent paralysis of the will to change, many theorists do share a sense that the Enlightenment projects of truth and reason are definitively over. And if representations, whether visual or verbal, no longer refer to a truth or referent "out there," as Trinh T. Minh-ha has put it, for us "in here" (83), then we seem to be plunged into a permanent state of the self-reflexive crisis of representation. What was once a "mirror with a memory" can now only reflect another mirror.

Perhaps because so much faith was once placed in the ability of the camera to reflect objective truths of some fundamental social referent— often construed by the socially relevant documentary film as records of injustice or exploitation of powerless common people—the loss of faith in the objectivity of the image seems to point, nihilistically, like the impossible memory of the meeting of the fictional Rambo and the real Roosevelt, to the brute and cynical disregard of ultimate truths. Yet at the very same time, as any television viewer and moviegoer knows, we also exist in an era in which there is a remarkable hunger for documentary images of the real. These images proliferate in the verité of on-the-scene cops programs in which the camera eye merges with the eye of the law to observe the violence citizens do to one another. Violence becomes the very emblem of the real in these programs. Interestingly, violent trauma has become the emblem of the real in the new verité genre of the independent amateur video, which, in the case of George Holliday's tape of the Rodney King beating by L.A. police, functioned to contradict the eye of the law and to intervene in the "cops'" official version of King's arrest. This home video might be taken to represent the other side of the postmodern distrust of the image: here the camera tells the truth in a remarkable moment of cinema verité that then becomes valuable (though not conclusive) evidence in accusations against the L.A. police department's discriminatory violence against minority offenders.

The contradictions are rich: on the one hand the postmodern deluge of images seems to suggest that there can be no a priori truth of the referent to which the image refers; on the other hand, in this same deluge, it is still the moving image that has the power to move audiences to a new appreciation of previously unknown truth.

In a recent book on postwar West German cinema and its representations of that country's past, Anton Kaes has written that "the sheer mass of historical images transmitted by today's media weakens the link between public memory and personal experience. The past is in danger of becoming a rapidly expanding collection of images, easily retrievable but isolated by time and space, available in an eternal present by pushing a button on the remote control. History thus returns forever—as film" (198). Recently the example of history that has been most insistently returning "as film" to American viewers is the assassination of John F. Kennedy as simulated by filmmaker Oliver Stone.

Stone's *JFK* (1991) might seem a good example of Jameson's and Kaes's worst-case scenarios of the ultimate loss of historical truth amid the postmodern hall of mirrors. While laudably obsessed with exposing the manifest contradictions of the Warren Commission's official version of the Kennedy assassination, Stone's film has been severely criticized for constructing a "countermyth" to the Warren Commission's explanation of what happened. Indeed, Stone's images offer a kind of tragic counterpart to the comic mélange of the *New York Times* photo of Groucho and Roosevelt. Integrating his own reconstruction of the assassination with the famous Zapruder film, whose "objective" reflection of the event is offered as the narrative (if not the legal) clincher in Jim Garrison's argument against the lone assassin theory, Stone mixes Zapruder's real verité with his own simulated verité to construct a grandiose paranoid countermyth of a vast conspiracy by Lyndon Johnson, the CIA, and the Joint Chiefs of Staff to carry out a coup d'état. With little hard evidence to back him up, Stone would seem to be a perfect symptom of a postmodern negativity and nihilism toward truth, as if to say: "We know the Warren Commission made up a story; well, here's another even more dramatic and entertaining story. Since we can't know the truth, let's make up a grand paranoid fiction."

It is not my purpose here to attack Oliver Stone's remarkably effective deployment of paranoia and megalomania; the press has already done a thorough job of debunking his unlikely fiction of a Kennedy who was about to end the Cold War and withdraw from Vietnam.[1] What interests me, however, is the positive side of this megalomania: Stone's belief that it is possible to intervene in the process by which truth is constructed; his very real accomplishment in shaking up public perception of an official truth that closed down, rather than opened up, investigation; his acute awareness of how images enter into the production of knowledge. However much Stone may finally betray the spirit of his own investigation into the multiple, contingent, and constructed nature of the representation of history by asking us to believe in too tidy a conspiracy, his *JFK* needs to be taken seriously for its renewal of interest in one of the major traumas of our country's past.

So rather than berate Stone, I would like to contrast this multimillion-dollar historical fiction film borrowing many aspects of the form of documentary to what we might call the low-budget postmodern documentary borrowing many features of the fiction film. My goal in what follows is to get beyond the much-remarked self-reflexivity and flamboyant auteurism of these documentaries, which might seem, *Rashomon*-like, to abandon the pursuit of truth, to what seems to me their remarkable engagement with a newer, more contingent, relative, postmodern truth—a truth which, far from being abandoned, still operates powerfully as the receding horizon of the documentary tradition.

When we survey the field of recent documentary films two things stand out: first, their unprecedented popularity among general audiences, who now line up for documentaries as eagerly as for fiction films; second, their willingness to tackle often grim, historically complex subjects. Errol Morris's *The Thin Blue Line* (1987), about the murder of a police officer and the near execution of the "wrong man," Michael Moore's *Roger & Me* (1989), about the dire effects of a General Motors plant closing, and Ken Burns's eleven-hour *The Civil War* (1990) (watched on PBS by thirty-nine million Americans) were especially popular documentaries about uncommonly serious political and social realities. Even more difficult and challenging, though not quite as popular, were *Our Hitler* (Hans-Jürgen Syberberg, 1980), *Shoah* (Claude Lanzmann, 1985), *Hotel Terminus: The Life and Times of Klaus Barbie* (Marcel Ophuls, 1987), and *Who Killed Vincent Chin?* (Chris Choy and Renee Tajima, 1988). And in 1991 the list of both critically successful and popular documentary features *not* nominated for Academy Awards—*Paris Is Burning* (Jennie Livingston), *Hearts of Darkness: A Filmmaker's Apocalypse* (Fax Bahr and George Hickenlooper), *35 Up* (Michael Apted), *Truth or Dare* (Alex Keshishian)—was viewed by many as an embarrassment to the Academy. *Village Voice* critic Amy Taubin notes that 1991 was a year in which four or five documentaries made it onto the *Variety* charts; documentaries seemed to matter in a new way (Taubin 62).

Though diverse, all the above works participate in a new hunger for reality on the part of a public seemingly saturated with Hollywood fiction. Jennie Livingston, director of *Paris Is Burning,* the remarkably popular documentary about gay drag subcultures in New York, notes that the out-of-touch documentaries honored by the Academy all share an old-fashioned earnestness toward their subjects while the new, more popular documentaries share a more ironic stance toward theirs (Taubin).[2] Coincident with the hunger for documentary truth is the clear sense that this truth is subject to manipulation and construction by docu-auteurs who, whether on camera (Lanzmann in *Shoah*, Michael Moore in *Roger & Me*) or behind, are forcefully calling the shots.

It is this paradox of the intrusive manipulation of documentary truth, combined with a serious quest to reveal some ultimate truths, that I would like to isolate within a subset of the above films. What interests me particularly is the way a special few of these documentaries handle the problem of figuring traumatic historical truths inaccessible to representation by any simple or single "mirror with a memory" and how this mirror nevertheless operates in complicated and indirect refractions. For while traumatic events of the past are not available for representation by any simple or single "mirror with a memory"—in the direct cinema sense of capturing events as they happen—they do constitute a multifaceted receding horizon that these films powerfully evoke.

I would like to offer Errol Morris's *The Thin Blue Line* as a prime example of this postmodern documentary approach to the trauma of an inaccessible past because of its spectacular success in intervening in the truths known about this past. Morris's film was instrumental in exonerating a man wrongfully accused of murder. In 1976, Dallas police officer Robert Wood was murdered, apparently by a twenty-eight-year-old drifter named Randall Adams. Like Stone's *JFK*, *The Thin Blue Line* is a film about a November murder in Dallas. Like *JFK*, the film argues that the wrong man was set up by a state conspiracy with an interest in convicting an easy scapegoat rather than prosecuting the real murderer. The film—the "true" story of Randall Adams, the man convicted of the murder of Officer Wood, and his accuser, David Harris, the young hitchhiker whom Adams picked up the night of the murder—ends with Harris's cryptic but dramatic confession to the murder on a taped phone conversation with Errol Morris.

Stylistically, *The Thin Blue Line* has been most remarked upon for its film-noirish beauty, its apparent abandonment of direct cinema realism for studied, often slow-motion, and highly expressionistic reenactments of different witnesses' versions of the murder, all to the tune of Philip Glass's hypnotic score. Like a great many recent documentaries obsessed with traumatic events of the past, *The Thin Blue Line* is self-reflexive. Like many of these new documentaries, it is acutely aware that the individuals whose lives are caught up in events are not so much self-coherent and consistent identities as they are actors in competing narratives. As in *Roger & Me*, *Shoah*, and, to a certain extent, *Who Killed Vincent Chin?* the documentarian's role in constructing and staging these competing narratives thus becomes paramount.[3] In place of the self-obscuring voyeur of verité realism, we encounter, in these and other films, a new presence in the persona of the documentarian.

For example, in one scene David Harris, the charming young accuser whose testimony placed Randall Adams on death row and who has been giving his side of the story in sections of the film alternating with Adams, scratches his head while recounting an unimportant incident from his past.

In this small gesture, Morris dramatically reveals information withheld until this moment: Harris's hands are handcuffed. He, like Adams, is in prison. The interviews with him are now subject to reinterpretation since, as we soon learn, he, too, stands accused of murder. For he has committed a senseless murder not unlike the one he accused Adams of committing. At this climactic moment Morris finally brings in the hard evidence against Harris previously withheld: he is a violent psychopath who invaded a man's house, murdered him, and abducted his girlfriend. On top of this Morris adds the local cop's attempt to explain Harris's personal pathology; in the end we hear Harris's own near-confession—in an audio interview—to the murder for which Adams has been convicted. Thus Morris captures a truth, elicits a confession, in the best direct cinema tradition, but only in the context of a film that is manifestly staged and temporally manipulated by the docu-auteur.

It would seem that in Morris's abandonment of voyeuristic objectivity he achieves something more useful to the production of truth. His interviews get the interested parties talking in a special way. In a key statement in defense of his intrusive, self-reflexive style, Morris has attacked the hallowed tradition of cinema verité: "There is no reason why documentaries can't be as personal as fiction filmmaking and bear the imprint of those who made them. Truth isn't guaranteed by style or expression. It isn't guaranteed by anything" (17).

The "personal" in this statement has been taken to refer to the personal, self-reflexive style of the docu-auteur: Morris's hypnotic pace, Glass's music, the vivid colors and slow motion of the multiple reenactments. Yet the interviews, too, bear this personal imprint of the auteur. Each person who speaks to the camera in *The Thin Blue Line* does so in a confessional, "talking-cure" mode. James Shamus has pointed out that this rambling, free-associating discourse ultimately collides with, and is sacrificed to, the juridical narrative producing the truth of who, finally, is guilty. And Charles Musser also points out that what is sacrificed is the psychological complexity of the man the film finds innocent. Thus the film foregoes investigation into what Adams might have been up to that night taking a sixteen-year-old hitchhiker to a drive-in movie.[4]

Morris gives us some truths and withholds others. His approach to truth is altogether strategic. Truth exists for Morris because lies exist; if lies are to be exposed, truths must be strategically deployed against them. His strategy in the pursuit of this relative, hierarchized, and contingent truth is thus to find guilty those speakers whom he draws most deeply into the explorations of their past. Harris, the prosecutor Mulder, and the false witness Emily Miller all cozy up to the camera to remember incidents from

The Thin Blue Line: The charming David Harris gives his side of the story.

their pasts that serve to indict them in the present. In contrast, the man found innocent by the film remains a cipher; we learn almost nothing of his past, and this lack of knowledge appears necessary to the investigation of the official lies. What Morris does, in effect, is partially close down the representation of Adams's own story, the accumulation of narratives from his past, in order to show how convenient a scapegoat he was to the over-determining pasts of all the other false witnesses. Thus, instead of using fictionalizing techniques to show us the truth of what happened, Morris scrupulously sticks to stylized and silent docudrama reenactments that show only what each witness claims happened.

In contrast, we might consider Oliver Stone's very different use of docudrama reenactments to reveal the "truth" of the existence of several assassins in the murder of J.F.K. and the plot that orchestrated their activity. Stone has Garrison introduce the Zapruder film in the trial of Clay Shaw as hallowed verité evidence that there had to be more than one assassin. Garrison's examination of the magic bullet's trajectory does a fine dramatic job of challenging the official version of the lone assassin. But in his zealous pursuit of the truth of "who dunnit," Stone matches the direct cinema style of the Zapruder film with a verité simulation which, although hypothesis, has none of the stylized, hypothetical visual marking of Morris's simulations and which therefore commands a greater component of belief. Morris, on the other hand, working in a documentary form that now eschews direct cinema as a style, stylizes his hypothetical reenactments and never offers any of them as an image of what actually happened.

In the discussions surrounding the truth claims of many contemporary documentaries, attention has centered upon the self-reflexive challenge to once hallowed techniques of verité. It has become an axiom of the new documentary that films cannot reveal the truth of events, only the ideologies and consciousnesses that construct competing truths—the fictional master narratives by which we make sense of events. Yet too often this way of thinking has led to a forgetting of the way in which these films still are, as Stone's film isn't, documentaries—films with a special interest in the relation to the real, the "truths" that matter in people's lives but cannot be transparently represented.

One reason for this forgetting has been the erection of a too simple dichotomy between, on the one hand, a naive faith in the truth of what the documentary image reveals—direct cinema's discredited claim to capturing events while they happen—and, on the other, the embrace of fictional manipulation. Of course, even in its heyday no one ever fully believed in an absolute truth of direct cinema. There are, moreover, many gradations of fictionalized manipulation ranging from the controversial manipulation of temporal sequence in Michael Moore's *Roger & Me* to Errol Morris's scrupulous reconstructions of the subjective truths of events as viewed from many different points of view.

Truth is not "guaranteed" and cannot be transparently reflected by a mirror with a memory, yet some kinds of partial and contingent truths are nevertheless the always receding goal of the documentary tradition. Instead of careening between idealistic faith in documentary truth and cynical recourse to fiction, we do better to define documentary not as an essence of truth but as a set of strategies designed to choose from among a horizon of relative and contingent truths. The advantage, and the difficulty, of this definition is that it holds onto the concept of the real—indeed, of a "real" at all—even in the face of tendencies to assimilate documentary entirely into the rules and norms of fiction.

As *The Thin Blue Line* shows, the recognition that documentary access to this real is strategic and contingent does not require a retreat to a *Rashomon*-like universe of undecidabilities. This recognition can lead, rather, to a remarkable awareness of the conditions under which it is possible to intervene in the political and cultural construction of truths which, while not guaranteed, nevertheless matter as the narratives by which we live. To better explain this point I would like to consider further the confessional, talking-cure strategy of *The Thin Blue Line* as it relates to Claude Lanzmann's *Shoah*. While I am aware of the incommensurability of a film about the state of Texas's near execution of an innocent man with the German state's achieved extermination of six million people, I want to pursue the comparison because both films are, in very different ways, striking examples of postmodern documentaries whose passionate desire is to intervene in the construction of truths whose totality is ultimately unfathomable.

In both of these films, the truth of the past is traumatic, violent, and unrepresentable in images. It is obscured by official lies masking the responsibility of individual agents in a gross miscarriage of justice. We may recall that Jameson's argument about the postmodern is that it is a loss of a sense of history, of a collective or individual past, and the knowledge of how the past determines the present: "the past as 'referent' finds itself gradually bracketed, and then effaced altogether, leaving us with nothing but texts" ("Postmodernism" 64). That so many well-known and popular documentary films have taken up the task of remembering the past—indeed, that so much popular debate about the "truth" of the past has been engendered by both fiction and documentary films about the past—could therefore be attributed to another of Jameson's points about the postmodern condition: the intensified nostalgia for a past that is already lost.

However, I would argue instead that certainly in these two films and partially in a range of others, the postmodern suspicion of overabundant images of an unfolding, present "real" (verité's commitment to film "it" as "it" happens) has contributed not to new fictionalizations but, paradoxically, to new historicizations. These historicizations are fascinated by an inaccessible, ever-receding, yet newly important past that does have depth.[5] History, in Jameson's sense of traces of the past, of an absent cause that "hurts" (*Political Unconscious* 102), would seem, almost by definition, to be inaccessible to the verité documentary form aimed at capturing action in its unfolding. The recourse to talking-heads interviews, to people remembering the past—whether the collective history of a nation or city, the personal history of individuals, or the criminal event that crucially determines the present—is, in these anti-verité documentaries, an attempt to overturn this commitment to realistically record "life as it is" in favor of a deeper investigation of how it became as it is.

Thus, while there is very little running after the action, there is considerable provocation of action. Even though Morris and Lanzmann have certainly done their legwork to pursue actors in the events they are concerned to represent, their preferred technique is to set up a situation in which the action will come to them. In these privileged moments of verité (for there finally are moments of relative verité) the past repeats. We thus see the power of the past not simply by dramatizing it, or reenacting it, or talking about it obsessively (though these films do all this) but finally by finding its traces, in repetitions and resistances, in the present. It is thus the contextualization of the present with the past that is the most effective representational strategy in these two remarkable films.

Each of these documentaries digs toward an impossible archaeology, picking at the scabs of lies that have covered over the inaccessible ordinary event. The filmmakers ask questions, probe circumstances, draw maps, interview historians, witnesses, jurors, judges, police, bureaucrats, and survivors. These diverse investigatory processes augment the single method of the verité camera. They seek to uncover a past the knowledge of which will produce new truths of guilt and innocence in the present. Randall Adams is now free at least partly because of the evidence of Morris's film; the Holocaust comes alive not as some alien horror foreign to all humanity but as something that is, perhaps for the first time on film, understandable as an absolutely banal incremental logic and logistics of train schedules and human silence. The past events examined in these films are not offered as complete, totalizable, apprehensible. They are fragments, pieces of the past invoked by memory, not unitary representable truths but, as Freud once referred to the psychic mechanism of memory, a palimpsest, described succinctly by Mary Ann Doane as "the sum total of its rewritings through time." The "event" remembered is never whole, never fully represented, never isolated in the past alone but only accessible through a memory that resides, as Doane has put it, "in the reverberations between events" (58).

This image of the palimpsest of memory seems a particularly apt evocation of how these two films approach the problem of representing the inaccessible trauma of the past. When Errol Morris fictionally reenacts the murder of Officer Wood as differently remembered by David Harris, Randall Adams, the officer's partner, and the various witnesses who claimed to have seen the murder, he turns his film into a temporally elaborated palimpsest, discrediting some versions more than others but refusing to ever fix one as *the* truth. It is precisely Morris's refusal to fix the final truth, to go on seeking reverberations and repetitions that, I argue, gives this film its exceptional power of truth.

This strategic and relative truth is often a by-product of other investigations into many stories of self-justification and reverberating memories told to the camera. For example, Morris never set out to tell the story of Randall Adams's innocence. He was interested initially in the story of "Dr. Death," the psychiatrist whose testimony about the sanity of numerous accused murderers had resulted in a remarkable number of death sentences. It would seem that the more directly and single-mindedly a film pursues a single truth, the less chance it has of producing the kind of "reverberations between events" that will effect meaning in the present. This is the problem with *Roger & Me* and, to stretch matters, even with *JFK*: both go after a single target too narrowly, opposing a singular (fictionalized) truth to a singular official lie.

The much publicized argument between Harlan Jacobson and Michael Moore regarding the imposition of a false chronology in Moore's documentary about the closing of General Motors plants in Flint, Michigan, is an example. At stake in this argument is whether Moore's documentation of the decline of the city of Flint in the wake of the plant closing entailed an obligation to represent events in the sequence in which they actually occurred. Jacobson argues that Moore betrays his journalist/documentarian's commitment to the objective portrayal of historical fact when he implies that events that occurred prior to the major layoffs at the plant were the effect of these layoffs. Others have criticized Moore's self-promoting placement of himself at the center of the film.[6]

In response, Moore argues that as a resident of Flint he has a place in the film and should not attempt to play the role of objective observer but of partisan investigator. This point is quite credible and consistent with the postmodern awareness that there is no objective observation of truth but always an interested participation in its construction. But when he argues that his documentary is "in essence" true to what happened to Flint in the 1980s, only that these events are "told with a narrative style" that omits details and condenses events of a decade into a palatable "movie" (quoted in Jacobson 22), Moore behaves too much like Oliver Stone, abandoning the commitment to multiple contingent truths in favor of a unitary, paranoid view of history.

The argument between Moore and Jacobson seems to be about where documentarians should draw the line in manipulating the historical sequence of their material. But rather than determining appropriate strategies for the representation of the meaning of events, the argument becomes a question of a commitment of objectivity versus a commitment to fiction. Moore says, in effect, that his first commitment is to entertain and that this entertainment is faithful to the essence of the history. But Moore betrays the cause-and-effect reverberation between events by this reordering. The real lesson of this debate would seem to be that Moore did not trust his audience to learn about the past in any other way than through the direct capture of it. He assumed that if he didn't have footage from the historical period prior to his filming in Flint he couldn't show it. But the choice needn't be, as Moore implies, between boring, laborious fact

and entertaining fiction true to the "essence," but not the detail, of historical events. The opposition poses a false contrast between a naive faith in
the documentary truth of photographic and filmic images and the cynical
awareness of fictional manipulation.

What animates Morris and Lanzmann, by contrast, is not the opposition between absolute truth and absolute fiction but the awareness of the
final inaccessibility of a moment of crime, violence, trauma, irretrievably
located in the past. Through the curiosity, ingenuity, irony, and obsessive-
ness of "obtrusive" investigators, Morris and Lanzmann do not so much
represent this past as they reactivate it in images of the present. This is
their distinctive postmodern feature as documentarians. For in revealing
the fabrications, the myths, the frequent moments of scapegoating when
easy fictional explanations of trauma, violence, and crime were substituted
for more difficult ones, these documentaries do not simply play off truth
against lie, nor do they play off one fabrication against another; rather, they
show how lies function as partial truths to both the agents and witnesses
of history's trauma.

For example, in one of the most discussed moments of *Shoah,* Lanzmann stages a scene of homecoming in Chelmno, Poland, by Simon Srebnik, a Polish Jew who had, as a child, worked in the death camp near that
town, running errands for the Nazis and forced to sing while doing so. Now,
many years later, in the present tense of Lanzmann's film, the elderly yet still
vigorous Srebnik is surrounded on the steps of the Catholic church by an
even older, friendly group of Poles who remembered him as a child in chains
who sang by the river. They are happy he has survived and returned to visit.
But as Lanzmann asks them how much they knew and understood about
the fate of the Jews who were carried away from the church in gas vans, the
group engages in a kind of free association to explain the unexplainable.

Lanzmann: Why do they think all this happened to the Jews?

A Pole: Because they were the richest! Many Poles were also exterminated.
Even priests.

Another Pole: Mr. Kantarowski will tell us what a friend told him. It happened
in Myndjewyce, near Warsaw.

Lanzmann: Go on.

Mr. Kantarowski: The Jews there were gathered in a square. The rabbi asked
an SS man: "Can I talk to them?" The SS man said yes. So the rabbi said
that around two thousand years ago the Jews condemned the innocent
Christ to death. And when they did that, they cried out: "Let his blood
fall on our heads and on our sons' heads." The rabbi told them: "Perhaps

the time has come for that, so let us do nothing, let us go, let us do as
we're asked."

Lanzmann: He thinks the Jews expiated the death of Christ?

The first(?) Pole: He doesn't think so, or even that Christ sought revenge. He
didn't say that. The rabbi said it. It was God's will, that's all!

Lanzmann [referring to an untranslated comment]: What'd she say?

A Polish woman: So Pilate washed his hands and said: "Christ is innocent,"
and he said Barabbas. But the Jews cried out: "Let his blood fall on our
heads!"

Another Pole: That's all; now you know! (Lanzmann 100)[7]

As critic Shoshana Felman has pointed out, this scene on the church
steps in Chelmno shows the Poles replacing one memory of their own witness of the persecution of the Jews with another (false) memory, an auto-
mystification, produced by Mr. Kantarowski, of the Jews' willing acceptance
of their persecution as scapegoats for the death of Christ. This fantasy,
meant to assuage the Poles' guilt for their complicity in the death of the
Jews, actually repeats the Poles' crime of the past in the present.

Felman argues that the strategy of Lanzmann's film is not to challenge
this false testimony but to dramatize its effects: we see Simon Srebnik suddenly silenced among the chatty Poles, whose victim he becomes all over
again. Thus the film does not so much give us a memory as an action, here
and now, of the Poles' silencing and crucifixion of Srebnik, whom they
obliterate and forget even as he stands in their midst (120–28).

It is this repetition in the present of the crime of the past that is key to
the documentary process of Lanzmann's film. Success, in the film's terms,
is the ability not only to assign guilt in the past, to reveal and fix a truth
of the day-to-day operation of the machinery of extermination, but also to
deepen the understanding of the many ways in which the Holocaust continues to live in the present. The truth of the Holocaust thus does not exist
in any totalizing narrative but only, as Felman notes and Lanzmann shows,
as a collection of fragments. While the process of scapegoating, of achieving premature narrative closure by assigning guilt to convenient victims,
is illuminated, the events of the past—in this case the totality of the Holocaust—register not in any fixed moment of past or present but rather, as
in Freud's description of the palimpsest, as the sum total of its rewritings
through time, not in a single event but in the "reverberations" between.

It is important in the above example to note that while cinema verité is deployed in this scene on the steps, as well as in the interviews
throughout the film, this form of verité no longer has a fetish function of

demanding belief as the whole. In place of a truth that is "guaranteed," the verité of catching events as they happen is here embedded in a history, placed in relation to the past, given a new power, not of absolute truth but of repetition.

Although it is a very different sort of documentary dealing with a trauma whose horror cannot be compared to the Holocaust, *The Thin Blue Line* also offers its own rich palimpsest of reverberations between events. At the beginning of the film, convicted murderer Randall Adams mulls over the fateful events of the night in 1976 when he ran out of gas, was picked up by David Harris, went to a drive-in movie, refused to allow Harris to come home with him, and later found himself accused of killing a cop with a gun that Harris had stolen. He muses: "Why did I meet this kid? Why did I run out of gas? But it happened, it happened." The film probes this "why?" And its discovery "out of the past" is not simply some fate-laden accident but rather a reverberation between events that reaches much further back into the past than that cold November night in Dallas.

Toward the end, after Morris has amassed a great deal of evidence attesting to the false witness borne by three people who testified to seeing Randall Adams in the car with David Harris, but before playing the audio tape in which Harris all but confesses to the crime, the film takes a different turn away from the events of November and into the childhood of David Harris. The film thus moves both forward and back in time: to events following and preceding the night of November 1976, when the police officer was shot. Moving forward, we learn of a murder in which David broke into the home of a man who had, he felt, stolen his girlfriend. When the man defended himself, David shot him. This repetition of wanton violence is the clincher in the film's "case" against David. But instead of stopping there, the film goes back in time as well.

A kindly, baby-faced cop from David's hometown, who has told us much of David's story already, searches for the cause of his behavior and hits upon a childhood trauma: a four-year-old brother who drowned when David was only three. Morris then cuts to David speaking of this incident: "My dad was supposed to be watching us. . . . I guess that might have been some kind of traumatic experience for me. . . . I guess I reminded him . . . it was hard for me to get any acceptance from him after that. . . . A lot of the things I did as a young kid was an attempt to get back at him."

In itself, this "getting-back-at-the-father" motive is something of a cliché for explaining violent male behavior. But coupled as it is with the final "confession" scene in which Harris repeats this getting-back-at-the-father motive in his relation to Adams, the explanation gains resonance, exposing another layer in the palimpsest of the past. As we watch the tape recording

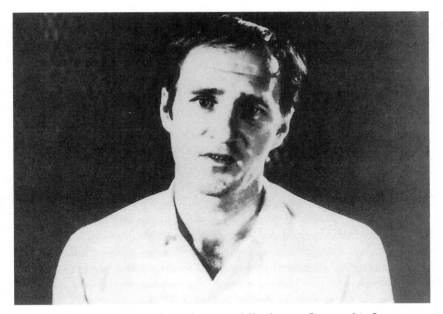

The Thin Blue Line: Convicted murderer Randall Adams reflects on his fate.

of this last unfilmed interview play, we hear Morris ask Harris if he thinks Adams is a "pretty unlucky fellow." Harris answers, "Definitely," specifying the nature of this bad luck: "Like I told you a while ago about the guy who didn't have no place to stay . . . if he'd had a place to stay, he'd never had no place to go, right?" Morris decodes this question with his own rephrasing, continuing to speak to Harris in the third person: "You mean if he'd stayed at the hotel that night this never would have happened?" (That is, if Adams had invited Harris into his hotel to stay with him as Harris had indicated earlier in the film he expected, then Harris would not have committed the murder he later pinned on Adams.) Harris: "Good possibility, good possibility. . . . You ever hear of the proverbial scapegoat? There probably been thousands of innocent people convicted."

Morris presses: "What do you think about whether he's innocent?" Harris: "I'm sure he is." Morris again: "How can you be sure?" Harris: "I'm the one who knows. . . . After all was said and done it was pretty unbelievable. I've always thought if you could say why there's a reason that Randall Adams is in jail it might be because he didn't have a place for somebody to stay that helped him that night. It might be the only reason why he's at where he's at."

What emerges forcefully in this near-confession is much more than the clinching evidence in Morris's portrait of a gross miscarriage of justice. For in not simply probing the "wrong man" story, in probing the reverberations between events of David Harris's personal history, Morris's film discovers an underlying layer in the palimpsest of the past: how the older Randall Adams played an unwitting role in the psychic history of the sixteen-year-old David Harris, a role that repeated an earlier trauma in Harris's life: of the father who rejected him, whose approval he could not win, and upon whom David then revenged himself.

Harris's revealing comments do more than clinch his guilt. Like the Poles who surround Srebnik on the steps of the church and proclaim pity for the innocent child who suffered so much even as they repeat the crime of scapegoating Jews, so David Harris proclaims the innocence of the man he has personally condemned, patiently explaining the process of scapegoating that the Dallas county legal system has so obligingly helped him accomplish. Cinema verité in both these films is an important vehicle of documentary truth. We witness in the present an event of simultaneous confession and condemnation on the part of historical actors who repeat their crimes from the past. Individual guilt is both palpably manifest and viewed in a larger context of personal and social history. For even as we catch David Harris and the Poles of Chelmno in the act of scapegoating innocent victims for crimes they have not committed, these acts are revealed as part of larger processes, reverberating with the past.

I think it is important to hold onto this idea of truth as a fragmentary shard, perhaps especially at the moment we as a culture have begun to realize, along with Morris, and along with the supposed depthlessness of our postmodern condition, that it is not guaranteed. For some form of truth is the always receding goal of documentary film. But the truth figured by documentary cannot be a simple unmasking or reflection. It is a careful construction, an intervention in the politics and the semiotics of representation.

Any overly simplified dichotomy between truth and fiction is at the root of our difficulty in thinking about the truth in documentary. The choice is not between two entirely separate regimes of truth and fiction. The choice, rather, is in strategies of fiction for the approach to relative truths. Documentary is not fiction and should not be conflated with it. But documentary can and should use all the strategies of fictional construction to get at truths. What we see in *The Thin Blue Line* and *Shoah*, and to some degree in the other documentaries I have mentioned, is an interest in constructing truths to dispel pernicious fictions, even though these truths are only relative and contingent. While never absolute and never fixed, this under-construction, fragmented horizon of truth is one important means of combating the pernicious scapegoating fictions that can put the wrong man on death row and enable the destruction of a whole people.

The lesson that I would like to draw from these two exemplary postmodern documentaries is thus not at all that postmodern representation inevitably succumbs to a depthlessness of the simulacrum, or that it gives up on truth to wallow in the undecidabilities of representation. The lesson, rather, is that there can be historical depth to the notion of truth—not the depth of unearthing a coherent and unitary past but the depth of the past's reverberation with the present. If the authoritative means to the truth of the past does not exist, if photographs and moving images are not mirrors with memories, if they are more, as Baudrillard has suggested, like a hall of mirrors, then our best response to this crisis of representation might be to do what Lanzmann and Morris do: deploy the many facets of these mirrors to reveal the seduction of lies.

Notes

I owe thanks to Anne Friedberg, Mark Poster, Nancy Salzer, Marita Sturken, Charles Musser, James Shamus, B. Ruby Rich, and Marianne Hirsch for helping me, one way or another, to formulate the ideas in this chapter. I also thank my colleagues on the editorial board of *Film Quarterly,* the journal in which this essay was originally published, whose friendly criticisms I have not entirely answered.

1. See, for example, Janet Maslin, "Oliver Stone Manipulates His Puppet," *New York Times,* January 5, 1992, 13; "Twisted History," *Newsweek,* December 23, 1991, 46–54; Alexander Cockburn, "J.F.K. and *JFK*," *The Nation,* January 6–13, 1992, 6–8.

2. Livingston's own film is an excellent example of the irony she cites, not so much in her directorial attitude toward her subject—drag-queen ball competitions— but in her subjects' attitudes toward the construction of the illusion of gender. See Caryl Flinn's essay on *Paris Is Burning* in this volume.

3. In this essay I will not discuss *Who Killed Vincent Chin?* or *Roger & Me* at much length. Although both of these films resemble *The Thin Blue Line* and *Shoah* in their urge to reveal truths about crimes, I do not believe these films succeed as spectacularly as Morris's or Lanzmann's in respecting the complexity of these truths. In *Vincent Chin,* the truth pursued is the racial motives animating Roger Ebens, a disgruntled, unemployed autoworker who killed Vincent Chin in a fight following a brawl in a strip joint. Ebens was convicted of manslaughter but only paid a small fine. He was then acquitted of a subsequent civil rights charge that failed to convince a jury of his racial motives. The film, however, convincingly pursues evidence that Ebens's animosity toward Chin was motivated by his anger at the Japanese for

stealing jobs from Americans (Ebens assumed Chin was Japanese). In recounting the two trials, the story of the "Justice for Vincent" Committee, and the suffering of Vincent's mother, the film attempts to retry the case showing evidence of Ebens's racial motives.

Filmmakers Choy and Tajima gamble that their camera will capture, in interviews with Ebens, what the civil rights case did not capture for the jury: the racist attitudes that motivated the crime. They seek, in a way, what all of these documentaries seek: evidence of the truth of past events through their repetition in the present. This is also, in a more satirical vein, what Michael Moore seeks when he repeatedly attempts to interview the elusive Roger Smith, head of General Motors, about the layoffs in Flint, Michigan: Smith's avoidance of Moore repeats this avoidance of responsibility toward the town of Flint. This is also what Claude Lanzmann seeks when he interviews the ex-Nazis and witnesses of the Holocaust, and it is what Errol Morris seeks when he interviews David Harris, the boy who put Randall Adams on death row. Each of these films succeeds in its goal to a certain extent. But the single-mindedness of *Vincent Chin*'s pursuit of the singular truth of Ebens's guilt and of his culture's resentment of Asians limits the film. Since Ebens never does show himself in the present to be a blatant racist but only an insensitive working-class guy, the film fails on its own terms, though it is eloquent testimony to the pain and suffering of the scapegoated Chin's mother.

4. Shamus, Musser, and I delivered papers on *The Thin Blue Line* at a panel devoted to the film at a conference sponsored by New York University, "The State of Representation: Representation and the State," October 26–28, 1990. B. Ruby Rich was a respondent. Musser's paper argued the point, seconded by Rich's comments, that the prosecution and the police saw Adams as a homosexual. Their eagerness to prosecute Adams, rather than the underage Harris, seems to have much to do with this perception, entirely suppressed by the film.

5. Consider, for example, the way Ross McElwee's *Sherman's March* (1985), on one level a narcissistic self-portrait of an eccentric Southerner's rambling attempts to discover his identity while traveling through the South, also plays off against the historical General Sherman's devastating march. Or consider the way Ken Burns's *The Civil War* (1990) is as much about what the Civil War is to us today as it is about the objective truth of the past.

6. Laurence Jarvik, for example, argued that Moore's self-portrayal as a "naive, quixotic 'rebel with a mike'" is not an authentic image but one Moore has promoted as a fiction. Quoted in Renee Tajima, "The Perils of Popularity," *The Independent* (June 1990): 30.

7. I have quoted this dialogue from the published version of the *Shoah* script but I have added the attribution of who is speaking. It is important to note, however, that the script is a condensation of a prolonged scene that appears to be constructed out of two different interviews with Lanzmann, the Poles, and Simon Srebnik before

the church. In the first segment, Mr. Kantarowski is not present; in the second he is. When the old woman says, "So Pilate washed his hands . . . ," Mr. Kantarowski makes the gesture of washing his hands.

Works Cited

Baudrillard, Jean. "Simulacra and Simulations." In *Jean Baudrillard: Selected Writings*, ed. Mark Poster, 166–84. Stanford: Stanford University Press, 1988.

Doane, Mary Ann. "Remembering Women: Physical and Historical Constructions in Film Theory." In *Psychoanalysis and Cinema*, ed. E. Ann Kaplan, 46–63. New York: Routledge, 1990.

Felman, Shoshana. "A l'age du temoignage: *Shoah* de Claude Lanzmann." In *Au sujet de Shoah: Le film de Claude Lanzmann*, 55–145. Paris: Editions Belin, 1990.

Grundberg, Andy. "Ask It No Questions: The Camera Can Lie." *New York Times*, August 12, 1990, sec. 2, pp. 1, 29.

Jacobson, Harlan. "Michael and Me." *Film Comment* 25, no. 6 (1989): 16–26.

Jameson, Fredric. "Postmodernism or the Cultural Logic of Late Capitalism." *New Left Review* 146 (1984): 53–92.

———. *The Political Unconscious: Narrative as a Socially Symbolic Act*. Ithaca, NY: Cornell University Press, 1981.

Kaes, Anton. *From Hitler to Heimat: The Return of History as Film*. Cambridge, MA: Harvard University Press, 1989.

Lanzmann, Claude. *Shoah: An Oral History of the Holocaust*. New York: Pantheon, 1985.

Lyotard, Jean-François. *The Postmodern Condition: A Report on Knowledge*. Minneapolis: University of Minnesota Press, 1984.

Morris, Errol. "Truth Not Guaranteed: An Interview with Errol Morris." Interview by Peter Bates. *Cineaste* 17, no. 1 (1989): 16–17.

Musser, Charles. "Film Truth: From *Kino Pravda* to *Who Killed Vincent Chin?* and *The Thin Blue Line.*" Paper presented at "The State of Representation: Representation and the State" conference, New York University, October 26–28, 1990.

Shamus, James. "Optioning Time: Writing *The Thin Blue Line*." Paper presented at "The State of Representation: Representation and the State" conference, New York University, October 26–28, 1990.

Taubin, Amy. "Oscar's Docudrama." *Village Voice*, March 31, 1992, 62.

Trinh T. Minh-ha. "Documentary Is/Not a Name." *October* 52 (1990): 77–98.

Chapter 24

DOCUMENTAPHOBIA
AND MIXED MODES

Michael Moore's *Roger & Me*

Matthew Bernstein

There was a startling vehemence to the journalistic critics' denunciation of *Roger & Me* (1989), Michael Moore's insightful and bitingly funny exposé of corporate greed in the 1980s. Pauline Kael accused Moore of "gonzo demagoguery," whereby "members of the audience can laugh at ordinary working people and still feel they're taking a politically correct position" (91, 92). Harlan Jacobson termed the film's rearranged chronology a cinematic Gulf of Tonkin resolution (Moore, interview with Jacobson 23).

The controversy demonstrated how difficult certain journalists find conceptualizing the documentary film. The *New York Times* queried whether the film was a documentary or a satire or both (R. Bernstein). Michael Moore, himself a journalist, defended *Roger & Me* by appealing to our sophisticated understanding of how knowledge is produced in the contemporary media: "All art, listen, every piece of journalism manipulates sequence and things." Moore proceeded to defend his film on generic grounds. *Roger & Me* is not a documentary, he asserted to Jacobson, but "a movie," "a documentary told with a narrative style." He wanted to avoid "a three hour movie," which presumably a more accurate documentary would become (interview with Jacobson 22, 23).[1] In other interviews, Moore has cited only Kevin and Pierce Rafferty and Jayne Loader's 1982 *The Atomic Cafe* as an inspiration for his work (Collins C20).

Unlike the journalistic discourse, academic discussion has acknowledged that defining the documentary is difficult, whether documentary is understood in terms of its formal features, its assumptions about the construction of knowledge, its approach to narration, its assertions of authority, the expectations it evokes in the audience—or all of the above.

That documentary is understood as all of the above is the contention of Bill Nichols's seminal 1983 essay "The Voice of Documentary," which he revised in his *Representing Reality* as "Documentary Modes of Representation." I propose to examine *Roger & Me* more closely as a documentary and to do so using Nichols's typology of documentary modes, which he defines as "basic ways of organizing texts in relation to certain recurrent features or conventions" (*Reality* 32).[2] Nichols's categories of expository, observational, interactive, and reflexive modes affirm what Moore and the journalists seem to have overlooked: there are many different kinds of documentary. I will argue that, in fact, one of the most interesting questions Moore's film raises involves the juxtaposition of conventions of the expository and interactive documentaries. First it is useful to review briefly Nichols's typology.

Nichols's Typology of Documentary Modes

In expository documentaries, Nichols notes, "Images serve as illustrations or counterpoint of the verbal argument." The visuals are "at the service" of the commentary, even if the latter is ironic and satirical, as in the case of Luis Buñuel's *Land without Bread* (1931) (*Reality* 34). This approach is also exemplified by the voice-of-God narration of *The March of Time* newsreels, the poetic cadences of the voice-over commentary in Pare Lorentz's *The River* (1937), and even the associative editing of Humphrey Jennings and Stewart McAllister's *Listen to Britain* (1942). Expository documentaries embody an epistemological assumption that knowledge about the world is readily accessible to the filmmaker. Such films thus give an impression of objectivity and of well-substantiated argument. Given the strident certainty of expository documentaries, ethical considerations (such as collaboration with participants in the film) become negligible. Subjects interviewed "give their testimony within a frame they cannot control and may not understand" (Nichols, *Reality* 37).

Nichols further distinguishes the expository mode from the "Observational Mode" of direct cinema typified by the Drew Associates' *Primary* (1960), the Maysles Brothers' *Salesman* (1969), and even D. A. Pennebaker's *The War Room* (1993). Lacking the accentuated presence of the filmmaker through (the expository mode's) voice-over narration, observational documentaries are frequently marked by long takes and by synchronous sound for "the exhaustive depiction of the everyday," as well as processes or crises. Sharing the expository mode's assumption of untroubled access to knowledge and understanding (Nichols, *Reality* 42–44), and deploying a style that aspires to immediacy and transparency, the observational films focus "on the activity of individuals within specific social formations such as the family, the local community, or a single institution or aspect of one" (Nichols, *Reality* 40).

The third documentary mode, "interactive," highlights "the processes of social exchange and representation" in the historical world (Nichols, *Reality* 56). (In the "Voice of Documentary" essay, Nichols had described this as "a return" to the direct address of expository filmmaking via the interview.) Most obviously, the interactive documentary acknowledges the filmmaker's presence in conducting interviews and gathering information. The filmmaker can be present onscreen as is Jean Rouch in his 1961 *Chronicle of a Summer;* in a voice-over; or as an intelligence overtly organizing the images, as in Julia Reichart and Jim Klein's *Union Maids* (1975) or Frederick Wiseman's films. Editing patterns do not efficiently present cause-and-effect relations among phenomena (as in expository films) but typically entail crosscutting among the different and often contradictory evidence offered by different subjects (Nichols, *Reality* 45).

Conflicting testimony and the on-camera appearance of the filmmaker lead the interactive film "to an emphasis on the act of gathering information or building knowledge, the process of social and historical interpretation" (Nichols, *Reality* 49). Consequently, the authority of the film to speak about the world is subdued. Nichols writes: "The mode introduces a sense of partialness, of *situated* presence and *local* knowledge that derives from the actual encounter of filmmaker and other" (*Reality* 44).

Finally, Nichols distinguishes a fourth mode of documentary, the "reflexive," typified by films such as Chris Marker's *Letter from Siberia* (1958) and Errol Morris's *The Thin Blue Line* (1987), which, unlike the other modes, questions the very ability of filmmakers to know—and cinema to represent any historical reality fairly and adequately (*Reality* 57). Such documentaries employ various modal conventions but disrupt them as a means of conveying their epistemological skepticism. In *The Thin Blue Line,* Morris's constant reenactment of the crime "reminds us of how every documentary constructs the evidentiary reference points it requires," as does his crosscutting among different "witnesses" to the crime who contradict each other (Nichols, *Reality* 58).

As Nichols emphasizes, there are many variations within each mode. Moreover, the four modes are historically and textually intertwined. While he outlines a historical dialectic (for example, the expository mode was a reaction against the fiction film, the observational film arose from new portable technologies and a rejection of the expository mode, and so forth), he also notes that "these modes have been potentially available from early in the cinema's history," so that the progression among preferred modes has not occurred in a linear fashion (*Reality* 33).

Documentary history is not Nichols's subject as such, so that detailing the historical relations among modes remains a task for future scholarship. It would be fruitful to explore films that exemplified transitions between—or modifications within—modes, as examples of competing documentary practices and rhetoric. In fact, Jeanne Hall's perceptive analysis of *Primary*—which shows how Robert Drew and his team frequently used sound-image relations in an expository mode instead of the observational manner that the rhetoric of their cinema verité movement championed—is an exemplary study of a transitional text that attempts to negotiate between different modes (cf. Hall).[3]

Yet if we bracket questions concerning the historical development of documentary, Nichols further notes that individual films feature a mixing and modification of modes (*Reality* 33). This is possible because the modes are, as noted above, "basic ways of organizing texts" (*Reality* 32) derived from "common ingredients," such as their textual features, their epistemologies, and their ethical assumptions. Nichols uses the term "mode" to make less rigid distinctions than other scholars might employ. For Nichols, the modes "partly serve as a heuristic model, drawing out more cleanly defined alternatives than we find in practice" (*Reality* 65).[4]

If the different modes are to be meaningful terms of analysis, however, one must at least acknowledge that certain modes are logically incompatible on epistemological grounds. A documentary cannot be said to present a consistently logical argument if it employs practices that embody both skepticism (as in the reflexive mode) *and* confidence (expository or observational mode) about its capacity to understand and represent the "real world."[5]

If epistemological categories are absolute, the other attributes of documentary modes are more easily intertwined. Most notably, different textual features of different documentaries can align those films with the same mode. For instance, the way Frederick Wiseman and Emile de Antonio frequently cut among the statements of different subjects provides an interactive dimension comparable to that which filmmakers such as Ross McElwee and Claude Lanzmann accomplish through probing, impertinent on-camera interviews.

Alternately, the same textual features, such as interviews, can have different valences in different films. For example, interviews in the interactive mode can, as Nichols puts it, "work reflexively to make us aware of the contingencies of the moment, the shaping force of the representational project itself, and the modification of action and behavior that it can produce" (*Reality* 73). Interviews "generally serve as evidence for an argument presented as the product of the interaction of filmmaker and subject" (*Reality* 48) and hence hold greater authority in the argument of the film. In expository films, by contrast, interviews buttress the film's thesis, providing important sources, but ones of secondary authority. Distinguishing among the different modes operative in a single film becomes a matter of detecting nuances in how various elements of the film are deployed and structured.

DOCUMENTARY MODES AND FICTION FILM GENRES

Why should we even bother to speak of Nichols's categories when discussing particular films? Because for all their characteristics as "tendencies" in filmmaking, these modes resemble fiction film genres. Documentary filmmakers acknowledge these modes (albeit with different nomenclature) as existing traditions. In fact, Nichols notes, "Attaching a particular text to a traditional mode of representation and to the discursive authority of that tradition may well strengthen its claims, lending to these claims the weight of previously established legitimacy" (*Reality* 34). In this light, for example, Michael Moore's claims of his and his crew's technical incompetence in making *Roger & Me*—Jesse Jackson had to tell Moore's sound crew that their recorder was not turned on—are highly significant, insofar as they enhance his eschewal of documentary affiliations.

The documentary modes further resemble fiction film genres in that viewers recognize them. Having pegged a documentary in terms of a certain mode's traditions, viewers maintain certain expectations of the film. Viewers of an expository film, recognizing the tradition's textual conventions and its epistemological assumptions, expect "a commonsensical world will unfold in terms of the establishment of a logical, cause and effect linkage of sequences and events" (Nichols, *Reality* 37). Viewers of observational films are encouraged to expect a virtual fiction film (Nichols, *Reality* 42–44). Interactive film spectators are challenged to infer the film's argument from the juxtaposition of admittedly limited perspectives. They are also more highly aware of the construction of the film and its argument (Nichols, *Reality* 48, 56). Reflexive films cue the spectator to "expect the unexpected, functioning not with a surreal intent to shock and surprise so much as to return the film systematically to questions of its own status and that of documentary in general" (Nichols, *Reality* 62). That viewers have these sets of expectations of different modes is one reason why critics can remain skeptical of Moore's rejection of the documentary label.

THE EXPOSITORY MODE IN *ROGER & ME*

In *Roger & Me,* Michael Moore works with and plays on these modes and the expectations they invite. *Roger & Me* establishes itself in its opening moments—in what theorists of narration call the primacy effect (cf. Bordwell 37)—as an interactive documentary, one that relies heavily on subject interviews and the filmmaker's openly acknowledged and limited understanding. But after the film's prologue, Moore settles into the expository mode of documentary, whereby his apparently objective narration asserts its absolute authority.

There is little argument that *Roger & Me* functions primarily in the expository mode. Moore has a thesis about why General Motors closed its manufacturing plants in and around Flint, Michigan, and he has a clear argument about its effects on the town. The film is rhetorically organized to support this thesis.

Roger & Me's expository ethos—whereby images illustrate commentary—is in constant evidence in the film: there is the sequence in which "Wouldn't It Be Nice" plays ironically over shots of abandoned homes and storefronts. There are Moore's introductions to various sequences such as his visits to the yacht club, the athletic club, and GM's Detroit headquarters. Like the most effective of such documentaries, Moore's commentary permits no ambiguity in terms of the audience's interpretation of the people, places, and events they see.

Similarly, Moore's editing strategies are a textbook case of what Nichols calls "rhetorical continuity" in the expository documentary. The images constantly corroborate his verbal statements—about everything from his move from the *Michigan Voice* to *Mother Jones* to the plant closings—with headlines and footage from the national and local news media. In this way, Moore offers "an economy of analysis," making his points concisely, "partly by eliminating reference to the process by which knowledge is produced, organized, and regulated" (Nichols, *Reality* 35) or reference to the fact that his corroboration comes from media corporations that themselves operate for profit.

Nowhere is Moore's allegiance to the epistemology and strategy of the expository mode more evident than when he lays out his interpretation of GM's corporate strategies. In roughly twenty-eight seconds, Moore explains to the accompaniment of a dazzlingly quick montage how GM closed its American plants, wrested concessions from the unions to open Mexican plants with seventy-cents-an-hour labor wages, and used the savings to fund corporate takeovers (the latter illustrated by an airborne missile firing). In de Antonio's films, Nichols once noted, "Not everyone can be believed. Not everything is true" (Nichols, "Voice" 25). The twenty-eight-second analysis of GM's motives encapsulates one of the major points of *Roger & Me:* only Michael Moore and those who share his views can be believed.

"Rhetorical continuity" is used not only to confirm Moore's arguments but to sabotage the opposing viewpoints through extensive crosscutting. Following the pattern codified in D. W. Griffith's *A Corner in Wheat* (1909), Moore time and again cuts from some upper-class setting, like the Great Gatsby party or the crowning of Miss Michigan as Miss America 1988, to Deputy Sheriff Fred Ross evicting someone. But Ross's workday is not the only term of comparison, and the juxtapositions gleefully contradict everything GM corporate officials have to say.

Early in the film, Moore cuts from Roger Smith's statements about GM's efforts to further its employees' job security to the day on which the last GM truck was assembled, and then to the expletives of the workers about to be laid off. After PR man Tom Kay's statement that GM does "what it has to do to stay competitive," Moore immediately shows us his friend who left the assembly line in a panic and turned on "Wouldn't It Be Nice?" on his car radio. Later in the film, when Anita Bryant and Pat Boone suggest that the unemployed should help themselves, Moore immediately shows us Janet, the feminist color analyzer; after Tom Kay asserts "there are all kinds of opportunities" for GM's newly fired employees, Moore shows us lint rollers, the infamous "pets or meat" woman, and the increasing violent crime rate in Flint.

During Flint's 1980s parade in honor(!) of the city's sit-down strikers, Moore asks political leaders (such as Michigan's governor) and a rank-and-file unemployed autoworker about the prospects of a sit-down strike in the 1980s; Moore crosscuts their answers. After UAW leader Owen Beeber dismisses strikes as ineffective and hopelessly idealistic, Moore cuts to a scantily clad baton twirler on a float—suggesting that Beeber's views are a diversionary tactic and that the rank-and-file member's earlier observation is correct: union leaders are too cozy with management.

After the next shot of a young baton twirler in the parade (after Beeber speaks of Flint's future "growth"), Moore then cuts to the same rank-and-file member, who says, "Some people know what time it is; some people don't." From here, Moore quickly gives us Miss Michigan's disastrously and spontaneously selfish on-camera comments as a perfect illustration of the aphorism. He then cuts from her crowning as Miss America to another eviction scene.

The crosscutting pattern reaches its rhetorical climax of course when Moore cuts back and forth between Roger Smith's Christmas party speech and Ross's eviction of one furious tenant before Christmas, using Smith's voice-over to accompany the scenes of eviction. If Moore's explanation of Smith's corporate policies in twenty-eight seconds is the film's strongest instance of the expository method (particularly with voice-over authority), this Christmas sequence is the high point of Moore's editing strategies. It is so effectively built up that even Moore does not feel the need to provide further commentary beyond the voice-over of Smith's hollow-sounding speech about holiday cheer and goodwill.

Although Moore has cited *The Atomic Cafe* as the documentary he most admires, the crosscutting in *Roger & Me* follows precisely the logic of Connie Fields's 1980 *The Life and Times of Rosie the Riveter*: institutional dogma, as expressed in newsreels in Fields's film is opposed to withering personal testimony from female home front workers that undercuts the bombast and exposes the duplicity of official representations of women's work during and after World War II. As in Fields's film, Moore's crosscutting becomes a stunning indictment of corporate malfeasance, constantly demonstrating the social and corporate elite's naive or thoughtless conceptions of

Roger & Me: Moore cuts to the spontaneously selfish Miss Michigan.

working-class social realities. The crucial difference from *Roger & Me* is that Fields's thesis arises from the materials she films and juxtaposes, not from the dicta of authoritative voice-over narration.

These textual features of the expository mode—authoritative voice-over and rhetorical continuity—are precisely what provoked audiences and critics like Harlan Jacobson into anger over Moore's creative chronologies. Moore provides a "logical, cause and effect linkage of sequences and events" (Nichols, *Reality* 37). Though Jacobson's outrage was strongly termed, it was a reasonable response to the chronological cues in Moore's voice-over narration. Some of these cues are trivial. For example, Moore tells us of the three-month gap between Janet's first and second color analyses. Less precise is the language in the segue from the sequence at the Grosse Pointe Yacht Club, when Moore tells us he has to "hurry back" to the county fair where diving donkeys and Bob Eubanks hold sway.

But Moore's use of voice-over narration offers temporal cues that are more significant. After the "Wouldn't It Be Nice" sequence, Moore introduces Ronald Reagan's visit to Flint with "just when things were beginning to look bleak." After the failed espionage session at the Waldorf Astoria, Moore has to head "back" to GM headquarters for another try at the fourteenth floor. The Hyatt Regency opening and tourism boost come "just when it appeared that all hope was lost." "With thirty thousand jobs now eliminated, the city decided to turn to that one event that had always made us so happy: the big parade." In other words, Moore relied on chronological cues, vaguely but explicitly, in presenting many major events. It is no wonder that some viewers felt betrayed by the revelation of the actual sequence of dates.[6]

THE INTERACTIVE MODE OF THE PROLOGUE

One strategy for defending Moore's creative chronology would rest on the grounds that Moore makes his point of view—and the very fact that he is presenting *his* own point of view—clear from the outset of the film. Indeed, *Roger & Me*'s prologue (and its title for that matter) clearly operates on the model of the limited knowledge and constrained perspective of the interactive mode of documentary. In other words, the opening (as well as its title) cues the spectator to expect a film that centers on Moore's perceptions and understanding of what has happened to Flint; that is, that it will be tentative, exploratory, and diffuse in organizing its materials. Thus its subsequent shift into the expository mode signals a change in the film's assertions about its own authoritative knowledge.

Roger & Me: Moore, "the strange child," mugs for the camera.

In the prologue, Moore generally situates himself as a small-town, working-class individual, subjected to all the media spectacles with which General Motors and Flint, Michigan, alternately disguise and proclaim their allegiance to American capitalism. The segment evokes what Nichols calls "a sense of constraint and over-determination" in the town's history and its residents' identity ("Voice" 23). Moore's narration ironically contrasts his childhood naïveté with his adult political sophistication. It also resembles the testimony of the subjects in any interactive film: Moore's narration acknowledges his limited perspective as a town resident. As the most complex sequence of the entire film, the exposition is worth considering in some detail.

Moore skillfully interweaves his personal and family background with that of his hometown and General Motors. He begins by noting in a confessional tone that "I was kind of a strange child" over shots of him making faces and gesticulating in a Popeye birthday costume. After more home movie footage of him swinging, walking in front of a baton-twirling sister, and (appropriately) bumping into the family Chevrolet sedan, Moore zooms into a close-up shot from his second birthday party, which he graphically matches with a close-up on a dancer-singer from the Pat Boone show.

He recounts how in his childlike innocence—precisely the response elicited by the Boone show and all of GM's visual spectacles—Moore thought that Boone, Dinah Shore, and his father were the only three employees at General Motors.

These images segue into Flint's parades to salute General Motors' fiftieth birthday. This includes hilarious footage from an industrial short film of marching spark plugs, Zorro, Miss America, the dancing Elks Junior Drill Team and the statue—like Mr. and Mrs. America, a middle-class family with two children on a float—all accompanied by orchestral Muzak meant to suggest industrial energy, thrills, and pride. Even Moore's voice-over humorously suggests the conquest of personal consciousness by municipal propaganda, as Moore intones the phrase repeated by the newsreel that "it's a great day alright" in Flint, Michigan. The GM publicity footage end credits appear, signaling the conclusion of the prologue's first phase.

During the second phase (in which marching Flint citizens are replaced by automotive parts on assembly lines), Moore articulates GM workers' relationship to the corporation while hilariously describing the development of his social consciousness. Again interweaving home movies and photographs, scenes from generic fiction films, and GM's promotional films, he recounts his family's history of employment at GM—his father's thirty-three years there, his mother's work for AC spark plugs, and, most notably, his Uncle LaVerne's participation in the 1937, forty-four-day sit-down strike that spawned the United Auto Workers' Union. Another General Motors promotional film speaks with dispassionate pride about the company's employees, "even those who at times cause problems."

Cutting to a home movie shot of a parent placing a crown on his head, Moore then expresses his desire to leave town, like Casey Kasem, Grand Funk Railroad, and the wives of Zuban Mehta and Don Knotts. His work at the *Michigan Voice* and *Mother Jones*, corroborated by news media reports, and his return to Michigan from San Francisco, hilariously parodied with a generic scene of a soldier returning home from World War II, complete his account of his personal history. The film suggests that the Flint layoffs began within days of his return home.

The prologue is then a quintessential instance of interactive documentary because the mix of recollections, home movies, Hollywood footage, and industrial films provide that "sense of partialness" we associate with films like *Union Maids*. Moore's sifting of material from his, Flint's, and GM's family histories is based in his particular experiences rather than in the authoritative narration of the GM documentaries. We are strongly aware here, as we cannot be in expository or observational films, of how Moore has constructed the film because of the intercutting of different kinds of footage and Moore's self-deprecating ironic narration.

It is worth noting, in passing, that this apparently free-associational collage functions like the newsreel in *Citizen Kane* (1941): it is a quick preview of the film to come, in this case providing a quick survey of how corporate capitalism *still* attempts to mystify its citizens visually and verbally, demonstrating the close intertwining of the political economy of Flint and the personal lives of its residents, and indicating the film's rhetorical organization of diverse materials. Specifically, the prologue presents events and motifs that get repeated constantly in the rest of the film. The parade with Miss America, Zorro, and the dancing Elks Club members is literally repeated with the 1980s parade that includes virtually the same elements (Zorro is replaced by Ronald McDonald; Miss America is now Miss Michigan, who is crowned Miss America after Flint's parade anyway). The old footage's marching spark plugs are echoed in the city's various spectacular schemes to lift itself up with tourism, the Auto World, and the Water Pavilion; and the narrators' blather about proud employees becomes the befuddled rationalizations of GM publicity man Tom Kay and other GM officials' statements to the press.

More important, the opening minutes demonstrate the intertwining of capitalism and the category of the personal. This is of course the crucial relationship that GM spokespeople and city officials are at pains to deny, particularly after GM's competitive policies devastate Moore's hometown. The materials out of which Moore constructs the interrelationship between personal and public spheres in the prologue—intercutting his home movies with GM's slickly produced industrial films and some newsreels—also establish Moore's adherence to the editing strategies of *Rosie the Riveter*, which set up a rhetorical contest between the statements of officialdom and the testimony of various "Rosies." The superior "truth" of Moore's home movies resides in their status as personal documents as opposed to city and corporate publicity.

More significant than the prologue's formal coherence in relation to the rest of the film is the fact that *Roger & Me* appears to sustain elements of the interactive mode, primarily through its narrative framework of a quest to meet Roger Smith and through Moore's on-camera presence. Both the quest format and Moore's appearances place "emphasis on the act of gathering information or building knowledge, the process of social and historical interpretation, and the effect of the encounter between people and filmmakers" (Nichols, *Reality* 49). Moore eschews the safety of remaining behind the camera to engage with security guards and other residents of Flint.

THE QUEST FRAMEWORK

Moore's personal audacity is admirable when he deploys it against the powerful and the privileged. He shows the debilitating effects of rampant corporate greed in the 1980s in part by demonstrating through interviews, which seem spontaneous, the callousness of the haves toward the have-nots. Whether Moore is on-camera at GM headquarters or off-camera with the wealthy women on the golf course, he is a provocateur. Many of the provocations in *Roger & Me* are delightful to watch, from the various attempts to meet Roger Smith at GM, the Grosse Pointe Yacht Club, and the Athletic Club, to the numerous confrontations with company flunkies like the woman who prevents Moore from shooting a plant closing by stating hypocritically that it is a "very private, personal time" for the GM "family." Moore here appears to be operating on the same principle of brash provocation as Ross McElwee when the latter enters his girlfriends' homes with his camera running in *Sherman's March* (1985) or as Jean Rouch when he asks the unsuspecting Landry about Marcelline's tattooed concentration camp numbers in *Chronicle of a Summer*.

The futility of Moore's quest—whereby, as in Maximilian Schell's *Marlene* (1987), the subject refuses to appear—is in Gary Crowdus's words, "an apt metaphor for corporate indifference to the public interest" (28). But as many critics pointed out, Moore's handling of less imposing interview subjects backfires. Moore's temerity at the yacht club becomes a form of verbal cruelty when he persists in questioning Miss Michigan or Flint matrons on the golf course. And as Richard Schickel observed, Moore's persona as a shuffling Candide rings absolutely false: "Far from being a hick, Moore is an experienced professional journalist who knows perfectly well that getting in to see the chairman of anything without an appointment is virtually impossible" (77).

Neither Moore nor we can know how the completely unprepared Miss America will respond to questions about plant closings or how the GM security guards will respond *precisely* to Moore's bravado. But the spontaneity of his encounters, which is rendered often in the observational aesthetic of "uncontrolled" reality in front of the camera, is undercut by our recognition that in fact Moore has orchestrated all but the fine details of this profilmic event. (Judging from *Pets or Meat*, Moore's short 1993 sequel to *Roger & Me*, Moore is irrevocably attached to the grand, apparently spontaneous yet implausible gesture. Where *Roger & Me* was organized around Moore's quest to meet Smith, *Pets or Meat* begins and ends with Moore considering whether or not to write Roger Smith a handout check for $100,000. I do believe, however, that on the evidence of his *TV Nation*, Moore's talents are best suited to the television magazine format. Here, his incisive twenty-minute demonstrations of the inanities of American life and of the mal-feasance of corporate capitalism do not have to withstand the scrutiny—or fabricate the large-scale narrative structure—that a ninety-minute feature film entails.)

At the crux of this difficulty with Moore's mixed modes are the multiva-lent functions of the interview we have noted in the expository and interac-tive modes. Ross McElwee may anticipate the response of various women to his omnipresent camera, but he is not out to prove anything in particular about the women he meets. Jean Rouch can guess that Landry doesn't rec-ognize the numbers on Marcelline's arm, but he does not ask the question to support any argument about race relations. In *Roger & Me*, however, every encounter serves to illustrate Moore's preconceived thesis about the people on-camera and their milieu. There is no possibility of contradicting or nu-ancing his position. Moore's use of interviews, combined with his voice-over, is clearly consistent with the expository mode, in which authority rests with the film and not its subjects. In short, after the prologue, Moore settles in, with all the self-righteousness of a formulaic 1930s Warner Bros. social problem film, on one villain and his unwitting underlings.

DOCUMENTAPHOBIA: SYMPTOMS AND DIAGNOSIS

Moore's use of a quest framework and the crosscutting and voice-over de-vices derive from his pathological fear of boring an audience with what he calls "a three hour movie." He suffers from what we might term "documen-taphobia." A "three hour movie" is a documentary in the expository mode, the much-maligned "illustrated lecture." "The reason people don't watch documentaries," Moore told Harlan Jacobson, "is they are so bogged down with 'Now in 1980 . . . then in '82 five thousand were called back . . . in '84 ten thousand were laid off.' . . . If you want to tell the Flint story, there's the Flint story" (interview with Jacobson 23).

Documentaphobia further led Moore to personalize Flint's story, showing that the wrong people have power. (For an incisive discussion of Moore's reductive version of events, see Bensman.) "Then why didn't I deal with the Japanese?" he asked Jacobson. "Why didn't I deal with the oil embargo? Why didn't I deal with all the other factors that aren't in the movie?" (interview with Jacobson 22). Because it would involve abstract complexities that would not have entertained the audience. Significantly, the brief passage explaining GM's strategies is the closest Moore comes to suggesting how impersonal forces (labor unions, trade and labor relations with foreign countries, the lack of government regulation, and ruthless corporate competitiveness) shaped GM's policies. This presumably is an unintentional homage to the "three hour" movie.

The illustrated lecture is, ironically, what Moore has produced. What obscures this fact is not only the interactive mode of the prologue (and its remnants in the rest of the film) but the comic tone of *Roger & Me*. The self-mocking tenor of the prologue sets up the double-edged comedy in the rest of the film: Moore may have been a "kind of a strange child," as he calls himself in the beginning, but he is nothing compared to the strange adults whom he subsequently introduces in deadpan. In fact, some critics see Moore as an ironic hero.[7] Paul Arthur is one of the most persuasive: "it is precisely Moore's confection of an ineffectual, uncertain, journalistic self that lends an Everyman quality to his social analysis" (128). Arthur further notes that after Moore has documented his own disappointments as a journalist in San Francisco, Moore's "new job as filmmaker is consistently identified with the conditions of the (often eccentric) unemployed workers; and it is predicated on their mutual failure to make the system work. Like the ex-worker who breeds rabbits to sell as either meat or pets, the filmmaker demonstrates expository skill by seeming to readjust the shape of his movie as he goes along" (Arthur 130).

The parallels Arthur suggests between Moore and Flint's unemployed are persuasive. As I have argued above, however, the improvisational nature of the film is superficial and Moore's everyman status is an improbable posture. Arthur notes this in passing by using the term "confection" to describe Moore's persona but emphasizes Moore's impostures to security guards and the like at the expense of Moore's pretenses in front of the audience. He claims that Moore "is at pains to demonstrate his good faith in meeting his announced goal" (129), but Moore's quest to meet Smith is what results precisely in a sense of Moore's bad faith.[8]

CONCLUSION

In summary, Nichols's notion of documentary modes helps us articulate some of the troubling aspects of *Roger & Me*. Michael Moore, in his attempt to escape documentary film entirely, fudges his affiliations with the expository mode. We have heard complaints like Moore's about expository documentary before, of course; they were the bread and butter of the direct cinema movement's rhetoric in the early 1960s.

Does Moore's position, filmmaking, and rhetoric signal yet another significant shift in documentary filmmaking? Paul Arthur suggests that *Roger & Me* is part of a new ethos—derived from poststructuralist thought and postmodernist form—that flouts "negative mastery" as a form of validity (*Sherman's March; Lightning over Braddock*, 1988; and *Driving Me Crazy*, 1990, are among his other examples). In all these works, the filmmakers engage in hybridization of "materials, techniques and modes of address" in an interactive mode. But their pastiche approach expresses a skepticism about "certain types of artistic mastery" and results from their self-presentation as ironic, uncontrolling antiheroes (Arthur 127), for these filmmakers gradually abandon their original projects and struggle, comically, with technical malfunctions and catastrophic setbacks. In contrast to the authoritative appeals to government agencies in 1930s government-sponsored films like *The River*, or to the power of personal perception apotheosized in direct cinema, the recent documentaries suggest that *"failure* to adequately represent the person, event or social situation stated as the film's explicit task functions as an inverted guarantee of authenticity" (Arthur 127).

Though I subscribe to Arthur's characterization of this distinctive trend (though, as he carefully notes, it is not a movement), I do not believe Moore's film is part of it. Arthur notes that "the impossible project" scheme of these films (in Moore's case, meeting Roger Smith) "disguises mechanisms of internal validation" of the film's representation of events (128). I would argue that Moore's "mechanisms of internal validation" are those devices associated with expository filmmaking (voice-over narration, crosscutting, and so on) and that they finally overwhelm Moore's localized failures (his technical difficulties and his inability to meet Smith) in the film. For despite the emphasis Moore places in his witty and complex exposition on his status as what Nichols calls "a participant witness and an active fabricator of meaning" ("Voice" 18), Moore's mastery remains intact. He is too univocal in his position, too reductive in his promotion of personal agency, and himself too conventional in his deployment of individual and media testimony to accomplish *either* a more complex film of negative mastery like *Sherman's March or* a more challenging political film like Christine Choy and Renee Tajima's sober and complex *Who Killed Vincent Chin?* (1988), which addresses the same working-class autoworker milieu as *Roger & Me*, to show how economics and politics engender the not-so-benign racist indifference of Vincent Chin's killers and their circle.

From a historical standpoint, Moore's choice of documentary modes to mix is perturbing. The interactive mode of documentary was revived in the late 1970s and early 1980s in films like *Union Maids* and *The Life and Times of Rosie the Riveter*, films that celebrated political resistance and activism as America negotiated the shift from the "me" generation's lingering aspirations for a meaningful life to the complacent Reagan era. In the prologue to *Roger & Me*, Moore similarly recounts his relatives' participation in Detroit labor activism with evident pride. Yet after everyone asked in the film dismisses the possibility of the solidarity that would make for another successful strike, the film provides no alternative point of view between the obliviousness or hot air of the members of the upper class on the one hand and the irrelevant Flint residents' struggle to survive on the other. Like *The Atomic Cafe*'s nihilistic cynicism in the face of Cold War officialdom (Glass 59), *Roger & Me* offers no hope.

Some critics have defended Moore's film on the grounds that the considerations like those I have raised about *Roger & Me* should not outweigh Moore's achievement in demonstrating vividly and humorously corporate America's indifference to the welfare of the communities in which it operates (cf. Orvell). Obviously I cannot agree. In fact, I would argue that one of the film's distinctive achievements resides in the fact that its most complex effects derive less from Moore's careful crafting of the film into a coherent whole or from his humorous attempts to overcome his "failed" mission than from Moore's unwitting alienation of even those viewers who applaud his film's politics.

NOTES

1. Moore's sentiments about documentary terminology have been echoed in Miramax's suggestion that the Academy of Motion Picture Arts and Sciences rename the "Best Documentary" award category as the "Best Nonfiction" category. Miramax apparently agrees with Moore that the term "documentary" has negative connotations and blames these connotations for the Academy's failure to nominate some of its more successful and unusual theatrical documentaries such as *Truth or Dare* (1991) and *The Thin Blue Line* (1987). See Michael Renov, "Towards a Poetics of Documentary," in *Theorizing Documentary*, ed. Michael Renov (New York: Routledge, 1993), 15.

2. There are of course alternative schemas for organizing the variety of documentary film practice: Erik Barnouw's vaguely descriptive categories such as "Prophet," "Explorer," "Reporter," "Painter" in *Documentary: A History of the Non-Fiction Film*, 2nd rev. ed. (New York: Oxford University Press, 1993); David Bordwell and Kristin Thompson's rigorous "categorical," "rhetorical," "abstract," and "associational" types of "Nonnarrative Formal Systems" in *Film Art*, 5th ed. (New York: McGraw-Hill, 1996), 128–65; or Michael Renov's more recent and functionalist

poetic typology: "to record/reveal/preserve," "to persuade/promote," "to analyze/ interrogate," "to express" (cf. Renov 12–36). While each of these models offers important insights, and many of them overlap (Bordwell and Thompson's "categorical form" is, for example, compatible with Renov's "to record/reveal/preserve" and "to analyze/interrogate"), Nichols's schema remains the most nuanced and most comprehensive available to documentary critics and historians. For a thoughtful critique of Nichols's work, see Carl Plantinga, "Blurry Boundaries, Troubling Typologies, and the Unruly Fiction Film," *Semiotica* 98, nos. 3–4 (1994): 387–96.

3. In his critique of Nichols's documentary modes, Carl Plantinga argues, among other things, that the difficulties we encounter in characterizing prevailing documentary practices in any period of documentary history undercut Nichols's chronology of modes and that Nichols's chronology/typology has a teleology that leads him to value reflexive documentary above all other modes on relatively arbitrary grounds. While I agree that elevating the reflexive documentary above all others is a product of our poststructuralist moment, I do not find that this completely invalidates Nichols's model. Since Nichols argues that all four modes have been available to documentarists throughout the form's history, I see Plantinga's insights as a reminder that Nichols's scheme should be employed with care (cf. Plantinga 1994).

4. Similarly, Renov notes that his typology of documentary impulses is also designated for conceptual clarity and subject to "friction, overlaps—even mutual determination" (21).

5. In Nichols's scheme, reflexivity—political, formal, and stylistic—can inform the expository and interactive modes. For example, *Listen to Britain* is an example of poetic exposition that emphasizes "the rhythmic and expressive elegance of [its] own form in order to celebrate the beauty of the quotidian and those values that unobtrusively sustain day-to-day endeavor" (*Reality* 35). Yet the film's poetic components also constitute a variant of stylistic reflexivity, "loosening the linkage to a historical referent in favor of more internally generated foci such as color, tonality, composition, depth of focus, rhythm, or the personalized sensibilities and perceptions of the author" (*Reality* 70).

The Jennings-McAllister film is typical of those films Nichols describes in which "rhetoric yields to poetic or evocative exposition, stressing the formal organization of the message rather than its persuasive effects; in other films representational strategies may give way to more reflexive ones, also calling greater attention to the message and the nature of argumentation than to a specific argument" (*Reality* 166n).

In short, the poetic features of *Listen to Britain* belong to two different modes, even though the expository film is informed by a confident epistemology that the reflexive film, in one of its varieties, answers with skepticism. One can reconcile these classifications by stressing the fact that *stylistic reflexivity* is not as stridently skeptical as other reflexive documentary forms. Alternately one could emphasize the sensibility of the filmmaker as a unifying factor that expresses the film's definite perspective on British wartime culture in an indirect manner. See Jim Leach's essay on *Listen to Britain* in this volume.

6. In a letter to *Premiere* magazine, Moore asked, "And where are the chronology stories from all the chronology nuts about this year's Academy Award–winning documentary feature, *Common Threads: Stories from the AIDS Quilt?* Did the people with AIDS in the movie die in the order in which they appear? Of course they didn't. But that discussion won't take place in *Premiere* or *The New Yorker* because it would be obscene. The point is, *those people died* and AIDS is a serious issue neglected by Washington" (Moore). Moore attributes the different standard for *Roger & Me* to the fact that his film deals with corporate America.

7. Carl Plantinga has mounted a similarly provocative analysis of *Roger & Me* as an inversion of the romantic/mythic quest narrative with "bankrupt donors, hopelessly incompetent helpers, and 'wise old men' who offer the worst sort of advice" (like the long-winded account of when the blood bank is open), as well as tricksters (Pat Boone, Ronald Reagan, Robert Schuller) who are supposed to heal the city and don't. Drawing on Hayden White's concept of tropes of discourse, Plantinga rightly sees the prevailing trope of the film as irony. Cf. Plantinga, "Roger and History and Irony and Me," *Michigan Academician* 24 (1992): 511–20.

8. Moore's bad faith is apparent as well in his treatment of his subjects. As Kael puts it, "Moore is the only one the movie takes straight. (Almost everybody else is a fun-house case.)" (91). By default, we side with the man beside and behind the camera, and at the editing bench, whose most compelling virtues are his political consciousness and his sense of humor. It is refreshing to see Moore treat the Flint residents with humor rather than with the paralyzing sentimentalism that Brian Winston locates in the Grierson movement's depiction of victims. But Moore takes the exploitative potential of the documentary film (as articulated by Calvin Pryluck) and puts it to a time-honored end: comedy's reactionary predilection for humor at the expense of the marginalized.

Miles Orvell has mounted a rousing defense of *Roger & Me*, pointing out that not all the laid-off workers in *Roger & Me* are ridiculed; some are shown with dignity and righteous anger at Smith and GM (for example, the lady who could use a "few choice words" about Smith after one of the plant closings). Making use in passing of Nichols's typology, he contrasts *Roger & Me* with Barbara Kopple's *American Dream* (1991), which in traditional documentary fashion elicits our sympathy for the unemployed strikers.

WORKS CITED

Arthur, Paul. "Jargons of Authenticity (Three American Moments)." In *Theorizing Documentary*, ed. Michael Renov, 108–34. New York: Routledge, 1993.

Bensman, David. "*Roger & Me:* Narrow, Simplistic, Wrong." *New York Times,* March 2, 1990, sec. A, 33.

Bernstein, Richard. "*Roger & Me:* Documentary? Satire? or Both?" *New York Times,* February 1, 1990, sec. C, 20.

Bordwell, David. *Narration in the Fiction Film.* Madison: University of Wisconsin Press, 1985.

Canby, Vincent. "An American Death in a Troubled Time." *New York Times,* March 11, 1988, sec. C, 22.

Collins, Glenn. "A Self-Taught Filmmaker Creates a Comic Hit." *New York Times,* September 28, 1989, sec. C, 15, 20.

Crowdus, Gary. "*Roger & Me.*" *Cineaste* 17, no. 4 (1990): 27–30.

Glass, Fred. "*The Atomic Cafe.*" *Film Quarterly* 36, no. 3 (1983): 51–59.

Hall, Jeanne. "Realism as a Style in Cinema Verité: A Critical Analysis of *Primary.*" *Cinema Journal* 30, no. 4 (1991): 24–50.

Hoberman, J. "Standing on Ceremonies." *Village Voice,* March 15, 1988, 62.

Kael, Pauline. "Melodrama/Cartoon/Mess." *New Yorker,* January 1990, 90–93.

Klawans, Stuart. "Films." *The Nation,* October 30, 1989, 505.

Moore, Michael. "Michael and Me." Interview with Harlan Jacobson. *Film Comment* 25, no. 6 (1989): 16–18, 20, 22–26.

———. "Who Framed *Roger & Me?*" *Premiere,* July 1990, 12.

Nichols, Bill. *Representing Reality: Issues and Concepts in Documentary.* Bloomington: Indiana University Press, 1991.

———. "The Voice of Documentary." *Film Quarterly* 36, no. 3 (1983): 17–30.

Orvell, Miles. "Documentary Film and the Power of Interrogation: *American Dream* and *Roger & Me.*" *Film Quarterly* 48, no. 2 (1994–1995): 10–18.

Plantinga, Carl. "Blurry Boundaries, Troubling Typologies, and the Unruly Fiction Film." *Semiotica* 98, nos. 3–4 (1994): 387–96.

Pryluck, Calvin. "We Are All Outsiders." In *New Challenges for Documentary,* ed. Alan Rosenthal, 255–68. Berkeley: University of California Press, 1990.

Renov, Michael. "Towards a Poetics of Documentary." In *Theorizing Documentary,* ed. Renov, 12–36. New York: Routledge, 1993.

Schickel, Richard. "Imposing on Reality." *Time,* January 8, 1990, 77.

Schwartz, John, with Louis Aguilar. "The Film That Ran over GM." *Newsweek,* January 15, 1990, 52.

Williams, Linda. "Mirrors without Memories: Truth, History, and the New Documentary." *Film Quarterly* 46, no. 3 (1993): 9–21. Reprinted in this volume as "Mirrors without Memories: Truth, History, and *The Thin Blue Line*" (chapter 23).

Winston, Brian. "The Tradition of the Victim in Griersonian Documentary." In *New Challenges for Documentary,* ed. Alan Rosenthal, 269–87. Berkeley: University of California Press, 1990.

Chapter 25

SILENCE AND ITS OPPOSITE

Expressions of Race in *Tongues Untied*

Sheila Petty

When Marlon Riggs's *Tongues Untied* (1989), a video by, for, and about black gay men, was broadcast on American public television in 1991, it unleashed a wave of unprecedented controversy and heated debate fueled by right-wing conservatives and their supporters in Congress. In an obvious attempt to win office by exploiting homophobia during his 1992 election campaign, candidate Pat Buchanan used a clip from the video in a television ad to accuse President Bush of misusing taxpayers' money to fund "pornographic art." Ironically enough, the clip chosen for the ad focused on white men's exposed buttocks, and neither the ad nor the media reports about it referred to the production context or the goals of the video itself. According to Riggs, this appropriation by white hegemony was also racist and "amounted to the erasure of black gay men from a work designed to empower and affirm us" (interview with Grundmann 53). Viewed today, *Tongues Untied* still possesses the power to challenge, shock, enrage, and reveal. The voice in which the video speaks is personal and confrontational. It interrogates rather than provides answers, and perhaps it is the passion with which the video questions black gay identity, and the maelstrom in which it is forged, that is the essential heart of the power of *Tongues Untied*.

When Marlon Riggs died on April 5, 1994, at the age of thirty-seven, he had directed, in addition to *Tongues Untied,* two other major documentary works, *Ethnic Notions* (1986) and *Color Adjustment* (1992), as well as several shorter videos. However, it was the highly political and lyrical form of *Tongues Untied,* with its open celebration of black gay content, that not only challenged contemporary notions of the documentary tradition but revolutionized black film- and videomaking in general. Indeed, the video moves beyond the tradition of black independent documentary realism pioneered by African American filmmakers such as William Greaves, St. Clair Bourne, Henry Hampton, Louis Massiah, and Carroll Parrot Blue (Mercer 22) by expanding the ways in which media are used to tell stories about "our lives as black people" (Riggs quoted in Mercer 23).[1]

The creation of *Tongues Untied* was inspired by Riggs's desire to make a video to illustrate "all the poetry that was coming out by black gay men" (Riggs interview with Kleinhans and Lesage 119). Interested in documenting the art and interaction taking place in such venues as the Other Countries Workshop in New York, Riggs wanted poems that would lend themselves to visual translation in a video medium.[2] Benefiting from interaction with poets like Essex Hemphill,[3] Riggs searched for works, conversational in structure and style, that expressed the same passion that he felt toward his own black gay identity. This search, in turn, inspired his own writing, and Riggs "wanted to use everything in the way the poems did, with words and phrases coded for the black community or the black gay community" (Riggs interview with Kleinhans and Lesage 120). Thus the concept of *Tongues Untied* expanded beyond that of a documentary dealing specifically with black gay poetry to include a deeply personal exploration of Riggs's own experience as a black gay man.

Tongues Untied is truly a breakthrough documentary, for it penetrated "the walls of silence by which oppressive norms and taboos erase any 'evidence of being' among black lesbians and gay men" (Mercer 22). Although Riggs is considered among the first to speak out and give open voice to the black gay male experience in Western cinema (Mercer 22), he does not construct a monolithic representation of black gay identity. Rather, Riggs advocates the construction of an "open-ended black sexuality" (Reid 124) that is in a constant process of (re)negotiation. Through the use of personal monologues placed at critical points in the video, Riggs foregrounds his personal journey toward black gay identity and provides a unifying frame for the video's multiple agendas. In fact, the monologues themselves, both his and others', are so integrated with the poetry in the text that the very notion of authorship is often blurred. This lack of distinction between poetry and personal recollection, between authorship and utterance, creates ambivalent narrative spaces that are at once confirmatory and confrontational. Riggs achieves this by politicizing silence and the act of speaking in order to structure representations and negotiations of race and sexuality. Thus Riggs's own experience, and those of the black poets, become universalized as metaphorical constructs of black gay identities. This leads to a proliferation of voices and gives the video its sense of polyphony.

The narrative premise of the video is very complex because Riggs negotiates not within one cultural space but four: black culture, white culture, gay culture, and black gay culture. This makes generalizations, either about his narrative structure or his thematic material, almost impossible. There is something musical in the video's structure, particularly evidenced by the interdependence of visual and auditory rhythms and the poetic use of language. *Tongues Untied* is at once a symphony on race, culture, and sexuality, and these threads are so tightly intertwined that it is virtually impossible to extricate a single thread and discuss it independently of the others.

It could be argued that the video possesses a literal symphonic form, complete with prelude, exposition, development, recapitulation, and coda.[4] In *Tongues Untied,* the "prelude" at the beginning of the video provides the general historical and cultural context in which black gay identities will eventually be located. Riggs creates a theme-and-variation structure: the "prelude" introduces themes that will be restated and transformed into layered variations by adding and changing textures and densities of narration, visual systems, and ideological structures. Most important, the use of repetition and restatement forges the central organizing principle facilitating Riggs's exploration of a wide variety of issues without sacrificing narrative clarity or cohesiveness.

In the "prelude," Riggs begins by hailing a specific audience through the use of voice-over narration.[5] The words "brother to brother" are chanted over a black screen that is disrupted by black-and-white images of young black men moving in slow motion. Having stated that his "intended primary audience was really focussed on black gay men" (Riggs interview with Kleinhans and Lesage 122), Riggs uses the images of young black men to initiate a process that will eventually posit specific black gay identities as natural expressions within the larger realities of African American culture.

The sequence further develops with a color long shot of young black men greeting each other on a basketball court. Riggs introduces the notion of ambiguous or contradictory space through narration of a poem: to the uninitiated eye, the images could be of any young black men, but the use of coded words such as "girlfriend" and "Miss Thang" suggests that these young men, the space they occupy, and the language itself might all possess double meanings. By employing several performers in the narration and subverting the notion of authorship, Riggs appears to be presenting the poem as both a singular and plural experience. This implies the existence of a cultural gestalt by underscoring the commonality and shared nature of African American experience.

The poem begins with an acknowledgment of the existence of a pattern of "silence" within African American culture. The speaker tells of being refused entry to a jewelry store because he is black and therefore a "thief." Riggs dramatizes the poem with visual irony: the racist incident is predicated on the depersonalized view that all black men are thieves. He then takes this example of systemic racism and places it in visual counterargument to a series of slow motion close-ups of young black men, some of whom address the camera directly. Thus the close-ups become personalized and the subjects are individualized in a way that is denied them by the dehumanizing racist incident.

The sequence also introduces the issue of silence versus the act of speaking out. The speaker of the poem is able to share with his intimates the ordinary details of life but feels constrained from discussing the racist incident, except in the context of anger. The hurt that such racism engenders is deeply internalized but not forgotten or forgiven: silence becomes a way to "grin and bear it"[6] but does not provide resolution. Riggs then politicizes the relationship between such silence and unresolved rage by associating its articulation with images of social unrest and police brutality directed at black males. The narration and the images become causally linked, suggesting that such hurt, thus internalized, translates into violence.

This is further illustrated as the sequence progresses and the camera slowly zooms in from a medium close-up to a close-up on a photo of a black man, again personalized through direct address. The zoom is spatially interrupted by intertitles—"Howard Beach, Virginia Beach, Yusef Murder, Crack, AIDS, Black Men, Endangered Species?"—each representing a landmark incident of violence or a social issue affecting African American culture. By interrupting the personal space of the photograph with the intertitles, Riggs suggests that individual identity is both disrupted and realized within larger cultural and political realities.

The "exposition" section of *Tongues Untied* begins with Riggs locating himself and his personal experience within the video's narrative space. Having posited a construction of passive silence that is culturally specific, Riggs catalyzes the construction by expanding on the ambiguity of its power. This is accomplished on both narrative and visual levels by positioning slow-motion, medium long shots of Riggs himself dancing naked contiguously with the following poem: "silence is my shield, it crushes, silence is my cloak, it smothers, silence is my sword, it cuts both ways, silence is the deadliest weapon." Riggs's nudity and well-muscled physical appearance skirt the stereotype of the brutish black man, but this is powerfully deconstructed by the vulnerability created as Riggs uses his hands to shield his face. Balanced between power and defenselessness, the movement is enhanced by slow motion and dramatically illustrates the ambiguity of the narration that describes silence as both protective and destructive. The sequence ends with a moving exhortation to black gay men to end the legacy of silence by speaking out together as a community. Thus Riggs takes the notion of silence as a passive coping mechanism and translates it into the action of "untying tongues."

Tongues Untied is a consequence of the absence, certainly in 1989, of black gay discourse in African American history and culture. This video reflects not only a personal struggle to legitimize identity but also the struggle of the entire black gay community to do so. However, in order to create a presence in the void, Riggs must first initiate a process of discarding codes and revealing the specifics of black gay realities. This community exists in an invisible relationship to the larger expression of African American culture, and in the "exposition" Riggs seeks to expose or "out" the community, much as he openly proclaims his own relationship to this narrative space.

Riggs uses codes both to situate his community in and to differentiate it from mainstream expressions of black culture. In the context of *Tongues Untied,* Riggs outs, or "reads," the black gay community by making transparent the coded act of "snapping" fingers: as Riggs has observed, "the Snap! can be as emotionally and politically charged as a clenched fist; can punctuate debate and dialogue like an exclamation point, a comma, an ellipsis; or can altogether negate the need for words among those who are adept at decoding its nuanced meanings" ("Black Macho" 392). Associated as it is with the "fine art of insults" (Becquer 8), the outing of Snap! and its identification as a uniquely black gay discursive practice is actually a declaration of defiance. Riggs is stating that the black gay community, with its own expressions of culture, exists whether or not its mode of being is recognized or accepted by the mainstream black community.

In the "Snap Rap" sequence, Riggs deconstructs the musical practice of "rap" and subverts the form for his own discursive practices by the infusion of black gay ideology. Riggs uses group shots of black gay men snapping in unison to visually underscore the notion of an invisible community suddenly choosing to visibly and defiantly declare their mutual association. This use of the group, or community, will come to have an enhanced meaning as the video unfolds because Riggs, having revealed the existence of an identifiable black gay community, will now proceed to demonstrate the cultural isolation experienced by its individual members.

Expanding, in the "exposition," on the devices of direct address and disruption of personal space first introduced in the "prelude," Riggs places his own personal experience of black gay reality within the larger expression of both black and white culture through a series of monologues that chronicles his struggle to establish a constructive black gay identity. Riggs is shot in direct address, in a loosely framed close-up, and positioned slightly left-of-center in the frame. He begins by stating, "I heard my calling by age six. We had a word for boys like me." The monologue space is disrupted by the intercutting of an extreme close-up shot of a young, black male mouth grunting out the word "Punk." The first disruption is unpleasant and intrusive, but not threatening. This swiftly changes as Riggs, now in a tighter close-up, reveals how he and his best friend "practiced" kissing until his friend's brother caught them. A new word, "homo," is introduced as the narrative space of the close-up is disrupted by a new and more mature black male mouth, which expands on the term, adding the invectives "punk, faggot, freak." As Riggs relates how "best friend became worst enemy," a third disruption occurs when a white, male mouth chants "mother-fuckin' coon." The monologue continues with Riggs's description of dislocation from both the black and white communities as he is bused to Hephzibah Junior High School and then placed as one of only two blacks in the advanced class. Tension rises with the incorporation of two additional disruptions: the first is a white mouth that spits out "Niggers, go home" and the second is a black mouth that declares "Uncle Tom." As the name-calling escalates into menace, Riggs's personal space contracts as he is framed in progressively tighter close-ups. In the final disruption sequence, the shots of the mouths are intercut, and the effect of collision between the angles is that of Riggs being crushed and pounded by the violence of the epithets.

In the final shot of this sequence, Riggs is fragmented by an extreme close-up that concentrates on his eyes as he rearticulates the notion of silence proffered in the "prelude" by declaring, "Cornered by identities I never wanted to claim, I ran fast, hard, and deep inside myself where it was still silent, safe." Here, Riggs actively demonstrates why the roots of silence grow in the black gay community and why they run so deep within it. The shots of mouths suggest that the prejudice and racism faced by black gay men are systemic and thus linked to the same dehumanizing processes exhibited by the racist jeweler in the "prelude." Riggs creates a variation on this theme by implying, through the combination of black mouths and white, that in the case of black gay men the prejudice is not only systemic but cross-cultural as well. Thus black gay men are isolated both by the inescapable racism of the dominant white culture as well as by "Black America's pervasive cultural homophobia" (Riggs, "Black Macho" 390) that make invisibility and deception seem inevitable, even desirable, as survival strategies. The fear of identification as a black gay is underscored by the sequence in which several black men attack and beat a gay brother while a voice-over poem bitingly observes: "Left, in a bloody pool, he [the victim]

Tongues Untied: Marlon Riggs addresses the camera directly, discussing his personal experience as a black gay man.

waited for the police, ambulance, the kindness of brethren, or Jesus to pick up his messages." This is clearly a society, both black and white, in which open declarations of sexual difference engender violence.

Since identification with mainstream black culture is problematic and potentially dangerous for black gays, gravitation toward white gay culture seems somewhat inescapable, as white gays theoretically share certain interests with them, at least in terms of surviving systemic homophobia and violence. But as Riggs illustrates in the developing "exposition," this is a troubled relationship fueled by, among other factors, the absence of positive black images with which black gays might identify. Beginning with a series of slow-motion color shots of white gays, which recall the black and white shots of young blacks from the "prelude," Riggs transforms the device from a statement of black male community to one of white gay community. He then offers a series of "positive" shots from *Blue Boy* magazine with its white icons and contrasts these with those of black "slaves" in chains and leather; "comic," grossly obese black women; and drawings of muscular black men with exaggerated penises. The implication is that power and desirability in gay reality are determined by the dominant white culture, just as they are in the heterosexual community, underscoring the ambiguities of identity and negative stereotypes that black gay men must negotiate. As Riggs's narration reveals, even though he is intent on his search for his "reflection, love and affirmation" in an environment of "vanilla," he is nevertheless aware of a deep dysfunction in his own cultural context. Despite "sharing" sexual orientation with white gays, Riggs reveals, again in tight close-up and direct camera address, that he remains "an invisible man. I had no shadow, no substance, no place, no history, no reflection. I was an alien, unseen and seen, unwanted. Here, as in Hephzibah, I was a nigger. Still." This realization becomes the central inquiry of the video's "development" section: can black gay identities find expression within the larger African American mainstream culture?

Beginning the "development" section with a series of quick shots, Riggs provides several views or constructions of homosexual stereotypes that occur in mainstream African American culture. These shots echo those of the "exposition" in that they are extreme close-ups of male mouths, and the attitudes of homosexuality they espouse are negative: a preacher quotes homophobic doctrine from the Bible; a black activist questions the inclusion of black gays in his cause; another man asks what type of role model black gays provide for children. Once these "voices" are introduced, they are intercut with a close-up of Essex Hemphill, whose personal space is disrupted by the intrusive editing.

The use of close-up and disruption of space is transformed by substituting the overlapping of voices from the extreme close-ups of mouths for the straight cuts of the "exposition." The poetry, presented in voice-over rather than actively articulated by Hemphill, questions his passive silence in the face of the negative stereotypes espoused by the mouths. Emphasized by waves of overlapping sound, the relationship of these elements to Hemphill's evocative close-up invokes a sense of identity adrift in a wave of political, social, and religious imprecations. When the black activist demands to know, "Come the final throw-down, is he black or gay?" the schism in which black gay identity exists is painfully exposed, just as it is in the "exposition" when Riggs realizes the meaning of "homo." As the voice-over narration dramatically illustrates, this question is fraught with impossibility: "How do you choose one eye over the other, this half of the brain over that or, in words this brother might understand, which does he value most? His left nut or his right?" The sequence offers Riggs's position that it is impossible in fact to separate the thread of race from the thread of sexuality and that the act of privileging one over the other leads to diminishment of identity.

Riggs adds to this a sharp critique of "Hollywood's Black Pack" (Riggs, "Black Macho" 392), African American artists who have the power to shape

public representations of black experience. Clips from homophobic rou-
tines performed by Eddie Murphy and scenes of homophobic content from
Spike Lee's *School Daze* (1988) reinforce the negative stereotypes with
which black gay men are burdened. The cumulative shame evoked by all
these judgments is accentuated by Hemphill's silence and his lowered,
averted gaze.

The sequence climaxes in a tightly structured montage that combines
the shots of the assault and robbery of the black gay man (from the "exposition") with shots of the preacher, the activist, Essex Hemphill's passive close-up, Eddie Murphy, and *School Daze.* By such an association,
Riggs suggests that the roots of violence against black gays are found in
both their own passivity and the unchallenged and glorified homophobia
within mainstream African American culture. When the montage ends,
Hemphill begins to speak on-camera, giving active voice and resistance
to these detractors and the anger they engender. It both reprises the discourse of anger and yearning introduced in the "prelude" and culminates
in multiple voices all expressing articulations of anger and cultural isolation as black and white photographs of black gay men follow one another
onscreen.

As Riggs has observed, "*Tongues Untied* tries to undo the legacy of silence about Black Gay life" (interview with Simmons 21), but it appears
that this cannot be achieved without black gay men assuming responsibility for empowering their own lives. In the "development" section, Riggs
asserts that the ultimate act of colonization occurs among/between black
gays themselves because of their refusal to acknowledge their own common existence. In a monologue, Riggs describes how, while walking in
the predominantly white gay community of the Castro, he noticed the approach of another black gay man but chose not to meet his eyes as they
passed. A slow-motion, long-to-medium shot of Riggs walking down the
street toward the camera dissolves into a close-up still shot of another man.
For an instant, both men appear suspended together on the screen, but the
shots "pass" from one to the other without any real contact.

Riggs problematizes the types of gazes and identification between black
gay men: the act of denial evoked by the physical action of looking away and
refusing eye contact is a recognition of shame and negation, an affirmation
of inferiority. For Riggs, it is an acknowledgment of all the ways in which
black gay men have internalized the negative valuations that dominant white
society and mainstream black culture have invested in them and thus become complicit with the shame of the moment (interview with Harris 9). By
employing a "disempowering" gaze, Riggs appears to suggest that black gay

men are encoding themselves as "Other": "an essential Other against whom Black men and boys maturing, struggling with self-doubt, anxiety, feelings of political, economic, social, and sexual inadequacy—even impotence—can always measure themselves and by comparison seem strong, adept, empowered, superior." The dismantling of this bias is critical and Riggs advocates that black gays construct a new, independent space, "not of peace, harmony, and sunshine, no, but truth. Simple, shameless, brazen truth. . . . Listen" (Riggs, "Black Macho" 390–91).

In the last major section of the video, the "recapitulation," and for the first time since the "Snap Rap" sequence in the "exposition," Riggs presents shots of black gay men as a cohesive social group, discussing issues and passions close to their community. By displacing articulations of anger and isolation with depictions of diverse black gay experiences, Riggs suggests that empowerment must come from within the black gay community through self-acceptance before social change can be effected. This is underscored as the group shots give way to a dolly shot of two black gay men walking and discussing voguing: as differences between practices in New York and Washington, D.C., become evident, one of the men comments, "Each state, each gay community does different things." As in the earlier "Snap Rap" sequence in the "exposition," Riggs "outs" the practice of voguing by creating in its slow-motion photography and distortion of movement a defiant embrace of all that is overtly black and gay. As Marcos Becquer remarks, "the elements united in voguing coalesce around a critique (and here also an appropriation) of dominant culture, while simultaneously connecting with popular African diasporic practices and gay-identified attitudes" (11). Riggs, therefore, issues a challenge and claims with pride specific "sexual" grounds for his community, as the video openly, perhaps even defiantly, identifies its unique cultural difference. Furthermore, through shots of gay activist marches and the explicit exhortation to "Come Out Tonight," Riggs urges the black gay community not only to proclaim its existence but to take responsibility for its own emancipation. This suggests that "ending the silence" has both personal and political responsibilities.

Building on the idea of community, Riggs initiates an exploration of black, gay desire or, as the voice-over poetry describes it, "the unending search for what is utterly precious." In a series of shots depicting gay black men in social environments such as clubs, Riggs shows men embracing, dancing, and exchanging looks of desire while poetic narration presents contrasting expressions of sexual desire. Combined with slow motion and the sound of a slow heartbeat, the digitized images invoke a feeling of time

Tongues Untied: Ending the silence—an exploration of male homoerotic desire.

and life suspended. This is reflected in the poetic narration as Essex Hemphill, again in close-up, provides a forthright celebration of love between black gay men as he asks, "Who dares tell us that we are poor and powerless? We keep treasure any king would count as dear." Riggs offers the explicit images, both visual and narrative, of black men making love without apology, rationalization, or justification for the existence of black gay desire. As he himself has commented, "There is no debate about whether my life is right or wrong. It is right—period!" (interview with Simmons 21).

But there are inherent risks attached to a black gay lifestyle, and Riggs demonstrates that he is very aware of them as he takes a lyrical exploration of personal power and sexual delight and transforms it, with bitter irony, into a somber discourse on AIDS. The sequence begins with a direct address close-up of a black man chanting, so quickly that the words are almost unintelligible, "Now we think as we fuck." This is disrupted by another direct address close-up, of Hemphill, as he relates how each sexual encounter results in the risk of a "lethal leak" in the condom and exposure to AIDS. These two elements are intercut for "orgasmic" rhythm, and as the sequence builds to climax, Riggs reprises a third element: a close-up image of himself being kissed, from the "exposition." It becomes graphically apparent that the landscape of black gay identity has been irrevocably transformed by the incurable virus.

Riggs builds this sequence by moving from the individual consequences of AIDS to the cost to the community at large. Starting with a close-up of himself, and the acknowledgment that "I found a time bomb ticking in my blood," Riggs fades to a series of brief, still shots of obituaries of black gay men, a restatement of a similar device used in the "prelude." The toll of AIDS is vividly illustrated as the sound of a heartbeat, which had begun with the explicit images of black men making love, fades and the obituaries fly by with increasing speed until only the ticking of a clock, the "time bomb," is heard. Riggs finally freezes on an extreme close-up of a black man, focusing on the eyes, as there is silence. Then, in voice-over, Riggs says, "I listen for my own silent implosion."

With the resumption of the heartbeat, Riggs begins the process of locating the struggle of the black gay community within the resonance of "older, stronger rhythms." Still images of black activists like Harriet Tubman and Frederick Douglass appear, culminating with that of Martin Luther King. As a black spiritual is heard, Riggs posits the black gay struggle for cultural autonomy as part of the ongoing historical struggle for political and cultural equality as being shared with the African American community generally. This is further reinforced as the video dissolves from stock footage of earlier civil rights marches to shots of more recent gay activist demonstrations.

The "coda" begins with a final blank screen after the credits fade, as words chanted on the sound track offer the spectator the heart of the video: "Black men loving black men. A call to action. A call to action." This fragment of theme extracted from the video as a whole is significant in identifying Riggs's artistic rationale. It underscores his desire to address the wrongs that have been done by his own community to black gay men (interview with Simmons 21) and to recoup black gay identity as a vibrant and constructive force.

Riggs is uninterested in either balance or objectivity but rather considers *Tongues Untied* as an attempt to counter what he views as the displacement of the black gay as "Other" within his own community ("Black Macho" 393). By "untying tongues" and daring to give voice and image to that which remains culturally taboo, Riggs succeeds in simultaneously exposing and dismantling cultural barriers. By closing with Joseph Beam's quote, "Black men loving Black men is *the* revolutionary act," Riggs invites controversy and demonstrates that *Tongues Untied* is uncompromising in its insistence that black gay men can and must take responsibility for declaring their worth to society.

Notes

I would like to thank V. Borden, C. Cunningham, D. L. McGregor, and C. Moore for discussing this essay with me and offering so many creative comments.

1. See Mark A. Reid, *Redefining Black Film* (Berkeley: University of California Press, 1993) and Gladstone Yearwood, ed., *Black Cinema Aesthetics: Issues in Independent Black Filmmaking* (Athens: Ohio University Center for Afro-American Studies, 1982) for further discussion on how black documentary filmmakers and their films became an important part of the American documentary tradition.

2. Information regarding Riggs's preference for working in video is sketchy. However, a reasonable inference can be made that his choice of video is linked to his extensive background in journalism.

3. The poetry and performance of Essex Hemphill play a prominent role in the video. Marlon Riggs has said that "Hemphill has probably published as much if not more than any other black gay poet in this country. His work moves me extremely just reading it, and it did so before I ever met or heard him" (interview with Kleinhans and Lesage 120).

4. The following are brief definitions of the musical terms used metaphorically in this essay: prelude—an introductory movement that sets the stage for a more substantial movement; exposition—the main thematic material of a movement; development—the further presentation of thematic material presented in the exposition; recapitulation—a return of the first theme and other material from the exposition; and coda—a short motif extracted from the exposition.

5. According to John Fiske, "In responding to the call, in recognizing that it is *us* being spoken to, we implicitly accept the discourse's definition of 'us,' or, to put it another way, we adopt the subject position proposed for us by the discourse" (Fiske 53).

6. All quotations, unless indicated otherwise, are taken directly from the video.

Works Cited

Becquer, Marcos. "Snap!thology and Other Discursive Practices in *Tongues Untied.*" *Wide Angle* 13, no. 2 (1991): 6–17.

Fiske, John. *Television Culture.* New York: Routledge, 1990.

Mercer, Kobena. "Black Is . . . Black Ain't." *Sight and Sound* 4, no. 8 (1994): 22–23.

Reid, Mark A. *Redefining Black Film.* Berkeley: University of California Press, 1993.

Riggs, Marlon T. "Black Macho Revisited: Reflections of a Snap! Queen." *Black American Literature Forum* 25, no. 2 (1991): 389–94.

———. "Cultural Healing: An Interview with Marlon Riggs." Interview by Lyle Ashton Harris. *Afterimage* 18, no. 8 (1991): 8–11.

———. "Interview with Marlon Riggs: Listening to the Heartbeat." Interview by Chuck Kleinhans and Julia Lesage. *Jump Cut* 36 (1991): 119–26.

———. "New Agendas in Black Filmmaking: An Interview with Marlon Riggs." Interview by Roy Grundmann. *Cineaste* 19, nos. 2–3 (1992): 52–54.

———. "Tongues Untied: An Interview with Marlon Riggs." Interview by Ron Simmons. *Black Film Review* 5, no. 3 (1989): 20–22.

Yearwood, Gladstone L., ed. *Black Cinema Aesthetics: Issues in Independent Black Filmmaking*. Athens: Ohio University Center for Afro-American Studies, 1982.

Chapter 26

Containing Fire

Performance in *Paris Is Burning*

Caryl Flinn

The question of the performative has always dogged documentary. Traditional wisdom maintains that one should not stage or imitate reality; instead, the documentary filmmaker is supposed to capture it. Conventional criticism takes documentary's more performative features—conspicuous signs of manipulation such as editing or restaging events—and places them against a stable, irrefutable "reality" believed to exist (indeed, preexist) beyond the text. Since the time of Flaherty, reenactments have been singled out for special opprobrium, as if a reproduced performance threatened the existence of documentary proper. As Bill Nichols notes, "Documentaries run some risk of credibility in reenacting an event: the special indexical bond between image and historical referent is ruptured. . . . It has the status of an imaginary event, however tightly based on historical fact" (21). Documentaries in the 1990s like Jennie Livingston's *Paris Is Burning* (1990) and documentary criticism—influenced by poststructuralist and postmodernist theory—have cast the concept of a preexisting "reality" and its attendant notions of authenticity, truth, and objectivity into permanent question (e.g., Allen, McGarry, Nichols, Rosenthal). In fact, it is no stretch to say that documentary films, in many ways more so than other cinematic forms, reveal the constructed—indeed, performative—nature of the world around us.

Paris Is Burning makes immediately clear the investment in performance. The film, which documents a Harlem subculture of gay Latino and black men, shows the men attending elaborate balls; there, dressed in extravagantly detailed outfits and makeup, contestants "walk," competing for awards in categories like "town and country," "schoolgirl," and "executive realness." As if aware of the uninitiated nature of its likely spectator, the film offers a lexicon of terms like "mopping," "voguing," and "realness," which are either explained or enacted. Reenactment and performance thus play center stage in the film, and the film's critics were quick to revel in its spectacular, stunning show.

While *Paris* appears to have no actual reenactments (the balls were recorded by Livingston as they occurred in New York City), the drag queens in the balls "reenact" social, sexual, racial, and economic identities (e.g., military officers, members of the leisure class) they have encountered countless times before in the media. In other words, the performances do not stage anything experienced by the ballgoers themselves: these sexual, economic, and racial roles are largely unavailable to them. The film shows how lifestyle, identity, and, indeed, "realness" are all based on the repetition of images, acts, and performances already in circulation. It tacitly assumes that performance is "real," that there is no such thing as a reality beyond performance. As Lisa Henderson writes, "The performances expose the constructedness of image and identity in the world at large. As the balls and the film make strikingly clear, everyone is in drag" (116). Perhaps nowhere is the point better made than in the glimpses we get of passersby in the street, which Livingston cleverly juxtaposes with scenes of the voguers. Because we have seen many identities acted out in the balls, these people, the purported norm against which the ballgoers are compared, look every bit as "made-up" as their flamboyant counterparts (where is "executive realness" best performed?). The effect is unsettling and, for the many critics who praised the sequence, humorous.

Initially, *Paris Is Burning* seems to accomplish two things: it disrupts the conception of a stable, preexisting reality that is neutral or unmediated—one need only consider "realness" as a key ballroom category. It also, by focusing on cross-gender, cross-class, and cross-race performances, challenges the notion of identity as natural, biologically guaranteed, or "real." In other words, gender, and perhaps racial identity (scholars have been more reluctant to argue the latter), is not something settled by the body. Like contemporary gender theory, *Paris* seems to posit that none of the various parts of the body "under" the clothes—skin, sexual organs, genetic codes "within" that body—guarantees our identities as women, men, gay or heterosexual, or as people of color. Livingston herself notes that she had always been "impressed by drag queens, because they prove that gender is a construction" (quoted in Bailey 26). The stakes in these assertions are considerable, not just for issues pertaining to documentary but for the very way our identities are carved out. As Livingston herself asserts, "the act of transforming yourself is a political act" (quoted in Bailey 26).

It is hard to disagree with Livingston on that point, but it is worth exploring how *Paris Is Burning* offers its particular transformations. "Who," as one scholar asks, "has historically had greater access to transformation?" (Cvetkovich 160). How is "successful" transformation measured? This essay will look at ways that *Paris* destabilizes conventional notions of reality, gender, and identity; we will see that it also reinscribes traditional perspectives on performance, keeping them separate from the realm of social effectivity. In this way, the film's treatment of performance, display, and theatricality suggests that *Paris* is not altogether as deconstructive as many have claimed.[1]

WHAT *PARIS* BURNS

Paris Is Burning was intensively covered and, for the most part, remarkably well received by the press. Critics lauded what they considered Livingston's unsentimental and nonjudgmental look into the "Paris" subculture. "Like the best documentaries," wrote Terrence Rafferty, "*Paris* does its subjects the honor of not understanding them too readily. . . . The movie is a sympathetic observation of a specialized, private world; it doesn't feel like a violation or an intrusion" (73). Livingston's ethnography was almost unanimously considered unpatronizing, one that gave voice to a community that, Madonna aside, would otherwise have gone unnoticed. "The result," wrote another critic, "could have been an exploitative freak show, but Livingston simply observes" (Travers 60). Several of *Paris*'s North American reviewers compared it favorably to Michael Moore's commercially successful *Roger & Me* (1989). The two documentaries, in fact, share a number of similarities, not the least of which is their send-up of images and behavior supported by corporate America. Both films highlight the elusive nature of their semiotic/corporate "sponsors": Moore doggedly and unsuccessfully pursues the man behind the economic and social devastation of Flint, Michigan; the white privilege and positions "vogued" in the Harlem balls are similarly unlocatable for most of their participants. Despite their invisibility, then, the "centers" of both films exert considerable effects, leaving marks and traces everywhere.

Just as the stabilizing center of the film is absent, so too no steady notion of reality or identity seems to be offered, particularly at the level of gender. The continual barrage of personalities on parade demonstrates the extent to which identity does not exist apart from what is "put on."

Paris Is Burning: The gay balls reveal gender as performance.

Considering the film's general challenge to authenticity, its "absent center" and lack of stabilizing terms and binarisms, it might be read as the quintessential postmodern text, blurring and complicating distinctions between real and constructed, natural and performed, as well as the codes sustaining sexual, racial, and class differences. Indeed, for many critics, *Paris* suggests just how fragile and tentative the boundaries between performance and the natural (or fiction and "realness") actually are. The film's apparent destruction of binary logic is noted by Jackie Goldsby, who writes that it "dislocat[es] the oppositions of male/female, colored/white, power/ disenfranchisement, margin/center" (110). This is not to say, however, that the film ignores the social effects that those differences produce. By emphasizing the ballgoers' fantasies and ambitions—qualities conventionally associated with individuality—*Paris* shows the extent to which desires are socially and commercially produced and consumed. The balls, says Pepper LaBeija, speaking not just for herself, exist as "our fantasies." And the film imputes a certain liberating quality to them, or at least this is what the majority of its critics maintain. To quote Rafferty again: "*Paris Is Burning* has its share of sobering, even tragic moments, but its spirit is buoyant, because it never strays too far from the crazy exuberance of the ballrooms" (73–74).

As Rafferty's remarks make clear, the film's "crazy exuberance" and presumed liberatory power (we shall question liberatory for whom) emerge from its performative dimension. Indeed, *Paris* lavishly organizes itself around spectacle and theatricality, spending most of its time in the balls, either in preparation for the competitions or in dramatizing performance categories. The film's sense of display is also crucial to its political endeavors, since the groups depicted have been, for all their bodacious flair, largely *invisible* to the mainstream world. The widespread assumption here is that to remain unseen is to remain voiceless and that to gain representation is to achieve a certain amount of power or self-determination. Indeed, a substantial tradition of cinema and literary criticism follows this idea, maintaining that a text that reflexively foregrounds its aesthetic and formal conventions *makes visible* ideological forces that conventionally go unseen. *Paris* certainly sits within this tradition, showing how the roles and rules we live by are not timeless, natural, or (invisibly) set in stone but are socially and historically derived, and thus open to change. Since subjectivity is standardly "produced through certain exclusionary practices that *do not 'show,'*" revealing them becomes a crucially important task (Butler 2, my emphasis).

Without question, the contestants at the Harlem balls offer reproductions of reproductions. Who looks most like the bangee boy who harassed them on the way to the ball? Here identities, like the notion of "realness," have no stabilizing point of origins, a perspective that enjoys particular currency in recent feminist and queer theories of identity. Judith Butler's *Gender Trouble,* for instance, places great weight on drag as a performative practice that disrupts authoritative, heterosexual models or norms.[2] For Butler, gender is a simulacrum based, much like the structure of documentaries such as *Paris,* on an unavailable center or absence. All gender identity—heterosexuality emphatically included—is nothing more than a series of repetitive acts, acts that copy a nonexistent original model. "Gender," Butler writes, "is . . . performatively produced"; it "is the repeated stylization of the body, a set of repeated acts . . . that congeal over time to produce the appearance of substance, of a natural sort of being" (Butler 24, 33). Livingston's film very much supports Butler's already classic contention that gay is to straight not as copy to original but as copy to copy. It, too, exposes the myth of a "proper" or "natural" (heterosexual) identity—even though this myth boasts considerable power (a point painfully made for some participants of *Paris*'s world). As Dorian Carey, one of the older drag queens, puts it: "Realness is to be able to blend. If you can pass the untrained or even the trained eye and not give away the fact you're gay, that's when it's real. . . . The idea of realness is to look as much as possible as your straight counterpart." And then, teasing out some of the disturbing implications of the equation of realness and heterosexuality, Carey notes: "It's really a case of going back into the closet . . . you erase all the mistakes, all the flaws, all the giveaways to make the illusion perfect."

As Carey's remarks begin to suggest, the mere display of ideological machinations does not guarantee their subversion: consider how realness involves "erasure" and a desire to blend in, so that one's gayness (and, one might add, one's racial and economic status) *doesn't* appear. Consider also, as noted above, the fact that white men are largely invisible in *Paris* and that gay men of color are socially and representationally invisible *but for* Livingston's film. The choice to place gay men of color "center stage" opens a number of questions concerning visibility and performance, especially given the film's concern with sexual, economic, and racial "passing." And what explains the straight, white, mainstream press's infatuation with the film? Were spectators supposed to appreciate the skill of the contestants' performances as women, all the while knowing that men are "really" underneath, as in *The Crying Game* (1992)? Or are they supposed to take in the spectacle in all its exotic ethnicity and "spirit"?

Who Is Watching?

A performance, as most theorists agree, is always *for* someone, and the issue of "who is watching, and how" becomes extremely important for ethnographic films—particularly those that, like *Paris,* concentrate on performance and theatricality. The film's status as an ethnographic text and its use of several traditional ethnographic techniques have in fact generated most of the criticism it has received. As Ann Cvetkovich argues, "The interview format, for example, draws upon realist and empiricist epistemologies that assume that truth can be obtained from the testimony of subjects speaking in their own voices" (Cvetkovich 163). For Bill Nichols, ethnographic filmmaking (which he compares to pornography) more generally works in an observational mode that sharply separates performer from spectator, obliging the observed group to function as Other (cf. Nichols, especially the coauthored chapter "Pornography, Ethnography, and the Discourses of Power"). Certainly this strategy is not restricted to the domain of documentary (or pornography)—one thinks of contemporaneous Hollywood films ostensibly sympathetic but ultimately patronizing to people of color, like *Mississippi Burning* (1988) or *Geronimo: An American Legend* (1994)—but the documentary, given its long association with the unadorned, the authentic, and the real, raises the issue with particular urgency. Ethnographic cinema always runs the risk of ethnocentrism, of affirming the power of the viewer at the expense of the Other, despite even the most sympathetic intentions.

For Peggy Phelan, ethnographic matters undermine the ambiguity that Livingston's film otherwise achieves; she notes that the spectators *within* the film are positioned and constructed quite differently than those *outside* the film watching: "In keeping with the law of the genre of ethnographic film, Livingston addresses her spectator as external to the community" (102). As we shall see, this issue of externality is extremely important to an analysis of the film.

In order to mask the implicit imbalance between spectator and observed, ethnographic films will often establish a protagonist whom Nichols labels "one of us" to lend order and establish the terms by which other characters' actions are made meaningful. In so doing, the character reconsolidates the power of observer over observed, since the spectator can now identify *with* the "Other" along with enjoying otherness at a distance. Now, while *Paris* gives us no clear leading character, plenty of character *traits* are offered up to viewers as points of "entry" and identification, leading one reviewer to argue that "we understand we are voyeurs, ultimately of ourselves, as reflected by the mirror the voguers are holding up to us" (Dunphy D6). The walkers' ambitions for self-invention and advancement, for instance, are disturbingly familiar. As Phelan explains, "The stories told in *Paris* are compatible with the myths of American identity—myths which center on white men's struggle to invent and reinvent their identities in the moment" (106). According to this position, the "us" to whom the film might point is the invisible white male of capitalist culture. bell hooks makes the point with even more force:

> The whiteness celebrated in *Paris Is Burning* is not just any old brand of whiteness but rather that brutal imperial ruling-class capitalist patriarchal whiteness that presents itself—its way of life—as the only meaningful life there is. What could be more reassuring to a white public . . . than a documentary affirming that colonized, victimized, exploited, black folks are all too willing to be complicit in perpetuating the fantasy that ruling-class white culture is the quintessential site of unrestricted joy, freedom, power, and pleasure. (149)

For hooks and Phelan, the whiteness underlying the ballgoers' fantasies reproduces the whiteness of the film's presumed spectator. Other critics have wondered whether Livingston's film should shoulder responsibility for the whiteness (and the heterosexuality) of the ballgoers' idealized images. As

Goldsby explains, for instance, the ballgoers' "desires are wholly logical within the scheme of consumer capitalism" (111).

UNHEARD/INVISIBLE PERFORMANCE

> The assumption of objectivity is false. . . . As soon as one points a camera, objectivity is romantic hype. With any cut at all, objectivity fades away.
>
> Emile De Antonio (quoted in Zheutlin 235)

The critical debate over objectivity leans heavily on the question of who speaks and how that speech is arranged by a particular film. With surprising frequency, the topic is perceived literally, that is, as an issue of voice-over narration, and the criticism surrounding *Paris Is Burning* proves no exception. Countless reviews of the film praised Livingston for "letting the participants speak for themselves" (Soehnlein 54), and even Livingston maintained "that in *Paris Is Burning* people are really speaking for themselves for the first time" (quoted in Ogilvie).

It is worth noting the irony in praising *Paris Is Burning* for letting the walkers "express themselves," since the film tries to destabilize the notion of an authentic self that might be expressed in the first place. Just *whose* self are we seeing, for instance, when Pepper LaBeija walks the runway or, for that matter, when she addresses the camera in her house? Acutely aware of the political sensitivities involved in the issue of appropriation, Livingston is at pains not to usurp her subjects' voices with her own. Her initial written project proposal states this aim clearly: "This documentary will allow individuals to tell their own stories in their own words, with little reliance on scripted narration" ("Proposal" 1).[3] But here as well the decision has repercussions, and Livingston has been roundly criticized for her failure to examine her own position as observer in *Paris:* Why does she leave her presence unacknowledged? Why does Livingston never emerge onscreen? Or, for the biographically inclined, why does Livingston's "identity" as a lesbian remain unremarked?

For bell hooks, this lack of self-consciousness gives grounds for considerable suspicion. "Since [Livingston's] presence as white woman/lesbian filmmaker is 'absent' from *Paris Is Burning*," she writes, "it is easy for viewers to imagine that they are watching an ethnographic film documenting the life of black gay 'natives' and not recognize that they are watching a work shaped and formed by a perspective and standpoint specific to Livingston. By cinematically masking this reality (we hear her ask questions but never see her), Livingston does not oppose the way hegemonic whiteness 'represents' blackness, but rather assumes an imperial overseeing position that is in no way progressive or counter-hegemonic" (hooks 151). hooks makes an important point here: because the observing gaze has been institutionally and historically aligned with whiteness, *not* to acknowledge it is in a real sense to reproduce it. (hooks doesn't explore, however, how homosexuality or the "queer look" complicates the hegemony of this dominant gaze.) She is one of the film's harshest critics; and while her argument raises crucial points, it occasionally confuses Livingston's position *within* racist culture with the director's own probable political position ("Her inability to assume such a position [as acknowledged outsider] without rigorous interrogation of intent is rooted in the politics of race and racism" [hooks 153]).

What ultimately concerns hooks though is not so much the absence of Jennie Livingston as the film's omission of an historical framework. For hooks, Livingston should have explored the African and African American contexts of the culture she was documenting.[4] But another critic suggests that it is precisely those historical contexts that trouble the film's "performance" of race: "The presence of a white filmmaker re-presenting a story of Harlem drag queens recalls the construction of the white 'editor' of the dictated slave narratives who 'arranges' the former slave's words for publication." With white "transcribers" of slave narratives, Shannon Sikes argues, "the 'authors' were obliged to . . . prove the authenticity and veracity of the accounts, foregrounding the 'truth' of the narratives, thereby concealing the inevitable control the intermediaries had over the slaves and the representations of slavery. One can find in numerous texts an expression similar to a 'plain, unvarnished' account taken 'from the slave's own lips' by the intermediary. Yet the intermediary nonetheless 'mastered' the words of the slave" (2–3). In this regard, *Paris*'s own relatively "unvarnished" status, with its participants "speaking for themselves," is a significant problem, as is Livingston's own somewhat shadowy status within the text.

Sikes compares other historical forms of white mastery with Livingston's film techniques, observing, for instance, similarities between the ball world of *Paris* and the Quadroon Balls of antebellum New Orleans, where "wealthy and cultured white men formally courted prospective mulatto mistresses" (Sikes 5). While the sense of spectacle was extreme in those balls, the "appearance" of women of color *outside* of these controlled spaces was strictly taboo: Louisiana law at the time actually prohibited mulatto women from "excessive attention to dress" (Sikes 5). The tragedy of Venus XTravaganza, killed by a john who discovers her "real" sex, suggests that things have not changed that much.

Such "excessive attention to dress" is still widely deemed taboo and/ or transgressive, particularly insofar as Western masculinity is concerned. Examples may be found in the racist zoot suit riots of the 1940s or in contemporary assertions of transvestism's subversive potential (cf. Garber). Men—and especially men of color—must not, it seems, be too "marked." As fashion historians have noted, modern apparel for men in the West has generally been characterized by an absence of decoration and stubbornly neutral colors, projecting an illusion of stability and "naturalness" unknown to the more erratic, decorated women's fashions (cf. Flugel). The business suit, for instance, virtually unchanged for generations, enjoys a kind of unmarked hegemony as the international outfit of "choice" of politicians and businessmen—the sartorial equivalent, one might say, of English.

Even when dressed as a man, then, as with the zoot-suiters, or with ball walkers doing "executive realness," the man who is "too much on display" assumes an otherly position that is, not coincidentally, aligned with femininity. Indeed, a battery of major theoreticians insists on the feminine status of spectacle: psychoanalyst Jacques Lacan argues that "virile display

Paris Is Burning: Venus Xtravaganza
wishes to be "a spoiled, rich white girl."

in the human being itself seem[s] feminine" (291); Laura Mulvey's classic essay, "Visual Pleasure and Narrative Cinema," aligns cinematic "to-be-looked-atness" with woman; and postmodernists like Jean Baudrillard feminize spectacle, denouncing its "seductive" capacities, and so forth. Given such elaborate discursive support, it would have been difficult for Jennie Livingston to undo the more pernicious connotations of spectacle. What remains to be seen, however, is how much of the tradition she reproduces.

It is important to underscore the extent to which race, along with fashion and gender, spectacularizes the performers and to note the degree to which whiteness remains a considerable "unsigned" presence. For while optics might teach us that blackness emerges from the absence of color, the lessons of North Atlantic culture would have whiteness function as the absence of color, beyond color: unraced. As Richard Dyer observes, "Black is always marked as a color (as the term 'colored' egregiously acknowledges), and is always particularising; whereas white is not anything really, not an identity, not a particularising quality, because it is everything—white is no color because it is all colors" (142). In this scheme, race becomes visible only on bodies of "color." Note also that the white roles emulated by the walkers in *Paris* are largely those of white women. It is not incidental that the female white body is obliged—both in the Harlem balls and elsewhere in North Atlantic culture—to signify "whiteness," for only white *male* power, disembodied and transcendent, eludes presence. The image of the white woman is necessary for the ballgoers to circulate in an economy of desire and capital, even if she is "biologically" absent in the film. Black and Latina femininity seems even more absent (and not in the least transcendent). Even though most of the *Paris* walkers are black or Latino, the vast majority of idealized images of recognizable stars or models discussed in the film's interviews or featured in its still photographs are white. As Dorian Carey wryly observes, early African American queens wanted to emulate Marilyn Monroe—not Lena Horne.

VISIBILITY

Livingston's subjects, she writes, were happy to comply with the filmmaking, being natural hams in front of mirrors and cameras:

> Certainly the people I filmed worked with me in part because I represented a chance to speak out, to be in front of a camera, to show off. Still, I hope I represented [to them] more than just a running camera, but an opportunity to begin to erase that invisibility by speaking out. I consider *Paris Is Burning* a collaboration

on the deepest level. The people who we filmed were articulate, funny and poised; while the editor and I made coherent form of all that we shot, *the documentary was truly written by the ball people themselves.* (Livingston, "Making" 2, emphasis added)

By exposing such an "invisible," marginalized culture, it might be said, after Livingston, that the film was made *for* its members, that she does not, in other words, subject them to the "discourse of domination" that scholars like Nichols associate with ethnographic filmmaking.

But Livingston's reference to the "coherence" she imposed on the film reveals the extent to which the documentary was not "written by the ball people themselves" and recalls Sikes's comments on the white editorializing of slave narratives. Indeed, two years after *Paris* was released, the *New York Times* ran a story revealing the participants' disappointment in the film, for not having given them a better shot at fame, and in Livingston, for not having compensated them better financially (Green).

Sikes and hooks raise the question whether *Paris* might be concerned less with the gratification of the desires, needs, and fantasies of the performers and spectators *in* the film than those of the spectators *outside* the film, which would confirm the apprehensions of ethnographic critics. Consider the repeated praise mainstream critics lavished on the film for its capacity to entertain: there is delight in its "buoyant" spirit (Rafferty 74) and praise for Livingston for not leaving the audience "bleak and powerless" (Webster 6). Such enthusiastic receptions of *Paris*'s feel-good pleasures rightly concern hooks, who was "disturbed by the extent to which white folks around us were 'entertained' and 'pleasured' by scenes we viewed as sad and at times tragic. . . . The laughter was never innocent. Instead it undermined the seriousness of the film, *keeping it always on the level of spectacle*" (hooks 154, my emphasis). From this perspective, the film's viewers and reviewers have responded more like excitable tourists than anything else, armed with a lexicon, their own Berlitz guide, to steer them through the foreign scenery. In fact, the intertitles comprising this lexicon provide more than terminology, since vocabulary ("mopping," "shade") is interspersed freely with characters' names (Pepper LaBeija, Octavia Saint Laurent), introducing both people and lingo as objects to get to know, facets of the same exotic show.

These are some of the concerns that show the problems in attaching a simple progressive or subversive label to Livingston's film—something many critics rushed to do. Such issues also reopen questions pertaining to performance and spectacle. What notions of performance is the film working with? What does it mean, for instance, that homosexuality be so heavily

cast in terms of role-playing? How might Livingston have contextualized
the role of theatricality in gay male culture and/or deconstructed some of
the clichés of that relationship? What is the place of *Paris* next to other pro-
drag films like *Outrageous* (1977) or *The Adventures of Priscilla, Queen of the
Desert* (1994)? We have also observed the spectacularization of race operating in the film. What of ethnicity? Latino, white, and African American cultures each have had very different historical and discursive relationships to
spectacle: how is this history repeated and/or repudiated by the film? What
relationships may be drawn among economic status, class, and spectacle?

Partly by sidestepping these questions, *Paris* raises another one: is it
enough for a subculture or a marginalized group simply to be "seen"? In
her critique of "visibility politics," Peggy Phelan argues that it is not: "While
there is a deeply ethical appeal in the desire for a more inclusive representational landscape and certainly underrepresented communities can be empowered by an enhanced visibility, the terms of this visibility often enervate
the putative power of these identities" (7). Similarly disturbed by *Paris*'s
sense of histrionic display, hooks opposes it to ritual, a term she characterizes as regionally and historically meaningful: "Much of the film's focus
on pageantry takes the ritual of the black drag ball and makes it spectacle.
Ritual is that ceremonial act that carries with it meaning and significance
beyond what appears, while spectacle functions primarily as entertaining
dramatic display" (150). Even a conservative reviewer—one of few writers
hostile to Livingston's basic ambitions—makes the same point: "The misery and alienation of these people [whom he calls "pathetic"] is *somehow lost
in the spectacle of their performances*" (Thorsell, my emphasis). Of course, as
we will see in a moment, to argue that spectacle is always and automatically vacated of meaning, or is antihistorical, is to court a certain essential-
ism. Yet the manner in which *Paris* constructs its own particular sense of
spectacle makes some of these critics' concerns understandable.

PERFORMANCE SEVERED FROM SOCIAL SPACE

Dorian Carey tells us that "The ball is a gay street gang—our street fight is a
ball." Reviewers for their part also drew parallels between the ball world and
life on the Harlem streets. Some, like Carey, stressed the competitive and
often violent nature of the two worlds; others made more general connections. "Actual life," writes one, "is never completely obliterated . . . [by the
film, whose strategies] make it something other than theater" (Howell 9).

But in fact *Paris* keeps the ball's performances and "actual life" quite
separate.⁵ Despite the considerable time spent there, the film ends up turning the balls into special, rarefied events. As Pepper LaBeija puts it, "[The

ball circuit] is like crossing into a looking glass, a wonderland. You feel 100 percent right about being gay, and that's not what it's like in the world." Presenting the ball as a refuge, a place quivering with utopian energy and desires, *Paris* carefully contrasts the world outside as a place of danger and dashed dreams. The runway category of "femme realness queen" acknowledges this, defined as it is as someone who can return home in her ball clothes unharmed. The street is where the bangees can get you, it is where you can be bashed or, as Venus XTravaganza's case makes brutally clear, killed. Significantly, though, the film shows that the threat of that outside world only affects some, and in this regard it is worth recalling the intercut footage of the white passersby. Uninvolved in anything but their own banal movement, they seem to dramatize—in a conspicuously undramatic way—the effortlessness with which their own identities, though indeed "constructed" and made up, move about the urban landscape. Their "easy casualness," as Phelan observes, "is the inimitable kernel of the Real that eludes the walkers" (104).[6] In this light, their images have little in common with those of the uptown runway performers: their "realness" is unstudied. Perhaps, then, the powerful, straight, white, middle-class norm they represent has not been as tampered with as some critics maintain.

The "outside" is also the place where success is measured, where hustling occurs, where money, images, and power circulate. Significantly, Willi Ninja is the sole voguer portrayed with a success record in this world beyond (others, like Jose XTravaganza, have done moderately well, but this is not documented by the film). *Paris* establishes Ninja's achievement through scenes of him working at a midtown dance studio, doing work for MTV, and discussing a recent tour in Japan—again, all spaces *outside* of the ball circuit. Redundantly enforcing this sense of success lying "elsewhere," a number of *Paris*'s reviewers go beyond the parameters of the film itself to track Ninja's achievements, acknowledging his work in Madonna's Blond Ambition Tour, for instance (although no one mentions his appearance in Pratibha Parmar's *A Place of Rage* [1990], an omission revealing how often "success" is measured in terms of white-sponsored culture).

That Ninja finds success "outside" of the Harlem balls is, in one sense, not surprising. But certain representational issues are nonetheless raised by situating success so squarely in the world "beyond" the balls. Despite its other boundary-bending elements, the film rather rigorously maintains certain binarisms, like that of exterior/interior. It is quite telling, for instance, that Ninja is one of the few voguers who does not cross-dress. With his masculinity coded as not "overly dressed," he appears less estranged from traditional (male, heterosexual, white) representations of power. Moreover, because Willi Ninja seems not to be "performing identity" like the others (the film shows him only as a voguer), our attention is focused on the physical skill and dexterity of his movement rather than his ability to "pass." He is also introduced differently from other house mothers in the film such as Angie XTravaganza and Pepper LaBeija. Whereas Angie and Pepper introduce themselves inside the enclosed, domestic spaces of their respective "houses," Willi is presented out of doors (Sikes 14–15), standing in front of a chain-link fence, as if defying its potential to enclose.

The effect of such details segregates the performative from the social. Indeed, Livingston's film rarely strays outside the space of the ballrooms or the houses and is largely devoted to three things: documenting the balls, showing participants as they prepare for the balls, or showing them as they dream of other performances down the road. Of itself, the focus on performance and spectacle does not automatically weaken the political or representational force of the film, for to argue that spectacle is essentially ahistorical (or mindless, colonizing, whatever) is, again, itself ahistorical and essentialist. But questions have been raised about Livingston's choice of such a spectacular subject. "Giving" (a problematic notion to begin with) such lavish representation to a disenfranchised group, as Phelan observes, does not guarantee empowerment: "If representational visibility equal[ed] power, then almost-naked young white women should be running Western culture" (10).[7]

The considerable weight *Paris Is Burning* places on contained spectacle makes its critique of "realness" difficult to situate in nonperformative situations. To be sure, allusions are made to them ("realness is when you get home without being mugged"), and other details are offered (one cross-dressed man responds to Livingston's questions while relaxing with other, noncrossdressed house members on an outdoor bench; a spirited drag queen "reads" a group of straight people taunting her in the street). And there are, of course, the whites walking about in the downtown area—for many writers the film's most dramatic crossover of artifice into a social, non-theatrical arena. But as we have had occasion to observe, there is a stubbornness with which these last figures remain untouched.

Rather than situating performance, identity, and social existence on a continuum, then, which is where the film's subject matter logically leads, *Paris* ends up generating distinctions among them. This is not to say that it fails to interrogate the put-on "realness" of reality, but there remains a sense in which the outside "real" remains less marked (indeed, according to the text's own devices, almost unmarked) than the feigned "realness" of the balls. Spectacle, in other words, is always designated as such. Performance—and its theoretical potential to denaturalize identity—is segregated, enacted only in rather internalized spaces and runways, much as the sequestered quadroon balls in the South had been.

The problem, then, is not in treating performance as a "show" but in removing it from a larger, social space.[8] We have already asked for whom that spectacular show is made, a question that revives the problem of re-enactment in documentary. To return to Nichols: "In a reenactment, the bond is still between the image and something that occurred in front of the camera but what occurred occurred *for* the camera. *It has the status of an imaginary event, however tightly based on historical fact*" (21, last emphasis added). Nichols's contention supports hooks's criticism of *Paris* for failing to historicize its subject matter; it also obliges us to consider the extent to which the important fantasies of *Paris Is Burning*'s characters are relegated to the status of "imaginary events" and consequently evacuated of social weight.

For as much as the constructed "nature" of reality or the performativity of representation and identity is asserted by documentaries—or the critics who analyze them—their actual deconstruction remains a far more elusive achievement. So, too, the emancipatory quality or progressive politics with which that deconstruction is often associated. As one critic puts the matter, "Gender is less malleable in practice than it is in theory" (Cvetkovich 158). The point is not to underestimate Livingston's attempts to explore the "political transformations" at work in the Harlem ball scene, nor is it to minimize her interest in dismantling binary structures. It is, however, to underscore the difficulty of such dismantling. It is also to note that even efforts as vital as Livingston's reproduce those structures in very significant ways.

NOTES

1. Since this essay was first written, an excellent piece on *Paris Is Burning* appeared that challenges the extent to which the denizens of *Paris* had access to subjective agency "within" the film, within the ball world, and within the legal world after the film was completed. Like the present essay, it questions the eagerness of critics to attach labels of "progressive" or "subversive" to a film perceived fundamentally as depriving its subjects of agency. See Phillip Harper, "'The Subversive Edge': *Paris Is Burning*, Social Critique, and the Limits of Subjective Agency," *Diacritics* 24, nos. 2–3 (1994): 90–103.

2. After the publication of her book, Butler frequently stressed that her notion of performance referred not to literal, theatrical performances, over which a subject would have facile control, but to performance as a discursive phenomenon. Drag, however, remains her key example.

3. While Livingston herself repeatedly stresses the expressiveness of her subjects in the film's press kit, she also acknowledges the "intense irony here, that people should express themselves by imitating a world that, if given half a chance, would spit on Black gays or at best ignore them" (Livingston, "Making" 1).

4. The film's press release shows that Livingston was aware of these historical influences (see Livingston, "Making" 4).

5. Livingston's initial ideas for the film give a similar impression: "The Children live in two worlds: the world of poor Blacks and Puerto Ricans in New York City, and the world of 'Realness,' where through costume and competition . . . they imitate and transcend—the powerful fantasy media that exclude them" (Livingston, "Proposal" 1).

6. Jami Bernard, "A Vogue's Gallery of Poses," *New York Post*, March 13, 1991, 32, writes that "it is both funny and poignant that the several 'realness' categories—Executive Realness, Schoolboy/Girl Realness—require contestants to try as hard as they can to pass for something the rest of society sees as so normal, so effortless."

7. For an approach to visibility and subculture that emphasizes visibility's potential to disrupt, see Dick Hebdige, *Hiding in the Light: On Images and Things* (London: Routledge, 1988).

8. In a similar way, some have criticized Judith Butler's position on performativity and gender identity for what they believe to be its emphasis on the private, quasi-individualistic, and volitional notion of subversive "performance" acts, in spite of Butler's efforts to discourage that reading. See, for example, Tania Modleski, *Feminism without Women: Culture and Criticism in a "Postfeminist" Age* (New York: Routledge, 1991), as well as Butler's own follow-up to *Gender Trouble, Bodies That Matter: On the Discursive Limits of "Sex"* (New York: Routledge, 1993), which includes a chapter on *Paris Is Burning*.

WORKS CITED

Allen, Jeanne. "Self-Reflexivity in Documentary." *Cine-Tracts* 1, no. 2 (1977): 37–43.

Bailey, Cameron. "*Paris Is Burning.*" *Now* (Toronto), June 13, 1991, 26.

Butler, Judith. *Bodies That Matter: On the Discursive Limits of "Sex."* New York: Routledge, 1993.

Cvetkovich, Ann. "The Powers of Seeing and Being Seen: *Truth or Dare* and *Paris Is Burning*." In *Film Theory Goes to the Movies*, ed. Jim Collins, Hilary Radner, and Ava Preacher Collins, 155–69. New York: Routledge/Los Angeles: American Film Institute, 1993.

Dunphy, Catherine. "Crossing over to Vogue Scene." *Toronto Star*, June 14, 1991, sec. D, 6.

Dyer, Richard. "White." In *The Matter of Images: Essays on Representation*, 141–63. London: Routledge, 1993.

Flugel, J. C. *The Psychology of Clothes*. London: Hogarth, 1930.

Garber, Marjorie. *Vested Interests: Cross-Dressing and Cultural Anxiety*. New York: Harper, 1993.

Goldsby, Jackie. "Queens of Language." In *Queer Looks: Perspectives on Lesbian and Gay Film and Video*, ed. Martha Gever, John Greyson, and Pratibha Parmar, 108–15. New York: Routledge, 1993.

Green, Jesse. "Film, Fame, Then Fade-Out: The Drag World in Collapse." *New York Times*, April 19, 1993, sec. B, 1, 4.

Henderson, Lisa. "*Paris Is Burning* and Academic Conservatism." *Journal of Communication* 42, no. 2 (1992): 113–21.

hooks, bell. *Black Looks: Race and Representation*. Boston: South End Press, 1992.

Howell, John. "Exits and Entrances: On Voguing." *Artforum* 27, no. 6 (1989): 9–11.

Lacan, Jacques. "The Signification of the Phallus." In *Ecrits*, trans. Alan Sheridan, 281–91. New York: Norton, 1977.

Livingston, Jennie. "Making *Paris Is Burning*." Production notes from press kit, n.d., n.p.

———. "*Paris Is Burning*: Proposal." Production notes from press kit, n.d., 1–4.

McGarry, Eileen. "Documentary, Realism, and Women's Cinema." *Women and Film* 2, no. 7 (1975): 50–59.

Nichols, Bill. *Representing Reality: Issues and Concepts in Documentary*. Bloomington: Indiana University Press, 1988.

Ogilvie, Dayne. "Tales from the Harlem Drag Balls." *XS* (Toronto), July 7, 1991, n.p.

Phelan, Peggy. *Unmarked: The Politics of Performance*. London: Routledge, 1993.

Rafferty, Terrence. "Realness." *New Yorker*, March 25, 1991, 72–74.

Rosenthal, Alan, ed. *New Challenges for Documentary*. Bloomington: Indiana University Press, 1991.

Sikes, Shannon. "*Paris Is Burning*, or Incidents in the Lives of Harlem Drag Queens as Dictated to Jennie Livingston." Unpublished ms., presented at University of Florida graduate seminar, "Cinema and Spectacle," spring 1992.

Soehnlein, Karl. "Pose, She Said." *Outweek*, June 13, 1990, 54–55, 62.

Thorsell, William. "Group Dynamics Give Rise to a New View of Morality." *Toronto Globe and Mail*, July 6, 1991, sec. D, 6.

Travers, Peter. Review of *Paris Is Burning*. *Rolling Stone*, April 4, 1991, 60.

Webster, Nancy. "Really in Vogue." *Festival Movie Listings* (Toronto), n.d., 3, 6.

Zheutlin, Barbara. "The Politics of Documentary." In *New Challenges for Documentary*, ed. Alan Rosenthal, 227–53. Berkeley: University of California Press, 1988.

Chapter 27

CONTESTED TERRITORY

Camille Billops and James Hatch's
Finding Christa

Julia Lesage

AUTOBIOGRAPHY AND THE TEXTUALITY OF DAILY LIFE

The self that everyone has is not singular but plural selves. And these selves change over time. Contemporary autobiographers, both in literature and the visual media, seek new formal strategies to bring into public consciousness images of and narratives about what some authors have called "the postmodern condition"—that is, the fact that we live in a rapidly changing world where we are multiply situated inside contradictory discourses and roles. In particular, women artists working in various media often take up the theme of the self's fragmentation, personae, layering, ambivalence, and contradictions, often refracted through the optic of interpersonal relations and the mundane business of daily life.

In the documentary film and video tradition, women making such autobiographical works thus face a specific conceptual problem. They must find formal means to "complicate" subjectivity, a strategy that goes against the grain of documentary's common incorporation of "witnesses" who speak in the first person and whom the documentarist uses to advance an argument. The documentary witnesses' most common function, then—to advance an explanatory or argumentative narrative—simplifies and reifies their subjectivity. In contrast, autobiographical documentaries by women characteristically layer contrapuntal dialogues between various voices, contradictory aspects of the maker's identity, and discrete moments of that identity across time, often a span of generations. Examples of such documentaries include Marilu Mallet's *Journal Inachevé* (*Unfinished Diary*, 1986), where Mallet, a Chilean in Quebec, examines the layers of her identity as a woman in exile, with husband and son speaking different languages; Sadie Benning's adolescent video diaries (1989–90), in which she experiments with self-definition by tracing the objects in her room, performing her image for the camera, and writing bits of social and political concerns on scraps of paper; and Rea Tajiri's *History and Memory* (1991), which examines her and her sister's need to create images to affix identity, the difficulty of doing that because of the parents' silence about their internment in the 1940s, and the historical paucity of images of the U.S. internment of Japanese Americans in World War II.

These and other contemporary autobiographical videos by women testify to the fact that the self is textual and, further, that the plurality of the self is related to its textuality. Not only do we need words and textual strategies to construct a sense of self, we also shape versions of social reality and especially the past as texts. For example, in the everyday world, this "textual" establishing of identity is accomplished by our looking at old family photos, listening to what the older generation has to say about the past, or participating in gossip, that is, asking about and adding to the stories that circulate about us and those we know. We do these things in order to establish continuity out of experience. We cannot face the succession of events as a string of discrete and discontinuous "presents," for that would render experience meaningless. In order to live in the present as persons with a continuous history, we constantly evoke memory to reexperience past images, events, and emotions (Eakin). We stubbornly persist in feeling ourselves to be "naturally" unitary, unique, and important even though this requires that we do much unconscious work to maintain ourselves as such.

Autobiography derives from our need to create a meaningful narrative of selfhood, but it also questions life's continuities. In particular, autobiographical works by women often question ideologies of the familiar, the family, and the natural, even as they evoke moments from the domestic sphere with great emotional impact. In exploring the domestic sphere, women's autobiography makes use of the daily textualizing of identity to develop aesthetic forms artfully drawn from a close observation of daily life. However, these autobiographical artists and writers also contest the bonds of domesticity. Their works detail the ideological and institutional limits on women's lives, and in this way they analyze how a woman's subjectivity is subjugated and acted upon. They record feminine masochism, the common wounding of a woman's spirit, her "colonized mind" (Lesage).[1]

FINDING CHRISTA

A contemporary documentary film that exemplifies some of these strategies of contemporary women's autobiographies is *Finding Christa* (1991), in which the mother-daughter "plot" itself becomes a figure for women's shifting subjectivities. The film's narrative, frequently an obvious dramatic reenactment, reveals the permeability of the self. African American director Camille Billops was pregnant with her daughter Christa and then raised the child for four years; the child subjected Camille to a way of life she did not want. As well, being abandoned by Camille "subjected" Christa to traumatic childhood memories that would affect the rest of her life. Each became the other's source of trauma, the other's object. As the film explores how the one's being the mother or child of the other shaped each in a way that was out of her control, *Finding Christa*'s dual story keeps challenging the "auto" in autobiography, alternately reducing one's "autobiography" to elements of the other's "biography" and vice versa.[2]

What makes this film so rich, and why it brings new concepts to light and elicits different emotions on each viewing, is that it combines so many modes of discourse. In a postmodern way, it is an unstable text, apt for representing selves in conflict and flux. The film shifts tone, from comic to thoughtful, without transition, and it incorporates many kinds of textual material: old home movie images, dramatic reenactments, songs by Christa (now Christa Victoria) and her adoptive mother (Margaret, a professional singer with the stage name of Rusty Carlyle), recollections from family and friends, orphanage records, photos as triggers for reflection, and Christa's reenacting her reunion with Camille (which had occurred about eight years before the film was made). The film is constructed around the theme of the strata and fragments of its characters' lives, and it accomplishes this theme with the structure of a mosaic.

In addition, *Finding Christa* asserts a relation between the crafting process and the fractured self: the act of re-visioning, so common in women's personal writing. As Christa enters Camille's life twenty years after Camille gave her up for adoption, the older woman can re-see herself. For Camille and perhaps also for her husband and co-director, James Hatch, making the film allows her to reconstruct something she had pushed out of her mind, a part of herself she had thought she had amputated or expelled. Her family members had condemned her for her act, and by including them as adversarial voices in this work, she looks back at how those stories had "fixed"

Finding Christa: Making the film allowed the filmmaker to reconstruct something she had pushed out of her mind.

her position in the family. She also thus disrupts any impulse to retell the story in a self-protective and unitary way.

For Christa, her primal self has been shaped by the formative effect of having been given up by her mother at age five, leading to her fractured self-image and sense of self-worth. Her getting in touch with Camille means narrativizing in a public way her old obsessive memory of loss and the limited history to which it confined her. Furthermore, the genre of a dual autobiography allows Christa a kind of retelling that is both "safe" (making a video as part of her career goal as artist/singer) and "true" (reenacting abandonment).

The film opens with this truth of abandonment. The title, *Finding Christa,* comes up over an image of a four-year-old's face, and we also see a photo taken of Christa just before she was left at the orphanage. "Christa" is written in a child's hand, and Christa's voice-over speaks the child's lament: "My last memory of you is when you drove off and left me at the Children's Home Society. I didn't understand why you left me and I felt so alone. Why did you leave me?" Yet the film's multiple discursive formations are manipulated so as to cast doubt on this scene's pathos, which offers a "simple" interpretation of the Camille-Christa story. We are asked to read the styles of filmed material complexly, judging the opinions of others for their truthfulness or bad consciousness, to fill in the life stories that are only suggested, to sympathize with people's periods of intense confusion at different moments of their lives. And the editing sets up different domains of meaning-making against each other. For some viewers, the "truth" lies in the characters' facial gestures or emotional coding of voice, and such viewers will pass much of the film looking for moments in which a character's personality will express itself most "authentically" (e.g., audio or visual signs read as indicating Camille's coldness, friends' and family members' sincerity, or Christa's petulance). Other viewers will appreciate the way that the text sets in motion multiple, conflicting narratives, perhaps seeing in the film a miniature version of domestic life, in which every family member has her own version of collective history.

Camille and Christa do not resolve their basic conflict, dating to the time Camille left Christa in the Children's Home. Their adult personalities are presented as fallible and contradictory. Instead of focusing just on the two women's motives and personalities, the film makes us equally consider how "a history" of self has to be constructed out of different vehicles of expression, ones that are motivated by forgetting, memory, and desire. Furthermore, the details in the film do not all fit together nor are all the most pertinent details about the people in the film ever given. We have only

Finding Christa: Every family member has her own version of collective history.

scanty referential information in some parts, and other segments are symbolic or inconclusive. In all its formal strategies, the film tries to preclude closure, even though desire for closure is what motivated Christa as she made contact with her birth mother, and perhaps it is also what motivated Camille as she undertook to make the film "about" that renewed contact.

Toward the end of the film, there is a key sequence between James Hatch and Christa that stages the old tensions between present and past, between what each character wants and what each gets:

Jim [reading]: "Camille signed over Christa today; the child was not concerned at all. We were rehearsing *Blackbird* those days. After rehearsing, Camille got on a crying jag about Christa. I went for a cold ten-minute walk to allow her the freedom of a real cry. And when I returned she had written a story into her journal about how a child loved a toy [Christa's eyes very wide, she looks up] but didn't care for it. So she took it to a toy doctor who fixed it but told her that if she took the toy home again [camera moving in slowly on Christa], she had to love and care for it. So the little girl, knowing she couldn't, left the toy with the doctor. [Christa's body is rigid. She puts her head down, looks up and away from Jim. He looks at her and then down, his face in shadow. He closes his book with a thump.] And that's how it was in 1961. Makes you feel abandoned all over?"

Christa: "Sometimes." [She wipes away a tear.]

Jim: "Well, I guess I read it because I feel bad sometimes, too." [He rocks, looking down at diary. She looks down, sad.]

The entire scene pits "staginess" against "authenticity." The theatricality negates our receiving Jim's diary as a simple document giving witness to the past; rather, the scene depicts how complex reading the diary becomes in the present. The composition in the frame here is as carefully planned as a portrait. Christa and Jim sit near a wall in an empty, tight space with her in center frame behind him. Christa is starkly lit with dramatic Rembrandt lighting as a stream of light from above illuminates Jim's journal and also her white blouse and face, leaving his face largely in shadow. The dramatic emphasis in the composition is on capturing her response. My own estimate as a producer is that Camille and Jim collaboratively staged the scene with Christa's participation but did not rehearse it. Christa's sad response seems too "authentic." The scene effectively plays off its tight composition against the narrative interest of Camille's diary and Christa's reexperiencing pain from the past.

In its construction and subject matter, the scene seems calculated to elicit strong emotion from Christa, but it also sets in motion a multivalent audience response. There is some hostility on both Jim and Christa's parts as they attempt to get together emotionally. Jim expresses fatherly concern toward Christa, demonstrates his ongoing support for Camille, and offers Christa the explanatory power of what he reads (the journal entry has explanatory power for the viewer as well). Christa seems forced back into reexperiencing the trauma while in a state of emotional isolation from Jim and Camille although temporarily residing in their home. As a viewer, I am torn between judging Jim and Camille harshly for staging a scene "to make Christa cry" and admiring them, especially Camille, for allowing us to see the depth of Christa's pain and for exposing us to Camille's ambivalent, even "bad," actions. To the extent that Camille here and elsewhere stages events that show her in a negative light, she earns a certain respect. The scene is staged in a minimalist yet emotionally moving way so that the audience is led to respond with their own conflicting emotions—sadness, condemnation, and respect—all at once.

We all cling to discrete images, moments, and experiences from the past. Beyond this, we develop unique ways of narrating these to others in personal conversation because we must use social life to write our personal histories, to make a story out of our life. The film here juxtaposes intersecting stories: three different people's frames of reference, emotions, and present situations in relation to their pasts. The combination of visual and verbal material in the scene hints at movements of emotion back and forth between different realms of each of the three's experiences, a choreography of interconnections. We intuit the characters' internal processes of change and loss. The story Camille had written is metaphoric, and we may attribute a range of ambivalent emotions to it. The scene itself represents Jim's contribution to Christa's understanding and emotional growth. The mixture of narratives in this scene represents different ways of knowing and remembering. For that reason, whatever interpretation we make of the scene, it is hard not to take sides with Camille, Christa, or Jim.

This scene, like many others in the film, demonstrates how family members can weave old stories into a new pattern, constructing a new collective memory. As represented in the work, and as evidenced in viewers' ambivalent and conflicted responses to it, revising family history is an edgy, painful, and incomplete process. *Finding Christa* is a public act of self-expression. In it, a reconstituted family rewrites the history of its members' personalities and constructs a public version of its mutual text. However, for the viewer, this film offers an uncomfortable "mutual" text since it is constructed around ambivalence, strong emotions, old grudges revivified, conflicting subjectivities, loss, stubbornness, and the pain of change.

Fifty Ways to Leave Your Daughter

Interviews with Camille Billops provide more information than the film does about her motives and her personal history at the time she gave Christa up for adoption in the late 1960s at age twenty-seven. As she has said:

> I went to art school at USC in 1954 after having gone to City College in Los Angeles. At USC you had the most classical education possible for artists. . . . It was a beautiful thing. Then I got pregnant, or as we say in *Finding Christa,* "knocked up." I had to change majors and go to another school. It threw me back three years, but I worked days, full time at the bank and went to school at night and finished. But at one point, I decided I didn't want to be anyone's mother. I wanted to go back to the place that I considered the crossroads. (Quoted in Meer)

> I wasn't mean; I just wasn't there. She was at a baby sitter's all the time. By the time I gave her up, I wasn't poor. I wasn't broke. I just didn't think that being an unwed mother was so special. I felt shackled. I wanted my life back. And I thought, if you care at all, then let her go. So I unmothered myself. I seized an opportunity to give her to someone who would provide a good loving home. ("Lost and Found")

In the opening section of *Finding Christa,* Camille remains content to let family members tell most of her tale. The images give a view of a middle-class black family, and the conversations among and interviews with relatives provide us with a view of the traditional black family in its moral cohesiveness and mutual love. Variously her relatives say that Camille could have let Christa stay with them, that they begged her to change her mind, that she could have let them and sitters care for the child, that she could have been known to Christa as just an aunt, or that they would have liked to visit the child in the orphanage on a regular basis. Camille says that none of them came forward to adopt the child except her brother-in-law. (That man, as told in her earlier film, *Suzanne, Suzanne* [1983], regularly beat his wife and daughter, although this information is not given in *Finding Christa.*) *Finding Christa*'s opening section is slanted to let the family tell the most damning story possible about Camille and her motives, since that is probably the story they have circulated about her in conversation for years.

Yet Camille resists others' definitions of her. Her behavior was that of an outlaw, and she made this decision just before leaving the country to travel to Egypt. Its consequences were far from tragic for her. She developed as an extremely talented artist, and she and her white husband, James Hatch, have become important archivists and historians of black arts in the United States (L. Jones, Lekatsas). Her public self in that community is another aspect of her life that she does not present, so as to set the positions in her family in sharp opposition to her from the beginning of the film.

She herself is the archetypal romantic hero, not usually seen in feminine guise. From the nineteenth century on, this figure has appeared in literature and later in film as an idealistic searcher or a creative genius who rejects established mores and lives as an outsider. Such heroes often ally themselves with political causes and are flawed, bear a wound, or act in self-destructive ways. When Christa finally meets Camille, Christa phones her mother Margaret to exclaim that Camille is a hippie (interviews confirm that Camille indeed was a flamboyant hippie in earlier years). In fact, Christa, too, is the wounded artist pursuing a quest. In presenting the lives and decisions of these two women, the film does not give either the traits of the virtuous or dutiful woman.

In many mainstream films, the main character is often a romantic hero, a reporter, detective, or artist—an outsider—who is allowed a complex subjectivity even though he may be flawed or an antihero. In many avant-garde films, which often use a diaristic or autobiographical, personal mode of address, the seer behind the camera and editing is implied to be such a person, and also implied is that he (it is usually a he) has a complex vision to which we should pay attention. When a film chooses to represent the subjectivity of someone from an oppressed group, it rarely assigns this person "the artist's" subjectivity. Camille's, and later Christa's, aggressive claim to this subjectivity, to that of artist and rebel, raises the question of whether or not ethnic subjects have the same cultural right to the ideology of individualism that has characterized the bourgeois era for several centuries. Or is the ethic of individualism and complex artistic sensibility somehow different when claimed by a person, especially a woman, of color (Mercer and Julien)?

Camille stakes out for herself the turf traditionally reserved for the white male romantic hero. She says the following about why women need to pursue this path as well as men:

Finding Christa is a plea for women to think about their choices. You should never let anyone take those choices away from you. The control words for women are moral words. They will call you a whore if you want to stand out on the street, just to find out the news. You can't hang out on that street. Men will circle and drive you away from public space. (Quoted in Meer 22)

See, that's the adventure they want to deny us, to hit the horses and ride the trail. And that's the information, that's where the news is. I don't think the news is all in the parlor; I think it's out there on the road. And those are the adventures. I mean women as adventuresome and adventurers—I like that idea. (Filmed introduction to *Finding Christa*'s television debut on PBS's *Point of View* series, 1992)

Finding Christa resists and seeks to change definitions of motherhood. For years before meeting Christa, motherhood for Camille had been what Jung would call her liminal or shadow self. The title of this section of the essay refers to a popular song, Paul Simon's "Fifty Ways to Leave Your Lover," but when I uncomfortably substitute the word "Daughter" for "Lover," the change in the phrase's connotation points to acute contradictions that often exist in the subjectivity of a "mother" but are rarely spoken, written about, or socially acknowledged. In interviews, Camille has said that she considers Margaret Liebig the hero of the film and of her life, since that woman could give Christa such a good home. The film valorizes Margaret by presenting her in a totally positive way. In particular, it is her spoken history of Christa's childhood and adolescence that is intercut against the comic montage representing Christa's failed marriage. I cite Margaret's interview at length here because within the film it represents, if not ideal family life, at least ideal motherhood:

I had my girl; I had raised her to the best of my ability, and she still was unhappy. She was jealous of everyone, she got mad about everything, but it was only because she wanted to have somebody to identify with. . . . I knew what she needed and I didn't know how to give it to her. And that was, she needed to know where her mother was, her family. . . . I said, Christa, there's something I want you to do for me. I want you to find your mother. And she was in shock. Of course, she tried to pretend that it was all right, she didn't need to do that, she was happy. And she went through this big spiel like Christa does. But all behind that, her eyes just lit up when I said that, and she said, "Do you really want me to do this?" And I said, "Yes, I want you to do this—for me."

Camille had left her address at the orphanage when placing Christa there, so the film, titled *Finding Christa,* is basically from Camille's point of view.[3] Indeed, at the end of the film, a scene showing the two mothers walking in a park arm in arm leaves Christa visually isolated. In voice-over Christa says, "You know, it's a blessing to have two mothers, but at times it can be difficult, especially when both are strong-willed people. Sometimes I feel as if I'm pulled apart, as if no one sees my side because there are two dominant sides, and I'm caught in the middle."

Camille and Margaret had agreed that because Christa wanted to become a professional singer, it was best if she moved to New York so that Camille could help her with her career. When the film concludes with the two mothers in friendship agreeing about Christa's needs, it eases the acuity of the contradictions the film earlier had presented around a mother's giving up a child. However, in interviews, Camille speaks of the new relation as still fraught with pain, ten years after her reunion with the adult child: "Whatever our relationship becomes over the years, it is something that has to be worked at very hard. We live quite separate lives. Our contact is very casual because there is still a perception of abandonment that will never be resolved. It is not simple and it is not without pain. There are days when I think, 'What did I do this for?' and days when I am sure she thinks the same thing" (quoted in Smith 38).

The whole first section of the film is echoed by a later section where Christa meets Camille's extended family. The film's emphasis on images of family, with people talking about their family memories as the mainstay of filmed conversation, has both a political and philosophical purpose. People look to families for self-definition but also rebel against them when the definitions imposed by others are too confining. In addition, for oppressed and poor communities, the family provides a network for survival, both physically and culturally. It maintains the minority culture as a culture because it preserves collective wisdom and memory. The film's layered, mosaic-like structure represents facets of identity formation and how these change historically. Its choreographing of a black family's voices is both a tribute to that kind of extended family and a challenge to it. *Finding Christa* looks at society's value systems, the values maintained by the black family, and the ones Billops wants to explore. She asserts her own story as a moral lesson about survival in contrast to the family's version of how it as a unit should survive, and of course, the family shifts with changes among its members. Earlier, Camille and James Hatch had made the film *Suzanne, Suzanne,* with accompanying music by Christa Victoria, about Camille's sister Billie and niece Suzanne. Those two women had to come to terms with the way that Suzanne's father's brutality had led to Suzanne's heroin addiction, with how his abuse was hidden behind the facade of middle-class prosperity, and with the failure of mother and daughter to unite against it or even to discuss it in private.

Both films use cinema's formal resources to choreograph the family, their voices and interpretations. As we see the many (mostly) women in the film discuss how they and others have acted, the film also uses many kinds of audio and video modes of presentation to expose both the ideology and the emotional urgency behind what they say. One of the functions of the film, it seems, is to elicit reflection on the discourses that shaped its participants. Furthermore, the collective family knowledge on which Billops builds the film is not something abstract but the negotiated, interactive, and painful process of face-to-face oral communication, something she is willing to confront again in the very making of the film.

All the talking in the film circles around the connections between love, obligation, and circumstance. Furthermore, the sometimes antagonistic positions and the back-and-forth of emotions expressed by Christa, Camille, and those who love them are often restated in a partisan way by audience members as they later discuss the film. In fact, such ambivalence and circularity characterize how we talk about family and about women's and children's roles. Camille's family had certain specific facts to discuss: the children's home, adoption, Camille's going with her lover to Egypt. Beyond that, cruel-mother stories often circulate orally among women, as well as stories of mean men and rebellious children. In recapitulating these themes, melodramas, soap operas, and talk shows draw a large female audience. This film, however, offers little of the familiar emotional frisson that such stories traditionally bring with them. For Billops, reshaping family memory is her goal as a feminist filmmaker, since she wishes to demonstrate in both *Finding Christa* and *Suzanne, Suzanne* how family memory works and what it silences.

Finding Christa creates a new way of speaking for and about African American women, especially about the black family structure and black women's experiences. African American women artists and writers have often shaped their narratives to echo patterns found in the extended family's conversation, which makes an intergenerational claim on the meaning of any one member's experience (Braham 118). A lot of work has been written on the strengths of the black family, noting how slavery kept it fragmented and how members migrated north looking for work (Davis, J. Jones, Stack). Billops considers another related aspect of the black family, that is, that men's picking up and moving on is a fact the community has tacitly accepted as a norm. For she demanded a kind of equity, reversed gender roles, and "walked out"—not knowing that she might later reinterpret this as a "feminist" act. *Finding Christa* explores what the implications of such a role reversal have meant for Camille, Christa, and Camille's extended family. Camille self-consciously reflects on her situation as a black woman artist, which she uses in the film as both a personal and cultural locus, a point from which she explores her personal history so as to trace out the social and psychic forces that have shaped her and those around her. Yet she resists being a group voice, and the film's fragmented structure precludes our coming to any concept of global identity that would characterize her or Christa.

SINCERITY, AUTHENTICITY, AND AUTHORIZATION

Ironically, at the same time that the film alternately elicits sympathy for Christa and for Camille, *Finding Christa*'s own "authority" or "sincerity" in terms of its relation to the viewer is problematic. It masks its timeline (made nearly ten years after Christa and Camille met) and mixes interview material, dramatic reenactments, family reunions, and what might be Christa's original tape recording sent to Camille as if they were all from the time that Christa first contacted Camille. My own judgment of dramatic reenactments comes from my knowledge as a video producer of how staged material looks. However, I did not know that much of the rest of the material was a reenactment until reading Camille's 1991–92 interviews, and I did not know it was almost all reenactment until Camille gave me feedback on a first version of this essay.

Some things are still unclear. For example, what parts of the film might be home movies? The section showing the family reunion where Christa meets Camille's relatives, who welcome her as kin, seems marked as original, spontaneously filmed material, showing mugging close-ups of Christa, holding her face next to each person in turn, as if to test whether they all had a family resemblance. It is impossible to judge whether this footage was shot at an originary event or staged as Christa's reunion with the relatives years after she had gotten in touch with Camille.[4] This question about home movie versus staged footage has ethical implications with which the film never deals.

At this point it is worth taking a close look at the dramatic reenactment in Camille's atelier, in which she tells her two friends that Christa has contacted her and wants to see her. In considering this sequence and, indeed, the film as a whole, I am fascinated with the probable timeline of the various kinds of filmic material used. In the studio, Careen, Camille's friend, tells the story of her own life, the pain of having her birth mother deny her the chance to enter the mother's life. If this is a performance, it is one that elicits the teller's own remembered hurt. George Wolfe tries to get Camille to respond to Christa's overture and Camille demurs. What is the date of this dramatic reenactment in Camille's work space? I assume it is a dramatic reenactment from internal visual evidence, such as change of shot setup to make traditional shot-reverse shot and over-the-shoulder-shot conversational patterns. But nowhere is it mentioned in the film that some sections are dramatic reenactments, nor is such an interpretation necessarily or even likely to be the response of viewers who see the film only once. If the date of that shoot was before Camille met Christa, which the film lets viewers easily assume, then it would mean that Camille had decided to make an autobiographical film on the subject of having abandoned her daughter before getting her not-yet-met daughter's assent.

Furthermore, we see shots of Camille greeting Christa in the airport that look like home movies of an important family event, capturing spontaneous emotional reactions. At that moment did Camille have Jim shoot such footage for a future documentary project that Christa did not know about yet? Since the film blurs all timelines and indications of the relation of its own production to originary documents, the viewer does not know. I assume that Christa did send a tape with her music on it to Camille: "I wrote a song for you," the taped phone message tells us. When Camille responds to Christa's overtures in a Christmas phone call, we hear the recording of Christa's excited voice answering the call. Is this original material or dramatic reenactment? The ethical implications are that if that were original material, it would have been illegally taped. And what hubris it would have been to tape such an intimate, spontaneous, emotionally important moment in Christa's, if not Camille's, life!

In this way, the film presents a particular problem I call the problem of "authorization." I have already indicated the way in which this work was never intended to be a culture's or group's version of the truth but rather that its makers authorized themselves to create an account of their mutual, interacting histories they deemed valuable enough to be made public. However, autobiography sets itself up in terms of what Phillipe Lejeune has called an autobiographical "pact" with the reader/viewer—that is, a pact that referential truth will be respected, that we will not be lied to. Of course, the facts of the past, what is being referred to, will be confused and mediated by texts—both present-day interviews and artifacts from the past. But as John Paul Eakin notes, the genre depends on not abusing our trust in reference.[6] This kind of trust in the authentic intentions of first-person narratives blinds even other artists to all the elements of "constructedness" in a film such as *Finding Christa*.

For example, I often teach media students, who have made documentaries and training in journalism, to respect the "facts"—that is, not to use fiction within a documentary. However, these students are often fooled by fictionalized documentaries, especially autobiographical ones or ones that seem to be made in a first-person voice. Thus, when I show certain films that seem autobiographical—for example, Jim McBride and L. M. Kit Carson's *David Holzman's Diary* (1968) or Michelle Citron's *Daughter Rite* (1979)—and then the end credits state that these works were acted, a good number of the film students in the class always express surprise because the films' setup had made them watch it according to the autobiographical pact even though their production savvy should have cued them that certain shots were impossible or improbable for autobiographical shooting. *Finding Christa* has no such information in the end credits, nor does it ever signal which shots or audio material are originary material from the time of the reunion in 1981.

The viewer receives all the interview material in the film as occurring in approximately the same time span, perhaps about a year. I think that viewers do not notice the time differences in gathering and shaping the material (which Camille said was reworked over a number of years because of the difficulty in getting funding). Most viewers probably never confront what for me as a media maker is a crucial question: at what time did the idea for the film, as it were, get born? On the sound track, the information that Camille, Christa, and Margaret give verbally provides the basic necessary exposition. The viewer, who receives the film in the span of an hour along with all of its ambivalent emotional moments, needs the exposition as the film unfolds before her so that the interviews and dramatic reenactments are all lent a certain aura of "simultaneity" and perhaps also spontaneity.

TAKING SIDES—FOR CHRISTA OR FOR CAMILLE

Finding Christa evokes a strong reaction especially since it takes as its subject matter shifting, strong, polarizing emotions. Audiences who get a chance to discuss the film are often vehemently divided, frequently siding with either Camille or Christa. I myself have widely different reactions to Christa and Camille at different viewings, reactions that call up memories of my own decision not to have children and my own ambivalent love-hate relationship with my mother. In this essay I have given a reading that favors

Camille, partly based on my reading her interviews in preparation for my writing. Furthermore, I am giving this reading as a white academic who eagerly reads works by women of color and seeks out their films and tapes to view and teach. I know that my reading cannot decode all the connotations of race and gender that the film contains, including assumptions about selfhood that circulate in the African American community the film depicts, nor can I fully appreciate how all the connotative elements are artistically worked.[7]

Rather, I have read the film for the pleasure and tension we anticipate from turning to a text by a woman that promises in its title and publicity to be about issues of motherhood and abandonment. From Christa's perspective, which I also share, the film echoes my own grudges that I carry around with me, my own stubbornness in recalling family pain, my own acute past desire for plenitude and closure in relation to my parents. Viewers who were abandoned may not get past that memory in their response to the work, while others who feel some distance from both Camille and Christa may find pleasure in viewing it as a performance and an artistic construct, enjoying its postmodern artifice.

Jeanne Braham analyzes how women's autobiography offers an invitation to women readers to enter the narrative in an emotional and analytic way. She says that the source of our empathy with the text is the way that it calls up responses in us. It resonates with our lived experience, psychological formation, or past history. In that way, an autobiographical text to which I respond, or, in this case, a viewer's strong response to Christa or Camille, interpellates or hails my subjectivity, indeed confirms it, in that another has publicly claimed what I have long known to be my truth.

Camille now considers herself a feminist but can see this decision to put Christa up for adoption as a feminist one only in retrospect: "That this was a feminist statement was a hindsight. Everyone had a problem with it. Men leave, but women are supposed to endure. Fatherless houses, unwed mothers—is that something attractive? I didn't think so, so I reversed it. They say you don't have a lot of choices but you do; you just have to have the courage to take them" (quoted in L. Jones).

For me, one of the film's virtues is that it makes viewers feel uncomfortable.[8] Camille is not a conventionally good woman, but an interesting one. The film pairs moral complexity with aesthetic richness. In terms of its themes, *Finding Christa* challenges assumptions and categories and shows alternative ways of expressing personhood, agency, and family. In viewing it repeated times, I take great pleasure in noting how the images, events, and persons are framed by the film, as well as how the people within the film frame their discussions of the past, each other, and themselves.

It is important in contemporary times that we look at the social and historical conditions that shape our caring about something, both what matters to the viewer and what matters to others, which the viewer might not under ordinary circumstances come to understand (Grossberg 82–85). Black families in the United States have always understood how their members must embrace multiple identities and how their children must learn what W. E. B. DuBois defines as "double consciousness," since all the family members will have one life inside the home and another "out there." While *Finding Christa* seems to be dealing primarily with Camille's personhood, someone who defines herself as a black artist, it is also socially mapping an intervention in the family, both the black family and everyone else's.

NOTES

1. See the application of Fanon's essay, "On Violence," from his book *The Wretched of the Earth* (1961), to the topic of women's rage in Julia Lesage, "Women's Rage," in *Marxism and the Interpretation of Culture,* ed. Cary Nelson and Lawrence Grossberg (Urbana: University of Illinois Press, 1989), 419–28.

2. I am indebted for this observation to my colleague Karen Ford. Readers who gave me important feedback include Ford, Mark Reid, Chuck Kleinhans, and Camille Billops herself.

3. The title *Finding Christa* implies that Camille found her daughter, though the film seems to belie this. In a phone conversation of January 22, 1996, Camille explained to me that the director of the Children's Home Society told her that girls in their late teens or early twenties often want to contact their birth mothers when they begin to think of marriage. When Christa was eighteen, Camille left her own and her mother's addresses with the orphanage, since the elderly mother lived only three blocks from the Children's Home. If Christa ever went back to the Children's Home seeking this information, Camille thought, she could meet her grandmother. Christa did that, though the elderly woman died before the film was made.

4. Camille later told me that the family reunions had to be restaged since the first "reunion" had occurred almost ten years earlier.

5. Again, in our conversation after Camille read this essay, she said that the audio used in the film of that Christmas phone call was original taped material from the time that Camille called Christa. In terms of the scene where Christa listens to Jim read from his diary from the time she was given up for adoption, Camille said that the shoot was staged but that Christa had never heard the material before they did the filming. Her reaction of grief was so excessive that they cut most of the crying out in the editing.

6. Autobiography criticism reflects a tension between critics who are primarily concerned with reference and those concerned with textuality. The former place an emphasis on autobiography's unique "authority" in promising the reader a "truthful," "authentic," or "sincere" version of the author's self and past (Eakin); the latter emphasize the discovery of self as the author articulates it more textually, with less importance attached to issues of verifiable reference. See Leigh Gilmore, *Autobiographies* (Ithaca: Cornell University Press, 1994) and Kathleen Ashely, Leigh Gilmore, and Gerald Peters, eds., *Autobiography and Postmodernism* (Amherst: University of Massachusetts Press, 1994).

7. I discussed with Camille whether or not she was uneasy with me as a white critic discussing the racial issues she deals with in the film, especially the black family. She indicated that she thought it was important for white critics to deal with works by artists of color. However, she said it was important for me as a white academic to acknowledge my privilege, my access to a wide range of topics to write about, my capacity to gain authority in a certain area and thus define its terms. She said a black writer cannot establish authority to study, write about, and so define white culture, Jewish culture, European culture, and so on. Black writers' authority is often limited to defining "ethnic" issues. She defined her own relation to the black community in this way: "Primarily I am what is called a border crosser. I have to go back into my ethnic group to feel good about myself, but that gets tiring. If you cross borders, you come up with a lot of information. If you stay inside, it becomes limited and uninteresting."

8. Camille said that the viewers who protest the most are adoptees. Now when showing *Finding Christa*, she asks immediately after the screening, "How many people in the room are adoptees?" acknowledging their unique perspective and inviting them to give their reactions first.

WORKS CITED

Billops, Camille. "Lost and Found." *Los Angeles Times*, June 28, 1992, "TV Times," 7.

Braham, Jeanne. *Crucial Conversations: Interpreting Contemporary American Literary Autobiographies by Women*. New York: Teachers College Press, 1995.

Davis, Angela. *Women, Culture, and Politics*. New York: Random House, 1989.

DuBois, W. E. B. *The Souls of Black Folk*. New York: Bantam, 1989.

Eakin, Paul John. *Touching the World: Reference in Autobiography*. Princeton: Princeton University Press, 1992.

Grossberg, Lawrence. *We Gotta Get out of This Place: Popular Conservatism and Postmodern Culture*. New York: Routledge, 1992.

Jones, Jacqueline. *Labor of Love, Labor of Sorrow: Black Women, Work, and the Family from Slavery to the Present*. New York: Basic Books, 1985.

Jones, Lynda. "Dream On, Dreamer." *Village Voice,* September 6, 1994, 60.

Lekatsas, Barbara. "Encounters: The Film Odyssey of Camille Billops." *Black American Literature Forum* 25, no. 2 (1991): 395–408.

Lejeune, Phillipe. *On Autobiography.* Ed. Paul John Eakin and trans. Katherine M. Leary. Minneapolis: University of Minnesota Press, 1989.

Meer, Annabelle. "Profiles and Positions." *Bomb* (1992): 22.

Mercer, Kobena, and Isaac Julien. "De Margin and De Center." *Screen* 29, no. 4 (1988): 2–10.

Smith, Patricia A. "Mother-and-Child Reunion." *Boston Globe,* June 29, 1992, 38.

Stack, Carol. *All Our Kin: Strategies for Survival in a Black Community.* New York: Harper and Row, 1974.

Chapter 28

Spike Lee's 4 *Little Girls*

The Politics of the Documentary Interview

Paula J. Massood

> I think this is a very political film. But to me, the most important
> story to tell was the story of these four little girls and let that be
> the focus. But the politics is there. It's not exempt.
>
> Spike Lee

In July 1997, Spike Lee released his first feature-length documentary film, *4 Little Girls*. Made with backing from the Home Box Office cable network, the film played briefly in theaters before it premiered on television in February 1998. Unlike the majority of Lee's fiction films about African American history, such as *Malcolm X* (1992) and *Miracle at St. Anna* (2008), *4 Little Girls* was notably lacking in controversy. In fact, it garnered wide critical acclaim, receiving Oscar and Emmy nominations among other awards. While the film's subject matter, the 1963 bombing of a southern church and the death of four young African American girls, is noteworthy in itself, its critical reception was most often based on its formal qualities rather than its content. Many critics noted, for example, Lee's "lean, straightforward documentary style" (Maslin), while others mentioned his directorial "restraint" (Armstrong) and the film's overall "lack [of] the stylistic idiosyncrasies for which the director is known" (McCarthy). In fact, Todd McCarthy of *Variety* went as far as describing the film's style as "a conventional, talking-heads-and-archival-clips approach."

In short, for what seemed like the first time, Lee had produced a conventional, noncontroversial film in which he took a back seat to his subject.

But is 4 *Little Girls* a departure from the director's more noticeably reflexive style—seen in such films as *Do the Right Thing* (1989), *Clockers* (1995), and *Bamboozled* (2000)—or does it play with documentary form less visibly? The answer to this question lies in two different, though related, factors: Lee's stylistic choices, which range from the less obvious to the blatantly self-conscious, and the press surrounding the film, which tended to deemphasize the director's role. Indeed, despite the effective removal, or "deauteuring," of Lee from 4 *Little Girls,* the film shares more similarities with than differences from his other films, both fiction and nonfiction, including a focus on African American history, a reflexive style, and an unmistakable directorial presence. The following discussion will consider this assertion by focusing on the film's formal components, especially its use and reinvention of the conventions of the documentary interview.

4 *Little Girls* opens with the strains of Joan Baez's voice performing Richard Farina's "Birmingham Sunday" (1964). The song commemorates the events of September 15, 1963, when four members of the local Ku Klux Klan set off a bomb in the basement of the 16th Baptist Church in Birmingham, Alabama. The blast killed four young girls—Denise McNair, Carole Robertson, Cynthia Wesley, and Addie Mae Collins—as they prepared to attend services that morning. This opening scene not only introduces the film's subject matter, it also sets the tone and style for what follows, in which image and sound collaborate to produce different textual meanings and audience responses.

In all, the opening to 4 *Little Girls* lasts the length of "Birmingham Sunday," or roughly four minutes. It starts with a black-and-white tracking shot of a cemetery and then cuts to archival footage of different moments in the community's history of civil rights struggles, most notably the "Children's Crusade" of May 3, 1963, when local police turned fire hoses and dogs on marchers, many of whom were children.[1] The film then cuts back to a medium long shot of the cemetery, which appears in color. As the song introduces the four girls by name, a shot of each girl's headstone appears, accompanied by a floating black-and-white cutout of her portrait. The images are intercut with more black-and-white archival footage of protests and marches, visually linking the girls' deaths to the larger political events in Birmingham from the time. As the song narrates the events, the footage alternates between historical images from the day of the bombing and present-day color footage of the church and a sculpture commemorating the tragedy. The moving camera comes to rest on a plaque dedicated to the four girls, after which the song ends and the screen cuts to black.

As Christine Acham suggests, the "the opening sequence of 4 *Little Girls* reveals the film's overall structure, which shifts between the personal history of the four families whose girls died in the bombing and the more recognizable public history of civil rights in Alabama" (163). This alternating pattern is used throughout the film; for example, the next scene focuses on Maxine and Chris McNair, Denise's parents, and starts with their recollections of meeting and falling in love while undergraduates at Tuskegee. Following this, the film switches to a section that describes the racial environment of Birmingham in the late 1950s and early 1960s. The alternating sections provide a chronological history of important people and places; for example, we are introduced to the four girls and then return to their families as they narrate different moments in their daughters' lives (including their activities on the day of the bombing and their funerals). The more "public" sections take a similar approach in introducing the history of Birmingham and explaining the black community's involvement in the civil rights movement. In other words, we are introduced to the city through the personal stories of individuals, just as we are introduced to each of the girls, suggesting the links between the private and the public in the film's representation of historical memory.

Each section, whether private or public, combines contemporary interviews with archival footage of the events or people under discussion. Like the Baez song opening the film, sound—music or speech—provides the blueprint for the accompanying images. Often scenes start with an interview subject offering insight or opinions about a particular topic (each section focuses on a single theme). Just as often, the talking head is replaced with visual evidence (in the form of either personal mementos and home movies or newsreel footage) supporting the speaker's observations, which continues in voice-over on the sound track.

The strongest examples of the complementary pairing of sound and image are found in the interviews with the girls' families that are interspersed throughout *4 Little Girls*. Following our introduction to Birmingham's history of segregation, for example, the film transitions into a section introducing Carole Robertson. The section starts with a cut to a snapshot of a smiling child and a voice-over saying, "I remember Carole as a very vivacious, lovable fourteen-year-old." The camera pans over the photograph before cutting to a medium shot of Carole's aunt, describing her niece. The section continues with this sound-image pattern—cutting to a snapshot accompanied by voice-over and then revealing the speaker in direct address—three more times (with Carole's sister, a childhood friend, and Carole's mother, Alpha) before settling on Alpha Robertson, who provides a more nuanced description of her daughter. Like the earlier reminiscences, Alpha's memories are introduced via voice-over accompanying a snapshot of Carole.

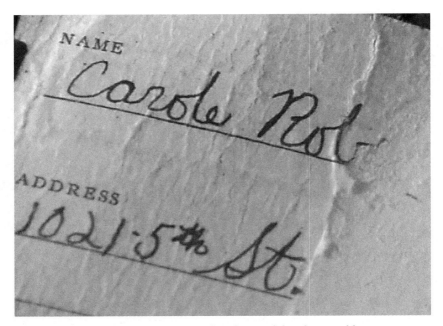

4 Little Girls: Alpha Robertson displays her deceased daughter's Bible.

The pattern of direct address–archival footage changes, however, as Alpha discusses her daughter more intimately. As she talks about Carole's involvement in the school band, for example, the images cut to close-ups of various mementos, such as the young girl's clarinet and a school scrapbook, thus providing the audience with a more personalized peek into Carole's personality. The section offers a similar treatment of Carole's involvement with the Girl Scouts. As Alpha talks, the image track cuts to close-ups of the young girl's sash and badges. The section ends as Alpha displays her daughter's Bible, which, as she explains, was with the young girl on the day of the bombing. As before, the visuals switch between close-ups of the Bible and medium close-ups of Alpha. As we watch Alpha's loving regard for these objects, Carole's presence is felt, along with her mother's overwhelming love and loss.

These more intimate sections introduce the victims and stress the trauma of the day's events and their aftermath. Interviews with former civil rights leaders and government officials, which introduce and describe the historical context, alternate with these sections. The majority of these interviews follow the same formal structure as the family sections, but they have a different function: they illustrate the forces that collided in Birmingham during the early 1960s that led to the girls' deaths. One such section occurs immediately following Alpha Robertson's discussion of her daughter, and it, like the sections on each of the girls, focuses on a single subject. In this case, the locus is Eugene "Bull" Connor, the former police commissioner of Birmingham and the individual responsible for maintaining law and order in the city at the time. The section starts with archival footage of protestors in and around the 16th Street Baptist Church and a voice-over describing one of the city's first civil rights marches. The image cuts to a close-up of the Reverend Wyatt Tee Walker (former executive director of the Southern Christian Leadership Conference [SCLC] and chief of staff for Martin Luther King Jr.) before cutting back to footage of protesters being threatened by police and dogs. This pattern continues until Walker says he told King that they could "count on Bull to do something silly."

Following Walker's statement, Connor appears in archival footage from the 1960s, giving a television address in which he details the police response to recent instances of civil disobedience in Birmingham. The section continues in a similar fashion as before as a variety of individuals describe Connor in a combination of talking heads (shot in close-up or medium close-up) or voice-over paired with archival footage or photographs. The stories are split between those focusing on Connor's reign of terror over the city's African American residents and those that attempt to understand his character. The former category includes Howell Raines, a journalist and former editor of the *New York Times,* who observes, "Bull was the manifestation of the perversity upon which segregation depended for its life . . . [he] was like the walking id of Birmingham."[2] Contrasted with such dispassionate—or theoretical—analyses of Conner are the memories of individuals directly affected by his actions, most of whom attempt to seek reasons for his behavior. For example, Tommy Wrenn, a former member of the SCLC, observes, "I used to be afraid of Bull 'til I discovered he was crazy," before relating a story of Connor arresting a blind man during a march (accompanied by archival footage).[3] In indicating the different responses of the community to Connor's actions—from outrage to puzzlement to humor—the section is tellingly poignant. Indeed, the combination of archival footage and sound succeed, through a focus on a single individual, in providing insight into the community.

Much of the archival footage in *4 Little Girls,* like that in the Bull Connor section, complements the speakers' observations, functioning in an evidentiary manner that supplements the oral histories with representations of actuality. Indeed, such sound-image stylistics are a long-established documentary convention. At key moments, however, the visuals contradict the speaker's words, thus offering a more explicit and visible model of authorial intervention than the more complementary pairings (the correspondences between image and sound are examples of Lee's less obvious manipulations). One instance of such a sound-image dialectic occurs near the beginning of the film, during one of the first times that historical context, specifically the history of Birmingham, is introduced. The section follows the introduction of Denise McNair's parents and opens with a medium shot of a train before cutting to an interview with Chris McNair. The train has no actual role in the section. Shots of it, paired with a blues sound track, metaphorically suggest the history of African American migration and set the tone for McNair's memories of moving to Birmingham in the 1950s. As McNair explains, his college degree was more of a detriment than an attribute for a black man trying to find a job and support a family in such a segregated setting.

McNair's story is followed by an interview with Circuit Judge Arthur Hanes Jr., the former defense lawyer for Robert Chambliss, one of the men found guilty of the bombing.[4] For Hanes, a wealthy white man, Birmingham was a place of economic opportunity during the 1950s and 1960s. During the interview, Hanes's direct address is replaced by voice-over paired with images of sparkling streets and bustling industry. His story is contradicted in the following interviews with Bill Baxley (former attorney general of Alabama) and Howell Raines, who discuss the city's violent past as a segregated union town. The former images of prosperity and peace are replaced by still photos of victims of lynching and other instances of racial violence. When we cut back to Hanes, who asserts that the 1950s "were a time of quietness . . . [during which Birmingham was] a wonderful place to live and raise a family," his memories are accompanied by archival footage of Klan marchers (including some children) and additional photos of lynching victims. By the time the section transitions into a selection of African American recollections of Birmingham's strict color line—"It was an awful time for young people to grow up in this city," recalls one speaker—the film's message is clear: attitudes from the past continue in the contemporary United States, at least in the form of Judge Arthur Hanes Jr. Indeed, in its *Rashomon*-like rendering of American history, *4 Little Girls* argues that racism continues to deform American life—a point more fully made in the film's references to a spate of suspicious fires that burned down black churches in the mid-1990s.

This observation is made all the more apparent in one of the film's most-discussed sections, an interview with George Wallace, former governor of Alabama, a famously adamant supporter of segregation and onetime presidential candidate.[5] Lasting a total of six minutes, the Wallace interview follows the Connor section, which ends on a close-up of Chris McNair suggesting, "Connor couldn't exist without the nods from the status quo people . . . the big boys." After the shot is held momentarily, the image cuts to archival footage of George Wallace's infamous 1963 inaugural speech in which he claimed "Segregation Now, Segregation Tomorrow, and Segregation Forever!" What follows first appears to be similar in format to previous sections: various individuals provide observations either in direct address or through voice-over accompanied by archival footage. But this is where the similarities end. Instead, the combination of personal memories and archival footage, along with Wallace's onscreen behavior, function dialectically to present a portrait of a man whose past views may not have evolved.

In order to grasp this observation, it is important to analyze the formal elements of the section, and here I've found Leger Grindon's "poetics" of the documentary interview to be a useful tool in understanding the dynamics of the interviews in *4 Little Girls*. Grindon's poetics consist of five categories, including "presence, perspective, pictorial context, performance, and polyvalence" (6) that contribute to the meaning and effect of the documentary interview. While the first four categories encompass the interview's style and content and refer to elements such as directorial presence and supporting materials, the last category, polyvalence, refers to its overall "effect" (Grindon 7). In other words, in what ways does the heteroglossia of stylistic choices contribute to the message one takes away from the film? While Grindon's categories may be somewhat deceiving in their focus on a documentary's form, they can be productively utilized—though in a different order here—to analyze the overall meaning of a specific interview and an entire film, particularly one like *4 Little Girls*, which critics have read as lacking Lee's customary didacticism but which the director characterizes as "a very political film."

A brief summary of the Wallace interview suggests the ways in which Lee utilized "pictorial context," or the inclusion of "independent imagery," as either a "complement [or] counterpoint to the verbal testimony of the speaker" (Grindon 7). The footage of Wallace's inauguration, for example, cuts to an extreme close-up of Reverend Shuttlesworth (former pastor of the 16th Street Baptist Church) observing, "George Wallace was the cause of many people's deaths." The following archival footage functions ironically by offering another Wallace public address in which the governor commends the white people of Birmingham for their restraint during the protests (protests, which we've seen from the Connor section, that included hoses and dogs, woundings and arrests). From here the section shifts to a close-up of Tommy Wrenn as he opines, "George Wallace was the dynamic expression of the derangement of white people." As Wrenn speaks, the film cuts to present-day footage of a now enfeebled Wallace, who appears

in close-up, first in color and then in a black-and-white film stock that resembles the archival footage in tone. The cut is emphasized aurally on the
sound track—which sonically accentuates Wallace's presence onscreen
with a discordant note—and visually through a rapid zoom into an extreme
close-up of his face. At this point, Wallace is silent, and the film cuts back to
archival footage of the then governor blocking the door of the University of
Alabama in order to fight the federal mandate for desegregation.[6] It is only
after a brief interview with former U.S. attorney general Nicholas Katzenbach, who expresses the irritation he felt toward Wallace on that day, that
the governor speaks.[7]

Wallace's interview takes up less than half the section's actual screen
time. His direct address is interspersed with archival footage and interviews
with other people, thus providing a similar effect as the earlier section on
segregation in Birmingham, in which multiple individuals voice often-
contradicting opinions on a subject. During his first speaking appearance,
the former governor is tightly framed in close-up with little background
showing. His speech is subtitled, suggesting the debilitating effects of the
Parkinson's disease that took his life soon after the film's release. Wallace,
addressing the camera, quickly switches from discussing segregation as
an accepted part of southern life during the 1960s and announces that
his "best friend is a black man" before introducing his personal assistant/
nurse, Ed Holcey. The film then cuts to Alpha Robertson, who observes,
"George Wallace was George Wallace. He's seeking redemption now, I understand." Her words act as a sound bridge to and voice-over for a mixture
of images of the governor from the past and present (some of the latter is
in black and white), and introduce a kernel of doubt regarding the governor's intentions in the interview. From Robertson's voice-over, we return to
Wallace (in close-up and color) explaining that he gave textbooks to black
children (in an attempt to suggest his political largesse) before the film
then cuts to Chris McNair, who begins to describe Wallace's personality.
The section returns to the former governor one last time, when he again
forces a visibly uncomfortable Holcey into the frame. The camera rests on
a medium shot of Wallace bracketed by Holcey (standing) on the left and
another assistant (sitting) on the right. Rather than punctuating the section further, the scene cuts to archival footage leading into another section
focusing on the civil rights movement in Birmingham.

What should be obvious from this description of the scene is that
Wallace's interview differs from most of the other historical accounts we see
and hear in 4 Little Girls. First, it is more self-contained than the other interviews, which tend to be spread throughout the film; for example, Chris and
Maxine McNair appear throughout 4 Little Girls, as does Alpha Robertson

(the setting and costume suggest one or possibly two interview sessions). Second, it also offers a more self-consciously visible perspective on its subject. Grindon identifies perspective as "setting and camera position" or, in other words, mise-en-scène and cinematography (7). Wallace first appears in close-up with little of his surroundings visible in the frame. In most of his following appearances onscreen Wallace appears primarily in close-up or extreme close-up. In many ways this continues with the film's overall treatment of interview subjects, most of whom are also framed in close-up unless they are displaying an object of interest. Much of the time such framing suggests a sense of intimacy and trust between filmmaker and subject, as in the interviews with the girls' families and friends. In the Wallace section, however, the shot composition, particularly the extreme close-ups of his cigar or portions of his face in combination with the shifts in film stock, have a discomforting effect by projecting a somewhat distorted and monstrous visage.

To understand the effect of such framing, it is helpful to compare it to the earlier interview with Alpha Robertson, Carole Robertson's mother. The only other time that extreme close-ups appear in *4 Little Girls* is during Robertson's discussion of her daughter's belongings. In that section,

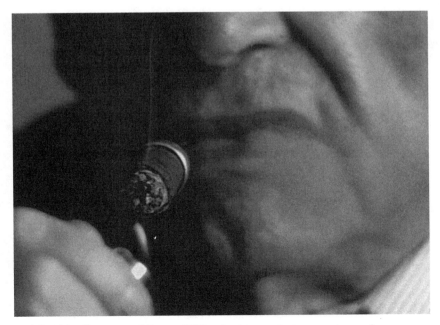

4 Little Girls: Close-ups of George Wallace's cigar project a monstrous visage.

the extreme close-ups function as punctuations to the subject's observations; for example, Alpha's discussion of Carole's involvement with the
Girl Scouts is accompanied by shots of her hands holding her daughter's
sash and her fingers pointing to various badges. In that context, the combination of extreme close-up and speech communicates a mother's love for
her lost child visually and verbally. In the Wallace interview, the extreme
close-ups are similarly anchored to speech; however, the subject is not the
speaker and the effect of the combination is different. The first time we see
Wallace in such a shot setup, for example, his face accompanies Wrenn's
words regarding the "mental derangement of white people." The second
time, Wallace's visage, intercut with an extreme close-up of his cigar, is
accompanied by Alpha Robertson's voice-over: "Sometimes I wonder if
he believed in all those things he did." The similarity in framing between
the sections—Alpha Robertson's memories of her daughter and George
Wallace then and now—ironically produces two different effects. In the
former example, we feel a connection with the dead girl; in the latter we
feel distance and, perhaps, disdain for a seemingly harmless old man who
is, nonetheless, dangerous.[8]

Near the end of the interview, Chris McNair speaks about the governor's
character and suggests that part of Wallace's behavior may have been a performance for the cameras. For Grindon, the category of performance is an
often overlooked, though central, component to the documentary film, and
many documentary filmmakers "welcome" the presence of a "star."[9] In a
number of the interviews in *4 Little Girls*, Lee "fashion[s] memorable performances" (Grindon 7) from his subjects, most notably (as is evident here)
from Chris McNair, Alpha Robertson, and Tommy Wrenn, who become the
film's stars (McNair and Robertson for their air of tragedy and Wrenn for
his humor). But Wallace's interview suggests a multiplicity of additional
meanings for documentary performance. First, Alpha Robertson and Chris
McNair's words already caution us to question Wallace's veracity by suggesting his skill as a performer. Second, Wallace himself invites such a reading
when he twice decides to pull Ed Holcey into the frame. By doing so, he
acknowledges his racist and violent legacy and gestures toward a possible
revision in which he becomes a benevolent patriarch. That he does so by
claiming interracial friendship, while casting a blind eye to the power relations involved in his relationship with Holcey, implies that he may not have
changed all that much in the intervening decades. In short, his performance
has the opposite effect of its intended purpose.

This particular interpretation returns to the question of cinematic perspective, particularly Lee's choices for shooting and framing the interview.
In the sections with Holcey, the focus shifts, by necessity, from a close-up

4 Little Girls: Spike Lee carefully frames the interview with George Wallace.

to a medium shot that allows the frame to accommodate the seated Wallace and his aide, who stands by the elder man's side. The second time we return to Wallace, the framing further expands and reveals another assistant sitting to the right of the governor. With the change in framing, Wallace's surroundings become more visible; for example, a state seal hangs on the wall behind him and a desk plate reading "George C. Wallace/Governor" is positioned prominently in the foreground. The framing at these moments has a somewhat contradictory effect. On the one hand, the presence of at least two assistants illustrates Wallace's diminished physical, if not mental, circumstances and a dependence on others (for example, his assistant on the right provides Wallace, who was hard of hearing, with written transcripts of Lee's questions). On the other hand, Wallace's surroundings suggest his continuing identification with the past, particularly with his position as governor (the plaque on Wallace's desk identifies him as governor, not the former governor, of Alabama). The mise-en-scène, therefore, subtly hints of a man still glorifying the past.

Returning to the subject of performance, it is important to note that Lee did not coax any particular reaction from Wallace during their question-and-answer session. Like many of the other interviews, the session with the former governor was shot in a single sitting with the subject answering a series of questions provided by the director (and visible on sheets of paper held in Wallace's hands). If one compares the original footage (available as a DVD extra) with its final cut, one can see that it was Wallace rather than Lee who determined the content of the section. Much like Frederick Wiseman's approach to the documentary interview in films like *Titicut Follies* (1967), Lee let his camera run uninterrupted during the sessions in *4 Little Girls*.[10] The effect of such an approach is that the filmmaker often captures revealing moments, whether intimate, emotional, social, or political. With Wallace, the long take reveals the former governor's inability to grasp contemporary race politics, despite his words to the contrary. Lee may have manipulated the look of the session through shifting color stocks and often ironic editing, but the uncut footage indicates that Wallace already had an agenda.[11]

One of the remaining categories in Grindon's poetics of the documentary interview is "polyvalence," which can be understood in two ways. First, polyvalence refers to the "overall formal effect" of an interview (Grindon 8). On its most basic level, the combination of interviews and archival footage in the section on George Wallace collapses distinctions between past and present and provides a "meta-commentary by suggesting a lack of change in Wallace's character" (Acham 171). But such a conclusion overlooks the density of the section's formal structure, whose cinematography, mise-en-scène, and performance qualities suggest a complexity of character that may even belie Lee's observation that Wallace was "pathetic."[12] Wallace appears at one and the same time as a feeble man who continues to wield power (at least over his assistants) and as a bigot who makes gestures toward political change yet resists those very same changes. In short, the Wallace section presents the former governor as a man torn between an urge to take pride in his legacy and the knowledge that his place in history may be problematic. The overall effect of the interview implies that Wallace's former urge won.

Polyvalence can also refer to the ways in which the documentary interview functions within the entire film. In *4 Little Girls,* much of the Wallace section comports with the film's other interviews, particularly those constructing a tension between differing versions of events or people. In its contradictory descriptions of the former governor, for example, the Wallace part resembles the earlier section describing the experiences of individuals on each side of the color line in Jim Crow Birmingham. But Lee's presence is more pronounced in the Wallace section than in other parts of the film. The section, for example, utilizes many of the formal strategies used elsewhere in the film, including talking heads combined with archival footage.

Most of the interviews are shot with the same camera setups—in close-up, with little surrounding space revealed in the frame—thereby focusing attention on the speaker rather than the location. While these elements suggest traces of a directorial presence behind the camera, in the Wallace section, Lee's "idiosyncrasies" become more pronounced through a collage of film stocks, varying shot composition, and performance, which destabilizes image and sound and constructs a challenging and complex representation of a seemingly harmless old man with a powerful and destructive past.

Grindon's first category—the one I've saved for last because it returns us to the subject of Lee's position as an auteur—refers to a director's presence in the documentary interview. Grindon's understanding of a filmmaker's presence is literal; a director appears in the film or not, and this has direct bearing on the final interview. Another position also exists, in which the director appears more intermittently, "occasionally acknowledging his presence with a question or offscreen comment but not intruding into the image," an approach that "allows the subject to reveal his or her personality to the viewer" (Grindon 7). This would seem to describe Lee's presence in *4 Little Girls*. In the majority of the interviews in the film, Lee has no visual or aural onscreen presence. In such scenes of directorial absence interview subjects directly address the camera and this, combined with the abundant use of close-ups and archival footage, provides the subjects with an authority over historical memory. But, as the previous discussion suggests, Lee is always present, choosing what to show and when to show it. In most of the scenes, he opts not to reveal himself literally.

In a few scenes, however, Lee is either seen or heard onscreen and each time his appearance has a different effect. The first time Lee's presence is known, for example, is in an early scene with Chris McNair, as the elder man recounts a time when he had to explain to his daughter that she was not allowed sit at a segregated lunch counter in a local department store. As McNair finishes his story, Lee is heard offscreen, asking his subject how Denise responded. As McNair answers, the camera zooms in for a tight close-up on his face and tear-filled eyes. In this case, the director's presence prompts a more emotional response from his subject. Lee's second appearance is more indirect and occurs during the Wallace interview, where the director appears symbolically, as questions on sheets of paper in the former governor's hand. In this example, we are made aware of the interaction between director and subject—and the fact that it is an interview—through Lee's traces as words and in Wallace's periodic glances at the filmmaker (rather than at the camera).[13] Lee's third and final appearance occurs late in the film in the interview with Alpha Robertson, during which she explains the anger and hatred she felt for years after the bombing. As she hesitates in her confession, Lee urges her to elaborate, much like he prompted Chris McNair in the earlier scene. The director's encouragement initiates a warm exchange between Alpha and Lee, during which their teasing repartee and the woman's observation that Lee's question "deserves an answer" suggests the trust that developed between them. In each case, Lee's literal presence tells us much about the relationship between director and subject. With McNair and Robertson, Lee's aural prompts add to the scene's intimacy and suggest an overwhelming trust and respect between the individuals engaged in the interviews. In the Wallace interview, by contrast, the director's visible presence sets up a distance the older man then awkwardly tries to bridge by reaching outside of the frame for his best friend Holcey. Like Chris McNair's tear-filled eyes in the earlier scene, the interview with Wallace is uncomfortable, but for different reasons.

But what of the other, less literal traces of the director's presence in *4 Little Girls*? Grindon's category of presence, while useful in creating an understanding of the way in which the documentary interview functions in terms of authority and legitimacy, is limited in its focus on the absence or presence of the director's body or voice within a text. As the preceding analysis of the film's cinematography, mise-en-scène, editing, and sound illustrates, Lee's fingerprints can be located all over the film, from the use of extreme close-ups in the interviews with Alpha Robertson and George Wallace, to the mixture of film stocks in a number of scenes to connect the past with the present, to the use of archival footage to either support or dispute different points in the film. While Lee may have chosen to absent himself from the screen in *4 Little Girls,* he is never absent from the frame.

The question of directorial presence returns us to the discussion of the critical responses to *4 Little Girls* and the number of reviews that credited Lee for his authorial restraint. Like Grindon's category of presence, many critics based their assessment of Lee's role in the film on his onscreen presence or absence rather than considering the film holistically. David Armstrong of the *San Francisco Examiner,* for instance, observed, "Lee's familiar face usually appears all over his movies. But this time, he has the great good sense to recognize the inherent drama of the story, and his restraint lends gravitas to a tale that has its own momentum and narrative contours." Sol Louis Siegel similarly argued that "Lee has often been a know-it-all talking down to his audience, but not here. [H]e's opted to keep his ego out of the way in organizing this emotional and volatile material." In each example, the author implies that the director's onscreen appearances are his films' weaknesses, while *4 Little Girls'* strength lies in Lee's absence.

The critical tendency to praise *4 Little Girls* because it is *not* like the director's other films has also been discussed by Jasmine Nicole Cobb and

John L. Jackson, who argue that (for the press) when "Spike 'documents' he is 'brilliant' at capturing the ostensibly real, but when he fictionalizes a black world of his own imagining, he is said to overreach . . . without a middle ground, this reading hardly ever renders Spike as an actual auteur participating in artistic expression" (253). For these authors, the film's positive reviews point to larger assumptions about documentary's connections to actuality. In such a scenario, they argue, Lee's documentary work is privileged because he "becomes a mere chronicler of fact, an emptied cipher, and not truly a self-conscious auteur" (Cobb and Jackson 255)—nothing more than a recorder of preexisting reality. In other words, Lee's politics are more legitimate when they refer to actual events than when he creates his own, equally plausible, though fictional, scenarios.

But what of Lee's position as an auteur? Is it any different here than in his fiction films? David A. Gerstner argues that during the early 2000s, certain directors "associated with urban subject matter, over-intellectualized or contemplative narrative style, personal scandal, or political interests viewed as discomfiting to 'mainstream audiences' [were] de-auteured" (244) by Hollywood. Films by directors like Lee, Woody Allen, and Robert Altman, according to Gerstner, were seen often as "box office poison" less for what they were about and more for who they were made by. Lee, for example, is often viewed as a controversial, "political" filmmaker, while Altman's films are stylistically strange for audiences accustomed to more conventional narrative filmmaking. As a result of such reputations, Gerstner argues, there was a general "de-auteuring" of a few directors, including Lee, as Hollywood's marketing machinery began to publicize films according to genre or as star vehicles rather than as products of a particular director.

Gerstner's discussion focuses on Lee's *Inside Man* (2007), a fiction film released a decade after *4 Little Girls,* but as Cobb and Jackson suggest, the seeds of this argument can be found in the marketing of and critical responses to the director's nonfiction film. Numerous promotional materials published at the time of the film's theatrical release, for example, focused on the director's relationship with the girls' families, particularly that of Chris McNair, whose acceptance of the project was what enabled Lee to make the film. According to McNair, in Lee "I found someone whom I could trust. If I didn't feel confident, I wouldn't have talked with him. It's very important that this be done accurately and correctly. In all his research he showed that he was objective and seeking a broad section of opinion. I'm a stickler for the facts" (quoted in Thomas). Lee also emphasized McNair's involvement in a number of interviews, including a July 1997 appearance on *The Charlie Rose Show* (1991–), in which the director stresses that McNair's support of the project ensured the participation of others in the Birmingham community.[14]

In addition, Lee effectively "de-auteured" himself by minimizing his role in the film's production. An interview between Lee and Gary Susman suggests the director's basic approach in discussing the film: "I didn't need to be in the film. I tend to like documentaries where you don't have a narrator, a voice-over. Just let the people tell the story." Such observations about directorial presence soon became metacommentaries on nonfiction film, the press, and the role of the director. On *The Charlie Rose Show,* for example, in response to a question regarding critical responses to the film, Lee discussed the number of reviewers who noted his seemingly more muted presence in the film and argued, "Forget about me. This film is not about me."

Indeed, *4 Little Girls* is not about Lee; it is about the events leading up to September 15, 1963, and the bombing at the 16th Street Baptist Church that left four young girls dead. It is also about the *girls,* and most of the interviews with their family members invite spectators to imagine who they were and what brought them to the church that fateful Sunday morning. The same could be said for how we get to know other figures in the story, including Bull Connor and George Wallace. But to say that Lee's presence is any more muted in this particular film would be disingenuous. As the interviews suggest—through cinematography, editing, and sound—Lee is a constant presence in *4 Little Girls.* Much like his fiction films, the director's formal choices in his first documentary feature create a dialectic, guide our responses to the story, and help us link the past to the present. In the end, *4 Little Girls* is a Lee film, even when the director's presence is less conspicuous than in his previous work.

Notes

I'd like to thank the students in my Nonfiction Film class at Brooklyn College (Spring 2011) for illustrating the usefulness of Grindon's categories in relationship to the interviews in *4 Little Girls.*

1. The Children's Crusade was spearheaded by SCLC staff member James Bevel as a means of supplementing the number of marchers with local high school students. The film suggests that many of the marchers were also younger children. The news footage of unarmed demonstrators being attacked by water hoses and dogs has become an iconic image of the civil rights movement.

2. Raines was born in Birmingham and spent much of his early life in the city. During the early 1960s he was a student at Birmingham Southern College. His career in journalism didn't begin until after the bombing. In 1983 he published "The Birmingham Bombing Twenty Years Later: The Case That Won't Close," the essay that first piqued Lee's interest in the subject. At that time, Lee contacted Chris McNair with the thought of making a fictional film about the bombing. The film

was never made and it wasn't until over ten years later that *4 Little Girls* was made. See Raines, "The Birmingham Bombing Twenty Years Later: The Case That Won't Close," *New York Times Magazine,* July 24, 1983.

3. The Southern Christian Leadership Conference traces its beginnings to 1955 and the Montgomery bus boycotts, when Revs. Martin Luther King Jr. and Ralph David Abernathy, among others, formed the Montgomery Improvement Association (MIA) as a support system for the boycott. The Southern Leadership Conference (SLC), formed from the MIA, was officially organized in 1957, with an executive board consisting of King, Abernathy, Rev. C. K. Steele, Rev. T. J. Jemison, and others. The SLC adopted its current name in 1957, at its first conference. The SCLC was a powerful force in civil rights efforts throughout the late 1950s and 1960s, organizing boycotts, voter registration drives, and other protests during this time. They also supported the demonstrations in Birmingham during the early 1960s.

4. Hanes appears in a medium shot, with the camera positioned slightly above and looking down on him. This shot stands out as one of the rare times that the framing allows for so much background.

5. George C. Wallace served four terms as governor of Alabama (1963–67, 1971–75, 1975–79, 1983–87) and unsuccessfully ran four times for president (1964, 1968, 1972, and 1976). Wallace's most enduring political legacy is his resistance to the Kennedy administration's desegregation legislation. In 1972, as Wallace was making his third run for president, he was shot five times. He survived the assassination attempt, but the shots left him paralyzed from the waist down. Despite his paralysis, he ran for president again in 1976 and served two more terms as governor of Alabama. In his last years he suffered from Parkinson's disease, the effects of which can be clearly seen in *4 Little Girls.*

6. On June 11, 1963, Wallace personally barred the entry of two black students, James A. Hood and Vivian J. Malone, from registering at the University of Alabama and desegregating the institution. As a result of Wallace's defiance of federal orders, President Kennedy mobilized the Alabama National Guard and moved some units to the campus. At this point, Wallace had no choice but to let the students register. This was just one of many of Wallace's attempts to stymie desegregation and voting registration activities in his state.

7. Katzenbach served as the deputy attorney general under President Kennedy from 1962 to 1965. In 1965, he became the attorney general for President Johnson. For more on SCLC's continuing work, see http://sclcnational.org/.

8. The extreme close-ups destabilize the world presented by the film in a similar manner as Dutch angles are often used to communicate a character's emotional or psychological distress in a fiction film. Lee uses Dutch angles liberally throughout his films for precisely this purpose.

9. In this context, a star isn't defined (necessarily) as a recognizable celebrity. Instead, it refers to an individual who becomes the defining character of the film.

10. See Barry Keith Grant essay in this volume for more on Wiseman's approach to the documentary interview.

11. In the uncut footage, Wallace admits that he wouldn't change anything from the past. It is unclear why Lee chose not to include this footage in the final version of the film; however, the governor's treatment of Ed Holcey makes a similar point in a subtler manner.

12. Lee used this term to describe Wallace's performance in an appearance on *The Charlie Rose Show*.

13. Wallace's references to Holcey may be directed at Lee—who was sitting across from the former governor during the interview—and less toward any presumed audience. In his *Charlie Rose* appearance, Lee explains that when he arrived to interview Wallace, the office was filled with media people. Lee didn't film the interview until the room was cleared. He also refused to have a photo taken with Wallace. This suggests that Wallace was hoping to use his interaction with Lee, an outspoken supporter of African American causes, to burnish his tarnished reputation.

14. Lee says something very similar in his interview with Susman and again in an interview included in the DVD extras.

Works Cited

Acham, Christine. "We Shall Overcome: Preserving History and Memory in *4 Little Girls*." In *The Spike Lee Reader*, ed. Paula J. Massood, 159–74. Philadelphia: Temple University Press, 2008.

Armstrong, David. "Lee's *4 Little Girls* Hits Mark." *San Francisco Examiner,* October 10, 1997. http://www.variety.com/review/VE1117911966?refcatid=31.

Cobb, Jasmine Nicole, and John L. Jackson. "They Hate Me: Spike Lee, Documentary Filmmaking, and Hollywood's 'Savage Slot.'" In *Fight the Power! The Spike Lee Reader,* ed. Janice D. Hamlet and Robin R. Means Coleman, 251–72. New York: Peter Lang, 2008.

"A Conversation about the Film *4 Little Girls*." *The Charlie Rose Show.* July 14, 1997. http://www.charlierose.com/view/interview/5458.

Gerstner, David. "De Profundis: A Love Letter from the Inside Man." In *The Spike Lee Reader,* ed. Paula J. Massood, 243–54. Philadelphia: Temple University Press, 2008.

Grindon, Leger. "Q&A: Poetics of the Documentary Interview." *Velvet Light Trap* 60 (Fall 2007): 4–12.

Lee, Spike. "With His New Documentary, *Four Little Girls*, Spike Lee Fulfills a Long-Standing Mission to Document the 1963 Birmingham Church Bombing." Interview with Gary Susman. http://industrycentral.net/director_interviews/SL01.HTM.

Maslin, Janet. "*4 Little Girls* (1997): Still Reeling from the Day Death Came to Birmingham." *New York Times*, July 9, 1997. http://movies.nytimes.com/movie/review?res=9500EED71439F93AA35754C0A961958260.

McCarthy, Todd. "*4 Little Girls*." *Variety*, July 20, 1997. http://www.variety.com/review/VE1117911966?refcatid=31.

Siegel, Sol Louis. "3 Little Girls." Philadelphia City Paper Archives. September 11–18. http://archives.citypaper.net/articles/091197/article033.shtml18.

Thomas, Chandra A. "McNair Will See Lee Film on Bomb." *Birmingham Post-Herald*, June 23, 1997. http://www.useekufind.com/peace/4littlegirls.htm.

Chapter 29

THE GLEANERS AND "US"

The Radical Modesty of Agnès Varda's
Les glaneurs et la glaneuse

Virginia Bonner

In both its formal and thematic choices, *Les glaneurs et la glaneuse* (*The Gleaners and I*, 2000) is one of Agnès Varda's most experimental films to date. The documentary's delicate themes of poverty, aging, filmmaking, and art warrant this shift toward a more unconventional style. *Gleaners* explores the agricultural tradition of gleaning, the legalized practice of culling leftover food from fields after the harvest. Varda journeys from France's rural fields to its urban markets to meet and, with her handheld DV camera, to chronicle the lives of gleaners of all sorts. Through her direct address to the camera, her voice-over commentary, and her associative editing choices, she reveals that some glean out of necessity while others glean as a lifestyle choice or in rebellion against commercialism and consumer waste. These diverse people, their life conditions, and their reasons for gleaning seem unrelated at first, but over the course of the film, Varda draws remarkable social connections among them. Such unusual associations question and upend conventions concerning subjects worthy of documentation, since Varda chooses to include not traditional documentary fare but quite the opposite: moments of banality, images of aging and decay, and interviews with social outcasts. *Gleaners* encourages viewers to connect the motives one might expect for gleaning, such as poverty and adversity, to more unexpected ones, such as resourcefulness, tradition, art, and activism.

Varda recognizes that her task as documentary filmmaker parallels that of other gleaners, though her voice-over says that instead of grains or fruit she gleans "acts, gestures, and information" with her camera. Moments selected from her travels and her many hours of footage self-reflexively acknowledge her own role as, in her words, a "gleaner of images": *la glaneuse*. By extension, Varda's methodology in *Gleaners* underscores that documentary filmmaking itself is always a form of gleaning, conditioned by what a filmmaker finds valuable while shooting on location, which footage the filmmaker selects for inclusion in a film, and how the filmmaker chooses to arrange those selections for an audience. Varda describes this approach to filmmaking as educational: "Every time you make a film, you learn something. You approach other people, other people's work, some landscape you never noticed before. It's like giving sudden life to what you see and capturing the beauty in it" (Anderson 27).

What makes *Gleaners* unique is Varda's profound manipulation of address in the process of achieving these effects. By modifying the modes of address, identification, and narration particular to the documentary genre, Varda hails both her viewers and the people she films—including herself— as active participants in *Gleaners*. This narrational style, which I call "filming in the second person," creatively locates Varda within her arguments while maintaining a firm commitment to the people she talks to, gleaners and viewers alike. As a result Varda's film conveys as much about herself and her spectators as her many acquaintances who glean. She draws poignant connections among these seemingly disparate groups, and the resulting eighty-two-minute film engenders a complex but direct circle of communication among filmmaker, filmed subjects, and viewing audience. In this essay I examine how Varda's filming in the second person contemplates the social politics of gleaning while simultaneously using her innovative filmic "you" to scrutinize the structures of documentary representation itself.

Indeed, the film is full of not only people revealing themselves but people revealing themselves *to each other*. With her onscreen presence, Varda connects with the gleaners she meets, and her physical proximity to them serves as a reminder that she shares in the conditions of their lives. Varda explains, "I asked people to reveal themselves, to give a lot of themselves; so I thought that the film should also reveal a little about the filmmakers, that I should just use a little bit of myself in it" (Havis). Underscoring this association is one of the film's most self-reflexive moments, one wherein Varda playfully adopts the pose of Jules Breton's *La glaneuse* for the camera, balancing a bundle of wheat proudly on her shoulder before dropping it in favor of her DV camera. Though seemingly whimsical, it is significant that she adopts the pose of the *subject* of the painting here: the gleaner herself, not the artist himself. In doing so, she creates an explicit connection with her interview subjects, breaking down the barriers between filmed subjects and filmmaker.

MEETING LA GLANEUSE AND LES GLANEURS

Furthering the investigative style she has practiced throughout her career—especially in Sans toit ni loi (Vagabond, 1985)—Varda is always present in Gleaners, whether she physically appears onscreen, asks questions off-screen, comments in voice-over, or frames the image as her point of view. Her insistence on placing herself within the film reminds us that Varda's gleaning and assembly of these images necessarily shapes the documentary story. Her connection to gleaning is further advanced by an onscreen interrogation of her own aging process. With clever wit and a good dose of humor, she often compares the rot of vegetables in fields or detritus in the streets with her own aging body, particularly her hands. These scenes are marked by an affable, bittersweet directness and by an extraordinary sense of visual and textural composition. Twice in the film, for example, the crisp, digital images slowly track over her wrinkled hands in close-up—first compared with the rotting, veined flesh of a potato and later with Rembrandt's mottled, aged flesh in a self-portrait. Varda's commentary makes the connections explicit: "That is to say, this is my project: to film with one hand my other hand. To enter into the horror [of it as it ages, decays], I find it extraordinary. . . . And here's Rembrandt's self-portrait, but it's the same thing in fact, it's always a self-portrait."

Similar moments feature highly abstracted close-ups of the roots of her graying hair, cabbages after the harvest, mangled cars after they have been crushed, a Lucite clock missing its hands. The film's voice-over and cutting always relate these moments back to Varda's self-portrait of her own aging process, as she dryly comments that "my hair and my hands tell me the end is near" or "a clock without hands, that suits me. You don't see time passing." Again, although somewhat whimsical, the ensuing pauses in her commentary and elevated minor-key music render each of these confessions disquieting; yet these explorations of her own aging approach a more fascinated than fearful tone. Her close framings in loving detail almost fetishize these harbingers of death and, in an adept feminist move, revalue the physical signs of age that society chooses to malign.

This exploration of aging parallels that of gleaning in powerful ways. Considered together, both themes mark an interrogation and revaluation of what society deems worthy of regard and respect. They embody a kind of eco-feminist subversion of aesthetics, of what Western society considers

Les glaneurs et la glaneuse: "This is my project: to film one hand with my other hand."

beautiful and therefore valuable. For in our capitalist patriarchy, one learns to prize the new, the young, the beautiful, the marketable; Varda instead revalues the used, the aged, even the unsightly. She rebelliously asserts that she likes to film "rot, waste, debris." She finds the "horror" of her aging hands "extraordinary," comparing it not to concepts of shame or use-lessness but to priceless artworks. She prefers the nonsalable, misshapen heart-shaped potatoes to the perfectly rounded ones. She praises the Musée en Herbe's program *Poubelle ma belle* ("my beautiful garbage can/trash"), which teaches children to recycle and to appreciate that which is not brand-new. The most sustained way in which she embraces this fundamental con-cept of "my beautiful trash," however, is by gathering the stories of those ig-nored by society, oppressed by corporations and governments. In short, she strives to increase social awareness of "waste and trash" but also to push that more important and compassionate question in gleaning embodied by "Who finds a use for it?" (Varda 1).

FILMING IN THE SECOND PERSON:
FROM "I" TO "YOU" TO "WE"

In hailing her audience as participants in an ongoing conversation about so-ciety's attitudes toward poverty, waste, and class, Varda is engaged in breaking the boundary between those onscreen and their viewers, and she does so by filming in the second person. Grammatical person, according to the *Oxford English Dictionary*, indicates a participant's role as either the speaker (I/we in first person), the addressee (you in second person), or someone or something spoken of (he/she/it/they in third person). Second-person address, rarely used in traditional literature, is most commonly found in travel guides, letters, lyrics, and games. Like literature, cinema traditionally prefers first- or third-person narration, and *Gleaners* employs these strategies as well. Varda occasionally narrates in third person ("they get all their food from trash cans"), though her first-person narration comprises most of the film's spoken commentary ("I wanted to talk to him," "I like filming rot, waste, debris") and nearly all of the film's interviews offer first-person accounts of gleaning.

The most distinctive mode of address in *Gleaners,* however, is the second person. Obvious cinematic uses of the second person include direct address through an eyeline match with the camera and voice-over commentary or dialogue that speaks to "you," the viewer. Varda sometimes narrates in second person ("you don't see time passing"), and she looks at the camera often, but most effective are the gleaners who look and speak directly to the camera/viewer, such as François in his rubber boots and Etienne-Jules Marey's grandson at his vineyard.[1] As the spectator becomes more involved in the stories of these gleaners, the lines between "you" and "them" begin to soften, and Varda thereby encourages her audience to participate in the film's conversations and to care about the people speaking.

But *Gleaners* is engaged in an even more radical project than speaking directly to individual spectators about social issues. Arguably the film's most important project is to interpellate you, the viewer, as an active participant and subject. This, however, is not Louis Althusser's repressive, dominant ideology hailing you (Althusser 174). Nor is it classical Hollywood's "textual hailing," as Kaja Silverman describes the "You are now in Bedford Falls" establishing shot of *It's a Wonderful Life* (1946) (49–50). That is, this is not an address that encourages you to adopt the false subjectivity of another—especially that of a fictional Hollywood character—or to be Althusser's "subjected being . . . freely accepting of his [sic] subjugation" or even to acquiesce to the subjugation of others (182).

Instead, *Gleaners* strives to raise your social consciousness in the Gramscian "spirit of scission [a redemptive break from social class, capitalism, or other forms of division] that must aim to spread itself from the protagonist class to the classes that are its potential allies" (390). Of course, many leftist propaganda films seek class reeducation and solidarity, but *Gleaners* differs in that it promotes a pensive, questioning spectator and a grassroots approach to social change that is *situated,* per Donna Haraway, and thus generative of "an epistemology and politics of engaged, account-able positioning" (196). By multiplying and revaluing the meanings of "gleaning," this documentary teaches us to recognize and reconsider our societal role in class, gender, and age practices, as well as in environmental, cultural, and filmmaking practices. Befitting Varda's lifelong commitment to countercultural activism, her film offers us an alternative, revolutionary model: *Gleaners* openly defies bourgeois ideologies by challenging class op-pression, environmental destruction, ageism, and rampant consumerism. The film's sociocultural critique teaches us to reject our prescribed role under consumer capitalism. It is a counterhegemonic second-person ad-dress that might more aptly translate: "Hey, you, gleaning comrade! Value your fellow humans and the environment!"

Toward this end, *Gleaners* strives not simply to target the second-person "you" but to inspire our embrace of a stronger, communal sense of the first-person plural, "we." The film's novelty and efficacy lie in its subtle inter-weaving of these modes of address, all designed to hail you in the second person, and through this hailing to lead you to a humanist awareness of the first-person plural. That is, Varda wants "you" to join "us," a community of gleaners, humanitarians, fellow humans, in order to shift from separatist ideologies of "I," "you," and "them" to the more inclusive "we."

One of Varda's most overt expressions of this humanitarian goal ap-pears not in *Gleaners* itself but in the DVD's follow-up documentary *Deux ans après* (*Two Years Later*, 2002), in which she revisits many of the original interviewees as well as other gleaners. Moving beyond a simple then-and-now update, Varda reverently tells us that it was the astounding number of letters, stories, and gleaned gifts sent to her after the release of *Gleaners* that prompted her to continue the film's project two years after its comple-tion. All of these letters share with the filmmaker how inspiring and life-changing her film is for their authors, and how it creates a new awareness and a sense of community among gleaners of all sorts. One viewer of *Glean-ers* interviewed in *Two Years Later* clearly summarizes the success of the film's humanitarian project: "It makes you want to be a better person, to pay more attention to other people." Confirming this response, Alain, the market gleaner first interviewed in *Gleaners*, reports that now more people stop to talk to him, praise his volunteer work, and buy his leaflets. Another interviewee who first appeared in *Gleaners*, the famous philosopher and psychoanalyst Jean Laplanche, compares gleaning to a radical practice of psychoanalysis; like gleaners who must be open to possibilities, the doctor "must give up what he knows so he can be receptive to something that is completely new." Yet another viewer describes her experience of *Gleaners* and the inspirational impact of Varda's role in it like this:

Delphine: Seeing this film was like a rebirth . . . this film just completely put us back in touch with ourselves, with life.

Varda: But it talks about leftovers, things that are abandoned.

Delphine: Yes, but it's made by someone who is very much alive.

The original *Gleaners* develops this inviting, communal tone in multiple ways. In the remainder of this essay, I will analyze how three of these methods raise awareness of social class: Varda's use of second- and first-person address, her unobtrusive DV camera coupled with her onscreen role, and her persuasively engaging sense of humor.

Raising Class-Consciousness: "Us" and "Them"

Clearly Varda's project seeks to humanize groups of people who are routinely ignored by more privileged members of society. She asserts in one promotional interview that gleaning "is a subject matter that is vaguely gray. When you see these people in the street, you don't look at them. My idea was not only to find them but to let them speak. To show that they have thoughts and feelings and intelligence—a luminescence" (Havis). Initially Varda's statement seems to take for granted a problematic position of dominance when she, as a middle-class film director, claims the authority to "let them speak."

By invoking the second person, however, she redirects that authority and addresses the very people who habitually ignore scavengers and gleaners. When she says, "you don't look at them" scavenging in the streets, she puts into question the identity of the "you." Most obviously, "you" refers to those who do not need to scavenge for food, who can afford to ignore gleaners in the streets and so choose to. Varda's statement implies that she herself was one of these people when she began her documentary project, since she needed "to find them" before she could "let them speak." Yet her strategic use of the second person groups her largely middle-class viewing audience in this category with her. She thereby implicitly slips into the deliberately absented first-person plural by hailing us as complicit, which perhaps initially incites a slight defensiveness about our privileged class position. Simultaneously, though, this subtle first-person-plural address encourages all viewers to open our eyes and minds, to acknowledge and accept a class of people whom society trains us to ignore.

In fact, Varda complicates such issues of class-consciousness throughout *Gleaners*. As one of her key political strategies, she strives to dismantle the lines that separate poor gleaners from higher-classed or recreational gleaners. As a shared practice, gleaning produces Antonio Gramsci's re-alignment of "potential class allies." The film's disjunctive editing facilitates this breakdown of class boundaries through its surprising and often humorous juxtapositions. For example, Varda's interview with Claude, the poor and dispirited yet persevering traveler who gleans from potato fields and trash cans, immediately cuts to the gourmet kitchen of four-star executive chef Edouard Loubet, who, the film soon reveals, also gleans. This shift from poverty-stricken traveler to gleaning gourmet chef broadens and revalues definitions of gleaning even as it offers a more comfortable point of identification for bourgeois audiences.

Since the film's release in 2000, I have viewed *Gleaners* with public audiences and with my undergraduate film students more than twenty times in Paris, New York, and Atlanta, and the response is unfailing: predominantly middle-class audiences always laugh at this comparison of a poor traveler and a gourmet chef. Considering the film's overt class analyses, I find this moment of laughter highly significant: Why do audiences feel compelled to laugh at this comparison? It is true that Varda's abrupt juxtaposition here creates a moment of visual shock as she cuts from Claude's dingy, cramped trailer to Edouard's bright, spacious, stainless-steel kitchen. The polar class associations of these locations alone locate a humorous irony in the moment. At a deeper level, however, the laughter may also originate in Varda's direct class comparison, one that necessarily calls attention to the viewer's own class position.

Varda's carefully edited juxtaposition of these two differently classed gleaners initially might seem designed to condemn middle-class viewers, as the comparison easily could have set up a biting criticism of the chef's, and the audience's, bourgeois privilege. More productively, however, this moment of awkwardness functions not as a slap at bourgeois audiences but as a gesture of inclusivity in the first-person plural: we must situate ourselves on a continuum of privilege ranging from the pristine, stainless-steel affluence of the chef as he prepares fetishized, expensive foods to the shabby, trailer-bound poverty of the traveler who must scrabble for leftover fish from garbage cans. Further, the surprisingly sensitive nature of Varda's interview with Chef Edouard quickly reveals that he gleans out of economic frugality as well, albeit under less dire circumstances. "Nothing should be wasted," he tells us. "We don't throw anything away [in my kitchen]. You have to be economical." This bourgeois chef gleans for his herbs and fruits because he refuses to pay for overpriced foods of lesser quality at the store. Moreover, through gleaning he can ensure the freshness of his ingredients and honor his grandparents, who taught him the tradition of gleaning when he was a boy. Through the sincerity and sensitivity of Varda's

interviews with both of these gleaners, the film allays any class defensiveness or judgment on the viewers' part and once again invites us to align
ourselves with all gleaners.

Varda's equal treatment of impoverished and bourgeois gleaners alike
creates a connection among diverse people because they value frugality and
resourcefulness. She accentuates this connection by cutting from the potato gleaner to the chef by way of a clever graphic match: the two scenes end
and begin, respectively, with similar shots of Claude and Edouard holding
food. Such visual rhymes typify the film's overall editing pattern, subtly
but effectively likening the motives for gleaning among poverty-stricken
travelers and gourmet chefs, as well as other gleaners. Through such parallel edits, *Gleaners* sutures us into identifying with all of the gleaners interviewed: the film's kaleidoscopic montage asks us to redefine gleaning by
drawing connections among its seemingly disparate motives of necessity,
tradition, kindness, activism, artistry, and resourcefulness, regardless of
class distinctions that would separate us from them.

In her interviews with gleaners Varda shows compassion and appreciation, trying to inspire a sympathetic response from viewers in turn. She
poses open-ended and concerned questions to the gleaners—"What happened to you [to necessitate gleaning for all of your food]?" or "Did you
know that once they're through picking potatoes, you're allowed to take leftovers?"—and devotes extensive screen time to their responses. In Beauce,
for example, she meets Claude's group of travelers, who must glean their
staple diet from leftover heaps of potatoes, several tons deemed unfit for sale
by corporate growers and so dumped in fields, left to rot. She conducts several lengthy interviews with these travelers. Close framings and longer takes
in this scene, particularly the tighter shots inside Claude's small trailer, reveal his dignity and resourcefulness. For almost six minutes of screen time,
Claude discusses the hardships of his living conditions, the wastefulness
of markets and corporate growers, and the difficulties of gleaning out of
necessity. Since Varda is posing her questions about gleaning to audiences
as well as to the gleaners, her second-person address of "you" during these
interviews invites a productive shift to first-person plural, carefully building a measure of intimacy among filmed subject, onscreen filmmaker, and
viewing audience.

DOCUMENTARY MODESTY AND DIGITAL VIDEO

Throughout *Gleaners*, Varda interrogates gleaning with a sense of wonder,
humility, and, as she puts it, "modesty": "The people I have filmed tell us
a great deal about our society and ourselves. I myself learned a great deal

while I was shooting this film. It confirmed for me that the documentary film is a discipline that teaches modesty" (2). She asserts that modesty, which she strives to inculcate in the audience, was one of her primary motivations for using a DV camera. Eyeline matches and slightly oblique camera angles stitch us into her conversations with her interviewees, but it is the small size and flip-out monitor of her handycam that allows us all to get physically closer to people during interviews without intimidating them: "to look them in the eye," she says, without having "to hide behind the camera" (Havis). Nothing inherent in digital cameras leads inevitably to changed relations between filmmaker and subject, but the DV camera's unobtrusive size and secondary viewscreen offer possibilities for such a difference, and Varda's film embraces these possibilities.[2]

The sense of connection enabled by Varda's technical choices extends to the viewer as well, creating the film's remarkable first-person-plural feel. In effect, the camera is "us," the viewing audience seated at the table or walking through the field with Varda and her interviewees. When the gleaners talk with Varda, they address the camera's presence and hence our presence, too. These choices turn the typical informant interview—a ubiquitous trope in documentaries—into something quite new. Varda's small DV camera, her casual on-location settings, and her onscreen presence trade not on the authority invested in the interviewer and the distanced objectivity of the staged third-person interview but on the situated communality and spontaneity among all conversing, including the overtly addressed viewer. *Gleaners* thereby fosters a more "modest" role for both the documentary *glaneuse* and the viewer, trying to sway our sensitivity subjectively toward the interviewees.

While *Gleaners* differs markedly from mainstream styles, so too does its mode of address differ from the subjective styles of other contemporary documentarians. As with these better-known filmmakers, Varda's own acknowledged presence as documentary director, aging persona, and gleaner of images helps flesh out her film's meanings, but in a personal appearance in Paris in July 2000, she preferred to emphasize the politics of poverty for the gleaners as the film's dominant theme. She is careful to avoid the pitfall of overemphasis on herself, a significant difference from other documentaries that prominently include their directors onscreen.

Ross McElwee's *Sherman's March* (1985), for example, humorously highlights its own derailment from its original topic (a historical documentary about Sherman's March) and its devolution into the director's "shameless alibi to pick up women," but it veers further into a masochistic, "hysterical" documentary, as Lucy Fischer terms it.[3] McElwee hides behind his camera for most of his film, often looking voyeuristically at women and then mocking himself for doing so. Varda, in contrast, conducts highly participatory onscreen interviews in *Gleaners* and engages far more explicitly with her film's political and social ramifications. In many ways her work is more akin to Michael Moore's documentaries. Like Moore, Varda wears her left-wing agenda on her sleeve and does not conceal her political biases during her interviews and voice-overs. But Moore often employs a rather egoistic and confrontational demeanor with his interviewees, one marked by "personal audacity," "self-righteousness," and a "principle of brash provocation," as Matthew Bernstein writes of *Roger and Me* (1989).[4] Moore's sense of humor often builds from the fallout from these confrontations, largely drawing on criticism and satire. Varda's sense of humor, on the other hand, stems mainly from her discoveries of odd, unexpected connections, found objects, and delightful absurdities.

HAILING US WITH HUMOR

Varda's use of humor in *Gleaners* is one of her crucial rhetorical tools when invoking her second-person address, and it strongly engenders the film's shift to the first-person plural. Through humor, the film engages us in a modest yet compelling way. Varda's witty asides and amusing anecdotes enable her to approach us more directly than a traditional documentary might, much in the way that the flip-out monitor of her small camera allows her to speak more intimately with the people she meets. Further, the candor of their stories is disarmingly funny and thus puts the viewer at ease with the different people interviewed.

Toward this end, *Gleaners* often inserts small gifts for our amusement: a dog inexplicably sporting an enormous red boxing glove strapped under its chin, a lawyer dressed in full judicial regalia standing in the middle of a cabbage patch, and a "dancing" lens cap. The latter is perhaps the best example of the film's strategic humor, since Varda uses it as gentle mockery of the presumed infallibility of the documentary genre and its director. Having forgotten to turn her camera off after an interview, she films "the dance of the lens cap." The camera swings at her side as she accidentally films the lens cap dangling above the ground. Rather than disregard or delete this extraneous footage, however, Varda embraces it. As the cap dances wildly for nearly fifty seconds, the director humanizes herself by admitting a moment of forgetfulness. She pushes the scene further, however, by scoring the shot with jazz music and transforming a delightful found object that she, too, has gleaned into a prized moment of beauty for us to share. In these gleaned moments of humor, the film winks at us and engages us on its own offbeat terms.

Les glaneurs et la glaneuse: The dance of the lens cap.

These funny asides and anecdotes strategically usher us into sympathy with the film's larger political issues, especially that we are all, in some sense, gleaners and therefore should not discriminate against those who glean out of poverty. Rather than lecturing, the film introduces us more fully to the gleaners Varda has met through its warm, humorous tone. Sometimes that humor simply entertains us while courting our political assent, as when Varda defiantly eats a stingy grower's figs; sometimes it relieves tension when comparing different living conditions, as with the potato gleaner and the chef. Most often, the film's humor serves as a common thread that unites the quirky *glaneuse* herself, the myriad interview subjects, and the film's diverse viewers—now reeducated as "modest" class allies—directly hailing us all as gleaners.

Notes

1. The *Gleaners'* shooting script (courtesy of Varda and Ciné-Tamaris) reads: "on ne voit pas le temps qui passe." My translation here to the second-person "you" follows the standard translation of the third-person French, "on" (one). The French "on" is commonly understood to address the reader in the second person, which the film's subtitles reflect as well.

2. For further reading on Varda's use of the digital camera in *Glaneurs*, see Homay King, "Matter, Time, and the Digital: Varda's *The Gleaners and I*," *Quarterly Review of Film and Video* 24, no. 5 (2007): 421–29.

3. See Lucy Fischer's chapter in this volume.

4. See Matthew Bernstein's chapter in this volume.

WORKS CITED

Althusser, Louis. "Ideology and Ideological State Apparatuses." In *Lenin and Philosophy and Other Essays*, trans. Ben Brewster. London: New Left Books, 1971.

Anderson, Melissa. "The Modest Gesture of the Filmmaker: An Interview with Agnès Varda." *Cinéaste* 26, no. 4 (2001): 24–27.

Gramsci, Antonio. "Cultural Themes: Ideological Material." In *Antonio Gramsci: Selections from Cultural Writings*, ed. David Forgacs and Geoffrey Nowell-Smith, trans. William Boelhower, 389–90. London: Lawrence and Wishart, 1985.

Haraway, Donna. *Simians, Cyborgs, and Women: The Reinvention of Nature*. New York: Routledge, 1991.

Havis, Richard James Havis. "Varda Gleans DV Style." *2-pop: The Digital Filmmaker's Resource Site Online*, May 30, 2001. http://www.2-pop.com/library/articles/2001_05_30.html.

Silverman, Kaja. *The Subject of Semiotics*. New York: Oxford University Press, 1983.

Varda, Agnès. Promotional materials for *Les glaneurs et la glaneuse*. Paris: Ciné-Tamaris and the Groupment National des Cinémas de Recherche, 2000.

Chapter 30

"You Must Never Listen to This"

Lessons on Sound, Cinema, and Mortality from Werner Herzog's *Grizzly Man*

David T. Johnson

Herzog: I think you should not keep it. You should destroy it.

Palovak: Yeah?

Herzog: I think that's what you should do.

Palovak: Okay.

Herzog: Because it will be the white elephant in your room all your life.

> Werner Herzog and Jewel Palovak, discussing the audio
> footage of the deaths of Timothy Treadwell
> and Amie Huguenard, in *Grizzly Man*

For all of the theories we have used to cocoon ourselves against the intrusion of reality in cinema, none has been able to expunge the fundamental sense of presence—or "presence of . . . absence," as Christian Metz so famously put it (57)—that the medium always returns us to. And perhaps no other experience accomplishes this effect better than seeing someone on film who no longer exists. Normally it is easy enough to repress or simply ignore the fact that many of the cinema's populace no longer have living, breathing counterparts. But when a film explicitly acknowledges the death of its inhabitants, then, in a very immediate way, we are forced to consider once again what it means to be recorded—and how those recordings function beyond one's death.

Perhaps no recent documentary confronts these issues more directly than Werner Herzog's *Grizzly Man* (2005). The film details the life and horrific death of Timothy Treadwell, a self-appointed savior to the Alaskan Grizzly who spent thirteen summers among the animals before being killed by one of them; his girlfriend, Amie Huguenard, also tragically lost her life on the same night. The film is a meditation on Treadwell's life and what led him to pursue the extreme lifestyle that he adopted, but the film is also as much about, if not more about, the facts surrounding Treadwell's and Huguenard's violent ends. Herzog underscores Treadwell's own death from the very beginning, with a subtitle in the first shot we see of him that could function as a modest grave marker: "Timothy Treadwell, 1957–2003." And the circumstances surrounding these deaths acquire even more weight when we learn that during the bear attack, which occurred in his tent, Treadwell turned on a video camera but never removed the lens cap. Thus the video recorded the sounds of the bear attack but not the images. We learn of the existence of this audio footage roughly fifty minutes into the film, during an oddly performative description from the pathologist about what must have occurred when the bear attacked the couple. But more disturbing is the scene that follows this one, a pivotal moment and perhaps the key scene of the entire film.

The scene begins with a shot of Jewel Palovak, one of Treadwell's friends, with a camera in her lap, as a man in the foreground, his back to the viewer, listens to headphones running from the camera. The man holds his left hand to his temple, and although we cannot fully see his face, we know that his eyes are closed in an attitude of concentration. "This is Timothy's camera," Herzog's voice-over states. "During the fatal attack, there was no time to remove the lens cap. Jewel Palovak allowed me to listen to the audio." Herzog—we now know that the man on camera is the filmmaker—hunches forward, intently listening to the audio, as the camera slowly zooms in on Palovak. "I hear rain, and I hear Amie, get away, get away, go away," Herzog notes, the camera holding on Palovak before swinging back to him. The film then cuts to a shot from the original position, and Herzog, after a long pause that prompts Palovak to laugh nervously, tells her, "Jewel, you must never listen to this." After she promises not to listen to the audio or look at the photos at the coroner's office, the film cuts again to the same shot, only now with the filmmaker and the subject holding hands. And now Herzog goes one step further than warning her against listening to the audio; here, Herzog actually advises her to destroy it, "because it will be the white elephant in your room all your life."

The narrative and dramatic logic of the scene is clear: here is the moment when one of our subjects, Palovak, will be both confronted with and

Grizzly Man: Jewel Palovak watches as filmmaker Werner Herzog listens to the audio recording of Timothy Treadwell's death.

denied access to evidence of the remaining minutes in her friend's life. Herzog need not prompt us any further in sensing the scene's importance, which accounts for its minimalist aesthetic (the long pauses, the relatively static camera). But the generative power of this scene rests not only in its functioning in this way. Rather, that power has everything to do with two other important aspects: (1) our perception that what Herzog is listening to—and what Palovak must not listen to—is *real;* and (2) our knowledge that Herzog is listening, not looking and listening, to a piece of video footage. These two aspects might simply be defined as the commingling of two theoretical veins, one archaic and the other still very young. They are the realist-theory tradition and the sound-theory tradition (though one hesitates to use the word "tradition" with the latter). Both meet here in this scene, and part of why the scene fascinates is because of the complex interactions between these two modes of discourse. "You must never listen to this," Herzog tells Jewel Palovak—and, by extension, the audience. Yet in doing so, he has already left an indelible impression of imagined trauma in the minds of viewers, who are forced to confront the simple reality that Timothy Treadwell and Amie Huguenard went into the wilderness and never came back.

REALISM, MORTALITY, AND THE CINEMA

With its equal interest in realist film theory and sound studies, this essay is indebted to the work of Jonathan Kahana, who identifies Herzog as one of a few recent documentary makers who explore older ideas about film realism, often ascribed to André Bazin,[1] while maintaining a critical sense of the inherent limits and pitfalls one encounters within them. Kahana begins his "Cinema and the Ethics of Listening: Isaac Julien's *Frantz Fanon*" with a brief history of film realism, showing how Bazinian ontology gave way to the film theory of the 1970s, which often set itself explicitly against what it saw in Bazin's work as an ultimately naïve understanding of cinema. Yet Kahana also shows how Bazin's questions have become relevant to a number of recent filmmakers: in addition to Isaac Julien, "Chantal Akerman, Werner Herzog, Errol Morris, and Trinh T. Minh-ha, to name only a few innovators," who wish to "challenge the importance of the documentary form while maintaining the importance of Bazin's question" (21). And that question, according to Kahana, is, "What kind of irrational desire makes the cinema real?" (21). While he sets up this theoretical tension to study the use of sound in Julien's *Frantz Fanon: Black Skin, White Mask* (1996), this essay, albeit interested in a similar tension, asks what happens when the sound in question is one that we cannot hear.

In terms of Herzog's work more generally, the idea of the irrational desire for realism cannot help but resonate with the dreamers that populate his fiction and nonfiction work, since they so often operate in an obsessive state the films find magnetic yet ultimately inaccessible. Timothy Treadwell, like Dieter Dengler (*Little Dieter Needs to Fly*, 1997) and Graham Dorrington (*The White Diamond*, 2004), is in this way very close to what Amos Vogel once called the "Holy Fool" in Herzog's work, or "the person considered a fool because outsider and eccentric, the one who dares more than any human should, and who is therefore—and this is why Herzog is fascinated by him—closer to possible sources of deeper truth though not necessarily capable of reaching them" (38). Herzog's oeuvre, while often unpredictable in its course from project to project, is nonetheless remarkably coherent, particularly in relation to this figure in both documentaries and fiction films. In the latter mode, one need only think of two of his most famous films, *Aguirre, the Wrath of God* (1972) and *Fitzcarraldo* (1982). It can even be tempting to read Herzog himself as a kind of "Holy Fool," with the exception that one feels he, in fact, is capable of reaching "sources of deeper truths," particularly since he so often addresses the concept of truth in his interviews and commentaries.

Such truth, however, is not what we might normally associate with documentary. For Herzog, a lie, in fact, may enable truth—at least the kind of truth he is after, or what he calls "ecstatic truth." Brad Prager's study of Herzog describes the moment we experience ecstatic truth as viewers; it is a moment that "exceeds our ability to assimilate it into the archive of what we have already seen and heard," an experience closer to poetry: "As a director, he is not reporting, but rather poeticising or rendering the world ecstatic. This capacity to transfigure reality is, in Herzog's view, what separates the poets from the accountants" (5). (Prager's use of "accountants" refers to Herzog's famous critique of cinema verité as "merely superficial truth, the truth of accountants" in his "Minnesota Declaration" [Herzog 301].) Such aesthetic aims allow Herzog to approach documentary in ways we might normally consider a violation of the viewer's trust; examples include a tendency to rehearse interviews as well as other more direct kinds of filmmaker intervention such as Herzog's invention of Dieter Dengler's desire for a tattoo, at the outset of *Little Dieter Needs to Fly,* as a way of narrating Dengler's hallucinations in Vietnam. Wisely recognizing Herzog's own ambivalence toward the terms "documentary" and "narrative," Prager chooses not to emphasize distinctions among the films along these lines. This ambivalence—or, rather, willingness to work in both documentary and narrative modes—is perhaps why Herzog has moved easily between them for his entire career, with documentaries returning to earlier narrative films (such as his Klaus Kinski film, *My Best Fiend* [*Mein leibster Feind—Klaus Kinski,* 1999], which explores Kinski's persona) and narrative films returning to documentaries (notably, the retelling of Dieter Dengler's story in *Rescue Dawn* [2006], with actor Christian Bale playing the lead). In light of this more poetic approach to truth, it should come as no surprise that Herzog's films both rely on and interrogate some of the central issues of cinematic realism.

To return to Kahana's question—"What kind of irrational desire makes the cinema real?"—André Bazin's own answers were complex and carefully articulated. While they resist any easy summary, we might say that at least part of his answer involved speculations on mortality. On this subject, Christian Keathley has noted, "It is remarkable, and often forgotten, that André Bazin—that theoretician who, more perhaps than anyone, celebrated film's force of realism, its life force—wrote just as much about film's relation to death" (158). Keathley has already treated some of the examples that follow, but they call for reexamination in the context of this essay. Bazin's foundational essay, "The Ontology of the Photographic Image," is probably most explicit in this regard, as he characterizes the history of art as an attempt by humanity to resist time and death, which "is but the victory of time" (*What Is Cinema?* 9). One of the central analogies of the essay is to the Egyptian process of embalming the dead; the cinema, he writes, is "change mummified as it were" (*What Is Cinema?* 15). He also cites, in explaining the irrational power of photography, "the charm of family albums" that conjure "the disturbing presence of lives halted at a set moment in their duration, freed from their destiny" (*What Is Cinema?* 14). Although his other essays are clearly not exclusively concerned with mortality, the subject often underpins his observations. The famous footnote to "The Virtues and Limitations of Montage," after all, is about an awareness of the *real* potential danger within a narrative film, when a montage cutting between a lion and a child gives way to a single shot in which viewers see lion, child, and parents. Here, "trickery is out of the question" (*What Is Cinema?* 49)—the threat of death seems real. Consider a similar moment in "Cinema and Exploration" when, in discussing a shot of a killer whale in *Kon Tiki* (1950), Bazin notes, "It is not so much the photograph of the whale that interests us as the photograph of the *danger*" (*What Is Cinema?* 161). And of his writings in English, perhaps no essay has as long a meditation on death as "Death Every Afternoon," about *The Bullfight,* where Bazin writes, "Death is surely one of those rare events that justifies the term, so beloved of Claude Mauriac, *cinematic specificity*"; "For every creature, death is the unique moment par excellence"; and "Death is nothing but one moment after another, but it is the last" (30).

Of course, Bazin's reflections on mortality and cinema also dovetail with the interests of *Grizzly Man* whenever he discusses examples of people interacting with animals (though the danger to Treadwell is much greater than to many of Bazin's case studies). In "The Screen of Fantasy (Bazin and Animals)," Serge Daney argues that among the many reasons Bazin cites for his investment in a cinema without montage—"no more cinema," as Bazin phrased it in his essay "*Bicycle Thief*" (60)—is "the *nature* of what is being filmed, the status of the protagonists (in this case men and animals) who are forced to share the screen, sometimes at the risk of their lives" (33). One thinks, again, of "The Virtues and Limitations of Montage" (an example Daney cites), where a sense of potential danger gives "immediate and retroactive authenticity to the very banal montage that preceded it" (49).

Bazin's careful analysis, however, notes that the people onscreen are not really in danger, since the animal had most likely been "half tamed" prior to filming, though he adds, "This is not the point"—it is the "respect for spatial unity" that matters (49–50). Still, the admission suggests more complexity in his realism than is often ascribed it, an impulse Daney draws upon when describing Bazin's "cinema of transparency" as one that "only desires whatever limits it, impedes it. It only worships transparency because it knows that—all the same—there is no such thing" (34). In other words, for Bazin, according to Daney, cinematic realism often depends on both a sense of unmediated access and, at the same time, an awareness of the limitations and artifice imposed by the film so that, in some cases, the spectator's encounter is enhanced, not muted, by the acknowledgment of those limitations. This paradox recalls Christian Metz's famous ideas about the cinema as an absent-present. In *The Imaginary Signifier,* he notes that in the cinema, unlike live theater, the spectator is a "voyeur, since there is something to see, called the film, but something in whose definition there is a great deal of 'flight': not precisely something that hides, rather something that *lets* itself be seen without *presenting* itself to be seen, which has gone out of the room before leaving only its trace visible there" (63). For Metz, a strong sense of presence and absence, in the same moment, defines cinema—the idea that a film is both "simultaneously very close and definitively inaccessible" (64). Metz's argument may lead him in quite different paths than Bazin (for Metz, a psychoanalytic reading of cinema indebted to Jacques Lacan; for Bazin, a humanist reading of cinema heavily influenced by Christian socialism and postwar French philosophy); but Daney's reading of Bazin's "cinema of transparency," one that only "desires whatever . . . impedes it," draws some useful parallels with Metz's sense of cinema as presence *and* absence.

When one turns to *Grizzly Man,* however, one might not at first expect a realist aesthetic to figure heavily into this film, given how self-aware and self-conscious Herzog's approach to "ecstatic truth" is throughout his filmmaking (recall his invention of Dengler's asking for a tattoo, for example). In other words, Bazin's ideas of a cinema of transparency, one that only "desires whatever . . . impedes it," do not immediately seem to present themselves, much less a realist aesthetic, however inflected by a Metzian presence-as-absence. And yet a realist aesthetic that trades on our sense of the subject's mortality saturates the film, making this key scene where Herzog plays the audio footage for Palovak even more compelling. In terms of subject matter, of course, mortality in *Grizzly Man* is rarely out of the spectator's mind, as Herzog constantly returns us to the facts of Treadwell's and Huguenard's death, whether through his interview subjects, his own voice-over, or the many shots of Treadwell interacting with bears. Interestingly, however, the scenes that seem to connect the cinematic image to reality most convincingly are the more quiet, reflective moments, when Herzog characterizes Treadwell's own aesthetic as itself dependent upon an inherent connection between camera and reality.

Several scenes make this connection explicit, both through the images and sounds of Treadwell's original footage and through Herzog's guiding

Grizzly Man: Timothy Treadwell records himself with the bears.

voice-over. In one scene, for instance, we see footage of a fox outside of Treadwell's blue tent and hear its paws scratch the surface, as Herzog describes Treadwell: "I, too, would like to step in here in his defense, not as an ecologist but as a filmmaker. He captured such glorious improvised moments, the likes of which the studio directors with their union crews can never dream of." Herzog here emphasizes the spontaneous aspects of the shot; the scratching sound of the paws and the fox's shadow are invested with a sense of material reality. In another scene, Treadwell is signing off, a bear in the background, when a fox and her pups come running through the frame, unplanned by Treadwell. Herzog remarks, "Now, the scene seems to be over, but as a filmmaker sometimes things fall into your lap, which you couldn't expect, never even dream of." He follows this remark with a line that could have been lifted from Bazin's "Ontology of the Photographic Image": "There is something like an inexplicable magic of cinema." And in yet another scene, Treadwell is setting up a shot where he will emerge from the brush and begin speaking to the camera. Because he does not have a film crew with him, however, he must start the camera rolling, walk up the path, out of sight, and then walk into the frame. Here, Herzog's voice-over emphasizes *not* the moment when Treadwell emerges from the brush but the moments preceding his entrance: "In his action-movie mode, Treadwell probably did not realize that seemingly empty moments had a strange, secret beauty. Sometimes images themselves developed their own life, their own mysterious stardom." As Herzog says these words, we simply see a shot of brush blowing in the wind (one thinks here of the subtitle to Christian Keathley's text, *The Wind in the Trees*). Watching such a moment onscreen, we are gently reminded that a camera makes no distinctions once it has been set in motion. For a viewer (or a filmmaker, for that matter) invested in film realism, brush in the wind can be as interesting as the person who emerges from it. Here, we find Herzog's interest in reanimating Bazinian issues, even if he does so only to question them further.

The more "quiet" scenes are thus complicit in—and not at all opposed to—developing a strong link between the cinematic image and mortality because they establish a fundamental link between Treadwell's camera and a spontaneous, uncontrollable reality that exists around him. Although the stakes are rather low in these scenes—a fox scratching his tent; foxes running through the frame; some excess footage of grass blowing in the wind—the connection of camera to reality sets up the existence of the videotape as *real*, even if it is only audio footage. And this deep association is part of what makes the scene between Herzog and Palovak so compelling.

The visual aesthetic of the scene adds to that awareness even further. Palovak holds the camera—Timothy's camera, Herzog tells us—in her lap. It is important that it is not simply *a* camera but *Timothy's* camera, the very one that recorded the death during the attack. Beyond the important connections that have already been established between Treadwell's camera and reality, this camera has been touched by Treadwell, which is now held by Palovak. Such tactile transference, if only imagined in the minds of viewers, is not unlike the sense of indexicality with which theorists of film realism invest the cinematic frame. And simply seeing a camera onscreen reiterates its recording function (think if Herzog had played the video on a Mini-DV deck, for instance, or simply had the camera placed offscreen—the effect would have been quite different). Herzog's posture, as well, indicates the intensity of the moment; his strain is apparent by his closing his eyes, his holding his hands to his head, and his leaning forward in an attitude of expectancy and alertness. Palovak nervously tries to read Herzog's face for signs of what he hears—much as we, too, scan all of these visual elements of the scene for evidence the film is never ready to yield. The camera imitates our own curiosity here, as it swings from Palovak to Herzog, trying to pick up some kind of clue. Finally, those brief cuts indicate ellipses and, by extension, what we cannot know—or what Herzog will not permit us to hear, which is the tape itself. The tape thus at once represents the strong connection of cinema to reality—the awful knowledge that what Herzog listens to is *really* the ultimate end of Treadwell and Huguenard both—and, at the same time, for viewers, does not exist insofar as we cannot hear it. If Bazin's cinema of transparency only "desires whatever . . . impedes it," what better metaphor might there be for it than the denial of access to the footage itself—evidence both present and absent that has, as Metz would put it, "gone out of the room before leaving only its trace" (63)?

Such complex but compelling invocations of cinema and the realist film tradition weight this moment as much as, if not more than, any other scene in the film with our sense of Treadwell's and Huguenard's mortality. But what also makes this scene so effective and affecting is that the footage is aural—and not visual *and* aural—evidence. While this fact is simply a matter of chance, in that the lens cap was never removed, it nonetheless is a major part of why the scene works in the way it does. It functions as evidence, but the fact that it is sound evidence necessitates further reflection.

SOUND AND THE CINEMA

Unlike the history we associate with theories of film realism—be they Bazinian or explicit rejections of that approach—cinematic sound has traditionally undergone less critical and theoretical consideration (though recent scholarship suggests this is becoming less the case). In 1992 Rick Altman raised the issue succinctly: "the image has been theorized earlier, longer, and more fully than sound"; therefore, "sound's importance has been recognized only belatedly, thus tending to make sound theory and analysis tributary of image theory and analysis (even if sound itself is not dependent on the image)" (171). Although Altman does not here speculate on the reasons behind this critical imbalance, his point is well-taken. A cursory glance through any critical or theoretical anthology shows how much our discipline relies on the image—and how little on sound—to construct its theories. The discipline itself, however, may not be at fault. It may simply be that the discipline's overemphasis on the image is symptomatic of the ways in which most spectators tend to absorb sound—as existing *only* in relation to the image, if it is acknowledged consciously at all.

For intelligent reflection on the relationship between sound and image, one need look no further than one of the only theorists of film sound, Michel Chion. Chion's work has been central to the development of scholarship on film sound, and his precision, clarity, and at times lyricism have made him an attractive theorist for anyone working in film sound in the past twenty to thirty years. Crucial to almost all of his major theoretical statements on sound has been the inherent bond between sound and image, with sound's legibility dependent upon its relation to image. For instance, in his *The Voice in Cinema,* he makes the following provocation: "*there is no soundtrack*" (3). Chion explains this odd formulation: "a film's aural units are not received as an autonomous unit. They are immediately analyzed and distributed in the spectator's perceptual apparatus according to the relation each bears to what the spectator sees at the time" (3). In other words, sounds are generally only processed in relation to visualized spaces, actual or imaginary (3). And one of the most important concepts running through his work is "synchresis," or "the spontaneous and irresistible weld produced between a particular auditory phenomenon and visual phenomenon when they occur at the same time" (*Audio-Vision* 63). Synchresis is crucial to the way we generally process sound in cinema, and what is interesting is the remarkable tolerance spectators have for sounds—*any* sounds—to seem as though they belong to the image. As he writes, "Synchresis is what makes dubbing, postsynchronization, and sound-effects mixing possible, and enables such a wide array of choices in these processes. For a single body and a single face on the screen, thanks to synchresis, there are dozens of allowable voices—just as, for a shot of a hammer, any one of a hundred sounds will do" (*Audio-Vision* 63). One cannot, however, think of such freedom with the visual. While one can make the sound of a hammer by hitting a wrench or a screwdriver against a board, for instance, the substitution of the same visuals would alter the meaning of the shot in a way that the sounds do not. Studio sound libraries, Foley artists, and the history of animation are a few examples that would seem to confirm the powerful effect of synchresis on audience reception of the cinema.

What happens, then, when we are confronted with cinematic sounds to which we have no images? Such an experience is more experimental than practical, since it would require that a viewer actually not watch the screen and listen instead—an experience that few moviegoers beyond critics interested in film sound would seek out. Yet these practices, even experimental ones, can be instructive. Consider the following description by Jeffrey K. Ruoff, discussing the uncanny experience of listening to an observational documentary, shot with location sound, without watching the images as well:

> listening to many of the scenes of observational films without watching the screen can be a dizzying experience. Without recognizable sources in the image to anchor the sounds, we hear a virtual cacophony of clanging, snippets of dialogue and music, and various unidentifiable sounds, almost an experiment in concrete music. Freed of their associations to objects, the sounds resurface in their phenomenological materiality. (221)

This materiality is not the materiality of sounds "attached" to their visual source but sounds in and of themselves, roaming free of any visuals
whatsoever.

It may be a conceptual leap to suggest that sounds without images are
necessarily anxiety producing, based on a brief discussion of Chion and
Ruoff, and counterexamples would certainly debunk any overly rigid theoretical approaches to those few occasions when we encounter cinematic
sound without image. Despite the tentative (and, potentially, theoretically
precarious) position, however, the remainder of this essay would like to take
up these ideas as they apply to *Grizzly Man,* because it is my contention that
part of the anxiety inherent in that scene is rooted in our knowledge that the
footage is sound without image.

Most of *Grizzly Man*'s use of sound confirms the desire for legibility, and while the two most identifiable and common sounds in the film
do not have onscreen visual counterparts, they are easily identifiable and
hardly anxiety producing: they are Herzog's voice-over and music. Very
little of the film unfolds without Herzog's voice, music, or both guiding
the spectator's experience. In many ways, these sounds provide an antidote to the often oppressive sense of mortality that suffuses the image;
both music and voice-over provide a critical distance, either in Herzog's
digressive, questioning rhetoric or in the music, which mimics Herzog's
digressions, its melodies tending to wander among various smaller themes
rather than play strictly structured songs. It would not be going too far to
say that sound and image in this film quite often have a dialectical relationship, with Herzog's voice-over and music pulling against the weight of
Treadwell's presence onscreen. As a result, the Bazinian questions about
cinema—its irrational power, often linked to the viewer's consciousness
about mortality—are not diluted so much as complicated by a critical distance that sound often provides. While it may be perfectly Bazinian, for
instance, to have an "empty moment" in one's film, it is hardly Bazinian to
point out that moment through voice-over, which is precisely what Herzog
does. *Grizzly Man*'s sounds rarely produce anxiety in and of themselves.

There is an early important exception, however, one that lingers and
complicates any easy associations of sound as somehow "safe." In the opening sequence of the film, a bear approaches the camera, quite docile, as we
hear Treadwell's voice say, "Go back and play." Previous images of the bears
have characterized them as tranquil and reflective, matching Treadwell's
own romanticized vision of the bears. The music has also encouraged this
reflective mood with a gentle melody led by acoustic guitar. But in one shot,
the bear comes close, and all at once, the sound cuts from the musical score
to direct sound. This cut happens as Treadwell loses his balance, either

because the bear has pushed him or because he has tripped. It may also simply be that Treadwell's camera has fallen, but his close proximity to the camera at this moment makes it seem as though any threat to the camera is a threat to him. In any case, the encroachment of real danger abruptly ends the reflective mood of the scene until this moment. Furthermore, part of what makes the shot so anxiety producing is that we cannot identify every sound within it, and the one we can, Treadwell's voice, has lost its gentle, high pitch and has deepened. He is scared, and we may feel fear as well, not only because Treadwell is in danger but because the sounds of that danger are beyond easy identification, making them all the more threatening. Herzog's inclusion of this early exception gives the rest of the film a certain instability, past violence always threatening to disrupt the order of the present and the documentary itself at any moment. In addition, we already know that Treadwell onscreen *has* died (in the present of our viewing, given the opening subtitle of the film) and *will* die (in the temporal present of the footage of Treadwell). Every potential eruption of violence thus becomes capable of fulfilling a dreadful promise—that Herzog might actually show us this death onscreen. That he does not comes as some initial relief, but it is quickly supplanted by another kind of anxiety, one related to sound itself.

In the scene in question, when Herzog sits with Palovak and listens to Treadwell and Huguenard's deaths, part of what makes the scene so difficult is that he is listening to sound without its accompanying image. So much of the visual and auditory information of the film at this moment emphasizes the unintelligibility of the sound that Herzog is listening to. He sits hunched over, clutching the headphones to his ears, and he says very little. At one moment, he even seems to tremble. Such aspects of the scene indicate both the brutality of the sound—its terrifying violence—and another terrifying aspect—that its sounds are incoherent and without easy identification. When he says, "I hear rain, and I hear Amie, Get away, go away, go away," it is as though he is listening to a corrupt transmission, as though those are the *only* sounds he can identify, the rest an inchoate auditory jumble evoking violence and death but ultimately incomprehensible. Sound produces anxiety here not only because it is divorced from the image but because it is, at least as interpreted through Herzog's own posture and speech, unintelligible.

The final turn in this scene, of course, and the most important one, is that this is a sound divorced not only from image but from sound itself. It is a sound that does not exist, at least within the world of the film, since we never actually hear it, and yet its absence echoes the absence of both Treadwell and Huguenard. For Herzog, who experiences the sound directly, the aural evidence is, in the Metzian sense, a presence that has "gone out of the room before leaving only its trace" (audible rather than "visible"); but for Palovak, one step further removed from the footage (given that she never hears it), the sound is a trace of a trace, an absence she experiences only through the gestures and fragmented speech of the filmmaker. For us, at an even further remove, this scene should yield a near kaleidoscopic effect of absences, traces, and echoes. And yet it is at this precise moment when the Metzian presence seems most compelling, or when the Bazinian real comes closest to seeming like an empirical, material fact. The lesson here is that rational awareness of the cinema's tenuous connection to reality sometimes falters in the face of the compelling irrational power of the medium when the mortality of its subjects is its main concern. As Bazin perhaps knew all too well, the absence always returns as a presence to be reckoned with. And although this particular recording was an accident, its existence as sound footage, and only sound, acts as an even more appropriate memorial to these figures, given that sound itself is an absent-presence within cinema studies—and given that, like death, it is a subject that still evokes mystery and anxiety, despite our rational apprehension of the material processes by which sound is made.

This scene's complex use of sound, however, is but one facet of Herzog's larger engagement with the documentary form, and his approach raises questions so many other essays in this volume ask: how can we represent the world in an ethical way when our ideas about truth and representation have been called into question by the intellectual, cultural, and aesthetic movements of the last and current centuries? What of the multifaceted media culture to which those movements have responded and of which they are ultimately a part? Can we recover a notion of truth and the real, and, furthermore, do we want to? *Grizzly Man* does not necessarily answer any one of these questions. Instead, Herzog's film is a dispassionate but empathetic investigation into the circumstances surrounding the deaths of Treadwell and his companion Huguenard, one that does not so much seek to form clear answers but rather to articulate its inquiry as carefully as possible, without reducing the complexity of what it is asking. If viewers wish to find such answers, they must ultimately look—and listen—elsewhere, for although his voice-over accompanies so much of the film, when it comes to certainty and closure in the culmination of his discourse, Herzog, like the audio footage he never provides us, remains silent.

NOTES

I am indebted to the *Film Criticism* reader and the current volume's editors for the insightful comments and suggestions on this essay.

1. So much has been written about André Bazin in the brief time since the first publication of this essay. For more, see especially Dudley Andrew, ed., with Hervé Joubert-Laurencin, *Opening Bazin: Postwar Film Theory and Its Afterlife* (New York: Oxford University Press, 2011).

Works Cited

Altman, Rick. "Introduction: Sound's Dark Corners." *Sound Theory/Sound Practice,* ed. Rick Altman, 171–77. New York: Routledge, 1992.

Bazin, André. "Death Every Afternoon." Trans. Mark A. Cohen. In *Rites of Realism: Essays on Corporeal Cinema,* ed. Ivone Margulies, 27–31. Durham: Duke University Press, 2003.

———. *What Is Cinema?* Vol. 1, ed. and trans. Hugh Gray. Berkeley: University of California Press, 1967.

Chion, Michel. *Audio-Vision.* Trans. Claudia Gorbman. New York: Columbia, 1994.

———. *The Voice in Cinema.* Trans. Claudia Gorbman. New York: Columbia, 1999.

Daney, Serge. "The Screen of Fantasy (Bazin and Animals)." Trans. Mark A. Cohen. *Rites of Realism: Essays on Corporeal Cinema,* ed. Ivone Margulies, 31–40. Durham: Duke University Press, 2003.

Herzog, Werner. "The Minnesota Declaration: Truth and Fact in Documentary Cinema." In *Herzog on Herzog,* ed. Paul Cronin, 301–2. London: Faber and Faber, 2002.

Kahana, Jonathan. "Cinema and the Ethics of Listening: Isaac Julien's *Frantz Fanon.*" *Film Quarterly* 59, no. 2 (Winter 2005–6): 19–31.

Keathley, Christian. *Cinephilia and History, or The Wind in the Trees.* Bloomington: Indiana University Press, 2006.

Prager, Brad. *The Cinema of Werner Herzog: Aesthetic Ecstasy and Truth.* London: Wallflower Press, 2007.

Metz, Christian. *The Imaginary Signifier: Psychoanalysis and the Cinema.* Trans. Celia Britton, Annwyl Williams, Ben Brewster, and Alfred Guzzetti. Bloomington: Indiana University Press, 1977.

Ruoff, Jeffrey K. "Conventions of Sound in Documentary." In *Sound Theory/Sound Practice,* ed. Rick Altman, 217–34. New York: Routledge, 1992.

Vogel, Amos. "Herzog in Berlin." *Film Comment* 13, no. 5 (September–October 1977): 37–38.

Chapter 31

Cultural Learnings of *Borat* for Make Benefit Glorious Study of Documentary

Leshu Torchin

Genre designations can reflect cultural understandings of boundaries between perception and reality, or more aptly, distinctions between accepted truths and fictions, or even between right and wrong. *Borat: Cultural Learnings of America for Make Benefit Glorious Nation of Kazakhstan* (Larry Charles, 2006) challenges cultural assumptions by challenging our generic assumptions. The continuing struggle to define the film reflected charged territory of categorization, as if locating the genre would secure the meaning and the implications of *Borat*. Most efforts to categorize it focused on the humor, referring to it as mockumentary and comedy. But such classifications do not account for how Borat Sagdiyev (Sacha Baron Cohen) interacts with people onscreen or for Baron Cohen's own claims that these encounters produce significant information about the world. Fictional genres always bear some degree of indexical relationship to the lived world (Sobchack), and that relationship only intensifies in a traditional documentary. *Borat,* however, confuses these genres: a fictional TV host steps out of the mock travelogue on his fictional hometown and steps into a journey through a real America. The indexical relationship between the screen world and the real world varies, then, with almost every scene, sometimes working as fiction, sometimes as documentary, sometimes as mockumentary. In doing so, the film challenges the cultural assumptions that inhere to expectations of genre, playing with the ways the West (for lack of a better shorthand) has mapped the world within the ostensibly rational discourses of nonfiction.

Documentary and mockumentary practices exist simultaneously in the film. Whereas a mockumentary sheathes its fictions within a documentary style, *Borat* sheathes its documentary elements (the interviews are perfectly real to the unwitting participants) within a fiction. Generic stability is complicated further when Borat drops his initial documentary plan of tracking down actress Pamela Anderson, whom he has seen as "CJ" in the television series *Baywatch* (1989–99). But from interviews with actual people and from news and clips of Anderson's pornographic home video, Borat is disillusioned, believing that he now knows the "true" Anderson behind the mediated form onscreen. One television program is thus exchanged for another, and this uneasy exchange throughout the film characterizes its unsettled nature in the context of genre and as a description of reality.

Borat's fictional voyage—complete with interviews, staged encounters, and provocations—is not so distant from the documentary tradition, which has been on shaky epistemological ground since Auguste and Louis Lumière staged their first actualities and Robert Flaherty enlisted Allakariallak to play Nanook in *Nanook of the North* (1922), a reenactment of past Inuit life. *Borat* bears a resemblance to a variety of documentaries—notably, to Jean Rouch's "ethnofictions" and to hoax documentaries. It also suggests the modes of documentary Bill Nichols has called "reflexive" and "performative" for the way they interrogate documentary authority, disorient the audience, and ask us to reconsider the premises that underpin the documentary's claim to truth and knowledge (Nichols, *Blurred Boundaries*). The film just as readily invokes Stella Bruzzi's "performative documentary" and, more important, the performance or "negotiation between filmmaker and reality" (186) embedded in many documentaries.

However, as a mockumentary and a documentary of a mockumentary, and even a fake mockumentary, the film continually retreats behind layer upon layer of reference, forging a recursive interrogation of American bigotry (Strauss) that implicates, by extension, the ostensibly rational technologies of knowledge production. The film elicits damning information by staging a series of intercultural encounters between American (Western) subjects and the racist, misogynist, anti-Semitic, homophobic, and socially ignorant Borat, the caricature of the Eastern foreigner, a modern-day Other. Sam Ali of the *Newark Star-Ledger* has expressed concern that this construction of the foreigner is dangerous to Muslims. In spite of Baron Cohen's (and Borat's) denial of any Muslim identity, Ali declares that Kazakhstan's predominantly Muslim population, combined with Borat's anti-Semitism and misogyny, is enough to cast Borat as Muslim in the American imagination. A fair enough point: Borat's rehearsals of Occidental xeno-phobia feed a stereotype, but they also clearly expose bigotries behind the rhetoric of enlightenment and equality. In this latter regard, the film may accomplish more than Baron Cohen set out to do. The performances do more than "let people lower their guard and expose their own prejudice," as Baron Cohen has explained (Parker). The meeting of "primitive" and "modern" subjects—in world fairs, museums, and documentaries—has frequently served to bolster the imagined superiority of the modern cul-ture and its claim on these institutions. *Borat* situates its modern subjects inside the presumed authority and possession of its own visual technology: a documentary film about America by a Third World admirer. And little by little, Baron Cohen undoes the authority of the subjects' knowledge along-side the authority of the documentary format and technologies' enlighten-ing claims. *Borat*, like "Borat" on- and offscreen, refuses to take the audi-ence backstage and end the charade. They may only exchange one form of programming for another. Americans are, in every sense, trapped by the technology of their understanding, unable to see Others beyond media stereotypes.

BORAT: THE MOCKUMENTARY

The mockumentary refers to a rapidly growing subgenre of the documen-tary. This form draws on recognizable documentary conventions to serve storytelling purposes. Examples range from the newsreel in Orson Welles's *Citizen Kane* (1941) to Christopher Guest's improvisational offerings of *This Is Spinal Tap* (1983), *Waiting for Guffman* (1996), *Best in Show* (2000), and *A Mighty Wind* (2003) to the television show *The Office* (BBC, 2001–3), whose format has since been imported to the United States, France, Ger-many, and Canada. The mockumentary format often explores mundane characters and situations, critiquing the limits of human empathy and imagination. The mockumentary also comments on the relationship be-tween the subject and the media itself, such as in the relationship between filmmakers and serial killer in *C'est arrivé près de chez vous* (*Man Bites Dog*, 1992). The subgenre can also resist the marketing conceits of Hollywood aesthetics and production. As Alexandra Juhasz notes, for example, the documentary pretense of Cheryl Dunye's *The Watermelon Woman* (1996) offered an affordable production style while countering the Hollywood histories that omitted lesbians of all races (17–18).

Amid these diverse practices and theories, mockumentaries "repre-sent a commentary on or confusion or subversion of factual discourse" (Roscoe and Hight 1). Alisa Lebow wonders if the notion of mockumentary "mocks . . . the very viability or sustainability of the documentary category" (228). The fake documentary, Juhasz argues, carries with it voices that simultaneously replicate and challenge the authoritative voice of the documentary, which figures for most historians as "discourses of sobriety" (Nichols, *Representing* 3) and "a tool of scientific inscription" (Winston).

To this end, *Borat* fits the mockumentary model. Borat travels through the United States to make a documentary with the help of his producer, Azamat Bagatov (Ken Davitian). Borat's unfocused and prejudicial interview style, however, quickly dispels any air of sobriety in this presumably authoritative voice. In the case of the interview with feminists, the misogynist Borat, obsessed with Pamela Anderson's voluptuous "CJ," rejects the women's political autonomy and cognitive capacity. Refusing to hear the women out, he cannot fully participate in the interview. Rather, he fantasizes about Anderson and turns the discussion from feminism to his own fixation. The failures of full participation and attention reemerge in his interview with conservative activist and two-time Republican presidential candidate Alan Keyes. Here the interruption becomes ours with cutaways that serve as flashbacks or shocking documentary B-Roll (that secondary footage often used to animate otherwise static and potentially repetitive

Borat: Borat (Sacha Baron Cohen) travels through the U.S. to make a documentary.

talking-head images). During the interview, scenes from the hotel room where Borat wrestled with men and brandished sex toys intrude on the setup. At no point is there any investigation of Keyes's own political life (a lost opportunity, in many ways) but instead only a discussion of Borat and his sexual preoccupations, reflected in speech and the image. Any knowledge to be gleaned in these encounters is unquestionably suspect, filtered as it is through Borat's narcissistic distraction. As much as Borat's behavior is intended to provoke (or, in some cases, incite), it equally calls attention to the limits of documentary interviews as a source of knowledge because, of course, the interview's structure and content are a function of the person holding the microphone. Borat's puerile obsession with Pamela Anderson, one that leads his documentary on an unplanned cross-country voyage, functions both as traditional plot device (the journey narrative) and as metanarrative critique of the vagaries, vicissitudes, and vices behind documentary production.

ETHNOGRAPHY AMOK

The most clearly mockumentary moment comes with the introductory tour of his hometown of Kuzcek. The format mimics the ethnographic film, and in this parody it produces a fantasy of the primitive Other so excessive that the documentary form becomes a sick joke and, more deeply, an absurdly grotesque specter of the Dark or Other Europe in the Western imagination. Like Luis Buñuel's *Las Hurdes* (also called *Terra sin Pan* or *Land without Bread*, 1932), *Borat* verges on surrealism imitating what Jeffrey Ruoff, in his discussion of *Las Hurdes*, calls "surrealist ethnography."[1] The ethnographic connection is important because *Borat* can be linked to a subversive genre that can be traced to a robust period of film history. In the 1920s, artists and anthropologists alike experimented with cultural codes and ideologies and produced startling juxtapositions intended to challenge the legitimacy of categorization and the authority of meaning-making (Clifford, "Ethnographic Surrealism").

The opening of *Borat* provides a mock-ethnographic sequence, mimicking the ethnographies and travelogues that have charted human knowledge. In doing so, much as *Las Hurdes* does, the sequence challenges the easy distinctions a modern documentary makes between us and them, between enlightened civilization and primitive culture. Unlike other ethnographies of its time, most plumbing Africa for subject matter, *Las Hurdes* finds its Other in Europe. As the opening intertitles explain, *Las Hurdes* is a "filmed essay in human geography" focusing on the Hurdanos, who inhabit a remote area between Portugal and Spain. *Las Hurdes* takes the viewer on a tour of "a sterile and inhospitable area" that holds "strange and barbaric" ceremonies and is home to extreme privation. The deadpan chronicle of utter abjection calls to our attention the delimiting, segregating power of narration and to the ethics of the objective encounter with death and disease. Viewers are presented with the death of a baby, with a "choir of idiots," and with dwarfism caused by "hunger, by lack of hygiene, and by incest." At one point, a bull exits a home. As religious as they are—a Buñuelian attack on Catholicism—the strictures of purity are grossly unsettled: the incest taboo is broken; humans and animals cohabitate. Meanwhile, the relationship between voice-over and image is broken: the voice-over explains that a goat has fallen off the cliff, but a telltale puff of smoke suggests otherwise; what appears clearly to be a child is called a dwarf and is, according to the narrator, twenty-eight years old; similarly, a woman who appears to be sixty (a hard sixty) is said to be thirty-six. Such jarring moments call into legitimacy the other claims, such as the statement that a child, still visible on-screen, died the following day. The combination of sound and image tests the authority that comes, in some ways, to be bolstered by the assumptions of impoverished primitivism.

Borat's tour of Kuzcek seems to draw directly from *Las Hurdes* in subject matter, theme, and style. Standing in front of his home, Borat kisses a woman he then introduces as his sister; incest pervades the town as we later learn that he and his wife, Oksana, share a progenitor in Boltok the Rapist (father to Oksana, grandfather to Borat). The proliferation of incest confounds the traditional ethnographic activity of charting kinship and presents a community forsaking even the most basic taboos. They are morally suspect or lawless, flouting traditional boundaries, defiling privileged spaces (Borat, for example, shushes a cow in his lounge). Borat is a primitive figure outside reason, unaware of law or structure. His mother, who appears to be in her seventies or eighties, is announced as the oldest woman in Kuzcek. "She is forty-two years old!" Borat proudly tells his audience, echoing the scene in *Las Hurdes*. Nightmares of archaic medicine carry on the surreal ethnography: the town mechanic is also the town abortionist. This introduction, following its ethnographic imperative, presents a barbaric ceremony as well, "The Running of the Jew." Borat's narration is as full of pride as Buñuel's, in *Las Hurdes*, is dry—both obtusely shameless and uncompassionate.

Meanwhile, Kuzcek, a fictional town in Kazakhstan, evokes the ready-made Western image of the barbaric post-Soviet Other. The "kindergarten" of children with guns suggests terrorist training camps. Kuzcek is as fictional a town as "Jewtown," name-checked in the fake Kazakh national anthem. Such fictions are hardly innocent, yielding real, lived effect. The town onscreen is Glod, Romania, and the sequence was made possible by the participation of the villagers, under the impression that they were part of a high-profile documentary. However, upon viewing the film, they learned of their depiction as abortionists and rapists. The response was one of outrage: "the villagers of Glod say they were tricked into appearing in Cohen's film. They claim they were told it was going to be a documentary, but instead have been portrayed as backward people and criminals" ("Village"). The lawsuits by Glod villagers, humiliated and outraged by their depiction in the film, reveal how deeply the trafficking of this grotesque European Other affects viewers on both sides of the camera.[2]

Baron Cohen is not Kazakh, nor does he resemble a Kazakh, but he does sport the uncertain appearance of a general Eastern stereotype, an easily "substitutable other" (Shohat and Stam 189), which is necessary for the film's effect on American audiences. Bobby Rowe, the rodeo manager, suggests Borat shave his moustache so as not to look Muslim, although Borat tells him that his people "follow the eagle." The point here is that Baron Cohen, though Welsh and Jewish, is mistaken for "Muslim" (both in the film, by Rowe, and outside it, by Ali) rather than for Iraqi, Iranian, Balkan, or any other genuine ethnicity. "Muslim" is not an ethnicity; it denotes a follower of a religion. But the term does refer to an established set of images that Americans use for categorizing the Dark side of Europe, as well as the Middle East. Borat is summarily converted into one of those "Muslim extremists" who occupy the lead stories of nightly newscasts. The term "Muslim" is a trope, not a religious or cultural category. It signals the enemy. Understanding here is quite beside the point. As punctuation to this theme, Borat does not even speak Kazakh; he speaks a mixture of Polish, Russian, and Hebrew. Ken Davitian's character, producer Bagatov, speaks Armenian, rounding out the Eastern pastiche. Meanwhile, the native Kazakh language exists only as a hypothetical trace of reality in the English subtitles onscreen. The musical sound track, too, is not Kazakh but mostly Balkan, with music provided by Sarajevan composer Goran Bregović and by the Macedonian Kočani Orkestar, among others. "Ederlezi," a traditional folk song of the Romani (and a piece refashioned by Bregović for Emir Kusturica's *Dom za vesanje/The Time of the Gypsies*, 1988), is used to represent Borat's own tormented emotional state. This use of Romani and Jewish culture to construct Borat's anti-Ziganist, anti-Semite persona dissolves the Kazakh fantasy back into the plural voices that simply do not exist to Westerners who see Eastern Europe and the Middle East on even the widest, brightest television screens money can buy. *Borat*'s projection of the West may be equally fraught, however. The film offers a skewed mapping of America, placing in Georgia a sequence filmed in Newton,

Massachusetts, while sequences from South Carolina and Texas are presented as if down the road from one another. This false mapping of actual encounters in the ascendant culture prevents Borat and *Borat* from achieving authority. At the same time, this distorted arrangement of place plays with the way documentaries can and do dispense with continuity editing in favor of "evidentiary editing"—editing that serves rhetorical logic (Nichols, *Introduction*, 30).

BORAT AND THE DOCUMENTARY TRADITION

Nanook director Robert Flaherty once explained that "sometimes you have to lie. One often has to distort a thing to catch its true spirit" (cited in Calder-Marshall 97). This distortion is reflected in John Grierson's phrase "the creative treatment of actuality," said to derive from Grierson's response to Flaherty's work (Winston 11–14). And, indeed, the work of the Grierson group is known for the reenactments and often poetic representations of social services and civic issues. Humphrey Jennings's film *The Silent Village* (1943) stands out as an exceptional example of early dramatic re-creation. The film stages the Nazi occupation of the Czech town of Lidice as the occupation of a Welsh village, with language prohibition and mass arrests. In doubled historical narration, the violence against Lidice articulates Britain's own violence against Wales, which, in turn, illustrates the Nazi occupation.

The place of fiction in documentary comes to the fore in the work of Jean Rouch. His "ethnofictions" brought together truth and fiction in "ethnographic fantasies built around historical and social realities, complete with a cast of 'fictional' characters" (DeBouzek 304). The improvisations were intended to reveal more about people's lives than any authoritative documentary could. In *Moi, un noir* (1959) day laborers in Treichville take names like "Edward G. Robinson," "Eddie Constantine," and "Dorothy Lamour." These names indicate the omnipresence of Western media culture and register the effacing impact on African self-representation. *Petit à petit* (1971) takes this encounter with the West in reverse, from Cote D'Ivoire up to Paris. Here actor Damouré Zika plays a character named Damouré who conducts an ethnographic expedition to France, studying the ways of the French people in order to assist in the development of office buildings back in Abidjan. The African actor, playing ethnographer, stands outside the Musée de l'Homme, attempting to take the measurements of passersby. The fictional pretense meets with a playful "reverse ethnography," turning the trip into a parodic pilgrimage that blurs the documentary boundaries between "us" and "them," between "science" and "art," and between sobriety and play (DeBouzek).

For Baron Cohen, the mixing of Eastern and Western spaces does not validate an inferior Other; it exposes the equivalent strangeness and otherness of those people whom Borat, the misogynistic, anti-Semitic primitive, is caricaturing. But their own caricatures prevent them from seeing that mirror. Like ethnographic surrealism, the film "attacks the familiar, provoking the irruption of otherness" (Clifford, *Predicament* 145). In other words, Borat's primitive figure encourages condescending instruction and complicity from people who themselves emerge as grotesque primitives.

A Documentary into Darkness

In its turn toward documentary, Borat leaves the fake Kazakhstan for the real world, making his way across America in a quest for knowledge. The tour begins in New York City but soon turns into a cross-country journey through the American South as Borat begins his pursuit of Pamela Anderson. Here the fictional reporter conducts interviews with politicians, a humor coach, and an etiquette coach, and he engages University of South Carolina frat boys, an American rodeo, a kosher bed-and-breakfast, teenaged hip-hop enthusiasts, and a Pentecostal service. Xenophobia, racism, anti-Semitism, homophobia, and misogyny make appearances, but so do surprising shows of good humor, courtesy, and willingness to indulge this stranger who aggressively tests their limits. Senator Bob Barr graciously, if awkwardly, swallows the "human cheese" he is offered. The southern hostess of a dinner party, perhaps believing this man has never seen a toilet, responds generously with a demonstration of the facilities. The tolerance may be born from condescension, but it is in equal measure kind. New Yorkers fare somewhat worse in their demonstration of stereotypical "uncivil" behavior: Borat is met with threats of violence and outbursts of obscenity.

The bulk of the voyage takes place in the American South, where the distinction between primitive and civilized is tested in each encounter with the natives. The New Yorkers, with their aggression and curses, illustrate an ignoble savage, to be sure, but it is the American South that will be the America of this trip, as storied with bigotry and violence as is the atavistic Kazakhstan the film imagines. Perhaps there is something cheap in this regional selection. Scenes from the South are selected for their focus on backward or religious attitudes, and this conviction is helped along by *Borat*'s imaginative geography, which unifies all southern states and even adds a sequence from New England into the southern trip, creating a "pastiched" American Other much like Kuzcek. But such pastiching and stereotyping are the rampant themes here and the film rather self-consciously participates in them.

The Pentecostal service offers a stunning occasion for collapsing distinctions between us and them, West and East, modern and primitive. The sequence presents a combination of religious and political fervor that viewers might easily associate with the Islamic East. The appearance of the politicians, including Congressman Charles "Chip" Pickering and a State Supreme Court Justice, erodes any pretense of a separation between church and state and, by extension, the notion that enlightened civilizations maintain a rational, secular distance from primitive religious fanatics. Pentecostal worship itself provides a considerable spectacle: its practitioners speak in tongues and swoon with the spirit. How is this Christian performance so different from the Kazakh ceremony depicted at the beginning of the film? If this is a congregation of savages, though, they are eminently welcoming and obliging toward Borat's provocative joking. "Nobody loves my neighbor," he answers to the claim that Jesus loves everyone. Yet they provide him with his ride to Los Angeles, where Borat is united with his producer, Azamat.

The complex, genteel primitivism of his southern dinner hosts and of the Pentecostal church is countered, however, with a more shameful heart of American darkness. At the Imperial Rodeo at the Salem Civic Center, Borat interviews manager Bobby Rowe. In passing, Borat refers to his country's practice of hanging homosexuals. "That's what we're trying to do here," responds Rowe, before continuing with his recommendation that Borat shave his moustache in order to appear less Muslim (and pass for Italian). Borat performs at the rodeo, too, and introduces his act with the claim, "We support your war of terror!" The crowd cheers, ignorant of or indifferent to the change of preposition from "on" to "of." Borat continues to test the limits of their support in his cry, "May George Bush drink the blood of every single man, woman, and child of Iraq!" The cheers subside, and the line is finally drawn: "May you destroy their country so that for the next thousand years, not even a single lizard will survive in their desert!" But the crowd's open hostility is reserved for the expression of Borat's nationalism. He sings the fictional Kazakhstan national anthem to the tune of the U.S. national anthem. The merger of the two testaments of national pride forces the audience to link Eastern primitivism to Western civilization and aggrandizement. Such heresy is not tolerated, and the crowd boos Borat from the stadium of sacred animal rites.

At other times, Borat fails to perturb, but the result is equally startling. A request for a gun to shoot Jews is met with seeming aplomb. In his encounter with University of Southern Carolina frat boys, casual misogyny and racism are met with enthusiasm as the students bemoan the end of slavery and complain that minorities now have all the rights. A used-car salesman sanctions the term "pussy magnet." For Baron Cohen, apathy is

as pernicious as open bigotry. This was his argument in response to the
Anti-Defamation League's complaint about an episode outside the film,
in which Borat performed his song, "In My Country There Is a Problem"
(alternately known as "Throw the Jew down the Well") to enthusiastic reception in a Tucson bar.[3] The willingness of the participants to accept this
warped character as a credible representative of Kazakhstan speaks to a
condescension that insulates them from their own primitive biases. *Borat*
reveals the West's cultural schizophrenia: one voice testifies to enlightened
democracy while the voice that testifies to tribal bigotry remains intact.

BORAT: HOAX DOCUMENTARY

Borat has much in common with documentaries that chronicle hoaxes,
such as Coco Fusco and Paula Heredia's *The Couple in the Cage* (1997), Chris
Smith, Sarah Price, and Dan Ollman's *The Yes Men* (2003), and Vít Klusák
and Filip Remunda's *Ceský Sen/Czech Dream* (2004). In these films, the stars
perform alternative identities (undiscovered Amerindians in *The Couple in
the Cage;* World Trade Organization officials in *Yes Men;* hypermarket indus-
trialists in *Ceský Sen*) to elicit truths about the institutions in which they appear. *The Yes Men* (whose UK DVD cover boasts similarities to Ali G, one of
Baron Cohen's other alter egos) chronicles the adventures of Mike Bonanno
and Andy Bichlbaum as they impersonate World Trade Organization rep-
resentatives on television and at conferences all over the globe. In these appearances, they make extreme claims and proposals—outsourcing slavery,
recycling food products for Third World distribution—intended to test the
limits of their audience. Armed with PowerPoint presentations, business jargon, and three-piece suits, the Yes Men mimic and decry corporate behavior,
showing the human cost of profit margins. Their mission is one of "identity
correction," which challenges the perceived superiority of the subjects.[4]

The Couple in the Cage chronicles the journey of Coco Fusco and
Guillermo Gomez-Peña in their "Guatanaui World Tour" exhibit, a critical response to the Columbus Quincentennial. In this exhibit, Fusco and
Gomez-Peña inhabit a cage as "undiscovered Amerindians" on display at
sites throughout the world, including the Smithsonian Museum of Natural
History in Washington, D.C.; the Plaza Colón in Madrid; and the Australian
Museum of Natural Science. The institutional sites were chosen for their
colonial legacies, where the "'savage' body" was produced from imperial
conquest (Taylor 165). While Borat's improprieties are designed to reveal
those of his subjects, the caged couple's are designed to "highlight, rather
than normalize, the theatricality of colonialism" (Taylor 167). Or, as Barbara Kirshenblatt-Gimblett observes, the "ethnographic burlesque" of *The*

Couple in the Cage "shifts the locus of repudiation and admonishment from the 'other' to the practices of 'othering'" (177).

In a sequence from television's *Da Ali G Show* (2000, UK; 2003–4, U.S.), Borat plays with this shift from "other" to "othering" when he tackles how one museum produces knowledge. Visiting Middleton Place Plantation in South Carolina, a living museum where actors play their historical roles by carrying out plantation work as if in the eighteenth century, Borat demonstrates how slavery can be written out of historical memory in the very act of preserving it. He marvels at the primitive culture before him and laments the state of U.S. technology, which he had held in such high esteem. Approaching one man, Borat attempts to help: there are now machines that can do this work, Borat tells him. Perhaps the poor man is a slave? The man attempts to explain: "This is the eighteenth century; I am a historic interpreter." Failing to make his point, the man tries again, stating that the museum is a historic site, a "time machine back to 1750 or 1760." "You make a time machine?" Borat asks, compelling the actor to ask his partner for help, but she can only complain, "I'm trying hard, but he keeps asking about buying a slave, and that hasn't been done since 1865!" The actor-educators have erased slave labor from their eighteenth-century lesson in plantation economies, but their conviction that Borat requires instruction in the museum's narrative blinds them to the obvious misrepresentation: 1865 is not the eighteenth century. As a result, the educational institution grows unstable and even anxious about the history it displays. In effect, the camera captures triple performances: their work performance as eighteenth-century characters, their instructional performance as live educators for Borat, and their performance for the camera as historically savvy Americans. All of these performances repudiate Borat, turning him into the primitive Other who must be taught how to see—or not see—history, nationality, and ethnicity.

By allowing a visitor to disrupt the proceedings, this encounter offers an appeal beyond that of *The Couple in the Cage*. Fusco and Gomez-Peña use the museum as part of their interrogation of colonial encounter and theatricality, so it is the museum visitors who bear the brunt of the interrogation, both in the live performance and in the video documentary. Gomez-Peña has stated that his ideal spectator would "open the cage and let us out" (Taylor 169). But, as Diana Taylor rightly notes, there is a "prohibition against uninvited intervention" (169), which would have been amplified for those who read *The Couple in the Cage* as performance art requiring protection. The exhibit effectively questioned the role of the museum visitor in the face of uncertain morality (two people caged). Museum protocol prevents contact with the exhibit, no matter how pernicious (or simply alive) its content might be. Borat is the inappropriate visitor who, in violating the limits of museum protocols,

Borat: Borat with the humor coach, Pat Haggerty.

contests the authority of its knowledge. He is the visitor who, by attempting to buy a slave, has opened the cage to let out captives.

This recursive play with epistemological framing appears again in *Borat* in the scene with the humor coach, Pat Haggerty. Borat wishes to learn about humor in order to better understand the United States and to better interact with its citizens. He asks if Haggerty laughs "on people with retardation," to which the humor coach answers that such jokes are not acceptable because this is a condition that one does not choose and that "causes pain and hardship." But perhaps they have not seen really funny retardation, says Borat, who then launches into a story about his sister, who teased his retarded brother, Bilo, mercilessly with her "vazhine" (vagina). "You will never get this!" she had taunted Bilo repeatedly, until one day he broke free from his cage and, in Borat's broken English, he "get this! High five!" There is a beat before Haggerty tells Borat that Americans would not find this joke funny. This is true and not true at the same time: the story, its impropriety, and Borat's apparent glee in the telling are hilarious in their excess, and the joke certainly had American audiences laughing from the safety of their seats. The advice that Haggerty gives seems quite sound, but performed at one register removed, the joke is once again funny. Haggerty's sober zone of repudiation—of Borat's backward sensibilities—is undone time and again by American audiences.

BORAT: RECURSIVE DOCUMENTARY

Although it is a chronicle of hoaxes, *Borat* differs from *Czech Dream, The Yes Men,* and *The Couple in the Cage* in its refusal to provide a clear backstage, where viewers can unproblematically assume complete knowledge of the identities and events. Viewers are not entirely in on the joke as Baron Cohen refuses to break with the character of Borat at any point. While the other films seek to expose the machinations and constructions of official institutions, commercial and corporate businesses, or educational resources like museums, *Borat* postures as transparent documentary. The pranksters of the other two films explain their processes to the camera, keeping the viewer in on the action—even if the Yes Men insist on using the names "Andy" and "Mike" (not their real names). *Czech Dream* incorporates the moment of deception and interviews the dupes who now know the truth. Even *The Couple in the Cage* provides interviews with the audience, an approach that Taylor and Kirshenblatt-Gimblett claim "makes explicit what was implicit in the live event, namely that the installation staged the viewer in ways that were unstable and untenable" (Kirshenblatt-Gimblett 177). But *Borat,* like the eponymous documentarian, refuses to tell the truth. Even when Borat is stripped naked and engaged in a gleefully real (if disgusting) nude wrestling match with Azamat, the charade continues. When the naked men run into the elevator, and into a meeting, audiences are not sure whether the event is staged. And that uncertainty situates them within the instability and untenability of performance itself: the film refuses to delimit knowledge—its documentation of America—according to the protocols of the cinema exhibit. The truth of the body is wrapped in the performance of an argument and carried out into a field whose truth-status has yet to be revealed.

Borat appears at first to work like documentary hoaxes with its bumbling mockumentarian spurring revelations through creative entrapment. Then there is the suggestion of the performative and reflexive documentaries as his encounters challenge the limits of documentary authority and the boundaries of truth and fiction, and of enlightened and primitive subjects, but *Borat* begins and ends with a fiction. The entire project is thrown into uncertainty as each sequence provides a step backward from verisimilitude, offering a performative documentary about performance and a mockumentary of a documentary of a mockumentary.

Rather than erasing the potential for documentary evidence, such recursive play instead amplifies our preoccupation with the factual, authentic
world of *Borat*. Audiences look all the harder for the truth. David Marchese
and Willa Paskin write that outing the figures in the film "has turned into
a mini-media craze, with tons of news outlets trying to sniff out the stories
behind the making of the film."[5] The film was comedy, it was documentary,
and it was performance art serving up metaphors of the truth: trying to sort
this out became sport not only in everyday conversation and news reports but
in the numerous lawsuits launched in the effort to "correct" misperceptions
of what people took to be true. This craze for determining the empirical, referential world of *Borat*, a compulsion known as "epistemephilia," is cousin
to "scopophilia," the voyeuristic compulsion to see (Nichols, *Blurred Boundaries*). Epistemephilia, though, connotes learning, whereas scopophilia connotes mere consuming. Epistemephilia suggests advancement; scopophilia
suggests appetite. The former marks the civilizing impulse, especially of empirical, technological acquisition, whereas the latter marks the atavistic impulse. Borat takes viewers voyeuristically into their society, revealing all manner of vice and virtue, but he refuses to satisfy their epistemic pleasures, and
so he leaves viewers dangling between atavistic glee and civilized revulsion.

Off camera, the dangling continued, as Baron Cohen refused to appear
as himself and instead appeared in character, forcing interviewers into playing along.[6] Late-night talk-show hosts were obliged both to affiliate with
and to disassociate themselves from Borat in order to appear cosmopolitan
and in on the joke yet politically tolerant (i.e., *not* "Borat"). "What do you say
to claims that your film was racist, homophobic, and misogynist?" asked
Jay Leno. "Thank you," answered Borat. Hosts struggled to find the right
tone. Ironically, some hosts took on the role of patronizing educator while
the other guests adopted a ridiculously tolerant posture, submitting to both
gropes and jibes as the man from Kuzcek took over the studio. Audiences
and guests could no longer determine what factual information or even
what performative information the talk show was delivering. The talk-show
genre itself had been hijacked, even within a context of reality television,
where real people perform versions of themselves for the representation of
life in a closed house or in the swap between families.

FROM *BORAT* TO *BRÜNO*

Borat's (and *Borat*'s) elegantly recursive performance takes no prisoners,
wickedly deconstructing and destabilizing the sites of cultural authority,
including popular authority. It is the absence of both the recursive performance and the willingness to target all classes that limits Baron Cohen's

subsequent project, *Brüno* (Larry Charles, 2009), which follows a flamboy-antly gay Austrian fashionista and erstwhile host of *Funkyzeit mit Brüno* to America in pursuit of fame. At first glance the film appears to continue in the vein of *Borat*, deploying a quest narrative that will interweave documen-tary encounters with fictional pursuits for self-improvement. Its unclear and unrealized commentary on homophobia aside, the film's mission to critique celebrity culture is hamstrung by the growing awareness of media pranking and culture jamming. Hence Baron Cohen relies more heavily on the overtly staged and fictional narratives, including a love affair and the adoption of an African child. This prevalence of the more overtly fictive ele-ments in *Brüno* diminishes the rich interplay of genres found in *Borat* that refuses complacency and promotes curiosity and critique.

In addition, the constraint imposed by savvy public relations person-nel turns Baron Cohen to less enfranchised targets for hoaxes: the working class, who become unwitting extras in his narrative. Brüno accompanies some men from Alabama on a hunting trip, attempting to provoke a re-sponse by comparing their grouping to the *Sex and the City* (1998–2004) women. As this fails to achieve more than a bemused silence, he pursues provocation in the form of a naked late-night visit to each man's tent. The angry rebuffs do little to reveal any hidden homophobia, while Brüno's own performance likely supports the paranoid stereotypes of gay men as flam-boyant sexual predators. In another case, Baron Cohen colluded with for-mer talk-show host Richard Bey to stage a fake talk show on the subject of "unusual parenting" for an unsuspecting audience.[7] Brüno joins the stage in a segment about single parents. At first the audience, a predominantly African American crowd, supports him, but they soon become increasingly upset by Brüno's revelations, beginning with his blithe announcement that he traded his son for an iPod. This claim excites already present anxieties raised by high-profile international adoptions and, more specifically, the very public celebrity concern around Africa that appears to some as "cul-tural colonialism masquerading as liberal multiculturalism" (Elkus). The invocation of a material exchange brings into sharp focus the slave trade that haunts this Western patronage that nonetheless traffics in children. Al-though this encounter presents an impressive opportunity to deconstruct celebrity charity and the platforms that fame allows, the sequence drops this thread in pursuit of the increasingly provocative. Brüno displays pho-tographs of him with his child, not only of his son posing as Christ on the cross or surrounded by bees but also of the child in a hot tub, surrounded by naked men (including Brüno) engaged in sex. The photographs chal-lenge few assumptions or stereotypes but instead confirm the worst fears of those in the audience convinced that children of gay parents are at risk.

Brüno further pokes at the audience by declaring he has given his son the "traditional African name: OJ," subjecting the audience to the (seemingly) casual racism of the ill-informed. Perhaps this is an attempt to address the challenges of cross-cultural adoptions, but the cavalcade of provocations diminishes the possibility of critique and seems only to serve the larger (staged) narrative in which a state authority removes OJ from Brüno's custody to the vigorous applause of the audience. The scene may drive Brüno's larger fictional quest for romance, family, and celebrity but does little to destabilize the presumed normativity of these goals.

In fact, celebrity is not so much deconstructed as bolstered. Baron Cohen toys with C-list celebrities (Paula Abdul and Republican congressman Ron Paul), but for the most part, the entertainment industry is invited backstage, their consent and complicity more or less assured. In one sequence, Brüno takes a job as an extra for the television show *Medium* (2005–11). Sitting in the jury box, he continually disrupts filming with distracting gestures, including the lighting of a cigarette. Actor Miguel Sandoval, who appears in this scene, reports that he was warned that an important person would be taking a seat in the jury box (the nephew of a network executive) and claims to have recognized Baron Cohen, stating, "It's one thing for Borat to go into an antique store in Georgia or Alabama. For Brüno to go on a TV show, he's among insiders. Most people knew who he was" ("Is *Brüno* Real or Fake?"). While Sandoval could have been attempting to perform himself as complicit after the fact, the power dynamic of inclusion (participation) and exclusion (extra in Brüno's narrative, subject to a hoax) is clear. A-list celebrities such as Bono and Sting are invited to participate in the narrative, contributing to the recording of Brüno's charity song "Dove of Peace." Bono and Sting might argue that they would not produce such a vapid song, but even so, they perform their already notorious political personas. They are not mocked but embraced and protected in the fictional finale as idealized versions of themselves: they represent Bruno's celebrity achievement while their cameos block genuine critique with a toothless play of their own culture of concern. In effect, the overall narrative of *Brüno* plays like *Borat* had Borat never left Kuzcek: it is a mockumentary that confirms rather than destabilizes problematic assumptions about the world.[8]

CONCLUSION

This essay charts the terrain of *Borat* in order to ask questions of genre and function. The category of the mockumentary begins to help us understand the work of the film, but it fails to account for the elements of cinema verité, the reportorial truth-claims, and clear documentary potential of Borat's interviews. All these components tip this film, however briefly, speciously, or unintentionally, back into the realm of the documentary, whose tradition is rife with fictions and hoaxes that produce dubious knowledge about the lived world, as well as critiques of the production of knowledge itself. What makes *Borat* intriguing is its recursive strategy and status. In an era in which digital manipulations and suspect documentary practices call the truth-status of the mode into doubt, *Borat* illustrates a difficult middle ground: a thrilling yet slippery territory that defies easy dichotomies of truth and fiction, us and them, primitive and civilized, mockumentary and documentary, reference and performance. This refusal of stable ground and clear referents does not encourage detachment and irony—the fail-safe position for those fraught with doubt.

The epistemological impasses of *Borat* instead taunt audiences as they struggle to know more than their basest impulses will let them see. Lebow observes that the mockumentary "adds a layer of fantasy, 'sexing-up' documentary" in the destabilization of references and thus returns interest to documentary, albeit "at the level of documentary studies" (225). But *Borat* suspends faith in the codes, the styles, and the politics of the traditional documentary, even as it promises to document what Americans fear most about themselves.

NOTES

1. Reporter Philip Martin described *Borat* as "vérité surrealism."

2. Mercedes Stalenhoef's documentary *When Borat Came to Town* (2008) tells the story of the villagers, focusing on the teenage Carmen and her family and neighbors, who meet with lawyers seeking to sue 20th Century Fox for misrepresentation.

3. The chorus of this song runs: "Throw the Jew down the well / So my country can be free / You must grab him by his horns / Then we have a big party."

4. See their website, http://www.theyesmen.org/.

5. Articles that address the real of *Borat* include: Adam Parker, "Comic Critic or Cruel? Charlestonians among Borat's Targets," *The Post and Courier* (Charleston, SC), December 17, 2006, G1; Devin Gordon, "Behind the Schemes" ("In *Borat* Sacha Baron Cohen Plays Unsuspecting Folks for Big Laughs. Meet the Real People Who Became Punch Lines"), *Newsweek*, October 16, 2006, 74; and Kathy Hanrahan, "Nation's Top Movie *Borat* No Laughing Matter for Some Mississippians," Associated Press News & Local Wire, November 12, 2006, unpaginated.

6. Borat's visits to *The Tonight Show with Jay Leno* and *Late Night with Conan O'Brien* have been included on the 20th Century Fox release of the DVD of *Borat: Cultural Learnings of America for Make Benefit Glorious Nation of Kazakhstan*. Also included in the DVD extras are Borat's own television show, *Sexy Drownwatch* (featuring

Lunelle), and news items of Borat's disruption of the rodeo—none of which is able to identify Baron Cohen and thus can do little more than report on the disruption we anticipate from the film that, even as fiction, provides more information.

7. The fact of the collusion was later revealed on Richard Bey's website where he posted the following on his message boards: "I signed a non disclosure agreement so I can't reveal much . . . but we shot 3 shows in Dallas last May. They built a Richard Bey show set and even had guards wearing the show's logo . . . the show was titled 'Unusual Parenting' and I warmed up the audience discussing the state of Texas taking custody of the children from the Mormon compound—When, if ever, does the state have the right to step in and tell a parent they are raising a child the wrong way? We had other guests—a Wiccan raising his son, husbands telling their wives to quit their jobs as strippers now that they were raising a child . . . and then of course, Brüno." Posted April 5, 2009, http://www.richardbey.com.

8. To be fair, *Brüno* approaches critique in the engagements in the performances of heteronormative masculinity. When Brüno engages in his mission to become straight, he visits a swingers club. Here he stands awkwardly as couples and threesomes have sex. After a pause, he gingerly reaches out to tickle the knee of a man in a couple. Bruno then attempts to make and hold eye contact with the man, an act that brings his participation to an end. The sequence hints at the potential of this film to function like *Borat*, challenging generic boundaries and tacit social assumptions. Baron Cohen, performing himself as Brüno, has entered a documentary space with a strong indexical link to the historical world: pornography (Nichols, *Representing* 163). He blurs and crosses boundaries by extending his touch to another man, joining their congress. At the same time, this act reveals the bisexual double standard of swingers clubs (and straight pornography): men are not allowed to have sex with men but women are encouraged to (or at least welcome to) have sex with other women.

WORKS CITED

Ali, Sam. "*Borat* Panders to Muslim Hatred." *Newark Star-Ledger*, November 21, 2006.

Bruzzi, Stella. *New Documentary*. 2nd ed. New York: Routledge, 2006.

Calder-Marshall, Arthur. *The Innocent Eye: The Life of Robert Flaherty*. London: W. H. Allen, 1963.

Clifford, James. "On Ethnographic Surrealism." *Comparative Studies in Society and History* 23, no. 4 (October 1981): 539–64.

———. *The Predicament of Culture: Twentieth Century Ethnography, Literature, and Art*. Cambridge, MA: Harvard University Press, 1988.

Cohen, Rich. "Hello! It's Sexy Time!" *Vanity Fair*, no. 556 (December 2006). http://www.vanityfair.com/culture/features/2006/12/borat200612.

DeBouzek, Jeannette. "The 'Ethnographic Surrealism' of Jean Rouch." *Visual Anthropology* 2, nos. 3–4 (1989): 301–15.

Elkus, Adam. "Babies and Banks: Celebrity Colonialism in Africa." *Counterpunch. org*, November 4–5, 2006. *http://www.counterpunch.org/elkus11042006.html*.

"Is *Brüno* Real or Fake?" *TV Guide* (July 27, 2009): 9.

Juhasz, Alexandra, and Jesse Lerner. "Introduction: Phony Definitions and Troubling Taxonomies of the Fake Documentary." In *F Is for Phony: Fake Documentary and Truth's Undoing*, ed. Alexandra Juhasz and Jesse Lerner, 1–35. Minneapolis: University of Minnesota Press, 2006.

Kirshenblatt-Gimblett, Barbara. "The Ethnographic Burlesque." *TDR: The Drama Review* 42, no. 2 (Summer 1998): 175–80.

Lebow, Alisa. "Faking What? Making a Mockery of Documentary." In *F Is for Phony: Fake Documentary and Truth's Undoing*, ed. Alexandra Juhasz and Jesse Lerner, 223–37. Minneapolis: University of Minnesota Press, 2006.

Marchese, David, and Willa Paskin. "What's Real in *Borat*?" November 10, 2006. http://www.salon.com/ent/feature/2006/11/10/guide_to_borat/.

Martin, Paul, "CRITICAL MASS: Borat's Hilarity Plays Off Our Capacity for Cruelty." *Arkansas Democrat-Gazette* (Little Rock), March 6, 2007, n.p.

Nichols, Bill. *Blurred Boundaries: Questions of Meaning in Contemporary Culture*. Bloomington: Indiana University Press, 1994.

———. *Introduction to Documentary*. Bloomington: Indiana University Press, 2001.

———. *Representing Reality: Issues and Concepts in Documentary*. Bloomington: Indiana University Press, 1991.

Parker, Adam. "Comic Critic or Cruel? Charlestonians among Borat's Targets." *The Post and Courier* (Charleston, SC), December 17, 2006, G1.

Roscoe, Jane, and Craig Hight. *Faking It: Mock-documentary and the Subversion of Factuality*. Manchester: Manchester University Press, 2001.

Ruoff, Jeffrey. "An Ethnographic Surrealist Film: Luis Buñuel's *Land without Bread*." *Visual Anthropology Review* 14, no. 1 (Summer 1998): 45–57.

Shohat, Ella, and Robert Stam. *Unthinking Eurocentrism: Multiculturalism and the Media*. New York: Routledge, 1994.

Sobchack, Vivian. "Inscribing Ethical Space: 10 Propositions on Death, Representation, and Documentary." *Quarterly Review of Film Studies* 9, no. 4 (Fall 1984): 283–300.

Strauss, Neill. "The Man behind the Mustache [*sic*]." *Rolling Stone*, November 14, 2006, 12–22.

Taylor, Diana. "A Savage Performance: Guillermo Gómez-Peña and Coco Fusco's *Couple in the Cage*." *TDR: The Drama Review* 42, no. 2 (Summer 1998): 160–75.

"Village 'Humiliated' by Borat Satire." *BBC News Online*, October 26, 2008. http://news.bbc.co.uk/1/hi/world/europe/7686885.stm.

Winston, Brian. *Claiming the Real: The Documentary Film Revisited*. London: British Film Institute, 1995.

BIBLIOGRAPHY

In addition to the works listed here, readers are also directed to the periodicals *Studies in Documentary Film* and *Journal of Visual Culture*.

Aitken, Ian, ed. *Encyclopedia of Documentary Film*. 3 vols. New York: Routledge, 2005.
———. *Film and Reform: John Grierson and the Documentary Film Movement*. New York: Routledge, 1990.
Alexander, William. *Film on the Left: American Documentary Film from 1931 to 1942*. Princeton: Princeton University Press, 1981.
Allen, Robert C. "Case Study: The Beginnings of American Cinema Verité." In *Film History: Theory and Practice*, ed. Robert C. Allen and Douglas Gomery, 213–41. New York: Knopf, 1985.
Armes, Roy. *Film and Reality: An Historical Survey*. Baltimore: Penguin, 1974.
Austin, Thomas. *Watching the World: Screen Documentary and Audiences*. Manchester: Manchester University Press, 2008.
Austin, Thomas, and Wilma de Jong, eds. *Rethinking Documentary: New Perspectives and Practices*. Berkshire, UK: Open University Press, 2008.
Baker, Maxine. *Documentary in the Digital Age*. Amsterdam and Boston: Elsevier/ Focal Press, 2006.
Barnouw, Erik. *Documentary: A History of the Nonfiction Film*. Rev. ed. New York: Oxford University Press, 1993.
Barsam, Richard Meran. *Nonfiction Film: A Critical History*. Rev. ed. Bloomington: Indiana University Press, 1993.
———, ed. *Nonfiction Film: Theory and Criticism*. New York: Dutton, 1976.
Beattie, Keith. *Documentary Display: Re-viewing Nonfiction Film and Video*. New York: Wallflower, 2008.
———. *Documentary Screens*. New York and Basingstoke: Palgrave-Macmillan, 2004.

Benson, Thomas W., and Brian J. Snee, eds. *The Rhetoric of Political Documentary.* Carbondale: Southern Illinois University Press, 2008.

Bignell, Johnathan. *Reality TV in the Twenty-First Century.* Basingstoke and New York: Palgrave-Macmillan, 2005.

Biressi, Andrea. *Reality TV: Realism and Revelation.* London and New York: Wallflower Press, 2005.

Bluem, A. William. *Documentary in American Television.* New York: Hastings House, 1972.

Bruzzi, Stella. *New Documentary.* 2nd ed. New York: Routledge, 2006.

Buchsbaum, Jonathan. *Cinema Engagé: Film in the Popular Front.* Urbana: University of Illinois Press, 1988.

Bullert, B. J. *Public Television: Politics and the Battle over Documentary Film.* New Brunswick, NJ: Rutgers University Press, 1997.

Burton, Julianne. *Cinema and Social Change in Latin America.* Austin: University of Texas Press, 1986.

———. *The Social Documentary in Latin America.* Pittsburgh: University of Pittsburgh Press, 1990.

Campbell, Russell. *Cinema Strikes Back: Radical Filmmaking in the United States, 1930–1942.* Ann Arbor: University of Michigan Press, 1981.

———. *Radical Cinema in the United States 1930–1942: The Work of the Film and Photo League, Nykino, and Frontier Films.* Ann Arbor: UMI Research Press, 1978.

Chanan, Michael. *The Politics of Documentary.* London: British Film Institute, 2007.

Chapman, Jane. *Issues in Contemporary Documentary.* Malden, MA: Polity Press, 2009.

Corner, John. *The Art of Record: A Critical Introduction to Documentary.* Manchester: Manchester University Press, 1992.

Cowie, Elizabeth. *Recording Reality: Desiring the Real.* Minneapolis: University of Minnesota Press, 2011.

Crawford, Peter, and David Turton, eds. *Film as Ethnography.* Manchester: Manchester University Press, 1992.

Cunningham, Megan. *The Art of Documentary: Ten Conversations with Leading Directors, Cinematographers, Editors and Producers.* Berkeley: New Riders, 2005.

———. *The Documentary Idea: A Critical History of English-Language Documentary Film and Video.* Englewood Cliffs, NJ: Prentice-Hall, 1989.

Ellis, Jack C., and Betsy A. McLane, eds. *A New History of Documentary Film.* New York: Continuum, 2005.

Ellis, John. *Documentary: Witness and Self-Revelation.* New York and London: Routledge, 2011.

Evans, Gary. *In the National Interest: A Chronicle of the National Film Board of Canada from 1949 to 1989.* Toronto: University of Toronto Press, 1991.

———. *John Grierson and the National Film Board: The Politics of Wartime Propaganda, 1939–1945.* Toronto: University of Toronto Press, 1985.

Fielding, Raymond. *The American Newsreel, 1911–1967*. Norman: University of Oklahoma Press, 1972.

———. *The March of Time, 1935–1951*. New York: Oxford University Press, 1978.

Friendly, Fred W. *Due to Circumstances beyond Our Control*. New York: Random House, 1967.

Geiger, Jeffrey. *American Documentary Film: Projecting the Nation*. Edinburgh: Edinburgh University Press, 2011.

Grant, Barry Keith, and Jim Hillier. *100 Documentaries*. London: British Film Institute, 2009.

Grierson, John. *Grierson on Documentary*. Ed. Forsyth Hardy. London and Boston: Faber and Faber, 1979.

Grindon, Leger. "Q & A: Poetics of the Documentary Film Interview." *Velvet Light Trap* 60 (Fall 2007): 4–12.

Gross, Larry, John Stuart Katz, and Jay Ruby, eds. *Image Ethics: The Moral Rights of Subjects in Photographs, Film, and Television*. New York: Oxford, 1988.

Guynn, William. *A Cinema of Nonfiction*. Rutherford, NJ: Fairleigh Dickinson University Press, 1990.

Hammond, Charles. *The Image Decade: Television Documentary*. New York: Hastings House, 1981.

Heider, Karl G. *Ethnographic Film*. Austin: University of Texas Press, 1976.

Hess, John. "Notes on U.S. Radical Film, 1967–80." In *Jump Cut: Hollywood, Politics, and Counter-Cinema*, ed. Peter Steven, 134–50. Toronto: Between the Lines, 1985.

Hight, Craig. *Television Mockumentary: Reflexivity, Satire and a Call to Play*. Manchester: Manchester University Press, 2010.

Higson, Andrew. "'Britain's Outstanding Contribution to the Film': The Documentary-Realist Tradition." In *All Our Yesterdays: 90 Years of British Cinema*, ed. Charles Barr, 72–97. London: British Film Institute, 1986.

Hill, Annette. *Reality TV: Audiences and Popular Factual Television*. London: Routledge, 2005.

———. *Restyling Factual TV: Audiences and News, Documentary and Reality Genres*. New York: Routledge, 2007.

Hockings, Paul, ed. *Principles of Visual Anthropology*. The Hague: Mouton, 1975.

Hogarth, David. *Realer than Reel: Global Directions in Documentary*. Austin: University of Texas Press, 2006.

Holmes, Sue, and Deborah Jermyn, eds. *Understanding Reality Television*. New York: Routledge, 2004.

Issari, M. Ali. *Cinema Verité*. East Lansing: Michigan State University Press, 1971.

Issari, M. Ali, and Doris A. Paul. *What Is Cinema Verité?* Metuchen, NJ: Scarecrow Press, 1979.

Iverson, Gunnar, and Jan Ketil Simonsen. *Beyond the Visual: Sound and Image in Ethnographic and Documentary Film*. Walnut Creek, CA: Left Coast Press, 2010.

Izod, John, and Richard Kilborn. *An Introduction to TV Documentary: Confronting Reality*. Manchester: Manchester University Press, 1997.

Jacobs, Lewis, ed. *The Documentary Tradition*. 2nd ed. New York: Norton, 1979.

Jones, D. B. *Movies and Memoranda: An Interpretive History of the National Film Board of Canada*. Ottawa: Canadian Film Institute, 1981.

Juhaz, Alexandra, and Jesse Lerner. *F Is for Phony: Fake Documentary and Truth's Undoing*. Minneapolis: University of Minnesota Press, 2006.

Kahana, Jonathan. *Intelligence Work: The Politics of American Documentary Film*. New York: Columbia University Press, 2008.

Kilborn, Russell. *Taking the Long View: A Study of Longitudinal Documentary*. Manchester: Manchester University Press, 2010.

King, Geoff, ed. *The Spectacle of the Real: From Hollywood to "Reality TV" and Beyond*. Bristol, UK: Intellect, 2005.

Lane, Jim. *The Autobiographical Documentary in America*. Madison: University of Wisconsin Press, 2002.

Leach, Jim, and Jeannette Sloniowski, eds. *Candid Eyes: Essays on Canadian Documentary*. Toronto: University of Toronto Press, 2003.

Levin, G. Roy. *Documentary Explorations: 15 Interviews with Film-Makers*. Garden City, NY: Anchor Doubleday, 1971.

Leyda, Jay. *Films Beget Films*. New York: Hill and Wang, 1964.

Lovell, Alan, and Jim Hiller. *Studies in Documentary*. New York: Viking Press/London: British Film Institute, 1972.

Macdonald, Kevin, and Mark Cousins, eds. *Imagining Reality: The Faber Book of the Documentary*. Boston and London: Faber and Faber, 1996. 2nd ed., 2005.

MacDougall, David. "Prospects of the Ethnographic Film." *Film Quarterly* 23, no. 2 (Winter 1969/70): 16–30.

Mamber, Stephen. *Cinema Verite in America: Studies in Uncontrolled Documentary*. Cambridge, MA: MIT Press, 1973.

Marcorelles, Louis. *Living Cinema: New Directions in Contemporary Film-Making*. New York: Praeger, 1973.

McCann, Richard Dyer. *The People's Films: A Political History of U.S. Government Motion Pictures*. New York: Hastings, 1973.

Murray, Susan, and Laurie Ouellette, eds. *Reality TV: Remaking Television Culture*. 2nd ed. New York: New York University Press, 2009.

Murrow, Edward R., and Fred W. Friendly. *See It Now*. New York: Simon and Schuster, 1955.

Nichols, Bill. *Blurred Boundaries: Questions of Meaning in Contemporary Culture*. Bloomington: Indiana University Press, 1994.

———. *Ideology and the Image*. Bloomington: Indiana University Press, 1981.

———. *Introduction to Documentary*. 2nd ed. Bloomington: Indiana University Press, 2007.

————. *Representing Reality: Issues and Concepts in Documentary*. Bloomington: Indiana University Press, 1991.

Ouellette, Laurie. *Better Living through Reality TV: Television and Post-Welfare Citizenship*. Malden, MA: Blackwell, 2008.

Plantinga, Carl. *Rhetoric and Representation in Nonfiction Film*. New York: Cambridge University Press, 1997.

Rabinowitz, Paula. *They Must Be Represented: The Politics of Documentary*. London and New York: Verso, 1994.

Rascaroli, Laura. "The Essay Film: Problems, Definitions and Textual Commitments." *Framework* 49, no. 2 (Fall 2008): 24–47.

Renov, Michael. *The Subject of Documentary*. Minneapolis: University of Minnesota Press, 2004.

————, ed. *Theorizing Documentary*. New York: Routledge, 1993.

Renov, Michael, and Jane Gaines, eds. *Collecting Visible Evidence*. Minneapolis: University of Minnesota Press, 1999.

Roscoe, Jane, and Craig Hight. *Faking It: Mock Documentary and the Subversion of Factuality*. Manchester: Manchester University Press, 2008.

Rosenthal, Alan, ed. *The Documentary Conscience: A Casebook in Film Making*. Berkeley: University of California Press, 1980.

————, ed. *New Challenges for Documentary*. Berkeley: University of California Press, 1988.

Rosenthal, Alan, and John Corner, eds. *New Challenges for Documentary*. 2nd ed. Manchester: Manchester University Press, 2005.

————, ed. *The New Documentary in Action: A Casebook in Film Making*. Berkeley: University of California Press, 1972.

Rotha, Paul. *Documentary Diary*. New York: Hill and Wang, 1974.

————. *Documentary Film*. New York: Hastings, 1952.

Rothman, William. *Documentary Film Classics*. New York: Cambridge University Press, 1997.

————, ed. *Three Documentary Filmmakers: Errol Morris, Ross McElwee, Jean Rouch*. Albany: SUNY Press, 2009.

Russell, Patrick. *100 British Documentaries*. London: British Film Institute, 2007.

Sarkar, Bhaskar, and Janet Walker, eds. *Documentary Testimonies: Global Archives of Suffering*. New York: Routledge, 2009.

Smail, Belinda. *The Documentary: Politics, Emotion, Culture*. Basingstoke and New York: Palgrave-Macmillan, 2010.

Sobchack, Vivian C. "Inscribing Ethical Space: Ten Propositions on Death, Representation, and Documentary." *Quarterly Review of Film Studies* (Fall 1984): 283–308.

————, ed. *The Persistence of History: Cinema, Television, and the Modern Event*. New York: Routledge, 1996.

Steven, Peter. *Brink of Reality: New Canadian Documentary Film and Video*. Toronto: Between the Lines, 1993.

Stott, William. *Documentary Expression and Thirties America*. New York: Oxford University Press, 1973.

Sussex, Elizabeth. *The Rise and Fall of the British Documentary Film Movement*. Berkeley: University of California Press, 1975.

Swallow, Norman. *Factual Television*. New York: Hastings House, 1966.

Swann, Paul. *The British Documentary Film Movement, 1926–1946*. Cambridge: Cambridge University Press, 1989.

Taddeo, Julie Anne, and Ken Dvorak, eds. *The Tube Has Spoken: Reality TV and History*. Lexington: University of Kentucky Press, 2010.

Trinh T. Min-ha. "Documentary Is/Not a Name." *October* 52 (Spring 1990): 76–98.

——. *The Framer Framed*. New York: Routledge, 1992.

——. *When the Moon Waxes Red: Representation, Gender, and Cultural Politics*. New York: Routledge, 1991.

——. *Woman, Native, Other*. Bloomington: Indiana University Press, 1989.

Vaughan, Dai. *For Documentary: Twelve Essays*. Berkeley: University of California Press, 1999.

——. *Television Documentary Usage*. London: British Film Institute, 1976.

Wahlberg, Malin. *Documentary Time: Film and Phenomenology*. Minneapolis: University of Minnesota Press, 2008.

Waldman, Diane, and Janet Walker. *Feminism and Documentary*. Minneapolis: University of Minnesota Press, 1999.

Ward, Paul. *Documentary: The Margins of Reality*. London and New York: Wallflower Press, 2005.

Warren, Charles, ed. *Beyond Document: Essays on Nonfiction Film*. Hanover, NH: University Press of New England, 1996.

Waugh, Thomas. *The Right to Play Oneself: Looking Back on Documentary Film*. Minneapolis: University of Minnesota Press, 2011.

——, ed. *"Show Us Life": Toward a History and Aesthetics of the Committed Documentary*. Metuchen, NJ: Scarecrow Press, 1984.

Waugh, Thomas, Michael Brendan Baker, and Ezra Winton, eds. *Challenge for Change: Activist Documentary at the National Film Board of Canada*. Toronto: McGill-Queen's University Press, 2010.

Winston, Brian. *Claiming the Real: Documentary Film Revisited*. London: British Film Institute, 1995.

——. *Lies, Damn Lies and Documentaries*. London: British Film Institute, 2000.

Wolfe, Charles. "The Poetics and Politics of Nonfiction: Documentary Film." In Tino Balio, *Grand Design: Hollywood as a Modern Business Enterprise, 1930–1939*, 351–86. Berkeley: University of California Press, 1993.

CONTRIBUTORS

MATTHEW BERNSTEIN teaches film studies at Emory University in Atlanta, Georgia. He is the author of *Walter Wanger, Hollywood Independent* (1994, 2000) and *Screening a Lynching: The Leo Frank Case on Film and TV* (2009), and editor of several volumes, including *Visions of the East: Orientalism on Film* (with Gaylyn Studlar, 1996), *Controlling Hollywood: Censorship and Regulation in the Studio Era* (1999), and *Michael Moore: Filmmaker, Newsmaker, Cultural Icon* (2010).

VIRGINIA BONNER is an associate professor of film and media studies at Clayton State University in metropolitan Atlanta, where she teaches courses in film studies, women's studies, art history, and media studies. She regularly presents papers internationally and for local arts organizations and curates film festivals in the Atlanta area. She has published essays on Chris Marker, Alain Resnais, and Agnès Varda in such journals as *Senses of Cinema, Scope: An Online Journal of Film Studies,* and in the anthology *There She Goes: Feminist Filmmaking and Beyond* (2009).

JOHN R. COOK is Reader in Media at Glasgow Caledonian University, Scotland, UK. The author of *Dennis Potter: A Life on Screen* (1995, 1998), he has done intensive research on the work of Peter Watkins. At Watkins's invitation, Dr. Cook wrote and provided voice-over commentaries for the DVD release of the director's 1964 *Culloden* (2006). He has also published several articles on Watkins and contributed an essay to the package for the first UK DVD release of Watkins's cult 1967 British feature film, *Privilege* (2010).

SETH FELDMAN is Professor of Film Studies and Director of the Robarts Centre for Canadian Studies at York University, Toronto, Canada. He is the author of *Evolution of Style in the Early Work of Dziga Vertov* (1977) and *Dziga Vertov: A Guide to References and Resources* (1979), coeditor (with Joyce Nelson) of *Canadian Film Reader* (1977), and editor of *Take Two: A Tribute to Film in Canada* (1984) and *Allan King, Filmmaker* (2002). Dr. Feldman is also the author of twenty-six radio documentaries for the CBC-Radio program *Ideas*. He is presently director of a major research project on the Canadian films of Expo '67.

LUCY FISCHER is Distinguished Professor of English and Film Studies at the University of Pittsburgh where she serves as Director of the Film Studies Program. She is the author or editor of *Jacques Tati* (1983), *Shot/Countershot: Film Tradition and Women's Cinema* (1989), *Imitation of Life* (1991), *Cinematernity: Film, Motherhood, Genre* (1996), *Sunrise* (1998), *Designing Women: Art Deco, Cinema and the Female Form* (2003), *Stars: The Film Reader* (2004), *American Cinema of the 1920s: Themes and Variations* (2009), *Teaching Film* (2012), and *Body Double: The Author Incarnate in the Cinema* (2013). She has held curatorial positions at the Museum of Modern Art (New York City) and the Carnegie Museum of Art (Pittsburgh), and has been the recipient of both a National Endowment for the Arts Art Critics Fellowship and a National Endowment for the Humanities Fellowship for University Professors. She has served as president of the Society for Cinema and Media Studies (2001–3) and in 2008 received its Distinguished Service Award.

CARYL FLINN is a professor in the Department of Screen Arts and Culture at the University of Michigan in Ann Arbor. She is the author of *Strains of Utopia: Gender, Nostalgia, and Hollywood Film Music* (1992), *The New German Cinema: Music, History, and the Matter of Style* (2004), and *Brass Diva: The Life and Legends of Ethel Merman* (2007), and coeditor (with James Buhler and David Neumeyer) of *Music and Cinema* (2000).

SANDY FLITTERMAN-LEWIS teaches English, cinema studies, and comparative literature at Rutgers University in New Brunswick, New Jersey. She is the author of *To Desire Differently: Feminism and the French Cinema* (revised ed., 1996) and coauthor of *New Vocabularies in Film Semiotics* (1992), as well as numerous chapters in anthologies on topics ranging from feminist film theory to television and cultural studies. Her current work, *Hidden Voices: Essays on Childhood, the Family and Anti-Semitism in Occupation France,* comes out of a conference she organized at Columbia University in 1998 concerning the Shoah and its repercussions in French culture.

BARRY KEITH GRANT is a professor in the Department of Communications, Popular Culture and Film at Brock University in Ontario, Canada. He is the author of *Voyages of Discovery: The Cinema of Frederick Wiseman* (1992), *Film Genre: From Iconography to Ideology* (2007), *Shadows of Doubt: Negotiations of Masculinity in American Genre Films* (2010), *Invasion of the Body Snatchers* (2010), and *100 Science Fiction Films* (2013) and coauthor of *The Film Studies Dictionary* (2001) and *100 Documentary Films* (2009). The editor of more than a dozen books, including *The Dread of Difference: Gender and the Horror Film* (1996), *Auteurs and Authorship: A Film Reader* (2007), *Britton on Film: The Collected Film Criticism of Andrew Britton* (2009), and the *Film Genre Reader* series, he edits the Contemporary Approaches to Film and Television series for Wayne State University Press.

WILLIAM GUYNN is Professor Emeritus at Sonoma State University in California. Principally concerned with the theory of nonfiction in the documentary and the history film, he is the author of *A Cinema of Nonfiction* (1990), *Writing History in Film* (2006), and numerous articles published in journals and anthologies in the United States and Europe. He is also the editor of *The Routledge Companion to Film History* (2010).

JEANNE HALL was Associate Professor in the College of Communications at Penn State University, where she taught film history, theory, and criticism. Coauthor, along with husband and colleague Ron Bettig, of *Big Media, Big Money: Cultural Texts and Political Economics* (2003), her work appeared in *Cinema Journal, Film Criticism, Film Quarterly, Creative Screenwriting*, and the *Journal of Communication Inquiry*, as well as in such volumes as *Critical Thinking about Sex, Love & Romance in the Mass Media* (2007) and *The Rhetoric of the New Political Documentary* (2008).

JOANNE HERSHFIELD teaches third world cinema, film criticism and theory, and film and video production in the Department of Communication Studies at the University of North Carolina at Chapel Hill. The author of *Mexican Cinema and the Myth of the Mexican Woman, 1940–50* (1995) and *Imagining la chica moderna: Women, Nation, and Visual Culture in Mexico, 1917–1936* (2008) and coeditor of *Mexico's Cinema: A Century of Film and Filmmakers* (1999), she has also published in *Wide Angle* and *Canadian Journal of Film Studies*. Her films include *Women in Japan: Memories of the Past, Dreams of* *the Future* (with Jan Bardsley, 2002), *The Gillian Film* (2006), and *Men Are Human, Women Are Buffalo* (2008).

DAVID T. JOHNSON is Assistant Professor of English at Salisbury University where he teaches courses in film and adaptation studies. He is the coeditor of *Literature/Film Quarterly* and (with Elsie M. Walker) of the collection *Conversations with Directors: An Anthology of Interviews from Literature/Film Quarterly* (2008). His essays have appeared in *Film Criticism* and *Adaptation: A Journal of Literature on Screen Studies,* as well as in the anthology *Lowering the Boom: New Essays on the Theory and History of Film Sound* (2008).

CHARLIE KEIL is Director of the Cinema Studies Institute and Associate Professor of History at the University of Toronto. He is the author of *Early American Cinema in Transition: Story, Style and Filmmaking, 1907–1913* (2001) and coeditor of *American Cinema's Transitional Era: Audience, Institutions, Practices* (2004), *American Cinema of the 1910s: Themes and Variations* (2009), and *Funny Pictures: Animation and Comedy in Studio-Era Hollywood* (2011). His writings on documentary include an essay in the anthology *F Is for Phony: Fake Documentary and Truth's Undoing* (2006).

JIM LEACH was Professor of Film and Communications Studies at Brock University, St. Catharines, Ontario, Canada. The author of *A Possible Cinema: The Films of Alain Tanner* (1984), a monograph on Tanner's *Messidor* (1996), *Claude Jutra: Filmmaker* (1999), *British Film* (2004), and *Film in Canada* (2006), and coeditor of *Candid Eyes: Essays on Canadian Documentaries* (2003), his work has also appeared in numerous anthologies and journals. His most recent book is a monograph on *Doctor Who* for Wayne State University Press's TV Milestones series (2009).

JULIA LESAGE is a documentary videomaker whose work includes *In Plain English: Students of Color Speak Out* (1992) and *Getting Around* (1995). The cofounder and coeditor of *Jump Cut: A Review of Contemporary Media,* she teaches in the Department of English at the University of Oregon, Eugene. The editor of *A Research Guide to Jean-Luc Godard* (1977) and coeditor of *Culture, Media, and the Religious Right* (1997), her writing has been widely anthologized in such works as *"Show Us Life": Toward a History and Aesthetics of the Committed Documentary* (1984), *Home Is Where the Heart Is: Studies in Melodrama and the Woman's Film* (1987), *Marxism and the Interpretation of Culture* (1988), *The Social Documentary in Latin America* (1990), and *Feminism and Documentary* (1999).

PAULA J. MASSOOD is a professor of film studies in the Department of Film, Brooklyn College, City University of New York, and on the Doctoral Faculty in the Program in Theatre at the Graduate Center, CUNY. She is the author of *Black City Cinema: African American Urban Experiences in Film* (2003) and *Making a Promised Land: Harlem in 20th Century Photography and Film* (2013) and editor of *The Spike Lee Reader* (2008).

JOAN NICKS is an adjunct professor in the Department of Communication, Popular Culture and Film, at Brock University, St. Catharines, Ontario, Canada. She is coeditor of *Slippery Pastimes: Reading the Popular in Canadian Culture* (2002) and *Covering Niagara: Studies in Local Popular Culture* (2010). Her writing on film and media has appeared in various anthologies including *Gendering the Nation: Canadian Women's Cinema* (1999) and *Candid Eyes: Essays on Canadian Documentaries* (2003) and in journals including *Post Script, Cinema Canada,* and *Canadian Journal of Communication.*

SHEILA PETTY is a professor of media studies at the University of Regina, Saskatchewan, Canada. She has written extensively on issues of cultural representation, identity, and nation in African and African diasporic cinema and new media, and has curated film, television, and new media exhibitions for galleries across Canada. She is author of *Contact Zones: Memory, Origin and Discourses in Black Diasporic Cinema* (2008) and editor of *A Call to Action: The Films of Ousmane Sembene* (1996) and *Canadian Cultural Poesis: Essays on Canadian Culture* (2006). Currently she is the leader of an interdisciplinary research group and New Media Studio Laboratory spanning computer science, engineering, and fine arts.

CARL PLANTINGA is Professor of Film at Calvin College in Grand Rapids, Michigan. He is the author of *Rhetoric and Representation in Nonfiction Film* (1997) and *Moving Viewers: American Film and the Spectator's Experience* (2009), and coeditor of *Passionate Views: Film, Cognition, and Emotion* (1999) and *The Routledge Companion to Philosophy and Film* (2009).

WILLIAM ROTHMAN teaches at the University of Miami in Florida. The author of several books including *Hitchcock: The Murderous Gaze* (1982), *The "I" of the Camera* (1988), and *Documentary Film Classics* (1996), he is also the editor of *Cavell on Film* (2005) and *Three Documentary Film Makers: Errol Morris, Ross McElwee, and Jean Rouch* (2009). His writing has appeared in such journals as *Quarterly Review of Film Studies, American Film,* and *East-West Film Journal.*

JEFFREY K. RUOFF, a film historian and documentary filmmaker, is Associate Professor in the Department of Film and Media Studies at Dartmouth College. The author of *The Memory of War: Hara Kazuo's "The Emperor's Naked Army Marches On"* (1997) and *An American Family: A Televised Life* (2001) and editor of *Virtual Voyages: Cinema and Travel* (2006) and *Coming Soon to a Festival Near You: Programming Film Festivals* (2012), his writing on film has also appeared in such journals as *Visual Anthropology, Wide Angle, Cinema Journal,* and *Film History.* His films and videos, including *Hacklebarney Tunes: The Music of Greg Brown* (1993) and *The Last Vaudevillian* (1998), have been shown at festivals and on television in the United States and abroad.

CATHERINE RUSSELL is professor of film studies at Concordia University in Montreal, Canada. She is the author of *Narrative Mortality: Death, Closure, and New Wave Cinemas* (1995), *Experimental Ethnography: The Work of Film in the Age of Video* (1999), and *Classical Japanese Cinema Revisited: A New Look at the Canon* (2011).

DIANE SCHEINMAN has taught at New York University and the New School for Social Research. Her publications include articles in *CVA Review* and *PRISM,* and booklets produced in conjunction with the exhibit "Ashanti to Zulu: A Collection of Traditional African Arts" at the Brooklyn Children's Museum.

JEANNETTE SLONIOWSKI is Associate Professor in the Department of Communication, Popular Culture and Film, and the Graduate Program in Popular Culture, at Brock University. The coeditor of *Slippery Pastimes: Reading the Popular in Canadian Culture* (2002), *Detecting Canada: Essays on Canadian Detective Fiction* (2014), *Canadian Communications* (2002), and *Candid Eyes: Essays on Canadian Documentaries* (2003) she also coedits the TV Milestones series for Wayne State University Press. Her work has also appeared in such journals as *Journal of Popular Film and Television, Journal of Canadian Studies, Canadian Journal of Film Studies,* and *Journal of Canadian Communications.*

VIVIAN SOBCHACK is Professor Emerita in the Department of Film, Television, and Digital Media and former Associate Dean at the UCLA School of Theatre, Film, and Television. She was the first woman elected president of the Society for Cinema and Media Studies and served many years on the Board of Directors of the American Film Institute. Her essays have appeared in journals such as *Film Quarterly, Film Comment, Quarterly Review* *of Film and Video, camera obscura,* and the *Journal of Visual Culture,* as well as in many anthologies. She is the author of *The Address of the Eye: A Phenomenology of Film Experience* (1982), *Screening Space: The American Science Fiction Film* (1987), and *Carnal Thoughts: Embodiment and Moving Image Culture* (2004), coauthor of *An Introduction to Film* (2002), as well as the editor of *The Persistence of History: Cinema, Television and the Modern Event* (1996) and *Meta-Morphing: Visual Transformation and the Culture of Quick Change* (1999).

ROBERT STAM is University Professor at New York University. His books include *Reflexivity in Film and Literature: From Don Quixote to Jean-Luc Godard* (1992), *Subversive Pleasures: Bakhtin, Cultural Criticism, and Film* (1989), *Tropical Multiculturalism: A Comparative History of Race in Brazilian Cinema and Culture* (1997), *Film Theory: An Introduction* (2000), *Literature through Film: Realism, Magic and the Art of Adaptation* (2005), and *Flagging Patriotism: Crises of Narcissism and Anti-Americanism* (2006), and he is the coauthor of *Unthinking Eurocentrism: Multiculturalism and the Media* (1994) and *Brazilian Cinema* (1995). He has taught in France, Tunisia, and Brazil.

BART TESTA teaches cinema studies and semiotics at the University of Toronto. He is the author of *Spirit in the Landscape* (1989) and *Back and Forth: Early Cinema and the Avant-Garde* (1992), and is coeditor of *Pier Paolo Pasolini: Contemporary Perspectives* (1994). He is a former book review editor of *Canadian Journal of Film Studies.*

FRANK P. TOMASULO was most recently Professor and Head of Film Studies in the College of Motion Picture, Television, and Recording Arts at Florida State University in Tallahassee. He has also taught cinema and television history and theory, as well as film production and screenwriting, at UCLA, Ithaca College, Cornell University, the University of California–Santa Cruz, Georgia State University, and Southern Methodist University. The coeditor of *More than a Method: Trends and Traditions in Contemporary Film Performance* (2004), he is the author of more than eighty scholarly essays. A former editor of *Journal of Film and Video* (1991–96) and *Cinema Journal* (1997–2002), in 2009 he was the first recipient of the annual University Film & Video Association Teaching Award.

LESHU TORCHIN is a lecturer in film studies at the University of St. Andrews, Fife, Scotland, where she teaches classes on film studies, documentary, and the use of screen media in social advocacy and human rights campaigns. The author of *Creating the Witness: Documenting Genocide on Film, Video and the*

Internet (2012) and coauthor of *Moving People, Moving Images: Cinema and Trafficking in the New Europe* (2010), her work has appeared in the journals *Third Text, American Anthropologist, Tourist Studies,* and *Cineaste.*

THOMAS WAUGH is Concordia University Research Chair in Sexual Representation and in Documentary in the Mel Hoppenheim School of Cinema, Montreal. Among his books are *"Show Us Life": Towards a History and Aesthetics of the Committed Documentary* (1984), *Hard to Imagine: The History of Gay Male Erotic Photography and Cinema from Their Origins to Stonewall* (1995), and *The Right to Play Oneself: Essays on Documentary by Thomas Waugh, 1976–2001* (2010), and the coauthor of *Challenge for Change: Activist Documentary at the National Film Board of Canada* (2010). He is currently completing *Joris Ivens: Essays on the Career of a Radical Documentarist.*

LINDA WILLIAMS is Professor of Film Studies and Women's Studies at the University of California, Irvine. She is the author of *Figures of Desire: A Theory and Analysis of Surrealist Film* (1981), *Hard Core: Power, Pleasure, and the "Frenzy of the Visible"* (1989), *Playing the Race Card: Melodramas of Race from Uncle Tom to O. J. Simpson* (2001), *Porn Studies* (2004), and *Screening Sex* (2009) and editor of *Viewing Positions: Ways of Seeing Film* (1994). In addition, she is the coeditor of *Revision: Essay in Feminist Film Criticism* (1984) and of *Re-Inventing Film Studies* (2000), and her writing has appeared in many journals and anthologies including *The Dread of Difference: Gender and the Horror Film* (1996) and *Film Genre Reader* (2003).

INDEX

Index